EVOLUTION
of
MIND, BRAIN, *and* CULTURE

Penn Museum International Research Conferences
Holly Pittman, Series Editor, Conference Publications

Volume 5: Proceedings of "Evolution of Mind, Brain, and Culture,"
Philadelphia, September 27–30, 2007

PMIRC volumes

1. *Landscapes of Movement: Trails, Paths, and Roads in
Anthropological Perspective,* edited by James E. Snead,
Clark L. Erickson, and J. Andrew Darling, 2009
2. *Mapping Mongolia: Situating Mongolia in the World from
Geologic Time to the Present,* edited by Paula L.W. Sabloff, 2011
3. *Sustainable Lifeways: Cultural Persistence in an
Ever-changing Environment,* edited by Naomi F. Miller,
Katherine M. Moore, and Kathleen Ryan, 2011
4. *Literacy in the Persianate World: Writing and the Social Order,* edited by
Brian Spooner and William L. Hanaway, 2012

EVOLUTION
of
MIND, BRAIN,
and
CULTURE

EDITED BY

Gary Hatfield and Holly Pittman

University of Pennsylvania Museum of Archaeology and Anthropology
Philadelphia

LIBRARY OF CONGRESS CATALOGING-IN-PUBLICATION DATA

Evolution of mind, brain, and culture / edited by Gary Hatfield and Holly Pittman.
  pages cm
  Includes bibliographical references and index.
  ISBN-13: 978-1-934536-49-0 (hardcover : alk. paper)
  ISBN-10: 1-934536-49-0 (hardcover : alk. paper)
  1. Human evolution. 2. Brain–Evolution. 3. Language and language–Origin.
  I. Hatfield, Gary C. (Gary Carl) II. Pittman, Holly.
  GN281.E8928 2013
  155.7--dc23
                    2012046591

© 2013 by the University of Pennsylvania Museum of Archaeology and Anthropology
Philadelphia, PA

Published for the University of Pennsylvania Museum of Archaeology and Anthropology
by the University of Pennsylvania Press.

Printed in the United States of America on acid-free paper.

Contents

Figures

Tables

Contributors

Robert Boyd
Department of Anthropology
University of California Los Angeles
Los Angeles, CA 90095

Peter Carruthers
Department of Philosophy
University of Maryland
College Park, MD 20742

Thierry Chaminade
Institut de Neurosciences de la Timone -
   UMR7289 - Aix-Marseille Université & CNRS
Faculté de Médecine
27 Bd Jean Moulin
13385 Marseille
FRANCE

Philip G. Chase
Penn Museum
University of Pennsylvania
Philadelphia, PA 19104

Dorothy L. Cheney
Department of Biology
University of Pennsylvania
Philadelphia, PA 19104

Contributors

Merlin Donald
Queen's University,
Kingston, Ontario K7L 3N6
CANADA
and
Case Western Reserve University
Cleveland, OH 44106

Peter Gärdenfors
Cognitive Science
Lund University
Lund
SWEDEN

Gary Hatfield
Department of Philosophy
University of Pennsylvania
Philadelphia, PA 19104

Jody Hey
Department of Genetics
Rutgers University New Brunswick
Piscataway, NJ 08854

Steven Mithen
School of Human and Environmental Sciences
University of Reading
Reading, Berkshire
RG6 6AH
England
UK

April Nowell
Department of Anthropology
University of Victoria
Victoria, British Columbia
V8W 3PS
CANADA

Peter J. Richerson
Department of Environmental Science and Policy
University of California – Davis
Davis, CA 95616

Theodore G. Schurr
Department of Anthropology
University of Pennsylvania
Philadelphia, PA 19104

Robert M. Seyfarth
Departments of Psychology
University of Pennsylvania
Philadelphia, PA 19104

Kim Sterelny
Research School of Social Sciences
Australian National University
Canberra ACT 0200
AUSTRALIA

Felix Warneken
Department of Psychology
Harvard University
Cambridge, MA 02138

Penn Museum International
Research Conferences

Foreword

For more than a century, a core mission of the University of Pennsylvania Museum of Archaeology and Anthropology has been to foster research that leads to new understandings about human culture. For much of the 20th century, this research took the form of worldwide expeditions that brought back both raw data and artifacts whose analysis continues to shed light on early complex societies of the New and Old Worlds. The civilizations of pharonic Egypt, Mesopotamia, Iran, Greece, Rome, Mexico, Peru, and Native Americans have been represented in galleries that display only the most remarkable of the Penn Museum's vast holding of artifacts. These collections have long provided primary evidence of many distinct research programs engaging scholars from around the world.

As we moved into a new century, indeed a new millennium, the Penn Museum sought to reinvigorate its commitment to research focused on questions of human societies. In 2005, working with then Williams Director Richard M. Leventhal, Michael J. Kowalski, Chairman of the Board of Overseers of the Penn Museum, gave a generous gift to the Museum to seed a new program of high-level conferences designed to engage themes central to the Museum's core research mission. According to Leventhal's vision, generating new knowledge and frameworks for understanding requires more than raw data and collections. More than ever, it depends on collaboration among communities of scholars investigating problems using distinct lines of evidence and different modes of analysis. Recognizing the importance of collaborative and multidisciplinary endeavors in the social sciences, the Penn Museum used the gift to launch a program of International Research Conferences that each brought together ten to fifteen scholars who had reached a critical point in the consideration of a shared problem.

During the three years until the spring of 2008, it was my privilege to identify, develop, run, and now oversee the publication of eight such conferences. The dozen or so papers for each conference were submitted to all participants one month in advance of the meeting. The fact that the papers were circulated beforehand meant that no time was lost introducing new material to the group. Rather, after each paper was briefly summarized by its author, an intense and extended critique followed that allowed for sustained consideration of the contribution that both the data and the argument made to the larger questions. The discussions of individual papers were followed by a day discussing crosscutting issues and concluded with an overarching synthesis of ideas.

Evolution of Mind, Brain, and Culture is the edited proceedings of a conference of the same name held in the fall of 2007. It is the fifth of the conferences to see publication. As Series Editor, I look forward to three more volumes that will appear over the next few years. The publication of the results of these conferences allows the new knowledge and understanding that they achieved to be shared broadly and to contribute to the uniquely human enterprise of self understanding.

HOLLY PITTMAN

Series Editor

Deputy Director for Academic Programs, Penn Museum 2005–2008

Curator, Near East Section

Professor, History of Art

Bok Family Professor in the Humanities, University of Pennsylvania

Preface

The present volume is the product of a multidisciplinary research conference on the evolution of mind, brain, and culture. It unites the efforts of psychologists, philosophers, neuroscientists, archaeologists, anthropologists, geneticists, and environmental scientists in seeking to understand the origins of the human mind and of its biological substrate, the human brain, and including the mind's expression in and formation by human culture. Together, the essays presented here cover the variety of methods and the diversity of theories at work in the resurgence of evolutionary approaches to the mind during the past two decades.

The volume is distinctive in uniting contributions in the biological and psychological sciences with those of archaeologists and paleoanthropologists. Such links have previously been forged by several of the authors in this volume and we now seek to broaden the connections and to move the dialogue forward. The chapters by Schurr, Donald, Gärdenfors, Mithen, Nowell, Richerson and Boyd, Sterelny, and Chase engage the archaeological record to find evidence of past patterns of behavior and the conditions in which they occurred and to compare human cognitive functions with those that may be ascribed to our hominin ancestors. We have considered it especially important that claims about changing behavioral patterns in hominin evolution take account of the body of archaeological knowledge. The chapters by Schurr and Hey examine the comparative genetic evidence for reconstructing the evolution of human cognition, taking into account the chimp and Neandertal genomes. The remaining chapters, by Seyfarth and Cheney, Chaminade, Warneken, and Carruthers, take a comparative look at cognition and behavior in humans and our living primate relatives among the monkeys and apes. Here again, we have favored work that directly reports or engages closely with ongoing empirical research.

Several of the chapters undertake methodological or theoretical reflection. Hey examines the logic of relating function, and especially cognitive function, to genetic data. Nowell closely examines the notion of "behavioral modernity" as applied to Neandertals and *Homo sapiens*. Sterelny examines the scope and limits of models that draw upon human behavioral ecology in accounting for the behavior patterns differential survival of these two species. The introductory chapter, composed by Hatfield as an expansion of his introductory remarks at the workshop, surveys the major theoretical approaches to the evolution of mind, brain, and culture and the variety of methods that have been employed, places recent work in historical perspective, and summarizes the main themes and points of agreement or disagreement in the remaining chapters. Hatfield pays particular attention to framing the debate on nonhuman "culture." This topic is further addressed by Chase, who investigates the apparently unique features of human culture that distinguish it from other instances in which behavioral patterns are socially transmitted from generation to generation.

The workshop from which this volume grew took place in the Penn Museum, September 27–30, 2007. The papers were predistributed. During the workshop, the authors summarized their papers and then two other participants offered critical responses to begin a more extensive discussion. In addition to the invited authors, each of whom served as a critic for one or, more usually, two of their colleagues, Mark Liberman (Penn Linguistics) was a discussant for the paper by Gärdenfors and Robert Seyfarth commented on Warneken. Pete Richerson was to have presented the paper by Richerson and Boyd, but he was unable to attend; in the workshop, the paper was summarized by Steve Kimbrough, a philosopher in the Department of Operations and Information Management of the Wharton School of Business. At the close of the workshop, the group invited Seyfarth and Dorothy Cheney to contribute a paper to the volume and, happily, they accepted.

The chapters were revised on the basis of the workshop discussions and, in some cases, additional written comments by discussants. Subsequently, the authors revised their chapters again in response to comments from two anonymous referees and from the volume editors. In these ways, the collaborative spirit of the workshop was carried into the editorial process.

In compiling the index for the volume, we have, as an aid to the reader, included brief glosses for some terms. In other cases, we have indicated where a term is defined or explained by a subheading under its index entry. The introductory chapter explains many of the important terms and concepts.

The editors are grateful to the Penn Museum International Research Conferences for funding the workshop and the production of the volume. Daniel Munoz-Hutchinson, a graduate student in philosophy, ably assisted in running the workshop. The initial editorial stages were overseen by Walda Metcalf, then Director of Publications at the Penn Museum. Jim Mathieu subsequently filled that role, and he arranged for the referees. As our editorial assistant, Victoria Carchidi did an excellent job in proofing the initial drafts and unifying the bibliography and system of referencing. Alistair Isaac was efficient and thorough in reading proof (and we acknowledge NSF grant 1028130 to the first editor in support of his work). Jennifer Quick ably saw the volume into print as copyeditor and designer. Lastly, our deepest thanks go to the participants themselves, who presented their research, and to the members of the Penn community who engaged in the memorable discussions that shaped the present volume.

GARY HATFIELD
HOLLY PITTMAN

Introduction: The Evolution of Mind, Brain, and Culture

GARY HATFIELD

Human beings possess tremendous capacities for passing on attitudes, skills, beliefs, and knowledge to others. These capacities extend not only to obviously human characteristics, such as the possession of syntactically complex languages and the absorption of complex belief systems. They are also present in the ability to imitate, on sight, the pattern of motion in a popular dance step, which sweeps the country in days. Or in the ability silently to discern the intention of a fellow carpenter in a home-improvement project and to move and hold a piece of lumber as needed. Together, these capacities and abilities have allowed human groups to spread across the globe while developing distinctive material and symbolic cultures. Manifestations of culture are everywhere: in six-inch platform heels, gothic tattoos, cummerbund and tails, hopscotch, jazz improvisations, evolution of mind conferences, and the subtle differences that make one painting worth millions and an identical-looking forgery—indistinguishable from the original to any but an expert eye—worth much less.

Many have held that the capacity to develop culture is distinctively human (e.g., Sahlins 1999). In recent years, this outlook has been challenged by claims that other animal species also possess cultural traditions that vary from group to group within the species. The proffered examples of such traditions include potato washing in certain troops of Japanese macaque monkeys (Watanabe 1994), variations in the use of ant and termite probes among distinct troops of chimpanzees (Boesch and Boesch 1990, Lonsdorf 2005), hand-sniffing in capuchin monkeys (Perry et al. 2003), whale songs

(Payne 1999), dolphin foraging traditions (Sargeant and Mann 2009), and tool use among corvids (New Caledonean crows, Hunt and Gray 2003). If culture is defined as socially transmitted, group-differential traditions within a species, then some nonhuman animals possess culture.

Nonetheless, human cultural processes and achievements remain distinctive. What, if anything, is unique about human cultures? How did the capacity for human culture evolve? In addressing these questions, we must draw on the techniques and findings of many disciplines: anthropology, psychology, philosophy, animal learning, evolutionary biology, neuroscience, genetics, environmental science, and Paleolithic archaeology. Our investigation must not only take the findings of these disciplines into account; it must also probe the framework within which the questions are posed. We need not only review basic findings about primate evolution, behavior, and cognition; we must also consider the concept of culture itself. In particular, we must ask whether the notion of culture as differential transmission that describes nonhuman animal traditions is adequate to human culture. We do this not out of a prior conviction that human culture must be unique, but from the empirical observation that human culture possesses distinctive characteristics that must be accounted for.

In investigating the evolution of culture, the chapters in this volume focus on the psychological or mental capacities (and their neural substrates) that make culture possible. Some species are better than others at imitating motor skills, at discerning the goal-directedness of others' behavior, at sharing attitudes and attention, or at perceiving social relations. Tracking the evolution of such differences is part of what is needed to better understand the origins of the ability for cultural transmission. Other capacities, including those for symbolic behavior, socially developed motivational norms, and socially created, all-encompassing webs of meaning, must be included in order to account for human culture (Chase 2006, Hill 2009, Perry 2009).

By way of introduction, in this chapter I survey some basic findings on primate evolution and the evolution of mind; examine socially transmitted traditions in relation to the concept of culture; recount the sources of evidence regarding the evolution of mind and culture; chart the history of evolutionary approaches to mind and behavior since Darwin; review several prominent theoretical syntheses concerning the evolution of the human mind and behavior; and, along the way, introduce the specific questions examined in the individual chapters.

THE HUMAN MIND IN EVOLUTIONARY PERSPECTIVE

Minds are remarkable, and in some ways mysterious. Everyone who reads this has a mind, but no one knows exactly what a mind is. The original *Oxford English Dictionary* (*OED*) defined a mind as "the system of cognitive and emotional phenomena and powers that constitutes the subjective being of a person" (Murray 1933, 6:461). This definition remains serviceable because it focuses on the functions of mind rather than its substantial character (as material or immaterial). In general terms, the cognitive functions include sense perception, learning, imagination, memory, motor capacities, and intellectual abilities such as classifying objects and events, recognizing dangerous or advantageous circumstances, planning how to obtain something, or, in the case of recent human beings, theoretical enterprises such as trying to understand what a mind is. The emotional phenomena mentioned in this definition must be understood broadly to include desires and other motivational states as well as feelings and other affective responses. This volume focuses primarily on cognitive abilities, but we do consider motivational and affective processes as well. Finally, the phrase "subjective being of a person" connotes a single unified consciousness in which cognitive and emotional phenomena come together.

The original *OED* definition restricted mindedness to persons, reflecting older beliefs that predominated prior to the 19th century but have since been challenged. The contributors to this volume accept that nonhuman animals have minds, even if they may not agree on which animals have minds or even on how that question might be decided. Some of the abilities noted so far, such as sense perception, learning, and behavioral guidance, are widely distributed among animals. Others, such as planning and unified consciousness, are more narrowly distributed, while certain abilities, such as the use of syntactically complex languages, the purposeful teaching of complex motor skills, or the pursuit of abstract theoretical reasoning and knowledge, are restricted to only one living instance, *Homo sapiens*.

Many factors come together to make a human mind. Each individual mind arises from biological capacities rooted in the brain, body, and environment, develops by learning the language and culture of its family and group, and manifests itself in a wide variety of psychological traits and behavioral patterns. We are interested in the basic, shared features of human mentality: the biologically based and culturally developed capacities that make human cognition unique. Our fundamental approach to understanding the human mind is comparative and evolutionary. We seek to understand the unique features of the human mind and its ancestors by comparing human psychology and behavior with the abilities of other anthropoid primates (monkeys and apes) and with previously existing members of the hominin line (our evolutionary ancestors and relatives after the ape-human split). This requires that we describe current human and anthropoid mental traits so as to compare them with each other and with the evidence that we have concerning the mental capacities of extinct ancestors.

In examining the origin of some basic features of anthropoid and specifically human psychology, we assume that these features have evolved—by which we mean, primarily, that they have undergone Darwinian natural selection.

Natural selection results from variation within the members of a species that is selectively transmitted and retained (Campbell 1965). It operates on heritable differences ("variation") among members of a population. If some members of the population possess genetically heritable traits that are better suited to the current environment, those members are expected, on average, to have better success at reproducing and to leave comparatively more descendants in the next generation than those lacking the trait. The variation occurs in genotypes and phenotypes: "genotype" refers to the genetic makeup of an individual; "phenotype" refers to the morphological and behavioral features of an individual that result as the genotype is expressed and develops in an environment. Variation may arise through genetic mutation and, in sexually reproducing populations, through genetic recombination during meiosis.

Genotypes that are selectively transmitted as a result of differential survival and reproduction yield changes in the phenotypes within the population over time. The relevant population may include all the members of a species or some subset that has become reproductively isolated (for whatever reasons). Evolutionary change by natural selection may alter the traits of a species or subspecies, or it may lead to the formation of new species, a process called "speciation."

Not all changes in genetic and phenotypic properties of a population over time result from natural selection; some arise by statistical chance, called "genetic drift." Because such changes initially are not selected, they may be neutral, beneficial, or harmful (and, in the latter two cases, may become subject to selection).

Many evolutionary thinkers call changes that are driven by natural selection "adaptations" because they better adapt successive generations to environmental conditions (Orzack and Sober 1994). A phenotypic trait becomes fixed in a population through natural selection because it adapts its possessors to the environment in a specific way. Such adaptations are characterized as performing a "function" that benefits their possessors. The function of a given anatomical or psychological trait is whatever the trait accomplishes that makes the organism "fitter" or more likely to survive and reproduce in a given environment than population members lacking the trait (Schwartz 2002, Walsh 1996).

A further factor in biological evolution is the effect that an animal population has on its environment. Called "niche construction," this factor has been receiving growing attention (Odling-Smee, Laland, and Feldman 2003). A standard example is earthworms, which have "kidneys" (nephridia) suited to a freshwater environment but live on land (or in land). They alter the soil in which they live so as to provide an environment that is more suited to their physiologies. Subsequent generations inherit the altered soil, not by genetic transmission, but by being born into it. This has been termed "ecological inheritance." It can take many forms. A beaver dam, used by subsequent generations of beavers, is an example. An abri, or rock overhang, inhabited by successive generations of early humans in France, is another. In such cases, the "selective retention" that defines natural selection arises from the population remaining in or otherwise interacting with the altered environment.

Characteristics of the population that are already in place constrain genetic evolution. The current characteristics of organisms in a population limit the variation that can arise in meiosis or through genetic mutation (Raff 1996: chap. 9). Too great a mutation may disrupt the developmental program that yields bodily structures; such mutations may be debilitating or lethal. Indeed, body plans are deeply conserved in the animal kingdom, through homologies (structures inherited from a common ancestor). Darwin (1859:434–50) referred to underlying similarities in structure among widely separated species, including limb structure, and to even deeper similarities among animal embryos. In recent decades, the field of evolutionary development has revealed that the genetic mechanisms underlying body plans and their expression during development are more deeply conserved than could have been imagined heretofore (e.g., Carroll, Grenier, and Weatherbee 2005).

Gary Hatfield

The evolutionary facts that are relevant to the development of anthropoid primates extend back to the origin of organic molecules and the first unicellular organisms, some 4 to 3.5 billion years ago (Fig. 1.1). The evolutionary pathway leads through the first multicellular animals (more than 600 million years ago, or mya); separation from the other major branch of animals, which includes mollusks, arthropods, and some worms (ca. 550 mya); the development of chordates (ca. 525 mya), with a dorsal nerve cord (nerve cord running along the back); the development of vertebrates (fish),

Era	Period	Epoch		mya	Some "Firsts"
			0		
		Holocene		0.006	First cities
			0.012	0.011	First farmers
	Quaternary			0.07–05	*Homo sapiens* spread from Africa
		Pleistocene		0.2	First *H. sapiens*
CENZOIC			1.7/ 2.58		
		Pliocene		2.6	Oldest known stone artifacts
			5.2		
		Miocene		7–5	First hominins (split from chimp-line)
			23.3		
	Tertiary	Oligocene		30–20	Apes distinct from Old World Monkeys
			34	50–45	First anthropoid primates
		Eocene		55	First primates of "modern aspect"
			56.5		
		Paleocene		65.5	First primates
			65.5	120	First placental mammals
MESO-ZOIC	Cretaceous			160	First birds
			145.5		
	Jurassic				
			199.5		
	Triassic			220	First mammals and dinosaurs
			251		
	Permian			320	Synapsids, or "mammal-like reptiles"
PALEOZOIC	Carboniferous		299		
			359.2		
	Devonian			370	First amphibians
			416		
	Silurian				
			443.7		
	Ordovician			518	First vertebrates (fish)
			488.3	525	First chordates
	Cambrian			550	Separation of ancestors of chordates from line of mollusks, arthropods
			542		
				800–600	First multicellular animals
PRECAMBRIAN				4–3.5 billion ya	First unicellular animals

1.1. Geologic ages. Evolution of some animal forms in relation to the geologic timescale (adapted and modified from Klein 2009: fig. 2.1; see also Gradstein et al. 2004, Walker et al. 2009). The more recent geologic epochs are discussed below in relation to hominin evolution. The table shows both the previously accepted date for the beginning of the Pleistocene (ca. 1.7 mya) as well as the newly accepted date of 2.58 mya, which was recently ratified by the International Union for Geologic Sciences based on the redating of a geologic marker for the start of a cooling trend (Gibbard and Head 2009). See Richerson and Boyd, this volume, for data on climatic variation.

with a spinal cord surrounded by segmented vertebrae (ca. 518 mya); and the further development of amphibians (ca. 370 mya), "mammal-like reptiles" (early synapsids, ca. 320 mya), and true mammals (ca. 220 to 120 mya, depending on the definition of "mammal"). The earliest primates, sometimes called "archaic primates" (Klein 2009:102), appeared at least 65 mya; primates of "modern aspect," which occurred in both lemur- or loris-like and tarsier-like forms, arose ca. 55 mya. Lemurs, lorises, tarsiers, and tree shrews are modern non-anthropoid primates.

It may seem as if these far-distant evolutionary events have little explanatory value in relation to the subsequently evolved anthropoid primates. Yet many aspects of the human form originated several hundred mya. Bilateral symmetry arose prior to separation from the line leading to mollusks and their relatives. The skeletal structures of vertebrates show deep homologies, from fish onward (Carroll, Grenier, and Weatherbee 2005). A long-noted example is the morphology of limb structure in tetrapods, or four-limbed creatures, including some fish and all amphibians, reptiles, birds, and mammals. The photosensitive pigments in the eyes of mammals may be descended from pigments in ancient green algae (Deininger, Fuhrmann, and Hegemann 2000). Binocular vision, which increases light sensitivity, contrast discrimination, and permits stereoscopic depth perception, evolved as early mammals adopted nocturnal, predatory lifestyles. Nocturnal visual predation may have been the driving force toward the increasingly frontal eye sockets found in primates (Heesy 2008). Nocturnal hunting is implicated in the evolution of binocular vision in owls (Pettigrew 1991), independently of mammals (a case of the convergent evolution of an analogous function).

A number of anatomical features distinguish primates from other mammals (Klein 2009). Many of these pertain to limb anatomy and related structures, including the preservation of the clavicle or collarbone, lost or modified in other mammals; the presence of grasping extremities (hands and feet) with five highly mobile digits, a distinct big toe, and an opposable thumb; and flattened nails replacing mammalian claws, with sensitive pads on the finger tips, equipped with friction-enhancing ridges (dermatoglyphs, i.e., fingerprints). Other distinguishing features pertain to head shape and the senses, including frontal eyes with elaborated eye sockets; a shortened muzzle, with a reduced sense of smell; and a characteristic bone structure in the middle ear. Primates have a reduced number of incisors and premolars compared with ancestral and many living mammals. Relative to body size, they tend to have larger brains than other mammals (which already tend to have relatively larger brains compared to non-mammals).

The anthropoid ancestors of monkeys, apes, and humans arose some 50–45 mya (see Fig. 1.2). Their teeth show a likely adaptation for a diet that includes nuts and fruit. They are quadripedal like their ancestors, but may also have walked on top of the branches in addition to leaping between them. As hominoid apes separated from Old World monkeys ca. 30–20 mya,

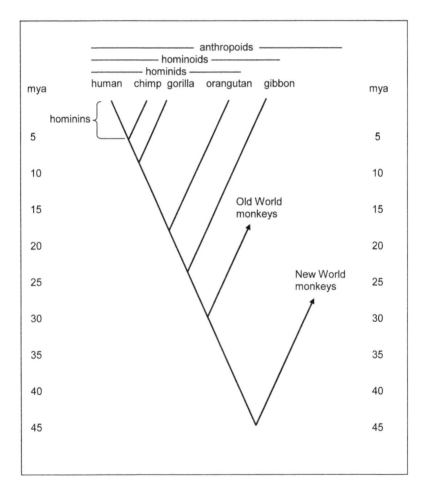

1.2. Branching of groups within the anthropoid primates (*Anthropoidea*). The dates of the branching become more tentative the farther back in time, but the order of branching is reasonably firm. The more recent branches within the hominins are shown in Figure 1.3.

the former continued to eat fruit and the latter specialized more on leaves. About 17–16 mya, some apes developed a more upright posture, greater shoulder mobility, and ability for hand-over-hand climbing. The still more upright-postured descendants of these apes provided the stock for the first hominin ancestors, who split with the line leading to chimpanzees and bonobos about 7–5 mya. A reduction in tree cover ca. 6 mya may have provided the impetus toward bipedalism in the first hominins (who are generically called australopiths).

The evolutionary lines related to modern humans have been redrawn in recent decades, to include more branchings than before. For present purposes, the main finding is that Neandertal is no longer regarded as a direct ancestor of *H. sapiens*. Generally, the taxonomy of the hominin line is a work in progress. In one current conception, shown in Figure 1.3, the primary line of descent runs from the australopiths to *H. habilis* (lived ca. 2.5–1.6 mya). The subsequent form, *H. erectus*, is characterized by modern body portions, a larger brain, and a fully terrestrial (vs. arboreal) life style. This ancestor is now sometimes divided to include an African form (*H. ergaster*, ca. 1.8–0.7 mya) from which Asian *H. erectus* evolved. The latter form lived until 100 thousand years ago (kya), or even later. *H. heidelbergensis* (arose ca. 600 kya) is now regarded as the common ancestor to *H. neanderthalensis* (ca. 400–28 kya in Eurasia) and *H. sapiens* (arose ca. 200 kya in Africa). Neandertals are sometimes divided into "early" and "classical," the latter extant from ca. 200 kya.

Once Neandertals are rendered as cousins rather than parents, the most widely accepted hypothesis is that *H. sapiens*, also called "anatomically modern humans" (AMH), arose in Africa ca. 200 kya and spread out from there about 50 kya (after an abortive entrance into the Levant ca. 100 kya). The hypothesis of a single African origin for AMH has replaced the multiregional hypothesis, according to which various populations of *H. sapiens* evolved separately and in parallel from local populations on different continents (from Neandertal in Europe and from distinct populations of *H. erectus* in Africa and Asia). In the single-origin scenario, as AMH spread into Europe and Asia they replaced Neandertal and *H. erectus* by causing their extinction and perhaps to some extent by absorbing them through interbreeding. The evidence for a single African origin includes fossils, artifact traditions, and genetic sampling. (See Schurr, this volume, on bipedalism, geographic dispersal, dietary changes, brain size, genetic evidence, and taxonomy in hominin evolution; see Klein 2009:714–21 on claims for an early arrival for AMH in

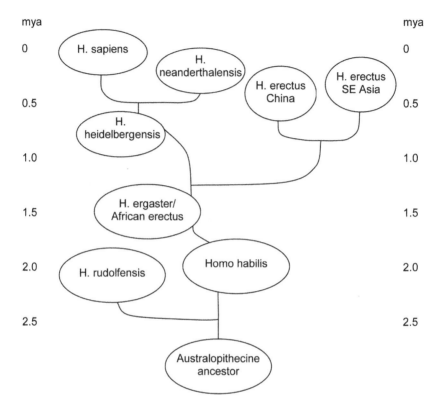

1.3. The evolution and branching of the genus *Homo* in the hominin line, starting from an australopithecine hominin ancestor (pre-*Homo*). Recent work suggests that *H. heidelbergensis* is the common ancestor of Neandertal and *H. sapiens. H. rudolfensis* may be a distinct species from *H. habilis* (see Klein 2009: chap. 4).

Australia, ca. 60 kya, requiring an earlier dispersal from Africa.)

By 2.6 mya, hominins were fashioning stone tools (Semaw 2000). The sequential development of stone toolkits, or "industries," over the subsequent 100s of millennia provides an important source of evidence for behavioral development. Over time, the toolkits show greater elaboration and precision of manufacturing technique. The earliest industry is the Oldowan, which consists of pebbles from which flakes have been removed and the flakes themselves. This toolkit, illustrated in Figure 1.4A, was present from 2.6 mya to 1.7–1.6 mya, and underwent little change during that period. It is associated with *H. habilis* (and perhaps with *Paranthropus robustus*, see Klein

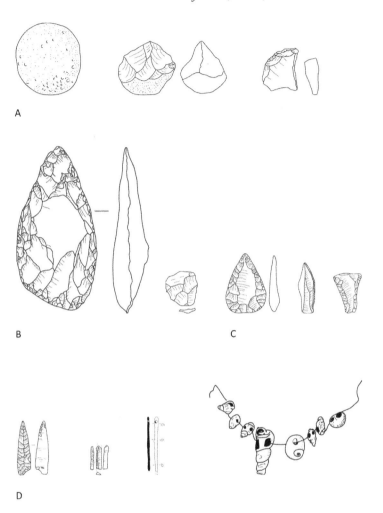

A

B

C

D

1.4. Examples of various artifact industries: (A) The Oldowan, showing a hammerstone, a bifacial chopper, and a flake scraper; the industry consists largely of pebbles from which flakes have been removed, and the flakes themselves. (B) The Acheulean, showing a bifacially symmetrical handax and a core with a Levallois flake (a late Acheulean technique); the industry includes a variety of axes, choppers, scrapers, and points. (C) The Mousterian, showing a Mousterian point, a double biconcave sidescraper, and a backed knife; the industry includes a variety of points, scrapers, borers, and backed knives, with great use of the Levallois method and frequent instances of retouch. (D) The LSA/UP, showing a shouldered point, some beads, and some backed microblades; the various LSA/UP industries include fine blade technology, many bone, ivory, and antler artifacts, and items of personal adornment. For a survey of the various industries and regional variations, see Klein 2009, chs. 4–7. (Artifacts redrawn from Klein 2009: Figs. 4.51, 5.51, 6.35, 7.10–7.11.)

2009:260). About 1.7–1.6 mya, the Acheulean industry appeared, which is best known for its bifacially symmetrical handaxes, although it included other forms (Fig. 1.4B). The Acheulean toolkit is associated with *H. erectus* (a.k.a. *H. ergaster*). A later and more refined version of the Acheulean, which used prepared cores to produce flakes of a desired size and shape (the "Levallois" technique), is perhaps associated with *H. heidelbergensis* (Klein 2009:379). These two industries, when found in sub-Saharan Africa, are termed Earlier Stone Age (ESA); in Eurasia and North Africa, they are termed Lower Paleolithic (LP). (Prehistoric archaeological periods are not defined by dates but by artifact types, which may then be dated using chronometric methods, such as radiopotassium or radiocarbon; consequently, period dates can change and can vary by region.)

About 250–200 kya, the Middle Paleolithic (MP) and Middle Stone Age (MSA) industries appeared. In Eurasia and Northern Africa, the MP industry is often called "Mousterian." The MP and similar MSA industries are associated in Europe and the Levant with Neandertal and in Africa with *H. sapiens* and its immediate ancestor. The MP and MSA are characterized by the use of prepared cores from which useable flakes are removed sequentially. The industries vary from region to region, and include triangular and elongated points, various scrapers, and some elongated flakes or blades. Some show "retouch," in which the cutting edge is sharpened, and "backing," in which an edge is dulled, presumably to allow a finger hold (Fig. 1.4C). Some points were hafted to wooden shafts.

Finally, Later Stone Age (LSA) and Upper Paleolithic (UP) industries appeared after 50 kya. LSA begins in sub-Saharan Africa ca. 50–45 kya and the UP in Northern Africa and Eurasia ca. 45–36 kya. LSA / UP artifacts are characterized by thin blade technology, finer and more standardized stone tools, the regular use of bone, ivory, and antler, and the unquestioned production of art and items of personal adornment (Fig. 1.4D). Some theorists hold that transition to the LSA / UP marks a "revolution" or "cultural explosion" that indicates the rise of "fully modern" humans (Coolidge and Wynn 2009; Klein 2009: chaps. 6–8; Mithen 1996)—or, on more recent data, that the revolution occurred earlier, ca. 70 kya (Mithen, this volume). Others maintain that LSA / UP-like material was produced significantly prior to 45 kya by AMH and after 45 kya by Neandertals (Nowell, this volume; for an overview, Klein 2009: chap. 6). The existence of fine blades, symbolic forms, and items of personal adornment across an earlier period and also associated with Neandertals argues against a revolutionary origin for fully modern humans and in favor of a gradualist account of the rise of AMH cultural patterns (Chase 2006, Gamble 2007, McBrearty and Brooks 2000).

Changes in limb structure, sensory systems, living environment (arboreal or savannah), diet (herbivorous, insectivorous, carnivorous), relative brain size, and tool use all have implications for the evolution of mind. An animal that takes to the trees requires the motor coordination and visual capacity to move from limb to limb. An animal that walks upright and uses its hands to make stone tools must have achieved new kinds of motor control. An animal that can learn stone toolmaking from a conspecific (or near taxonomic relative) requires further sensorimotor and cognitive changes. In addition, the demands of troop social life, characteristic of anthropoids, require cognitive skills that may have prepared the way for some of these other changes. Or so it has been argued, as we will find in subsequent references to other chapters in this volume.

SOCIAL TRANSMISSION AND THE CONCEPT OF CULTURE

Another potential source of change in the behavioral profile of a population over time is the cultural transmission of behavioral patterns and cognitive attitudes from one generation to another. Such transmission is extra-genetic: it relies on social transmission from the individuals in one generation to those of another. A prime example is the transmission of the attitudes and behavioral patterns that constitute human culture. The acquisition of a culture depends on cultural setting, not genes: infants that are adopted across cultural boundaries grow up speaking the language and sharing the customs of their adoptive parents. Changes in culture over time are thought of as cultural evolution.

Some of the causal mechanisms of cultural evolution can be compared to natural selection. In this analogy, the notion of variation with selective retention is applied to cognition and behavior (Campbell 1965, Mesoudi, Whiten, and Laland 2004). Innovations that are advantageous in a given environment and that are socially transmitted because they are advantageous are more heavily represented in the next generation. Some theorists speak of a "dual inheritance" system, genetic and cultural, for species that show differential social transmission (Richerson and Boyd 2005). Cultural evolution can yield significant changes in behavior in the absence of biological evolution (beyond the capacities underlying cultural transmission). Such changes need not be biologically adaptive; as a result of fads, fashions, or random variation (Bentley 2007), attitudes and behaviors may spread through a population that either have no effect on survival or that actually reduce the fitness of the members of a population. Further, cultural change can arise through processes of conscious decision making or "guided variation" (Richerson and Boyd 2005:69). Not all cultural evolution need be driven by (nongenetic) natural selection.

Although culture previously was viewed as the specific preserve of humans (with animal traditions labeled as "protoculture"—e.g., Gerard and Veith 1960:197), in recent decades numerous investigators claim to find culture proper in nonhuman animals (Bonner 1980 is an early instance). This extension of the notion of culture has met with both enthusiasm and skepticism. Some find the extension obvious, others view it as unwarranted (the contributions to Laland and Galef 2009 provide an overview).

The underlying disagreements are both empirical and conceptual. Investigators disagree over the extent that social transmission is found in the animal kingdom, and also over its consequences for the concept of culture (Galef 1992, 2009). Some find that social transmission is a very common phenomenon and that any group-distinctive behavior created by such transmission counts as culture. Accordingly, fish that are translocated from one population to another and then follow the schooling sites, migration routes, and mating sites of their new group exhibit "culture" (reviewed by Laland, Kendal, and Kendal 2009:190). Other theorists distinguish various forms of social learning and animal tradition, calibrating various concepts of culture accordingly (Boesch and Tomasello 1998, Whiten and van Schaik 2007).

In distinguishing forms of social learning, let us consider behavior that arises in relation to a model instance, since this type of transmission has been emphasized in previous discussions. Such socially aided learning is classified into four types, according to the cognitive interaction between model and learner. In the first type, the actions of the model simply draw the attention of the learner to the environmental elements that can be used to achieve a desired outcome. This is called "social enhancement" (Galef 1996), or sometimes "local enhancement" (Thorpe 1963:134) or "social facilitation" (Zajonc 1965). It does not imply a tendency or a desire to imitate the actions of the model; rather, the learner has its perceptual attention drawn to environmental circumstances and then, on the basis of its own individual learning capacity, sees (e.g.) that food can be obtained in a certain location. Tomasello (1999:26–28) suggests that potato washing in Japanese macaques may result from such a process, which he terms "stimulus enhancement." A second form involves a desire to "emulate" the effect of the behavior: one chimp can see that another has attained food using a stick and seeks to use the stick to achieve the same outcome, but without copying the exact motor procedures—the sequence of movements—that produces it. A third form of social learning involves copying the precise motor procedures; this is called true "imitation" (Whiten, Horner, and Marshall-Pescini 2004). A fourth form involves active intervention on the part of a teacher in order to improve the performance of the learner. This is called "active teaching" or "intentional instruction" (Kruger and Tomasello 1996).

Culture is ascribed to nonhuman animals (hereafter, "animals") either on grounds of behavioral differences alone or in connection with evidence for particular types of social learning. In either case, the attribution depends on the concept of culture that is applied. This has led to extensive discussions of the concept of culture and its proper definition.

The attribution of culture to animals may start from observations that some populations exhibit distinctive behaviors in comparison with other populations of the same species. However, such differences need not arise from cultural transmission, but may reflect genetic or ecological differences. For example, different feeding practices may be due to innately specified preferences in genetic subpopulations or to ecological differences in food availability. But the differences may also arise through social transmission; for example, when one or more members of a local population hit upon a way of cracking nuts with stones or of dipping ants with twigs that is passed on through social learning to become a "tradition" in that population (Avital and Jablonka 2000, Fragaszy and Perry 2003). Evidence of socially transmitted traditions has been found in birds, dolphins, whales, and anthropoid primates, among others. Some instances have been challenged by arguing that genetic and ecological factors have not been ruled out (Galef 1992, 2009). Recent findings suggest that in the celebrated case of tool use among New Caledonian crows, a genetically inherited action pattern is involved (Kenward et al. 2006) and ecological factors (foraging niches) may also play a role (Hunt and Gray 2007). Nonetheless, social transmission may remain as a further cause of variation. In any event, at least some animal behaviors do arise from social transmission rather than from genetic or ecological factors.

How are these discussions relevant to the evolution of mind, brain, and culture in humans? Our interest in this volume is primarily in the evolution of human cognitive capacities, including the capacity for complex human culture. We want to know what makes humans distinct in their ability to develop and transmit culture, and how these distinctive traits have arisen in the hominin, anthropoid, or mammalian lines. For this purpose, a comparative perspective is of great use. The comparisons must extend to both similarities and differences between human and nonhuman abilities and patterns of behavior. A framework of description that extends to nonhuman social transmission can provide a benchmark for what is the same and what is different in the human case.

Consider the control of motor function in human beings. A person can stand in front of a group and go through a multi-step dance routine, involving five or six moves. Most if not all persons in the group will be able to repeat this sequence on their first try and in the correct order of steps. On the part of the leader, this action involves planning the sequence before or as it is executed. The imitators must then recognize each part of the routine as it is performed, remember the order, and then execute and monitor their own performances. Human beings find it easy to imitate motor sequences. Whether chimps and other apes engage in true imitation is controversial (Call, Carpenter, and Tomasello 2005, Whiten, Horner, and Marshall-Pescini 2004). There is agreement, however, that chimps and other apes focus more on outcomes than on imitating motor procedures. As we will see, some theorists believe that the human ability to think about, plan, and control complex motor sequences is a key difference between human beings and our distant hominin ancestors as well as our living anthropoid relatives.

The ability to transmit improvements in complex skills marks a difference between chimp and human traditions of tool use. Chimps do not regularly notice and transmit improvements in tool design. If a human being discovers a better widget, the discovery need not be lost to the next generation. The discoverer can teach the technique to his or her compatriots. Improvements can be cumulative. Tomasello (1990) has termed this aspect of social learning the "ratchet effect." Although some (disputed) cases of ratcheting are reported in ape learning (McGrew 2004), so far as is known humans alone exhibit ongoing and widespread instances of the effect. In Tomasello's view (1999, Tomasello, Kruger, and Ratner 1993), ratcheting is central to the human ability to develop complex culture.

Among living primate species, the teaching and learning of complex techniques and knowledge schemes is distinctively human (Kruger and Tomasello 1996). The cumulative acquisition of improvements in hunting, cooking, tool-design, knowledge of plants and animals, and use of natural materials is a hallmark of human culture, eventually resulting in agriculture, city-building, and complex societies. The advances in agriculture and in building techniques have allowed human beings to alter their environments in dramatic (and in some cases ultimately detrimental) ways so as to permit human beings to inhabit the far reaches of the earth, from tropical climes to arctic cold.

Culture is a product and a facilitator of the human ability to cooperate. Other animals, including wolves and chimps, cooperate in chasing prey or enemies (Mech 1970, Watts and Mitani 2002). But they do not form complex plans for cooperative hunts. Modern human foragers use game drives to collect and kill large number of animals. Such drives require elaborate coordination and adjustments (Blehr 1990). Archaeological evidence shows that MP Neandertals (Scott 1980) and MSA *H. sapiens* (Klein and Cruz-Uribe 1996) engaged in such drives. It has been argued that such coordinated hunts require some form of language (Chase 2006:115).

Linguistic ability is a boon for human cooperation. However, it is not plausible that cooperation springs from language. Rather, it is more likely that cooperation evolved first in the hominin line and syntactically complex language came second (see Gärdenfors, this volume). Syntactically complex language is unique to humans. While many animals communicate via calls (Cheney and Seyfarth 2007: chaps. 10–11) and birdsong may possess basic syntax (Balaban 1988), no other living animal is known to acquire complex language in its natural environment. More generally, no other living animal is known to exhibit culturally acquired collective schemes of thought that define their world.

In studying the evolution of human culture, we need a culture concept that distinguishes various types of culture and cultural transmission. In the literature on animal culture, proposed definitions abound. Some offer a single comprehensive definition of culture, based on differential social transmission alone (Laland and Hoppitt 2003). Others distinguish different levels or types of culture, which is a more useful approach for studying the evolution of cultural abilities, since the resulting taxonomy reflects the unique aspects of human culture.

Whiten (2009) distinguishes four different levels of social and cultural transfer: mere social information transfer; formation of traditions; groups having multiple traditions; and cumulative culture, involving the ratchet effect (also Whiten and van Schaik 2007). Social information transfer is widespread, as when mother mice take their pups on a specific route to a grain bag, and they learn the way (Avital and Jablonka 2000:105–7). Traditions may arise in populations, as with potato washing or bird songs. Whiten does not think that a short-term behavioral change or the transmission of a single tradition warrants the term "culture." He restricts that term to groups with multiple group-distinctive traditions, such as Whiten et al. (1999) report in chimpanzees (they identified 39 variant traditions, including tool usage, grooming, and courtship). Finally, the fourth level is cumulative culture, which involves the acquisition, transmission, and retention of improvements to techniques and implements over time (the ratchet effect).

Whiten's distinction among various sorts of social transmission is useful because it distinguishes cumulative culture from other instances of tradition. Whiten (2009:120) believes that cumulative culture is distinctively human. Nonetheless, his distinctions are not sufficiently fine-grained for our purposes. Human culture is not merely the accumulation of improved techniques. It also involves shared meaning and culturally created systems of motivation. The various schemes of human culture determine which proffered foods can actually be eaten, which individuals are allowable mates, what sorts of dwellings are acceptable, what an eclipse of the moon means, and much more. An account of the evolution of the human capacity for culture must seek the origin of shared symbolism, culture-specific motivation, and all-encompassing systems of meaning (Chase 2006, Hill 2009, Perry 2009). Even accounting for these might not be sufficient, since human cultures also have developed the ability to store symbolic codes materially, in the form of images, writing, and electronic symbols, enabling new forms of cognition (Donald 1991). The ability for and the effects of external symbolic storage must also be accounted for.

Other animals do exhibit behavioral patterns that are like human behaviors. Some animals change their environments to their benefit (think of beavers' dams, birds' nests, and ants' trails); some animals use calls to warn or otherwise inform conspecifics; some animals use tools; some animals cooperate in the hunt. But human beings mold their environments more profoundly, improve their tools through cultural transmission, engage in social cooperation, develop cultural categories and conceptions of the world, and pass on systems of belief and knowledge in unprecedented ways.

EVIDENCE FOR THE EVOLUTION OF MIND, BRAIN, AND CULTURE

Efforts to trace the evolution of cognitive abilities in the hominin line must seek to describe changes in basic cognitive abilities in now extinct human ancestors. What sorts of evidence could be available for such an undertaking? Minds themselves leave no fossil remains—although some skulls, which housed the brains that supported the minds, have survived. Minds express themselves in behavior, and patterns of behavior can be inferred from archaeological evidence of habitation, hunting, butchering, toolmaking, tool use, and symbolic acts. Further, a baseline from which hominins evolved can be inferred from the cognitive capacities of our living anthropoid relatives, the monkeys and apes. The neural bases of such capacities can be studied comparatively. The lifeways of current human populations who live in the bush and survive by hunting and gathering (or who did so in previous centuries) provide a comparison for interpreting the lifeways of ancestral hunters and gatherers. Environmental science charts changes over millions of years, revealing patterns of climate change during hominin evolution. Finally, genetic techniques allow investigators a further source of evidence for relations among monkeys, apes, Neandertals, and humans, as well as a means for estimating the age of significant genetic alterations.

The interpretation of archaeological, genetic, paleontological, environmental, neuroscientific, and psychological data draws on techniques and theories across the sciences. Investigation into the evolution of mind must therefore call upon and synthesize results from various disciplines, as when it seeks to link genetic structure to brain function and to behavior, or to infer cognitive changes from changes in toolmaking or hunting practices. The chapters in this volume exhibit the full spectrum of these methods and results. It may be helpful to illustrate some of them here.

Using new genetic techniques for assessing how various species are related, the family tree for apes and humans has been redrawn (Pilbeam and Young 2004). Comparison of human, chimp, and other anthropoid DNA resulted in reclassifying the great apes and humans into the same family, distinct at this level from the lesser apes (gibbons and siamangs). This led to the proposal (followed herein) to expand the term "hominid" to include great apes (orangutan, gorilla, and chimp) and humans, to place humans and chimps together in a subfamily, and to call the specifically human lineage "hominins" (see Klein 2009:71–75). These techniques use the "molecular clock," which assumes that the genetic material of species that share a common ancestor changes at a constant rate for each species after their separation. This technique can be applied to nuclear DNA or to mitochondrial DNA (mtDNA), the latter inherited from mothers in cellular material outside the nucleus. Comparison of mtDNA in human and Neandertal specimens, together with additional fossil evidence, resulted in the out-of-Africa hypothesis for human origins described above, as well as the acceptance of Neandertal as a related rather than directly ancestral species (Stringer 2002).

In addition to providing assessments of relatedness and estimates of time-since-separation, genetic evidence is used to infer the timeframe for functional differences among separated species. Because of its role in the genetic control of brain development, great attention has been paid to estimating how and when a variant of a gene that causes microcephaly (MCPH1) entered the human line. Similarly, because of its role in speech pathology in modern humans, the timeframe for changes in the forkhead-box P2 (FOXP2) gene has been of great interest. The issues and assumptions involved in using genetic change to infer functional change are intricate, as are those involved in using the molecular clock more generally; the chapters by Schurr and Hey (this volume) provide complementary discussions of the relevant methodologies. Schurr reviews a variety of genetic techniques, including chimp-human genetic comparisons, surveying the implications for taxonomy and for the development of specific human functions. Hey provides a tutorial on the logic for inferring function from genetic change, including a discussion of the MCPH1 and FOXP2 genes.

The molecular clock is checked and calibrated in relation to other established and newly found dating methods. Geological dating provides the basic temporal frame for evolution. It is, in the first instance, organized into periods based on the relation between levels or strata in the Earth's crust. The strata define a relative time scale, and chronological ages are provided by other methods of dating. The numerical dates are therefore subject to revision. For hominin evolution, the relevant geologic epochs are the Miocene (ca. 23.3–5.2 mya), Pliocene (ca. 5.2–2.58 mya), Pleistocene (ca. 2.58 mya to 12 kya), and Holocene (from 12 kya). Until recently, the beginning of the Pleistocene was dated at 1.7 mya; in this previous dating scheme, the epoch was further divided into Lower (ca 1.7 mya to 780 kya), Middle (ca. 780–127 kya), and Upper (ca. 127–10 kya). (On the newly accepted earlier boundary for the Pliocene/Pleistocene transition, see Fig. 1.1.)

Climate and vegetation varied during these periods. The Miocene was on average warmer than subsequent periods. The later Miocene saw cooling and the formation of polar ice in Antarctica with an expansion of grasslands ca. 7–6 mya. On average, climate continued to cool during the Pliocene, becoming drier and seasonal, the Arctic ice cap and the Greenland glacier formed, the sea level fell, and deserts formed in Asia and Africa. The continents largely took on their present positions, with a land bridge exposed between Siberia and Alaska. The Pleistocene saw repeated glaciations and retreats, extending well into Europe at their peaks. The last ice age marks the end of the Pleistocene, after which climate stabilized in the Holocene. On climate change and measurements of temperature, see Richerson and Boyd (this volume); on techniques for determining the ages of inorganic and organic materials, see Klein (2009: chap. 2).

Stone tools are the oldest surviving type of human artifact, and they provide the most persistent source of evidence for human behavioral change throughout the Paleolithic ("old stone") era, which runs from 2.6 mya (pending discoveries of still earlier tools) to 12 kya. Prior to the beginning of the UP (after 45 kya), stone tools, bones (of human ancestors and animals), and (more recently) fire sites (or "hearths") are the primary sources of evidence. These sources of data have proven to be surprisingly rich as interpreted through archaeological and paleoanthropological methods. Archaeologists have not been content simply to classify stone tools by shape and potential function (as in Oldowan, Acheulean, Mousterian, and so on). In some sites, they have been able to glean information about the process of toolmaking, by examining discarded flakes and also by fitting flaked tools back into the their original cores (Andrefsky 2009). Further, by seeking to recreate the tools themselves, they have learned much about the motor and cognitive skills that go into knapping (see Roux and Bril 2005).

The re-creation of knapping techniques also supports comparative neuroscientific investigation of the brain areas active during toolmaking. By comparing brain activity of a macaque monkey perceiving and manipulating objects with the brain areas activated when humans make Oldowan and Acheulean tools, investigators can explore whether early toolmaking draws upon areas of the brain that expanded in hominin evolution or instead on development in areas for the sensorimotor control of object-directed actions that are homologous in monkeys. Initial results suggest that for the Oldowan industry, the relevant areas of activation occur in the premotor areas homologous to monkey areas rather than in the posterior parietal and prefrontal areas associated with cognitive functions, and that both the homologous premotor areas and the expanded parietal and prefrontal areas are involved in the Acheulean industry (see Chaminade, this volume).

Patterns of brain expansion in the hominin line are established through comparison of human brains with present-day monkey and ape brains, and through endocasts (both fossil and modern) showing the interior shape of various fossil skulls. I have already mentioned the trend toward encephalization, which is measured by brain size in relation to body size. Endocasts allow paleoneurologists to chart changes in the shape of the brain, including the relative location of sulcuses, or major creases in the exterior surface of the brain. In the course of hominin brain evolution, the relations among the occipital, parietal, temporal, and frontal regions of the brain have changed, with a decrease in the occipital lobe in *H. sapiens* and a comparative increase in the frontal and parietal areas (see Holloway 1999, and Chaminade, Chase, and Nowell, this volume).

Habitation and hunting patterns can also be inferred from the patterning of stones, bones, and hearths. The practice of game driving, previously mentioned, was inferred from bone collections found at the foot of cliffs. The age profile of the animals provides evidence for large-scale game drives in which an entire herd suffers a "catastrophic" death, by contrast with bones accumulated over time through isolated hunting by "attrition." A herd of animals that is killed all at once should exhibit young animals and adults in their prime, with older animals more scarce (Klein, Allwarden, and Wolf 1983).

Paleoanthropologists assess evidence of human occupation for patterns that would indicate the existence of "home bases" around which a group organizes its subsistence activities. The interpretation of the evidence remains controversial, with some arguing that *H. habilis* used home bases, others questioning the evidence, and others wondering how distinct such a behavior is from that of anthropoid primate groups that recongregate in the same sleeping areas each night (Chase 2006:112–14; Isaac 1983, Potts 1987). These arguments depend in part on comparisons with habitation patterns known from recent ethnographic study. Ethnographic comparisons have also been applied to the interaction between Neandertals and invading AMH (O'Connell 2006) and to the social organization of comparatively high-density UP populations (e.g., Richerson and Boyd, this volume).

The archaeological record provides evidence of changing human behavior patterns over time, and these changes may in turn provide evidence for evolving human cognitive abilities and brain structures. The reasoning that infers cognitive and neural evolution cuts across disciplines. A necessary condition for such reasoning is a description of current human psychology and neural structure. Psychology, cognitive science, and neuroscience are working on this characterization, which is far from complete. Evolutionary thinkers apply current theories of mind to the cognitive features of human mentality that are thought to make us distinctively human or that permit the development of human culture (Carruthers, Donald, and Mithen, this volume). Some theorists use the archaeological and paleoneurological evidence to propose developmental sequences for human cognitive capacities over time (Chase, Donald, Gärdenfors, and Mithen, this volume).

A further point of reference for cognitive evolution in humans is provided by a comparison between human and monkey or ape psychology. Chimp behavior may provide a window into the psychology of the last common ancestor shared by chimps and humans (hominins), some 7 mya. Abilities that humans have but chimps lack presumably were also lacking in the last common ancestor. Only presumably, because chimps have also undergone evolutionary change in the past 7 my (indeed, more changes than humans according to genetic measures; see Hey, this volume), and they could have lost traits that were possessed by the common ancestor. Warneken (this volume) examines differences in helping behavior between chimps and human children and finds that only human children share the intentions of the other.

Some check on the relation between chimp and human psychology is provided by expanding the comparison to include other apes and also monkeys. If a trait is found in gorillas and humans, but not chimps, the most likely explanation is that this trait existed in the hominid (great ape and human) line and was lost by chimps but retained by humans. Again, the inference is not certain, because gorillas and humans may have evolved the trait independently. Nonetheless, comparisons among human, chimp, and other anthropoid (or even mammalian) psychologies provides a framework for isolating the new cognitive mechanisms found in humans. The association of the new cognitive mechanisms with comparatively expanded brain regions in hominins can also support the attribution of human novelty (see Chase, Chaminade, Hey, and Schurr, this volume).

In recent years the discovery of "mirror neurons"—neurons that fire not only when one performs a motor action, but also when one observes that action in another—has seemed to reveal a basis for the learning of motor skills as well as for mindreading and social cognition in anthropoid primates, including humans. In this volume, Chaminade reviews the neuroscientific evidence for mirror neurons in humans and monkeys. He also seeks to make the notion of a mirror neuron more precise. Drawing on brain imaging studies of human motor activity and perception and direct recording from the cortex of behaving monkeys, he concludes that in order to explain various phenomena of social cognition and the teaching and learning of tool use, there is no need to posit innately specified mirror neurons. Instead, he invokes the more general phenomenon of cognitive and neural resonance to explain how we (or monkeys) might learn to respond to motor actions and social attitudes in others.

Seyfarth and Cheney (this volume) examine evidence for social cognition in baboons. They report experiments on baboon social perception in the wild, which rely on carefully recording calls that occur during baboon interactions. Using a system of speakers, investigators play back combinations of sounds that should, if baboons have a detailed cognitive ordering of social dominance relations, either be surprising or unsurprising to individual baboons. By noting responses to surprising and unsurprising combinations, the experimenters establish that baboons have extensive knowledge of dominance and familial relations which they apply perceptually. Seyfarth and Cheney conclude that baboons possess conceptual knowledge that is representational, categorically discrete, hierarchically structured, rule-governed and open-ended, quasi-propositional, and independent of sensory modality. Structured social knowledge of this type, which probably is present across the anthropoid primates, might serve as a basis for the evolution of hominin linguistic abilities; that is, they suggest that linguistic ability evolved from nonlinguistic social cognition. In Cheney and Seyfarth (2007), they speculate that abilities originally supportive of social cognition enabled homonoid primate and specifically chimp tool-using abilities, and that further selection of these tool-using abilities was the basis for hominin cognitive evolution.

What, if anything, do these various bodies of evidence, from a diversity of disciplines, *dictate* about the evolution of mind, brain, and culture? Not much. In order to develop an account of the evolution of mind, brain, and culture, this evidence, which typically is already the product of interpretation within its home discipline, must be further interpreted in a synthetic manner. Several of the most prominent theoretical syntheses are represented in this volume. The theoretical viewpoints show disagreements and divergences. Some theorists find a few central evolutionary developments, in motor coordination, representation, and planning, to be fundamental (Donald, this volume). Others think that the basic human adaptation is for mindreading and shared intentions (Tomasello 2000b; represented by Warneken in this volume). Others find that the evolution of human mentality arises from the development of a plurality of distinct cognitive abilities in concert, such as mindreading, language, creativity, fine motor coordination, innate physical conceptions, new inferential abilities, and norms for cooperation (Carruthers). Still others see human evolution as consisting first in the evolution of innate "intelligences"—technical, linguistic, social, and for local natural history—among earlier hominins, with *H. sapiens* becoming distinct by evolving "cognitive fluidity" among these intelligences (Mithen).

Considering the interpretive difficulties surrounding the sources of evidence, and faced with the theoretical diversity just scouted, one might conclude that it is too soon to seek synthetic accounts of the evolution of human cognitive and cultural capacities. However, acting on such doubts would make it less likely that an adequate account of that evolution would ever be obtained. It is the business of science to go beyond the data. This is trivially true in the sense that some sciences seek to determine universal constants, such as boiling points or specific heats, on the basis of finite numbers of measurements; they make an inductive leap from finite data to universal statements. Nontrivially, theoretical frameworks that go beyond the data are used to interpret that data and may suggest new questions for empirical testing. Leaps beyond current viewpoints are not trivial at all, as when new theoretical outlooks and syntheses are proposed. Successful leaps become legendary, as with Newton, Darwin, and Einstein. At all levels of ongoing science, progress demands a steady diet of theoretical proposals.

Data remain largely mute and meaningless without theoretical interpretation. Because Einstein proposed his general theory of relativity, astronomers could look for evidence to confirm or disconfirm it. Without his proposal (or a related one), there would be no reason to look for the evidence of stellar shift. Even incorrect theories can serve to organize data and guide its collection; Newton's theory of absolute space and time, which proved to be incorrect, provided the framework of theory and data from which Einstein began. Isaac's (1976) proposal of early hominin home bases, though controversial, stimulated an elaboration of the evidential profiles that would be required to infer their presence (Potts 1987).

Faced with theoretical diversity concerning the evolution of mind and culture, what shall we do? We should encourage a variety of integrative approaches that respond to as broad a swathe of the evidence as is feasible. In this volume we have favored work that is rigorously comparative or that includes archaeological, paleontological, and environmental evidence interpreted from biological, cognitive, and anthropological perspectives. By way of background to the theories that are discussed in the subsequent chapters, I survey the history of evolutionary approaches to mind and behavior and then sample some recent approaches.

EVOLUTIONARY APPROACHES TO MIND AND BEHAVIOR SINCE DARWIN

From the beginning, Darwin applied his theory of "descent with modification" to the "mental qualities." In early drafts and in the *Origin* itself, Darwin used the evolution of instincts as his primary example of a mental quality (1842[1909]: Pt. 1, sec. 3; 1844[1909]: chap. 3; 1859: chap. 7). In the conclusion of the *Origin*, he foresaw extension of his theory to human origins (which he had already begun) and the remaking of psychological theory:

> In the distant future I see open fields for more important researches. Psychology will be based on a new foundation, that of the necessary acquirement of each mental power and capacity by gradation. Light will be thrown on the origin of man and his history. (1859:488)

Subsequently, he published *The Descent of Man* (1871) and *The Expression of the Emotions in Man and Animals* (1872), each of which examined mental faculties and qualities in human and nonhuman animals, and argued for the gradual development of human mentality from ancestral primates.

Darwin's call for an evolutionary psychology was taken up in subsequent decades. Hiram Stanley pursued a (rather notional) account of the emotions in his *Evolutionary Psychology of Feeling* (1895). In England and America, Frances Galton, George Romanes, C. Lloyd Morgan, William James, John Dewey, and James Mark Baldwin pursued the implications of Darwin's theory for the evolution of mind and its application within psychology. Romanes (1889) and Morgan (1894:ix) developed a "comparative psychology" for studying "mental" or "psychical" evolution. The evolutionary outlook of James entered American psychology through the functionalism of James R. Angell and Harvey Carr (Wagner and Owens 1992). Dewey (1894, 1895) held that Darwin's conception of emotion required adjustment in light of James's theories. The behaviorist J.B. Watson was initially enthusiastic about instinct and evolutionary explanation, but he subsequently came to emphasize learning and environmental factors over instinct and evolution. This outlook characterized mainstream American behaviorism, which therefore did not emphasize evolutionary considerations (Boakes 1984: chap. 8; Richards 1987:505–9).

Perhaps ironically, in Watson's home field of comparative psychology evolutionary considerations were prominently invoked throughout the 20th century (Warden, Jenkins, and Warner 1934, Stone 1943; see Dewsbury 1984:235–38, 334–35), sometimes from a cognitive or mentalistic viewpoint (Köhler 1925, Tolman 1932).

In 1953, the American Psychological Association and the Society for the Study of Evolution initiated planning for conferences on behavior and evolution, which brought together biologists, psychologists, and anthropologists during 1955–56. The conferences yielded a multidisciplinary volume (Roe and Simpson 1958), which promoted an "evolutionary psychology" (p. 3). The participants included leading and emerging figures in evolutionary biology (George Gaylord Simpson and Ernst Mayr; Julian Huxley sent a paper); behavioral genetics (Ernst Caspari); paleontology (Edwin Colbert, Alfred Romer); ecology (Alfred Emerson); animal behavior and ethology (Donald Griffin, Robert Hinde, Niko Tinbergen); comparative psychology (Harry Harlow, Henry Nissen); physiological psychology and psychobiology (Karl Pribram, Roger Sperry); physical anthropology (S.L. Washburn); and cultural anthropology (Margaret Mead). The papers surveyed the evidence for the evolution of behavior across the animal kingdom, including paleontological and archaeological evidence. Several acknowledged that the mechanisms for learning have themselves evolved as has also the capacity for culture. The comparative psychologists Nissen and Harlow were among the authors using cognitive language (as did Huxley and Mead).

The discipline of anthropology received the theory of evolution with initial enthusiasm, which cooled and then rekindled. Darwin had apprised himself of such anthropological and archaeological knowledge as was available when he wrote. Later 19th-century anthropologists, including John Lubbock with his culture stages, embraced the Darwinian perspective. The excesses of social Darwinism caused a reaction in the early 20th century. The anti-evolutionism of Boas and his influential students prevailed for a time (Oldroyd 1980), extending to both physical (or biological) and cultural anthropology, more so in America than in Europe.

The middle decades of the 20th century saw a great surge of evolutionary thinking in anthropology. In paleontological physical anthropology, Louis Leakey pursued research from the 1920s onward in Kenya, joined by Mary Nicol (from 1936, Mary Leakey) in 1934 (e.g., Leakey 1934). Franz Weidenreich was based first in Germany and then China (e.g., Weidenreich 1946). In America, S.L. Washburn (1953) reoriented physical anthropology away from racial theory toward the evolution of human beings, consolidated its relations with primatology, and encouraged what later was called a paleoanthropological perspective (that is, the interpretation of Paleolithic archaeological evidence in relation to the development of social organization and culture; e.g., Washburn and Howell 1960). Observations of primate behavior in the wild, already undertaken by the comparative psychologist Nissen, now also fell within physical anthropology as conceived by Washburn. Leakey subsequently encouraged Jane Goodall to undertake her extensive study of chimps, which began in 1960.

Within cultural anthropology, an appreciation for Darwinian evolution and a concern for processes of cultural evolution grew from the 1920s on. This can be seen in the works of major cultural anthropologists, including Kroeber (1923, 1928), V. Gordon Childe (1936), Leslie White (1949), A. Irving Hallowell (1955), and Julian H. Steward (1955). Prehistoric archaeology, long attuned to the notion of cultural stages in the Paleolithic, had by the 1950s become more interested in multilinear, ecologically specific cultural evolutionary processes (as emphasized by Steward) and less devoted to a unilinear scheme of artifact classification (Braidwood 1959). Gordon R. Willey (1960) applied this approach to New World Pleistocene archaeology.

No group celebrated the centennial of Darwin's *Origin* more thoroughly than anthropologists in America. Three edited collections stemmed from anthropological meetings: Spuhler (1959), from a session of the American Anthropological Association in 1957; Meggers (1959), largely from papers presented to the Anthropological Society of Washington in 1957–58; and Tax (1960), arising from the most ambitious celebration of all, held at the University of Chicago to include the centennial date of 24 November 1959. These volumes brought together biologists, geneticists, primatologists, physical and cultural anthropologists, archaeologists, neurophysiologists, and psychologists, among others.

The topics and themes they discussed are remarkably similar to those found in the recent debates over cultural evolution in humans and animals. They comprise similarities and differences between biological and cultural evolution, including the non-particulate nature of some cultural evolution; interactions, in both directions, between genetic and cultural evolution; speculations about the evolution of the capacity for culture; socially transmitted behaviors in animal populations (including Japanese macaques and English titmice); the claim that cumulative culture is unique to humans; discussion of whether chimps symbolize; and claims that human culture is unique in developing systems of meaning. The earlier skepticism of many anthropologists toward cultural evolution was now described as a thing of the past (Kluckhohn 1959). Mainstream cultural anthropologists, including Kroeber, Steward, and White, advanced their agendas for evolutionary studies of culture. (See especially panels 3–5 in Tax 1960, vol. 3.)

Clyde Kluckhohn concluded the Washington Anthropological Society volume by listing desiderata for the "role of evolutionary thought in anthropological studies":

1. More attention to the evolution of behavior and the psyche;

2. Still greater fusion of biological with cultural-social-psychological dimensions;

3. Bold and imaginative focus upon the constant interactions between the environment (both physical and cultural) and the constitution and experience of individuals;

4. The creation of models that are as embracive as possible. (1959:154) He indicated that the range of discussion must include nonhuman primate behavior and social organization. His list would seem prescient, if it weren't for the fact that these directions were already emerging in the

1950s, in the literature just reviewed.

Work on the evolution of behavior and psychological capacities continued in the 1960s and 1970s. In psychology, Munn reviewed work in "psychology, zoology, genetics, paleontology, archaeology, and anthropology" on "how the human mind evolved" (1971:vii). Jerison (1973) scrutinized the fossil evidence for interspecific differences in brain size together with evidence of ancient environments and selection pressures in studying the evolution of intelligence from an information-processing point of view. Work on the human emotions continued to look to Darwin for inspiration (Plutchik 1980), and Gibson treated the senses from an evolutionary and ecological perspective (1966: chap. 11). In anthropology, research went forward on various aspects of human evolution, physical and cultural, including the evolution of language (P. Lieberman 1975). Among cultural anthropologists, Geertz (1962, 1966) sounded the theme of biology-culture interaction in the evolution of humankind. The New Archaeology continued the "neoevolutionary" functionalism of the 1950s and 1960s, insisting on an anthropological archaeology (Binford and Binford 1968, Flannery 1972). Several evolutionary approaches vied in the archaeology of the 1970s and 1980s (see Shennan 2009 for an overview).

During the 1970s, three lines of evolutionary thinking about human and nonhuman behavior emerged from the fields of ethology, comparative psychology, and animal behavior. Evolution and an emphasis on instinct had been central in the ethology of the Austrian zoologist-turned-psychologist Konrad Lorenz and the Dutch ornithologist Tinbergen. Their work was somewhat coolly received in American psychology (Oldroyd 1980). In England, Hinde (1970, 1982) successfully combined ethology with comparative psychology and animal behavior, acknowledging the need for a cognitive perspective (1970:585–93). He trained generations of students who worked in an evolutionary and cognitive framework (e.g., Cheney and Seyfarth 1990, 2007).

In America, the Harvard entomologist E.O. Wilson, inspired by ethology and his studies of social organization in insects, founded the sociobiology movement (Wilson 1975). Sociobiologists held that social behavior can be explained in terms of inclusive fitness, kin selection, and reciprocal altruism—selection pressures operating on closely related individuals or on population members that aid one another. They generally opposed group selection—natural selection operating on groups of individuals, including non-kin, or on group-related behaviors rather than simply on individuals. Wilson's book initiated a "land rush of biologists into the human sciences," who expected that explaining human behavior from a genetic perspective would be "easy pickings" (Laland and Brown 2002:71). Some anthropologists welcomed the new outlook (Chagnon and Irons 1979). The claims of sociobiology generated vigorous discussion and criticism from philosophers (Kitcher 1985), psychologists (Tobach 1976), and anthropologists (Sahlins 1976), sometimes quite heated (for a personal review, see Irons and Cronk 2000).

A third stream of work applying biological ideas to human behavior arose in anthropology. Human behavioral ecology (HBE) applied theoretical models from ecologically oriented ethology and from animal behavior studies to past and present human populations (Winterhalder and Smith 1981, Smith and Winterhalder 1992). Paradigmatically, this approach applies optimal foraging theory to human foragers (Smith 1983). HBE accounts for behavioral diversity among populations through each population's socioecological environment. It emphasizes the plasticity of behavioral response to environmental change, but is agnostic about the mechanisms (genetic, cognitive, or cultural) that produce observed behavioral patterns (Smith 2000).

During the 1980s, two additional streams of investigation emerged, one in anthropology and environmental science, the other in psychology. The first is the dual inheritance view of cultural evolution, mentioned above. It began in the late 1970s and was consolidated in Boyd and Richerson (1985). Their outlook differed from sociobiology and HBE in insisting on a significant role for culture in human adaptation and evolution. They postulated that the social learning mechanisms that allow cultural transmission evolved to permit behavioral plasticity. They modeled cultural evolution partially on analogy with gene-based evolution, while recognizing forms of social transmission not analogous to genetic transmission. In this way their approach differed from earlier attempts to use genetics to model cultural evolution, which were inspired by Richard Dawkins's (1976) notion of the "meme" as the unit of cultural evolution. Boyd and Richerson (1985) rejected the meme-based view.

The other stream arose when psychologists adopted aspects of sociobiology in framing evolutionary explanations of human behavior. These self-styled "evolutionary psychologists" accepted kin selection and retained the sociobiological emphasis on mating. As psychologists, they posited that primate and specifically human behavioral capacities are governed by a multitude of domain-specific, innate psychological mechanisms, called "modules" (Cosmides and Tooby 1987, Daly and Wilson 1988, Buss 1989). Unlike sociobiology and HBE, this approach wants to infer psychological mechanisms. In contrast to the dual inheritance approach, it downplays the role of culture and learning in explaining human behavior.

In this section, I have ascribed the renewed application of evolutionary thinking to human behavior and cognition as stemming from the 1950s, led by anthropology (both physical and cultural). In psychology, beginning in the 1950s, Harlow, Pribram, Sperry, and then Gibson pursued evolutionary thinking, but such ideas spread more slowly in that discipline.

Others ascribe the re-invigoration to sociobiology (e.g., Laland and Brown 2002:21). The difference may partly stem from my giving greater emphasis to the development of evolutionary approaches to cognition, rather than simply to behavior. Some overviews of recent work (e.g., L. Barrett, Dunbar, and Lycett 2002: chap. 2) limit the major current positions in the evolution of human behavior and cognition to HBE and the evolutionary psychology of Barkow, Cosmides, and Tooby (1992). As will become apparent, I disagree with this assessment as well. However, because these last named positions are prominent in the literature, it is worth looking at them more closely before surveying what I consider to be more promising approaches.

"EVOLUTIONARY PSYCHOLOGY," HBE, AND THEIR CRITICS

The "massively modular evolutionary psychology" of Barkow et al. (1992) was the most visible form of evolutionary psychology during the 1990s. It had both negative and positive agendas. Negatively, it opposed the so-called Standard Social Science Model (SSSM), which emphasized behavioral plasticity and the importance of learned behaviors over innate mechanisms. Positively, it suggested that the human mind evolved in the Pleistocene period and contains many specific psychological adaptations fitted to the hunting and gathering lifestyle of hominin ancestors. Pleistocene conditions formed the Environment of Evolutionary Adaptedness (EEA). Psychological adaptations to EEA are realized as cognitive and motivational modules.

A module is a domain-specific mechanism that is aimed at a certain problem: "cheater" detection in social circumstances, so that no one gets more than their due; nubile-female detection for males seeking mates; high-status-male detection for females seeking mates.[1] There are many such modules, "hundreds or thousands" (Tooby and Cosmides 1995:1189). The modules are discovered by working from two sets of constraints. First, the EEA provides a set of problems, such as mate detection, that must be solved. Ostensibly, the human mind hasn't evolved since the EEA, so its structure has been fixed in relation to those problems. Theorists can then reverse engineer from the problems to an expected set of module-based capacities, which are presumed to be innate or biologically primitive. The latter assumption is supported by the "poverty of the stimulus argument," according to which the problems confronting the human mind are too hard to be solved by general-purpose learning mechanisms.[2] They require specialized mechanisms that provide a head start through innate knowledge or problem-specific structure. The hypothesized modules are tested against current behavior in the human population. In a modern setting, these Pleistocene modules often may be maladaptive. For instance, one claim is that humans in the EEA would evolve to help closely related individuals instead of more distantly related (or apparently unrelated) individuals. Accordingly, today's step parents would more regularly abuse their children in contrast with biological parents (Daly and Wilson 1985). However, this claim has not withstood empirical scrutiny (Buller 2005: chap. 7).

Because this particular brand of "evolutionary psychology" is characterized by commitment to massive modularity and appeal to the EEA, I abbreviate it as MMEEA-EP, for "massively modular, environment of evolutionary adaptedness evolutionary psychology." The first element, MMEEA, when pronounced phonetically, is a reminder of the individualistic or egoistical outlook of MMEEA-EP, which rejects the notion that selection could fix group-level forms of altruism. MMEEA-EP differs from other evolutionary approaches considered below in showing little concern for archaeological, paleontological, and geological evidence concerning the EEA or for comparative psychology.

MMEEA-EP has been critically evaluated by sociologist Christopher Badcock (2000), psychologist Cecilia Heyes (2000), and philosophers Kim Sterelny (2003), David Buller (2005), and Robert Richardson (2007). These critics convincingly object to the idea of a single Pleistocene EEA, to the requirement that domain-specific knowledge entails massive modularity, and to the specific empirical claims of MMEEA-EP. Buller (2005) and Richardson (2007) question whether sufficient evidence can ever be found for testing hypotheses about the evolution of mind and cognition. However, in focusing on MMEEA-EP, they do not address more integrative theoretical positions that engage the archaeological, genetic, comparative, and geological evidence.

As regards HBE, from the outset it applied its models of behavioral strategy not only to present-day populations, but also to the archaeological evidence for past patterns of subsistence behavior (Yesner 1981). Characteristically, this meant applying optimal foraging theory (OFT) to archaeological data. OFT examines the relations among food preferences, foraging patch selection, and allocation of time among patches. It seeks to model the optimal allocation of these three factors in relation to the available resources in the environment. Some resources may be easy to get but offer relatively modest value; others may be more difficult to obtain but higher in value. Differing patterns of food preference, patch selection, and time allocation constitute various "strategies" or "decision rules."

Despite its focus on "decisions," HBE does not examine or posit particular cognitive mechanisms or knowledge bases to underlie the behavioral strategies it examines (Smith 2000). Rather, it assesses the relation between observed behavior and "optimal" strategies. If observed behavior approaches optimality, this suggests that the predicted behavioral strategy is in play. HBE does not assume that human actors actually think in terms of the strategies or that they are utility optimizers. It assumes that a correlation between behavior and reproductive success explains why the behavioral pattern has evolved. Consequently, HBE pays scant attention to culture as a conveyor of strategies or as an explanation of behavioral differences.

During the 1980s, archaeologists developed other ecological approaches, including "community ecology" (Foley 1984) and "socioecology" (Standen and Foley 1989). These approaches again tended to eschew cognitive mechanisms. Where they invoked culture, it was in terms of differential social transmission.

Mithen (1990) criticized standard HBE, optimal foraging theory, and related ecological approaches on three accounts. First, he argued that OFT is essentially static: it assumes that environments remain constant. As an archaeologist, Mithen was interested in applying ecological decision models to changing patterns of behavior as revealed by the archaeological record. Second, Mithen criticized the lack of engagement with actual psychological processes of information flow and decision making. Study of psychological processes can reveal the reasons that a pattern of behavior fails to reach optimality. A change in a cognitive strategy, such as the use of external aids to memory, may explain a change in behavioral pattern. Mithen thus sought to examine the development of cognitive abilities and mechanisms across time periods. This led to his third departure from standard HBE: he rejected the optimality assumption. As he rightly pointed out, a cognitive strategy need only yield better fitness over its rivals to yield an adaptive advantage. Mithen (1990) offers a distinctive "evolutionary ecological" approach to human cognitive and behavioral evolution. Citing Hodder (1985), he also noted that explanations cannot be limited to the interaction between cognition and environment; historical context (his counterpart to culture) must also come into play.

As we turn to examine some major theoretical syntheses in the evolution of mind from the 1990s and after, I note that the relevant authors (several of whom contributed to this volume) do not describe themselves as "evolutionary psychologists" or as engaging in "human behavioral ecology" (although Sterelny claims partial affinity to HBE). Unlike HBE, the positions considered below pay attention to cognition and culture. Their authors do not call themselves "evolutionary psychologists" perhaps because they accede to the proprietary claims made by adherents of MMEEA-EP, which include a false claim that the movement coined the term "evolutionary psychology" (Plotkin 2004:123).

Be that as it may, it is not a happy use of terminology to use a phrase such as "evolutionary psychology," which should name a field, for one particular theoretical position in the field. Heyes (2000) proselytizes for an "evolutionary psychology in the round": an investigation of the evolution of human psychology that accommodates phylogenetic development, comparative psychology, and ecological variation from a selection-theoretic standpoint. This inclusive attitude has been adopted by authors who previously focused on MMEEA-EP (Dunbar and Barrett 2007). From this perspective, many of the contributors to this volume are engaged in evolutionary psychology, even if they prefer to avoid the older (MMEEA-EP) connotations of the label.

PROMINENT THEORETICAL SYNTHESES ON THE EVOLUTION OF HUMAN MIND AND BEHAVIOR

The past two decades have seen new theoretical conceptions of the evolution of human cognition that take an *integrative approach*. Their authors seek to integrate psychology (cognitive, comparative, and developmental), neuroscience, evolutionary biology, archaeology, paleoanthropology, and, in some cases, genetic and geological streams of evidence.

The first such integrative work was Donald's *Origins of the Modern Mind: Three Stages in the Evolution of Culture and Cognition* (1991). Reviewing evidence from psychology, neuroscience, paleontology, and archaeology, Donald concluded that the main biological changes in hominin cognition occur in motor skill and memory and that further changes are cultural. He posited four stages in hominin development, starting from the common ancestor with chimps. In the first stage, the cognitive structure of the common ancestor is *episodic.* Chimps and other anthropoids perceive and remember events but have poor autorecall (ability to remember them at will). In the second stage, expanded hominin capacities for representation evolved through changes in the ability to plan and execute motor sequences; planning and auto-cuing of motor sequences requires abstract representation of possible but not yet effected sequences. This change in the hominin line allowed mimetic communication to develop and the teaching and learning of motor skills. In Donald's scheme, this second, *mimetic* stage peaks with *H. erectus.*

With the subsequent development of complex language, a new level of cognitive capacity arises: the *mythic* stage, characterized by lexical invention and phonological apparatus allowing for complex phonetic mimicry (a specialized mimetic system), which peaks in AMH. Donald contends that the language ability must spring from pre-linguistic, mimetic representations, which he locates in systems of gesture and the perceptual abilities that guide them and read them. With the development of language came the possibility of extended narrative structure and the web of contextual cultural meaning.

Whereas the first two transitions involved biological evolution and changes in the structure of the body and brain, Donald proposes that the final stage is a product of cultural development alone. The final transition is to the *theoretic* stage, characterized by visuosymbolic invention (images and writing), external memory, and theory creation, the latter arising in Greece ca. 450 BC. By contrast with the oral-mythic culture of earlier *H. sapiens,* this new stage brings new cognitive manifestations through graphic invention (image-making, symbol-making, script-making), the resultant external memory (symbolic coded and written forms of memory storage), and theory construction (critically honed theoretical traditions, formal thought). Donald's concept of external memory inspired the philosophical notion of the "extended mind" (e.g., Clark 1993, Clark and Chalmers 1998), which makes external media such as images and writing constitutive parts of the mind. This conclusion is not in Donald's original thesis, which contends that external aids alter the memory capacity of human beings and thus augment their cognitive abilities without supposing that one's written notes literally constitute a part of one's mind.

Donald's discussion of the transition between the mythic and theoretic stage and his notion of external memory storage formed the subject of a conference at the McDonald Institute for Archaeological Research in Cambridge in 1996, resulting in Renfrew and Scarre's 1998 volume. Renfrew (1998) argues that between the origin of language and the invention of writing, material culture, in the form of images and artifacts, formed a distinct stage in the development of external symbolic storage. Renfrew (1982) was a pioneer of "cognitive archaeology" and he continues to discuss the role of cultural, as opposed to purely biological or genetic, aspects of the development of the modern mind (Renfrew 2009).

Although Donald (1991) stresses the role of motor representations in the first two transitions, he is also favorable toward Dunbar's (1993) social intelligence hypothesis of anthropoid and hominin evolution. The increasing size of the social group requires an increased capacity for representing (pre-linguistically, at first) members of the group and their relations, and, ultimately, for sharing knowledge through mimetic exchange. Unlike Dunbar, Donald seeks to specify the cognitive mechanisms that would make social intelligence possible. His chapter in this volume re-examines his particular conception of mimesis, a central mechanism in his account.

Mithen's *Prehistory of the Mind* (1996) also combined archaeological, paleontological, and psychological lines of evidence. Mithen sought to infer the evolution of psychological mechanisms from changes in toolmaking, patterns of hunting and gathering, and social structures. Like MMEEA-EP, he invoked poverty-of-the-stimulus arguments to infer domain specific psychological structures. However, his position differs considerably from "massive modularity." Drawing on the work of Howard Gardner (1983, 1993), he describes his domain specific structures as "intelligences." In the hominin line, Mithen divides these intelligences into four super-categories: social intelligence, natural history intelligence, technical intelligence (e.g., toolmaking), and linguistic intelligence. He posits three broad phases in the evolution of mammalian and primate minds: general intelligence (nonprimate mammals); encapsulated central intelligences (falling under the four categories); and cognitive fluidity (specific to modern humans).

Mithen likens the evolution of the mind to the construction of a cathedral. General intelligence—the learning and problem-solving abilities found in all nonprimate mammals—forms the central nave. The inputs to general intelligence are Fodor's (1983) sensory modules, which are specialized, encapsulated sensory systems (the visual system with its subunits, auditory system with its subunits, etc.), and general intelligence is like Fodor's central systems. The four intelligences are added as chapels around the central nave. In earlier hominins, these chapels are encapsulated (insulated) from one another and from general intelligence. In the modern human mind, the walls are breached between nave and chapels and among the chapels themselves, allowing general intelligence to engage in cross-domain thinking and problem solving. Drawing on developmental psychologist Annette Karmiloff-Smith (1992), Mithen argues that modern human intelligence is not modularly isolated but creatively combines knowledge and abilities across domains.[3]

The chapels are added sequentially, starting from the last common ancestor (inferred from today's chimps). This ancestor possesses social intelligence; *H. habilis* adds natural history and technical intelligences (to account for foraging patterns and the Oldowan industry); *H. erectus* (or *H. ergaster*) gains in technical intelligence (to account for the Acheulean toolkit). Neandertal, whose behavioral repertoire approaches that of early AMH, has increased natural history, technical, and social intelligence, with language being parasitic on and largely limited to social intelligence.

Mithen (1996) divides the biological evolution of the mind of *H. sapiens* into two stages. Early modern humans basically have Neandertal minds, with language use focused on social relations. Sometime after 60 kya, further biological evolution breaches all the chapel walls, yielding the cognitive fluidity of (fully) modern humans. Language becomes general purpose, yielding symbolic cognition. Mithen (1996:151) argues that this additional biological change is needed to explain the "cultural explosion" of the LSA/UP. Subsequently, he pushes back the date of the transition to fluidity to sometime after 100 kya (Mithen 2005:266). Cognitive fluidity allows for the beginning of history, or the "cumulative development of events and knowledge," including cultural identities that are expressed in artifact traditions

(Mithen 2003:3 and n9). In this volume, Mithen discusses the current status of his cathedral model with its emphasis on human cognitive fluidity.

Mithen and Donald present contrasting views of hominin cognitive evolution. As opposed to Mithen's specialized super-modules, Donald posits enhanced motor control and memory capacity as the gateway to representational meta-cognition and the ability to teach and learn, which yields culture as an engine of cognitive development. Their positions are part of a larger theoretical landscape containing an array of positions, with some authors defending multiple modular approaches and others arguing that a small number of crucial cognitive changes can explain the diversity of hominin cognitive evolution and human abilities.

Tomasello (1999) invokes the ability for cultural transmission as the key element, which he at first explained by joint attention and subsequently by shared intentionality (Tomasello 2000b). Joint attention is the ability to recognize not only what someone wants you to attend to, but that the person wants you to attend to it and that both of you are focused on the same item. It facilitates teaching and learning. The ability to share intentionality is a more cognitive version of joint attention, involving awareness of what the other believes or desires in the current situation and what the other wants you to believe or desire. Joint attention and shared intentionality enable knowledge and skill to be transmitted with high fidelity through teaching and learning (Tomasello, Kruger, and Ratner 1993, Tomasello et al. 2005b). In Tomasello's view, the creative capacity of chimps and early hominins allowed them to make isolated discoveries concerning tool use and the like; but they lacked the high-fidelity transmission required for the ratchet effect.

In this volume, Warneken examines helping behavior in chimps and young children in relation to shared intentions. He distinguishes "instrumental helping behavior" from truly collaborative activity. Instrumental helping requires discerning what the other is aiming to do so as to permit intervention if the other is stuck (unable to reach something, needs a latch opened, and the like). Chimps are capable and disposed toward such helping (even if unrewarded), but only human children show genuine collaboration in coordinated activities to achieve a goal, with differentiated individual roles and a realization that both parties are seeking the same outcome. Warneken concludes that shared goals and shared intentions are unique to humans. He discusses this finding in the context of the possibility that group selection has yielded the human ability for shared intentions.

Carruthers (2006) defends massively modular evolutionary psychology. His main concern is with current evidence for modularity in human and comparative psychology. His notion of a module is, in his terms, considerably weakened from the notion of a Fodor module. Fodor (1983) held that modules are domain specific in their inputs and in their task (e.g., color perception, shape, face recognition); automatic ("operation is mandatory"); insulated (central systems have access only to the output); informationally encapsulated (receive inputs from sensory transducers but have no access to central information or other modules); conceptually shallow in their output (e.g., representation of color and shape, but not object-kind); innate and hardwired; and fast. Fodor further argued that modules are restricted to input-systems (sensory systems) and motor routines (though he has virtually nothing to say about the latter).

Carruthers (2006) drops several of these specifications. In particular, he allows that modules need not be domain specific in their inputs, but might accept any input that is relevant to their task. He emphasizes that modules may have domain specific "on" switches: they may be activated by motivational states (e.g., hunger), but then use any available information to find food. Modules must have an innate basis, but their task may be learning, so that adult modules are constructed through modularized learning routines. Integration across modularized capacities allows flexible cognitive responses.

In this volume, Carruthers eschews the terminology of "modularity" and speaks instead of seven central "pillars" of human cognition that constitute innate, domain-specific cognitive mechanisms with specific motivational triggers. He focuses on pillars that would sustain the evolved human capacity for cultural transmission. The seven pillars are: imitation, shared intentionality, and mindreading; language; creativity; fine motor coordination; innate naive physics; the ability to make inferences to the best explanation; and the ability to form and enforce social norms. Of course, other theorists would accept that human beings have the capacities named here. The point in dispute concerns their cognitive or psychological bases, with Carruthers arguing for what he had earlier termed a weakly modular and innate basis.

In their treatment of the evolution of mind, Boyd and Richerson (1985) and Richerson and Boyd (2005) are concerned especially with the origins of the capacity for culture. They stress the changing character of environmental circumstances over the past 14 million years, focusing on the

2.5 my in which the genus *Homo* has existed. They contend that different cognitive strategies and hence different cognitive mechanisms would be favored by different rates of environmental change. Long periods of environmental stability would favor the evolution of innate cognitive mechanisms. Our hominin ancestors did not enjoy such periods of stability. They were subjected to fairly rapid changes (with transitions measured in a few thousands of years) from moderate climate to ice age and back again. Boyd and Richerson argue that, in these conditions, cognitive flexibility would be favored over innate fixity. The mechanisms for such flexibility include imitative learning and tribe-oriented values, which might be subject to group selection. Group selection for tribal values would be an instance of gene-culture interaction and co-evolution. Richerson and Boyd's chapter in this volume applies their models to questions of the evolution of cognition and culture.

Other syntheses have been offered by Sterelny (2003), Gärdenfors (2003), Coolidge and Wynn (2009), and Chase (2006). Sterelny emphasizes the importance of the evolution of cognitive bases for cooperation in the hominin line. Cooperation yields niche construction, in which human populations alter their environments, both social and natural. By contrast with the cognitive fixity of massive modularity, Sterelny suggests that cognitive plasticity would be favored in hominin evolution. His contribution to this volume applies thinking about niche construction and optimal foraging theory to two cases: !Kung foraging behavior, and local fitness maxima in the subsistence strategies of AMH and Neandertal. He contends that the differential survival of the latter two groups need not reflect fundamental cognitive differences, but may have resulted from Neandertal getting stuck on a relative fitness peak.

Gärdenfors (2003) uses the conceit of a talking monkey named Egon to focus on the sensory, motor, and cognitive differences between humans and nonhominin anthropoids. Key cognitive differences are in imagination, planning, mindreading, self-consciousness, and linguistic abilities. He argues that mental simulation and planning explain many of the new hominin capacities. In this volume, he maintains that an ability for intersubjective cognition underlies hominin symbolic behavior and the evolution of cooperation. He distinguishes the intersubjectivity needed for shared intentions and future planning from that for "indirect reciprocity" (I'll help you on the assumption that someone else will help me). He maintains that future planning requires only protolanguage and that indirect reciprocity requires full predicative language.

In a recent book, Coolidge and Wynn (2009) survey hominin cognitive evolution in the spirit of Donald (1991) and Mithen (1996). Like Mithen, they introduce a biological step that occurs after early AMH evolved. In their scheme, previous hominin ancestors showed improvements first in sensorimotor abilities (*H. erectus*) and then cognitive enhancements including shared attention and indexical signaling, involving some symbolic behavior and a form of protolanguage (*H. heidelbergensis*). Neandertal further develops technical competency (procedural memory), symbolism, language, and social cognition, but with no difference in kind. Prior to 45 kya, early AMH are like Neandertal, with the possible addition of symbolic social marking (Coolidge and Wynn 2009:244). A genetic mutation in AMH then yields a small but significant cognitive addition: enhanced working memory (Coolidge and Wynn 2005). This change brings a suite of other cognitive enhancements, including increased phonological storage and more extensive recursive linguistic processing; cross-modal thinking; technology involving long-range planning; planned voyages to unseen destinations; and symbolic art. These result in the LSA/UP cultural explosion ca. 45 kya.

Nowell's contribution offers another perspective on the cognitive differences between AMH and Neandertal. Reviewing the evidence for symbolic behavior in Neandertals and AMH prior to the extinction of Neandertals, she concludes that there is no evidence to establish a difference in kind. As a result, she contends that the evidence is consistent with the hypothesis that Neandertals and AMH did not differ cognitively in significant ways. She then attributes the evidence of rapid cultural innovation in AMH after the extinction of Neandertal to a multiplier effect of increased group size. On this scenario, population density increases the likelihood that cultural innovations will be preserved and transmitted. Her conclusion is consistent with a gradualist approach to the development of AMH culture. Her position ascribes the surge in UP culture (occurring after Neandertal are extinct, in her estimation) to cultural rather than biological evolution.

Chase (2006) seeks to isolate what is empirically unique about human culture. As we have seen, he holds that even if cumulative cultural transmission were unique to humans, it would not adequately describe other apparently unique features of human culture. He finds that human culture creates *social codes* that can exist only as possessions of groups, such as the rule for driving on the right, the rules of chess, and the requirement of celibacy in some religious groups. Socially created codes condition the *motivation* of individual behavior, and such codes form an *all-encompassing system* that assigns meaning and value to nearly all aspects of human life. From his survey of the archaeological evidence, he concludes that the ability for social coding, including referential language, entered the hominin line no later than the late Middle Pleistocene (some 150 kya) and that cultural motivation and the formation of complex worldviews arose later.

In this volume, Chase examines the distinctive features of culture as a group rather than an individual-level phenomenon, and recounts the evidence for the timing of its evolution. If Donald (1991) is correct, Chase's account of the unique aspects of human culture must be supplemented to include new cognitive abilities that arose with external symbolic storage and theoretical modes of discourse.

DISPUTED QUESTIONS

Recent decades have witnessed an explosion of interest in the evolution of mind, cognition, and their neural bases, as well as in the evolution of culture and the underlying mechanisms of social learning. This increased research activity, across a span of disciplines from molecular genetics to philosophy, has produced much new data and many new theoretical proposals but no abiding theoretical consensus. That is as it should be for an ambitious research enterprise focused on a difficult problem that requires the synthesis of data and theories from a wide spectrum of disciplines.

The contributors to this volume share no single theoretical perspective, but they do concur on some points. They acknowledge the need to bring all potential sources of evidence and theory to bear on the problem of hominin cognitive and cultural evolution, including archaeological, environmental, cultural anthropological, and comparative perspectives. The contributors who offer theoretical syntheses also agree on the importance of social cognition and cooperation in hominin evolution, even if they differ in their accounts of how these elements evolved. They disagree on gradualism vs. revolution in the rise of AMH culture, biological change vs. cultural change to explain the UP, many vs. few cognitive adaptations in the hominin line and their timing, the selection pressures that yielded syntactic language, the distance between AMH and Neandertal cognition, and the definition and import of culture.

The workshop from which this volume arose took the form of an extended dialogue, in which individual speakers summarized their papers (which had been predistributed) and two members provided commentary. In the course of the discussions, disagreements concerning theory and data were aired with intensity and good humor. I invite the reader to join the dialogue that unfolds in the following chapters.

NOTES

1.1 The notion of a module was introduced into cognitive science by Jerry Fodor (1983) for sensory and motor programs. The idea is that some functions need to be carried out by specialized mechanisms that have innate structure which is specialized for certain types of problems (see my discussion of Carruthers, below, for further specification of Fodorean modules). Fodor restricted modules to input systems (sensory systems) and motor routines, as opposed to central systems or "higher" cognition, which he believed lacked modular features (being domain neutral, catholic or "isotropic" in its consideration of evidence, and conceptually complex). Barkow, Cosmides, and Tooby (1992) posit modules for central cognitive functions such as mate selection, thereby applying Fodor's concept to "higher" cognition. Such modules might be termed "central modules," to distinguish them from Fodor's input-output modules.

1.2 The poverty of the stimulus argument was made popular by Noam Chomsky (1980: chap. 1), who argued that children learn language too easily for this learning to occur through general-purpose mechanisms. Rather, we should attribute to all human beings knowledge of an innate, universal grammar, which allows them to solve quickly the difficult problem of learning their own natural languages (such as English or Chinese). The argument depends heavily on the notions of "quickness" and "difficulty," and is not universally accepted. Some critics contend that general purpose mechanisms can suffice and that the learning path toward syntactically complex sentences is longer than linguists had presumed (e.g., Tomasello 1999: chaps. 4–5).

1.3 Mithen (1996) sometimes speaks of his "intelligences" as modules and perhaps as containing more specialized modules. Nonetheless, his four intelligences are distinct from the massive modularity of MMEEA-EP, which does not incorporate the Gardner-inspired notion of intelligences (Gardner 1983, 1993), which are like "super-modules" that stand above the insulated, "massive" (in number) central modules of MMEEA-EP. Because Mithen's intelligences or super-modules significantly differ from the encapsulated modules of MMEEA-EP, I do not classify him with the latter.

2

When Did We Become Human?
Evolutionary Perspectives on the Emergence of the Modern Human Mind, Brain, and Culture

THEODORE G. SCHURR

One of the most longstanding debates in the field of biological anthropology is when members of our lineage became "human." There is keen interest in knowing when we evolved the characteristics seen in our species, and which of these features truly makes us distinctive from other primates and especially earlier forms of hominins. Language, culture, tool use, brain size, and bipedalism have all been cited as traits that differentiate modern humans from other primate species. While it was once thought that these traits were uniquely human, we now understand most of them to be elaborations of similar features in other species, although with some specific manifestations for modern humans.

Counterexamples to modern human uniqueness seem to proliferate every day. For instance, chimps and orangs are now viewed not only as having "culture" (Whiten et al. 1999, Whiten, Horner, and Marshall-Pescini 2003, Hohmann and Fruth 2003, van Schaik et al. 2003, Whiten 2005, Lycett, Collard, and McGrew 2007, Horner et al. 2010), but, in the case of chimps, also an extensive cultural repertoire (Boesch, Hohman, and Marchant 2002, Boesch 2003) (Fig. 2.1). Field researchers have noted cultural patterns in chimps in 30 different behaviors, including anting, greeting gestures, and reconciliation (Whiten, Horner, and Marshall-Pescini 2003, Whiten 2005, Schöning et al. 2008). However, as S.E. Perry (2006:171) has noted, the evolution of culture in these species cannot be fully explained without determining "(a) how socioecological variables affect

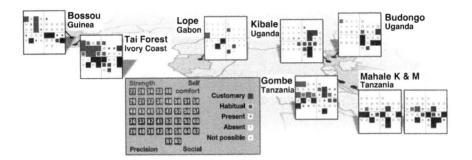

2.1. The cultures of wild chimpanzees. Each chimpanzee community has its own unique array of traditions that together constitute the local "culture." "Customary" acts are those typical in the community, "habitual" ones are less common but consistent with social transmission, and "absent" acts are those missing with no apparent straightforward environmental explanation. Traditions are defined as behavior patterns that are customary or habitual in at least one site but absent elsewhere. Transmission is attributed to social learning on the basis of a complex of circumstantial evidence. The numbers in cells refer to behavior patterns catalogued in Whiten et al. (2001:1489–1525). (Reprinted by permission from Macmillan Publishers Ltd: *Nature* 437 [2005], A. Whiten, pp. 52–55, Fig. 1.)

cultural transmission dynamics, (b) the proximate mechanisms by which social learning is achieved, (c) developmental studies of the role of social influence in acquiring behavioral traits, and (d) the fitness consequences of engaging in social learning."

Through numerous experimental studies, it is also clear that apes have incipient language abilities (Patterson and Linden 1981, Savage-Rumbaugh, Rumbaugh, and McDonald 1985, Savage-Rumbaugh et al. 1986, Miles 1990). Most apes have the capacity to comprehend and manipulate symbols, with some understanding of syntax. At the same time, apes cannot produce articulate speech like humans, and have a rudimentary understanding of grammar, although they are clearly able to communicate various emotions through vocalizations (Premack 2004, P. Lieberman 2007). Others suggest that clues to the emergence of human language may be found in the manual gestures, facial expressions, and vocal signals of chimps and bonobos (Pollick and de Waal 2007) or gorillas (Forrester 2008). Yet, it is still not clear whether apes understand anything about the unobservable mental states of other individuals (Penn and Povinelli 2007) or have shared intentionality as seen in humans (Tomasello et al. 2005b).

Aside from cognitive abilities, there has also been a concerted effort to link social behavior and brain evolution. A number of studies attempted to associate the expansion of the neocortex to the social group complexity for different species (Humphrey 1976, Byrne and Whiten 1988, Dunbar 1992, 1993, 1995, 1998; but cf. L. Barrett, Henzi, and Rendall 2007). According to this social brain hypothesis, in a population containing multiple members of different sexes and ages, individuals need to understand the social relationships in the group, including both kin and non-kin (Byrne and Whiten 1988, Byrne 1996, Byrne and Bates 2007). Selection favored those individuals who were able to keep track of this complex set of relationships and remember information about others' demeanor, rank, kinship, and past history of give-and-take, while using this information in social problem-solving. Since it is the location where such higher cognitive functions take place, neocortex size and complexity would have been selected for under these conditions.

In addition, there is the issue of tool use by different primates, and the implications of deliberate manufacturing or employment of tools for the evolution of the brain. Indeed, thanks to many years of field research with wild populations of apes and monkeys, we now know that tool use occurs in most ape species (Fox, Sitompul, and van Schaik 1999, Hohmann and Fruth 2003, van Schaik et al. 2003, Breuer, Ndoundou-Hockemba, and Fishlock 2005, Mulcahy, Call, and Dunbar 2005, Hernandez-Aguilar, Moore, and Pickering 2007). There is more extensive use of tools for various purposes by chimps than by other great apes (e.g., Sanz, Morgan, and Gulick 2004, Sanz and Morgan 2007), which is consistent with chimps being our closest hominoid cousins. In fact, it appears that at least certain chimpanzees were capable of producing stone tools (Mercader et al. 2007). However, researchers have also observed tool use in certain New World monkey species, indicating that these behaviors are not confined to the Family Hominidae (e.g., Visalberghi et al. 2007). It further appears that tool use can be "taught" or transmitted between individuals, although not in as clearly a deliberate manner as with human teaching (Premack 2004).

All of this new evidence would seem to diminish the assertion of modern human uniqueness, despite clear quantitative differences between *Homo sapiens* and other primate species. In light of the changing perspective on human nature, this chapter provides an evolutionary context for assessing the evolution of mind, brain, and culture in modern humans, which is addressed in various ways in the chapters of this volume. It presents a view of human and primate evolution that reflects our current understanding of bio-behavioral variation in these species. Yet, even as these words are being written, this view is shifting very quickly with new information from ethology, neurobiology, genetics, and paleoanthropology. Even so, it is possible to highlight the major transitions in the evolution of primate and hominid species and explore their implications for the emergence of modern human behavior and cognitive capacities.

HOMININ PHYLOGENY

There have been many attempts to construct a phylogeny of fossil humans in an effort to determine the place of modern humans in nature. These trees have continued to change as new fossils are discovered and old fossils are reanalyzed, and the absolute dating of these fossils provides new insights into the chronological context of speciation events. One could rightly state that recent paleoanthropological research has been remarkably successful in providing new information about human ancestry and evolution and in filling some of the gaps in the hominin phylogeny that had persisted for some time.

The general outline of the evolution of hominin species[1] is largely agreed upon. As illustrated in Figure 2.2, there are relatively few straight lines between the identified species, and more of a gradation between the different forms through time. We observe some correlation between brain size, tooth size, and bipedalism for all of these species, and that brain size increases while tooth size diminishes in the modern human lineage (genus *Homo*) over the past several million years.

In addition to discussions of the shape and complexity of hominin phylogeny, there is great interest in defining the starting point for this tree. Recent fossil discoveries have pushed back the origin of the hominin clade[2] into the late Miocene, to 6–7 million years ago (mya). The oldest known potential hominin fossils have been attributed to *Sahelanthropus tchadensis* and come from Toros-Menalla in Chad (Brunet et al. 2002, 2005). This finding was unexpected because of the fact that so few hominin fossils had previously been discovered there. Some researchers assert that *Sahelanthropus* belongs to the stock that gave rise to both chimps and humans and is not the beginning point for the human lineage (e.g., Wolpoff et al. 2002).

The next-oldest species, *Orrorin tugenensis*, has been dated to 6.0 mya

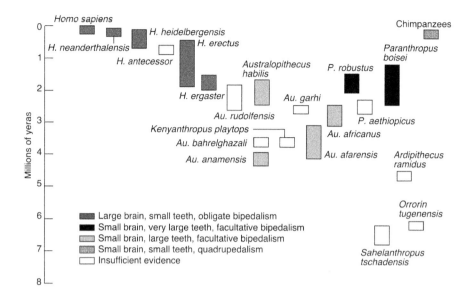

2.2. A current hominid phylogeny based on fossil evidence. Modern humans are shown at top left and the chimpanzee at top right. Extinct species are indicated with the dates of the earliest and latest fossil evidence; these are likely to change with the accumulation of more fossil evidence. Species are assigned to one of four categories, based on brain and cheek-tooth size, and inferred posture and locomotion. A fifth category, "insufficient evidence," indicates species that cannot be readily classified based on these features. (Modified after B. Wood, *Nature* 418 [2002]:133–35, Fig. 2; used with permission.)

(Senut et al. 2001, Pickford et al. 2002). As will be discussed below, this species shows clear postcranial evidence for bipedalism in the shape of the proximal femur, an adaptation seen as distinctive in hominins. This observation is quite important because it establishes the fact that upright posture and locomotion occurred very early in the evolution of the hominin lineage. There is debate over whether this "Millennium Man"—as well as *Sahelanthropus*—belongs to the human or human-chimp lineage (Haile-Selassie 2001).

Shortly after the appearance of *Orrorin* the earliest forms of *Ardipithecus* arose between 5.2–5.7 mya (Haile-Selassie, Suwa, and White 2004, Semaw et al. 2005). This species persisted until around 4.0 mya before giving way to australopithecines. The exact taxonomic status of this hominin is vigorously debated. These questions have arisen in part due to the fragmentary nature of the fossil evidence, and because this species seems to have both primitive and advanced features relative to later hominins and chimpanzees (Haile-Selassie, Suwa, and White 2004, Semaw et al. 2005).

Various forms of australopithecines emerged around 4.4 mya and persisted until some 1.0 mya (White et al. 2000, 2006). These species included both the more gracile forms of the genus *Australopithecus* and more robust forms in the genus *Paranthropus*.[3] There is no clear consensus on the species that gave rise to *Homo*. Some favor *A. garhi* because of its possible association with Oldowan stone tools (Asfaw et al. 1999, de Heinzelin et al. 1999), although this view is not uniformly accepted. Others have suggested that a separate species (and genus), *Kenyapithecus playtops*, could be the precursor to the genus *Homo* (Leakey et al. 2001).

Regardless of its ancestor, the earliest forms of *Homo* appear to have evolved from an australopithecine stock around 1.8–2.3 mya (Gabunia et al. 2001, Vekua et al. 2002, Antón and Swisher 2004, Lordkipanidze et al. 2007). This transition is marked by a number of changes, such as the appearance of stone tools, an increase in brain size beyond the chimpanzee and australopithecine range, and other skeletal and behavioral attributes (McHenry and Coffing 2000). Meanwhile, the chimpanzee lineage continued to evolve and diverge, producing a number of subspecies over the course of the next several million years.

There is still considerable debate about the exact phylogenetic relationships among the early forms of *Homo*. This uncertainty arises in part because of fossils that were recently found in Dmanisi, Georgia. Attributed to *Homo erectus*, these fossils date to 1.8 mya and appear to have characteristics similar to both *H. habilis* and *H. erectus* (Gabunia et al. 2001, Vekua et al. 2002, Lordkipanidze et al. 2007). Some investigators have suggested that variation in early *Homo* may be partly ecogeographic in nature—that is, the Dmanisi specimens are simply smaller than those found in Africa—or that early African *H. erectus* fossils represent different populations of a single, highly variable species (Ruff 2002, D. Lieberman 2007). Alternatively, the Dmanisi fossils may represent a different species altogether (e.g., Vekua et al. 2002). In either case, early *Homo* probably had substantial levels of sexual dimorphism,[4] as also seen in members of the genus *Australopithecus* (D. Lieberman 2007).

Given the temporal overlap in the appearance of *H. habilis* and *H. erectus* and their seemingly similar cognitive capabilities, as indicated by the use of simple stone tools by both taxa, there is some uncertainty about which hominin represents the precursor to *H. erectus*. For some time, *H. habilis* had been considered to be ancestral to *H. erectus* due to its having a vertical face, teeth of intermediate size between those of *Australopithecus* and *H. erectus*, and an intermediate-sized brain. One problem with this interpretation was that, until recently, the oldest fossils definitively attributed to *H. habilis* were only 1.9 million years old (Leakey, Tobias, and Napier 1964), a date which was not much earlier than the appearance of the oldest *H. erectus* fossils.

The discovery of a new *H. habilis* upper jaw dated to 1.44 mya (Spoor et al. 2007) further complicates the picture. The comparison of this specimen with other examples of early *Homo* demonstrates the distinctiveness of *H. habilis* and *H. erectus* regardless of their relative cranial size. This evidence plus the dates of the new fossils suggests that these taxa lived sympatrically[5] in the same area for nearly 500,000 years (Spoor et al. 2007). However, it remains possible that *H. habilis* evolved before 2 mya, as a 2.33 mya upper jaw (AL 666) from Hadar, East Africa, is thought to belong to this species (Kimbel, Johanson, and Rak 1997).

Homo erectus represents a major transition in the genus *Homo* (Wood and Collard 1999, McHenry and Coffing 2000). This species took on modern human stature and limb proportions, became habitually bipedal, and began the ontogenetic[6] shift that led to modern human life history (Leigh 1996, Bogin 2001, Aiello and Wells 2002). It has sometimes been subdivided into *H. ergaster* in Africa (ancestral form) and *H. erectus* in East Asia (derived form) to reflect subtle morphological and apparent behavioral differences between the specimens across the species' range, although not all investigators make this distinction (Antón and Swisher 2004). In addition, this species appears to have undergone major physiological changes to allow for greater mobility, changing dietary strategies, and new reproductive demands (Aiello and Wells 2002, Antón and Swisher 2004).

Current studies have also raised questions about the degree of behavioral and morphological modernity exhibited by early *H. erectus*. The species had small teeth, suggesting a more human-like diet, and relatively long legs and other features suited to walking and running (Wood and Collard 1999, McHenry and Coffing 2000, Pearson 2000, Ruff 2002, Bramble and Lieberman 2004), although these traits may also have been present in the Georgian hominins (Lordkipanidze et al. 2007). However, it appears that they matured more rapidly than modern humans do (Antón 2003), although some disagree with this interpretation (e.g., Clegg and Aiello 1999), and large increases in brain size occurred well after the species originated (Antón 2003, Antón and Swisher 2004, Schoenemann 2006). It is also likely that *H. erectus* was more sexually dimorphic than modern humans (Antón 2003, D. Lieberman 2007). These observations have important implications for reconstructing the bioenergetics, reproductive ecology, and social organization of this species.

During the later phases of *H. erectus*, the ancestral stock for later *H. sapiens* emerged. Called *H. heidelbergensis* by some, *H. rhodesiensis* by others (Hublin 2009), these archaic humans appeared by 600,000 years before present (ybp) in Africa, and then spread to other parts of the Old World. *H. heidelbergensis* in Africa continued to evolve in Africa, and eventually gave rise to anatomically modern humans (AMH), *H. sapiens* (Rightmire 1998, 2004, Stringer 2002a,b). According to Rightmire (2004), the changes in absolute and relative brain size in hominins from the Middle Pleistocene point to a speciation event in which *H. erectus* produced a daughter lineage, represented by *H. heidelbergensis*. Archaeological evidence from this period also indicates that these species differed in their technology and behavior from earlier hominins (Thieme 1997, Klein 2000b).

There is still some debate as to whether earlier archaic humans in Europe are related to *H. heidelbergensis* or instead represent a separate and earlier species of hominin, called *H. antecessor* (Bermúdez de Castro et al. 2004, Carbonell et al. 2008). This hominin form shows some differences from *H. erectus,* although being more archaic in some of its features from later *H. heidelbergensis* and Neandertals. Even if this species entered Europe some 800,000 years ago, it is not certain that this hominin eventually gave rise to the ancestral stock of Neandertals (Rightmire 2004, Bermúdez de Castro et al. 2004). "Classical" Neandertals lived in Europe and West Asia from ~200,000–28,000 ybp before disappearing, probably due to challenges presented by climate change, demography, and pressure from expanding AMH (Gravina, Mellars, and Ramsey 2005, Finlayson et al. 2006, Kuhn and Stiner 2006, Tzedakis et al. 2007).

There has been tremendous debate over the phylogenetic status of Neandertals relative to AMH. The range of opinions includes Neandertals being the same species as AMH (Trinkhaus 1983, Wolpoff et al. 2001) or a separate species entirely (Tattersall and Schwartz 1999, Stringer 2002a,b). Most of the recent genetic data available from Neandertals and AMH—

mitochondrial DNA, Y-chromosome, and autosomal DNA—indicate that there is considerable distance between these two hominins, perhaps at the species level (Serre et al. 2004, Caramelli et al. 2003, Green et al. 2006, Krause et al. 2007a).

The examination of craniofacial traits in these hominins also supports the view that Neandertals were a species distinct from early modern humans (Harvati, Frost, and McNulty 2004, Weaver, Roseman, and Stringer 2008), and had different developmental trajectories with taxon-specific patterns of ontogeny (Ponce de León and Zollikofer 2001, Ramirez Rossi and Bermúdez de Castro 2004). Collectively, these data imply that Neandertals were not the direct ancestors of any extant human populations, even if limited interbreeding were to have occurred between them (Duarte et al. 1999, Zilhão 2006).

However, more recent studies now suggest a somewhat different picture of the biological relationship between Neandertals and modern humans. Thanks to the technological advances of next generation sequencing, researchers have obtained a draft sequence of the Neandertal genome and compared it to those of modern humans and anthropoid primates to better define the genetic relationships between them. This research suggests that modern human and Neandertal DNA sequences diverged between 500,000 and 706,000 years ago based on genomic sequence data (Green et al. 2006, 2010, Noonan et al. 2006), and between $660,000 \pm 140,000$ years based on whole mtDNA genome sequence data (Green et al. 2008). However, the human and Neandertal ancestral populations appear to have split between 270,000 and 444,000 years ago (Noonan et al. 2006, Green et al. 2010), well before the emergence of modern humans in Africa.

Furthermore, the genomic analysis points to a low level of gene flow between Neandertals and modern humans, perhaps 1–4% (Green et al. 2010). Interestingly, Neandertals share more genetic variants with present-day humans in Eurasia than with those in sub-Saharan Africa (Green et al. 2010). This finding suggests that gene flow from Neandertals into the ancestors of non-Africans occurred before the divergence of Eurasian groups from each other, although other scenarios have been proposed (Green et al. 2010). This genetic exchange could possibly have occurred as modern humans first moved into the Middle East before 100,000 years ago, when Neandertals existed in the same region after this time, and probably until 50,000 years ago (Shea 2003b, Hublin 2009).

As for our own species, various lines of evidence indicate that anatomically modern humans arose in East Africa some 200,000 years ago. The dating of the Omo fossils from Ethiopia indicates the antiquity of early anatomically modern *H. sapiens* at 195,000 ± 6,000 ybp (McDougall, Brown, and Fleagle 2005). Genetic data also indicate similar time depth for modern humans based on mtDNA and Y-chromosome phylogenies (Chen et al. 2000, Ingman et al. 2000, Gonder et al. 2007, Behar et al. 2008). However, genetic data also demonstrate that AMH did not begin to expand out of Africa until approximately 60–70,000 years ago (Ingman et al. 2000, Forster 2004, Macaulay et al. 2005, Kivisild et al. 2006), meaning that *H. sapiens* existed in Africa for some 100–130,000 years before leaving the African continent. This expansion is also marked by the appearance of UP-like complexity in 70,000 year-old tools at MSA sites in South Africa (Henshilwood and Marean 2006, Backwell, d'Errico, and Wadley 2008), and its spread around the globe after that time (Foley and Lahr 2003, Shea 2003b).

How one makes taxonomic and evolutionary sense of this wide array of fossil hominins depends in part on one's predisposition to lump or split taxa. It is also contingent on the model of human origins and the early stages of hominin evolution that one accepts. For example, according to the linear model (Asfaw et al. 1999), the distinctive hominin anatomy evolved only once, and was followed by a ladder-like ancestor-descendant series, or anagenesis. In this model, there is little to no branching, or cladogenesis, until well after 3 mya.

In contrast, the so-called bushy model views hominin evolution as a series of successive adaptive radiations. During these moments of evolutionary diversification in response to novel circumstances, anatomical features present in these hominins may have been mixed and matched, producing the mosaic of traits seen in some fossils (Wood and Collard 1999, Leakey et al. 2001, Foley 2002). In fact, this model suggests that, due to the independent acquisition of similar shared characters (homoplasies), key hominid adaptations such as bipedalism or a large brain may have evolved more than once in the human lineage (Collard and Wood 2000).

Judging from the current fossil evidence, there may well have been considerable taxonomic diversity during hominin evolution around 5–7 mya. These species probably exhibited various and perhaps unknown combinations of hominin, chimp, and even novel features (Wood 2002, Wolpoff et al. 2002). However, due to homoplasy in these traits, certain of them may not be especially useful for phylogenetic reconstructions, since different species could possess these features without sharing a common ancestor (D. Lieberman 2000, 2007).

The complexity of hominin phylogeny has implications for how we model the evolution of the brain and mind, and think about the cultural and cognitive capabilities of our hominin ancestors. As indicated above, the evolution of our lineage was not likely to have followed a strict unilineal path but instead a reticulate branching process. The difficulty in finding a direct line linking earlier hominins with modern humans means that we must examine evidence for the emergence of human traits across the entire hominin lineage, and within the primate order, as well.

GENETIC VARIATION IN HUMANS AND OTHER PRIMATES

An important source of information about the evolution of modern human characteristics comes from studies of genetic variation in different primate species and, in particular, the great apes and humans. These studies, and especially those focusing on the comparison of human and chimpanzee genomes, have yielded new and fascinating insights into the phylogenetic relationships among primate species, and also the way that selection has shaped the evolution of coding sequences in these species. The detection of selection on certain loci is crucial because these changes in functional genes have likely led to the anatomical, behavioral, and cognitive differences that we see in monkeys, apes, and humans. What follows below is a summary of studies of the human and primate genomes and a discussion of their implications for the emergence of our species.

Primate Cytogenetics

Prior to the use of the polymerase chain reaction (PCR) and high throughput sequencing methods to analyze genetic variation, research-ers characterized chromosomal banding patterns and compared segmen-tal positions in different primate species to understand phylogenetic and functional differences between them. These structural features of chromo-somes revealed information about the genomic similarity of different spe-cies. These studies did not generate direct genealogical insights into the phylogenetic relationships between species as do studies of single copy nuclear genes or uniparentally inherited genetic systems, such as the mitochondrial DNA (mtDNA) or the Y-chromosome, in large part due to re-combination and other rearrangements that have taken place over many millions of years. However, they demonstrated the relative similarity of the genomes of these species, and identified sorts of evolutionary processes that they have experienced over the past 10–20 million years.

In reviewing one cladogram based on chromosome banding patterns (Fig. 2.3), we can see that there have been a number of significant changes in chromosome structure over the past 14–25 million years, including fissions, fusions, and inversions. Gibbons have undergone tremendous chromosome rearrangements, and they also show a range of karyotypes, while the branch leading to the orangutan and African apes has undergone two fissions to produce the 48-chromosome karyotype. In the human lineage, there has been a fusion of two chromosomes present in chimpanzees and other primates to create the human chromosome 2, thereby reducing the human karyotype to 2n=46 (e.g., Ferguson-Smith and Trifonov 2007). A recent survey of sequence variation of the >600 kb surrounding this fusion

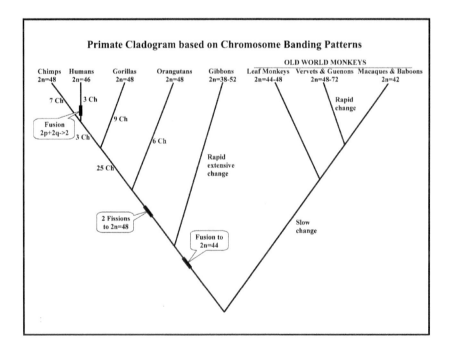

2.3. Primate cladogram based on chromosomal banding patterns. (Modified after S. Jones et al. 1992, Chap. 8.2, J. Marks, p. 301.)

point revealed multiple duplications of large sequence blocks that originated on other chromosomes (Fan et al. 2002), some of which may be associated with breakpoints of inversions that occurred during primate evolution, or with recurrent chromosome rearrangements that have taken place in humans.

Overall, both cytogenetic and molecular data indicate that genomic rearrangements have occurred frequently during primate genome evolution and significantly contributed to the DNA differences between these species (Fan et al. 2002, Frazer et al. 2003, Ciccarelli et al. 2005, Ferguson-Smith and Trifonov 2007). Because they are often found in intergenic regions, such rearrangements may play a role in gene expression differences between humans and other primates (Frazer et al. 2003).

Primate Genome Expansion

Recent work at the genomic level has confirmed the dynamic quality of primate genomes, as well as the extent of chromosomal rearrangements and expansion implied by earlier cytogenetic work. Compared to those of other mammalian species, the genomes of humans and other primates are enriched with large, interspersed segmental duplications (SDs) with high levels of sequence identity. These SDs appear to have arisen in waves of duplication during different phases of primate evolution. These genomic comparisons also point to a strong association between duplication, genomic instability, and large-scale chromosomal rearrangements. More important from an evolutionary standpoint, the occurrence of these SDs may have generated novel primate gene families, as well as significantly influenced human genic and phenotypic variation (Bailey et al. 2002, Bailey and Eichler 2006, Eichler 2006) (Fig. 2.4).

Why is this feature of SDs so important? Compared to single copy nuclear genes, SDs are 5–10 times as likely to show interspecies and intraspecies structural and/or copy-number variation (Fortna et al. 2004, Cheng et al. 2005, Tuzun et al. 2005). These copy number variants (CNVs) have, in turn, been correlated with differences in mRNA expression levels, and, thus, appear to exert an influence on normal gene regulation (Hollox, Armour, and Barber 2003, Khaitovich et al. 2004, Cheng et al. 2005). Strong signatures of positive selection are also common in segmentally duplicated genes (Johnson et al. 2001, Semple, Rolfe, and Dorin 2003, Birtle, Goodstadt, and Ponting 2005, Chimpanzee Sequencing and Analysis Consor-

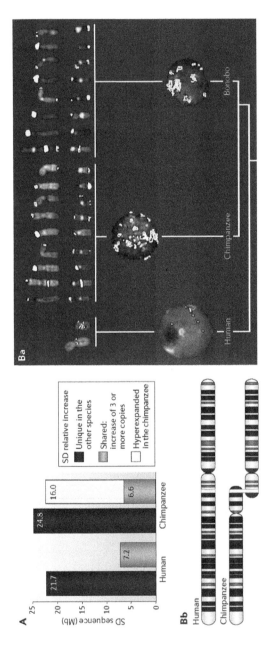

2.4. Variation in genomic segmental duplication (SD) content between chimpanzees and humans. Panel A: A comparison of duplicated sequence from the chimpanzee and human genomes allowed the identification of regions of shared duplication and those that contain human-specific or chimpanzee-specific multicopy sequence (>94% identity and >20 kb). An estimated 60% represented duplicative gain, whereas 40% of the change occurred as a result of deletion of ancestral duplications. Overall, as shown in the graph, a minimal estimate of 76 Mb is differentially duplicated between humans and chimpanzees, corresponding to 3–5 Mb duplication gain per million years. Panel B: Hyperexpansion of an SD in the chimpanzee lineage. Fluorescence in situ hybridization staining (white) is shown in panel **Ba** for an SD duplicon of ~40 kb, revealing an expansion to 400–500 copies of this sequence in the chimpanzee and bonobo, mainly near telomeres (only chromosomes that carry the duplicon are shown). This expansion added ~16 Mb of duplicated sequence in a common ancestor of chimpanzees and bonobos that is not present in gorillas and humans. As shown in panel **Bb**, the same SD underlies an association between duplication and rearrangement: it is associated with a large-scale chromosome fusion event that produced human chromosome 2 (this chromosome is shown next to the two orthologous chimpanzee chromosomes; the SD lies 40 kb proximal of the fusion point). (Reprinted with permission from Macmillan Publishers Ltd: *Nature Reviews Genetics 7* (2006), J. Bailey and E. Eichler, pp. 552–64, Fig. 5.)

tium 2005, Ciccarelli et al. 2005).

Furthermore, it has been noted that several functional categories are enriched among these genes, including loci involved in immune response, xenobiotic recognition (e.g., olfactory reception), and reproduction (Clark et al. 2003a). These findings suggest a very important role for SDs in primate and human adaptive evolution. In support of this view, polymorphic insertions, deletions, and inversions in humans are non-randomly distributed, with a 4–12-fold greater frequency near sites of SD (Sebat et al. 2004, Iafrate et al. 2004, Feuk et al. 2005, Sharp et al. 2005, Tuzun et al. 2005, Eichler 2006). Similarly, in chimpanzee populations there is an almost 20-fold enrichment of copy-number variation for regions in which duplications arose in the human-chimpanzee ancestor (Bailey and Eichler 2006, Perry et al. 2006, 2008). These data further indicate that duplicated regions are continuing to rearrange and evolve in contemporary primate populations.

The human genome has also grown in size over the past 50 million years through retrotransposition (Liu et al. 2003). Retrotranspositions are a subclass of transposons, or jumping genes, that can amplify themselves in a genome through self-replication. They are ubiquitous components of the DNA of many eukaryotic organisms, and comprise around 42% of the human genome (Lander et al. 2001). While rates of single-nucleotide substitution remain relatively constant in different primate lineages, those for retrotransposition have not. These evolutionary differences have led to a 15–20% expansion of the human genome size over the last 50 million years of primate evolution, 90% of it being attributable to new retroposon insertions. Within the last 6–8 million years, the human chromosomes have expanded 30 megabases (Mb) compared to the primate genome of the chimpanzee (Liu et al. 2003). In fact, it appears that our genome continues to significantly expand due to shifts in retrotranspositional activity. The exact implications of this chromosomal expansion for selection and adaptation in the human and chimp lineages have yet to be fully elaborated.

Nuclear Gene Variation

Much work has been done with functional genes in humans, apes, and monkeys to clarify their evolutionary relationships prior to the emergence of genomic sequences. Since that time, data obtained from comparative and functional genomics has elaborated on the initial findings obtained through traditional sequencing and chromosomal mapping approaches.

PRIMATE NUCLEAR GENETIC TREE

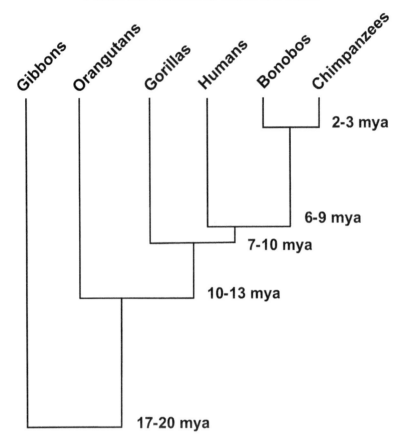

2.5. A phylogeny showing the evolutionary relationships between different hominoid species. The numbers indicate estimated millions of years (myr) from the last branch point to the present along particular lineages. The time estimates are based on both fossil evidence and genetic data from the species represented in the tree. (After Klein and Takahata 2002.)

Various nuclear gene sequences have been used to reconstruct phylogenetic relationships of humans and hominoid ape species. In the phylogeny shown in Figure 2.5, there is a clear separation of the human-chimp lineage from that uniting gorilla with human-chimp. The human-chimp split dates to 5.4 mya and human-gorilla to 7.3 mya, while the common chimp-bonobo split occurred around 2.5 mya. The human-chimp split is somewhat later than other estimates of the genetic divergence of these species (e.g.,

Arnason et al. 2000), but is consistent in showing a shallower subdivision of these hominoid lineages than was once supposed based on morphological and fossil evidence (Klein and Takahata 2002).

These kinds of phylogenetic reconstructions are now being investigated at the genomic level through sequence comparisons involving multiple different primate species. In one such study of four genomic regions from human, chimp, gorilla, and orangutan comprising ~2 million base pairs, Hobolth et al. (2007) estimate the human-chimp speciation event at 4.1 ± 0.4 mya and fairly large ancestral effective population sizes (65,000 ± 30,000 for the human-chimp ancestor). Interestingly, they noted that approximately half of the human genome coalesced with chimpanzee after speciation with gorilla. Through their comparison of genomic segments from humans, chimpanzees, gorillas, orangutans, and macaques, Patterson et al. (2006) suggested that the apparently short divergence time between humans and chimpanzees on the X chromosome was explained by an interspecific hybridization event in the ancestry of these two species. Their data also indicated that hominin-chimp gene flow ceased and final speciation occurred as recently as 4.0 mya. This date is generally consistent with the hominin fossil record, in particular, the emergence of the genus *Australopithecus*, and suggests that, while basal to the hominin clade, *Orrorin* and *Sahelanthropus* may not demarcate the exact starting point of the human lineage.

A similar effort to determine the genomic divergence among hominoids and estimate the effective population size of the common ancestor of humans and chimpanzees involved the analysis of 53 autosomal intergenic nonrepetitive DNA segments from a human, a chimpanzee, a gorilla, and an orangutan (Chen and Li 2001, Chen et al. 2001). The average sequence divergence was only 1.24% ± 0.07% for the human-chimpanzee pair, 1.62% ± 0.08% for the human-gorilla pair, and 1.63% ± 0.08% for the chimpanzee-gorilla pair. When these DNA segments were subjected to phylogenetic analysis, they strongly supported the *Homo-Pan* clade. However, when each segment was analyzed separately, about 42% of them produced a phylogeny that was inconsistent with the species tree (Chen and Li 2001).

These results were interpreted as revealing a large effective population size (N_e) of the common ancestor of *Homo* and *Pan* (between 52,000 to 96,000), as also seen by Hobolth et al. (2007). Interestingly, these estimates are 5–9 times larger than the long-term effective population size of humans (~10,000) estimated from genetic polymorphism data and linkage disequilibrium studies (Zietkiewicz et al. 1998, Wall 2003, Zhivotovsky, Rosenberg, and Feldman 2003, Tenesa et al. 2007). Thus, the human lineage appears to have experienced a large reduction in effective population size after its separation from the chimpanzee lineage some 4.6–6.2 mya (Chen and Li 2001).

Primate mtDNA Evolution

Much has also been learned about primate evolution from the analysis of mtDNA. The phylogenetic analysis of hominid mtDNAs shows a clear differentiation of each species in terms of its maternal lineage(s) and differing degrees of branching within each species-specific clade (Gagneux et al. 1999) (Fig. 2.6). The hominin lineage is distinct from the chimpanzee lineage in having very short branches at its terminus and lacking any truly archaic branches, aside from that leading to Neandertals.

By contrast, chimpanzees show far greater mtDNA diversity than humans in terms of the number and antiquity of the branches at both the species and

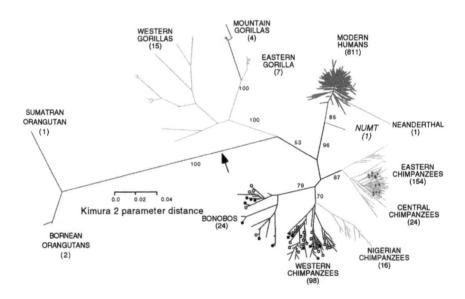

2.6. An unrooted neighbor-joining tree of hominid mtDNA sequences. The numbers of samples per species or subspecies represented in the tree are shown in parentheses. Bootstrap values ≥50% for the primary internodes are shown along the branches. The position of the midpoint root is indicated by an arrow. (From P. Gagneux et al. 1999:5077–82, Fig. 1. © 1999 National Academy of Sciences, USA.)

the subspecies levels. This pattern of branching implies long-term occupation of the species range, the maintenance of population structure over time, and the preservation of much of the genetic diversity that had accumulated over the past 3–5 million years, not to mention a larger effective population size of chimpanzees relative to hominins (Gagneux et al. 1999).

FUNCTIONAL DIFFERENCES IN HUMAN-CHIMP GENOMES

The previous discussion of genetic variation in primates and humans sets the stage for a review of analyses of human and chimp genomes, which have now been completely sequenced, at least in draft form. This analysis is facilitated by the availability of genomic sequence data from other species such as rat (Rat Genome Sequencing Project Consortium 2004), *Drosophila* (Adams et al. 2000), rhesus macaque (Rhesus Macaque Genome Sequencing and Analysis Consortium 2007), and others. Based on the comparison of genomic data, human and chimpanzee gene sequences are nearly 96% identical, implying close phylogenetic links between them (e.g., Clark et al. 2003a).

However, these two genomes also exhibit biologically important changes that have occurred since the ancestral lineages of these species diverged. Studies of primate genomes have identified hundreds of genes that show a pattern of sequence change consistent with adaptive evolution occurring in human ancestors. These data have also allowed researchers to estimate the extent and regional variation of the mutational forces shaping these two genomes. The patterns of evolution in human and chimpanzee protein-coding genes are also highly correlated and dominated by the fixation of neutral and slightly deleterious alleles.

Through using the chimpanzee genome as an outgroup taxon in studies of human genetic variation, researchers have been able to identify signatures of selective sweeps in recent human evolution. These selective sweeps facilitate a greater understanding of the molecular basis of adaptive evolution. As previously noted, the rapidly evolving categories of genes within the hominin lineage are primarily related to immunity and host defense, reproduction (especially spermatogenesis), and sensory perception (especially olfaction). These are the same categories that are known to be undergoing rapid evolution within the broader mammalian lineage, as well as more distantly related species (Chimpanzee Sequencing and Analysis Consortium 2005, Clark et al. 2003a, Sabeti et al. 2006, Nielsen et al. 2005, Williamson et al. 2007, Bustamante et al. 2005).

We also see evidence for accelerated evolution in several functional classes of genes involved in nuclear transport, cell adhesion, ion transport, and sound perception that have undergone accelerated divergence in both human and chimpanzee (Clark et al. 2003a, Chimpanzee Sequencing and Analysis Consortium 2005), while other candidates for positive selection have novel, as-yet-unknown functions (Clark et al. 2003a, Nielsen et al. 2005, Bustamante et al. 2005). There is further evidence that, in addition to being influenced by positive selection, certain genes have experienced particularly strong relaxation of constraints in hominins. On the other hand, roughly 13.5% of potentially informative loci exhibited few amino acid differences between humans and chimpanzees. This observation indicates that weak negative selection and/or balancing selection has operated on mutations at these loci (Bustamante et al. 2005).

Several studies have also noted that X-linked genes are significantly overrepresented among rapidly evolving genes in humans and chimps (Chimpanzee Sequencing and Analysis Consortium 2005, Nielsen et al. 2005). The increased selection on the X chromosome is undoubtedly related to the fact that it contains a large number of sperm- and testis-associated genes (Nielsen et al. 2005), which are frequent targets of selection. In addition, the hemizygosity of the X chromosome in males exposes recessive alleles to selective pressure, which may further promote rapid evolution (Schaffner 2004).

Human-chimp genome comparisons have also permitted a closer examination of regions of the human genome that may reflect recent adaptive evolution. For example, a recent study of different human populations revealed regions of the human genome with strong evidence of a recent selective sweep, with the estimated position of the selective sweep falling within 100 kb of a known gene (Williamson et al. 2007). Within these regions, a number of loci of biological importance were identified, including ones involved in pigmentation pathways, components of the dystrophin protein complex, clusters of olfactory receptors, genes involved in nervous system development and function, immune system genes, and heat shock genes. Overall, Williamson et al. (2007) noted that as much as 10% of the human genome had been influenced by linkage to a selective sweep.

Olfaction

Having described the overall patterns of genetic divergence and selection in the human and chimp genomes, I will now focus on several key genetic adaptations in the hominin lineage and explore their relationship to other anatomical, physiological, and behavioral characteristics.

One set of genes that has undergone very rapid change in the chimpanzee and especially the human lineage are those involved with olfaction. Nearly 50 such genes linked to smell show evidence of positive selection (relaxed selection) in humans (Chen and Li 2001, Clark et al. 2003a, Gilad et al. 2003a, 2003b, Chimpanzee Sequencing and Analysis Consortium 2005). These differences probably reflect the reduced importance of smell in the human lifestyle relative to that of chimpanzees.

One of the largest gene families influencing the sense of smell, the olfactory receptors (OR), is known to be undergoing rapid divergence in primates. OR genes are encoded by the largest mammalian gene superfamily of >1,000 genes (Ben-Arie et al. 1994, Gilad et al. 2003a, 2003b). Analysis of these genes in the draft assembly of the human genome has suggested that more than 100 functional human ORs are likely to be under no evolutionary constraint (Gilad, Man, and Glusman 2005).

Bipedalism

Bipedalism is a key human adaptation and a defining feature of the hominin clade. It is marked by a series of skeleto-muscular, neurological, postural, and developmental changes that permit habitual movement and balance on two legs (Lovejoy 1981, Alexander 1992, Jablonski and Chaplin 1993, Spoor et al. 1994, 1996, Fitzpatrick et al. 2006). The anatomical changes involved in supporting bipedal creatures include changing pelvic structure, angled knees, curved lumbar region, reorientation of muscle attachments, and adducted large toes, among others (Lovejoy 1981, Alexander 1992, Jablonski and Chaplin 1993). Within the hominin clade, researchers have recognized two forms of bipedalism, termed "facultative" (i.e., optional) or "obligate" (habitual) (Wood 2002). As indicated in Figure 2.2, these forms imply different degrees of adaptation to this locomotory pattern, hence, the presence of the anatomical, behavioral, and physiological changes associated with it.

The anatomical changes involved in supporting bipedalism also posed challenges to hominins that were undergoing increasing encephalization from about 2.0 mya to the present. The problem of birthing increasingly large-headed infants necessitated changes in the pelvic structure and shape of the birth canal, which, in turn, created obstetric complications (Trevathan 1987, Whitcome, Shapiro, and Lieberman 2007). The trade-off between being fully bipedal and becoming larger brained resulted in delayed prenatal development and significant post-natal brain growth in hominin offspring (Bogin 2001, Aiello and Wells 2002). It also appears that the growth in size and complexity of neuronal connectivity in the human cerebellum compared to chimps may be related to upright posture and modulation of muscle movements and timing, not to mention aspects of language processing (Gazzaniga, Ivry, and Mangun 1998, Schoenemann 2006). Therefore, in addition to being an adaptation with important anatomical and physiological consequences, bipedalism also likely had an important influence on the development of human cognitive abilities.

Comparative genomic work has indicated that certain selective changes may have occurred in genes that influenced the evolution of bipedalism. These include loci that may be involved in long-bone growth (cytoskeletal proteins) and hair loss (thermoregulation) (Winter et al. 2001, Clark et al. 2003a), as well as other loci involved with actin binding, cytoskeletal formation, and ectoderm development and which may be under weak negative selection (Clark et al. 2003a, Bustamante et al. 2005). Cytoskeletal protein genes in particular show extensive amino acid polymorphism within humans but limited amino acid divergence between humans and chimpanzees (Bustamante et al. 2005).

These new genetic data provide a new context in which to understand the emergence of bipedalism in the hominin lineage based on fossil evidence. To date, *Sahelanthropus* is only known from craniodental evidence (Brunet et al. 2002). Therefore, while the position of its foramen magnum suggests that it was bipedal (Zollikofer et al. 2005), postcranial fossils from this taxon are needed to confirm its bipedal status. Fossil femora discovered in the Lukeino Formation of Kenya and attributed to *Orrorin tugenensis* (Senut et al. 2001) purportedly provide the earliest postcranial evidence of hominin bipedalism at 6 mya (Pickford et al. 2002). However, there has been considerable debate over the functional and phylogenetic significance of these femora in relation to those of other hominin forms (e.g., Begun 2004).

Subsequent analysis of hominin and ape femora has provided additional insights into the emergence of bipedality in the hominin lineage (Richmond and Jungers 2008). This study has shown that the *O. tugenensis* femur differs from those of apes and *Homo,* and most strongly resembles those of *Australopithecus* and *Paranthropus.* Femoral morphology also indicates that *O. tugenensis* shared distinctive hip biomechanics with australopithecines. This evidence suggests that the morphological complex involving the pelvis and femora evolved early in hominin evolution and persisted for almost 4 million years until additional modifications of the hip appeared in early *Homo.*

However, the similarities in femoral morphology among the early hominins do not exclude the possibility that they also engaged in other forms of locomotory behavior. In fact, the upper limb fossils of *O. tugenensis* exhibit morphological features related to arboreal climbing, such as curved proximal manual phalanges (Senut et al. 2001). The presence of these features in a species close to the chimp-human split implies that bipedalism evolved from a hominin ancestor that was adapted to orthograde and vertical climbing. This interpretation, in turn, indicates that the ancestor had a climbing and knuckle-walking repertoire (Richmond, Begun, and Strait 2001) rather than being an orangutan-like arboreal specialist (Thorpe, Holder, and Crompton 2007).

The comparative biomechanical anatomy of *O. tugenensis* femora suggests that this species is a basal hominin adapted to bipedalism (Senut et al. 2001, Richmond, Begun, and Strait 2001, Thorpe, Holder, and Crompton 2007). In addition, current evidence suggests that an *Australopithecus*-like bipedal morphology evolved early in the hominin clade and persisted successfully for most of human evolutionary history. However, truly obligate bipedalism apparently did not arise until the emergence of *Homo erectus*, in contrast with the facultative bipedalism of early hominids. Regardless of the exact time when obligate bipedalism took root in the hominin lineage, the anatomical changes underlying this locomotory adaptation were substantial (Fig. 2.7).

There is also the matter of the bioenergetics of bipedal locomotion. Various studies have attempted to quantify the energetic costs of quadrupedal versus bipedal locomotory patterns in humans, hominins, and chimps to determine whether bipedality conferred some benefit to those species that habitually employed this pattern of movement (Pontzer and Wrangham 2004, Steudel-Numbers 2006, Sockol, Raichlen, and Pontzer 2007). One such study examined stride lengths, speed, and energy costs in the walking of *Australopithecus afarensis*, based on the Laetoli footprints. These investigators noted that, by 3.5 mya, at least some early hominins, despite their small stature, could sustain efficient bipedal walking at absolute speeds within the

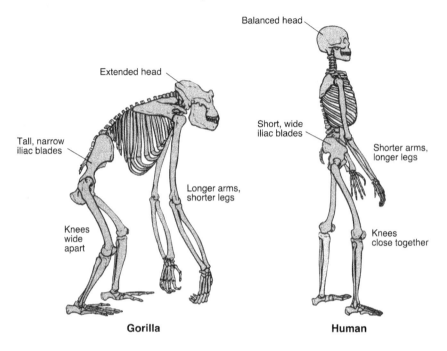

2.7. Human bipedality and ape anatomy. A comparison of gorilla and human anatomy and stature. (From Bernard G. Campbell, James D. Loy, and Kathryn Cruz-Uribe, *Humankind Emerging,* 9th ed., © 2006, Fig. 13.16. Printed and electronically reproduced by permission of Pearson Education, Inc., Upper Saddle River, New Jersey.)

range shown by modern humans (Sellers et al. 2005).

Walking on two legs also produced certain thermoregulatory demands that had to be compensated for physiologically. The need for hominids to walk long distances upright probably led to the loss of much of their body hair and the emergence of an extensive system of sweat glands to remove excess heat through transpiration (Wheeler 1984, 1991), and perhaps also darker skin pigmentation to protect the skin from excessive UV light (Jablonski 2004). In fact, according to the thermoregulatory model, the increased heat loss, increased cooling, reduced heat gain, and reduced water requirements conferred by a bipedal stance in a hot, tropical climate was the primary selective pressure leading to bipedalism (Wheeler 1991). However, others have suggested other possible selective forces, such as ecological adaptations for feeding (Hunt 1996) or the social, sexual, and reproductive conduct of early hominids (Lovejoy 1981). In any case, the shift from a quadrupedal to a bipedal locomotory adaptation led to a major transformation of hominins at anatomical, behavioral, cognitive, and physiological levels.

Dietary Changes

Comparisons of the human and chimp genomes have also indicated that nearly 80 genes used to digest proteins also differ between these two species (Clark et al. 2003a, Chimpanzee Sequencing and Analysis Consortium 2005). These differences likely reflect how the human diet has changed in the 5 million years since hominins split from chimpanzees. The most significant dietary change occurring during this time period was the greater reliance on meat in the diet, which is evident in the taphonomic record for early *Homo* (Stanford 2001, Foley 2002, Dominguez-Rodrigo and Pickering 2003). This evidence marks a major shift in subsistence strategy to one focusing on acquisition of fats and proteins in meat, whether through scavenging or hunting (Stiner 2002).

The transition to a diet consisting of greater amounts of meat and fats is also reflected in changes in gut morphology in apes and hominins (Aiello and Wheeler 1995, Milton 1999) (Fig. 2.8). Concurrent with increasing encephalization in the hominin lineage, within the genus *Homo* (see below), the hominin digestive system also underwent a major transformation. Chimps (and most probably early hominins) have a longer large intestine and a shorter small intestine, as needed by an omnivorous species with a significant intake of vegetative matter and fibrous food sources. By contrast, humans have the opposite configuration, a shorter large intestine and longer small intestine, allowing them to absorb more of nutrients, minerals, and fats in the food sources that they consume (Aiello and Wheeler 1995, Milton 1999). This remodeling of the body had significant bioenergetic implications, as both the brain and the stomach are metabolically costly organs, although it was possibly mediated by changes in the proportion of body weight comprised of fat (Milton 1999, Aiello and Wells 2002). Overall, *H. erectus* exhibits features more similar to those of modern humans than those of earlier and contemporaneous australopithecines and paranthropines, such as larger relative brain sizes, larger bodies, higher energetic needs, slower rates of growth and maturation, obligate bipedalism, and smaller teeth and jaws (Aiello and Wells 2002, Antón and Swisher 2004).

There has been considerable effort to understand the conditions under which these morphological and dietary changes took place. According

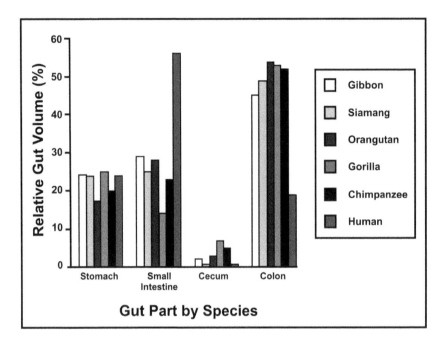

2.8. Relative gut volume proportions for some hominoid primate species. (Redrawn after Milton 1999:488–98, Fig. 1.)

to the turnover-pulse hypothesis, the emergence of the genus *Homo* was linked to climatic fluctuations and habitat disruption about 2.5–2.0 mya, which coincided with the initial transition of forests to open grassland in Africa (Stanley 1992, Vrba 1994, deMenocal 1995, Larick and Ciochon 1996). Under these conditions, long-term directional selection related to lower temperatures and increased aridity may have favored ecological generalization in early hominins (Potts 1998). In addition, the emergence of numerous savannah-adapted antelope species during this time would have provided diverse food resources for hominin scavengers, who were beginning to exploit prey taken by large cats and hyenas (Vrba 1985, Larick and Ciochon 1996, de Heinzelin et al. 1999, Teaford, Ungar, and Grine 2000).

Others view the role of dietary change in the origin and early evolution of the genus *Homo* in Africa slightly differently. For example, based on craniodental remains of early *Homo*, Ungar, Grine, and Teaford (2006) see no simple transition from an australopithecine to a *Homo* grade of dietary adaptation, or from closed forest plant diets to reliance on more open-country plants or animals. In their view, early *Homo* species more likely had adaptations for flexible, versatile subsistence strategies that would have served them well in the variable paleoenvironments of the African Plio-Pleistocene. This view is echoed by Wood and Strait (2004), who suggest that it was the dietary and behavioral flexibility exhibited by early *Homo*, not the narrowing of its ecological niche that enabled this lineage to persist.

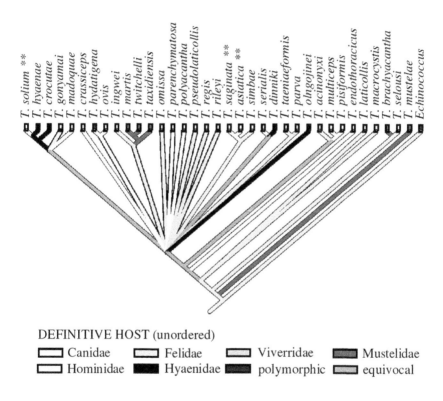

DEFINITIVE HOST (unordered)

☐ Canidae ☐ Felidae ▨ Viverridae ▨ Mustelidae
☐ Hominidae ■ Hyaenidae ▨ polymorphic ▨ equivocal

2.9. Phylogenetic relationships and host associations among species of *Taenia* (tapeworms). The majority rule consensus tree is based on analyses of 35 species-level taxa. Species of *Taenia* in human definitive hosts (asterisks) can be divided into two sub-clades: the "*T. solium* sub-clade" containing *T. solium, T. hyaenae, T. crocutae, T. gonyamai,* and *T. madoquae*; and the "*T. saginata* sub-clade" including *T. saginata* and its sister species, *T. asiatica* and *T. simbae*. Parsimony mapping was used to examine the putative relationships for *Taenia* spp. and definitive hosts. Not all host families are depicted on the tree due to multiple host groups and polymorphic coding in terminals for some species of *Taenia* (i.e., Suidae, Procaviidae, Canidae and Primates for *T. solium*). (From Hoberg et al., Out of Africa: Origins of the Taenia Tapeworms in Humans, *PRSB* 268 (2001): 781–87, Fig. 1a; used with permission.)

We also have indirect evidence for this shift in subsistence strategy to one focusing on acquisition of fats and proteins in meat, whether through scavenging or hunting. This evidence comes in the form of morphological and genetic data from different species of tapeworms (genus *Taenia*). Based on these data, it appears that these parasites colonized early hominins at least twice around 2.0–2.5 mya during hominins' dietary and behavioral shifts, from herbivory to scavenging and carnivory in the Plio-Pleistocene (Hoberg et al. 2001) (Fig. 2.9). Phylogenetic analysis indicated that the immediate ancestors of these tapeworms used carnivores (hyaenids, canids, or felids) as definitive hosts and bovids as intermediate hosts.

At a behavioral level, the practice of scavenging and hunting implies the coordination of group actions to procure food sources. Some form of communication must have been involved in these activities, particularly since they involved either chasing felids and hyenids away from freshly killed animals, or stalking herd animals that were highly mobile. In this regard, comparisons between chimp and human hunting practices reveal considerable differences between them, including the types of prey taken, the coordination of group action, and the sharing of meat after an animal is killed (Stanford 2001). The lack of coordinated group actions in chimps implies that the hominin form of scavenging, and later hunting, probably began during the Plio-Pleistocene period (Foley 2002, Stiner 2002, Dominguez-Rodrigo and Pickering 2003).

EVOLUTION OF LANGUAGE

What do we mean when we say language evolution? How different are language abilities between apes and humans? To begin with, humans have voluntary control of the voice, face, and hands, whereas chimps and monkeys show deliberate control only of their hands. Both humans and apes are capable of learning and imitation, but only humans can clearly teach others how to do tasks, while apes require human training to repeatedly perform imitative behaviors. While great apes can clearly master the use of hundreds of symbols and rudimentary grammar, humans are capable of learning a far greater vocabulary and symbolic repertoire (Premack 2004). In addition, humans have both recursive and non-recursive theories of mind, and the capacity to understand recursive and non-recursive grammars, whereas apes or monkeys are limited to non-recursive grammars (Premack 2004). Moreover, as P. Lieberman (2007:39) notes, "speech also requires a brain that can 'reiterate' or freely reorder a finite set of motor gestures to form a potentially infinite number of words and sentences." This appears to be lacking in chimps and other nonhuman primates.

While there must be a genetic basis to the differences in cognitive and language abilities observed in different primate species, we have also learned much about them through the analysis of brain anatomy, neuronal complexity, and vocal tract anatomy in these same taxa. Whereas language abilities were once thought to reside mostly in Broca's and Wernicke's areas in the left hemisphere of the brain, we now understand that many different parts of the brain are involved in speech production and comprehensive and symbolic behavior. Comparative studies of primate and human brain anatomy viewed in the context of new genetic data have also given us insights into aspects of brain growth and development. Furthermore, research on genes affecting brain size and studies of neuronal connectivity and morphology suggests different kinds of wiring in primate and human brains.

Language, Hearing, and Vocal Apparatus

Human-chimp genome comparisons have identified changes in 21 human genes that are linked to hearing. Such genes not only enable humans to understand speech in the brain, but also are involved in hearing and are likely related to the linguistic abilities of modern humans. One particular locus, the alpha tectorin gene, shows considerable differences between chimps and humans. Interestingly, this locus is expressed in the brain and in the hearing apparatus itself in a membrane of the inner ear (Clark et al. 2003a). Its importance for hearing had previously been known, as mutations in this gene cause congenital deafness in humans (e.g., Verhoeven et al. 1998).

Language or speech production also relies on having the appropriate anatomical features of vocal apparatus. As noted in Figure 2.10, humans and apes differ considerably in the size and shape of the vocal tract, the position of the tongue in the oral cavity, and the location of the larynx in the throat. In apes, we observe the higher position of the larynx, a longer and shallower tongue and oral cavity, and the inability to use tongue and oral cavity to produce vowel sounds. By contrast, the human tongue's shape and position creates 1:1 oral-to-pharyngeal proportions of the supralaryngeal vocal tract. Overall, "the chimpanzee lacks a vocal tract capable of producing the 'quantal' sounds (regions of acoustic stability) that facilitate both speech production and perception, and a brain that can reiterate the pho-

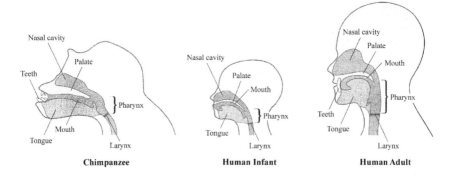

2.10. A comparison of chimpanzee and human vocal anatomy. (From Bernard G. Campbell, James D. Loy, and Kathryn Cruz-Uribe, *Humankind Emerging,* 9th ed., © 2006, Fig. 13.5. Printed and electronically reproduced by permission of Pearson Education, Inc., Upper Saddle River, New Jersey.)

netic contrasts apparent in its fixed vocalizations" (P. Lieberman 2007:39).

There has been considerable interest in understanding the ontogenetic aspects of language abilities in humans and apes. One possibility is that the developmental sequence that gives rise to the adult human vocal apparatus follows a general ape trajectory until shifting into a more human track. In this model, the human child has its larynx situated higher in its throat like apes until 2–3 years of age, when it begins producing articulate speech, at which time several developmental changes take place, including the descent of the larynx into its adult position in the throat. Thus, both anatomical and cognitive changes mark the emergence of the human ability to comprehend and produce semantically meaningful sounds (P. Lieberman 2007).

While this scenario may be generally accurate, a recent study of the ontogenetic trajectories of craniofacial traits for humans and apes revealed the existence of developmental differences even earlier in life. In this analysis, Mitteroecker et al. (2004) carried out a geomorphometric analysis of 96 traditional three-dimensional landmarks and semi-landmarks on the face and cranial base from adult *H. sapiens, Pan paniscus, Pan troglodytes, Gorilla gorilla,* and *Pongo pygmaeus.* They observed that *H. sapiens* specimens were clearly separated from the great apes in shape space and size-shape space. At birth, *H. sapiens* infants were already markedly different from the great apes, which overlap at this age but diverge among themselves post-natally. Hence, there are distinct ontogenetic trajectories in humans and apes that begin early in development and cannot be explained as differences arising through heterochrony (changes in timing in the appearance of these features).

FOXP2 Gene and Language Abilities

Additional clues about the evolution of language abilities in humans come from genetic studies of loci that are involved in the production and comprehension of speech. Many of these genes have been identified through studies of speech and language comprehension deficits in different human populations. The mutations underlying these disorders likely influence the areas of the brain that are most centrally involved in speech and language processing, namely Broca's and Wernicke's areas.

Broca's area, located in the inferior frontal gyrus (IFG) of the human brain, is one of several critical regions associated with the motor planning and execution of language. Wernicke's area, located on the posterior section of the superior temporal gyrus, on the Sylvian fissure, is known to be involved in the comprehension of spoken language. Based on current evidence, the neural circuits linking these cortical regions with the basal ganglia and other subcortical structures help to regulate motor control, including speech production, as well as syntax and other cognitive processes (P. Lieberman 2007).

Recent studies with nonhuman primates have revealed the importance of these brain areas for communication in both ape and monkey species. For example, PET scans of chimpanzees engaged in vocalization showed activity in the IFG as well as other cortical and subcortical regions (Taglialatela et al. 2008). These findings were taken as implying that the neurological structures underlying language production in the human brain may have been present in the common ancestor of chimps and humans. Related studies with monkeys have shown that the homolog of Broca's area in monkey brains corresponds to a region involved in the control of the monkey's face, larynx, tongue, and mouth (Petrides, Cadoret, and Mackey 2005, Gil-da-Costa et al. 2006). In addition, the homologous Wernicke's area was involved in the recognition of sound sequences and calls of other monkeys (Gil-da-Costa et al. 2006). However, as noted above, humans' ability to develop articulate speech relies on capabilities such as fine control of the larynx and mouth that are absent in apes and monkeys (Premack 2004, P. Lieberman 2007).

Several years ago, researchers identified a gene that is central to the human ability to develop language, due to its role in governing the embryonic development of subcortical structures of brain involved with speech production and comprehension. They noted that a point mutation in the forkhead-box P2 transcription factor gene (FOXP2) co-segregated with a disorder in a family in which half of the members have severe articulation difficulties accompanied by linguistic and grammatical impairment (Specific Language Impairment Consortium 2002). The predominant features of the FOXP2 phenotype of affected individuals were an impairment of both the selection and sequencing of fine orofacial movements underlying fluent speech, and the linguistic processing for both spoken and written language (Enard et al. 2002, Specific Language Impairment Consortium 2002, Groszer et al. 2008). Two functional copies of FOXP2 were required for the acquisition of normal spoken language, as the disease appears to be caused by the haploinsufficiency of gene expression.[7] However, it should also be noted that other genes may also be involved in language production, such as loci on chromosomes 16 and 19 (SLI Consortium 2002).

Because of this gene's significant impact on speech production and language comprehension, particularly on fine orofacial movements that are typical of humans and not great apes, there was speculation about its possible role in the emergence of the human capability to develop proficient spoken language (Enard et al. 2002). Were this true, the time at which this FOXP2 variant became fixed in the human population could be linked to the evolution of human language.

To investigate this question, Enard et al. (2002) sequenced the FOXP2 gene in humans, a number of nonhuman primate species, and the mouse as a mammalian outgroup. They then analyzed the phylogenetic relationships among these sequences. They observed that nearly all mutations in this gene were synonymous nucleotide changes, with the branches leading to the orangutan and the mouse each having a single non-synonymous mutation (Fig. 2.11). By contrast, the human lineage exhibited only two mutations, both of which are non-synonymous changes. Enard and colleagues concluded that this gene has been the target of selection during recent human evolution, although they were not able to exclude the possibility that relaxation of constraints on FOXP2 specific to the human lineage produced this pattern of nucleotide changes (Enard et al. 2002). Their data also suggested that the fixation of the mutations in the human form of the gene occurred during the last 200,000 years of human history, that is, concomitant with or subsequent to the emergence of anatomically modern humans. These findings suggest that expansion of modern humans was

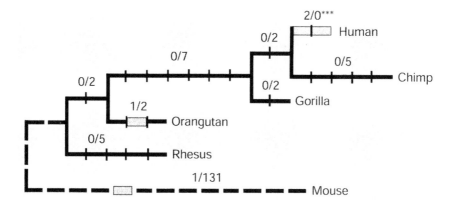

2.11. A phylogeny of the FOXP2 gene in primate species. Silent and replacement nucleotide substitutions are mapped onto this phylogeny. The horizontal bars represent nucleotide changes, while the gray bars indicate amino-acid changes. (Reprinted with permission from Macmillan Publishers Ltd: *Nature* 418 [2002], Enard et al., pp. 869–72, Fig. 2.)

stimulated by the emergence of a more-proficient spoken language.

Yet, while these non-synonymous changes were clearly unique to the human lineage compared to apes, it is possible that other hominin species had the same allelic variants in this gene, hence, shared a common capacity for speech production. Recent genomic sequencing of a Neandertal specimen (Green et al. 2006) has provided huge amounts of autosomal data that allow this possibility to be tested. In their examination of these data, Krause et al. (2007a) observed that the Neandertal individual shared the two mutation changes in the FOXP2 gene that are implicated in the development of speech and language in modern humans, and that these mutations appeared on the widespread modern human haplotype.

How did modern humans and Neandertals come to share the same FOXP2 haplotype? There are at least three different scenarios that can explain these findings. One is that the positively selected FOXP2 haplotype could have been transferred into Neandertals from modern humans or vice versa through gene flow. This model is now tentatively supported by genomic data from these hominins (Green et al. 2010), although mtDNA (Caramelli et al. 2003, Serre et al. 2004) and Y-chromosome (Krause et al. 2007a) data for modern humans and Neandertals reveal no gene flow between them.

Alternatively, the FOXP2 haplotype could have been present in the ancestral population of modern humans and Neandertals and then was positively selected in humans after their divergence from Neandertals. In this case, the relevant haplotype must have been present at a considerable frequency in the ancestral population in order to occur at relatively high frequencies in Neandertals. However, if alleles or haplotypes grow to high frequencies before being positively selected, it becomes difficult to detect a genetic signature of selective sweep (Wall and Przeworski 2000). Thus, this scenario seems implausible, as well.

The most likely scenario is that the selective sweep started prior to the divergence of the ancestral populations of Neandertals and modern humans around 300,000–400,000 years ago (Fay and Wu 2000). Assuming a human-chimp divergence of 6.5 mya, the fixation of the sweep would have occurred within the last 260,000 years (Enard et al. 2002). Hence, based on these findings, it would appear that Neandertals were capable of some kind of language, although how similar it was to that of modern humans is, of course, entirely speculative.

As it turns out, the FOXP2 transcription factor is also extremely similar in many vertebrate species, showing conserved expression in neural circuits related to sensorimotor integration and motor learning (Vargha-Khadem et al. 2005, Fisher and Marcus 2006). This finding makes it possible to examine the function of this gene in other nonhuman species, and determine the phenotypes produced by mutated forms of the gene. In one such study, Groszer et al. (2008) created transgenic mice with the identical FOXP2 mutation seen in humans having specific language impairment (SLI). The resulting homozygous mutated mice showed severe reductions in cerebellar growth, but were able to produce complex innate ultrasonic vocalizations. Heterozygous mice were seemingly normal in brain structure and development and basic motor abilities, but they exhibited significant deficits in species-typical motor-skill learning, accompanied by abnormal synaptic plasticity in striatal and cerebellar neural circuits (Groszer et al. 2008). These findings reinforce the clinical data obtained in studies of SLI patients (Specific Language Impairment Consortium 2002), and emphasize the crucial role that single genes may play in normal brain development and function.

Encephalization in the Hominin Lineage

It has long been assumed that relative brain size was a primary trait demarcating differences between humans and apes, and between the different hominin taxa present in the human lineage (Dunbar 1995, Kappelman 1996, Wood and Collard 1999, McHenry and Coffing 2000). Size seems to generally correlate with subsistence practices and technological shifts, as well as evidence for greater mobility, and, ultimately, symbolic behavior and language (Foley 2002, Foley and Lahr 2003, Rightmire 2004). Figure 2.12 shows the overall trend in encephalization that accompanied human brain evolution. While relative size does have some relationship to certain aspects of language ability, cultural behavior, and symbolic use (Dunbar 1995, Kappelman 1996, Wood and Collard 1999), primate species with smaller brains show some abilities to communicate, comprehend symbols, express cultural traditions, and recognize members of their social groups. Thus, both relative size and also neurological organization and development must be crucial variables in the emergence of large-brained hominins and the complex linguistic and cognitive functions that humans are able to perform.

Nevertheless, various researchers have begun searching the human

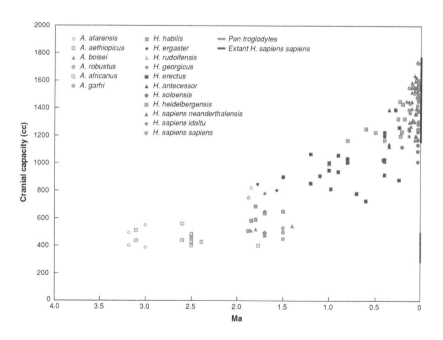

2.12. Cranial capacity in fossil hominids over time. Extant chimpanzees (*Pan troglodytes*) and humans (*Homo sapiens sapiens*) are included for comparison. Fossil data and species designations are from Holloway et al. (2004). (From Schoenemann 2006:379–406, Fig. 2; used with permission.)

genome for genes related to brain growth and development whose sequences show evidence of positive selection in the human lineage. Such loci are viewed as potentially contributing to the emergence of modern human cognition. This search has identified two genes associated with primary microcephaly (small cerebral cortex), the first being abnormal spindle-like microcephaly associated (ASPM) and the second being microcephalin (MCPH1) (Bond et al. 2002, Evans et al. 2004a, 2004b, 2005, 2006, Kouprina et al. 2004, Wang and Su 2004, Mekel-Bobrov et al. 2007). Microcephaly reduces the human brain to 50% or less of its normal mass, i.e., to about the size of the brain of chimpanzees or early hominin ancestors.

Recent work on the microcephalin gene in humans and other primates has provided some very interesting insights into the evolution of the hominin brain. This gene is highly polymorphic in human populations, with most mutations being non-synonymous in nature (Wang and Su 2004). In fact, researchers have identified, within modern humans, a group of closely related haplotypes at MCPH1, called haplogroup D, and found that it arose from a single copy ~37,000 years ago and subsequently swept to a very high frequency. These changes probably resulted from the effects of recent population expansion for modern humans and also selection in the lineage leading to *H. sapiens* (Wang and Su 2004, Evans et al. 2005, 2006). They suggest that this haplogroup originated in a hominin lineage that had diverged from modern humans around 1.1 mya and then introgressed into humans by ~37,000 years ago. If true, then this finding would imply that admixture occurred between archaic and modern humans (Evans et al. 2005, 2006).

ASPM has also undergone strong positive selection over the course of human and primate evolution. Its sequence shows evidence of accelerated evolution in the African hominoid clade, which preceded hominin brain expansion by several million years, as well as during recent human evolution (Evans et al. 2004b, Kouprina et al. 2004). In fact, it has been estimated that, on average, ASPM fixed one advantageous amino acid change in every 300,000–400,000 years since the human lineage diverged from chimpanzees some 5–6 mya (Evans et al. 2004b, Kouprina et al. 2004). Furthermore, the regions of the ASPM gene under positive selection in primates are also the most highly diverged regions between primates and non-primate mammals (Kouprina et al. 2004). Therefore, current data indicate that the ASPM gene has undergone adaptive evolution in the hominin lineage. Moreover, these findings indicate that brain size seems to be controlled in part through the modulation of mitotic spindle activity in neuronal progenitor cells (Bond et al. 2002).

A third gene that may be of some importance for human brain evolution is the Abelson Helper Integration Site 1 (AHI1) locus. This gene is essential for axon path finding from the cortex to the spinal cord and, thus, for normal coordination and gait (Hill and Walsh 2005). It, too, causes severe neurological disease when mutated, including mental retardation and sometimes autism-like symptoms, such as anti-social behavior and perhaps even schizophrenia (Ingason et al. 2007, Alvarez Retuerto et al. 2008). This gene also shows evidence for positive selection in the lineage leading to humans (Ferland et al. 2004). Together, these observations have been interpreted as suggesting that sequence differences in AHI1 may relate not only to human patterns of gait, but also to species-specific social behavior (Ferland et al. 2004, Hill and Walsh 2005).

Brain Systems for Language

When it comes to modeling brain evolution in apes and humans, relative size does seem to matter. There is a general relationship between brain size and the complexity of hominin behavior as viewed through the lithic production, faunal analysis, coordination of group activities, language ability, and adaptability to numerous different environments. However, more recent studies of brain anatomy employing modern imaging techniques are showing that expanding brain size is only part of the story behind the emergence of modern human cognitive function and behavioral capacities.

Various reports have shown that there are different systems for language in the left hemisphere in the brain (Schoenemann 2006). These include word- and sentence-implementation structures and mediation structures for lexical items and grammar (Fig. 2.13). In addition, the sets of neural structures that represent the concepts themselves are distributed across both right and left hemispheres in many sensory and motor regions. In addition, researchers have identified a parallel pathway to the classical arcuate pathway connecting Broca's and Wernicke's areas (Catani, Jones, and ffytche 2005). Interestingly, this parallel pathway, called Gerschwind's territory, may be important for the acquisition of language in childhood. It is the last area in the brain to mature, and the completion of its maturation generally coincides with the development of reading and writing skills in young children (Catani, Jones, and Ffytch 2005).

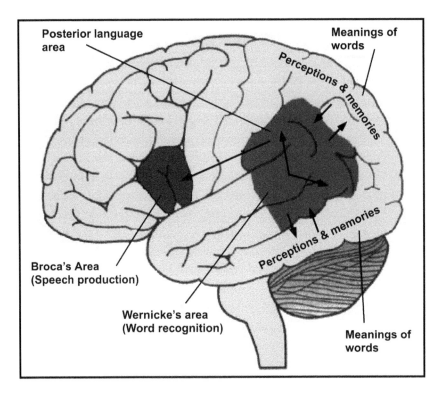

2.13. Language areas of the brain. (Modified after image from http://emedia. leeward.hawaii.edu/hurley/Ling102web/mod5_Llearning/5mod5.2_disorders. htm.)

The identification of different parts of the brain that are involved in language production and comprehension, as well as the evolution of the different parts of the brain in humans and other primates, has been made possible by the use of modern imaging technologies, such as computer tomography (CT) and magnetic resonance imaging (MRI). Studies employing these methods have greatly facilitated cross-species comparisons of brain size, and the examination of developmental features of brain function.

In one such study, Gogtay et al. (2004) investigated the developmental features of brain maturation in apes and humans. Their primary goal was to better understand the anatomical sequence of human cortical gray matter development between the ages of 4 and 21 years. MRI scans showed that higher-order association cortices matured only after the development of the lower-order somatosensory and visual cortices, the functions of which they integrate. In addition, the phylogenetically older areas of the brain matured earlier than the newer ones.

In a similar study, Schoenemann, Sheehan, and Glotzer (2005) investigated the extent to which different parts of the brain increased in hominins compared to apes. They focused on the prefrontal cortex, which mediates evolutionarily important behaviors such as planning complex cognitive behaviors, personality expression, decision making, and controlling social behavior, while also generally orchestrating thoughts and actions in accordance with internal goals (Miller and Cohen 2001, Krawczyk 2002, Lebedev et al. 2004). Through the MRI imaging of 11 primates species, Schoenemann, Sheehan, and Glotzer (2005) were able to measure gray, white, and total volumes for both prefrontal and the entire cerebrum for each taxa. They found that the prefrontal white matter showed the largest difference between apes and humans, while gray matter showed no significant difference at all. Schoenemann, Sheehan, and Glotzer (2005) interpreted these results as suggesting that connectional elaboration, as indicated by white matter volume, played a key role in human brain evolution.

Although these studies show that relative brain size, the nature and extent of neuron connections, and the comparative volumes of white and gray matter are of great evolutionary and functional importance in apes and humans, they did not specifically examine the changes in sizes of different parts of the brain through time and across species. In an effort to understand these aspects of hominoid evolution, Rilling (2006) analyzed brain structure sizes across the primate order to determine whether human, ape, and other anthropoid brains are allometrically scaled versions of the same generalized design. His MRI results showed that both human and ape brains exhibited specializations with respect to other anthropoid brains. More specifically,

[a]pe specializations include elaboration of the cerebellum (all apes) and frontal lobes (great apes only), and probably connectivity between them. Human brain specializations include an overall larger proportion of neocortex, with disproportionate enlargement of prefrontal and temporal association cortices, an apparent increase in cerebellar connections with cerebral cortical association areas involved in cognition, and a probable augmentation of intracortical connectivity in prefrontal cortex. (Rilling 2006:65)

These quantitative and qualitative differences in the brain are undoubtedly linked to the species' cognitive abilities, while the dramatic expansion of higher-order association cortices in humans would have supported the emergence of language abilities in the hominin lineage (Rilling 2006).

Moving from the structural to the cellular level, recent neuroanatomical studies have also yielded insights into the expansion of the brain in apes and humans, and, in particular, developmental aspects of neuron formation. For example, it has been noted that the enlarged cortex of hominoids reflects a longer period of neuronal formation during prenatal development, meaning that each dividing progenitor cell undergoes more cell cycles before stopping cell division (Kornack and Rakic 1998). In addition, the longer period of neurogenesis adds novel neurons to the cortex, thereby allowing the cortical circuit diagram to develop differently in primates compared to other mammals. Upper cortical layers, generated late in neurogenesis, are overrepresented in the primate cerebral cortex, especially in humans (Marin-Padilla 1992). Additionally, special cell types, such as spindle cells (specialized, deep-layer neurons), are unique to primates (Allman, Hakeem, and Watson 2002). Thus, the primate brain is noteworthy not only for its size and complexity relative to other mammalian species, but also for the nature and extent of neuronal connections within the brain itself (Hill and Walsh 2005).

Myosin Gene Evolution

While most studies of the emergence of language production and comprehension have focused on genes influencing brain anatomy or the analysis of cognitive and neurological phenomena underlying its function, other researchers have taken a different approach to understanding the evolution of large brains in hominins. In one such study, Stedman et al. (2004) examined the masticatory muscles in humans and several primates, as well as one of the genes involved in producing them. They noted that powerful masticatory muscles are found in most primates, including chimpanzees and gorillas, and were a prominent part of the adaptive strategies of *Australopithecus* and *Paranthropus*. In contrast, these muscles are considerably smaller in both modern and fossil members of the genus *Homo*. The evolving hominin masticatory apparatus, which can be traced back to a Late Miocene, chimpanzee-like morphology (White et al. 2000), shifted toward a pattern of gracilization nearly simultaneously with accelerated encephalization in early *Homo* (Tobias 1991, Schoenemann 2006).

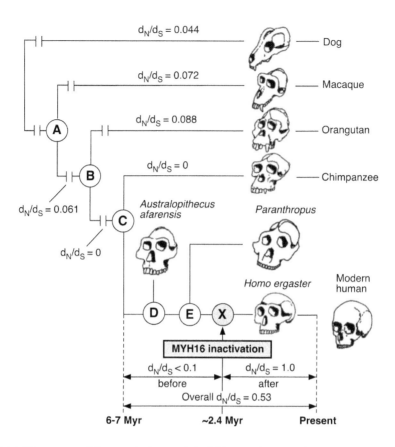

2.14. Divergence of the myosin heavy chain 16 (MYH16) gene. The data are based on nucleotide sequences for the six largest exons in the rod-coding domain. Individual mutations are indicated by N for non-synonymous or S for synonymous. d_N and d_S refer to the mutational rates normalized to the number of relevant sites (840 N, 225 S) in pairwise comparisons between MYH16 orthologues of extant species and inferred ancestors at nodes A, B, and C. The atypically high d_N/d_S in the human ancestral lineage (significant, $P = 0.0527$) indicates a loss of negative Darwinian selection approximately 2.4 million years ago (Myr). (Reprinted by permission from Macmillan Publishers Ltd: *Nature* 428 [2004], H.H. Stedman et al., pp. 415–18, Fig. 4.)

In support of this view, Stedman et al. (2004) found that the gene encoding the predominant myosin heavy chain (MYH) expressed in these muscles was inactivated by a frameshift mutation after the lineages leading to humans and chimpanzees diverged. Based on histological comparisons, they noted that the mutation was associated with marked size reductions in individual muscle fibers and entire masticatory muscles in modern humans compared to great apes (Fig. 2.14). Coalescence estimates using primate and human MYH sequences indicated that the frameshift mutation appeared approximately 2.4 mya. This date predates the appearance of modern human body size (Walker and Leakey 1993, Pearson 2000, Aiello and Wells 2002, Antón and Swisher 2004, Ruff 2008) and the emigration of *Homo* from Africa (Vekua et al. 2002, Antón and Swisher 2004). Given these findings, Stedman et al. (2004) asserted that the reduction in the mass of the temporalis muscle allowed the cranium/brain to expand in size. Thus, in their view, the MYH mutation facilitated greater encephalization in the hominin lineage due to removing physiological and structural constraints on brain and cranial growth.

It should be noted here that the proposed date for the MYH mutation coincides with the timing of several key transitions in hominin biology and behavior. The first of these is the beginning of the Oldowan lithic tradition in east Africa, which is generally viewed as being initiated by early *Homo* (Haile-Selassie 2001, Panger et al. 2002). The use of tools is viewed as being significant in that it demonstrates the existence of mental templates in the minds of early hominins, not to mention the more systematic use of raw materials, the processing of food, and task specialization.

Sexual Selection

Yet another factor that may be relevant to understanding the process of increased brain size in humans is sexual selection. Schillaci (2006) examined the relationship between brain size and sexual selection in terms of sperm competition and male competition for mates. While observing no significant relationship between relative brain size and sperm competition as measured by testis size in primates, he did find a significant negative relationship between relative brain size and the level of male competition for mates. These results suggested to him that the largest relative brain sizes among primate species are associated with monogamous mating systems, suggesting that primate monogamy may require greater social acuity and abilities of deception.

SUMMARY

This chapter outlines the major evolutionary events in modern human evolution, including the transitions between different hominid and hominin forms. We have also evaluated the emergence of human characteristics in the context of broader primate and mammalian evolutionary patterns. The totality of the evidence shows that, while having roots in primate and hominin prehistory, modern humans have undergone significant biological and behavioral changes over the last 2 million years.

Overall, genomic comparisons clearly show that the human genome has undergone profound changes in terms of its size, content, and regulation relative to those of chimps, gorillas, and other primate species. While these interspecific comparisons have identified a number of genes that have undergone selection, or relaxed selection, in the hominin lineage, ongoing analysis may well identify additional loci of similar evolutionary importance. New sequence data will also help to improve estimates of the neutral substitution rate, i.e., the rate at which fixed differences between species accumulate under neutral evolution, hence, the timing of the divergence of ape and human lineages (e.g., Sabeti et al. 2006). Furthermore, we need to improve our understanding of the likely functional outcomes of these genetic changes, such as the effects of specific mutations on protein structure and function, and the way that noncoding regulatory regions of the genome work.

While there is close genetic affinity betweem apes and humans, such that these taxa share over 96% of their genomic sequences, it is also increasingly evident that there are significant differences in the expression and regulation of these genes in the two species, as well as specific allelic and chromosomal changes (e.g., segmental duplications) that led to the phenotypic, physiological, and behavioral differences seen in them. Each lineage has also been affected by selection in different ways, and, for humans, the extent to which cultural and sexual selection have shaped genetic variation requires fuller resolution.

Current evidence gives us a better sense of the basis of cognitive differences between apes and humans, and the evolutionary forces that have influenced them. While relative brain size is clearly one feature that distinguishes humans from apes, it is only one dimension of the transformation of the hominid brain. In fact, we observe the expansion of different areas of the brain in humans relative to other primates, including the cortical areas related to higher cognitive function, as well as differences in neuronal density and neuroanatomical architecture. Although it is possible to infer when some of the changes occurred in the hominin lineage, e.g., the emergence of the genus *Homo* in the Pliocene-Pleistocene boundary, the timing of most of these transitions remains speculative. However, it is clear that the hominin brain has been transformed in a manner that now allows us to have articulate speech, abstract reasoning, and complex cultural behavior in contrast to other hominoid apes.

The conditions under which the transformation of the genus *Homo* took place—which shaped the evolution of the species or lineage—are still incompletely understood. Major climate changes may have triggered a shift in subsistence towards broader spectrum diet and greater consumption of meat, and accompanying behavior changes (hunting/scavenging). This dietary shift led to the transformation in gut morphology of hominids, setting the biological foundation for the later encephalization of the lineage, and perhaps also the bioenergetic basis for more hominin-like forms of bipedalism, which permitted the expansion of the lineage outside of its Africa homeland.

Even though these findings have helped us reconstruct the emergence and evolution of the hominin lineage, there are still many questions and issues concerning this process that remain to be resolved. Among these are the timing of emergence of modern human language, the selective forces that promoted rapid brain size growth, and the relationship between brain size and complexity and primate and hominin linguistic and cultural abilities. Ongoing and future work, particularly research at the genomic level, should provide new insights into these questions and tell us more about the evolution of the modern human mind, brain, and culture.

NOTES

2.1 Hominins are humans or human ancestors. They include all of the *Homo* species (*Homo sapiens, H. ergaster, H. rudolfensis*), all of the australopithecines (*Australopithicus africanus, A. boisei*, etc.), and other ancient forms like *Paranthropus* and *Ardipithecus*.

2.2 A clade is a group of species whose members share homologous features derived from a common ancestor.

2.3 Gracile and robust australopithecines are differentiated by the size of their jaws, teeth and cranial features, among other traits.

2.4 Sexual dimorphism refers to the difference in size between males and females of a species; males are usually slightly to considerably larger than females in hominid and hominin species.

2.5 Sympatry refers to species whose ranges overlap or are even identical such that they occur together, at least in some places. If they are closely related, they may have arisen through sympatric speciation.

2.6 Ontogeny is the origin and development of an individual organism from embryo to adult.

2.7 Haploinsufficiency is the situation where the total amount of a gene product (protein) produced by cells is half of the normal amount, thereby causing the cell to function abnormally. It usually occurs when one of two functional copies of a gene is inactivated by mutation, with the resulting reduction of gene function producing an abnormal phenotype.

3

What Genetics Can Tell Us about the Origins of the Modern Human Brain

JODY HEY

Today genetic methods are so powerful, and genetic databases so informative, that it is now possible to identify genes, and regions of the human genome, that have experienced positive Darwinian selection (i.e., adaptation) during the evolution of modern humans. What is more difficult than identifying the genes that experienced adaptation, is figuring out the basic functions of these genes. And more difficult still is figuring out just what the functional differences were between the ancestral form of a gene and the more adaptive form that replaced it. For adaptive traits that can be studied at the physiological or cellular level, it is sometimes possible to connect genetic changes to adaptive phenotypic changes. However for cognitive or behavioral adaptations, like many of these thought to be associated with the evolution of the modern human brain, it is acutely difficult to identify the genetic changes underlying the adaptations.

Because humans differ from other species in having high intelligence, language, and an array of behaviors that facilitate complex, culturally based societies, it seems reasonable to suppose that our species has experienced a lot of adaptive evolution that uniquely shaped our cognition, behavior, and sociality. If this is true then some of our genes are different from those of our distant ancestors in the way that they now encode such traits.

Evidence of a genetic basis underlying human cognitive and behavioral traits comes from several different sources. Certainly the observation that all humans (even infants) have capacities for reason and language that appear to differ sharply from those of other animals is strong prima facie evidence of an evolved genetic basis for such abilities. A different kind of insight comes from cases when genes are disrupted. Many of our cognitive and social abilities can be strongly affected or eradicated by genetic mutations (McKusik 1998), suggesting (though not proving) that genes are responsible for some of our unique abilities. Another kind of evidence for a genetic basis of many behavioral and social traits comes from findings of behaviors that are not known in other animals but that seem to be common to all human societies, even those long separated from one another (Brown 1991).

Notwithstanding the uncertainty and complex debate that surrounds questions about the adaptive nature of particular cognitive traits (see, e.g., Hauser, Chomsky, and Fitch 2002, Fitch, Hauser, and Chomsky 2005, Jackendoff and Pinker 2005, Pinker and Jackendoff 2005), this review supposes that many of our unique abilities do have a basis in genetic adaptations. We can survey the issues that arise when trying to identify and study genes that carry adaptations for human cognitive and social traits, even if there is debate about the degree to which evolution by natural selection has shaped or caused these traits.

CONTRASTING ADAPTATION AT THE GENETIC LEVEL WITH ADAPTATION AT THE PHENOTYPIC LEVEL

At the DNA level a change in a species that is wrought by natural selection will be manifested as an alteration in one portion of the DNA sequence of the genome of each of the organisms of the species. At this level, adaptation begins with a mutation that alters the DNA sequence of a gene; proceeds through a process of natural selection, whereby the altered copy of the gene replaces other forms of the gene in the species; and is complete when all copies of that gene in the species bear the DNA sequence that resulted from the original mutation.

The contrast between this highly reduced view of adaptation and what is typically meant by "adaptation" as applied to phenotypic traits is considerable. A phenotypic adaptation is usually considered to be an inherited trait that is characteristic of a species and that came into existence through natural selection (Tooby and Cosmides 1992, Buss et al. 1998). The requirement of inheritance demands that a phenotypic adaptation has some basis in the DNA, but otherwise there is little need for any kind of one-to-one correspondence between adaptations at the DNA level and at the phenotype level.

One phenotypic adaptation could be caused by one or more DNA adaptations. This will certainly be true of large phenotypic changes that are the result of many DNA changes over a period of time, but it can also happen through the simultaneous fixation of multiple DNA adaptations that contribute to the same phenotypic trait.

Similarly, one single DNA adaptation may affect a great many aspects of the phenotype (a process called *pleiotropy*). When a DNA mutation becomes fixed by natural selection it is because of the overall net effect of that change on the fitness of the organism throughout the life cycle, and not just because of its contribution to a salient trait that an investigator might identify. This last point concerning pleiotropy is especially relevant when considering traits of the mind or brain, for it is the brain tissue that expresses more genes than any other tissue. Adult human brain tissue expresses approximately 75% of all known genes at least to some degree (Franz et al. 2005). This means that for most genes a DNA adaptation is expected to lead to either an altered protein that is expressed in the brain (and typically other tissues) or an altered expression pattern in the brain (and typically other tissues). The point is somewhat rhetorical since many genes are expressed in contexts where they are not required, but it nevertheless serves to highlight the discontinuity between DNA adaptations and phenotypic adaptations. Those phenotypic adaptations for which a basis in DNA has been found are likely far more complex at the phenotypic level than may appear, simply because most genes are expressed in many tissues and many stages of the life cycle.

THE DIFFERENCE BETWEEN HUMAN TRAITS AND VARIATION FOR HUMAN TRAITS

When considering questions about genes for human traits it is important to highlight the distinction between traits for which humans differ from other great apes, and traits for which humans are themselves variable. To develop the point we can use language as an example and suppose that some fundamental aspect of language, which humans have and apes to do not, is an adaptation caused by natural selection since we last shared a common ancestor with chimpanzees (including both chimpanzee species, the common chimpanzee and the bonobo). But in addition to this human/ape difference, we can also note that some humans are more versatile with language than others, and it is possible that some component of this variation has a genetic basis (i.e., it is possible that there is genetic variation that explains some of the phenotypic variation among people in language versatility). Then for the sake of the argument suppose for both of these cases (i.e., the human/ ape difference and the differences among humans) that the differences in language ability are caused by genetic differences.

Both of these situations are interesting, and for various reasons we might want to find the genes underlying both kinds of genetic differences (i.e., the genes underlying the human/chimpanzee difference, and the genes that affect language and that vary in humans). However the contrast between these two situations is an important one for several reasons. First, the genes associated with the human/ape difference might rightly be said to be the site of adaptations that make us who we are—they set us aside from other animals. This is simply not the case for genes that are variable and that contribute to variation among people in some part of language, however interesting they may be. Second, there is no necessary association between that subset of our genes which experienced adaptations for language since our genetic separation from other apes and that hypothetical subset of genes which is variable for language among humans.

A third contrast that becomes apparent when considering these two categories of variation is a great disparity in our capacity to identify genes associated with a trait of interest. In the case of human/chimpanzee differences there are few tools available for discovering such genes. The geneticists' favorite method for identifying genes that affect a trait is genetic mapping. This method relies upon being able to compare large number of individuals with varying degrees of genetic similarity *and* varying amounts of sharing of the target phenotype. In the case of humans and chimpanzees, all humans differ from all chimpanzees to some degree at virtually all of our genes, and of course at all of the cognitive traits associated with humans' unique cognitive and behavioral traits. The massive correlation of all genes with all traits, when considering humans and chimpanzees, summarily halts any genetic mapping project that one might suppose, particularly given the ethical issues that immediately arise under some possible experimental designs. In contrast it is often possible, and increasingly less difficult, to map genes for traits that vary among humans, and today it is done routinely to identify genes that contribute to diseases.

Recent research on the microcephalin gene (MCPH1) highlights some of the issues that arise when considering human/chimpanzee differences and when considering variation among humans. Mutations at the MCPH1 gene are known to cause a harmful condition of reduced cranial capacity called microcephaly. The simple fact of such mutations suggests a role in brain development for the product of this gene, and it suggests the possibility that the gene might be among those at which humans have experienced adaptations affecting cognition. Evans et al. (2004a) and Wang and Su (2004) compared the DNA sequence of the human form of the gene with that of other primates, and showed that several branches of the gene tree had experienced accelerated rates of amino acid change—a clear sign of adaptation. However the branch of the tree that separates humans from chimpanzees did not have an unusually high rate. So on the basis of this evidence, this gene does not appear to be the site of a uniquely human brain even though it does appear to have undergone adaptation during primate evolution.

Another study of the MCPH1 gene looked within human populations, and in this case did find indirect evidence of different functional forms of the gene in human populations (Evans et al. 2004b). This finding was controversial, and it was argued by some to have been over-interpreted by the authors and possibly to be mistaken (Balter 2005). But suppose for the sake of the argument that it is true. Even if present-day people do vary for functional alleles at this gene, and even if there is evidence of cognitive differences associated with those alleles (although newer evidence seems to refute this, Mekel-Bobrov et al. 2007), the observation only concerns variation *within* our species. In other words, even if the finding were true it would not bear directly on the evolution of cognitive traits that separate us from apes.

THE AGE OF UNIQUELY HUMAN ADAPTATIONS

Based on fossil and genetic evidence the date of the last common ancestral species to humans and chimpanzees is in the range of 4 to 7 million years ago (Chen and Li 2001, Brunet et al. 2002, Hobolth et al. 2007). This age marks the lower temporal boundary of when adaptations could have occurred in the history of humans, and yet not be shared with related species. Of course, there were almost certainly a great many adaptations shaping cognition and behavior that happened in the ancestry of humans before the time of the last common ancestral species leading to humans and chimpanzees. But since

TESTING FOR GENETIC ADAPTATIONS

The test for adaptation that was used for the MCPH1 gene is based on the genetic code and the fact that in gene regions that code for proteins, some mutations will affect the protein by causing a change in the sequence of amino acids in the protein, and other changes will have no affect on the protein, because they are redundant within the genetic code. The former changes, called non-synonymous changes, are potentially more common (more random mutations will affect the amino acid sequence than will not), but because most non-synonymous changes are harmful (i.e., they cause reduced Darwinian fitness) these types of changes are relatively rare. In contrast the redundant changes, called synonymous changes, are likely to have little or no affect on gene function and to be selectively neutral. The synonymous changes are usually observed to be more common than non-synonymous changes when the DNA sequences of the same genes are compared in related species. For any pair of gene copies it is possible to calculate the ratio of the non-synonymous changes to synonymous changes, called the K_a/K_s or the D_N/D_S ratio. Both types of changes are calculated per position that could potentially have a change of that type. A ratio of 1 suggests that the sites that could have an amino acid change are evolving just as fast as the sites that can have synonymous changes and that are supposedly selectively neutral. It follows that a gene with a value of K_a/K_s that is statistically significantly greater than 1 can be inferred to have experienced a higher rate of amino acid sequence evolution than is expected based on sites at which mutations are neutral (Hughes and Nei 1988). In other words, a gene with a finding of $K_a/K_s > 1$ over some portion of its evolutionary history is considered to have experienced adaptation during that time. Genes with values of $K_a/K_s \leq 1$ may well have also experienced adaptive amino acid changes, but that cannot be detected on the basis of this simple kind of test.

such adaptations would have been present in the ancestors of humans and chimpanzees, they would also have been passed on to chimpanzees.

To assess the upper, recent time boundary of the interval in which uniquely human adaptations may have occurred we need to figure out when was the last time it would have been possible for a beneficial mutation to arise and spread throughout the entire human population. This could possibly happen today because humans, in the past few hundred years, have been migrating at increasing rates. But before that it is likely that many human populations were isolated from one another for very long periods of time.

One way to assess the upper time boundary is to consider the age of fossils and artifacts associated with the earliest known modern humans. The oldest known skulls that look like those of present-day people, more than they resemble archaic hominins, have been found in Ethiopia with an estimated range of dates between 150,000 and 200,000 years (White et al. 2003, McDougall, Brown, and Fleagle 2005). Archaeological evidence from one of these sites reveals a Middle Stone Age culture and apparent modifications of some of the skulls point to mortuary rituals (Clark et al. 2003b). Given the skull morphology and the snippets of insight into the culture of these people there seems to be a fair chance that we would recognize in them many, if not all, of the mental traits we associate uniquely with humans.

From living humans we can also get a time point that brackets the age when all modern humans possibly were not isolated from one another (and thus could share in a common process of adaptation). It happens that Australia was populated by people perhaps fairly soon after some modern humans first migrated out of Africa, 40 to 50 kya (Bowler et al. 2003, Hudjashov et al. 2007). Genetic evidence from the mitochondrial genome and the Y chromosome suggests that Australians share alleles with New Guineans, and thus that genetically they are related to other Asians. This means that they are probably part of the same out-of-Africa migration event that lead to the peopling of Asia (Hudjashov et al. 2007). However, the genetic evidence also suggests a long-term isolation from other Asians. In other words, adaptations that are shared by all humans, including Aboriginal Australians, would have arisen not later than the time of the populating of Australia.

From these different reference points we can see that uniquely human adaptations would have occurred between about 6 million years ago and not later than the populating of Australia 40 to 50 kya. A somewhat different time range is arrived at if we wish to focus on adaptations that were also shared by the earliest known modern humans. In this case, uniquely human adaptations would not have arisen more recently than the age of the early modern skulls from Ethiopia, that is between about 150,000 and 200,000 years ago.

The draft sequence of the Neandertal genome suggests that we last shared a common ancestor with Neandertals between 270 and 440 kya, although there is also a signal in the genomic data of limited gene flow from Neandertals into modern humans (Green et al. 2010). These genomic data provide an additional opportunity to estimate dates of genetic changes on the lineage to modern humans. However, our knowledge of Neandertal phenotypes is limited to inferences from bones and archaeological evidence. While these reveal Paleolithic cultures, many questions about Neandertal culture and language remain open to speculation.

When the MCPH1 gene was examined in the Neandertal genome it was found to have the ancestral form of the gene (Green et al. 2010, Lari et al. 2010), which is not surprising given the recent estimated age of the other form of the gene (Evans et al. 2005). However the finding is not consistent with the possibility that had been suggested that the derived form of the gene that is found in many modern humans entered the population via gene exchange with Neandertals (Evans et al. 2006).

IT IS EASIER TO FIND ADAPTING GENES THAN IT IS TO KNOW WHAT TRAITS WERE UNDER SELECTION

Paradoxically, it is easier to identify genes that have undergone adaptation than it is to figure out what those adaptations are, or which phenotypic traits are involved. Consider again the MCPH1 gene and Figure 3.1 which indicates the branches on the primate evolutionary tree that show evidence of adaptation at this gene. This evidence comes from an analysis of the coding sequence of the gene and a finding of high ratios of changes that affected the MCPH1 protein, to DNA sequence changes that did not (see box). However, DNA sequences by themselves do not reveal the role that a gene plays in development. Even if a detailed role for a gene is known, DNA sequence evidence of adaptation is unlikely to reveal the nature of the trait differences between the old (before the adaptation) and the new (after the adaptive change) forms of the gene.

Now that both the human and the chimpanzee genomes have been sequenced it is relatively straightforward to align their genes and to assess the amounts of different types of changes at every gene. Roughly 10% of human protein coding genes are estimated to have undergone adaptive evolution at the amino-acid level since the time of common ancestry

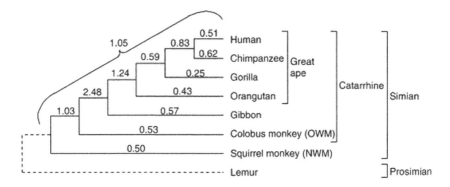

3.1. Evolution of microcephalin within primates. The Ka/Ks ratios of individual phylogenetic segments are indicated. The Ka/Ks of the entire lineage from simian progenitors to humans is also indicated. OWM: Old World monkey; NWM: New World monkey. (From P.D. Evans et al. *Human Molecular Genetics* 2004b 13:1139–145, fig. 1; used with permission.)

with chimpanzee (Clark et al. 2003a, Bustamante et al. 2005, Nielsen et al. 2005). Given that the human genome contains about 25,000 protein coding genes (International Human Genome Sequencing Consortium 2004), these findings implicate a couple of thousand genes as having been shaped by considerable adaptive evolution in the time since common ancestry with the chimpanzee. Also given that these studies report only those genes that show a clear statistical signal, it is likely that there are many thousands more of beneficial mutations that have occurred at individual genes but that went undetected given the statistical power of the tests being used.

But simply having found the genes that have experienced adaptations tells us nothing about the phenotypic traits that changed as those genes evolved. Humans can be expected to have experienced adaptations in the entire panoply of phenotypic traits, not just the minority of phenotypes associated with intelligence or language or behavior. The point is brought home particularly by the recent observation that chimpanzees have experienced more adaptation in protein coding genes than have humans, over precisely the same time period (i.e., since our common ancestor) (Shi, Bakewell, and Zhang 2006, Bakewell, Shi, and Zhang 2007).

Another approach to identifying genes that have experienced recent adaptation relies upon patterns of variation within a species to reveal the imprint of a mutation that has recently become fixed within a species. Figure

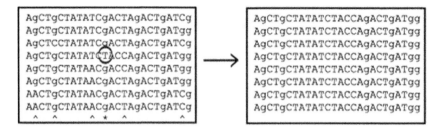

3.2. An illustration of selective sweep and genetic hitchhiking. On the left is a set of aligned gene copies. Base positions that are variable are indicated by a caret "^". At one base position, indicated by an asterisk, "*", one of the sequences has a base value that confers a selective advantage on individuals with that form of the gene. After the selected mutation becomes fixed in the population (right panel), all forms of the gene carry the selected form of the base and all of the sequence that was linked to that selected base. The effect is the removal of variation at other sites within the gene. In effect the sequences linked to the favored mutation have hitchhiked to fixation in the population by being physically linked to the selected base, and the gene has been swept clean of variation.

3.2 shows how a beneficial mutation (indicated on the left with a circle) can lead to a removal of variation in a population in the region of the chromosome that is near a gene. When the beneficial mutation replaces other forms of the gene in the population, all of the DNA sequence that was originally physically linked to that mutation also becomes fixed in the population. The next effect is a removal of variation that was present in the population before the selective event. This kind of removal of variation is called a "selective sweep" and the fixation of sequences linked to the beneficial mutation is called "genetic hitchhiking" (Maynard Smith and Haigh 1974).

The potential for selective fixations to remove variation from populations immediately reveals an approach to identify recent selective events by looking for regions of the genome that have unusually low levels of variation. To date, millions of variable positions in the human genome have been identified and this large database of single nucleotide polymorphisms (or SNPs) can be used to search for regions of unusually low variation (Williamson et al. 2007). This approach is particularly interesting because it is directly targeted at recent adaptations—regions of the genome that experienced adaptations and selective sweeps long ago are expected to have rebounded in the amount of diversity. In fact, it is possible to catch selective sweeps "in the act" by identifying genomic regions that are significantly depauperate of variation in just one or some human populations. Recently, Williamson and colleagues (2007) used this approach and identified over 100 regions of the genome that appeared to have experienced a recent selective sweep. However the large majority of these affected only one or two of the three human populations considered. Only 21 genomic regions showed evidence of a sweep that affected all three populations (one each representing Europea, Asia, and Africa) in the study (Williamson et al. 2007).

A key limitation of using genetic polymorphisms to identify recent selective sweeps is that the analysis cannot offer information about the functional role of the adaptation that caused the sweep. Indeed, the situation is even worse when a gene is highlighted on the basis of high rates of amino acid polymorphism. In that case, at least the investigator knows what gene is involved, if not the functional differences that underlay the adaptation events. However, screens for apparent selective sweeps reveal only the general genomic regions that have low variation. If a region of low variation is long, as it may be if the selective sweep happened quickly, then there may be multiple genes contained within it, each of which could have been the one that experienced the beneficial mutation that caused the sweep.

HOW CAN WE IDENTIFY THE PHENOTYPES ASSOCIATED WITH ADAPTATIONS IDENTIFIED IN THE GENES?

The classical way to do genetics is to start with a phenotype of interest and to try and find the gene(s) responsible. As described above, this requires some variation for the trait, in which case the situation lends itself to genetic mapping methods. However, it is not possible to map genetic differences between humans and chimpanzees for two reasons: (1) all humans differ from all chimpanzees at all genes *and* all traits that uniquely distinguish humans from animals, so that there is no scope for identifying particular associations between genes and traits; and (2) there are strong ethical prohibitions against developing methods that might overcome this.

The other modern (as opposed to classical) approach to connecting phenotypes to genotypes is to begin with the genes rather than the traits, and to try and figure out the function of genes and what phenotypes they affect. With the rise of molecular and cell biology, and with vast genetic and genomic resources for humans and many other organisms, it is today a simple matter to begin an investigation of a particular phenotypic trait by starting with the genes that *might* be associated with that trait. The emphasis on "might" is used here to highlight the uncertainty of this approach. Investigators, knowledgeable of their phenotypes of interest, can come up with lists of genes that could possibly be involved with that trait. The sources of information used to make such connections are many and diverse, and ultimately dependent on the investigators' level of knowledge of their phenotype of interest.

A relatively straightforward example of this "candidate gene approach" is the FOXP2 gene, which encodes a transcription factor protein of 715 amino acids. Mutations in this gene have been shown to cause a speech and language disorder (Lai et al. 2001), suggesting that the gene might be a site of functional changes associated with the evolution of language in humans. Soon after the Lai et al. paper appeared, two groups of researchers compared the human form of this gene with those of other mammals and discovered that humans had two amino acid changes in this gene, whereas only one amino acid change had occurred in this gene since the common ancestry of apes and the mouse (see Fig. 3.3) (Enard et al. 2002, Zhang, Webb, and Podlaha 2002). In other words, the FOXP2 gene seems to evolve very slowly at the amino acid level and yet has had a relative burst of change on the branch leading to modern humans.

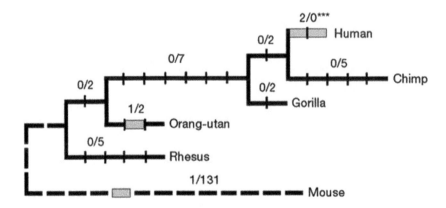

3.3. The gene tree for the FOXP2 gene is shown, with branch lengths among primates corresponding to the number of synonymous changes (dark bars) and non-synonymous changes (light bars). (Reprinted with permission from Macmillan Publishers Ltd: *Nature* 418 [2002], Enard et al., pp. 869–72, Fig. 2.)

From low levels of variation among humans at the FOXP2, it has been estimated that our current form of the gene became fixed in human populations within the past 200,000 years (Enard et al. 2002, Zhang, Webb, and Podlaha 2002). For insight into when the human form of the gene first arose, researchers turned to the Neandertal genome and found that both modern humans and Neandertals share the same form of the FOXP2 gene (Krause et al. 2007a).

The FOXP2 discoveries have triggered an explosion of research trying to discern just what it is that the gene does. Such studies include knocking out function in nonhuman model systems (French et al. 2007), more behavioral studies on individuals with mutations in FOXP2 (Liegeois et al. 2003, Hamdan et al. 2010), and studies of the location of FOXP2 proteins in cells in culture (Mizutani et al. 2007), among others. Recent studies of the affect of the human and the chimpanzee forms of FOXP2 on gene expression of neuronal cells in culture reveal that the human form of the gene alters the expression of over 100 other genes (Konopka et al. 2009).

CONNECTING MOLECULAR PHENOTYPES TO COGNITIVE AND BEHAVIORAL PHENOTYPES

Molecular biologists are rapidly discovering the genes that have experienced adaptation in the evolutionary history of modern humans. Yet they are limited in the tools they can use to identify what traits were affected by those adaptations. In the case of the FOXP2 gene we have a useful example of the panoply of methods that creative investigators are likely to employ. How long will it take to find the higher-level traits, above the level of gene expression, that are associated with the adaptations at these genes? What kind of traits will these be?

A mirror set of questions arise with regard to language, and other cognitive traits, for researchers who study cognition and language and other human behaviors. In areas of psychology, cognitive philosophy, and anthropology there are long-running debates about the nature of human cognition. For example, some scholars of language insist on a very limited role for Darwinian adaptation in the origins of human language (Hauser, Chomsky, and Fitch 2002, Fitch, Hauser, and Chomsky 2005), whereas others disagree strongly (Jackendoff and Pinker 2005, Pinker and Jackendoff 2005). Similarly, the focus in Evolutionary Psychology on identifying those components of present-day human behavior that have evolved and that distinguish us from apes is controversial and generally lacking in consensus on just what components of human behavior can be singled out as indicative of adaptation (Buller 2005). A more hopeful approach links evolutionary changes in hominin cognition and behavior to the archaeological record and to such knowledge as is available about climate change, hunting patterns, social groups, and toolmaking; the chapters by Donald, Gärdenfors, Mithen, Nowell, and Richerson in this volume provide examples. Similarly, comparative studies of monkey, ape, and human behavior, as exemplified in the chapters by Chaminade, Seyfarth and Cheney, and Warneken in this volume, may help identify common adaptations shared by primate subgroups as well as species specific differences.

It is tempting to wonder, Who will get there first? Will molecular biologists, having identified the genetic targets of selection, find a way to get back to the phenotypic traits that were actually selected? Or will social scientists find a way to figure out what are the key components of cognition, language, and culture that are likely to have a basis in genetic adaptations?

4

The Primate Mind before Tools, Language, and Culture

ROBERT M. SEYFARTH AND DOROTHY L. CHENEY

Plato says in Phaedo that our "necessary ideas" arise from the preexistence of the soul, are not derivable from experience—read monkeys for preexistence.

We can thus trace causation of thought...it obeys the same laws as other parts of structure.

— Charles Darwin, 1838 [1987]: Notebook M

INTRODUCTION

Beginning with the arrival of the first stone tools, roughly 2.3 million years ago (Semaw 2000), the archaeological record provides a rich source of data from which to reconstruct the evolution of human mind and behavior. Supplementing these historical data, some living monkeys and apes, particularly chimpanzees, make tools (McGrew 1994, Matsuzawa 1994, Yamakoshi 2001) and exhibit a limited form of culture (Whiten et al. 1999), allowing these species to be used as points of comparison when developing theories about human cognitive evolution.

But what about the period before tools and culture appeared? Regardless of whether they were made by early hominids or modern chimpanzees, tools and culture did not emerge *de novo*—they were, instead, the product of minds that had been evolving for millions of years in response to a variety of selection pressures. What were these selective forces and what kind of cognition did they produce? To reconstruct the evolution of mind before tools and culture, our hypotheses must come primarily from the behavior and cognition of modern primates—a much more speculative enterprise since these species have themselves undergone their own evolutionary changes during the millions of years since they diverged from the common ancestor of monkeys, apes, and humans (the anthropoid primates).

Baboons and other Old World monkeys rarely if ever manufacture tools. Unlike chimpanzees, they have few if any traits that could be called cultural. Yet they, like other primates, have larger brains than non-primate mammals of a similar size (Martin 1990). Why? In *Baboon Metaphysics* (Cheney and Seyfarth 2007), we argue that the baboon mind—and, by extension, that of other nonhuman anthropoid primates—has been shaped by natural selection acting in a complex social environment. Baboons live in a society where reproductive success depends on social skills. As a result, natural selection has favored a mind that is specialized for observing social life, computing social relations, and predicting other animals' behavior.

Here we offer three additional speculations concerning the evolution of human cognition, based on our research on baboons. First, long before the evolution of language and culture, the demands of social life created primates who recognized others as individuals and arranged them into groups according to an implicit set of rules. These ancestors had, in effect, a theory of social organization. Second, the prior evolution of social cognition created individuals who were, in some important respects, preadapted to develop the cognitive skills that would eventually underlie language. The discrete, compositional structure we find in modern language did not first appear there, but arose instead because understanding social life and predicting others' behavior requires discrete, compositional thinking. Third, as Alison Jolly first proposed in 1966, the technological skills and cultural traits evident in rudimentary form in chimpanzees—and hyperbolically so in humans—have their historical roots in the evolution of social skills. In this chapter we review some of the data that lead to these speculations and discuss them in greater detail.

SOCIAL KNOWLEDGE IN BABOONS

Baboons (*Papio hamadryas*) are Old World monkeys that shared a common ancestor with humans roughly 30 million years ago (Steiper, Young, and

Sukarna 2004). They live throughout the savannah woodlands of Africa in groups of 50 to 150 individuals. Although most males emigrate to other groups as young adults, females remain in their natal groups throughout their lives, maintaining close social bonds with their matrilineal kin (Silk, Seyfarth, and Cheney 1999, Silk, Altmann, and Alberts 2006a, 2006b). Females can be ranked in a stable, linear dominance hierarchy that determines priority of access to resources. Daughters acquire ranks similar to those of their mothers. The stable core of a baboon group is therefore a hierarchy of matrilines, in which all members of one matriline (for example, matriline B) outrank or are outranked by all members of another (for example, matrilines C and A, respectively). Ranks within matrilines are as stable as those between matrilines: for example, A1>A2>A3>B1>B2>C1, where letters are used to denote matrilineal kin groups and numbers denote the different individuals within them (Cheney and Seyfarth 2007).

Baboon vocalizations, like those of many other primates, are individually distinctive (e.g., Owren, Seyfarth, and Cheney 1997; Rendall 2003), and playback experiments have shown that listeners recognize the voices of others as the calls of specific individuals (reviewed in Cheney and Seyfarth 2007). The baboon vocal repertoire contains a number of acoustically graded signals, each of which is given in predictable contexts. Because calls are individually distinctive and each call type is predictably linked to a particular social context, baboon listeners can potentially acquire quite specific information from the calls that they hear. Experiments that test what information actually is obtained are thus, in effect, tests of social cognition.

Throughout the day, baboons hear individuals giving vocalizations to each other. Some interactions involve aggressive competition; for example, when a higher-ranking animal gives a series of threat-grunts to a lower-ranking animal and the latter screams. Threat-grunts are aggressive vocalizations given by higher-ranking to lower-ranking individuals, whereas screams are submissive signals, given primarily by lower-ranking individuals to higher-ranking ones. A threat-grunt-scream sequence, therefore, potentially provides information not only about the identities of the opponents involved but also about who is threatening whom. Baboons are sensitive to both types of information. In playback experiments, listeners respond with apparent surprise to sequences of calls that appear to violate the existing dominance hierarchy. They show little response upon hearing the sequence "B2 threat-grunts and C3 screams", but respond strongly—by looking toward the source of the call—when they hear "C3 threat-grunts and B2 screams" (Cheney, Seyfarth, and Silk 1995a). In addition, between-family rank reversals (C3 threat-grunts and B2 screams) elicit a stronger violation of expectation response than do within-family rank reversals (C3 threat grunts and C1 screams) (Bergman et al. 2003).

A baboon who ignores the sequence "B2 threat-grunts and C3 screams" but responds strongly when she hears "C3 threat-grunts and B2 screams" reveals, by her responses, that she recognizes the identities of both participants, their relative ranks, and their family membership. Baboons who react more strongly to call sequences that mimic a between-family rank reversal than to those that mimic a within-family rank reversal act as if they classify individuals simultaneously according to both rank and kinship (Bergman et al. 2003). In both of these cases, listeners act as if they assume that the threat-grunt and scream have occurred together not by chance, but because one vocalization caused the other to occur. Without this assumption of causality there would be no violation of expectation when B2's scream and C3's threat-grunt occurred together.

Baboons' ability to deduce a social narrative from a sequence of sounds reveals a cognitive system in which listeners extract a large number of complex, nuanced messages from a relatively small, finite number of signals. A baboon who understands that "B2 threat-grunts and C3 screams" is different from "C3 threat-grunts and B2 screams" can make the same judgment for all possible pairs of group members as well as any new individuals who may join. This open-ended system of classification is, in at least one respect, abstract, because the categories of rank and matrilineal kinship persist despite changes in the individuals who comprise them (Cheney and Seyfarth 2007: chaps. 6, 7).

In addition to making judgments based on social causation, rank, and kinship, baboons appear to recognize other individuals' intentions and motives. Baboon groups are noisy, tumultuous societies, and a baboon would not be able to feed, rest, or engage in social interactions if she responded to every call as if it were directed at her. In fact, baboons seem to use a variety of behavioral cues, including gaze direction and the memory of recent interactions with specific individuals when making inferences about the target of a vocalization. For example, when a female hears a recent opponent's threat-grunts soon after fighting with her, she responds as if she assumes that the threat-grunt is directed at her, and she avoids the signaler. However, when she hears the same female's threat-grunts soon after grooming with her, she acts as if the calls are directed at someone else and ignores the calls (Engh et al. 2006a).

The attribution of motives to others is perhaps most evident in the case of 'reconciliatory' vocalizations. Like many other group-living animals, baboons incur both costs and benefits from joining a group. In an apparent attempt to minimize the disruptive effects of within-group competition, many primates 'reconcile' with one another, by coming together, touching, hugging, or grooming after aggression (Cheney, Seyfarth, and Silk 1995b). In baboons, reconciliation among females occurs after roughly 10% of fights, and typically occurs when the dominant animal grunts to the subordinate (Cheney, Seyfarth, and Silk 1995b, Silk, Cheney, and Seyfarth 1996). Playback experiments have shown that, even in the absence of any other behavior, grunts alone function to restore former opponents' behavior to baseline levels. When a subordinate female hears her opponent grunt soon after a fight, she approaches her opponent and tolerates her opponent's approaches at a rate that is even higher than baseline rates (Cheney and Seyfarth 1997). In contrast, hearing the grunt of another, previously uninvolved high-ranking female unrelated to her opponent has no effect on the subordinate's behavior.

In some cases, the behavior of subordinates after aggression seems to involve more complex and indirect causal reasoning about both other animals' motives and their kinship bonds. Playback experiments have shown that baboons will accept the 'reconciliatory' grunt by a close relative of a recent opponent as a proxy for direct reconciliation by the opponent herself (Wittig et al. 2007). If individual D1 has been threatened by individual A1 and then hears a grunt from A2, in the hour that follows she is more likely to approach, and more likely to tolerate the approaches of, A1 and A2 than if she had heard no grunt or a grunt from another high-ranking individual unrelated to the A matriline. Intriguingly, D1's behavior toward other members of the A matriline does not change. Subjects in these experiments act as if they recognize that a grunt from a particular female is causally related to a previous fight, but only if the caller is a close relative of her former opponent.

THE FUNCTION OF SOCIAL COGNITION

Baboons live in a society where reproductive success depends upon social skills. Among female baboons living in Kenya, longevity and infant survival are the best predictors of reproductive success, and the best predictor of infant survival is the extent of a female's social integration (Silk, Alberts, and Altmann 2003). Females are strongly motivated to form close social bonds (as measured by frequent proximity and grooming) with others, particularly their matrilineal kin. When a mother dies, females respond by strengthening their bonds with other matrilineal kin. When few or no matrilineal kin are available, they form bonds with paternal sisters and/or unrelated individuals (Silk, Altmann, and Alberts 2006a, 2006b).

In our study group, females experienced the greatest stress (as measured by elevated glucocorticoid levels; Sapolsky 2002) from predation and infanticide—the two events that exert the greatest effect on their own and their infants' survival and reproduction. When infants were threatened with infanticide, their mothers alleviated stress by forming a temporary pair bond, or 'friendship' with an adult male; when a close female companion was killed by a predator, females alleviated stress by broadening and extending their network of bonds with other females (Beehner et al. 2005, Engh et al. 2006b, 2006c). During a "calm" period without infanticide or predation, females whose grooming networks focused on a few preferred partners had lower baseline glucocorticoid levels than did females whose grooming was spread more widely among others (Crockford et al. 2008). When the same females were subsequently challenged by the threat of infanticide, individuals with the most focused grooming networks and the lowest baseline levels showed the smallest increase in glucocorticoid levels (Wittig et al. 2008).

A female's ability to form stable, persistent bonds with other females had a direct effect on her reproductive success. Lifetime reproductive success was most strongly influenced by a female's lifespan and the survival of her infants (Cheney et al. 2004). Females with stronger, more stable, and more enduring social bonds exhibited significantly higher infant survival (Silk et al. 2009) and lived longer (Silk et al. 2010) than females with weaker, less stable social bonds. Dominance rank also affected females' longevity (high-ranking females lived longer), however, the strength of a female's social bonds and her dominance rank had independent effects on longevity. Results suggest that the ability to form strong, enduring social bonds—an indication of social intelligence (see below)—may have allowed low-ranking females to overcome at least some of the limitations imposed by their social status.

In sum, a female baboon's social skills affect her reproductive success. Under these conditions, an individual must know as much as possible about other animals' relations—that is, she must have a sophisticated understanding of the individuals in her group, their long-term associations, short-term bonds, and the motivations that underlie them. Natural selection has thus favored the evolution of skills in identifying and classifying conspecifics because these skills are essential to survival and reproduction (Cheney and Seyfarth 2007).

THE ORIGIN OF SOCIAL CONCEPTS

A variety of research suggests that the mind of a human infant is not a *tabula rasa*. Instead, infants begin life with what Carey (2011:113) has called "a set of innate conceptual representations...that guide an infant's expectations of which objects go together and how they are likely to behave." In Keil's words, they "embody systematic sets of beliefs [that are] largely causal in nature" (1989:1).

How do infants bring together their knowledge of 'what objects go together' and how these objects behave? Reviewing studies of children's cognitive development, Keil (1994) distinguishes between two broadly different hypotheses: "One strongly empiricist account argues that early concepts are devoid of a theory, which then gradually gets overlaid. The other view, which will be called the primal theories account, argues that concepts are embedded within theorylike relations from the start" (1994:235). According to the latter hypothesis, "even in infancy, some very crude theoretical biases start to be abstracted away" from the regularities observed in the social and physical world (1994:238). In Gopnik and Wellman's (1994) terms, an empiricist child may be able to make generalizations that allow her to predict behavior, but these generalizations do not yet constitute a theory because they "are not far removed from the evidence itself." Theories, in contrast, make "predictions about a wide variety of evidence, including evidence that played no role in the theory's initial construction" (1994:261).

Of course, it would go far beyond the evidence to suggest that baboons have the same kind of theories or concepts we see in young children. Nonetheless, there are points at which baboons appear to make deductions that go beyond the mere observations of behavior—deductions that suggest that they have some underlying theory about individuals, their motives, and how these motives are likely to be expressed.

For example, consider the phenomenon of individual recognition, which is widespread among animals (Tibbetts and Dale 2007). Nonhuman primates—and perhaps many other species—have neural structures that appear to be specialized for identifying individual faces and voices (reviewed in Seyfarth and Cheney 2008). Individual recognition is also cross-modal: when a female baboon hears her offspring's call she looks toward the source of the sound (e.g., Cheney and Seyfarth 1999), as if the sound has created an expectation of what she will see if she looks toward its source. Dogs and squirrel monkeys associate the faces and voices of their caretakers (Adachi, Kuwahata, and Fugita 2007, Adachi and Fujita 2007), while horses associate the whinny of a specific herd member with the sight of that individual (Proops, McComb, and Reby 2008). Humans, of course, do this routinely, integrating information about faces and voices to form the rich, multimodal percept of a person (Campanella and Belin 2007).

Taken together, these results suggest that individual recognition in many animals involves the formation of a concept—the concept of animal X—that cannot be reduced to or defined in terms of any single sensory attribute. It involves, instead, the integration of many different attributes into a single percept, such that the sound of X's voice creates an expectation of what one will see and the sight of X creates an expectation of what one will hear. These concepts are formed without language: animals do not give names to each other. How they develop is unclear. Obviously, animals require experience to recognize the members of their group and any new animals who join or are born into it. But neural structures specialized for the recognition of individual faces, voices, and their cross-modal integration suggest that animals in some species have an innate predisposition to form the concept of an individual—an innate conceptual representation that parallels those found in human infants. Finally, individual recognition has a long evolutionary history, appearing throughout the animal kingdom. Perhaps one of the earliest concepts—whenever it appeared—was a social one: what in our species we call the concept of a person.

Building on the recognition of individuals, baboons go on to recognize what human observers describe as "close associates." Here the animals act as if they have a theory: one that is causal because it is based on assumptions about why individuals behave the way they do ("because they are members of the same matriline, or close associates"), and one that has generality because it makes predictions about a wide variety of evidence, some of which played no role in the theory's initial construction. On the basis of some minimal observations (as yet unknown), baboons conclude that, if A1 and A2 interact in certain ways in some contexts (when feeding, for example), they can therefore be counted on to behave in predictable ways in many other contexts—when forming an alliance, or grooming, or reconciling with each other's former opponents. In apparently predicting how matrilineal kin will interact under a wide variety of circumstances, baboons act as if they have a theory about "matrilineal families"—how they should be recognized and how, once identified, individuals within them are likely to behave. The baboons then use this theory to predict behavior.

When it comes to recognizing matrilineal kin groups, baboons are "essentialists" (Gelman, Coley, and Gottfried 1994). They act as if the members of kin groups "have essences or underlying natures that make them the things that they are." These essences cannot be based on physical appearance, because members of the same matriline do not look alike (think of mothers, their infants, and their adolescent sons) or share any other physical features that distinguish them from the members of other matrilines. Baboons' classification of others must be based on something more abstract. It constitutes a kind of implicit theoretical knowledge because "one of the things that theories do is to embody or provide causal linkages from deeper properties to more superficial or surface properties" (Medin 1989:1476).

Consider, as another example, the baboons' ascription of motives to others. When a baboon hears the sequence "Sylvia threat-grunts and Hannah screams," she responds as if she assumes a causal relation between the two events: the threat-grunt and the scream occurred together not by chance but because the former caused the latter. The listener has no other evidence on which to base this assumption because she cannot see the animals interacting. Only her memory of past interactions can guide her perception of current events. And yet she makes the assumption of causality not just for Sylvia and Hannah but for every combination of females whose calls she hears. The listener acts as if she has a general theory about how individuals—all individuals—interact.

In much the same way, recall that, in several experiments, a baboon who grooms with X and then, some minutes later, hears X's threat grunt shows little if any response. She acts as if the threat grunt is not directed at her. In contrast, if the baboon has recently fought with X and then hears X's threat grunt, she responds strongly, as if the threat is meant for her. These results hold across many different trials in which many different individuals were substituted for X (see references above). The subject, in other words, acts as if she has a theory that can be applied to all individuals in her group—not just X. Individuals with whom you groom are kindly motivated toward you and this motivation is likely to persist over time, whereas individuals who have recently threatened you are not kindly motivated and this, too, predicts their subsequent behavior. Of course, these expectations probably begin with the formation of relatively simple, Pavlovian associations between, say, grooming with X and subsequent friendly behavior with X. But these associations are not enough to explain the baboons' behavior. Instead, as they develop into adults baboons seem to develop some very crude generalizations—or "theoretical biases" (Keil 1994) that allow them to organize what they know about other individuals.

Lastly, it is interesting to note that as children's conceptual skills develop they begin to formulate many different concepts in parallel—concepts that can differ widely in both the objects they include and the causal mechanisms that underlie them (Carey 1985). The formation of multiple concepts helps elucidate the children's growing skill because, as Keil (1989:1) points out, "no individual concept can be understood without some understanding of how it relates to other concepts." Here again, baboons provide us with a rich source for speculation because they appear to have different social concepts that follow different rules. Individuals grouped together in the same matriline are assumed, by virtue of this grouping, to behave in certain ways toward each other. Individuals arranged in a linear dominance hierarchy follow different rules. The concepts 'matrilineal kin group' and 'dominance hierarchy' thus differ in their essential properties, but they can also be merged to form a more complex concept of 'ranked matrilines' (Bergman et al. 2003).

IMPLICATIONS FOR RESEARCH ON THE EVOLUTION OF HUMAN COGNITION

We propose that, long before the evolution of human language and culture, natural selection favored individuals who could predict each other's behavior and form social relationships that returned the greatest benefit to them. In doing so, selection favored skills in recognizing and classifying individuals along multiple abstract dimensions (rank, kinship, and so on). Because these skills evolved long before the appearance of tools, culture, or language, they acted as important "prime movers" in human evolution, preadapting individuals for the evolution of more advanced abilities, such as shared attention, a full-blown theory of mind, teaching, and cultural transmission.

PREADAPTATIONS FOR LANGUAGE

Darwin believed that the course of evolution could be revealed through the comparative method—by contrasting similar traits in related species, examining their common properties, measuring their differences, and searching for branching points in the fossil record. When the trait in question is language, the Darwinian approach might logically begin with a comparative study of human language and the vocalizations of nonhuman anthropoid primates. But this technique has not proved very successful, because the two sorts of communication are so different that comparison between them reveals little about their common ancestry. The differences are most pronounced in call production. Nonhuman primates have a relatively small repertoire of calls, each of which is closely linked to particular social circumstances and shows little modification during development (see Hammerschmidt and Fischer 2008 for a review). With some intriguing exceptions (Zuberbuhler 2002, Arnold and Zuberbuhler 2006), nonhuman primate signalers do not combine different call types to create new meaning.

We suggest, however, that for those interested in reconstructing the evolution of language these differences in production have been overemphasized, distracting attention from studies of perception and cognition where continuities with language are more apparent. Here nonhuman primates have a much larger repertoire and an almost open-ended ability to learn new sound-meaning pairs throughout their lives (Seyfarth and Cheney 2008). And while, for the most part, they do not create call combinations, nonhuman primates hear them all the time, whenever two individuals vocalize to each other. Their interpretation of the information contained in these call sequences reveals a discrete, computational mode of thinking that shares several properties with human language processing.

It is now well accepted that before a child can learn language she must have some experience with the objects, events, and relations that make up her world. As Noam Chomsky has put it, "If you couldn't pick pieces of meaning out of the world in advance, before you learned a language, then language couldn't be learnt" (Fisher and Gleitman 2002:447; Chomsky 1982:119). The same argument appears in theories of language evolution. Pinker and

Bloom (1990), for example, propose that "grammar exploited mechanisms originally used for…conceptualization," and Newmeyer (1991) suggests that "[t]he conditions for the subsequent development of language…were set by the evolution of…conceptual structure. A first step toward the evolution of this system…was undoubtedly the linking up of individual bits of conceptual structure to individual vocalizations" (for similar views, see Jackendoff 1987, 2002, Kirby 1998, Newmeyer 2003, Hurford 1998, 2003).

The hypotheses that a certain kind of thinking appears before the emergence of language in young children, and evolved before spoken language in our hominin ancestors, are widely accepted but rather vague. What kind of conceptual thinking? Concepts about what? We propose that nonhuman primate social knowledge shares several properties with human language that may be relevant to theories of language evolution.

First, primate social knowledge is representational. When one baboon hears another's vocalization she acquires information that is highly specific—about a particular sort of predator, or about a particular individual and her motivation to interact in specific ways (threaten, appease, or reconcile) with another.

Second, social knowledge is based on properties that have discrete values (Worden 1998). At least in baboons, each individual is unique and unambiguously associated with a specific dominance rank. Ranks are not "fuzzy" categories: an individual ranked third always defers to those ranked first and second but never defers to those ranked fourth or below. Matrilineal kin associations have boundaries that are slightly less precise (e.g., Dasser 1988), but they still constitute a category to which an individual either belongs or does not.

Third, nonhuman primates combine these discrete-valued traits to create a representation of social relations that is hierarchically structured. Baboons, for example, create a nested hierarchy in which others are placed in a linear rank order and simultaneously grouped according to matrilineal kinship in a manner that preserves ranks both within and across families.

Fourth, social knowledge is rule-governed and open-ended. Baboons recognize that vocalizations follow certain rules of directionality that must, for instance, correspond to the current dominance hierarchy. Threat-grunts are given only by dominant animals to subordinates, fear barks are given only by subordinates to dominants, but grunts can be given in either direction. Knowledge is open-ended because new individuals can be added or eliminated without altering the underlying structure, and because the set of all possible interactions is very large (Worden 1998, Seyfarth and Cheney 2003). Taken together, the rule-governed and open-ended properties of primate social knowledge lead to a cognitive system that allows animals to comprehend a huge number of messages from a finite number of signals. If a baboon understands that "Sylvia threat-grunts and Hannah screams" carries a different meaning from "Hannah threat-grunts and Sylvia screams," she can make the same judgment for all possible pairs of individuals in the group, including any new individuals who may join.

Fifth, knowledge is, loosely speaking, propositional. Baboons evaluate the meaning of call sequences in terms of other individuals' identities, motives, and the causal relations that link one individual's behavior with another. That is, they represent in their minds (albeit in a limited way) the individuated concepts of "Sylvia," "Hannah," "threat-grunt," and "scream," and they combine these concepts to create a mental representation of one individual's intentions toward another. In so doing, they interpret a stream of sounds as a dramatic narrative: "Sylvia is threatening Hannah and causing her to scream" (for an empirical test of the hypothesis that baboons listeners know when a vocalization is directed at them and hence recognize another's intention to communicate, see Engh et al. 2006c).

Sixth, knowledge is independent of sensory modality. While playback experiments allow us to explore the structure of primates' social knowledge and demonstrate that such knowledge can be acquired through vocalizations alone, social knowledge is also obtained visually. Indeed, we now know that, at the neurophysiological level, visual and auditory information are integrated to form a multimodal representation of call meaning (Ghazanfar and Logothetis 2003, Gil-da-Costa et al. 2004, Ghazanfar et al. 2005, Barsalou 2005).

In sum, when they hear and interpret a sequence of calls, baboons recognize individuals, assess their motives and behavior, and evaluate the entire call sequence in light of what they know about the dominance hierarchy in their group. Elements of the sequence—the individual calls—retain their own separate meaning, but taken together they convey a meaning that is more than the sum of its parts.

Some Caveats

There are important limits to the parallel we have drawn between non-human primate social cognition and the cognitive operations that underlie language. Note, for example, that agents, actions, and recipients in a baboon call sequence are not coded in the way we usually encounter them in language. For baboon listeners, agent and action are coded in the threat-grunts, which are recognizable as aggressive vocalizations and identifiable as Sylvia's. The same holds for Hannah's screams. Although the precise order of calls seems relatively unimportant in listeners' assessment of the event, their temporal and spatial juxtaposition is not. Listeners behave as if they assume that the calls do not occur together by chance, but instead are juxtaposed because Sylvia's threat-grunt *caused* Hannah's scream. We suggest, therefore, that the propositional information baboons acquire when they hear vocalizations includes an understanding of the causal relations that link an actor's threat-grunts and a recipient's screams.

Perhaps more important, none of the call sequences we describe was produced by a single individual. In their manner of production, therefore, baboon vocalizations could hardly be more different from language. Despite this difference, however, listeners interpret the meaning of a sequence in ways that bear important resemblances to the meanings we express in language, which are built up by combining discrete-valued entities in a structured, hierarchical, rule-governed, and open-ended manner. This leads to the hypothesis that the internal representations of language meaning by humans initially built upon our pre-linguistic ancestors' knowledge of social relations (Cheney and Seyfarth 1998, Worden 1998). Indeed, as Worden (1998:156) argues, "no other candidate meaning structure has such a good fit to language meanings."

Lastly, we are not suggesting that all of the syntactic properties found in language are present in nonhuman primate social knowledge. Such a claim would be entirely unjustified, given the many features of language—like case, tense, subject-verb agreement, open- and closed-class items, and recursion—that have no counterpart in the communication or cognition of any nonhuman primate and almost certainly evolved long after the divergence of the hominin line from the common ancestor of humans and chimpanzees (for recent discussions see Jackendoff 1999, Calvin and Bickerton 2000, Hauser, Chomsky, and Fitch 2002, Burling 2005, Johansson 2005, Hurford 2007). Instead, focusing on the early, prelinguistic stages of language evolution, we suggest that primates—including Old World monkeys, apes, and our hominin ancestors—evolved in a social environment that created selection pressures favoring structured, hierarchical, rule-governed intelligence.

Because this social intelligence exhibits, in simpler form, several language-like features, many of the rules and computations found in human language first appeared as an elaboration of the rules and computations underlying social interactions.

First Thought, Then Language

The "social cognition" hypothesis adds a slightly new wrinkle to theories of language evolution because it proposes that some precursors of grammar may have been part of the cognitive abilities of our prelinguistic ancestors. In a widely cited hypothesis, Bickerton has proposed that language evolved in two stages: first "protolanguage" and then modern language (1990, Calvin and Bickerton 2000). Bickerton's model of protolanguage is drawn from four sources: pidgin languages (Bickerton 1981), the language of individuals who have been isolated from adults during childhood (Curtiss 1977), children's language at the one-word stage; and the signing of captive apes (e.g., Savage-Rumbaugh 1986). In essence, protolanguage is language without syntax (Jackendoff 1999, 2002).

By contrast, the social cognition hypothesis suggests that some of the cognitive operations that underlie modern syntax were among the earliest precursors of language. Specifically, before language appeared, natural selection favored individuals who, upon hearing a sequence of calls, could combine several discrete, meaningful elements in a rule-governed manner to create a complex, propositional representation of events. In Bickerton's hypothesis, protolanguage is grammatically impoverished, making it difficult to imagine a gradual transition from protolanguage to language. The social cognition hypothesis may in some respects help to alleviate this problem.

The social cognition hypothesis also makes chronological sense. If we assume that social complexity favored increasingly sophisticated cognitive abilities, we can imagine how these skills might have created an environment in which natural selection favored more flexible articulation, a full-blown theory of mind, the ability to generate new words, and the ability to create sentences. By contrast, it is difficult to imagine how—or why—these uniquely human skills would have evolved if humans had not first possessed the conceptual capacity that made them adaptive. Indeed, if one accepts the view that there are parallels between primate social cognition and the mechanisms that encode meaning in language, and agrees that the former is a generalized primate trait while the latter are unique to humans, it is hard to imagine that the earliest forms of human syntax did *not* build upon these pre-existing cognitive skills. Before hominids produced syntactic utterances, they assigned meaning to other individuals' calls and extracted syntactic, rule-governed, propositional information from the vocal interactions of others.

Talmy (2006) suggests that during the course of evolution a crucial bottleneck was overcome when our ancestors' vocal communication changed from analog to digital, and he poses the question: Where did language get its digitalness from? The answer, we believe, lies in social cognition. Long before they could engage in the computations that underlie modern grammar they performed the computations needed to understand their societies. As a result, the discrete, compositional structure we find in spoken language did not first appear there. It arose, instead, because understanding social life and predicting others' behavior requires discrete, compositional thinking.

Similarly, Hurford (1990) asks whether propositional structures (among other features) are "elements of the structure of languages" or whether they "somehow existed before language" in another domain. Here again, data on primate social cognition provide an answer: The propositions that are expressed in language did not originate with language. They arose, instead, because to succeed in a social group of monkeys or apes one must understand an elementary form of propositional relations.

The linguistic revolution thus occurred when we began to express this tacit knowledge, and to use our cognitive skills in speaking as well as listening. The earliest syntactic utterances, however, were not entirely original. They described relations that their speakers already understood and had a formal structure that grew out of their speakers' knowledge of social relationships.

SOCIAL COGNITION AND THE EVOLUTION OF TECHNOLOGY

Finally, the social cognition hypothesis may help explain how social complexity and technological complexity—the use and manufacture of tools, for example—may have interacted to shape human evolution. Extrapolating from our research on baboons, it seems likely that social complexity and social intelligence are widespread among monkeys and apes. By contrast, the use and manufacture of tools is restricted almost entirely to two of the great apes, chimpanzees and orangutans. With the exception of one New World monkey species, the capuchin, tool use among monkeys is decidedly unimpressive. It therefore seems probable, as Jolly (1966) first proposed, that the technological and innovative skills found in chimpanzees (and greatly elaborated in humans) have their roots in the selective forces that originally favored the evolution of social skills. Although innovation, tool use, and technological invention may have played a crucial role in the evolution of ape and human brains (Reader and Laland 2002), these skills were probably built upon mental computations that had their origins and foundations in social interactions.

5

Functions of Premotor Cortices:
From Motor Control to Social Cognition

THIERRY CHAMINADE

INTRODUCTION

The development of fine motor skills and complex action sequences and their cultural transmission by imitation are distinctively human. In the course of human evolution, areas of the brain controlling motor functions have developed to support such distinctively human behaviors as language and the ability to fashion stone tools. A collection of areas known generically as premotor cortices are particularly relevant to understand how the brain controls these sequentially and hierarchically structured actions. The archaeological record provides a sequence of the types of tools used by our successive human ancestors, and modern techniques of neuroimaging allow us to study directly the brain areas that serve the different types of toolmaking in modern humans. By comparing these brain areas with homologous areas in other primates, we can begin to sort out the evolution of human premotor cortices.

Recently, startling claims have been made concerning the role of "mirror neurons" in the development of anthropoid primate motor skills and social interactions, including the phylogenetic acquisition of language in the hominin line. The assessment of such claims requires an overview of neurophysiological studies of the operation of "mirror neurons" paired with a reexamination of the anatomy of premotor cortices in a functioning context. This chapter aims to provide such an assessment. Reviewing the monkey electrophysiology literature, we will find that, under strict definition, there are very few true mirror neurons. Further, the chapter questions the notion of a "human mirror system" and proposes to replace it by the concept of "motor resonance" to avoid misunderstanding of the neural principles underlying the participation of premotor cortices in the evolution of the social and linguistic capacities that have been associated with mirror neurons.

ANATOMY OF THE PREMOTOR CORTEX

The brain region now referred to as "the premotor cortex" was originally called the "intermediate precentral cortex" (Campbell 1905), while Brodmann (1905) emphasized the idea that this area, numbered 6 in his map of the human brain, is devoted to motor functions. Fulton (1935) reported that ablations in the homologous region in monkeys altered the execution of skilled movements. These early findings supported the concept of a "non primary" motor cortex with distinct motor functions (reviewed in Wise 1985). Subsequent work discredited this concept: electric shocks to the monkeys' premotor cortices did not elicit movement (Woolsey et al. 1952). The characterization of the motor functions of the "intermediate precentral cortex" had to wait until the early 1980s, when a renewed interest confirmed and extended its motor properties.

Taken as a whole, motor cortices cover a large strip of frontal cortex anterior to the central sulcus and comprise a mosaic of anatomically and functionally distinct areas (Fig. 5.1, CS). Characterization of a brain area is based on cytoarchitectonics, the characterization of gray matter neuronal composition under the microscope, that also informs us about the connectivity (Barbas and Rempel-Clower 1997) and the type of processing taking place (Shipp 2005) in this area. The presence of star-shaped interneurons, called granule cells, in the internal layer IV is particularly useful: a cortical area with a thick layer IV is known as a granular cortex, and is usually a magnet for feed-forward connections for sensory or higher-order processing. In contrast, the a-granular primary motor area (Fig. 5.1, M1) has the richest pool of upper motor neurons, which project to the lower motor neurons controlling muscles through cortico-spinal tracts, in the anthropoid primate's brain. It sends very few projections to other cortical areas (Shipp 2005) but stands at the top of the motor hierarchy, controlling motor output. Considering the lack of association properties of the

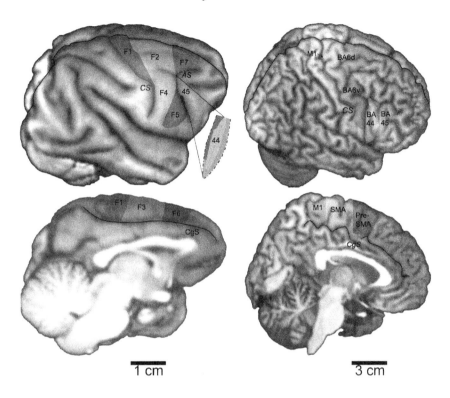

5.1. Anatomy of macaque and human premotor cortices. The depiction of the right hemisphere (top row) and of the medial view (bottom row) of macaque (left column) and human (right column) brain anatomy is labeled with the functional parcellation of motor cortices. CS = Central Sulcus, CgS = Cingulate Sulcus. More details available in the text.

primary motor cortex, we will not discuss its functions in the rest of this chapter.

The premotor cortex is a dysgranular, transitional area between the primary motor cortex posteriorly and the granular prefrontal cortex anteriorly. In Brodmann's (1905) cytoarchitectonic parcellation of the human brain, the original "intermediate precentral cortex" comprises Brodmann Area 6 (BA6) posteriorly and extends, ventrally, to BA44 and BA45, discussed later. BA6 was further divided in Vogt and Vogt (1919) on the basis of myeloarchitecture. More recently, premotor cortices were mapped in macaque monkeys using electrophysiology (Rizzolatti, Luppino, and Matelli 1998), and we will use the parcellation scheme derived from this group. It presents several advantages. First, its main premise is that a mosaic of anatomically and functionally distinct areas forms premotor cortices. Second, it is primarily interested in characterizing frontal and parietal areas' involvement in motor control, focusing on the functional division of labor between parietofrontal control loops relevant to motor control. Last, the use of macaque monkey anatomical and functional data offers a better spatial resolution than human data. Several observations support a good homology between human and macaque brain structures. For instance, a progressive increase in the morphological complexity of pyramidal cells from area 4 to area 6 is preserved in humans, macaques, and vervet monkeys, suggesting that regional microcircuitry was present in a common ancestor of anthropoid primates (Elston et al. 2005). The ratio between the size of the frontal lobe, which includes motor and premotor cortices, and the size of the whole brain is also preserved between humans and other great apes (Semendeferi et al. 1997), suggesting that the increase of absolute brain size preserved the relative sizes of brain lobes.

According to Rizzolatti's group parcellation scheme, premotor cortices can be divided along two axes. The mediolateral axis can roughly be described as the medial wall controlling sequential actions, the lateral cortex controlling actions related to the surrounding space, and the ventral divisions involved in fine-grained motor control. Along an anteroposterior axis, the anterior cortex has closer connections with prefrontal cortices while the posterior cortex has closer connections with the primary motor cortex (Picard and Strick 2001, Rizzolatti et al. 1998). This latter axis is particularly well established in the medial premotor cortex, in which a clear division between an anterior and a posterior region was demonstrated in humans using the tracking of white fibers originating from these medial premotor areas. The posterior region is connected to the primary motor cortex and the corticospinal tract while the anterior region is connected to the frontal cortex (Johansen-Berg et al. 2004), similar to the anatomical division between the caudal supplementary motor area (SMA proper in humans, or F3 in macaques, see Fig. 5.1) and the rostral presupplementary motor area (pre-SMA, or F6) in the macaque brain.

This anatomical division is reflected in functional differences between F3 and F6. Monkey electrophysiology (Nakamura, Sakai, and Hikosaka 1998) and human neuroimaging (Hikosaka et al. 1996) studies suggest that the anterior medial premotor area (F6) is involved in the learning of an arbitrary sequence of movements, while the posterior area is involved in motor aspects of the task. Receiving and processing associative cues is thus preferentially implemented in the anterior F6, where activity can be recorded even in the absence of actual movement, for example associated with the switching of action rules (Rushworth et al. 2004). Motor execution in contrast involves the posterior F3 (Hoshi and Tanji 2004). Altogether, functional results confirm the anatomical report of closer ties with motor cortices in posterior premotor cortices, related to motor execution, and closer ties with prefrontal cortices in anterior premotor cortices, related to information processing.

Rizzolatti and colleagues accordingly further divided the lateral premotor cortices along the anteroposterior axis. The dorsal premotor cortex consists of an anterior area F7 and a posterior F2. It was proposed, on the basis of ablation studies in monkeys, that area F7 would play a role in conditional stimulus-response association tasks (Passingham 1993), while F2 would be involved in preparing and monitoring arm and leg movements in space on the basis of somatosensory and visual information. A comparable distinction was reported in humans (Boussaoud 2001). The anterior lateral premotor cortex was associated with the sensory attentional demands of a task, i.e., processing of the visual cues indicating which action to perform, while the posterior lateral premotor was associated with the motor intentional demands of a task, i.e., preparing the appropriate motor response given the visual cues.

Similarly, the ventral premotor cortex area has been divided into a caudal region F4, encoding peripersonal space for action control, and a rostral region F5, devoted to relationships between objects and body parts (Rizzolatti et al. 1988). Importantly, these neurons respond not only during movement, but also to certain sensory, in particular visual and somatosensory, stimuli. For example almost all F4 neurons respond to sensory stimulation, half in response to somatosensory stimuli, and the other half responding to both visual and somatosensory stimuli. Similarly F5 neurons, that typically code goal-directed actions such as manipulating objects with hand or mouth movements, also respond to the observation of three-dimensional objects (canonical neurons, encoding a pragmatic representation of the object's properties relevant for action), or to the observation of the actual action encoded by that neuron. The latter class of F5 neurons have been called "mirror neurons."

MACAQUE MONKEY MIRROR NEURONS

The definition of mirror neurons is therefore based on their physiological response. Thus characterization of mirror neurons is based on monkey electrophysiology, the recording by intracerebral electrodes of single neurons' action potentials while the macaque monkey performs a given task. The discovery of mirror neurons was serendipitous: as a researcher grasped some food in front of a monkey being recorded in the premotor area F5, the neuron fired despite the absence of motor activity from the monkey. Following this anecdotal finding of a premotor neuron response to the observation of an action, a series of studies investigated their properties more thoroughly. In the first report (di Pellegrino et al. 1992), a total of 184 F5 neurons were recorded, of which 48 responded to simple visual stimuli (i.e., target object), and 39 fired in response to complex stimuli showing the experimenter interacting with objects. This last category was divided into four groups according to their properties: roughly one fourth had no recordable motor properties, another fourth was also affected by motor execution, another category responded more to the observation than to the execution of actions, and for a last fourth of the neurons, there was a logical relation between the action they encoded motorically and their visual response. For example, neurons in this later category fired during the execution of a grasp and during the observation of a graspable object. The neuronal response persisted when visual feedback was hidden during the monkey's action, demonstrating that the response is not purely visual.

A subsequent and more thorough investigation of F5 neurons (Gallese et al. 1996, Rizzolatti et al. 1996b) reported very similar properties and proportions: out of 532 neurons recorded, 92 responded to complex stimuli and 29 were strictly congruent. Thus, "stringent" mirror neurons, in which the observed and the executed actions most effective to elicit a mirror neuron activity match perfectly, are scarce: 12 out of 184 or 6.5%, 29 out of 532 or 5.5%. More frequent are F5 neurons whose visual properties involve observing an experimenter's actions irrespective of the neurons' motor properties ("loose" mirror neurons; 39 of 184 or 21.2%, 92 out of 532 or 17.3%). In addition, only a restricted set of actions, believed to trigger activity in the recorded region, were tested, and nothing precludes that other actions are as or even more effective in eliciting a response when presented visually, without necessarily having a counterpart in the animal's motor repertoire. It is impossible in practice to demonstrate the direct correspondence, i.e., that a mirror neuron encodes a single action both in motor and visual terms. Hence considering mirror neurons as neurons activated when the macaque executes and observes an identical action as in a mirror is misconstrued; they are neurons active when the monkey executes an action as well as when the monkey observes an experimenter executing an action, whether or not the action effective in triggering the motor and the visual responses is unique, or even the same in both modalities.

Mirror neurons also show the ability to "infer hidden goals" (Umilta et al. 2001). Activity of F5 mirror neurons was recorded as a grasping action was shown in its entirety or hiding the goal, and the object was present or absent. Half of 37 "loose" mirror F5 neurons recorded responded similarly when the final part of the action was hidden from the monkey's vision, suggesting that their responses incorporate the monkey's knowledge about the world.

Another important finding concerns the sensory modality mirror neurons respond to. If a mirror neuron encodes the abstract representation of a given action, it is quite likely that any sensory input eliciting an internal representation of this action will cause the mirror neuron to fire. In the previous examples vision was the only sensory modality tested, but nothing precludes other modalities, such as audition, having a similar effect. Activity of F5 mirror neurons was recorded in response to action-related sounds, for example the sound associated with breaking a peanut (Kohler et al. 2002). More than 1 out of 10 neurons tested fired both during the execution of an action and in response to action-related sounds. Some of these neurons responded to the same action during execution, vision, and audition of action sounds, making them stringent multimodal mirror neurons. All mirror neurons described previously are concerned with hand actions, but one class of mouth-related mirror neurons has also been described in the mouth sector of F5 (Ferrari et al. 2003). One fourth of recorded neurons were categorized as "mouth mirror neurons" in agreement with their firing in response to the execution and to the observation of ingestive actions such as sucking from a syringe and lip-protrusion.

Mirror neurons were also reported in a brain area other than F5, the inferior parietal lobule area PF (Fogassi et al. 2005). Such a finding had been expected as areas PF and F5 are anatomically connected (Rizzolatti, Luppino, and Matelli 1998). Roughly a fourth of recorded neurons responded to the execution and to the observation of a grasping action. Interestingly, some neurons responded differently depending on the ultimate goal of actions. Some neurons fired when the monkeys grasped an object to place it into a container, but not into the mouth, and also responded when monkeys observed the experimenter grasp an object to place it into a container but not when he placed it in his mouth (Fogassi et al. 2005). Despite the actions having similar movements, PF mirror neurons responded to one goal (place in container) and not the other (place in mouth), both in the motor and visual modalities.

The previous paragraphs summarize most of our knowledge on "mirror neurons." First, it is generally believed that mirror neurons are neurons firing when the monkey executes an action and when he observes the same action. Such neurons have been recorded in the ventral premotor region F5 and inferior parietal lobule PF. Comparing the various reports, it is reasonable to assume that around 20% of recordable neurons in these areas have mirror properties (in a loose sense), and a lower percentage, around 5%, can be described as stringent mirror neurons according to the criteria used here. There is a discrepancy between the idea conveyed by the name "mirror neurons" and the experimental data—most of the neurons reported as "mirror" are only loosely congruent in terms of the action most effective in activating them during observation and execution. They might better be described as premotor neurons responding to the observation of actions. A second point is that all actions were performed by a human experimenter in front of the monkey, implying that agents from different species suffice to elicit mirror responses. It was reported anecdotally that mirror neurons fire when a monkey observes another monkey acting, but there is a lack of experimental data concerning mirror neurons responses to conspecifics; a stronger response to humans than to monkey actions would imply that the properties of mirror neurons derive from the monkeys' contacts with their humans caregivers, and are likely to result from associative learning of action routines during their daily interactions, in particular feeding. This leads to a third important point: all actions for which neurons with mirror properties were reported were object-directed, concerned the hand or, in one case, the mouth, and were most of the time related with feeding. There is no evidence from the monkey's electrophysiological data pointing to a generic mirror system in which neurons respond to a variety of actions, irrespective of their relation to feeding, their goal-directedness, or the effector used. These points highlight the sharp contrast between the actual findings and the popular description of a mirror neuron as "a neuron which fires both when an animal *acts* and when the animal observes the *same* action performed by another (*especially conspecific*) animal."[1] Italics were added to emphasize generalizations of the experimental results that are questionable: (1) only a very limited set of actions were proven to be mirrored, (2) similarity of action is stringent only for a maximum of one fourth of so-called mirror neurons, (3) response to conspecifics, in particular the fact that they would be in any way stronger or more systematic, is not backed up experimentally. Nevertheless, the finding and characterization of mirror neurons has renewed interest in perception-action matching mechanisms, and their putative role in human cognition.

MIRROR NEURONS IN HUMANS?

Mirror neurons, and their human counterpart the "human mirror system," are prevalent in the contemporary cognitive literature. In August 2010, a simple search using these two terms ("mirror neuron" and "mirror system" in the title, abstracts, and keywords) in Medline, the online repository of medical abstracts yielded almost 450 publications in the last fifteen years. Yet a more scrupulous look gives surprising results: almost a half of these publications can be considered as reviews or commentaries. The monkey electrophysiology summarized previously accounts for a small percentage of the literature. The human physiological data, using the brain imaging techniques which emerged in the last decades such as positron emission tomography (PET), functional magnetic resonance imaging (fMRI), electroencephalography (EEG), magnetoencephalography (MEG), and transcranial magnetic stimulation (TMS), and the investigations of normal or pathological behaviors interpreted in relation to mirror neurons account for almost another half of the manuscripts. More is written speculating about possible functions of the mirror neurons than on the properties of the mirror neurons themselves, even when both human and monkey physiological studies are considered together.

The first thing expected from an investigation of mirror neurons in humans is to reproduce, as closely as possible, the results obtained in monkeys. As it is ethically unacceptable to record systematically single cell activity in the human premotor cortex, any evidence has to be indirect, using non-invasive neuroimaging techniques. Yet the paucity of neurons with stringent mirror properties in area F5 sheds doubt on the possibility of recording their activity using a global signal such as the blood oxygenation level used in human fMRI. In order to be comparable to monkey experiments, a "mirror neurons" neuroimaging experiment in humans should (1) record activity during execution and observation of action, (2) use grasping of objects by hand, and (3) present live full-body actors as stimuli for observation. Most PET and fMRI experiments don't meet these requirements. Point 3 has been tested only once in a PET experiment (Rizzolatti et al. 1996a), mainly because of the lack of control associated with having a live element during a neuroimaging recording. Only two studies particularly aimed at identifying the region containing mirror neurons in humans conformed to points 1 and 2. In the first (Rizzolatti et al. 1996a), volunteers were PET-scanned during the observation and the execution of grasping. When compared to the observation of static objects, the observation of object-directed actions activated significantly an anterior region of the inferior frontal gyrus estimated to be BA45. No other premotor regions were reported for action observation. When contrasted to the observation of objects, action execution yielded significant activity around the central sulcus, with premotor activity more dorsal and posterior than the region found in action observation. Highly relevant for the current discussion, no overlap between response to action observation and action execution, expected if mirror neurons were present, was reported in this study. This negative finding was attributed to technical limitations. As objects were presented visually in the control condition, PET measurements were not sensitive enough to differentiate between signals caused by the firing of two types of F5 neurons—canonical neurons in response to static objects in the control condition and mirror neurons in response to action observation. Another possible limitation is the lack of spatial resolution of PET.

An fMRI study searched for human brain regions with functional properties similar to monkeys' F5 (Grezes et al. 2003). Volunteers were asked to perform a grasp adapted to different objects, to observe a grasp on the same objects, or to observe the object. A cluster of activity in the left inferior frontal gyrus, localized in the ventral premotor area BA6, was found during the execution of action (mimicking the action, acting towards an object, or imitating). But this cluster did not respond specifically to the observation of a gesture. Activity was higher for the observation of the object alone or the observation of the gesture alone than for the condition supposed to elicit mirror neurons activity, observation of a gesture towards an object. The response of the premotor cluster in this last condition was comparable to the activity reported for the observation of the background, a clear breach of expectations regarding factors influencing mirror neurons firing. Taken together these two studies did not identify a region in the ventral premotor cortex or in the more anterior inferior frontal gyrus in which responses to the observation and to the execution of grasping actions overlap in humans.

More recent experiments use repetition suppression, a measure of functional specificity based on the observation that the repetition of the same feature in consecutive stimuli induces a reduction of the activity in regions specifically involved in processing this feature (Dinstein et al. 2007, Kilner et al. 2009). The experimental paradigm was based on the chifoumi ("rock-paper-scissor") game. Volunteers for this experiment observed one of the three actions, and executed them on instruction or in the course of a game. Repetition suppression was observed when the same gesture (closed fist, open hand, index or middle fingers extended) was observed or executed twice in a row. Overlap between repetition suppression for action execution and observation was found in the left ventral premotor cortex and anterior inferior frontal sulcus, corresponding roughly to BA6 and BA44 or 45. In addition to these, other regions of overlap were reported, along the intraparietal sulcus, in the visual cortex, and in primary sensorimotor and secondary sensory cortices (Dinstein et al. 2007). As a consequence, if we accept that regions in which activity for observing and for executing actions overlap constitute the human mirror system, then it is not restricted to a particular area of the premotor cortex but distributed across several areas involved in sensorimotor transformations, including primary sensory and motor areas.

HOMOLOGIES OF HUMAN AND MONKEY PREMOTOR CORTICES

It becomes obvious then that the question of homologies between human and monkey premotor cortices is crucial. As a matter of fact it is surely the most potent source of confusion between the scarce monkey electrophysiology literature and the overwhelming human neuroimaging one. And it is far from trivial, as suggestions that mirror neurons have a role in the evolution of language (Rizzolatti and Arbib 1998) stem in part from the assertion that they were found in the homolog of Broca's area, a key region for human language. Broca was a 19th century neurologist who found in a post-mortem examination that a speechless and hemiplegic patient had a lesion in the third frontal convolution of the left inferior frontal cortex, "Broca's area." The extent of this area varies according to authors between one to all of ventral BA6, BA44, and BA45. Broca's area was further parceled following the emergence of human neuroimaging. There is a growing consensus in favor of a functional anteroposterior gradient, with semantic rostrally (roughly BA45), syntactic in the middle (BA44), and phonological aspects of language caudally in the ventral premotor cortex (Hagoort 2005). Does the parcellation of the macaque monkey ventral premotor cortex overlap with the human one, as suggested in Figure 5.1?

A cytoarchitectonic investigation of areas buried within the macaque's arcuate sulcus was conducted to better understand homologies between monkey and human ventral premotor cortices (Petrides 2005). On the basis of granulometry, brain areas homologous to BA44 and BA45 in humans were described in the fundus of the arcuate sulcus, anterior to the convexity of BA6 where mirror neurons were recorded (F5), with BA44 located caudally at the bottom of the sulcus and BA45 located rostrally at the top of the sulcus (see Fig. 5.1). Single neuron microstimulation indicated that neurons in BA44 exercise high-level control over the orofacial musculature, a likely precursor of language. Therefore the assumption that macaque area F5, containing mirror neurons, evolved into human Broca's area, involved in abstract action representation including language, is not supported by the anatomical data. In contrast, anatomy suggests that F5 is homologous to the anterior part of ventral BA6 in humans, and regions homologous to humans' BA44/BA45 are found within macaques' arcuate sulcus.

Another way to assess homologies of brain areas between human and macaque is to characterize the areas functionally, using the same techniques and paradigms. As human intracerebral recordings are rare, a solution is to use brain tomography techniques with macaque monkeys. A first study used fMRI to investigate macaques' whole brain response to the perception of actions (Nelissen et al. 2005). The posterior bank of the arcuate sulcus in which mirror neurons were recorded (F5) responded to full-body depictions of transitive actions, stimuli comparable to those used to investigate mirror neurons with single-cell recordings. But this region did not respond to the same grasping actions shown without the full body, which are usually used in human neuroimaging experiments, and it was more active when the object was presented alone than when the hand interacted with an object. More anterior areas buried within the arcuate sulcus responded not only to the full-body depictions of actions, but also to stimuli showing only the hand grasping an object, even when the hand was robotic or the object was absent (mimicking). These anterior regions, putatively homologous to BA44/BA45 (Petrides 2005), are more likely to contain abstract, i.e., context-free, representations of action than the posterior premotor area F5, and were found associated with a number of functions in human neuroimaging experiments.

Two conclusions can be drawn. First, in macaques, F5 response to action observation is context-dependant, requiring the presence of the full body and of the grasped object. In contrast, more anterior regions buried in the arcuate sulcus are activated even in the absence of a body and of the target object, consistent with abstract representations of actions in Broca's area. Second, no human neuroimaging experiment has reproduced yet the specific properties of mirror neurons in the ventral premotor area (i.e., ventral BA6). In the absence of systematic human electrophysiology studies, it is thus reasonable to assume that while mirror neurons can be found in monkeys' F5 and humans' BA6, we have no argument in favor of a similar neuronal mechanism to explain results of macaque monkey or human fMRI, in which the more anterior inferior frontal areas, BA44 and 45, respond to abstract, context-free presentations of actions.

FROM THE "HUMAN MIRROR NEURON SYSTEM" TO "MOTOR RESONANCE"

The majority of the studies that introduced the human "mirror neuron system" have used action observation and imitation. Of particular interest is Iacoboni and colleagues' study in which volunteers scanned using fMRI had to lift the index or the middle finger in response to an abstract cue (a cross on a gray background), to the observation of the target finger lifted by a model, or to the observation of a static image showing the target finger lifted (Iacoboni et al. 1999). The imitation task compared to a simple observation task was associated with increased activity in three cortical regions: the left inferior frontal cortex, the right anterior parietal region, and the right parietal operculum, which were attributed to the human mirror system. A first criticism of this interpretation is theoretical: the conclusions are based on the hypothesis that as mirror neurons in monkeys would match observed and executed action, they must be used in imitation, therefore brain regions subserving imitation must be populated with mirror neurons. This reasoning is questionable because its main premise, that mirror neurons are involved in imitation, has not been demonstrated. On the contrary, most specialists agree that macaque monkeys do not perform full imitation in the wild (Tomasello and Call 1997). They are more likely to reproduce the goal of conspecifics, a process named emulation that could be the source of cultural transmission of motor skills such as the use of tools in animal communities (Whiten et al. 1999), but without copying the motor acts used by the model to achieve this goal (Whiten et al. 1996). Thus the equation of mirror neurons with imitation is speculative, and can amount to circular reasoning.

The second criticism concerns the results themselves. Looking closely at the data reported in the original publication (Iacoboni et al. 1999), one can see that during the observation phase and in the absence of motor response, the frontal region proposed to possess mirror neurons has similar responses for the abstract cue and for the stimuli showing finger movements. In other words, the brain activity is not modulated by the presence of an action in the stimulus. This is not compatible with the definition of mirror neurons as responding when an action is executed and when it is observed.

Experiments investigating the brain bases of action observation, such as the work of Buccino and colleagues (2001), are also difficult to interpret in terms of mirror neurons due to the lack of condition of action execution. Participants in this fMRI study observed object-related or intransitive actions performed either with the hand, the foot, or the mouth, such as grasping an object or mimicking its grasp, kicking a ball or mimicking the kick, and biting an apple or chewing. Irrespective of the presence of an object, activity was reported in premotor cortices during action observation. This activity was segregated along a lateral axis similar to the motor homunculus, with the mouth actions yielding a response in the ventral part of BA6 extending towards BA44 and 45, response to hand actions being located in the lateral part of BA6 and BA44, and foot action in the dorsal regions of BA6. These results have been used to suggest the premotor cortices have mirror properties, with a somatotopic organization reproducing the properties of the motor cortex. Taken literally, they imply that the whole premotor cortex, and not just its ventral part, has "mirror neuron" properties.

These examples bring about an important conclusion: premotor cortices, usually considered for their role in motor control, are also active during observation of action in the absence of any action execution (Chaminade and Decety 2001). What remains unsupported by experimental data is whether these premotor cortices activated by the observation of action are populated with mirror neurons. For this reason we propose to use the concept of motor resonance—motor cortices are activated by the performance of an action as well as by the perception of the sensory consequences of an action—to replace the "mirror neuron system" concept in order to make sense of human imaging results while avoiding confusion between known properties of mirror neurons in monkeys and the lack of knowledge about putative mirror neurons in humans.

Experimental psychology provides behavioral confirmation of the neurophysiological concept of motor resonance. Motor interference is the influence the perception of another individual's action has on the execution of action by the self as a consequence of the overlap between brain structures devoted to the observation and execution of actions. When volunteers are asked to raise their fingers in response either to a symbolic cue appearing on a fingernail or to a movement of the finger of a hand presented visually (Brass et al. 2000), the observation of a finger movement influences the reaction time to the symbolic cue, but the reverse effect is not significant. In other words, producing an action similar to an observed action is a prepotent response that interferes with the correct response to the cue. This motor interference was found when humans were facing another human (Kilner, Paulignan, and Blakemore 2003), and also, though reduced, when facing a humanoid robot having an anthropomorphic shape (Oztop et al. 2005), suggesting that motor resonance is influenced by the human appearance of the agent. This is correlated to the finding of a reduced response in the human inferior frontal cortex in response to humanoid compared to human actions (Chaminade et al. 2010).

Resonance has more recently been generalized to a number of other domains of cognition. For example, an fMRI study investigated the perception of touch by looking for overlap between being touched and observing someone being touched (Keysers et al. 2004). An overlap of activity was found in the secondary somatosensory cortex, a brain region involved in integrating somatosensory information with other sensory modalities such as touch. Another study reported activity in the primary sensory cortex during the observation of touch (Blakemore et al. 2005). Thus, there is resonance for touch, by which observation of someone else being touched recruits neural underpinnings of the feeling of touch. In the same vein, observation of the expression of disgust activates a region of the insula also activated during the feeling of disgust caused by a nauseating smell (Wicker et al. 2003). A neuron in the anterior cingulate cortex involved in pain perception fired when a patient experienced pinpricks and when he observed the examiner receiving the same painful stimuli (Hutchison et al. 1999). Another example comes from the study of emotions: the amygdala, a brain structure involved in the feeling of primary emotions such as fear, is fundamental in recognizing fear from observed facial expressions (Adolphs 2002).

All these examples support a generalization of the concept of motor resonance to other domains of cognition in humans. Resonance hence describes a general mechanism by which the neural substrates involved in the internal representation of an action, but also a feeling, an emotion, or a sensation, experienced in the first person are also recruited when perceiving another individual, at the third person, experiencing the same action, feeling, emotion, or sensation. In the domain of action, similar ideas can be traced back as far as William James in the 19th century (James 1890) or, more recently, identified in the motor theory of speech perception (Liberman and Mattingly 1985; see below for details). In this framework mirror neurons, defined and investigated in macaque monkeys' premotor area F5, are a very specific case of motor resonance, and offer an outstanding demonstration that the concept of resonance has underpinnings at the cellular level. At the same time, no experimental data supports that single neurons with mirror properties exist for cognitive functions and in brain regions in which resonance has been demonstrated in humans.

The choice to consider mirror neurons as a very specific case of the more general phenomenon of resonance has two theoretical consequences. First, functions purportedly supported by resonance systems are not necessarily located in the ventral premotor cortex. Second, resonance systems do not require "mirror neurons," and resonance properties can emerge at the level of localized brain networks assessable with human neuroimaging techniques. In the next section, we will present a simulation of this emergence we performed with a robotic device.

ONTOGENIC ORIGIN OF THE RESONANCE SYSTEM

The question of the innateness of motor resonance has been highly contro-versial following the seminal paper reporting neonatal imitation (Meltzoff and Moore 1977). The finding that "neonates between 12 and 21 days of age can imitate both facial and manual gestures" is often cited as evidence of innate resonance. Yet despite its elegance, this finding has been criti-cized (Anisfeld 1996).

Meanwhile, simple associative learning could support the formation of a resonance network (Heyes 2001). Links between sensory and motor representations of actions are formed through co-activation of motor and sensory representations during the execution of actions. Hebbian learning, which proposes that when two connected neurons fire simultaneously, the connection between them is increased, could support such associative learn-ing (Keysers and Perrett 2004). To illustrate this possibility of resonance emerging from self-observation, we showed that a simple associative net-work controlling a robotic hand and provided with a visual feedback of the hand posture could acquire low-level resonance abilities (Chaminade et al. 2008). The network showed the ability to imitate hand gestures, and even to generalize to new gestures. Cells in the network behaved like mirror neu-rons in that they could fire in response to either the motor command being sent to the hand or to the visual feedback of the moving hand. Such Hebbian learning, based on the co-occurrence of the execution of an action and of the perception of the sensory consequences of this action, is direct for body articulators with perceivable sensory consequences, the hands in the visual domain and the vocal tract in the auditory domain, but can make use of sensory feedback from a caregiver, for example when a mother imitates her baby's facial expressions (Heyes 2001).

The existence of tool mirror neurons (Ferrari, Rozzi, and Fogassi 2005) supports the Hebbian learning hypothesis: as the authors point out, exten-sive exposure to humans using tools created a "visual association between the hand and the tool." This learning of an association between a visual stimulus (an experimenter using a tool) and a motor action (grasping the object with the hand) emphasizes that far from being a static "mirror" bind-ing sensory and motor representations of actions, motor resonance makes use of brain plasticity to form new associations. We will now discuss three intertwined domains of human cognition pertinent for human evolution that are likely to make use of motor resonance: toolmaking, social cognition, and finally language.

PREMOTOR CORTICES AND TOOLMAKING

It has been advocated that integrating archaeological and neuroscientific approaches will help in understanding the evolutionary origins of the uniquely human technical ability of using tools to make tools (Toth and Schick 1993). We used this approach in a series of studies of Oldowan and Acheulean stone toolmaking (Stout and Chaminade 2007, Stout et al. 2008, Stout and Chaminade 2009, Stout et al. 2011). The appearance of stone tools over 2.5 million years ago, roughly concurrent with the origins of genus *Homo*, is a turning point in human evolution. The Oldowan technology includes sharp-edged stone flakes produced by striking a core with a hammerstone (Toth and Schick 1993). Although conceptually simple, stone toolmaking requires sensorimotor skills and an understanding of the physical properties of stones (Ambrose 2001). Despite the wealth of behavioral evidence provided by the archaeological record of toolmaking, it remains controversial whether it is associated with existing primate capacities or required a radical transformation of these capacities. For example, does the appearance of stone toolmaking in early humans reflect simple enhancements of motor control (Maravita and Iriki 2004) or the development of causal reasoning (Wolpert 2003)?

The identification of the cognitive foundations of stone toolmaking with neuroimaging addresses this question. In order to identify the unique demands of Oldowan flake production, Positron Emission Tomography (PET) data from six previously inexperienced human subjects making Oldowan tools were recorded before and after practice sessions and contrasted with simple percussion of stones (Stout and Chaminade 2007). Task-related activations were expected in the dorsal and ventral premotor cortices belonging to parietofrontal prehension circuits that support human (Johnson-Frey 2004) and monkey (Obayashi et al. 2001) tool use. The hypothesis was that activations restricted to these premotor regions would be in line with the observation that Oldowan stone tools preceded hominin brain expansion (Holloway 1999). In contrast, activations in dorsal prefrontal (Semendeferi et al. 2001) cortices, major sites of brain expansion during human evolution that do not belong to the premotor cortices, would imply reliance on new cognitive abilities for Oldowan toolmaking.

Our results indicated that Oldowan toolmaking is primarily supported by parietofrontal perceptual-motor systems. Oldowan toolmaking activated the left dorsal and ventral premotor cortices, brain regions involved in tool use in monkeys (Obayashi et al. 2001). This result supports the continued reliance on a cortical system that performs sensorimotor transformations for object manipulation and is conserved in primates. Bilateral clusters of activity were also found in the dorsal intraparietal sulcus. These clusters overlap with phylogenetically recent, i.e., not found in the monkey, functional areas that support increased sensitivity to the extraction of three-dimensional form from motion (Orban et al. 2005). This provided evidence that novel task demands, possibly in relation with extraction of depth information from the visual input, engaged recently evolved functional brain areas (Stout and Chaminade 2007).

Medial premotor cortices were also strongly activated in Oldowan toolmaking before practice. Their activation attests a complex organization of Oldowan toolmaking, which requires the coordination of cobble support, positioning and orientation in the non-dominant hand, with accurate, high velocity strikes by the dominant hand. Participants with no experience of toolmaking were challenged by the motor demands of the task and pursued a proximal solution relying on visual processing of the target to produce flakes. In line with the hypotheses, the absence of prefrontal activity supports the absence of higher reasoning in Oldowan toolmaking.

Practicing Oldowan stone toolmaking resulted in a posterior shift of the left ventral premotor cortex activity. The region is located in left anterior BA6, identified as homologous to monkey F5, where canonical neurons encode the appropriate grasp in response to visually presented objects, a finding reproduced in humans (Chao and Martin 2000). The shift of activity in this region was interpreted as a change of strategy in the handling of the hammerstone following practice (Stout and Chaminade 2007).

In a follow-up experiment, three professional archaeologists were scanned while making Oldowan flakes, Acheulean handaxes (roughly symmetrical, teardrop-shaped stone tools), or simply hitting stones without breaking them (Stout et al. 2008). In comparison to Oldowan, Acheulean toolmaking requires greater motor skills and more elaborate planning of complex action sequences, putatively increasing demands on the prefrontal cortex. Results from this experiment confirmed an activation of the left ventral premotor cortex for both conditions, in the close vicinity of the region activated for Oldowan toolmaking. Taken together, the two sets of results demonstrated that the ventral premotor cortex is differentially activated depending on expertise and the type of stone tool being made, and given the role of this area in representing object-related actions, this effect likely reflects different strategies in the handling of the hammerstone (Stout and Chaminade 2009).

Acheulean toolmaking was also associated with a number of additional premotor clusters, in the right ventral and in the bilateral dorsal premotor cortices, supporting the increase of motor skills required for Acheulean toolmaking. Note that given the functional anatomy of premotor cortices discussed earlier, the finding of lateral but no medial increases of premotor activations suggests a reliance on proximal cues on the next action according to rules that change in the course of the handaxe production (i.e., the aspect of the section following a hit guides the next hit) instead of a fixed planning of long sequences of actions (Stout et al. 2008). In summary, our results support that primates' capacities for sensorimotor transformation, rather than abstract planning, were central in the initial stages of stone toolmaking.

More recently, we investigated using fMRI whether the reliance on sensorimotor transformation demonstrated in stone toolmaking would also be involved, by virtue of motor resonance, in the observation of stone toolmaking (Stout et al. 2011). In this experiment, participants observed video clips of an expert demonstrator knapping Acheulean and Oldowan tools. Compared to Oldowan, Acheulean toolmaking was associated with activation of left anterior intraparietal and inferior frontal sulci, indicating the relevance of motor resonance mechanisms. We found different activated regions between Acheulean and Oldowan stimuli between two levels of expertise; while naïve subjects' increased activation of premotor cortices suggests reliance on motor resonance to understand unfamiliar actions, experts also employed mentalizing, i.e., thinking about the intention of the agent they were observing, as demonstrated by the medial prefrontal cortex activity. A third group, naïve subjects who had followed a training program, showed no specific response in the contrast between Acheulean compared to Oldowan, but heightened responses, in but not limited to premotor cortices, to both toolmaking conditions compared to control. These findings indicate that motor resonance is at play during the observation of toolmaking, especially when the observer has no a priori knowledge of the actions he is watching, is increased during training, and completed by higher-order mentalizing in experts. This result suggests that the transfer of sensorimotor capabilities involved in stone toolmaking between individuals makes use of motor resonance, which in turn raises questions about the social cognition of early toolmakers (Stout 2005).

MOTOR RESONANCE AND SOCIAL COGNITION

Intuitively, motor resonance offers a parsimonious system to automatically identify with conspecifics. But does this effect have a significant impact in everyday life? The chameleon effect was named to describe the unconscious reproduction of "postures, mannerisms, facial expressions and other behaviors of one's interacting partner" (Chartrand and Bargh 1999). In one of Chartrand and Bargh's experiments, subjects unaware of the purpose of the experiment interacted with a confederate of the experimenter who performed one of two target postures, rubbing the face or shaking the foot. Analysis of the behavior showed a significant increase of the tendency to engage in the same action. This effect can be experienced in face-to-face interactions: when one person crosses his arms or legs, it increases the probability that his partner swiftly and unconsciously performs the same action. In addition imitating partners were rated as more likable than non-imitating partners. These examples of motor resonance during interactions suggest that they are likely to be involved in social bonding, the identification with conspecifics (Decety and Chaminade 2003).

The main social function attributed to motor resonance is action understanding (Rizzolatti and Craighero 2004). We saw in a previous example that activity in premotor cortices is organized in a somatotopic manner depending on the body part being observed (Buccino et al. 2001). In addition, the content of the action being observed also influences the location of the activity. Observing a dot reproducing the kinematics of a pointing movement activates dorsal premotor regions, while a writing movement activates ventral areas (Chaminade et al. 2001), reproducing the specialization of premotor cortices for pointing and writing. The same premotor region is activated when producing a speech sound and when perceiving the same speech sound (Wilson et al. 2004). We previously showed the same result, overlap between action execution and observation, in the ventral premotor cortex for stone toolmaking. Yet these inferences do not demonstrate that premotor cortices have a role in action perception. The most convincing

argument can be found in neuropsychology, the study of cognitive impairments consequent to brain lesions. Neuropsychological findings hinted, in
the early 1990s, that gesture perception and limb actions share the same
cortical circuit (Rothi, Ochipa, and Heilman 1991), but it was only recently
reported that lesions of premotor cortices impair the perception of biological motion presented using point-light displays (Saygin 2007).

Another social function frequently associated with motor resonance is
imitation. Imitation covers a continuum of behaviors ranging from simple,
automatic, and involuntary action contagion to intentional imitation and
emulation (Byrne et al. 2004). Jacobs and Jeannerod recently emphasized
that "[imitation] is a folk psychology concept whose boundaries are pres-
ently too ill-defined for scientific purposes" (Jacob and Jeannerod 2005). A
large number of mechanisms are involved in imitation, from body correspondence to extraction of task-relevant features (Billard et al. 2004). Despite these caveats, it was shown that two regions involved in human imitation are the ventral premotor cortex (Iacoboni et al. 1999), homologue of
the macaque monkey area F5, and the inferior parietal lobule (Decety et al.
2002), homologue of the macaque monkey area PF, in which mirror neurons were described.

An important finding in relation to the use of motor resonance in
human evolution is its proposed role in imitative learning, the transformation of a newly seen action into an identical motor action done by the observer, that could explain the results from fMRI investigation of toolmaking
observation (see above). Motor resonance in response to the elementary
motor acts of a newly observed action can facilitate the execution of these
motor acts, but not necessarily of the full action itself. A complex action
needs to be parsed into its elementary motor acts. This form of learning
was investigated using fMRI to record brain activity during the acquisition
of guitar-playing skills (Buccino et al. 2004). Activity in both the ventral
and dorsal premotor cortices was stronger when participants observed an
action in order to imitate it later than when they observed it for no or for
an unrelated purpose. The anterior medial premotor cortices (pre-SMA or
F6) were active during the pause phases in the imitation conditions. Their
activity could reflect the sequential assemblage of the elementary motor
acts isolated by resonance in lateral premotor cortices. A medial prefrontal
activity was recorded in an imitation experiment requiring subjects to reproduce an action in which the goal (final placing of an object on a board)

was hidden, but could be extrapolated from the observation of the means of the action (the hand grasping the object and moving it towards its final position; Chaminade, Meltzoff, and Decety 2002). One could speculate that the response of a brain region involved in sequential action control during observational learning of sequential actions is a form of resonance at the level of the sequence itself.

Altogether, a large amount of data, from the chameleon effect to imitative learning, supports the view that motor resonance is involved in various aspects of humans' social cognition, and possibly in humans' evolution.

MOTOR RESONANCE AND LANGUAGE

The evolutionary origin of language remains a controversial issue. One proposal is that the ability to process complex hierarchical structures is a uniquely human ability (Hauser, Chomsky, and Fitch 2002). While non-human primates can acquire a simple grammar ability, they are unable to achieve mastery of the "phrase structure grammar level" which is characteristic of human languages (Fitch and Hauser 2004). Another proposal supposes that motor skills involved in making and using tools are related to language evolution as both are sequential and hierarchically organized behaviors (Greenfield 1991). Mirror neurons were also proposed for the origin of language (Rizzolatti and Arbib 1998). Mirror neurons provide a match between action execution and internal representation of actions, endowing the sender of a message (the acting agent) and the receiver of the message (the observing agent) with a shared meaning. Indeed, mouth mirror neurons, which would be active during the production and the auditory perception of articulated speech, would provide a physiological ground to the syllabic elements of the motor theory of speech perception (Liberman and Mattingly 1985). Anatomical and functional properties of premotor cortices reviewed in this chapter, together with recent human and monkey data, can help in understanding the physiology and the origins of language.

First, the motor theory of speech perception claims, on the basis of experimental data, that the objects of speech perception are not sounds, but the phonetic gestures of the speaker. Brain imaging reveals an overlap between premotor activities resulting from listening and from executing meaningless monosyllables (Wilson et al. 2004). The bilateral overlapping clusters are located in a ventral premotor region also responding to the observation of human (Buccino et al. 2001), but not monkey or dog (Buccino et al. 2004), mouth gestures. The application of resonance to phonetic gestures proposed in the motor theory of speech perception is thus validated experimentally on phonological aspects of language.

Resonance has also been proposed to participate in understanding the meaning of words. Remember that mirror neurons in monkeys also respond to the sound of actions such as cracking a nut open. In humans, listening to action words and producing movements elicit overlapping activity in premotor cortices (Hauk, Johnsrude, and Pulvermuller 2004). Different parts of the premotor cortex respond when a person listens to verbs implying mouth, hand, or leg actions (Tettamanti et al. 2005). Listening to leg-action verbs elicits dorsal premotor activity, while mouth-action verbs are associated with ventral premotor activity, in accordance with the somatotopy of the premotor cortex in action perception (Buccino et al. 2004). These results suggest that semantic understanding of action-related words utilizes motor structures involved in the execution of the actions.

While there is theoretical and experimental support for motor resonance in phonological processing and semantics, a question arises for grammar. Language production and comprehension relies on the sequential application of syntactic rules to combine a finite number of symbols in order to form and understand sentences (Hauser, Chomsky, and Fitch 2002). It was recently reported that an area of the inferior frontal gyrus, BA44, is involved in these syntactic aspects of language (Sakai 2005), with activity increasing with grammatical complexity of the sentence (Friederici et al. 2006). This conforms with the parcellation of Broca's area into several functional regions according to an anteroposterior gradient from semantic (roughly BA45) to syntactic (BA44) to phonological (BA6) aspects of language (Hagoort 2005). The fact that the expression and the perception of language utilize the same functional areas supports a resonance interpretation of language perception. An open question then is, what is the type of information used for grammatical aspects of language that resonates?

One possibility stems from the hypothesis that tool and language skills are evolutionary related because both are sequential and hierarchically organized behaviors (Greenfield 1991). If human grammar is functionally derived from primates' tool-related skills (Ferrari, Rozzi, and Fogassi 2005), then neural resources involved in both language and tool-use tasks should be shared in BA44. In contrast, if the processing of complex syntactic structures for sentence comprehension is a unique human specialization (Sakai 2005), there should be no tool-related activity in BA44. To distinguish between these two hypotheses, brain correlates of language and of tool-use tasks were measured in the same subjects using fMRI with a focus on the inferior frontal region. We (Higuchi et al. 2009) found an overlap between speech perception and the use of tools in the dorsal part of BA44. A cluster of overlap between the complementary tasks, i.e., verb generation and action observation, was previously reported in Broca's area (Hamzei et al. 2003). Since the application of sequentially organized rules is a common feature between language understanding and tool-use tasks used in this experiment (e.g., moving beads with chopsticks), the overlap of brain activity suggests that this region is part of a resonance system devoted to the processing of complex hierarchical structures. BA44 has indeed been reported in a number of functions that could have in common the processing of hierarchically structured behaviors (e.g., Koechlin and Jubault 2006).

Is this processing unique to humans? In the original description, only meaningful interactions between the hand and the object, but not interactions using a tool such as pliers, were sufficient to activate mirror neurons. More recently though, it has been reported that F5 neurons recorded in monkeys accustomed to observing humans using tools to feed them respond to the observation of tool actions on a target and do not respond without the target object, to the tool alone, or to a new tool (Ferrari, Rozzi, and Fogassi 2005). The frequency of tool-responding mirror neurons increased with exposure to tool use, and tool-responsive neurons had a stronger response to tool actions than to actions made with a biological effector. Monkeys in this experiment did not use tools, so that these tool-responsive F5 neurons can't be considered as "tool mirror neurons." In addition, most of the recorded neurons were buried within the arcuate sulcus, and could belong to the homolog of BA44 flanking F5 anteriorly (Petrides, Cadoret, and Mackey 2005). Neuroimaging experiments in monkeys demonstrate that tool use (Obayashi et al. 2001) activates a region within the arcuate sulcus, and that complex sequential tool use causes increased activity in this region compared to simple tool use (Obayashi et al. 2002). Thus, the processing of sequential information common to language and tool use and activating BA44 can be evidenced in macaques.

Activation of the anterior premotor cortex during Acheulean knapping by experts (Stout et al. 2008), as well as during observation of stone tool-knapping (Stout et al. 2011), provides a direct connection between language and early humans' toolmaking skills (Greenfield 1991). The location of this activity, in the anterior part of the ventral premotor cortex or Broca's area, suggests that the fine motor control and the sequential structure processing required by toolmaking skills could have contributed to the extended syntactic processing in human language. In addition to the phonological aspects highlighted in the motor theory of speech perception, the concept of resonance offers a generalization for semantics, more specifically to understand the meaning of action words, and for grammar, possibly an exaptation of the processing of hierarchical and sequential structures from tool use and toolmaking to the production and perception of language, though this latter point is still speculative.

CONCLUDING REMARKS

Resonance, derived from a description of the properties of mirror neurons, has been generalized to brain regions distinct from the human homolog of F5, across premotor cortices, and to other cognitive domains—emotional, social, and language. The use of a common system for the execution and the perception of actions may maximize the computational power of available neural resources. To better understand human unique cognitive abilities, the importance of premotor cortices might not lie in "mirror neurons" as much as in the capacity of associative learning to establish resonance systems effective to transfer motor skills and information between humans. While we haven't conclusively established a specific role for resonating systems in human evolution, the results reviewed here strongly support such a connection.

Acknowledgment

   I thank Chris Frith for continuous, very helpful discussions on mirror neurons, and Dietrich Stout for comments on this manuscript.

NOTE

5.1 http://en.wikipedia.org/wiki/Mirror_neurons

6

The Origins of Human Cooperation from a Developmental and Comparative Perspective

FELIX WARNEKEN

Humans readily help others with their problems, even in the absence of an obvious return-benefit. Humans also pool their efforts in collaborative enterprises to produce outcomes that lie beyond the capabilities of any one individual, such as sailing a ship across the ocean, building belltowers, and forming an army to fight for independence. Various disciplines investigate these phenomena by exploring how cooperation can emerge through natural selection, describing its historical development and its role in economic exchange. In this cross-disciplinary enterprise, psychological research highlights that human cooperation often requires sophisticated cognitive and motivational processes. For instance, in order to help someone with a problem, the helper must have the cognitive capacity to understand the goal the other is trying to achieve, as well as have the motivation to act on behalf of the other. Furthermore, participants of a collaborative activity must integrate their individual actions by way of some division of labor, and align their own interests with that of others in a collective enterprise aimed at a collective goal.

What are the ontogenetic and phylogenetic origins of these forms of human cooperation? As is the case for virtually all complex human behaviors, the emergence of these forms of cooperation is only possible because humans go through an extended ontogeny in which they gradually develop the necessary capacities to engage in such social interactions. Therefore, it is important to investigate this development by determining what children are equipped with early in ontogeny, and elucidating the interplay between such biological predispositions and (social) learning, which together enable children to become successful participants in human social life. In addition, by combining this developmental approach with a comparative one, we can investigate which elements of human cooperation we share with our primate relatives from aspects that are unique to humans. This is of particular importance because several researchers have claimed that humans cooperate in ways that even our closest primate relatives do not: that is, there is a species-unique psychology underlying cooperative behaviors that we find in humans, but not in other great apes. However, as studies that directly compare cooperation in humans and other great apes are scarce, this claim is mainly derived from supposition. Thus, comparative studies of human children and other great apes are needed to disentangle aspects of cooperation that humans share with their closest living evolutionary relatives from aspects that are unique to humans.

Therefore, I will begin by outlining how psychological research can contribute to an evolutionary understanding of cooperation. Evolutionary models are mainly concerned with the question of how cooperative behaviors—especially altruistic behaviors—can evolve in terms of long-term fitness costs and benefits. However, what I will advance in this chapter is the notion that for a comprehensive understanding of cooperative behavior, it is equally important to identify and investigate the psychological mechanisms by which different kinds of cooperation are instantiated. By studying these, we can learn more about the factors that enable and constrain certain types of cooperative behavior and explain its presence or absence in different animals. Specifically, I will argue that one crucial aspect of cooperation in humans is the ability to understand other people's intentions, that is, the ability to interpret and predict other people's overt behavior as actions executed in pursuit of a goal. The capacity to determine other people's intentions allows humans (and to some extent other primates) to act cooperatively in a much more flexible manner than found elsewhere in the animal kingdom.

In a second step, I will propose a classification of different kinds of cooperative behaviors based upon the underlying social-cognitive understanding of intentions. Namely, I will introduce a distinction between *individual* intentions and the formation of *joint* intentions (see also the terminology used by Gärdenfors, this volume). The main argument is that an understanding of individual intentions is necessary to perform acts of altruistic helping, whereas the ability to form shared intentions is critical for individuals to engage in collaborative activities with others.

Last, but not least, I will review recent findings from experimental studies with young children and chimpanzees in two particular types of cooperative behaviors: altruistic helping and joint collaborative activities. In these comparative studies, chimpanzees were chosen as subjects because they are, together with bonobos, the closest living relatives of humans. Several animal species perform cooperative behaviors of some form (see Cheney and Seyfarth 2007:64, 134), but I will focus on studies with humans and chimpanzees because such comparisons can distinguish those aspects of human cooperation that date back at least to the common ancestor of humans and chimpanzees from those that evolved only in the human lineage.

THE BIOLOGICAL STUDY OF COOPERATION

A crucial distinction for the study of cooperative and other behaviors is that between ultimate function and proximate causation (Mayr 1961, Tinbergen 1963). The study of ultimate function is concerned with the question of how a certain trait contributes to the survival and reproduction of the organism in terms of fitness costs and fitness benefits. This is complemented by the study of proximate causation which examines, for example, the hormonal or neurological mechanisms by which these characteristics become instantiated in the organism. Regarding cooperative behaviors, the issue of ultimate function poses a fundamental problem for evolutionary theory because some cooperative behaviors appear unlikely to evolve. Namely, altruistic traits, which in evolutionary terms lower the fitness of an individual in comparison to selfish individuals with whom they interact, should be eliminated by natural selection. However, we find several behaviors in humans and other animals that might qualify as altruistic in an evolutionary sense, such as the sting of a honeybee or alarm-calling in birds. Already Darwin saw that such behaviors cannot be easily explained by the usual process of natural selection as competition among individuals within a group (Darwin 1871). Since then, several alternative models have been proposed to integrate such behaviors within the framework of natural selection.

The premise of models such as inclusive fitness or reciprocal altruism is that behaviors that are costly to the actor in the short term can be beneficial for the actor in the long term or through some indirect process. Thus, a proximate mechanism such as an altruistic motivation to care about the welfare of one's offspring by providing them with food or feeling obliged to help other members of one's group when they encounter a problem can result in (or *has to* from an evolutionary standpoint) some ultimate fitness benefit to the actor. Because of this intricate relationship between short-term costs that result in long-term benefits, some are tempted to argue that, for example, caring for one's offspring or helping with the expectation of reciprocation are not "truly" altruistic. "Truly" altruistic would be only those behaviors that result in ultimately reducing a fitness outcome. Ironically, the term "true altruism" would then be reserved for something that cannot possibly exist. Correspondingly, should we refer to behaviors with short-term costs as "false altruism"? I think the problem here is that the proximate-ultimate distinction should not be conflated with the distinction between true and false. Although a proximate mechanism can only evolve if it does not result in a fitness disadvantage, proximate mechanisms are not false or merely epiphenomenal. Rather, the question is how certain ultimate mechanisms become instantiated in the organism by different equally "true" proximate mechanisms.

Although the biological explanation of cooperative behaviors, especially altruism, is framed as a challenge for evolutionary theory aimed at explaining the ultimate evolutionary function of cooperative behaviors in terms of fitness costs and fitness benefits, it is equally challenging to explain what the proximate mechanisms are that bring these behaviors about. For instance, if it is revealed that a certain cooperative behavior can be explained by mutualism because all interactants profit from the act, the investigation of the evolutionary function has come to an end. However, another important question remains unanswered: How was it possible for the individuals to produce these mutually beneficial outcomes in the first place? Brett Calcott calls this question about the generation of benefit the *"other* cooperation problem" (Calcott 2008). Evolutionary approaches primarily focus on the ultimate payoff of certain cooperative behaviors, abstracting away from the way in which the individuals actually produced them. One example is cooperative hunting, which has been described to result in mutualistic outcomes (Boesch and Boesch 1989, Boesch 1994, 2002, Muller and Mitani 2005). Cooperating with another is always the best option, because if both individuals defect, neither gets anything. Accordingly, as the individuals directly benefit from the interaction and potentially increase their fitness, this behavior is not puzzling with regard to their evolutionary significance. Nevertheless, the necessity of coordinating behavior in a hunt with that of others remains a serious challenge. Doing so can require quite advanced behavioral and cognitive capacities of the organism, reaching far beyond what is necessary for kin-selection or reciprocal altruism. Individuals must recognize that they are in a mutualistic situation and have to act jointly and adjust to each other at least to some extent in order to benefit mutually. This poses interesting questions for the study of the proximate mechanisms underlying mutualistic behaviors because species might differ enormously in their skills to create and engage in cooperative interactions with mutualistic outcomes.

THE ROLE OF INTENTIONALITY FOR HELPING AND COLLABORATION

Altruism, in terms of fitness costs and fitness, does not necessarily depend on psychological mechanisms: "A mindless organism can be an evolutionary altruist." (Sober 2002:17). However, the behaviors of such "mindless altruists" are confined to a very restricted set of situations and cannot be modified when confronted with novel exigencies. Humans (and potentially other animals, especially nonhuman primates), on the other hand, possess psychological processes to perform variable situation-specific cooperative behaviors. Namely, humans developed extraordinary skills in reading other people's intentions that are utilized to help others and collaborate with others. Instances of helping commonly require that the helper is able to identify the goal the helpee is trying to achieve. Interpreting others' behaviors as intentional actions with individual goals is a prerequisite for what I call "instrumental helping," that is, performing an instrumental act to help the other bring about his goal (rather than changing their emotional state as in the case of empathic concern). When I see a person bending down and stretching one arm towards the ground, I can interpret this behavior in many different ways. But certain contextual and behavioral cues will lead me to the interpretation that this person is not performing a stretching exercise, but is unsuccessfully reaching for an object: the person accidentally dropped an object just before starting to bend down, there is an expression of frustration on the face of the person, or the fact that the person is holding a bottle and the object on the ground is a lid. Whatever the cues are that guide my interpretation, the central point is that they allow me to identify the goal the other is trying to achieve. In experimental studies it is often taken for granted that the subjects understand the goals or desires of the other individuals they interact with. This is rather unproblematic in the case of behavioral economics studies with adults, in which all participants know that the other participants are interested in gaining money. However, in the case of studies with young children and especially nonhuman primates, this is not a trivial problem. Individuals might fail to help others not because they are selfish, but because they do not understand the other's goal.

Yet although understanding another's individual goal is sufficient for helping to occur, collaborative activities are based on the formation of a *joint goal*. Beyond the understanding of another's behavior in terms of individual goals and intentions ("She intends to do x by means of y."), people can form 'we-intentions' to engage in genuinely collaborative activities ("We intend to do x by means of me doing y1 and you doing y2."). The works of Bratman (1992), Gärdenfors (this volume), Gilbert (1990), Rakoczy (2006), Searle (1990, 2005), and Tomasello et al. (2005b) highlight three criteria that have to be met for a social behavior to qualify as a cooperative activity: (1) The participants must be mutually responsive to each other, so that each participant's behavior is at least in part influenced by the actions of the other; (2) they must be able to understand each other's behavior as actions directed at a goal; and (3) they must be committed to a joint goal in the sense that all pursue the same goal and perform their respective roles in pursuit of the joint goal by mutually adjusting their individual actions.

The critical problem is to distinguish actions exhibiting joint intentionality from mere social coordination. To take a slightly modified example from Searle (1990), imagine a group of people sitting in various places on the lawn in a park. When it suddenly starts to rain, they all run towards a shelter at the center of the lawn to take cover. This occurs in an almost perfectly coordinated fashion, with all individuals beginning to run at the same time towards the same location. The people are also responsive to each other in that they make sure not to run into each other, and adjust their running when another person is about to cross their way. We might even assume that the people act in mutual knowledge of each other's actions, with everybody knowing that everybody else has the same goal of taking shelter. Nevertheless, this does not qualify as a joint collaborative activity because each individual's intention is independent of the others' intentions. The sequence of individual acts only happens to converge on the same goal, because everyone has the same individual goal of escaping the rain, and therefore starts running at the same time when the rain begins. If, however, the same exact behaviors occur as part of a dance performance, Searle argues, it qualifies as a collaborative activity because each individual's intention to run towards the shelter derives from the joint intention to perform a dance together: "I am doing what I am doing as part of our doing what *we* are doing." (Searle 2005:6).

This conceptual distinction between helping others with their individual goals and collaborating with others towards joint goals enables us to examine cooperation in new ways. Specifically, we may ask when these skills develop during ontogeny and how unique they might be phylogenetically by looking for their existence in chimpanzees and other great apes.

EMPIRICAL EVIDENCE: HELPING IN CHILDREN

Can young children engage in acts of instrumental help? With regard to the social-cognitive component of helping, it is a well established finding that infants from around 12 to 18 months of age understand other people's behaviors in terms of their intentions. For instance, infants can differentiate accidental from purposeful actions (for an overview see Tomasello et al. 2005b). They can determine whether a similar environmental outcome was either the result of a purposeful act (when the outcome matches the goal) or an accident (when goal and outcome do not match). Similarly, they can infer the goal another person was trying to achieve without actually witnessing the intended outcome (Meltzoff 1995). Thus, already infants appear to possess the crucial social-cognitive component necessary for instrumental help.

With regard to the motivational component of helping, children as young as 12 months begin to show concern for others in distress and sometimes intervene by comforting them (for an overview see Eisenberg, Fabes, and Spinrad 2006). However, these instances are all based upon the infant's empathic responses to the emotional needs of another person. In contrast to these instances of empathic intervention or what one could also call "emotional helping," little is known about whether infants would also perform acts of instrumental helping: helping another person achieve their unfulfilled goal.

To explore this issue, we presented 18-month-old infants with ten different situations in which an adult was having trouble achieving a goal (Warneken and Tomasello 2006). This variety of tasks presented the children with a variety of difficulties in discerning the adult's goal. For instance, an experimenter used clothespins to hang towels on a line, then accidentally dropped a clothespin on the floor and unsuccessfully reached for it. In this case, the child had the opportunity to help by picking up the clothespin and handing it to the experimenter. In the "cabinet task" the experimenter was trying to put a stack of magazines into a cabinet, but he could not open the doors because his hands were full and the child could thus potentially help by opening the doors for him. Control conditions for each of the ten tasks ruled out the possibility that children would perform the target behavior irrespective of the other's need, e.g., because they like to hand things to adults or just like to open doors when their attention is drawn to it. In these control conditions, the same basic physical situation was presented to the infants, but with no indication that the experimenter needed help.

The finding of this experiment was that children display spontaneous, unrewarded helping behaviors when another person is unable to achieve his goal (but performed these behaviors significantly less often in control conditions where no help is necessary). Virtually all children helped at least once. They did so without being explicitly asked for help and never being rewarded or praised for their effort. Moreover, helping was observed in diverse situations. Infants handed the experimenter out-of-reach objects; they completed an action after his failed attempt of stacking books; they opened the door of a cabinet for him and they brought about the other's goal by different means such as accessing a box by lifting a flap (rather than doing it the way the adult was trying it by unsuccessfully reaching through a tiny hole). This initial experiment showed that 18-month-old infants spontaneously provide instrumental help and do so in a wide range of situations.

In a follow-up study we tested even younger infants on several of these tasks and found that 14-month-old infants also helped under some circumstances (Warneken and Tomasello 2007). Namely, they reliably helped with out-of-reach objects such as the "clothespin task," but did not help in the other types of tasks such as the "cabinet task." One possible interpretation for this finding is that they are willing to help, but can do so only in cognitively less demanding situations with more obvious goals such as a person reaching for an object, but fail to do so in situations with presumably more complex goals and more complex types of intervention. Thus, even 14-month-old infants help spontaneously in situations in which they are able to determine the other person's goal.

These findings shed light on young children's cognitive capability to read the intentions of others. Their social-cognitive understanding emerging in the second year of life enables them to intervene with increasing flexibility in various situations in which others fail with instrumental problems. With regard to the motivational aspect of helping, these results speak in favor of the view that a motivation to care about the welfare of others is already present early in human ontogeny (Eisenberg 1992, Hoffman 1981, 2000). This motivation becomes apparent not only in acts of emotional helping such as comforting, that is, not only as a response to the emotional needs of a distressed person, but also as an instrumental act of helping other persons with their unfulfilled goals. Thus, children's ability to read intentions, together with their altruistic motivation, enables acts of instrumental helping.

These acts of instrumental helping are some of the earliest manifestations of altruism in human ontogeny: children acting on behalf of others without a benefit for themselves. To further examine this interpretation, we tested children's helpfulness by on the one hand manipulating the costs for helping, and on the other hand varying whether the helper would benefit from this helpful act. Young children helped even when the costs for helping are slightly raised. In one study, we once again tested 18-month-old infants in a situation in which an object was on the floor and the experimenter was unsuccessfully reaching for it (Warneken et al. 2007:Experiment 2). But this time the children had to surmount an array of obstacles to pick up the object for the other. This can be quite effortful for toddlers who have just started to walk. But even these obstacles did not hinder them from helping the other person over a test session of ten trials. A similar result was obtained when we made the helping act costly in a different way. In this experiment, we gave 20-month-old children the opportunity to play with attractive toys in one corner of the testing room (Warneken and Tomasello 2008). The experimenter was located in the opposite corner, so that when she encountered a problem and needed help, the child had to stop playing and leave the toys behind in order to provide help. Again, children continued to help in the majority of cases and did so over repeated trials—even when they had the alternative to play an attractive game.

Children are thus willing to put some effort into helping—but do they expect to be rewarded in return? In one experiment we directly contrasted whether 18-month-old children are motivated by the other person's goal or an immediate benefit for themselves (Warneken et al. 2007:Experiment

1). We experimentally varied whether the helpee would or would not offer a reward in return for the helper's effort. The results could not be clearer: Children once again helped by picking up objects the experimenter was unsuccessfully reaching for—and did so irrespective of being rewarded for it. Rewarding was neither necessary nor did it increase the rate of helping. Thus, what determined children's helping was the other's unfulfilled goal, not an immediate benefit for themselves.

This suggests the possibility that young children have a genuine motivation to act altruistically. Using a crucial distinction from motivational psychology, we may thus ask whether such acts of altruism are intrinsically or extrinsically motivated: Do children help because the helpful act itself is inherently rewarding, or only because the helpful act is instrumental in bringing about separate outcomes such as material rewards? To test this empirically, we took advantage of a curious feature of intrinsic motivation. It is a well-established phenomenon that intrinsic rewards can be undermined by salient extrinsic rewards—what has also been called the "overjustification effect" (Deci 1971, Lepper 1981). In a seminal study, Lepper, Greene, and Nisbett (1973) tested 3- to 5-year-old children who took pleasure in drawing. One group of children was tested in a condition in which they engaged in drawing with the expectation of a concrete reward. Subsequently, when these children had the opportunity to draw in a free-choice period, they were less motivated to do so (as compared with children who had been tested in a condition with no expectation of a reward). Social-psychological theories suggest that this new extrinsic motivation to perform the activity in order to receive a reward supplants the previously intrinsic motivation, so that when the extrinsic reward is no longer forthcoming, the motivation for the activity decreases.

Would we find such an undermining effect of extrinsic rewards also in the case of altruistic helping? To investigate this possibility, we used the basic procedure from the overjustification-effect research in an experiment with 20-month-old children by varying the way in which the experimenter had responded to the helping act in previous encounters (Warneken and Tomasello 2008). The critical comparison was between children tested in the reward condition—in which the experimenter offered them a toy for helping, and children from a neutral condition—in which the experimenter did not reward them. In a subsequent test phase, all children had the opportunity to help over consecutive trials, but received no reward for doing so. The main finding was that children who had previously received a material reward helped significantly less often than children from the neutral condition. This provides further evidence for the claim that children's spontaneous helping is driven by an intrinsic rather than an extrinsic motivation. Rewards are often not only superfluous, but can have even detrimental effects as they can undermine children's intrinsic altruistic motivation.

In sum, this series of studies demonstrates that the ontogenetic origins of altruistic helping are apparent in early childhood. Infants as young as 14 months of age display spontaneous, unrewarded helping behaviors when another person is unable to achieve his goal. Throughout the second year of life, children become increasingly more flexible in their ability to read the other's intentions and intervene in different kinds of situations. Human infants use their emerging mindreading capabilities not only for their own ends, but also to help others. They are willing to help multiple times and continue to help when the costs for helping are raised. Further experiments confirm that infants are actually motivated by the other's goal and not an immediate benefit for themselves, as rewarding is neither necessary nor does it increase the rate of helping. On the contrary, children appear to have an initial inclination to help, but extrinsic rewards may diminish it.

EMPIRICAL EVIDENCE: HELPING IN CHIMPANZEES

Would chimpanzees perform such acts of altruistic helping? There is converging evidence that chimpanzees have the social-cognitive capacity to infer other people's goals—and therefore possess one crucial component for such acts of helping (Tomasello et al. 2005b, but see Povinelli and Vonk 2003 for an opposing view). However, when it comes to the motivational aspect of helping, the issue becomes more controversial. The predominant view is that chimpanzees are guided solely by self-interest: altruistic behaviors are thought to be unique to humans, emanating from a species-unique psychology (e.g., Boyd and Richerson 2006, Henrich et al. 2005, Silk et al. 2005). This view is supported by two recent experiments in which chimpanzees did not seem to care about the welfare of another individual (Jensen et al. 2006, Silk et al. 2005). In particular, they did not reliably pull a tray with food within reach of a conspecific if they themselves would not benefit from the act. The individuals were self-regarding and did not seem to pay attention to the needs of the other in this food-retrieval context. But this context might not be representative of all potential helping situations. In fact, there are a number of anecdotal observations which suggest that chimpanzees might on occasion act altruistically (for an overview see de Waal 1996). In particular, it has to be pointed out that chimpanzees are very competitive with each other about monopolizable food. It is thus possible that when the individuals are preoccupied with retrieving food for themselves, this might preclude altruistic behaviors. Moreover, in these experiments with negative results, the recipient chimpanzees remained rather passive during the test. That is, they were not actively trying to solve a problem such as failing to retrieve the piece of food in which the other could help. The situation was thus more a test of generosity than a test of instrumental helping. This allows for the possibility that when the constraints related to food are lifted and the problem situation is made more salient to the potential helper, a different picture might emerge.

Therefore, we adapted the instrumental helping tasks from the infant studies for a series of experiments with chimpanzees. In an initial study, we tested three human-raised chimpanzees who interacted with their primary human caregiver (Warneken and Tomasello 2006). The caregiver enacted ten different helping-situations in which she was unable to achieve her goal (including out-of-reach objects; physical obstacles such as a closed door; using the wrong means to open a novel box, etc.). No help was needed in the corresponding control conditions. Importantly, the tasks involved objects other than food and the caregiver never rewarded the chimpanzees. The intriguing finding was that all three chimpanzees helped in out-of-reach tasks. They reliably handed the caregiver objects she was unsuccessfully reaching for (and did not do so in the control condition in which she was not reaching for them). These chimpanzees were thus able to determine her goal and had the motivation to help her with the goal in the absence of a reward. However, in contrast to the out-of-reach tasks, we did not find any reliable helping in the other types of tasks (opening a door for the other; using different means to open the novel box for the other, etc.). Perhaps importantly, this discrepancy between types of tasks parallels the finding with the 14-month-old human infants whose helping was also limited to the tasks involving out-of-reach objects. This may thus reflect a difference between types of tasks in the complexity of the goal-structure and the type of intervention necessary: in the out-of-reach tasks the recipient's goal is in principle easier to identify (an outstretched arm oriented towards a visible object) and the intervention follows straightforwardly. In the other types of tasks, the goal might not have been obvious to them or they did not know how to intervene. This once again shows the importance of taking into account the social-cognitive demands of certain tests of altruism. These human-raised chimpanzees were in principle willing to help, but showed this behavior only in contexts in which the other's goal was easy to identify.

These were the first experimental demonstrations of altruistic helping in chimpanzees. It has to be noted, though, that the subjects were human-raised chimpanzees who helped a caregiver with whom they maintained a close relationship. Thus, it is possible that human-reared chimpanzees present a special case. Chimpanzees with such a rearing-history often possess superior social-cognitive skills and develop behaviors not found in individuals with less human contact (Bering 2004, Call and Tomasello 1996, Tomasello and Call 2004, Tomasello, Carpenter, and Hobson 2005a). Of particular importance for current purposes is that our chimpanzees helped a human who had reinforced their compliant behavior in other contexts. From this initial experiment it thus remains unclear whether helping is confined to interactions with highly familiar individuals who had rewarded them before or—as has been shown in studies with humans—extends also to unfamiliar individuals.

We had the unique opportunity to investigate this question by testing a sample of semi–free-ranging chimpanzees born in the wild who live in a sanctuary in Uganda. These chimpanzees spend the day in the forest of the island and come to a human shelter for feeding and sleeping. They thus had regular contact with humans, but were not exposed to comparable human schooling attempts and rearing practices as the three human-raised chimpanzees from the initial helping study. Most importantly, they were tested by a human who had not interacted with them before the experiment (no training, no feeding, no previous testing). In a first experiment, we wanted to investigate whether chimpanzees are actually motivated by another person's unfulfilled goal or a benefit for themselves (Warneken et al. 2007:Experiment 1). Thus, we tested 36 chimpanzees and compared their behavior with that of 36 human children at 18 months of age in the helping situation described above: We varied whether the human experimenter made an unsuccessful attempt to get at an out-of-reach object (reaching vs. no reaching for it) and whether he rewarded the subjects in exchange for the object (reward vs. no reward). In the case of the chimpanzees, the reward was a piece of food, in the case of the children, the reward was an attractive toy. The major finding was that just like the infants, chimpanzees helped by handing the out-of-reach object when the experimenter indicated that he was trying to get the object—and did so irrespective of being rewarded. Rewarding their helping was unnecessary and did not even raise the rate of helping. This indicates that the chimpanzees were motivated to help the experimenter with his unachieved goal, but did not aim at retrieving a material reward for themselves.

In this experiment the chimpanzees did not have to do much more than to pick up an object from the floor and hand it to the human. But when we made helping slightly more costly by putting the object in a location 2.5 meters above the ground, so that the chimpanzees first had to climb up to retrieve the object for the other, they still helped (Warneken et al. 2007:Experiment 2). Thus, the chimpanzees continued to help even when helping was made energetically more costly. Taken together, this shows that semi–free-ranging chimpanzees also perform acts of helping towards a human stranger, even when helping is made effortful and they receive no immediate benefit for themselves.

Despite the fact that subjects helped without prior or current rewarding by the same individual in a different situation, or a different individual in the same situation, it is conceivable that infants and chimpanzees had been rewarded in the past for the general behavior of handing over objects to humans. Therefore, an even more stringent test might be one with a novel task with no potential reward-history at all. Human infants help in such novel tasks (Warneken and Tomasello 2006), but there is as yet no such experimental evidence with chimpanzees. Moreover, these positive instances of chimpanzee helping all involved chimpanzees helping humans. The use of a human as the recipient allows us to experimentally manipulate otherwise uncontrollable factors (such as the exact behavior of the recipient or him offering a reward or not) and it can reveal what behaviors chimpanzees are in principle capable of performing. But the crucial test-case for social behaviors still is a situation in which chimpanzees interact with a conspecific. Therefore, the question remains: Would chimpanzees help other chimpanzees? As mentioned before, studies with conspecifics came to a negative conclusion, using experimental setups in which the chimpanzee subjects could generously pull food within reach of another individual who was not actively trying to solve an instrumental problem (Jensen et al. 2006, Silk et al. 2005). Thus, because in these experiments the need for help might not have been obvious to the subjects, we created a situation in which the need for help would potentially be more salient by having a chimpanzee actively struggle with a problem (Warneken et al. 2007). Specifically, we put chimpanzees in a situation in which one chimpanzee (the recipient) was faced with the problem that a door leading to a room with a piece of food was fixed with a chain that he could not unlock. Only if the other chimpanzee (the subject) released this chain from another room could the recipient enter. In individual pretests, chimpanzees had demonstrated that they were able to manipulate this chain-door mechanism when they themselves were trying to enter through the door. But they had never encountered this mechanism as part of a social situation with another chimpanzee. All chimpanzees were genetically unrelated group-members and roles of subject and recipient were not switched within a pair to exclude short-term reciprocation within the same context. Results showed that chimpanzees helped by releasing the chain in the majority of cases. They did so significantly more often than in control conditions in which releasing the chain would either not help the recipient or no recipient was present. This shows that subjects were attentive to the recipient's goal: They were more likely to release the chain if the recipient was unsuccessfully trying to enter through that door. Importantly, there was also no begging or harassment by the subjects after they helped, ruling out the possibility that they opened the door only to have the recipients access the otherwise unobtainable food and then try to coax it from them. Thus, this experiment showed that when the problem is made more salient, chimpanzees use a novel skill to help conspecifics gain access to food in a novel situation.

Taken together, the current results indicate that the altruistic tendency seen in early human ontogeny did not evolve in humans de novo. Chimpanzees also appear to have a basic motivation to act altruistically for others. Moreover, the fact that they show some flexibility in helping (towards different recipients who pursued different goals) indicates that chimpanzees utilize their social-cognitive skills in reading others' goals also for altruistic purposes. Thus, the origins of human altruism may date as far back as to the last common ancestor of humans and chimpanzees.

COLLABORATIVE ACTIVITIES

Humans not only show exceptional social capabilities for interpersonal interactions such as helping a person with her individual goal, but also engage in collective activities such as building houses, playing sports, or forming

governments. What psychological abilities allow children to become competent participants in these practices? As described previously, over and
above an understanding of individual goals, these collective activities require the formation of joint intentions. As illustrated by Searle's example of
people running to a shelter in the park (Searle 1990), participants must not
only be responsive to each other and able to understand the other's goals
and intentions, they must incorporate the other's intentions in their own
intentions. A promising area to investigate this in children is to look at social
activities like joint problem-solving or social games. These small-scale collective practices might serve children as an entry point into large-scale collective practices, as they share key characteristics with their adult counterparts (such as division of labor, behavioral coordination, social roles). From
a developmental perspective, the investigation of problem-solving and
social games can thus provide insight into young children's engagement in
and understanding of collective interactions. Additionally, from a comparative perspective, such situations allow for a comparison with chimpanzees
to explore the phylogenetic roots of group-level activities. Chimpanzees
show several complex social behaviors, such as group hunting in the wild
(e.g., Boesch and Boesch 1989, Muller and Mitani 2005) and collaborative
problem-solving in experimental situations (Melis, Hare, and Tomasello
2006a, 2006b). These situations most likely result in mutualistic outcomes
for the participants and therefore are not puzzling with regard to ultimate
function in terms of fitness costs and benefits. However, with regard to the
proximate psychological mechanisms producing mutualistic benefits, it is
currently unresolved whether chimpanzees view their own and their partners' actions as part of a collaborative activity with joint goals, or as independent means to individual goals.

How can we know that people engage in a collaborative activity with a
joint goal? Adults are able to express their intentions verbally and can produce explanations when asked what they are doing. This is obviously not
possible in the case of human infants and chimpanzees. But the aforemen-
tioned three criteria—mutual responsiveness, understanding of goals, commitment to a joint goal—can be adapted to create a test of joint intentionality that does not necessarily rely on language. It is uncontroversial that both
human infants and chimpanzees display mutual responsiveness, and it has
also been shown that they have an understanding of goals (see Tomasello
et al. 2005b). Thus, both appear to have the capabilities that are required to

meet the first two criteria. The critical issue is to examine whether the participants meet criterion 3, a commitment to perform their respective roles in pursuit of a joint goal. One example might illustrate this point (as an extension of Gilbert 1990). When two strangers are walking side by side towards a cinema, they might have the same goal of watching the same movie. They might even know from each other that each one has the same goal because they see each other's movie ticket or chatted about it. The two strangers might even be responsive to each other and coordinate their behaviors by e.g., one holding the entrance door open for the other or getting up from one's seat so that the other can pass. However, this can all be framed in terms of two individuals having two independent individual goals that happen to be the same goal. The goals are independent in the sense that it will not matter to either one of the strangers if the other one changes her mind (i.e., her goal), falling asleep or leaving the movie theater during the film. This turns into a totally different situation, however, if these two people are friends who agreed to watch the movie together. In this case, each individual's actions are partly governed by the joint goal of watching the movie. For instance, it is not legitimate if one friend suddenly walks away to rent the film on DVD and watch it at home. Although one could say that both friends have achieved the goal of watching the film, the friend's behavior has jeopardized the joint goal of watching the film *together*. Thus, once a person has agreed to engage in a joint collaborative activity, her individual actions are constrained by the joint commitment to contribute to a joint goal. Thus, one empirical way to identify social behaviors that are not only coordinated but collaborative is to investigate how one participant responds to instances in which the other participant disengages from the activity. If one of them views the task as collaborative, she should be displeased with a partner that disengages from the joint activity and try to redirect him towards it.

EMPIRICAL EVIDENCE: COLLABORATIVE ACTIVITIES IN CHILDREN AND CHIMPANZEES

To investigate these questions, we conducted a series of studies with young children and chimpanzees in situations in which they had the opportunity to collaborate with others in various ways. In particular, we tested children at 14, 18, and 24 months of age in four different collaboration tasks and compared their performance with that of the same three human-raised chimpanzees from the helping study discussed earlier (Warneken, Chen, and Tomasello 2006, Warneken et al. 2007). The rationale of all these tasks was that they could not be performed successfully by one individual alone but required the joint activity of two individuals. Two of these tasks were collaborative problem-solving tasks (e.g., two people had to perform complementary roles like one person holding a container open so that the other person could retrieve an object from inside), and two others were social games with no external goal other than playing together (such as a "trampoline" in which two people had to hold a large piece of cloth and make a toy bounce on it). First, we found that infants at 14 months of age begin to participate in these activities with an adult partner. At this early age, however, their skills in coordinating their actions with that of the partner remain rudimentary. Through the second year of life, children become considerably better at coordinating their actions with their partner spatially and temporally. For example, the older children would position themselves in the correct location more quickly and adjust their actions to their partner temporally by holding the container open until the other had completed his action. When approaching 2 years of age, children engage successfully in a variety of tasks (games and problem-solving), switching between roles if necessary (Brownell and Carriger 1990, Brownell, Ramani, and Zerwas 2006). Second, and of particular interest for the issue of joint intentionality, were the observations of children's behaviors when the adult partner interrupted his participation. Children at 18 and 24 months often communicated to the partner in an attempt to request his collaboration. All children produced at least one such communicative attempt. They frequently used gestural communication like pointing to the apparatus or placing the apparatus in front of the partner, and at 24 months they often accompanied this with verbalizations. This shows that the children understood their own and their partner's action as interconnected parts of a joint activity. Moreover, this can also be taken as evidence that the children were trying to redirect their partner towards a joint goal, insisting on the commitment to support each other's actions in a collaborative activity.

When the three human-raised chimpanzees interacted with a human caregiver in the same tasks, they were able to succeed in a problem-solving task such as lifting a door so that the partner could retrieve a piece of food from inside. In contrast, they showed no interest in cooperating in the social games, such as the trampoline game which had no other goal beyond doing something together. Most importantly, they never once attempted to reengage their partner when she refrained from cooperating during interruption periods (although the necessary gestures are part of their repertoire as known from other studies not involving cooperation; Tomasello, Carpenter, and Hobson 2005a). The chimpanzees instead tried to solve the task alone, or else disengaged from the task completely, suggesting that they had not formed a joint goal with the other.

Taken together, young children and chimpanzees are probably not so different in their ability to coordinate actions with a partner. In fact, Melis and colleagues demonstrated in studies on collaborative problem-solving that chimpanzee conspecifics are able to coordinate their actions in a very sophisticated manner, choosing between situations in which partners are needed or not, waiting for their partner until the other is ready to manipulate an apparatus in synchrony, and remembering who had been a skillful or an unskillful partner based upon previous interactions (Hare et al. 2007, Melis, Hare, and Tomasello 2006a, 2006b). The experimental investigation of collaboration in chimpanzees has only begun in recent years, especially concerning the question of joint intentionality. Thus, all conclusions can only be tentative at this point. However, at least from the limited evidence on chimpanzees that we have available at the moment it seems there may be a potentially major species difference in the way they collaborate: children—but not chimpanzees—appear to view their own and their partner's actions as integral parts of a collaborative activity with a joint goal that they try to reinstate when necessary.

CONCLUSION

The reported studies demonstrate that both human infants and chimpanzees are able and willing to altruistically help other individuals with their individual goals. They possess both a social-cognitive understanding of intentions and an altruistic motivation which together enable acts of instrumental helping. With regard to the ontogenetic origins of altruism, these results challenge the view that altruism is imposed by the social environment. Infants show altruistic tendencies at an age when socialization could not yet have had a major impact on their development. Also the internalization of norms or value systems is inapplicable to one-year old children. Moreover, these infants just did not have many opportunities for helping and its reinforcement. And even if that is the case under some circumstances, they also help in novel situations with unfamiliar adults. Thus, this early achievement cannot readily be explained by socialization alone. A more plausible approach is to assume that these early altruistic acts reflect a natural predisposition to develop these altruistic behaviors—and socialization processes build upon this tendency.

This altruistic tendency is not unique to humans: chimpanzees show altruistic behaviors as well. The phylogenetic roots of human altruism may thus go deeper than previously demonstrated, reaching as far back as the last common ancestor of humans and chimpanzees. The fact that chimpanzees display crucial components of human altruism is further evidence for the notion of a biologically based predisposition for altruism. Human culture may have created unique social mechanisms to preserve and foster these altruistic tendencies, resulting in forms of altruism not found outside the human species. But these cultural mechanisms appear to have cultivated rather than implanted the propensity to act altruistically in the human psyche.

In contrast to this commonality of human infants and chimpanzees in altruistic helping, they appear to differ in their prerequisites for collaborative activities. In other words, both humans and chimpanzees act *for* others, but possibly only humans act collaboratively *with* others. In mutualistic situations, chimpanzees are able to coordinate their behaviors with another individual, but the first study addressing collaboration in chimpanzees experimentally indicates that they do not view their own and the other's action as part of a collaborative activity with a joint goal. By contrast, human infants display this capacity in the second year of life. Therefore, humans appear to have a possibly species-unique capacity to engage in collaborative activities, which emerges early in ontogeny and lays the foundation for complex cultural practices.

7

Mimesis Theory Re-Examined, Twenty Years after the Fact

MERLIN DONALD

This review will cover the current status of the theory of mimesis, and attempt especially to clarify two issues: (1) the very broad nature of the adaptation that resulted in mimetic capacity in hominins, and (2) the particular importance of metacognition—that is, executive and supervisory skills—in the evolution of mimetic capacity and cultural evolution.

This chapter focuses on one aspect—mimesis—of a comprehensive theory of human cognitive evolution (Donald 1991). A mimetic act is a performance that reflects the perceived event structure of the world. It has three behavioral manifestations: (1) rehearsal of skill, in which the actor imagines and reproduces previous performances with a view to improving them; (2) mime, in which patterns of action, usually of others, are reproduced—for example, a child pretending to act like a puppy; and (3) nonlinguistic gesture, where an action communicates an intention through resemblance—for example, miming a facial expression of disgust. The contents of mimetic acts are observable by others, which makes them a potential basis for a culturally accepted "mimetic" vernacular, enabling members of a group to share knowledge, feelings, customs, skills, and goals; and to create group displays of emotions and intentions that are conventional and deliberate, for example, of shared aggression or grief.

Mimesis was conceived as an archaic (more than 2 million years old) neuro-cognitive adaptation that formed the initial foundation of a distinctively human mindsharing culture. This innovation ultimately enabled hominins to create the rudiments of a community of mind (or more properly, a community of brains). Although it was primarily an adaptation for refining skill, it was also the first step toward the formation of shared cognitive-cultural networks, so characteristic of human beings, which would serve as a means of accumulating culturally stored knowledge and skill. This had consequences for the future evolutionary trajectory of the hominin brain and the eventual shape of human culture. It also established the social conditions in which the later evolution of language became possible.

A METHODOLOGICAL CAVEAT

The human evolutionary scenario is well documented, and dotted with numerous hominin species that emerged over a period of over 5 million years. Australopithecines and archaic *Homo* each generated several subspecies. The line that led to modern humanity generally favored the more gracile subspecies, but there were many false starts, and many twists and turns, in the human lineage.

Speciation is not a small thing. New species typically emerge along many different dimensions, and the sole survivor of this sequence of speciation events, anatomically modern humans, is distinctive from its ancestral species in anatomy, diet, mating behavior, energy generation and consumption, heat dissipation, social life, and, of course, cognition. All of these features underwent significant modification in the human speciation process. This is normal. Organisms adapt to selection pressures in very complex ways, and single variables are seldom, if ever, adequate to account for speciation events. A satisfactory theory of human cognitive evolution should begin with this realization: cognition did not evolve in isolation of these other dimensions.

Nor did it evolve in a simple linear manner; theories of cognitive evolution should be subjected to a mandatory methodological caveat: Avoid oversimplifying the nature of major adaptations that culminate in a new species. Unfortunately, despite this much repeated caution, there has been a strong tendency to reduce human cognitive uniqueness, so dramatic and obvious even on a superficial examination, to the evolution of a single variable; that is, to one parameter of a complex system. It has been common for theorists in this field to propose any one of the following variables as *the* breakthrough that explains the special cognitive abilities of modern humans: imitation, generativity, spoken language, universal grammar, altruism, shared intentionality, prosociality, gesture, anticipation, mental time travel, skill, theory of mind, joint attention, blending, latching, symbolization, or even representational culture itself. Previous generations of scholars singled out other variables for their fifteen minutes of fame: stone toolmaking, speech, the opposed thumb, symbol use, the descent of the larynx, voluntary vocal control, and erect posture were all proposed as key variables that somehow typified or epitomized human uniqueness. Many single-variable neuroscientific theories have also been proposed; and they have emphasized variables such as encephalization, mirror neurons, spindle cells, increased cerebral plasticity, fourth-order dendritic arborizations, expanded fronto-cortical executive capacities, the re-differentiation of perisylvian and fronto-cortical regions, and so on.

In fairness, many of these variables were proposed with a narrower aim than a comprehensive theory, and it may well be that many, or most of them, will prove relevant to the definition of human uniqueness. In fact, there are major differences between apes and humans, and the list grows longer every year. Within the relatively narrow domain of executive brain functions alone, I was able to list at least a dozen significant differences between apes and humans—the so-called Executive Suite (Donald 1998b). All of these, and probably many more that have not yet been identified, may play a useful role as defining features of the human species. However complex our adaptation may have been, the bottom line for theorists is simple: Take an inclusive approach to human cognitive evolution, with a sufficiently broad theoretical reach to accommodate change along many dimensions. Mimesis theory was an attempt to achieve this kind of breadth.

This approach is consistent with Darwinian principles. The most salient aspect of Darwinian thought has been the complexity of the details of evolutionary change, especially of the massive patterns of change that lead to new species. The principle of natural selection is simple enough, but the details of any adaptation are usually extremely complex, and there is simply zero evidence for one-dimensional saltations in hominin evolution, especially at the level of speciation.

My initial proposal for an archaic mimetic adaptation was pitched at the broad integrative level of human cognitive-cultural co-evolution, with accumulated cultural knowledge gradually being drawn into the heart of the cognitive evolutionary scenario. The transitions and stages of cognitive hominin evolution listed in that proposal were all multi-dimensional adaptations that led to speciation, and involved many parameters that impinged on the survival strategies and social lives of hominins, including modifications to the brain, body anatomy, diet, survival strategy, and cognitive system. The targeted outcome of this complex adaptive process may have been a qualitative change in cognition, but the evolutionary changes that accompanied this development involved many other defining aspects of the species as well (bipedality is perhaps the most salient of these, but there were many others, such as heat dissipation and basal metabolism).

The central thrust was both social and cognitive. Human beings evolved a cognitive survival strategy that gradually made the species better able to perform cognitive work in groups (including the work of managing the increasingly complicated political intrigues of human society). This strategy involved so many radical changes to the primate template we inherited that there is no alternative but to view it as a multi-staged adaptive process, in which each stage had to be self-justifying and self-sufficient. Since the evolutionary process lacks foresight, every stage must convey some immediate and enduring advantage. While such a process could (and did) involve preadaptation, this only becomes clear in hindsight; each stage must have conveyed a complete adaptive scenario, with a credible survival strategy for each species as it emerged. Those constraints cannot be avoided, and they served as a selection standard for developing every stage of the theory.

I am emphasizing this at the beginning of this article, because my theory has at times been caricatured as something that it was never intended to be: a series of one-dimensional adaptations. Rather, it was designed as a comprehensive adaptive scenario that placed cognition at the top of the hierarchy of selection criteria. At each stage, hominins had a complete and self-sufficient survival strategy. At each stage, they were moving closer to group cognitive strategies—symbolic communication, cooperative cognitive work, and public sharing and trading of ideas.

We know, from comparing humans with our closest relatives (gorillas, bonobos, and chimpanzees), that hominin evolution has been characterized by many changes, including such diverse adaptations as altered skeletal morphology, a greatly modified digestive apparatus, novel ways of generating the metabolic energy needed to support a larger brain, radically different mating strategies, and a novel emotional repertoire (for primates) that includes laughing, grieving, and long-term pair bonding. The cognitive dimension of our adaptive process is diverse and complex, touching on virtually every aspect of mental function, from attention, memory, and thought, to gesture, imitation, and, of course, symbolic communication. This massive pattern of change developed over a very long time, in a complex, changing ecology that engaged all the variables listed above, and undoubtedly many more.

For this reason, my theory explicitly embraced the full complexity of the adaptive process that led to the modern human mind. In this, it is different from many other theories that have focused exclusively on a single variable, such as shared attention, symbolic communication, or imitation. There is no single variable that can be said to constitute the irreducible cognitive "atom" of a uniquely human mental substance, and the cognitive end result of very broad adaptive shifts emerged primarily on the level of culture. Hominins went through a series of evolutionary changes that were especially evident at the level of shared culture, but that also involved many detailed changes in anatomy, cognitive function, and social structure. The archaeological record testifies that, at certain key times in the 5 million year scenario of hominin emergence, those changes coalesced into the massive speciation events that gradually and cumulatively defined human nature. For this reason, and for the very good reason that the evidence is compelling only at this level, I felt it necessary to focus on transition periods that led to speciation events.

CORE PROPOSALS

The central proposals for an archaic mimetic adaptation were a response to three basic questions, all related to hominin uniqueness or exceptionality: (1) Humans have special mental powers, in particular those related to symbolic processing, which are barely detectable, or completely absent, in wild-reared apes. What is the nature of the neuro-cognitive adaptation that made the hominin brain capable of these achievements? (2) When compared to the cultures of other species, human culture is unique in its cognitive aspect, especially in its important epigenetic role in mental development. What is its appropriate place in theories of human cognitive evolution? (3) Unlike any other known species, humans are able to think and remember in organized groups, aided by technology, and this arrangement constitutes a distributed cognitive system with special properties, an unprecedented "hybrid" arrangement of mind, brain, and culture. Can we specify the origins of this distributed cognitive system, its evolutionary trajectory, and its key features?

Although we are a long way from having detailed answers to these questions, some of my original proposals might be evaluated in terms of current progress in various relevant fields. I make no pretence at comprehensiveness here; there is far too much exciting research going on, and too many competing unresolved issues, for anyone to track in detail at this point.

My model is the outcome of a cross-disciplinary project that attempted to trace the broad features of the cognitive trajectory from Miocene apes to modern humans. It was constructed from "big facts"; that is, the most enduring, and relatively stable, knowledge emanating from such fields as cognitive science, evolutionary biology, developmental psychology, comparative neuroanatomy, paleontology, archaeology, psycholinguistics, and anthropology. The notion was to maximize return and minimize risk. Convergences between so many disciplines, themselves so far apart in their methods and theories, are unlikely to be accidents, and very likely to point the way to an optimally robust theory (see Donald 2004). And, most importantly, it was not a one-dimensional theory. The stages proposed were all complex and multi-dimensional in cause and effect.

The chronology of the model lies in the internal logic of the phylogenetic sequence, rather than in specific dates. The latter have yet to be firmly established, although the paleontological database on human origins has produced a remarkably stable core body of facts. Judging from these, and accepting the fact that there is some serious disagreement about the details of succession of various hominin species, the basics of the human story have not changed in a fundamental way in the past 20 years. In general terms, the line of descent of the human species is much better established now than it was then, and, for the most part, it confirms and fills in the wider trends discovered by an earlier generation. This is reassuring.

While the fossil record tells a fairly stable story, the question of mental origins is a more difficult one. We do not have direct access to soft tissue in fossils, or to the past behavior of extinct species, and there are no surviving hominin species that evolved between Miocene apes and modern humans. However, we know a lot about the intervening hominin species that are human ancestors, especially about their life style, diet, technology, and survival strategies. We also know much more about paleoclimatology and paleoecology than we did 20 years ago (e.g., Richerson and Boyd 2005), and it has been possible to construct better theories of the ecological factors that contributed to the selection pressures affecting hominin adaptation.

Moreover, our comparative theories of cognition have progressed. We cannot measure the mental skills of human ancestors directly; nor are we ever likely to be able to achieve such a thing. But we know a great deal more about primate and human cognition, about the brains of chimpanzees, monkeys, and humans, and by extension, about the hominin ancestors of anatomically modern humans. In addition, recent genetic research has proven to be quite consistent with our established knowledge, while refining and deepening it, and has added significant depth to our speculations.

Overall, there is less uncertainty in this field than may seem to be the case to the outside observer, especially on first impression. First, the functional anatomy of the primate brain has changed very slowly, and the basic brain design of humans remains close to that of other primates. For this reason, neuropsychological comparisons of apes and humans can be quite informative, greatly narrowing the range of feasible theoretical options available to those who build models of nervous systems. Second, there is significant overlap between the behavioral repertoires of primates and humans. This reinforces the utility of cross species comparisons that employ behavioral and cognitive testing, and helps us single out those cognitive features that are species specific. Third, the mapping of primate and human genomes promises to yield a great deal of information about the complex triadic relationships between genes, functional neuroanatomy, and behavior in the primate line. Finally, the range of social cognitive behaviors available to humans is clearly derivative of equivalent behaviors in primates. This allows us to build reasonably convincing, biologically based models of human culture, with roots in evolution. By putting together specific findings from these and other fields of research, it is possible to build a larger view of human cognitive emergence that will have both heuristic and theoretical value.

At the time my theory was initially formulated, both cognitive neuroscience and genetics were much less developed than they are today, and there was more urgency to some issues than may be the case today. For example, mental modularity was a major concern at that time, and I took a strong stance against the Chomsky-Fodor notion that language was effectively a new module in the mental apparatus of the primate line (Chomsky 1984, Fodor 1983). In my view, that battle has been won, not only due to the efforts of such developmental researchers as Tomasello (1999) and

Nelson (1996), but also because the facts of modern cognitive neuroscience strongly support the idea that most brain regions, including those normally engaged in language, serve multiple functions. In effect, the hominin adaptation for language looks increasingly like a "kluge" cobbled together from various modifications to the existing primate brain apparatus.

The focus of my model was not on language as the *ne plus ultra* of hominin evolution. On the contrary, it was on mental models and knowledge representation, and particularly on the ability to capture, or express, that knowledge in public, or potentially public, motor actions. Language was one way of advancing this agenda but not the only, or even the primary, way. Social cognitive skills were more important in establishing the intersubjective cognitive domains out of which language eventually emerged. Moreover, I was convinced that hominin mental capabilities could not have improved in a narrow manner, but that they were part of a much broader adaptive shift, in the direction of increased hominin interdependency and sociality. This idea, that language emerged from a broad advancement in primate cognitive skills rather than from a new language module, has been strengthened by Savage-Rumbaugh's demonstration of nascent linguistic capacities in her bobono protegé Kanzi (Savage-Rumbaugh, Shanker, and Taylor 1998).

These shifts toward a cooperative and much more complex society were the surface outcome of tremendous changes in the way early hominins thought and acted; and the criterion for identifying the major "stages" of hominin evolution was to conceptualize major changes to hominin survival strategy to the level involved in speciation itself. Hence, the key transitions in the scenario were speciation events. They were inevitably complex, and closely allied to changes in the early evolutionary environment of hominins. A shift on such a global level, leading to a new species, is always more than purely cognitive. This is true of all species; cognition does not usually change in a major way without corresponding changes in life style, anatomy, sexual behavior, and social life.

The stages of hominin emergence also had to be durable, because any major shift away from the cognitive repertoire of ancestral apes must have been self-sufficient and effective for the long-term survival of the species, without further major modification, under the conditions of hominin life at that time. Thus, although preadaptations are a logical possibility from a retrospective vantage point, they cannot be projected into the future; every change had to stand on its own when it emerged.

Table 7.1 illustrates the basic proposal, which has been presented in various other publications (e.g., Donald 1998a), and is reproduced here for the convenience of the reader. The three stages were each the outcome of a transition period. These were inferred or, more accurately, massively induced from a very broad evidential base. The theory made use of any and all data, and of a range of other theories that might yield insights into the human mind's emergence over time. The cognitive core of the representational model driving the three-stage theory was social, and focused in particular on the process of social event–perception and social event–knowledge, which are highly developed in both chimpanzees and gorillas, and thus likely to have been present in the Miocene ancestors of hominins.

Table 7.1. Three stages of human cognitive evolution, tracing the path from the Miocene primate ancestors of hominins to anatomically modern humans in literate societies.

Stage	Species/period	Novel forms of representation	Manifest change	Cognitive governance
EPISODIC	primate	complex episodic event-perceptions	improved self-awareness and event-sensitivity	episodic and reactive; limited voluntary expressive morphology
MIMETIC (1st transition)	early hominins, peaking in *H. erectus;* 4M–0.4 Mya	nonverbal action-modeling	revolution in skill, gesture (including vocal), nonverbal communication, shared attention	mimetic; increased variability of custom, cultural "archetypes"
MYTHIC (2nd transition)	sapient humans, peaking in *H. sapiens sapiens*; 0.5 Mya–present	linguistic modeling	high-speed phonology, oral language, oral social record	lexical invention, narrative thought, mythic framework of governance
THEORETIC (3rd transition)	recent sapient cultures	extensive external symbolization, both verbal and nonverbal	formalisms, large scale theoretic artifacts and massive external memory storage	institutionalized paradigmatic thought and invention

CONFIRMING THE CHRONOLOGY OF MIMESIS:
STONE TOOLMAKING

The most important confirmatory proof of the chronology of mimesis in the past decade has perhaps been our improved understanding of the difficulty of learning, teaching, or imitating through observation, the craft of stone toolmaking. Chase (2006) and Toth et al. (1993, 2003) have shown that the making of relatively simple Oldowan cutting tools, similar to those identified with habilines, is a challenge, and typically takes numerous rehearsals over a period of weeks to perfect, even when the student is a biologically modern human being.

The earliest Oldowan artifacts, reliably dated to 2.3 million years ago, have finished edges that cannot be manufactured simply by the trial-and-error banging together of two rocks. Moreover, the chosen materials matter. Certain types of rock do not yield a sharp edge. Nor can a hammer stone be softer than a core. In addition, the correct sequence of knapping must be learned, so that a second round of strikes will sharpen rather than dull the first-struck edge. Chase (2006) has argued that the correct angle of striking the stone is particularly critical and requires considerable practice before the learner can produce a useful cutting edge. The fact that this skill was successfully transmitted over countless generations so long ago testifies to the mimetic capacity of the first toolmakers. On present evidence, the first users of stone tools were australopithecines; but the data linking a specific australopithecine subspecies to the earliest stone tools is not yet sufficiently clear to resolve this issue. A recently reported microscopic examination of cut-marks on two bones found in Ethiopia (McPherron et al. 2010) indicates that *afarensis* australopithecines were using stone tools as early as 3.4 million years ago. Even though no exemplars of those tools have yet been found, it is now clear that the emergence and initial refinement of stone tools predated *Homo*.

The skill gap between humans and archaic hominins (such as australopithecines), and present-day apes, in fashioning stone tools is not trivial. The enculturated ape Kanzi learned how to produce crude but serviceable stone tools (Toth et al. 1993) and has continued to manufacture and use these in order to gain access to food. However, even in this highly unusual single case, Kanzi never mastered the principle of striking the stone at the optimal angle, so as to enhance the resulting sharpness of the flake and produce it more reliably. Kanzi still relies on happenstance outcomes that work. He does not practice systematically to improve his skill. As a result, his tools have never reached the level of refinement found in the earliest Oldowan tools. In contrast, ancient hominins invented and transmitted their toolmaking skills in the wild, and also learned to select the right materials needed for butchering (Toth, Schick, and Semaw 2003).

The spread of stone toolmaking throughout archaic hominin culture suggests that they were much better than their ancestors at all aspects of this particular skill, and that they did not rely on chance outcomes, but rather refined their skills over time. This involved (1) planning and imagining the motor act; (2) executing it under conscious metacognitive supervision; (3) analyzing the outcome and noticing the conditions for a better outcome; (4) practicing and refining the final form of the action-pattern; and (5) if necessary, copying and profiting from the skill of others. Above all, stone toolmaking was these hominins' own innovation, achieved in their natural environment. This fact, combined with evidence of the extraordinary sustainability of this skill over many millennia, suggests that some pedagogical capacity accompanied the emergence of mimetic skills, as suggested in my initial proposal. This would have distanced these hominins even further from their primate forebears. Premack (1993) has suggested that pedagogy is one of the traits that distinguishes human beings from other primates.

Stone toolmaking was further advanced within the *ergaster* branch of the hominins. *Ergaster* produced Acheulian tools, starting about 1.8–1.6 million years ago, in Africa. These tools were significantly more complex to manufacture. The Acheulian industry did not appear in European or Asian branches of *Homo* until much later, approximately 1 million years ago. In the absence of evidence for a major biological difference between the Eurasian hominin subspecies and *ergaster,* this suggests that Acheulian toolmaking skill was culturally transmitted.

These findings confirm the following conclusions about mimesis. (1) At this early stage, hominins could *rehearse and refine* action. This confirms the most fundamental postulate of mimesis theory, that hominins advanced beyond primates in their ability to refine skill very early in their evolution. (2) The species could also *transmit and maintain* skills accurately across generations through a combination of imitation and practice, and possibly pedagogy as well. (3) The species was already moving toward a *group cognitive strategy,* in which the talents of individuals were transformed into shared resources within a group of hominins. (4) Because mimetic expression is regulated by essentially the same neuro-cognitive system that produces skill, it is very likely that hominins at this early stage had evolved a degree of *communicative capability,* especially in the domain of vocal modulations and whole-body gesticulation. This may well have been an exaptation, as initially proposed. The research of the past 20 years thus strengthens and enriches the original proposal for an archaic mimetic adaptation very early in the hominin scenario.

BRAIN MECHANISMS, EVENT-REPRESENTATION, AND MIMETIC ACTION

What of the underlying cognitive mechanism of mimesis? My proposal focused on two cognitive mechanisms in particular. The first is sophisticated event-representation, which implicates the tertiary regions of the parietal lobes; and the second is metacognition, or self-monitoring, which depends upon the executive or supervisory systems of the prefrontal cortex. Working together, these two cortical regions are essential, inasmuch as their breakdown causes executive supervision to deteriorate greatly.

Event-representation is the cognitive foundation of mammalian social life. The cognitive "atoms" of social life consist of events, or complex dynamic stimuli, batched in episodes that can extend over a considerable period of time. An example of an episode would be a dog fight, or an attempt to mate. Both of these behaviors can involve a considerable amount of judgment and negotiation, and take time, sometimes a relatively long time. Such episodes consist of brief sensory stimuli and motor acts strung out in a series of micro events—growls, bites, attacks, withdrawals, and so on. These are the source of numerous dynamic sensory stimuli that unfold over time. They often involve several simultaneous streams of events, because many social events engage several players, as well as a variety of other elements in the environment related to goals, terrain, and the larger social context. While engaged in a fight, participants must track time, place, and context, while keeping in mind what they have learned from previous encounters. They must also remember exactly what was done, and by whom, because these have important future implications.

The survival imperative is paramount here. In a social mammal such as a dog or an ape, the political ramifications of a fight must be understood and remembered, since they can have life-threatening importance. Social events are critical in securing food and shelter, resolving rivalries, asserting dominance, and forming affiliations, among other things. In other words, understanding them is a vital survival skill. For this reason, event-representation is highly evolved in all social mammals. Humans are, in many ways, the culmination of this trend, the ultimate social mammals. We appear to be the most social creatures in the biosphere.

Since its first formulation, this idea has also received considerable support from developmental researchers. The development of event-representation has been thoroughly studied in human children in the pioneering developmental work of Nelson (1986). She has explicitly acknowledged the close similarity of her observations on the unfolding of cognitive ontogenesis with the evidence for the evolutionary unfolding of mimetic skill in hominins (Nelson 1996). Importantly, Nelson explicitly avoided the recapitulatory fallacy, emphasizing that the useful parallels between ontogeny and phylogeny in the sequencing of cognitive change does not imply a similar mechanism. The additional work of Tomasello (1999) and others has further reinforced the importance of interrelating research on human child development with studies of ape cognition.

Social event–representation is the most abstract and complex achievement of the brain's perceptual systems. It is a necessary, but not sufficient, condition for mimetic event-representation, as seen in the fact that most social mammals are incapable of any degree of mimesis. They lack the ability to "read out" their social insights onto their action repertoire, even in the form of the simple event repetition needed to practice a skill.

My human evolutionary model was really about how the hominin event-representational hierarchy evolved, over a period of 5 million years, in such a way as to enable human beings to express their knowledge about events in actions of the musculature. A succession of evolutionary changes kept increasing the power and range of the event-representational machinery of hominins. This evolutionary trend began with the emergence of mimesis, and expanded greatly with the advent of speech and language. It later evolved even further with the advancement of material culture, and particularly with the invention of various forms of external symbolic representation, including writing. This sequence of changes equipped human beings to represent events that were more abstract and extended in space and time than the sensory and perceptual system alone could capture.

The starting point of this process was to transform the simplest event-perceptions of archaic hominins into actions, in the form of simple re-enactments. Rehearsal of skill is a re-enactive capacity, and one that cannot be limited to a single modality on either the perceptual or the motor side. Skills typically engage several sense modalities simultaneously, including both interoception and exteroception. Once this capacity had evolved, it produced a byproduct, or exaptation, inasmuch as the same system can reduplicate a wide variety of events, including social events. Very young children manifest this ability long before they have language; in fact, it is a prerequisite for practicing speech and other forms of language. Human children copy and mime their parents and their peers, and reflect the mimetic expressions of their social environment with remarkable accuracy, without always understanding the wider social implications of what they are doing.

A key consideration in any theory of mimesis is that human mimesis is not modality-specific, like, say, birdsong. It is not even limited to one cognitive domain. It exploits the whole body as an expressive device across any number of communicative domains, including emotional, locomotor, and object-oriented actions. The epitome of mimetic expression in modern humans is probably the art of dance, or acting, where the whole body is used to portray the characters of a scenario. Pantomime is the prototypal, and most ancient, form of theatrical performance. It is pure mimesis.

Executive supervision of behavior is at the heart of mimesis, and this implicates the prefrontal cortical regions and the cerebellum. The whole-body, or supramodal, nature of mimesis fits in well with the broad reach of the dorsolateral prefrontal system. The well-documented expansion of the prefrontal executive system in the hominin brain is consistent with this unique cognitive advantage of *Homo*. The prefrontal system is widely interconnected with many brain structures, and is coordinated from the lateral prefrontal regions of the cerebral cortex. This interconnectivity is wider and deeper in humans than in apes. Moreover, the pathway between the frontal lobes and the lateral cerebellum, which is crucial in motor learning and the refinement of skill, is many times larger in humans than it is in apes.

This is a crucial factor in terms of brain mechanisms, because mimesis is basically a capacity for selective event re-enactment, or pantomime, *using the whole body, including the voice*. Mimesis builds on the entire voluntary motor repertoire of the primate line, and entails an embodied style of expression, which produces actions that reflect and vary the patterns of previous actions, whether of self or of others. It must be regarded as a high-level action system that is mapped systematically onto an abstract imaginative model of events. This places the cognitive control of mimetic action very high up in the hierarchy of neural function, and the prefrontal area is well situated for this role, since it receives inputs from the event-sensitive parietal cortex, and sends outputs to the premotor and motor systems, which are richly connected to the lateral cerebellum (Stuss and Benson 1986, Thatch 1998).

For the mammalian brain, the emergence of mimetic capacity in hominin evolution was not a small innovation. It was a radical change. Previously, in every known mammalian species, the brain's action systems were focused outside, on the environment, rather than internally, on action itself. Animals could move, chase, hold, chew, and so on, in flexible and clever ways. But they could not focus on their own actions in detail in order to evaluate and improve them. In effect, mimesis requires an actor to attend to the exact form of his own actions in fine detail, and to parse his own movements, in order to bring a performed action sequence into conformity with an imagined ideal. This imagined ideal of movement might originate in the acts of another actor, or in the event structure of the environment. It could even originate in an event structure that was completely imaginary. In either case, in order to achieve this, the anterior and posterior cerebral cortices must interact in a way that was evolutionarily new.

A possible clue to how this happened has emerged out of the work of Deacon (1997). He proposed that the human prefrontal cortex evolved in such a way as to develop far more connections, both within the cerebral cortex (especially with the posterior association regions) and with various subcortical nuclei. This places the human prefrontal region in a powerful location, relative to other high-level cortical integration zones. Prefrontal expansion was apparently achieved through a relatively straightforward modification of the genes regulating cortical epigenesis. Although Deacon did not propose this idea in the context of a theory of mimesis, but rather of language, it seems a better fit to existing neuroscientific evidence on mimetic action than it does to language proper, which seems tied more closely to the expansion of the perisylvian regions.

Another clue comes from the literature on so-called "mirror" neurons (Rizzolati et al. 1996b, Gallese et al. 1996). These neurons are present in large numbers in primates that have very limited imitative ability, so we may conclude that they are not sufficient for mimesis, let alone language.

However, mirror neurons, or more properly the neural networks in which they are embedded, appear to have been a necessary preadaptation for the later evolution of mimesis in the primate phylum, since such neurons are the first step toward integrating the larger cognitive context of a movement sequence into the planning of specific acts. However, as Chaminade (this volume) has pointed out, their distribution and properties in humans are still not well documented, and there is very little direct evidence on their specific role in mimetic action.

Regardless of the final details of the brain mechanism involved, humans outperform modern apes on a wide variety of metacognitive and executive tasks. Some of these are listed in Table 7.2, in order of difficulty for apes, with the most demanding tasks at the bottom of the list. Note that apes have some success at all these tasks. This provides an evolutionary stepping-stone, or wedge, for the Miocene apes, pointing in the direction of mimesis, and makes the proposed first transition quite feasible for archaic hominins, given the right selection pressures. Even though it still constituted a major change, the raw materials on which natural selection could act were already present in primates. When combined with Deacon's evidence on the distinctive pattern of frontal ontogenesis in humans, and the reliably dated

Table 7.2. The executive suite: A comparison of basic features in related species. In *Homo* all these features are fully evolved.

	Monkeys	Wild apes	Enculturated apes
Function			
Self-monitoring	Yes	Yes	Yes
Divided attention	No	Maybe	Some
Self-reminding	No	Maybe	Maybe
Autocuing	No	No	Yes
Self-recognition	No	Yes	Yes
Rehearsal/Review	No	Maybe	Yes; limited
Imitation	No	Partial	Yes; limited
Mindreading	Minimal	Minimal	Yes
Pedagogy	No	Maybe	Yes
Gesture	No	Doubtful	Some
Symbolic invention	No	No	Proto-gesture
Skill hierarchies	No	No	Some

stone tools found in various African sites, this makes a good case for an archaic mimetic adaptation quite early in hominin evolution.

We might conclude: Case not yet proven, but still promising.

MIMETIC CULTURE

The concept of mimetic culture was first developed in the context of building a co-evolutionary theory that took into consideration the social and cultural implications of cognitive evolution. Mimesis was first conceived while I was trying to construct a theory of how language evolution might have become possible. At first, the gap between humans and apes seemed too large to bridge. A necessary first step in the direction of language would have been a change in the evolutionary environment in such a way as to increase the importance of culture, indeed a qualitative change in its role, so that culture would become a major influence in shaping the cognitive demands imposed by the environment. Such a development would have generated the kind of selection pressure that would favor a more powerful and precise mode of communication, namely language.

The hypothesis of an archaic mimetic stage was thus initially a largely unwanted and unanticipated necessity on the way to the evolution of language capacity. I was trying to find the cognitive "missing link" that might bridge the enormous gap between ape vocalization and human speech. Condillac ([1746] 1756) and Darwin (1871) had earlier made some useful suggestions about this necessity; both suggested gesture as the precursor to language. Apes are known to gesticulate, and their rather stereotyped gesticulating serves their purposes well enough; but it was not at all obvious why ape gestural ability, per se, would have been under the kind of selection pressure that would lead to a major cognitive change such as language entailed. Moreover, in terms of the genome, language was far too complex an adaptation to emerge suddenly.

On reflection, from examining the organization of the human nervous system, it became clear that an improved capacity for the refinement of skill would have provided the neural foundation for much more than skill. It was potentially the basis for a cultural shift of some magnitude, that is, for a change in the hominin survival strategy that added a shared and highly social dimension to cognition itself. This included the acquisition, transmission, and elaboration of skill by populations, rather than by individuals.

This might have been the first way in which there was a largely cultural accumulation of detailed knowledge that was important for survival. But, because skilled rehearsal requires an elementary form of event-representation, the representational genie would have been let out of the bottle, albeit inadvertently. This very basic form of event-representation itself would have improved the social coordination of behavior and led to mutual cognitive activities, such as demonstrating a skill to children, and eventually, to the conventionalization of simple voluntary emotional expressions, creating the possibility of local traditions that would have distinguished the nonverbal culture of one local community from that of another. For example, there would have emerged different and idiosyncratic ways of communicating deference to authority, marking status, and expressing intimacy or approval. While not yet language, this would have added greatly to the existing primate repertoire, and made hominin social life more complex and cognitively demanding. All of this is a good match to the way of life identified with early hominins.

To a degree, the possibility of such a scenario has been validated by recent developmental research, as summarized by Katherine Nelson (2007). Although Nelson places more weight on language as the primary mediator that enables children to enter into the larger "community of mind" in which they grow up, mimetic play, fantasy, and role-playing have also been shown to be crucial factors in both joining and mastering our shared culture.

The mimetic dimension of culture endures, and in fact flourishes, in modern society. Human social life still begins with role-playing, which begins with simple mimetic action and gradually expands to include more elaborate social scenarios, such as becoming a mother, a soldier, a doctor, a victim. All these are modeled by role-playing children. Humans are unique in their tendency to experiment with the potential forms a given action might take in the future. This is especially evident in children, who routinely play with creating variations on their routine action patterns. An example might be to practice standing on one foot, making faces, crying, laughing attractively, or generating aggressive or intimidating sounds. Many games, even adult games, capitalize on this spontaneous motor generativity, and one of the consequences is the existence of mimetic "wit" as seen in games such as peek-a-boo, or in generating funny ways of falling down when struck. The facial exaggerations of silent film are perfect examples of mimetic wit. Such scenarios are common among children, and even adults, in human society.

The capacity for this kind of expressive play, and for refining skills, implies a major change in the executive management of action. This change created a channel, or mechanism, for the generation of a different kind of hominin culture, one where there was an incipient mechanism for capturing intentions and emotions in action, and thus "escaping" the solipsism of the central nervous system, through public action–modeling. This provided a means of achieving some degree of coordination and ritualization of group behavior. It also created the potential for rudimentary iconic and metaphoric gestures, including vocal gestures, which, in groups, can create elementary rituals, as in demonstrations of grief or triumph.

The vocal aspect of mimesis did not have to evolve as such. A supra-modal mechanism for rehearsing and refining skill would have recruited the existing vocalization repertoire of archaic hominins, just as it recruited all other aspects of voluntary action. Long before hominins had any social need for a powerful phonetic mechanism for communication, a general system for refining action would have produced voluntary modifications of their hereditary (largely primate) vocal repertoire, enabling mimetic vocalizations. I have argued elsewhere that these rudimentary vocal abilities necessarily preceded the evolution of speech, for the simple reason that they are preconditions for generating any kind of morpho-phonology, even in its simplest form (Donald 1998b). The conditions for evolving vocal language could not have emerged without having already evolved a mimetic vocal capacity. The modern manifestation of that capacity survives in various vocal expressions (such as tones of voice that express culture-specific signals of hierarchy, intimacy, or approval), and especially in the prosodic envelope that normally surrounds speech. One corollary of this idea is that speech emerged in two major stages: a mimetic stage, which set the stage for prosodic modulation of the voice; and a linguistic stage, where lexical invention created selection pressures favoring a wider and more flexible range of sounds, as in phonology. Deacon (1997) has adopted a somewhat similar two-stage stance on the evolution of speech.

Finally, the adaptive cultural scenario that accompanied the emergence of mimetic skill is outlined in Table 7.3, which is a slightly modified version of the table presented in the original 1991 proposal (Donald 1991:198). Note that mimetic culture evolved on the platform of episodic culture, on the assumption that basic primate cognitive skills, shared by all modern primates, are already in place in the Miocene ancestors of humans. I will not try to recapitulate the properties of episodic culture here; suffice it to say that it is an abstraction drawn from common characteristics shared by modern chimpanzees, bonobos, and gorillas.

Added to an episodic mind and cultural context, mimetic skill would have immediately altered the array of available action patterns and collective cognitive strategies available to the members of a group of hominins.

Table 7.3. Elements of an archaic hominin mimetic adaptation, in which language is completely absent. In a group context, the presence of mimetic skills in individuals would combine and interact to produce mimetic culture.

EPISODIC CULTURE (Primates)

   +

MIMETIC SKILL

      - intentional representations

      - generative, recursive capacity for mime

      - voluntary, public communicative system

      - differentiation of reference

      - unlimited modeling of episodic events

      - voluntary, autocued rehearsal

   +

SOCIAL CONSEQUENCES

      - shared model of social customs

      - reciprocal mimetic games

      - conformity/coordination

      - group mimetic acts

      - slow-paced innovative capacity

      - simple pedagogy and social attribution

   =

MIMETIC CULTURE

      - toolmaking, eventual fire-use

      - coordinated seasonal hunting

      - flexible, rapid adaptation to ecology

      - more complex social behavior

      - primitive ritual (group mimetic acts)

Reciprocity is at the heart of this; mimetic interactions would engender replies and reactions. Reciprocal mimetic exchanges would ensue, leading to customs, informal games, novel skills, and representations. Added to a pre-existing episodic culture, mimesis would necessarily lead to cultural innovation. It would also necessitate new forms of social control. Some of the properties of mimetic culture are listed below.

1. *Modeling of Social Structure.* Mimetic skill results in the sharing of knowledge about society, without every member of a group having to re-invent that knowledge. Mimetic skill, extended to the social realm, results in a collective conceptual "model" of social behavior, expressed in shared ritual and play, and in social structure. To quote from my original proposal:

> Social roles, in a complex society, can only be defined with reference to an implicit model of the larger society. Mimetic representations would thus be tremendously important in building a stable social structure.
>
> All higher mammals possess social knowledge; young chimps learn about dominance hierarchies in their play, for instance. But chimps only learn how to react to each individual in the larger group; human children model the group structure. A significant part of childhood is spent rehearsing and modeling society, and children can act out, not only their own roles, but those of other players. Human children can "model" an interchange between parents, for example, taking either role; or play act a game with friends, taking various sides. This is clear evidence that they are implicitly modeling the larger social structure. Once again, this demands a break with the egocentric episodic view of the world. (1991:173–74)

This insight has been strongly reinforced by Nelson's (1996) comparative review of research on children's acquisition of social skills, especially on their use of mimetic expressions prior to their mastery of speech and language.

2. *Reciprocal Mimetic Games.* Reciprocal games involve a minimum of two players. One player generates a mimetic act, and another replies with the same, or another, mimetic act. Someone invents a move; the next one imitates it, and perhaps adds something new. And so on. People in every culture, especially young children, indulge in this type of play. Mimetic games often help to define roles, especially gender roles. Such games can be played

in the absence of language, as seen in non-signing deaf children, who play essentially the same games as hearing children. With mimetic games, it is possible to model adult roles and activities. This affords a very efficient way to acquire important social knowledge.

3. *Conformity and Coordination.* Mimetic cultures are highly conformist. Reciprocal mimetic exchanges can lead to regular, repetitive patterns of group behavior that resemble ritual.

4. *Group Mimetic Acts.* Mimesis can take the form of a collective, or group, action. One common form of group mimesis is found in mass displays and rituals, such as war cries or ritualized grieving. Ritual differs from most other forms of mimetic representation in that it is a collective act, in which individuals play out different roles. The carefully orchestrated action of a crowd can be interpreted as a mimetic act, representing such things as the consensus, fury, or power of a group.

5. *Innovation.* A purely mimetic culture can evolve. Mimetic acts are expressive and thus inherently inventive and creative. The implicit model of the social world projected by the customs and rituals of a society may change from one generation to the next. However, such societies, especially in the absence of language, would change slowly. The mimetic dimension of culture, even as manifest in modern human society, tends to be conformist and conservative, as seen in such things as religious ritual, royal coronations, and deep cultural habits such as ways of greeting, attitudes to authority, and so on.

6) *Pedagogy.* In mimetic culture, some degree of pedagogy is likely, given that one of the defining advantages of such cultures is precisely their success at transmitting skills and knowledge across generations. This would complicate the process of acculturating the young, and require more time. Practical skills would have been the basic reason driving pedagogy: the use and manufacture of domestic tools and weapons, methods of hunting, construction of simple shelters, the use of fire, weapons, and fighting. Pedagogy requires not only some form of mimetic skill, but also the ability of the adult to sense what the child can, and cannot, learn. In Vygotsky's (1978) words, the teacher must estimate accurately the student's "zone of proximate development," that region, close to what is already known, where the probability of new learning is optimal. Rituals, games, folkways, and mores would also have required the systematic mimetic transmission of knowledge.

Research on hominin intelligence, as carried out by archaeologists, paleontologists, and cognitive scientists during the past two decades, has taken several directions, and cannot be properly summarized in this brief article. Much of the work suggests that we probably underestimated the capacities of both Miocene apes and early hominins (Byrne 1995, Russon and Begun 2004). If anything, this strengthens the case for mimesis. The demands of the early evolutionary environment of hominins were daunting, to say the least, and mimetic culture seems a reasonable and conservative proposal. There has been no strong evidence that language itself was either necessary to explain the cognitive achievements of archaic hominins, or likely to have been present in their society. The latter seems especially unlikely in view of the slow cultural evolution of early *Homo* for more than a million years. There is good reason to propose that an archaic preadaptation was necessary for the later evolution of language, and that this preadaptation might have been implicit in mimesis. Two recent summaries of research on language evolution support this possibility, (Tomasello 2008, Fitch 2010.)

We may still be some distance from a finished theory, but the central point of mimesis theory as a preadaptation for language evolution—that it set the stage for distributed cognition, creating a need for a more efficient medium of hominin communication—seems still to stand.

SUMMARY AND CONCLUSION

Mimesis was a radical, species-defining adaptation that emerged as the central cognitive component of a speciation event that changed many variables in the hominin line more or less simultaneously, including skeletal anatomy, diet, social life, and reproductive behavior.

The prime adaptive significance of mimesis was in the refinement and rapid transmission of skill; that is, in evolving the basic mechanisms of procedural learning that we see in modern humans—the ability to rehearse and re-enact past behaviors with a view to improving performance. This is a highly complex capacity, involving major changes in primate metacognitive and supervisory abilities, and memory retrieval.

Stone tools provide the earliest archaeological evidence for refined skills in hominins. They now point to an origin of mimetic capacity in australopithecines. The cognitive systems supporting skilled rehearsal in biologically modern humans depend on a number of subtle changes in the connectivity of the cerebral cortex that are considered crucial for procedural learning. These include increased mutual interactivity between the structures defining what might be broadly termed the "action brain" (especially prefrontal and premotor cortex, lateral cerebellum, and basal ganglia), and the "event-perception brain" (especially posterior cortex and hippocampus).

It is likely that these changes took place in several sub-stages that are not yet transparent in the archaeological record, but may become clearer as the methodology of genetic analysis becomes more powerful. The evidence for some significant mimetic capacity in late australopithecines is now much stronger than it was 20 years ago, and recent work suggests that the afarensis australopithecines were already using stone tools to butcher game 3.4 million years ago. This pushes the origins of mimesis back before the emergence of *Homo*, as much as 1.5 million years before the emergence of *Homo ergaster,* and the more complex Acheulian toolkit associated with that species.

Mimetic capacity seems to have evolved over a very long period, appearing earlier than previously thought, with hominin skill improving gradually over a period of at least two million years. This is consistent with the chronological sequence first proposed in 1991, but greatly extends the time course of mimetic evolution, possibly implying a multi-staged emergence of mimesis.

Although the emergence of mimesis was primarily about the refinement and expansion of the skill-set of hominins as a species, by its nature it was also a potential channel for representing reality and communicating ideas. Once hominins were able to imagine actions and events, and re-enact what they imagined, groups of hominins would have had an elementary capacity for communication, improved imitation, and distributed cognitive events, such as sustaining toolmaking industries and maintaining fire.

It is not yet clear exactly when this aspect of mimesis—improved representation and communication—became a part of its legacy. As we reconstruct the genomes of ancient hominins, it may be possible to pinpoint the finer stages of mimetic evolution more precisely.

8

The Role of Cooperation in the Evolution of Protolanguage and Language

PETER GÄRDENFORS

COOPERATION AS AN EVOLUTIONARY FACTOR

The most common description of the uniqueness of *Homo sapiens* is that it is the only extant species with a symbolic language. According to evolutionary theory, there should be some selective advantage that has fostered the development of language among humans. There are many proposals for such an evolutionary force. Some of the major ideas have been that (1) language brings with it the ability to convey information, for example about prey or other food or about dangers of different sorts; (2) language is a result of sexual selection (first proposed by Darwin 1871); (3) language replaces the social grooming found in monkeys and apes as an instrument for building coalitions and other social bonds (e.g., the so-called gossip theory proposed by Dunbar [1996] and Worden's [1998] theory of social intelligence); (4) language is a "mother tongue" that evolved among kin for "honest" communication (Fitch 2004); and (5) language makes it possible to cooperate about common future goals (Brinck and Gärdenfors 2003, Gärdenfors 2003, 2004, Gärdenfors and Osvath 2010).

In the case of adaptations like language that are unique to humans, it is not enough to present an evolutionary scenario showing how useful language would have been for our ancestors. We need to ascertain not just why the hominins evolved language, but also why chimps and other apes did not, even though we share a fairly recent common ancestor. It must be shown that language was useful and adaptive specifically for proto-humans and not for proto-chimpanzees. Many hypotheses concerning the origin of language fail this test (Bickerton 2002, Gärdenfors 2004, Johansson 2005, Dessalles 2007). In the list above, it can be argued that only (5) clearly passes it.

Recent research on animal cognition has, to a large extent, focused on the deceptive capacities of different species—often in terms of Machiavellian intelligence (Whiten and Byrne 1988, 1997). This tendency has spilled over to the debate on the evolution of human cognition. In contrast, the perspective of this chapter will be that the development of advanced forms of *cooperation* is more important when explaining the evolution of language.

I will take a further step towards an ecologically grounded explanation of the function of human language (see also Bickerton 2002, Gärdenfors and Osvath 2010). I will continue on the theme of language as a tool for human cooperation. In particular, I shall discuss the role of two kinds of cooperation that are uniquely human: cooperation for future goals and indirect reciprocity.

As regards indirect reciprocity, a related form of cooperation, reciprocal altruism ("You scratch my back and I'll scratch yours"), is found in several animal species. It is possible to show that this principle is an evolutionarily stable strategy, given certain assumptions about the cognitive capacity of the individuals. However, indirect reciprocity, which appears to be unique to humans, is a more extreme form of altruism: "I help you and somebody else will help me." Recently, the conditions for indirect reciprocity to evolve as an evolutionary stable strategy have been modeled (e.g., by Leimar and Hammerstein 2001, Nowak and Sigmund 2005). The aspect that is crucial for my argument is that these conditions include the existence of advanced forms of communication.

I shall follow Bickerton's (1990) distinction between protolanguage and language with syntax, and use Dessalles' (2007) corresponding distinction between protosemantics and semantics as two stages in the evolution of human communication. One of the central theses of this chapter is that protolanguage is an efficient system for communication about cooperation for future goals. The other is that language with syntax is an efficient system for communication that results in indirect reciprocity.

Developing my argument involves a triangulation of cognition, cooperation, and communication. In the first sections of the chapter, I will present two aspects of cognition, namely prospective cognition ("mental time travel") and intersubjectivity ("theory of mind"), that are particularly well developed in humans and crucial for advanced forms of cognition. Then I discuss the two forms of cooperation—cooperation for future goals and indirect reciprocity. I will argue that these have emerged along the hominin line. This leads to an analysis of which cognitive and communicative capacities are required for these forms of cooperation. In brief, the argument is that along the hominin line, the ecological setting has generated evolutionarily selective forces that have fostered new forms of cooperation, which in turn have led to more advanced forms of cognition and communication, first protolanguage and then language with a syntax. However, it is difficult to untangle the evolutionarily causal links between these components and the process is probably best seen as a co-evolution between cooperative, cognitive, and communicative factors, with a basis in hominin ecology.

PROSPECTIVE COGNITION

In order to understand the functions of most of the higher forms of cognition, one must rely on an analysis of how humans and other animals *represent* various things, in particular the surrounding world and its possibilities.[1] For an accurate analysis of many phenomena in animal and human cognition, it is necessary to distinguish between two kinds of mental representations: *cued* and *detached* (Gärdenfors 1996, 2003).

A cued representation stands for something that is present in the current situation of the representing individual. When, for example, a particular object is categorized as food, the animal will then act differently than if the same object had been categorized as a potential mate. In general, the represented object need not be actually present in the actual situation, but the representation must have been triggered by something in a recent situation.

In contrast, detached representations may stand for objects or events that are neither present in the current situation nor directly triggered by some recent situation. A memory of something that can be evoked independently of the context where the memory was created would be an example of a detached representation. For example, consider a chimpanzee, who performs the following sequence of actions: walks away from a termite hill, breaks a twig, peels its leaves off to make a stick, returns to the termite hill, and uses the stick to "fish" for termites. This behavior seems very difficult to explain unless it is assumed that the chimp has a detached representation of a stick and its use.

The notion of detachment is related to Hockett's (1960) "displacement" which is one of the criteria he uses to characterize what constitutes a language. But the notion of a detached representation is not the same as "displacement." The reason is that he includes the following under "displacement": "Any delay between the reception of a stimulus and the appearance of the response means that the former has been coded into a stable spatial array, which endures at least until it is read off in the response" (Hockett 1960:417). His description has a clear behavioristic ring to it, and it means that every signal that is not an immediate reaction to a stimulus would be counted as an example of "displacement" according to his criterion.

The collection of all detached representations of an animal or a human and their interrelations will be called *the inner world* of the individual. There is strong evidence that humans have richer inner worlds than other animals (Gärdenfors 1996, 2003). Gomez (2004:20) argues that the prolonged immaturity in the children of apes and in particular humans results in a greater flexibility in forming representations, which in turn leads to greater cognitive and behavioral flexibility. For example, Donald (1999:143) argues that something like an inner world is a precondition for *rehearsing a skill:* "Hominids had to *gain access to the contents of their own memories.* You cannot rehearse what you cannot recall."

The ability to use the inner world to envision various actions and their consequences is a necessary requirement for an animal to be capable of *planning.* There are several clear cases of planning among primates and corvids and less clear cases in other species (see, e.g., Ellen and Thinus-Blanc 1987, Gulz 1991, Byrne 1995, Suddendorf and Corballis 1997, Hauser 2000). The termite fishing of chimpanzees is one such example.

The plans of apes and other animals depend in most cases on their current drive states: they plan because they are hungry or thirsty, tired or frightened. Bischof (1978) and Bischof-Köhler (1985) hypothesize that animals other than humans cannot anticipate future needs or drive states (see also Gulz 1991). Gulz (1991:55) calls planning for present needs *immediate planning* while planning for the future is called anticipatory planning. Here I will refer to anticipatory planning as *prospective planning.* Humans can predict that they will be hungry tomorrow and save some food, and we can imagine that the winter will be cold, so we start building a shelter already in the summer. The crucial distinction is that for an individual to be capable of prospective planning, it must have a detached representation of its *future needs*. In contrast, immediate planning only requires a cued representation of the current need.

In general, the cognition of other animals concerns here and now, while humans are mentally here, in the past, and in the future. The squirrel that is gathering and storing food for the winter is not engaged in prospective planning because it is not planning at all. It has no representation of the winter, let alone its future needs. The gathering behavior is an innate complex behavior pattern that is stereotypical without sensitivity to varying circumstances (cf. Gulz 1991:62).

However, recent results indicate that great apes and corvids under experimental conditions have a rudimentary capacity to act in order to fulfill future needs (Mulcahy and Call 2006, Correia, Dickinson, and Clayton 2007, Osvath and Osvath 2008). They are however not known to use this capacity in the wild, which implies that prospective cognition plays a minor or non-existing role in the life of great apes. More studies are required to determine to what extent it can be said that the apes are on the cognitive brink of prospective planning. In spite of these surprising results, the human capacity for prospective planning seems to be far more advanced, in particular when it comes to cooperation.

Prospective planning is a component in a more general prospective cognition that is a hallmark of *H. sapiens*. It also includes episodic memory (Tulving 1985) and other aspects of "mental time travel" (Suddendorf and Corballis 1997, Suddendorf and Busby 2003). A central question is what factors along the hominin line have created selective evolutionary forces that have resulted in prospective cognition in general (including episodic memory) and prospective planning in particular (also cf. Savage-Rumbaugh 1994).

Following Osvath and Gärdenfors (2005), I suggest that the Oldowan culture (2.5–1.6 million years ago) created an ecological niche that led to the evolution of prospective planning.[2] Osvath and Gärdenfors write:

> The appearance of the first sharp edged stone tools in the archaeological record roughly coincides with a series of other relevant events in the human evolution. Ice sheets started to grow in the northern parts of the world, and Africa experienced deforestation and expanding savannas. The increased grasslands reduced the floral food resources for the

hominids, as the savannah is only about half as productive as a tropical forest. On the other hand, the production of herbivores on the savannah is almost three times as high, yielding a markedly larger mammal biomass...These ecological changes resulted in selective pressures on the hominids that lead them to change their diet from predominantly vegetarian to more protein and fat based. (2005:5)

Bickerton (2002:213–14) argues that the savannah conditions forced the hominins to use a wider variety of food sources than the other primates and that these food sources were more transient and scattered than the predominantly vegetarian food sources exploited by the other primates. From this he concludes that the daily traveled ranges of the early hominins must have been larger than those of extant apes. In particular, there is clear evidence that *transport* of the artifacts (at least the stone tools) was an important trait of the Oldowan culture (Toth 1985).

Following Plummer (2004), the main components of the Oldowan culture can be recognized as: (1) the manufacturing and use of stone tools; (2) the transport of artifacts (at least the stone tools); (3) the transport of pieces of carcasses; and (4) the use of accumulation spots. The most significant advantage of this culture is that it enabled a much wider exploitation of species that provided meat. It is not quite clear who manufactured the Oldowan tools, but Plummer (2004:127) concludes his analysis by saying that *H. habilis* were probably the makers 2.3–2.0 million years ago and *H. erectus* 2.0–1.6 million years ago.

I am not suggesting that the Oldowan culture initially required agents with advanced prospective cognition. Rather, the development of this culture and of prospective cognition should be viewed as a form of co-evolution. Osvath and Gärdenfors (2005:8) write: "The Oldowan life style was in a way signified by an extension in time and space. For example, there were long delays between the acquisition and the use of a tool, as well as considerable geographical distances between the sources of tool raw material sources and killing sites. The fitness of the hominids in this niche would increase with adaptations for long ranging, as shown in the morphological remains. These morphological adaptations must also have been related to behavioral adaptations." It is reasonable to assume that the behavioral adaptations were mainly a result of an evolving prospective cognition.

Another aspect of prospective thinking that is important from a collaborative point of view concerns *division of labor.* Dividing tasks within the group could solve a multitude of needs at once. Some individuals might carry throwing stones, some might carry sharp edges, and others could carry water or wooden tools. It is a way of optimizing the carrying resources of the group, which is probably already burdened with carrying infants. Such cooperation requires a shared representation of a future goal, and, as I shall argue, it is dependent on being communicated via protolanguage.

The modern human form of hunting and gathering is heavily dependent on prospective cognition. The individual must in some sense be able to imagine other individuals currently outside his or her immediate sensory scope doing their part of the common tasks. This awareness does not allow that the individual immediately consumes all the obtained food, but involves a future sharing of the food that results from the group efforts.

These considerations present some reasons why complex prospective cognition evolved within the Oldowan culture (for a more detailed account, see Osvath and Gärdenfors 2005). Once the period of the Acheulean tools is reached, beginning about 1.57 million years ago, it is apparent that prospective cognition was in full use, making it possible for *H. erectus* to spread over the Old World. Overall, it can be said that prospective cognition fits well with the lifestyle of the hunter/scavenger-gatherer and highly energy-consuming *H. erectus* (Plummer 2004:128).

INTERSUBJECTIVITY

The second form of cognition that, in comparison to other animals, is well developed in humans is intersubjectivity, which in this context means *the sharing and understanding of others' mentality.* The term "mentality" is taken here to involve not only beliefs, but all sorts of forms of consciousness such as emotions, desires, attentional foci, and intentions. In the philosophical debate, intersubjectivity is often called having a "theory of mind" (see e.g., Premack and Woodruff 1978, Tomasello 1999, Gärdenfors 2003). I will avoid this term since it often presumes that one can understand the beliefs of others, something that, on the account presented here, is but one aspect of intersubjectivity.

A prerequisite for an animal (or a human) to entertain any form of intersubjectivity is that it has an inner world. The crucial issue is whether an individual has any representation of other individuals' inner worlds. The question of whether a nonhuman animal or a child exhibits intersubjectivity does not have a simple yes or no answer. For this purpose, intersubjectivity will here be decomposed into five capacities. In Gärdenfors (2001, 2003), I discussed four: representing the emotions of others (empathy), representing the attention of others, representing the intentions of others, and representing the beliefs and knowledge of others (theory of mind). To these I now want to add one more: representing the desires of others.

From the analysis of these five factors it will be clear that humans exhibit more intersubjectivity than other animals. In particular, we have a well-developed competence for representing the beliefs of others, but we also excel at forming joint intentions (Tomasello et al. 2005b) and joint beliefs. As I shall argue, these differences are crucial for advanced forms of cooperation and for the emergence of language.

1. Representing the *emotions* of others. At this level one can, for example, understand that someone else is in pain. This is what is usually meant by *empathy* (Preston and de Waal 2003). Even though one can understand others' emotions, it does not mean that one understands what they believe or want.

Bodily expressions of emotions have a communicative purpose. The expressions are most obvious among social animals. The evolutionary explanation for this seems to be that a capacity for *empathy* leads to greater solidarity within the group.

2. Representing the *desires* of others. This involves understanding that the other may not like the same things as you do. Emotions concern the inner state of an individual, without reference to an external object. A desire is a positive attitude towards some external object or event. Understanding that somebody has a desire for something therefore involves more than understanding emotions. Results from child development studies suggest that at 18 months old children can understand that others have different desires than they have themselves (e.g., Wellman and Liu 2004, Gopnik and Meltzoff 1997).

3. Representing the *attention* of others. This means that one can understand, for example, what someone else is looking at.

Humans, other primates, and some other mammals are good at following the direction of other individuals' gazes (Emery 2000, Kaminski et al. 2005). Even very young children can understand where other people are looking. A more sophisticated form of attention is to succeed in drawing *joint attention* to an object. If I see that you are looking at an object and you see that I see the same object, we have established joint attention. This presupposes that both you and I can achieve second-order attention. To achieve joint attention is a necessary condition for deliberate cooperation.

4. Representing the *intentions* of others. This capacity means, above all, being able to understand the objective that may lie behind another individual's behavior.

As Kant and others have argued, humans have a powerful inclination to look for *causes* in the world. By reasoning about causes and effects, we become better at predicting the future. The ability to distinguish phenomena caused by other agents underpins the capacity of understanding intentionality in other individuals' behavior. When we see that something is caused by an agent, our cognitive system presumes that there is some purpose for the act, in other words, that it is intentional. Humans thus find it very easy to create a representation of the objective of an action—we see other people's behavior as being goal-directed.

Tomasello et al. (2005b) strongly emphasize the role of *sharing intentions.* They write that "the crucial difference between human cognition and that of other species is the ability to participate with others in collaborative activities with shared goals and intentions: shared intentionality" (Tomasello et al. 2005b:675). At around 9 to 12 months of age, infants begin to understand other individuals as intentional and then they can begin to interact with them in activities with shared goals. For example, an adult and an infant can create a shared goal to build a tower of blocks together.

An even stronger form of intersubjectivity is to achieve *joint intention.* This involves an individual understanding the plans of somebody else and coordinating its own intention with the goals of the other. This involves that "I intend that you intend" and that "you intend that I intend" and that both are aware of these second-order intentions. When one can coordinate roles in working towards a goal, then joint intention is achieved. For example, in building a tower of blocks the child may understand that the adult holds the tower steady while the child places new blocks. In human children, joint intentions seem to develop between 12 and 15 months of age. This capacity is obviously important for advanced forms of cooperation.

5. Representing the *beliefs* and *knowledge* of others. This ability involves, among other things, understanding that others do not know the same things as you do.

Several experiments have been performed to test whether apes and monkeys can represent the beliefs of others. Most experiments focus on whether they understand that "seeing is knowing." So far the outcomes are negative and therefore there is nothing to suggest that nonhuman primates have representations of others' beliefs and knowledge.

It is easier to test whether young children can understand that "seeing is knowing," since one can communicate with them through language from a fairly early age. A common type of test of children's understanding of other people's beliefs concerns whether they can understand that someone else has a *false* belief about what the world is like. This is one of several types of experiments that suggest that a representation of others' beliefs and knowledge develops in humans at the age of three to four (see e.g., Perner, Leekam, and Wimmer 1987, Gopnik and Astington 1988, Mitchell 1997). Variations of the false belief tasks have also been performed with chimpanzees, but so far there is no indication that they understand the beliefs of others (Call and Tomasello 1999).

Humans do not only know that someone else knows, that is have second-order knowledge. They can also have higher orders of knowledge and belief, such as "Of course I care about how you imagined I thought you perceived I wanted you to feel." This capacity forms the basis for *joint beliefs,* which is often called *common knowledge.* I argue (2007a) that the capacity for joint beliefs facilitates advanced forms of human cooperation, such as cooperation based on conventions and cooperation based on contracts.

In the discussion on intersubjectivity, or "theory of mind," in ethology and animal psychology, the focus has been on animals' and humans' capacity for *deception.* This has also been dubbed the Machiavellian intelligence of animals (Whiten and Byrne 1988, 1997). It is argued that this escalation of deceptive strategies and counter-moves creates a long-term evolutionary pressure that makes individuals better able to interpret each other's intentions and beliefs (Dennett 1988).

In contrast, I focus on the role of *cooperation* in hominin societies as a selective factor behind the evolution of human intersubjectivity. I shall argue that the two forms of cooperation that will be presented in the following section presume joint intentions and beliefs and then argue that this in turn facilitates the evolution of protolanguage and language with syntax. Since the current evidence concerning the intersubjectivity of other animals does not indicate that they can achieve joint intentions or joint beliefs, this will explain why only humans have developed protolanguage and language.

TWO UNIQUELY HUMAN FORMS OF COOPERATION

Humans as well as some animals cooperate in order to reach common goals. There are many ways of cooperating, some of which are not cooperation in the literal sense of the word. Among these one may count more or less instinctive coordination of behavior, such as that seen among termites building hills or honeybees gathering food. At the other end of the scale, we find human cooperation that depends on elaborate long-term planning and negotiation. In this section, I shall describe two forms of cooperation that seem to be unique to humans and that require prospective cognition as well as advanced forms of intersubjectivity.

There are many ways of defining cooperation. A broad definition is that it consists of joint actions that confer mutual benefits.[3] A more narrow definition concerns situations in which joint action poses a dilemma, the paradigmatic example being "the prisoner's dilemma," so that in the short run an individual would be better off not cooperating. Here, I will focus on the more narrow definition.

Collaborating for Future Goals

For many forms of cooperation among animals, it seems that representations are not needed. If the common goal is *present* in the actual environment, for example food to be eaten or an enemy to be fought, the collaborators need not focus on a joint representation of it before acting. If, on the other hand, the goal is detached, that is, distant in time or space, then a *joint* representation of it must be produced before cooperative action can be taken. For example, building a common dwelling requires coordinated planning of how to obtain the building material and advanced collaboration in the construction. Among other things, this depends on forming joint intentions, which is an advanced form of intersubjectivity that seems to be unique to humans.

Another problem concerning collaboration in order to reach a future goal is that the *value* of the goal cannot be determined from the given environment, unlike a goal that is already present on the scene. The value of the goal has to be estimated by each individual or communicated between individuals. The suite of behavioral adaptations of early hominins such as *H. habilis* opened up new forms of future-oriented cooperation. For example, Plummer (2004:139) writes: "Given that body size often predicts rank in the carnivore guild, an individual *H. habilis* would likely not have fared well in a contest with many of its contemporary carnivores. Competition with large carnivores may have favored cohesive groups and coordinated group movements in *H. habilis,* cooperative behavior including group defense, diurnal foraging (as many large predators preferentially hunt at night) with both hunting and scavenging being practiced as the opportunities arose, and the ability (using stone tools) to rapidly dismember large carcasses so as to minimize time spent at death sites."

In general terms, cooperation about future goals requires that *the inner worlds of the individuals be coordinated,* in other words, that they can *share visions.* Some visions are about rather concrete goals. For instance, the chief of a tribe can try to convince the inhabitants that they should cooperate in digging a common well that everybody will benefit from or in building a defensive wall that will increase the security of everybody. The goal requires efforts by the members of the community, but it can still have a positive net benefit for all involved. The central question, that will be addressed below, is what kind of communication is required to make it possible to share visions within a community.

Indirect Reciprocity

In a social species, an individual often faces a decision whether to cooperate or not. In game theory, situations of the prisoners' dilemma type have been analyzed. However, in these analyses your potential collaboration partners are determined in advance. Most of the game theoretical modeling does not consider that the most important question is: How do you know *whom* to cooperate with? Here I agree with Dessalles (2007:360): "Some of our ancestors who belonged to the first species of *Homo,* say, began to form sizeable coalitions. In such a 'political' context, finding good allies becomes essential."

In an iterated game of the prisoners' dilemma type, one player can retaliate against another's defection. Trivers (1971) argues that this possibility can make cooperation more attractive and leads to what he calls *reciprocal altruism.* This form of cooperation can be formulated as a slogan: "You scratch my back and I'll scratch yours."

Reciprocal altruism is found in some animal species (Wilkinson 1984, de Waal and Bosnan 2006)[4] and is common among humans. However, in humans one often finds more extreme forms of altruism: "I help you and somebody else will help me." This form of cooperation has been called *indirect reciprocity* and it seems to be more or less unique to humans. A possible exception comes from a study by Warneken and Tomasello (2006). They let three human-raised juvenile chimpanzees watch when a human attempted, but failed to achieve different goals. The chimps sometimes helped the humans, but mainly in situations where the humans reached for but failed to grasp objects. However, it is not clear that these cases of helping are indirect reciprocity since the chimpanzees can perhaps expect reciprocation on part of the human. In contrast, Warneken and Tomasello (2006) also showed that 18-month-old human infants helped an adult experimenter in various scenarios. In a follow-up experiment, Warneken et al. (2007) showed that the children helped irrespective of being rewarded for it. Thus the evidence that their behavior is true indirect reciprocity is quite strong.

Nowak and Sigmund (2005) show that, under certain conditions, indirect reciprocity can function as an evolutionarily stable strategy. However, as we shall see, their explanation depends on strong assumptions concerning the communication of the interactors. The key concept in Nowak and Sigmund's evolutionary model is that of the *reputation* of an individual.[5] The reputation of individual *i* is built up from some members of the society observing *i*'s behavior towards third parties and the observers spreading this information to the other members of the society. In this way a level of reputation for *i* being a cooperator can be, more or less, known by all the members of the group. Then the level of *i*'s reputation is used by any other individual when deciding whether to help *i* or not in a situation of need. It should be noted that reputation is not something that is visible to all others, unlike status markers such as a raised tail among wolves, but each individual must keep a private account of the reputations of all others. In support of the evolutionary model, Semmann, Krambeck, and Milinski (2005) demonstrate experimentally that building a reputation through cooperation is valuable for future social interactions, not only within but also *outside* one's own social group.

In these interactions it is important to distinguish between *justified* and *unjustified* defections. If a potential receiver has defected repeatedly in the past, the presumptive donor can be justified in defecting, as a form of punishment. However, the donor then runs a risk that his own reputation drops. To prevent this, the donor should communicate that the reason that she defects is that the receiver has a bad reputation, which will make it possible for other individuals to understand the intentions of the presumptive donor.

Nowak and Sigmund (2005) say that a strategy is first order if the assessment of an individual *i* in the group depends only on *i*'s actions. More sophisticated strategies distinguish between justified and unjustified defections. A strategy is called second order if it depends on the reputation of the receiver, and third order if it additionally depends on the reputation of the donor. Nowak and Sigmund show that only eight of the possible strategies are evolutionarily stable and that all these strategies depend on the distinction between justified and unjustified defection.

The trust that is built up in reciprocal altruism is dyadic, that is, a relation between two individuals. In contrast, reputation is an emergent *social* notion involving everybody in the group. On this point, Nowak and Sigmund (2005:1296) write: "Indirect reciprocity is situated somewhere between direct reciprocity and public goods. On the one hand it is a game between two players, but it has to be played within a larger group."

Nowak and Sigmund note, without spelling out any details, that indirect reciprocity seems to require some form of "theory of mind." An individual watching a second individual (donor) helping a third (receiver) (or not helping a third in need) must judge that the donor does something "good" (or "bad") to the receiver.[6] The form of intersubjectivity required for such comparisons includes empathy, but also, more importantly, the ability to understand the *intention* of the donor (Gärdenfors 2003, 2008).

There may exist still other mechanisms that influence the reputation of an individual. In many situations people are not only willing to cooperate but they also punish free riders, that is, individuals who benefit from the cooperation of others without cooperating themselves. The punishing behavior is difficult to explain because the punishment is costly and also the cooperative non-punishers benefit (Fehr and Gächter 2002). Barclay (2005) presents some evidence that the reputation of a punisher increases and that people are more willing to cooperate with punishers. In combination with the mechanisms presented above, this indicates that punishing behavior is rewarded in the long run (see also Sigmund et al. 2001) and can stabilize cooperation in iterated interactions of the prisoners' dilemma type (Lindgren 1997). In contrast to human behavior, there is no evidence for altruistic punishment among animals in nature (van Schaik and Kappeler 2006), although de Waal and Brosnan (2006) report experimentally induced refusal to cooperate that is costly for the non-cooperative individual.

SYMBOLIC COMMUNICATION: PROTOLANGUAGE AND LANGUAGE WITH SYNTAX

To sum up, I have argued that the evolution of prospective cognition and intersubjectivity facilitated more advanced forms of cooperation among the hominins. I next turn to the types of communication that are relevant for an analysis of the demands of the two types of cooperation presented in the previous section. A decisive difference between a language and the signals employed by animals is that signals only refer to what is present in the environment of the animal. Bees only dance directly after having returned to the hive when they have found nectar. Vervets only signal when danger is immediate. In contrast, with the aid of a language humans can communicate about things that are not here and now or that may not even exist. Following the previous terminology, one can say that the symbolic words of a language stand for detached representations. The use of representations replaces the use of environmental features in communication. Language is also the tool by which humans can make their desires, intentions, and beliefs known to each other. It therefore builds on a rich inner world.

In order to formulate this idea more succinctly, I shall distinguish between *signals* and *symbols*.[7] Both signals and symbols are tools of communication that can be expressed in various ways, for example by sounds or gestures. Signals are about the surrounding world, while symbolic language is often about our inner worlds, i.e., about our imaginations, memories, plans, and dreams. An important consequence of this is that symbolic communication can be used to offload the demands of intersubjective understanding. With the aid of symbols, I can communicate my desires, intentions, and beliefs to you, so you do not have to rely on mindreading only.

The signals of an animal species are more or less identical in all members of the species (barring sexual and age differences). In contrast, a symbol is an arbitrary convention that you must *learn* in order to use it as a communicative tool. Using the Saussurian distinction between signifier and signified, Dessalles (2007:180) expresses the evolutionary importance of this point as follows: "The reason why some authors…see the relaxing of the signified-signifier link as a decisive moment in the evolutionary history of language is no doubt that at the one and the same time it originates ambiguity and semantics. Meaning ceases to be a simple reflex association and requires some cognitive processing."

The transition from a signaling system to a symbolic language was, most likely, not made in one step. Bickerton (1990) and other researchers (e.g., Dessalles 2007) propose that there was a stage in the evolution of language when a *protolanguage,* containing only the semantic components of language, was used. Bickerton (1990:117) says that protolanguage is "something other than full human language—an alternative means of communication that incorporates some features of language but rigorously excludes others." According to Bickerton, *H. erectus* mastered a protolanguage and it is not until *H. sapiens* that one finds a language with a grammatical structure.

In fact, the transition from a signaling system to protolanguage presumably went through several steps. Partly following Donald (1991) and Zlatev et al. (2005), I want to use the following seven criteria to characterize different types of systems of signs ("sign" is here used in Peirce's [1931–35] sense including signals, icons, and symbols):

1. *Cross-modality.* The signs involve a cross-modal mapping between proprioception (experience of the body) and exteroception (experience of the external world—normally dominated by vision).

2. *Volition.* Signs are realized by actions that are under volitional control.

3. *Representation.* A sign corresponds—either indexically, iconically, or symbolically—to some action, object, or event, but is at the same time differentiated from it by the subject.

4. *Communicative sign function.* The subject intends the sign to stand for some action, object or event for an addressee, and for the addressee to understand this.

5. *Compositionality.* Some signs are composed by meaningful sub-acts that relate systematically to each other and to other similar acts.

6. *Conventionality.* A sign is conventional, that is, a part of mutual knowledge, and must be learned.

7. *Grammaticality.* The system of signs contains syntactic markers and positions.

A signaling system satisfies only the first condition. Zlatev et al. (2005) call a communication system that satisfies criteria 1–3 a system of *dyadic mi-*

mesis and a system that satisfies criteria 1–4 a system of *triadic mimesis.* Examples of dyadic mimesis are imperative pointing and do-as-I-do-imitation; and examples of triadic mimesis are joint intention, declarative pointing, and pantomime.[8] It is important to note that protolanguage, as described by Bickerton (1990) and others, satisfies criteria 1–6 and that full language satisfies all seven criteria.

As a complement to the separation between protolanguage and (syntactic) language, Dessalles (2007) introduces a distinction between *protosemantics* and (predicative) *semantics.* According to him, protosemantics consists of joining the images evoked by words into *scenes.*[9] The scenes that are construed are to a large extent dependent on the context of an utterance. Even so, protolanguage is hampered by a manifold of semantic ambiguities. If a 2-year-old girl comes home from kindergarten and says "not eat fish," we do not know whether she, or one of her friends, has not eaten the fish (or did not want to eat it) or whether it is the fish in the aquarium that did not eat the candy offered by the girl.

What Dessalles partly misses in his description of protosemantics is that describing a scene is mostly valuable *when the scene is not present* in the communication situation. If the scene to be described is present, then a signaling system—for instance, pointing—could do much of the job. Thus protosemantics is primarily advantageous where non-present situations, for example future situations, are to be described.

In semantics proper, individuals, objects, properties, and relations are not just named, but properties and relations are predicated of individuals and objects (Hurford 2003, Dessalles 2007). In my opinion, Dessalles puts too much emphasis on predication, since it seems possible to express predication also in protolanguage. What is important is that in full language, the syntactic tools can be used to mark different kinds of *roles* that relate the elements of a statement, for example agent versus patient, and temporal relations. The resulting grammatical structure gives much less leeway for ambiguities in meaning. Dessalles (2007:219) notes that "syntax can establish dependences among predicates without any need of a system of variables. It does this by bringing together in a single phrase the two predicates to be linked."

Dessalles (2007) also argues that language with syntax opens up the possibility of *thematic segmentation,* that is, making distinctions between the theme and the reference point in a particular space. Thematic segmentation can occur in time as well as in ordinary space. Dessalles argues that the semantics of a syntactically full-blown language is a combination of the scenes created by protosemantic mechanisms and different kinds of thematic segmentation.[10]

I find the sequence of going from signaling systems to protolanguage to language with syntax and the parallel development of meaning systems from stimulus-response couplings to protosemantics to semantics very useful as a description of the steps in the evolution of human communication. However, in addition to describing the characteristics of a particular system of communication, it is desirable to give an independent evolutionary (ecological or cultural) explanation of why this particular kind of system has arisen. Along this line, Dessalles (2007:173) requires that it must be shown that protosemantics and full semantics are "functionally and locally optimal." This means that protolanguage must function for a particular communicative purpose that cannot be achieved with a signaling system, and that it is a local equilibrium for this purpose. The next section will be devoted to presenting my answer to what are the ecological and social forces that have generated the protolanguage and language as unique human systems of communication.

THE COGNITIVE AND COMMUNICATIVE DEMANDS OF HUMAN COOPERATION

The concepts and material from the preceding sections will now be brought together to analyze the cognitive and communicative demands of two forms of cooperation discussed in a previous section, namely, cooperation about future goals and indirect reciprocity. I will argue that a major reason for the evolution of language is that it enhances cooperation.

Cooperation about Future Goals Requires Protolanguage

In previous work (Brinck and Gärdenfors 2003, Gärdenfors 2003, 2004, Osvath and Gärdenfors 2005), it has been proposed that there is a strong connection between a lifestyle dependent on prospective cognition and the evolution of symbolic communication. In brief, the argument is that symbolic language makes it possible to *cooperate about future goals* in an efficient way. The detached goals and the means to reach them are picked out and externally shared through the symbolic communication. This kind of sharing gives humans an enormous advantage concerning cooperation in comparison to other species.

If somebody has an idea about a goal she wishes to attain, she can use protolanguage or language to communicate her thoughts. In this way, language makes it possible to share visions about the future. It should be noted that this involves establishing joint attention to elements of the inner worlds of the interlocutors, which is a fairly advanced form of intersubjectivity.

The question that has to be answered is why protolanguage is necessary for this kind of communication. If the communicated entity is not present, direct signaling will not work. If I want to refer to a deer that I saw down by the river yesterday, merely pointing will not help, nor will a call signal. Communicating about non-present entities clearly requires detached representations. As Dessalles (2007) argues, the crucial feature of protolanguage is that it makes it possible to *describe non-actual scenes*. He writes: "[T]he words put together in protolanguage are a way to bring to mind concrete scenes, either experienced or imagined" (2007:174). It is interesting that Arp (2006) also argues, from a different perspective, that scene visualization is unique in the *Homo* line.

Now, describing imagined scenes is a *sine qua non* for cooperation about future goals. The goal is not present, the actions leading to it must be imagined, and their consequences must be evaluated. There is no way a signaling system can achieve this. A minimal requirement is that the communicator can form combinations of the detached symbols of a protolanguage. For example, by uttering "Meet mountain well sunset" one individual can convey to another an image of a scene that constitutes a plan for a future goal that is of mutual benefit for both individuals. A particular form of cooperation for the future is division of labor. With the aid of protolanguage simple commands can be expressed and generate various ways of dividing the tasks within a group.

In brief, the long-ranging lives of the hominins during the Oldowan culture resulted in a selective pressure for a communicative system that made it possible for the members of a group to share visions of future collaborative scenes. The evolution of protolanguage and its corresponding protosemantics can have led to a locally evolutionarily optimal solution for a society that was built around cooperation about future goals.[11] In other words, my thesis is that there has been a co-evolution of cooperation about future goals and protolanguage. However, without the presence of prospective cognition, the potential for cooperation and the ensuing selective pressures that resulted in protolanguage would not have emerged.

In contrast to most other theories of the evolution of language, the ideas presented here also explain why only humans have language. Being able to cooperate about future goals requires prospective planning as well as an advanced theory of mind. Both these cognitive capacities are far more developed in humans than in other animals.

Indirect Reciprocity Requires Predicative Language

It can be argued that indirect reciprocity is a way of preparing for future cooperation, since it is a mechanism for finding out whom one can trust to be cooperative. However, the success of indirect reciprocity depends heavily on the mechanism of reputation. Indirect reciprocity, according to the model presented by Nowak and Sigmund (2005), requires several cognitive and communicative mechanisms. The minimal cognitive requirements are that one should be able to: (a) recognize the relevant individuals over time, (b) remember and update the reputation scores of these individuals, and (c) exercise empathy and understanding of intentions to judge whether a particular donor action is "good" or "bad." In addition to this, the communication system of the individuals in the group must be able to (d) refer to individuals in their absence, e.g., by names, and (e) express that "x was good to y" and "y was bad to x."[12] The latter expressions are clear examples of ascribing roles to persons. They are also difficult to convey without ambiguity within a protolanguage: without markers for roles, "x was good to y" cannot be distinguished from "y was good to x." In this context it should also be noted that Nowak and Sigmund's (2005) model considers only two kinds of reputation—"good" or "bad." It goes without saying that in real groups communication about reputation builds on finer nuances.

In general, the communication required for functioning forms of indirect reciprocity concerns different aspects of whom you can trust. This involves assigning various properties and roles to different individuals. The information is often conveyed in the absence of the individual discussed—and it can hence be characterized as gossip. Gossip normally contains expressions of the form "who did what to whom," which involves identifying thematic roles. Thus gossip plays a central role in the evolution of language according to the theory presented here, but it does not function as a replacement for grooming as Dunbar (1996) suggests.

A general feature of language with syntax is that it contains much more binding of variables—properties to objects and relations between entities—than can be accomplished in a protolanguage. As Dessalles (2007:72) points out, without syntax "it can be a tricky business even to explain a situation involving three characters." The upshot is that the communicative requirements for cooperation about the future are weaker than those for indirect reciprocity. The hypotheses put forward in this chapter are that they correspond to the expressive powers of protolanguage and syntactic language, respectively.

Of course, the need for communication is dependent on the size of the group facing the potentially cooperative situations. In a tightly connected group where everybody sees everybody else most of the time, there is no need for a reputation mechanism. However, in large and loosely connected groups, these mechanisms are not sufficient, but some form of communication about non-present individuals is required. A consequence of this argument is that the evolutionary mechanisms favoring reciprocal altruism will be stronger when the population density rises and when there are increasing distant contacts between people (Leonard and Robertson 2000). It seems that the conditions for reciprocal altruism are similar to those cultural innovations as analyzed by Shennan (2001). However, since hominid populations have probably been sparse with bottlenecks (Ambrose 1998, Richerson, Bettinger, and Boyd 2005), the full significance of reciprocal altruism may only have applied during the last 50,000 years, which coincides with the major cultural expansions.

CONCLUSION

The evolutionary relationships between cooperation, symbolic communication, prospective cognition, and intersubjectivity are intertwined in complicated co-evolutionary processes. These relationships have been important for human evolution, but they must be further analyzed in order to get a better understanding of the evolution of human communication.

The argument in this chapter has been that prospective cognition and increased intersubjectivity open up new forms of cooperation involving future goals and indirect reciprocity. Such cooperation has resulted in selective advantages for the most successful hominin groups. The new forms of cooperation created a need for more advanced communication in order to *share* visions about the future goals. I have argued that the required form of communication is symbolic since this form makes it much more efficient to communicate about detached needs and goals.

The main argument has focused on two uniquely human forms of cooperation: cooperation for future goals and indirect reciprocity. Partly building on Dessalles' (2007) analysis of the mechanisms of protolanguage and syntactic language, the two new theses of this chapter have been that protolanguage is an efficient system for communication about cooperation about future goals and that language with syntax is an efficient system for communication about indirect reciprocity.

So far, the two theses presented here are mainly speculative just-so stories. However, it is possible that they can be given further empirical support by new analyses of the available archaeological data concerning hominins. As regards the role of cooperation for future goals, we find evidence for prospective cognition already in the Oldowan culture, but it would be helpful for our understanding of when protolanguage evolved if evidence for cooperation about the future could be established.

There are three areas that seem to be particularly relevant for this problem.[13] First, signs of *cultural division of labor* (e.g., Hawkes et al. 1998, O'Connell, Hawkes, and Blurton Jones 1999, Bliege Bird 1999) would indicate communication about future cooperation. Second, *big game hunting* also seems to require such communication. The spears found at Schöningen (Thieme 1999) seem to be an indication of such hunting by *H. heidelbergensis* 400 kya. The findings from this site are still awaiting a detailed analysis concerning the cognitive and communicative implications. Third, *large constructions,* dwellings or others, would also be indications of communication about future cooperation. Although disputed, the Terra Amata construction (Villa 1983), which has been estimated to have been built 400 kya, is a possible candidate. Another relevant question is: if the predecessors to *H. floresiensis* crossed the strait to Flores by collaboratively constructing a raft or something similar, what kind of communication would be required for this task?

If my argument concerning protolanguage is correct, it is sufficient that there is clear evidence for one of these three areas. All in all, I believe the available archaeological evidence supports that cooperation for future goals and thus protolanguage was established at least 400 kya and thus well before the evolution of *H. sapiens.* This conclusion accords with Bickerton's

(1990) proposal that protolanguage emerged with *H. erectus,* although my argument is different from his. Similarly, it would be interesting to find out during which evolutionary period evidence for indirect reciprocity can be established in the archaeological data, for example in the form of an individual's reputation being of social importance. If the second thesis of this chapter is correct, this could be a clue to knowing when language with syntax evolved among the hominins.

NOTES

8.1   There is an extensive debate in the literature on what the appropriate meaning of "representation" is in this context (see e.g., Roitblat 1982, Vauclair 1990, Humphrey 1993, Gärdenfors 1996, 2003, Grush 1997).

8.2   For the classic analysis of the Oldowan culture, see Isaac 1977.

8.3   A stronger criterion, focused on human cooperation, is formulated by Bowles and Gintis (2003:429–30): "An individual behavior that incurs personal costs in order to engage in a joint activity that confers benefits exceeding these costs to other members of one's group."

8.4   Although this is disputed by Stevens and Hauser (2004).

8.5   A precursor to this concept is that of Sugden's (1986) "good standing".

8.6   This is in contrast to altruism towards kin, where an individual can experience as "good" that which improves its own reproductive fitness.

8.7   Following Peirce (1931–35), one could also discuss communication systems based on icons (see also Gärdenfors 2003). Icons also have a detached meaning and are partly conventional, so in this context they will be put on par with symbols.

8.8   Zlatev, Persson, and Gärdenfors (2005) argue that at least apes can communicate via dyadic mimesis (e.g., by gestures) and not only via signaling.

8.9   Images should be taken in a comprehensive sense so that forces (Talmy 1988, Gärdenfors 2007b) and emotions are also parts of the scenes that are created (see Dessalles 2007:249).

8.10   "Meaning is not limited either to thematic relations or to a mental scene stimulated by words. The interpretation of language results in two representations which are different in kind, one of them being a thematic representation and the other a representation which, in concrete contents, consists of a scene" (Dessalles 2007:248).

8.11   This kind of local optimality is one of the four conditions that Dessalles (2007:173–74) presents for protolanguage.

8.12   In contrast, van Schaik and Kappeler write: "The three basic conditions for reputation are individual recognition, variation in personality traits, and curiosity about the outcome of interactions involving third parties" (2006:15). In my opinion, however, these criteria are too weak since they do not include that reputation is communicated.

8.13 I am grateful to Steven Mithen and April Nowell for helpful discussions on this topic.

9

The Cathedral Model for the Evolution of Human Cognition

STEVEN MITHEN

INTRODUCTION

In my 1996 book entitled *The Prehistory of the Mind* I used the analogy of building a cathedral for how the modern mind evolved. More than a decade has passed since this model was proposed during which there has been substantial new research concerning the evolution of the mind. So in this chapter I will reflect on the "cathedral model" with regard to its status as a viable interpretation for human cognitive evolution. To do so, I will initially provide a brief summary of the model and then consider three areas of research and their impact on the model: new archaeological discoveries, research on the evolution of language and music, and changing conceptions of material culture.

THE PROBLEM

The fundamental problem we need to tackle is how can modern humans be so biologically similar to our extant primate relatives, notably the chimpanzee, and yet also be so vastly different with regard to our behavior and culture? Simply stating that this is because our brains are three times larger than those of chimpanzees is not sufficient, primarily because so too were the brains of the Neandertals whose culture was also radically different from ours today.

The most notable aspect of modern human cognition is its diversity and creativity: we think and do all sorts of novel and often rather bizarre things for which there often appears to be no cultural, let alone evolutionary, precedent. In the mid 1990s this simple fact challenged the arguments for massive mental modularity being proposed by a particularly provocative group of self-styled Evolutionary Psychologists including Symonds, Cosmides, Tooby, and Pinker (e.g., Barkow, Cosmides, and Tooby 1992, Pinker 1994, 1997). The core of their argument was that the human mind evolved by the gradual accumulation of mental modules, each being selected in light of adaptive problems faced by our ancestors in the so-called environment of evolutionary adaptedness (EEA).

Two things were strikingly absent from their work and model: first, any consideration how such evolved minds could come up with novel ideas unrelated to those of relevance to the EEA (e.g., second law of thermodynamics, Bach's Cello Suites); second, any reference to the archaeological and fossil record, i.e., the actual evidence for past behavior and thought. Indeed such reference was almost universally absent from the writings of psychologists and others addressing cognitive evolution, with Donald (1991) providing a significant exception.

What was evident from the archaeological record in the mid 1990s was a dramatic change in the nature of past behavior (and thereby thought) at a relatively late stage in human evolution. This was once referred to as the "cultural explosion" and dated to between 50,000–30,000 years ago, as primarily manifested in the appearance of the Upper Paleolithic in Europe (Mellars 1973, 1989, Mellars and Stringer 1989). Just as important, however, was the dramatic change in behavior that occurred at the start of the last (and on-going) interglacial (ca. 11,600 years ago) with the independent origin of farming lifestyles in several areas of the world, the rapid spread of this lifestyle, soon followed by the emergence of so-called "civilization" (see Mithen 2003 for a review). The Evolutionary Psychologists' massive modularity model neither drew upon nor had any explanation for such radical changes in human behavior.

Despite the neglect of the archaeological evidence by the Evolutionary Psychologists, their arguments in the mid 1990s against the existence of a content-free, general purpose learning mechanism were highly persuasive (to me at least; see, e.g., Tooby and Cosmides 1989, H. Barrett, Cosmides, and Tooby 2007). Moreover, there were numerous lines of evidence from neuroscience and developmental psychology for at least some degree of modularity in the human mind (as reviewed in Mithen 1996: chap. 3). So the key problem was how to reconcile the arguments for mental modularity with the evidence from both the recent (i.e., post 50,000 years ago) archaeological record and the present day that modern humans are behaviorally and cognitively radically different from other animals, being capable of an unprecedented degree of creative thought.

THE CATHEDRAL MODEL

I proposed reconciliation in *The Prehistory of the Mind*. The essence of the cathedral model is to recognize that the Evolutionary Psychologists' model for a modular human mind appeared to be a far better fit to that of our large-brained hominin ancestors, such as *Homo heidelbergensis* and *neanderthalensis,* than it is for modern humans. The archaeological record of those hominin species, whom I collectively refer to as "Early Humans," suggests high levels of expertise in numerous areas of behavior, such as toolmaking and foraging, but provides no evidence for creative thought in terms of entirely novel ideas. As such, the "multiple mental module" model for the human mind, as proposed by the Evolutionary Psychologists referred to above, might be viable for these species. Personally, I would prefer to see bundles of these modules operating closely together and forming discrete and isolated cognitive domains or multiple intelligences. This would be the case of the immediate ancestor of modern humans in Africa. The cathedral model proposed that all that was required to achieve the cognitive creativity that characterizes modern humans was the addition of cross-modular integration, or what I described as cognitive fluidity (Mithen 1996).

The term 'cathedral model' derives from an analogy I used to explain the process of cognitive evolution. I compared this to the construction of a complex building, with evolution having to always tinker with a previous phase of the building rather than starting with a blank slate for each hominin species. The modular mind of early humans appeared to me to be rather like an architecturally complex Romanesque church, with numerous isolated chapels each of which represented a specialized cognitive domain. I suggested the evolution of the modern mind was akin to walls being knocked down between these chapels or at least windows being inserted in their walls: "To constitute the modern mind, the thoughts and knowledge

located in all of these chapels must be allowed to flow freely around the cathedral…harmonizing with each other to create ways of thought that could
never have existed within one chapel alone" (Mithen 1996:151).

More specifically, I proposed that the evolution of the mind occurred
by the gradual evolution of isolated cognitive domains, notably those for
interacting with the social world, the natural world, and material objects; I
referred to these as social, natural, and technological intelligences, having
been influenced by Gardner's (1983) theory of multiple intelligences in the
modern human mind. I conceived each of these "intelligences" as bundles
of modules of the type that Cosmides and Tooby had been describing, although I proposed that the modules interacted within—but not between—
each of the intelligences. Each of these would have constituted an isolated
"chapel" within the early human mind. By the time of the emergence of
Homo ergaster, soon after 2 million years ago, complex behavior was being
exhibited in the domains of social life, hunting and gathering, and the manipulation of objects—in some respects little different to that of modern
hunter-gatherers. But there was very limited, if any, interaction between
the cognitive domains within the mind of *Homo ergaster.*

This type of domain-specific mentality proved to be a remarkably successful adaptation. It enabled technological developments such as Acheulian
and Levalloisian technology, big game hunting, and dispersal into Eurasia,
requiring the exploitation of new types of environments. However, it also
acted as a severe constraint on the levels of invention and creativity. Consequently the archaeological record shows a long time-period of minor adaptive variation around a limited number of behavioral themes; at a coarse
scale of analysis this appears as gross cultural stability. Even though we are
dealing with a sequence of radical glacial-interglacial cycles, and populations that would have had both within and between group competition, we
see hardly any behavioral innovation in material culture, subsistence, or any
other form of behavior for more than a million years. There are no traces
of unambiguous symbolic activity. There are certainly several claims (see
Nowell, this volume) and some of these (e.g., Zilhão et al. 2010) may indeed
relate to the emergence of symbolic behavior from the final Neandertals in
Europe as discussed below.

The usual caveat has to be made here that the Paleolithic archaeological
record is poorly preserved and dated; while stone tool technology may display such cultural stability, there may have been an exotic and ever-chang-

ing range of artifacts made from organic materials. And while we lack any traces for body ornamentation such as shell beads and pendants, rock art or sculpture, there may have been an array of tattoos, ice carvings, and sand paintings. This might indeed be the case; but it appears intuitively unlikely that such artistic and symbolic activities might have been expressed in such inorganic and non-enduring material without having been expressed in bone and stone.

The domain-specific mentality appeared to reach its apogee with *Homo neanderthalensis.* The Neandertal archaeological record from Europe and Western Asia is known in considerable detail and demonstrates high levels of technical skill, big game hunting, and survival in a wide range of environmental conditions. A novel feature of the European/West Asian Middle Paleolithic (i.e., Neandertal) archaeological record is the presence of human burials. This is most likely a reflection of intense social relationships resulting in the mourning, memory of, and care for the deceased. Otherwise the essential characteristics of the record are not too dissimilar from the rest of the early Paleolithic in terms of a gross cultural stability and an absence of symbolic behavior. When writing *The Prehistory of the Mind,* attributing the Neandertals with a domain-specific mentality seemed the only feasible interpretation for the type of behavior manifest in their archaeological record—in some ways as complex as that of modern humans, while in others radically different.

One set of particularly telling pieces of evidence in support of this model was that concerning Neandertal demography and health (Trinkaus 1995). This indicated that they were a marginally viable population: if there was ever a population that could have benefited from some cultural innovations—spear throwers, projectile points, fish hooks, sewing needles, stone-built dwellings—it must have been the Neandertals. The fact that such innovations did not occur suggests not only a major cognitive constraint but the precise constraint that the domain-specific mentality would propose: the lack of cross modular/domain thought.

Neandertal domain-specific mentality evolved from that of *Homo heidelbergensis,* which was also the direct ancestor of *Homo sapiens.* The cathedral model suggested that cognitive evolution took an alternative direction within the African *Homo* lineage, with the emergence of links between what had been isolated cognitive domains/intelligences. Hence stores of knowledge and ways of thinking that had evolved for use in one specific behavioral domain could be integrated with those from others to generate new ways of thinking and behaving. This was used to explain the cultural innovations that were particularly evident in the Upper Paleolithic of Europe. The manufacture of bead necklaces, for instance, required the integration of social and technical intelligence, while that of specialized hunting tools required the integration of technical and natural history intelligence. Anthropomorphic thinking—as evident from imagery on cave walls such as the bison/woman of Chauvet—required the integration of natural history and social intelligence.

The cathedral model proposed that the evolution of fully modern language played a causal role in the emergence of cognitive fluidity. While some linguistic ability had been attributed to the Neandertals, this was largely restricted to communication about the social world, with the linguistic capacity being seen as evolving within the domain of social intelligence. The presence of "snippets of non-social information" in the utterances of modern humans was claimed to have been significant in the transition from a domain-specific to a cognitively fluid mentality. Also integral to this cognitive change was the emergence of fully modern consciousness regarding the non-social domain. This too had been proposed as originally evolving in the domain of social intelligence and hence the Neandertals had limited, if any, conscious awareness about their own knowledge regarding, say, toolmaking and natural history.

While the emergence of fully modern language and consciousness were regarded as important, it was proposed that the critical feature of the modern human mind was cognitive fluidity as this provided the capacity for analogy and metaphor. These were seen as the basis for the origin of art, religion, and science. As such, it appeared particularly appropriate to use an analogy itself when explaining the origins of the modern mind, that of the gradual construction of the cathedral of the mind.

The Prehistory of the Mind had an epilogue that considered the origins of agriculture. It was proposed that this was effectively an inevitable outcome of the cognitively fluid mind, once the appropriate environmental conditions appeared at the end of the Pleistocene. With the fluidity between natural history and social intelligence, for instance, plants and animals could be treated as children in terms of being cared for and fed, ultimately leading to domesticated strains. The Neandertals and other hominins with domain-specific mentalities would never have been able to develop such social relationships with animals and plants and hence never entered into the domain of farming lifestyles.

FOURTEEN YEARS ON

During the last fourteen years there have been significant developments in our knowledge of the archaeological record and understanding of human evolution. There has also been a veritable explosion in the quantity and quality of research on the evolution of the human mind, especially with regard to language. Many areas of the cognitive sciences have advanced considerably, especially neuroscience.

My own ability to keep pace with all of the new research has been limited, my focus having primarily been on archaeological fieldwork, especially with regard to the origins of agriculture (Finlayson and Mithen 2007), by which I am seeking to develop the ideas within the epilogue of *The Prehistory of the Mind* (e.g., Mithen 2007). But none of the research with which I am familiar has led me to question the essence of the cathedral model: that there was a shift from a domain-specific to a cognitively fluid mentality at a relatively late stage in human evolution. Indeed I have become more persuaded of the veracity of this model, it seeming to have been supported by new lines of evidence and ideas, some of which have resolved weaknesses in the original proposition or extended its breadth. So I will now discuss some of this new research that has challenged, enhanced, or extended the cathedral model for human cognitive evolution.

NEW ARCHAEOLOGICAL, FOSSIL, AND GENETIC EVIDENCE

Fourteen years ago there was still a valid debate to be had between those who favored the hypothesis that modern humans had origins in several distinct geographical regions in and out of Africa and those who held to a single African origin—although I was always committed to the latter. The weight of evidence is now so fully towards the single African origin that there is no further room for such debate. While this is perhaps primarily because of the astonishing development of human evolutionary genetics, there has also been a convergence between the dates for modern human origins based on the fossil (White et al. 2003, McDougall, Brown, and Fleagle 2005) and genetic (Ingman et al. 2000) evidence at ca. 200,000 years ago. Moreover, the pattern of loss of genetic diversity out of Africa has now been shown to be mirrored by the lost of phenotypic diversity in terms of craniometric measurements (Manica et al. 2007).

Perhaps of greater significance for cognitive evolution is that the earliest evidence for symbolic behavior is also now found in Africa and has been pushed back to at least 70,000 years ago, and possibly earlier in the African Middle Stone Age (MSA). Incised ochre fragments with repetitive geometric patterns from Blombos Cave (Henshilwood et al. 2002, 2004) provide unambiguous evidence for such symbolism, while a case can also be made for symbolic behavior in terms of the shell bead necklace from the same site and date (Henshilwood et al. 2004). The production of such objects requires cognitive fluidity, just as I originally argued in *The Prehistory of the Mind* for similar types of objects from the Upper Paleolithic of Europe. A similar case can be made for the bone tools and bifacially worked points from the Middle Stone Age (e.g., Henshilwood and Sealy 1995)—artifacts that most likely functioned in the social as well as the natural history and technical domains and that had required the integration of technical and natural history intelligence for their design and manufacture.

The finds from Blombos contributed to the review of Africa evidence published by McBrearty and Brooks (2000) provocatively entitled "The Revolution that Wasn't." This article claimed that there is a long-term gradual emergence of symbolic and complex behavior in the African record, challenging both the notion of a "cultural explosion" and that this had happened at the start of the Upper Paleolithic in Europe. Neither point is particularly contentious or challenging to the cathedral model as that had proposed at least a two-stage emergence of cognitive fluidity and had simply used the European Upper Paleolithic as an example, not the source, of new types of thinking. It does remain striking, however, that there still exists a significant time lag between the earliest unambiguous symbolic behavior at 70,000 years ago and the likely date for the origin of modern humans at 200,000 years ago. As the out-of-Africa dispersal appears to start soon after 70,000 years ago (Mellars 2006), a case might still be made for a significant cognitive change at that time. Indeed, I would now want to attribute this date to the emergence of fully modern cognitive fluidity.

These developments in our understanding of modern human origins and the MSA of Africa are compatible with the cathedral model. Indeed, they enhance the model by bringing the key behavioral and cognitive changes associated with modern humans into Africa and closer to the genetic and fossil evidence for modern human origins. Developments in our understanding of pre-modern humans have done likewise, although there remains room for alternative interpretations. In *Prehistory of the Mind* I argued that the cathedral model was falsifiable simply by the discovery of unambiguous symbolic behavior by pre-modern humans, ideally a figurine in an incontestably Lower or Middle Paleolithic context in Europe. Claims for such symbolic behavior by pre-modern humans continue to be made, notably for the Berekhat Ram "figurine" (d'Errico and Nowell 2000, Nowell, this volume). But none of these have been convincing—with the possible exception of recent finds from Cuevo de los Aviones and Cueva Anton, Iberia (Zilhão et al. 2010).

These finds are perforated and pigment-stained marine shells dated to 50,000 years ago, which are claimed to indicate the symbolic use of ornaments and body painting by Neandertals (Zilhão et al. 2010). That interpretation remains contentious: pigment use need have no symbolic purpose and the shells may have been naturally perforated. If Zilhão et al.'s (2010) interpretation is correct, this would suggest an emergence of some elements of cognitive fluidity in the late Neandertals, perhaps comparable to those traces in the early modern humans from the Near East (e.g., Qafzeh), as described in *The Prehistory of the Mind* (Mithen 1996:202ff.).

Two discoveries of an equally contentious nature are the Schöningen spears (Thieme 1997) and *Homo floresiensis* (Brown et al. 2004). Some extravagant claims have been made regarding the 300–400,000 year old spears, most likely made by *Homo heidelbergensis,* and their cognitive implications (e.g., Dennell 1997). The extent to which they really were designed and manufactured to be the equivalent of Paleolithic javelins remains to be established. A more parsimonious interpretation is that they are little more than sharpened sticks with their seemingly perfectly designed weighting being a by-product of the raw material from which they were made. In this regard they certainly do not appear to be any more complex to manufacture than an Acheulian biface or a Levallois core and certainly within the capacity of a technical intelligence isolated from the rest of cognition.

The remains of *Homo floresiensis* come from Flores Island, Indonesia, and are characterized by small bodies, small brains, and a range of novel anatomical features, dating from at least 40,000 years ago to 12,000 years ago (Brown et al. 2004). Numerous interpretations have been offered; I find the most compelling suggestion to be that this is a dwarfed form of *Homo erectus,* originating from the arrival of a small population of that species on Flores Island at or around 800,000 years ago—the likely date for the stone artifacts on the island described by Morwood et al. (1998). If this is the case, it poses two potential challenges to the cathedral model. First, if *Homo erectus* had used a raft, or even a boat, to cross to Flores Island, such a construction might be beyond what is feasible with a domain-specific mentality. The alternative is that no such "artifact" was constructed and a natural raft was used, either deliberately or "accidentally" as the product of a tsunami event. The very fact that a dwarfing process occurred indicates that there was no regular contact between Flores and other islands and hence makes the likelihood of a one-off chance crossing the most likely.

The second potential challenge to the cathedral model from Flores arises from the stone tools that are claimed to be associated with *Homo floresiensis* (Morwood et al. 2004). These have been described as blades and hence far beyond what would have expected from the capacity of a 417cc. brain, one smaller than that of a chimpanzee. There are three problems here. First, the association between the stone tools and the fossils remains unclear: were they really made by *Homo floresiensis?* Second, we lack detailed technical descriptions of the so-called blades to assess the skill required in their production. Are they, for instance, from prepared platform cores? We should note that blades in general are no longer taken as a significant marker for modern human cognition (Bar-Yosef and Kuhn 1999). Third, we simply do not understand what happens to a brain and cognitive ability during the dwarfing process: would this necessarily destroy the brain structures that had evolved within the normal-sized *Homo erectus?*

In summary, the discoveries of the last decade have all been compatible with the cathedral model. We continue to have an archaeological record of pre-modern humans that shows gross cultural stability and the absence of symbolic behavior, both of which are most effectively explained by a domain-specific mentality, while the increased convergence between the archaeological, fossil, and genetic data for modern human origins enhances the veracity of a shift to cognitive fluidity at this stage of human evolution.

NEW MODELS IN PALEOANTHROPOLOGY FOR THE EVOLUTION OF THE HUMAN MIND

Here I should briefly comment upon three of the new models for the evolution of the human mind that have made extensive use of the old and new archaeological and fossil evidence and how they challenge or complement the cathedral model.

Dunbar and his colleagues have promoted the "Social Brain" hypothesis, this having been the subject of a major research program funded by the British Academy (Dunbar 2003). This is a development of the gossip theory for the evolution of language (Aiello and Dunbar 1993, Dunbar 1996), and argues that the complexities of hominin social life drove the evolution of the early hominin brain from its ape-like beginnings to its modern form. It focuses on explaining the emergence of large cooperating groups, the evolution of theory of mind and intense social relationships based on intimacy and trust. In this regard it complements the cathedral model by elaborating on the evolution of social intelligence, a key element of both domain-specific and cognitively fluid mentalities. What the social brain hypothesis appears to lack is an adequate explanation for the non-social achievements of pre-modern humans, such as their hunting and gathering and toolmaking behavior, and why the most significant changes in human behavior (i.e., post 70,000 years ago) occurred long after modern-sized brains had evolved by 250,000 years ago.

Wynn and Coolidge (2004, Coolidge and Wynn 2001) have argued that the key cognitive constraint on Neandertal thought and behavior arose from a limited capacity for working memory as compared to modern humans. Their argument integrates evidence and ideas from archaeology, cognitive neuropsychology, and cognitive anthropology. Wynn and Coolidge claim that by lacking the ability to maintain diverse sources of information within active memory, the Neandertals were constrained in their abilities for innovation and creativity. They speculate that a genetic mutation in the African *Homo* lineage resulted in an "enhanced working memory" and hence the cultural developments of the Middle Stone Age and European Upper Paleolithic. This model is entirely compatible with the cathedral model. Indeed, by stressing the cognitive role of working memory rather than language the model is simply proposing an alternative mechanism by which cognitive fluidity might arise.

Finally, Miller (2000) has argued that the key driver in the evolution of the human mind, and especially creativity, has been sexual selection. Building on the arguments originally presented by Charles Darwin, Miller used sexual selection to explain why our ancestors—especially male ancestors—would have engaged in novel behaviors, notably art, music, and language. While the major weakness in Miller's work was his almost entire lack of reference to the archaeological record, indeed effectively any chronological framework at all for the evolution of the human mind, his argument that sexual selection played a significant role is generally persuasive. Indeed, I have drawn on that to explain some of the peculiar characteristics of Acheulian handaxes (Kohn and Mithen 1999) and cited it as playing a role (though not the only role) in the evolution of music (Mithen 2005). While sexual selection theory is not as integrated as is entirely desirable, it appears at least compatible with the cathedral model for the evolution of the human mind.

LANGUAGE AND MUSIC

The last decade has seen an astonishing quantity of research and publication regarding the origins and evolution of the human language capacity (e.g., Hurford, Studdert-Kennedy, and Knight 1998, Knight, Studdert-Kennedy, and Hurford 2000, Christiansen and Kirby 2003). Whereas language had been given a central role in the emergence of cognitive fluidity, the cathedral model had dealt with the linguistic capacities of pre-modern hominins in a rather unsatisfactory manner. Attributing them with a language that related entirely to the social world alone was not particularly persuasive.

That fully modern language played a role in the emergence of cognitive fluidity has received strong support from the work of the philosopher Peter Carruthers (2002, 2006), who independently reached the same conclusion (although with different terminology) informed by linguistics, neuroscience, and psychology. He has defended the "massive modularity thesis" and argued that "inter-modular integration" (i.e., cognitive fluidity) arises from the imagined sentences we create in our minds that allow the output from one module to act as the input to another. Carruthers has a much more sophisticated scenario for the relationship between language and inter-modular integration / cognitive fluidity than I was ever able to develop (and as summarized above). The key point is that his work had lent significant credence to the cathedral model.

This has also come from the discovery and dating of the most recent mutation on the FOXP2 gene. This has been described as the "language gene"—an absurd suggestion as language can only be based on the activity of a multitude of genes (Bishop 2002). Nevertheless FOXP2 appears to play a crucial role in turning other genes on and off, some of which seem vital to the development of neural circuits for some aspects of language (Lai et al.

2001). The finding that the most recent mutation on this gene, that which presumably provides it with this linguistic function, occurred concomitant with or subsequent to the emergence of anatomically modern humans (Enard et al. 2002) supports the idea that the evolution of modern language is indeed inextricably linked with that of modern cognition and behavior.

While the proposed role that the evolution of language played in the emergence of cognitive fluidity has been substantiated by such recent research, the proposed nature of language-like communication by pre-modern, domain-specific mentality has been subject to some revision. Although the social language proposal gained support from the influential "gossip" or vocal grooming theory for language origins (Dunbar 1996), that seems most appropriate for early hominins rather than the large-brained species such as *Homo heidelbergensis* and *Homo neanderthalensis.*

One of the key reasons for having proposed a social language hypothesis in 1996 was that there did not seem to be any alternative: the evolved vocal apparatus and large brains of Early Humans suggested advanced vocal communication, but the absence of symbolic behavior and cultural change implied the absence of linguistic communication. As a consequence there had to be some form of communication that was complex but nevertheless did not constitute modern language. Bickerton's proposal of a "proto-language" (e.g., 1995, 2000), one with words but lacking in grammar was, and remains, unconvincing. The key problem is that if this did exist at, say, 2 million years ago, why would it not have rapidly evolved into fully modern language. Computational studies, such as by Kirby (2000, 2001), have indicated that as soon as a protolanguage is subject to inter-generational transition, such complexity becomes an emergent property.

During the last decade there have been two key developments that have allowed a new model for Early Human communication to be developed—or rather a model that was originally proposed in the late 19th century to be revived. First, there have been the arguments that Early Human communication (vocal and otherwise) was holistic rather than compositional in character (Wray 1998, 2000, 2002, Arbib 2003). By this is meant the use of phrases with fixed semantic meanings that could not be ordered by rules to create a second level of meaning, in the manner that grammar does for words. The communication systems of apes—and indeed all nonhuman animals—are holistic in nature so this proposal is simply arguing that this continued for much longer in human evolution than had previously been proposed.

The second key development was a return to viewing the evolution of language as inter-related with that of music—an idea promoted by Rousseau (1781, see Thomas 1995), Jespersen (1895), and others, but curiously neglected in almost all of the recent literature on the evolution of language. Music had been regrettably neglected in *The Prehistory of the Mind,* even though musical activity is found in all known and historically documented societies. The last decade has seen a surge of interest in the evolution of music (e.g., Wallin, Merker, and Brown 2000, Cross 1999, 2001), and I drew on some of that material and combined it with arguments regarding the holistic nature of protolanguage, along with recent research in neuroscience and developmental psychology to develop the Hmmmmm model for Early Human communication in my 2005 book *The Singing Neanderthals.*

Hmmmmm stands for Holistic, manipulative, multi-modal, musical, and mimetic—these features having been argued to characterize the communication by pre-modern humans, consisting of a limited set of phrases with fixed meanings that could nevertheless be nuanced by changes in pitch, rhythm, timbre, and tone. The mimetic quality of such communication had been previously appreciated by Donald (1991) but neglected within the cathedral model. By now including this within the range of behavior of pre-modern humans, along with the other aspects of Hmmmmm, a more complete (and surely accurate) picture of pre-moderns is created—lives that were enriched not only by complex (domain-specific) thought, but by elaborate communication, music, and dance and enthused with emotion.

Many of the communications of nonhuman primates—and by implication the common ancestor—can be characterized as Hmmmmm-like and so the critical question is at what date did this type of communication become transformed into a compositional form in which a fixed number of words could be recombined into an infinite set of utterances. Bickerton suggested this transition occurred early in evolution, but a likely scenario (for reasons stated above) is that this was in fact a late occurrence. Indeed the so-called segmentation (Wray 2000, or "fractionation" in Arbib's 2003 terminology) of holistic utterances to create words and ultimately compositional language (and music) would have been the process that created cognitive fluidity of the modern mind, and hence I date it to between 200,000 and 70,000 years ago in the African *Homo* lineage (Mithen 2005).

In summary, research during the last decade has enabled the characterization of Early Human communication within the cathedral model to be significantly enhanced, replacing a socially dedicated language with Hmmmmm, which also enables the evolution of music and Donald's (1991) arguments regarding mimesis to become an integral part of the model. The emergence of fully modern language (leading to cognitive fluidity) is now characterized as arising from the segmentation of Hmmmmm, which also led to the emergence of music as a distinct form of activity.

THE ROLE OF MATERIAL CULTURE AND THE EXTENDED MIND

If the argument for a socially dedicated language for early humans was one weakness of the original cathedral model, another was the relationship between material culture and mind. The cathedral model used the notion of cognitive fluidity to explain how ideas about entities that do not exist in the real world could arise which then became manifest in material culture. A classic example is the Hohenstadel lion-man—a half human, half lion anthropomorphic figure—that could only have arisen from the integration of social and natural history intelligences. It is likely that many of the abstract and even the simplest of images in Upper Paleolithic and earlier "art," such as the engravings from Blombos, may have had complex symbolic meanings about beings or events within an imaginary world. As such they too would have required cognitive fluidity for the ideas to have arisen prior to becoming manifest in material form. In this regard the cathedral model implied that material objects were simply the products of mental ideas.

The weakness in this proposition became especially apparent in the late 1990s from the publications of Andy Clark regarding the extended and/or external mind (Clark 1997, Clark and Chalmers 1998), and then variously developed such as by Sterelny (2004) and Knappet (2005). Rather than material objects simply being products of ideas, they must be seen as playing integral roles in the maintenance, manipulation, and transmission of those ideas, and the formulation of new ideas. In other words, among modern humans material culture had become a tool for thought, especially when thinking about cognitively fluid ideas. Those thoughts about supernatural beings, for instance, are evolutionarily "unnatural" with no deeply embedded modules in either social, natural history, or technical intelligences. Hence material paraphernalia of religion—figurines, symbols, beads and so forth—acts as a cognitive anchor for such ideas (Mithen 1998). Without these, they are simply too hard to maintain, manipulate, and transmit. As Day has recently argued (2004), this material paraphernalia is an integral part of the machinery of religious thought itself.

So rather than the complex items of material culture simply being products of cognitively fluid minds, as originally proposed in the cathedral model, I would now see these as integral to creating, or at least sustaining, the cognitive fluidity itself (Mithen 1998). And this is not just within one individual for, just like spoken utterances (Clark 1997), items of material culture allow the migration of ideas between minds and exponentially increase the range of conceptual spaces within which new ideas can be formed.

In this regard the term cognitive fluidity takes on a broader meaning. Whereas within the cathedral model cognitive fluidity referred to the flow of information and ways of thinking between cognitive domains within a single brain, we should now extend this by also referring to not only the fluidity between human brains created by language and material culture, but also to the fluidity between brains and the material world: material culture had become as much a part of the modern mind as the brain itself.

SUMMARY

Fourteen years after it was first proposed, I remain fully persuaded by the essential features of the cathedral model: that there was a transition from a domain-specific to a cognitively fluid mentality in the African *Homo* lineage, that this was related to the evolution of fully modern language and created the capacity for analogy and metaphor in the human mind. I am, of course, biased, but this model appears to continue to explain the variation and patterning in the archaeological record for pre-modern humans and *Homo sapiens* more effectively than its alternatives. Indeed, Dunbar's "Social Brain" hypothesis and Wynn and Coolidge's "Enhanced Working Memory" hypothesis are compatible with the cathedral model and may enhance certain of its specific aspects. The significance of metaphor for modern human thinking has been elaborated on by Lakoff and Johnson (1999), while even the Evolutionary Psychologists have now recognized that modern minds need more than dedicated mental modules and use the term "improvisational intelligence"—which sounds rather like cognitive fluidity in what it can achieve (see H. Barrett, Cosmides, and Tooby 2007).

New archaeological discoveries and interpretations have shown that the transition from domain-specific to a cognitively fluid mentality should be set in Africa at some time between 200,000 and 70,000 years ago. New research on the evolution of language and music has developed the model for pre-modern hominin communication that was proposed in *The Prehistory of the Mind,* this now recognizing the importance of mimesis, as originally proposed by Donald (1991), and musicality. Indeed the origin of music has now become a core element of the cathedral model. With these developments has come a much more explicit concern with the emotional lives of both pre-modern and modern humans.

With regard to cognitive fluidity, the new research has enabled this notion to be extended beyond the fluidity within a single mind to that between minds and between minds and material culture. Indeed, rather than simply being characterized as a product of thought, the material culture of modern humans is now recognized as an essential element of the machinery of thought itself, playing a key role in creating cognitive fluidity itself.

Acknowledgments

I would like to thank the organizers of the "Evolution of Mind, Brain, and Culture" conference at the University of Pennsylvania, September 2007, for the invitation to participate in the meeting and contribute to the publication. I would also like to thank all of the participants for such extremely stimulating presentations and discussions throughout the conference.

10

Cognition, Behavioral Modernity, and the Archaeological Record of the Middle and Early Upper Paleolithic

APRIL NOWELL

The study of the evolution of human cognition has a long history in archaeology (see Nowell 2001 for a review) but in the last decade this area of research has often been reframed as a question of "behavioral modernity" (Klein 2000a, Wadley 2001, Bar-Yosef 2002, d'Errico 2003, Henshilwood et al. 2002, Henshilwood and Marean 2003, Shea 2003b, Bower 2005, Hovers and Belfer-Cohen 2006, Zilhão et al. 2006, Zilhão 2007, d'Errico 2007; see also McBrearty and Brooks 2000, Shennan 2001). Some authors are explicitly cognitive in their use of the term "behavioral modernity" while others are not. In either case, it is often implicit in their writings that the emergence and timing of modern behaviors and the degree to which they are shared with other hominin species besides anatomically modern humans (AMH) have ramifications for our understanding of the evolution of human cognition (Nowell 2010a).

What exactly "cognition" refers to in these studies is not always clear, but the most common models of the cognitive underpinnings of modern behavior focus on factors such as a fully phonemic, syntactical, and symbol-based language, symbol-use and self-reflexivity, enhanced working memory, multiple intelligences, or the incorporation of "different minds," with each model allowing for some degree of greater communication, forethought, planning, and creativity that conveyed an advantage on our ancestors over other hominins (e.g., Donald 1991, 2001, Davidson and Noble 1989, 1993, Byers 1994, Noble and Davidson 1996, Deacon and Wurz 2001, Lewis-Williams 2002,

Klein 2003b, Mithen 1996, 2005, 2010, Wynn and Coolidge 2003, 2004, 2007, 2010, Bickerton 2007, P. Lieberman 2007, Rossano 2009, Spikins 2009).

In this chapter, I briefly review the evidence for behavioral modernity among Neandertal and AMH populations in the Middle Stone Age (MSA)/ Middle and Early Upper Paleolithic (M/EUP). I then discuss whether a cognitive framework is necessary for understanding the behavioral similarities and differences between these two populations or whether an alternative model based on social, cultural, historic, and demographic factors fits the available data more parsimoniously.

BEHAVIORAL MODERNITY AND MODELS OF HOMININ COGNITIVE EVOLUTION

While there is considerable debate concerning what exactly is meant by "behavioral modernity," the term acts as a useful heuristic, in the context of this chapter, for comparing the behavior of Neandertals and AMH, because for many researchers the study of "modern behavior" is a search for the essence of what makes modern humans unique (see Nowell 2010a). In a seminal paper by McBrearty and Brooks (2000; following d'Errico 2003: fig. 3), behavioral modernity is defined as four sets of behaviors: (1) abstract thinking; (2) planning depth; (3) behavioral, economic, and technological innovativeness; and (4) symbolic behavior. The archaeological signatures or correlates of these behaviors can also be divided into four groups (McBrearty and Brooks 2000; following d'Errico 2003: fig. 4): (1) ecology (e.g., "range extension of previously unoccupied regions [and] increased diet breadth"); (2) technology (e.g., new technologies and the use of new materials such as bone, standardization of tool forms, evidence of hafting and composite tools, the development of specialized tools, geographic and temporal variation in tool forms, and greater control of fire); (3) economic and social organization (e.g., long-distance exchange networks; use of exotic materials; "specialized hunting of large, dangerous animals[,] scheduling and seasonality in resources exploitation[,] site reoccupation[,] intensification of resource extraction (aquatic and vegetable), long distance exchange networks[,]...[and] structured use of domestic space"); and (4) symbolic behavior (e.g., "regional artifact styles[,] personal adornment[,] use of pigments[,] image and representation[,] notched and incised objects[,] and burials with grave goods" and/or a ritual dimension).

While a number of models have been proposed to explain the evolution of hominin cognition and by extension the cognitive underpinnings of modern behavior, I will briefly discuss some of the more influential ones. Mithen (1996, 2005, 2010), for example, has argued for a modular approach (see Gardner 1983, Fodor 2000a). According to Mithen, the hominin mind prior to AMH was initially characterized by a generalized intelligence and then over time was divided into separate modules or intelligences (technical, social, and natural intelligences). Pre-modern hominins, including Neandertals, were unable to combine intelligences. For example, Neandertals would not have been able to integrate technical knowledge with natural history knowledge and could not have created bone tools. It is not until the emergence of modern humans that the "walls" between these intelligences were "broken down" and the different types of knowledge could be integrated. This integration is responsible for archaeological patterning of AMH populations in the Middle Paleolithic/Middle Stone Age and Upper Paleolithic/Later Stone Age. According to Mithen, fully modern cognitive fluidity emerged 70,000 years before present (ybp). In this approach, the modern mind is (1) the result of cognitive processes that are unique to modern humans, (2) fundamentally different from that of all pre-modern hominins including Neandertals, and (3) the result of a significant reorganization of the brain. Evidence of the combination of "intelligences" by Neandertals would significantly undermine this model.

Similarly, Klein (2000a), in his "spontaneous mutation" model, argues that 50,000 ybp an unspecified genetic mutation occurred in African "near-modern" populations that is directly responsible for modern behavior. Evidence of modern behavior among anatomically modern humans prior to this period or in other hominin species at any time would disprove this model.

McBrearty and Brooks (2000) also see modern human behavior originating in Africa, but they view it as emerging during a speciation event that gave rise to AMHs. The same biological processes that selected for modern anatomy 160,000–200,000 years ago (White et al. 2003, McDougall, Brown, and Fleagle 2005) also resulted in language, the capacity for symbolic behavior, and other modern behaviors.

Perhaps the most clearly articulated model of the emergence of modern human cognition is the one proposed by Wynn and Coolidge (2004, 2010, Coolidge and Wynn 2005, 2007). Specifically, they argue for the importance of enhanced working memory. Working memory is involved in sequential memory, the integration of information over space and time, the ability to override competing attentional or behavioral responses and to stay on task or to return to a task if distracted, among other abilities (Casey, Giedd, and Thomas 2000, Coolidge and Wynn 2005, 2007, Wynn and Coolidge 2010). These are all necessary for sequencing activities in their proper order to attain a goal. Working memory is correlated with other abilities such as emotional reasoning, storytelling, general intelligence, and the ability to solve new problems (Wynn and Coolidge 2010). While other hominin species are believed to have possessed forms of working memory, only anatomically modern humans are characterized by an enhanced working memory.

PALEONEUROLOGICAL, GENETIC, AND LIFE HISTORY DATA RELATED TO COGNITION AND LANGUAGE

In the context of the above models, it is useful to consider data from fossil endocasts, genetics, and life history studies. According to the paleoneurological evidence, Neandertals had cranial capacities that overlapped with or exceeded those of modern humans. Detailed studies of fossil endocasts demonstrate that 1.5 million years ago (mya) the hominin brain underwent modifications in cortical organization that led to the modern *Homo* pattern (Holloway, Broadfield, and Yuan 2004). Holloway and colleagues (2004) acknowledge that brains of *Homo erectus* and later *Homo* species show cerebral asymmetries and Broca's cap regions that are modern in form, but they cannot exclude the possibility that slight changes in the brain leading to modern cognition occurred subsequently. This is consistent with Wynn and Coolidge's (2010) model, for instance. Still, Holloway, Broadfield, and Yuan (2004:287) emphasize that they *"see absolutely nothing, however, in these later forms of* Homo *that would, based on neuroanatomical evidence alone, lead us to conclude that language behavior was not possible*...most emphatically, we see no differences in the morphology of the prefrontal portion of the frontal lobe [of Neandertals]" (emphasis in the original). They further argue (2004:288) that the behavioral and underlying neurological morphological evidence supports the separation of Neandertals from modern humans at the subspecies rather than the species level. In an indirect reference to Klein's (2000a) mutation model (and by extension Mithen's 1996 and Wynn and Coolidge's 2010 models as well), they write that, considering the degree of cultural change that has taken place since the Neolithic without a concomitant change in the brain, "one should be skeptical about underlying mutations subserving cognitive abilities that conveniently sprang into being some 50,000 years ago" (Holloway et al. 2004; see also Speth 2004, Wolpoff et al. 2004).

Similarly, in the process of sequencing the Neandertal genome, Krause and colleagues (2007a) discovered that Neandertals possessed the derived modern human form of the FOXP2 gene. While language and speech are the result of a variety of processes, this gene is the only one known to be directly involved in the development of language and speech (Krause et al. 2007a). The human form possesses two amino acid substitutions that are not in the nonhuman primate form (Trinkaus 2007). According to Krause et al. (2007a), the genetic changes predate the last common ancestor of Neandertals and AMH.

More evidence of the close genetic relationship between Neandertals and modern humans comes from the recent publication of a draft sequence of the Neandertal genome (Green et al. 2010). Scientists found that non-Africans (Eurasians) share 1–4% of their nuclear DNA with Neandertals suggesting that after the divergence of modern humans and Neandertals approximately 270,000–440,000 ybp, but before modern humans reached Eurasia, gene flow occurred from Neandertals into early modern human populations (Green et al. 2010). This likely took place in the Levant (Hawkes 2012), a region populated alternately or concurrently by Neandertal and AMH populations between 130,000–45,000 ybp (Shea 2010). Unlike earlier findings based on mtDNA (Serre et al. 2004), this research offers strong evidence of interbreeding between these populations and the contribution of Neandertals to the modern human genome (Abi-Rached et al. 2011; Yang et al. 2012).

A complementary way of considering the biological similarities and differences between Neandertals and modern humans is from the perspective of life history. Life history is sometimes referred to as reproductive turnover or "the speed of life" (Stearns 1992). Following this metaphor, it is often said that primates have the slowest life histories of all mammals and that humans in turn have the slowest life histories of all primates (Harvey and Clutton-Brock 1985, Robson and Wood 2008, Zimmermann and Radespiel 2007); but, in actuality, the human condition is at once more elegant and more complex (Nowell 2010b and references therein). The advantage of a slowed life history is that it allows for "higher quality offspring" that are larger, more intelligent, and more social; the disadvantage is that you risk dying before you reproduce (Dean and Smith 2009:101; Robson and

Wood 2008). In conjunction with derived features such as concealed ovulation, helpless (secondarily altricial) young, and a vigorous post-menopausal life, humans have evolved a unique pattern of "living fast" (e.g., decreased birth spacing, early weaning, greater number of offspring for an "ape" that matures at the age we do) within an overall pattern of "living slow" (long gestation, large brain, slowed maturation, delayed age of first reproduction, etc.) (Nowell 2010b and references therein).

A significant divergence from an ape-like life history pattern begins with *Homo erectus* (Nowell 2010b), and recent evidence suggests that Neandertals more closely resembled the modern human pattern. Based on a study of a Neandertal neonate from Mezmaiskaya Cave (Russia) and two Neandertal infants from Dederiyeh Cave (Syria), researchers have concluded that Neandertal brain size at birth was the same as recent humans and that they, like we, experienced rapid brain growth during the first year after birth but at a slightly higher rate leading to larger adult brain sizes. Based on their findings, they suggest that "because large brains growing at high rates require large, late maturing mothers,...it is likely that Neandertal life history was similarly slow, or even slower-paced, than in recent *H. sapiens*" (Ponce de León et al. 2008:137–64; but see Smith et al. 2010 and references therein).

These findings corroborate earlier research conducted by Hemmer (2007). Based on the relationships between brain size, body size, and a suite of other variables (see Zimmerman and Radespiel 2007 for a detailed discussion), and on dental eruption and bone fusion sequences, it is estimated that the pace of growth and development for these two populations was similar (Hemmer 2007). For example (all data from Hemmer 2007, table 19.14), the age at eruption of the first lower molar is 5.75 years for Neandertals and 5.4 for AMH. Age at sexual maturity is estimated at 16 years for Neandertals and 16.5 years for AMH. Age at first reproduction is estimated at 19.5 years for Neandertals and 19.3 years for AMH. According to O'Connell (2006:44, and references therein), these patterns "imply close similarities in other aspects of life history, including gestation length, weaning age, duration of post-menopausal longevity and absolute life-span."

Taken together, the paleoneurological data, the FOXP2 genetic data, the draft sequence of the Neandertal genome, and the life history data suggest that while differences exist, there is a strong similarity between Neandertal and AMH populations, yet the models described above assume that the perceived behavioral differences between them are so significant that they must be explained within a cognitive framework. *While I am not arguing that there were no cognitive differences between these two populations,* I am asking whether it is possible that the patterning in the archaeological record (discussed below) is more likely the result of separate, historically situated cultural trajectories than differences in cognitive abilities. I will now briefly consider the archaeological evidence using the criteria devised by McBrearty and Brooks (2000) and I will argue that time and population dynamics may be better predictors of "behavioral modernity" than species affiliation (see also Riel-Salvatore and Clark 2001).

ARCHAEOLOGICAL SIGNATURES OF BEHAVIORAL MODERNITY

Ecology

Dietary Breadth

While early interpretations of archaeological data depicted Neandertals as obligate scavengers (e.g., Binford 1989), the growing consensus is that there is little to distinguish the subsistence strategies of Neandertals and AMH populations during the MSA/MP and EUP (Gaudzinski and Roebroeks 2000, d'Errico 2003, 2007, Bar-Yosef 2004, Burke 2004, Bocherens and Drucker 2006, Zilhão 2007, Shea 2010). According to Stiner and Kuhn (2006), during the MP similar subsistence strategies were practiced by all Paleolithic peoples. Both Neandertals and AMHs relied heavily on hunting large game animals, focusing on prime adult prey, while small game exploitation accounted for about 3% of their diets. Thus while Neandertals, like their AMH counterparts, hunted large game animals, there is evidence that they also ate small animals such as tortoise (Israel) (Speth and Tchernov 2002), turtle and rabbits (Portugal), birds (Russia), and mollusks (Italy and Gibraltar) (d'Errico 2003).

Neandertals also ate a variety of plants and seeds (Madella et al. 2002), including wild olive, date palm, roots, tubers, legumes, acorns, and pistachio nuts and stone pine nuts (D. Henry et al. 2004, Lev, Kislev, and Bar-Yosef 2005). In a recent study of phytoliths and starch grains recovered from the dental calculus of both European and Levantine Neandertals, A. Henry and colleagues (2011:486) found that their subjects not only consumed a variety of plant foods but "transformed them into more easily digestible foodstuffs in part through cooking them, suggesting an overall sophistication of the Neandertal dietary regime." Hardy (2010) argues that plant foods not only would have been an important "fall back," but also would have provided essential compounds and nutrients not available from meat. Furthermore, plant foods and, in particular, underground storage organs (USO) would have been available throughout the Neandertal range even during the cold-est periods, but their importance is often overlooked because plants can be completely consumed and their remains do not preserve in the archaeologi-cal record as readily as those of animals (Hardy 2010).

While it is now well known that MSA AMH populations consumed aquatic resources (e.g., Marean et al. 2007), it is less well known that Ne-andertals did as well. This is based on plentiful remains from sites such as Grotte XVI in the Dordogne region of France where evidence suggests that they may have been smoking fish to preserve them for future consumption (Karkanas et al. 2002). Further evidence comes from the sites of Vanguard and Gorham's caves on Gibraltar. At these sites, there is evidence for sys-tematic and repeated exploitation of both terrestrial and marine mollusks, pinnepeds (e.g., seals), and cetaceans (Stringer et al. 2008). Large mollusks were carried 3–4 km and opened using heat from a hearth (Barton 2000). At nearby sites, Neandertals exploited coastal water fowl and seabirds such as the great auk (Stringer et al. 2008). According to these authors, "the range of species exploited and the age distribution pattern of the prey strongly indicate that the coastal exploitation of resources by Neanderthals was not a sporadic and isolated occurrence but one that required a knowledge of the life history of prey and its seasonality" (Stringer et al. 2008:14323). Further evidence of the consumption of aquatic resources by Neandertals comes from St. Césaire where fish is thought to have accounted for up to 30% of the diet (Balter and Simon 2006; see also Erlandson 2001).

According to Stiner and Kuhn (2006:699), it is not until after 15,000 ybp that the proportion of biomass represented by small game increases to 17% of the diet of AMH. From this perspective, a true shift in diet occurs late in the Upper Paleolithic, long after Neandertals had disappeared from the fossil record and well after modern humans were established in Europe. At the same time, they argue that by 45,000 ybp modern humans living in Africa began to increase the number of prey types that accounted for the small game biomass in their diet (Stiner and Kuhn 2006). Thus while small game continued to represent a fraction of the AMH diet, the variety of small prey species consumed increased and this may have had important ramifications for their survival—a point to which I return below.

Geographic Range

In terms of geographic range, Neandertals were not as widely dispersed as AMH populations. Nonetheless, recent research has now extended the known Neandertal range 2000 km further east than was commonly assumed (Krause et al. 2007b). mtDNA studies were conducted on specimens from Uzbekistan and the Altai region of Siberia. The identification of these remains as Neandertal supports earlier work based on archaeological data by Pavlov and colleagues (2001). This has been further corroborated by the discovery of hundreds of Mousterian tools near the Arctic Circle (Slimak et al. 2011). Thus, while AMH were much more widely dispersed than Neandertals, both hominin species spread across vast landscapes and inhabited a wide variety of ecological and biogeographical zones and they both lived through cycles of glacial and interglacial periods (e.g., see d'Errico 2003).

Technology

The Howiesons Poort industry of southern Africa, dating to the MSA, is considered by many researchers to be the first stone tool industry that is essentially "modern" in character. In particular, the variety of geometric backed microblades are taken as evidence of innovation in tool type, regional difference in tool morphology, composite tools, and the use of non-local raw materials and the existence of long-distance exchange networks (Singer and Wymer 1982, McBrearty and Brooks 2000). Until now, this industry has been unquestionably associated with AMH but the fossils from Klasies River Mouth (100,000 ybp), the only site where hominin remains have been found in association with the Howiesons Poort, have recently been re-analyzed by Trinkaus (2005). Trinkaus (2005) states that the lack of comparable material precludes assigning them to either AMH or some form of African archaic sapiens. The resolution of this issue is significant because of the fossils' association with what is considered to be the first behaviorally modern industry.

Other African industries also contain elements of modern behavior as defined by McBrearty and Brooks (2000). These are the bone tools and tanged points of the Aterian industry in North Africa, the bone tools from Katanda in the Democratic Republic of Congo, and bone tools of the Still Bay industry in southern Africa. There are AMH hominin remains with "archaic" features associated with the Aterian.

What is most interesting about the industries of MSA Africa is that many of the innovations or pulses of "modern behavior" such as heat treating (Brown et al. 2009) and pressure flaking (Mourre, Villa, and Henshilwood 2010) do not persist uninterrupted into later periods but seem to disappear from the archaeological record for long periods of time. As Soriano and colleagues (2007:700) note in relation to the Howiesons Poort industries at Rose Cottage Cave, "the HP was a very original and innovative industry; but it did not persist and it did not give rise to the LSA. In a sense it was both "modern" and "non-modern." This is an important point to which I return below.

In the MP of the Levant both modern humans and Neandertal remains have been found in association with Levantine Mousterian industries. In fact, it is impossible to distinguish sites belonging to Neandertals from those belonging to modern humans based on lithics alone (Lieberman and Shea 1994, Shea 2003a, 2003b, 2003c, 2006). The only recourse is to use chronotypology. In Israel early forms of AMH at the site of Skhul are broadly contemporaneous with the Neandertal female from Tabun, both dating between 130,000 to 100,000 ybp; the AMH fossils at Qafzeh are slightly younger dating to 90,000 ybp (Shea 2010 and references therein). All other Levantine Neandertals (e.g., Amud, Kebara, Dederiyeh), cluster between 70,000 and 45,000 ybp (Shea 2010). Based on current evidence it appears that the initial colonization of the Levant by modern humans was not successful as they disappear from the fossil record from ca. 75,000 ybp– 45/38,000 ybp. They either abandoned the Levant or they were driven into local extinction. If the latter is the correct interpretation, then it would be the only known occurrence of modern humans being replaced by another hominin species (Shea 2010).

Blades and blade technology, once defining features of the Upper Paleolithic, are known from the Levant dating back to the Lower Paleolithic (Bar-Yosef and Kuhn 1999). Similarly, prismatic blade technology was practiced by Neandertals in northern Germany and in northeastern France some 90 millennia prior to the onset of the Upper Paleolithic (Conard 1990, Ameloot-van der Heijden 1993) and then simply disappeared (Hopkinson 2011).

In the Levant, there are no hominin fossils associated with the transitional lithic industries that bridge the MP and UP beginning at 45,000 ybp, making attribution of this transition to either species speculative; however, the Early Upper Paleolithic Ahmarian industry (ca. 38,000–26,000 ybp) is definitely associated with AMHs (Bergman and Stringer 1989, Bisson et al. 2007, Shea 2010). It is therefore generally assumed that the transitional industries were made by AMHs as well (Bisson et al. 2007).

In Europe, there is evidence of Neandertals in association with variants of the Mousterian industry from approximately 250,000 until 25/30,000 ybp and with "transitional" industries such as the Uluzzian, Bachokirian, Szeletian, Bohunician, and Châtelperronian industries from 45,000–35,000 ybp (Zilhão 2007). Because Neandertals evolved in Europe and there is little evidence of AMH on the continent until 35,000 ybp at the Romanian site of Oase (Trinkaus et al. 2003 but see Higham et al. 2011), most researchers attribute the transitional industries including the Châtelperronian (45,000–35,000 ybp) to Neandertals and associate the Aurignacian and subsequent Upper Paleolithic industries (36,500–28,000 ybp) with AMH populations. Neandertal remains have been found in association with the Châtelperronian at Arcy-sur-Cure (e.g., Bailey and Hublin 2006) and St. Césaire (France) (Lévêque and Vandermeersch 1980).

With respect to MP/MSA tool industries much of the research into modern behavior has focused on the relationship between the Châtelperronian and Aurignacian. The Châtelperronian industry is an in-situ development from local Mousterian industries whereas the Aurignacian industry is intrusive to western Europe, probably originating somewhere in the Zagros Mountains (Olszewski and Dibble 1994), and is associated with the migration of AMHs into Europe. The main question in this debate concerns whether or not the Châtelperronian represents an autonomous transition to the Upper Paleolithic by Neandertals or whether it is a result of acculturation from modern humans. The Châtelperronian shows clear affinities with the preceding Mousterian industry, but, like other transitional industries, it also includes Upper Paleolithic elements such as backed bladelets. At Arcy-sur-Cure, for instance, excavators uncovered 142 bone tools (some of which were decorated; see below) and numerous personal ornaments made from teeth, ivory, bone, and shell (Klein 2009).

Some have argued for an independent development of the Châtelperronian citing debitage analysis detailing bone and lithic manufacturing techniques that "do not display any apparent affinity with the techniques introduced into Europe" by AMH populations (d'Errico 2007:127; see also d'Errico et al. 1998b). Others counter that "if the Neanderthals *did* independently develop the whole range of behavior that traditionally has been regarded as the hallmark of fully 'modern' humans, this would arguably be the most important thing we have learned about the Neanderthals since their original discovery more than 150 years ago" (Mellars 2005:12). Mellars (2005) refers to this as the "impossible coincidence."

The difficulties of dating Aurignacian and Châtelperronian sites with sufficient resolution are a significant factor in this debate (Nowell 2010a). For some, the Châtelperronian is consistently older than the Aurignacian (Zilhão 2006); for others, the industries are broadly contemporaneous (Mellars 2005); while still others maintain the dates are too imprecise to take sides in this debate (Weniger 2006). Klein (2009), for his part, makes a distinction between older Châtelperronian industries that are more Mousterian in character and younger ones that are clearly the result of acculturation with modern humans. Mellars (2005) argues that even if the Châtelperronian industries are in fact older than Aurignacian industries it is possible that "modern ideas" reached the shores of Europe before "modern people" did. This is what Mellars (2005) calls the "bow wave" effect. But even if we take the contemporaneity of the industries and the suggestion of extensive cultural contact at face value, the fact that Neandertals could make and use personal ornaments and "Upper Paleolithic" tool types speaks to their cognitive capacity for modern behavior as defined by McBrearty and Brooks (2000; see Chase 2007 for an excellent discussion).

New evidence from the Uluzzian, a transitional industry in southern Italy associated with Neandertals, is adding to this debate. This industry is characterized by bone implements, true projectile technology, and personal ornaments made of shell and colorants (Riel-Salvatore 2010). According to Riel-Salvatore (2010), in order for acculturation to be the most parsimonious explanation for the origin and development of the Uluzzian there must be evidence of temporal and geographic proximity between the Uluzzian and Aurignacian cultures. While they are contemporaneous, there is what he calls a Mousterian "buffer" in the center of the Italian peninsula where Neandertals continue to make Mousterian tools, separating the Aurignacian in the north from the Uluzzian in the south.

An important MP innovation associated with Neandertals is the manufacture of a birch bark pitch as an adhesive to haft stone knives at the Königsaue site in Germany dating to ca. 80,000 ybp (Koller, Baumer, and Mania 2001, Haidle 2010). One sample of the pitch has an impression of a wooden handle in it (d'Errico 2003), as well as a fingerprint (Koller et al. 2001). According to a detailed analysis (Koller, Baumer, and Mania 2001) Neandertals would have had to carefully control the temperature between 340 and 400 degrees Celsius while making the adhesive. Not only is this pitch an important technological innovation but it also speaks to their pyrotechnical skills. According to Zilhão (2007:40), this "example of Pleistocene high-tech could not have been developed, transmitted, and maintained in the absence of abstract thinking and language as we know them; it certainly requires enhanced working memory whose acquisition, according to Coolidge and Wynn (2005), is the hallmark of modern cognition." Bitumen adhesives were also found on five lithic artifacts dating to 60,000 ybp at a Mousterian site in Syria (Boëda, Connan, and Muhensen 1998). There is evidence that AMH populations at MSA South African sites also produced a variety of adhesives (Wadley 2005), which attests to similar abilities in this population.

This brief review of MSA/MP technologies suggests that among both Neandertal and AMH populations there is ample evidence of new technologies, standardization, hafting, and composite tools and the creation of special purpose tools (e.g., awls). Both species used novel materials for making tools, such as bone. They also used wood for tools as evidenced by the impression in the birch bark pitch (d'Errico 2003), phytolith studies at Amud (Madella et al. 2002), and use-wear analyses on stone tools (Klein 2009). There is evidence of geographic and temporal variation in tool morphology, with some Neandertals making Châtelperronian and other transitional industries while others continue to make Mousterian tools. There is also geographic variation as outlined above. Similarly, in the MSA, AMH populations are associated with the Still Bay and possibly Howiesons Poort industries and in the MP with the Levantine Mousterian. They are later associated with the transitional UP industries of the Levant and the Aurignacian industries. With both populations there is evidence of the greater control of fire. Finally, the manufacture of adhesives by both Neandertals and AMH is further evidence of innovation.

Economic and Social Organization

There is evidence that both Neandertals and modern humans reoccupied sites (e.g., Speth 2006) and moved sites to take advantage of seasonal migrations of herds and other seasonally available foods. The use of domestic space by Neandertals is also more complex than once thought (Henry

1995, Henry et al. 2004, Speth 2006). Until recently, Molodova I, Layer IV, was perhaps the best known example of a possible open-air dwelling constructed by Neandertals, but it is controversial as a number of taphonomic explanations for the association of mammoth bones and tools have been advanced (e.g., Stringer and Gamble 1993, Hoffecker 2002). A detailed taphonomic study of the site must be undertaken before its significance in this context can be understood (see Nowell and d'Errico 2007).

Stronger evidence comes from the Neandertal site of Kebara, where Speth (2006) has shown repeated use of the site and continuity in the way in which domestic space was divided into activity areas and in the manner in which the space was managed. A newly discovered Neandertal camp in Germany dating to 120,000 ybp that contains hearths, postholes representing three separate shelters, and 400 tools may shed further light on this topic (Spiegel 2007). We must await full publication of the site before drawing conclusions from this provocative find.

Some of the best evidence we currently have of the discreet use of domestic space by Neandertals comes from the Jordanian site of Tor Faraj (69,000–49,000 ybp) (Henry et al. 2004, Henry 2012). Tor Faraj is a rare example of two large, well stratified living floors (67 m²) and, based on chronotypology, is associated with Neandertals. Henry et al. (2004) studied the spatial distributions of lithic tool types, phytoliths, and features such as hearths. Employing various methods, they discerned dedicated areas of use within the cave. In Area A they found grasses that were used as bedding and placed inside the drip line along the back wall near a row of sleeping hearths. In Area B they identified food preparation and cooking areas near a domestic hearth, as well as evidence of maintenance tasks, what Henry et al. (2004) refer to as "end of stream" lithic processing (retouching, resharpening, and maintenance). There were also refuse disposal areas.

Further evidence of Neandertal use of space comes from the Spanish site of Abric Romani, dating to approximately 55,000 ybp (Vallverdú et al. 2010). At this site, researchers identified sleeping areas similar to those used by modern hunter-gatherers, 19 hearths that attest to the reoccupation and use of the site for brief periods of time, and a 5 m long wooden pole that had been modified and likely was used as a tent-pole (Vallverdú et al. 2010).

A related issue is the evidence for the paving of living spaces. According to Mellars (1996:301–2 and references therein), pebble or stone paving has been documented at many Upper Paleolithic sites. It is believed that paving was used to make living surfaces drier or more regular. It appears that paving of occupation surfaces also occurred in the MP at several sites including at Baume-Bonne cave (Mellars 1996, Pettitt 2005). According to de Lumley and Boone (1976a, cited in Mellars 1996:302), in clearly defined areas of approximately 10 m² each "contiguous and densely packed concentrations of quartz and quartzite pebbles derived from the adjacent gravels of the Verdon river in densities of up to 185 of these cobbles per square meter" were documented. Evidence that these are intentionally paved areas comes from the fact that all the stones had to be carried into the site; they were uncovered in sharply defined areas; and most of the broken pebbles were laid with the convex sides (smoother sides) facing upward. De Lumley (cited in Mellars 1996) argues that the paved areas are located in places where muddy water would naturally pool.

In summary, based on these observations and those discussed under the heading of ecology, it can be argued that Neandertal and AMH populations engaged in specialized hunting of large, dangerous animals. They employed a level of scheduling and seasonality in the exploitation of resources. Further, there is evidence of site reoccupation and the structured use of domestic space, as well as the intensification of resource extraction (aquatic and vegetable). Evidence of long-distance exchange and self-identification through artifact style is discussed below.

Symbolic Behavior

Burials

Burials of AMH have been found in the MSA of Africa (but see Belfer-Cohen and Hovers 1992), the MP of the Levant, and the late Aurignacian of Europe. In Africa, the best example of AMH remains with any recognizable symbolic dimension to their disposal comes from the site of Border cave (75,000 ybp) where one bead has been found in association with an infant. There is debate over whether or not these remains are *in situ*, but if they are, then this is evidence of AMH in Southern Africa in association with personal adornment by 75,000 ybp (Zilhão 2007).

In Ethiopia, cutmarks were found on three skulls from the Herto site and one from the site of Bodo, all dating to approximately 150,000 ybp, that may represent ritual defleshing of a corpse (White et al. 2003). Similar claims have been made for Neandertal remains from the Croatian site of

Krapina (Russell 1987a, 1987b, Pettitt 2010) based on the location of cut-marks on the bone but Orschiedt (2008), in a recent, detailed taphonomic analysis of these finds, argues that the vast majority of this material was altered by nonhuman agents although there may be one example of scalping.

There are burials associated with both Neandertals and modern humans in the Levantine MP. The oldest known burial is at the Neandertal site of Tabun in Israel dating to approximately 122,000 ± 16,000 ybp (Grün and Stringer 2000:610). There is, however, very little evidence of a symbolic or ritual dimension to the burials of either species in this region. At the AMH site of Qafzeh, in Israel, ochre was found in association with the burials. *Glycymerys* shells were also uncovered. They are naturally perforated (Tabourin 2003, Zilhão 2007) but bear evidence of having been strung (Bar-Yosef Mayer, Vandermeersch, and Bar-Yosef 2009). Also at Qafzeh in association with AMH remains is a piece of cortex (the outermost layer or "rind" of a piece of flint, showing weathering), 6.2 cm in maximum length, that has been incised. A microscopic analysis of the lines (e.g., order in which the lines were drawn, curvature of the lines, etc.) suggests that these lines were not produced through use of the cortex as a cutting board (Nowell, d'Errico, and Hovers 2001, d'Errico et al. 2003a). At the same time, there is little evidence to support that they were deliberately made to create some type of pattern.

Perhaps the best known and most contentious Neandertal burial in the Levant comes from the site of Shanidar that dates to 60,000 ybp. In the sediment surrounding Shanidar I, clusters of pollen from brightly colored flowers (grape hyacinth, bachelors buttons, hollyhock, groundsel) and medicinal herbs were found in abundance (Leroi-Gourhan 1998). According to Leroi-Gourhan (1998), the body was laid to rest on a bed of pine boughs and then flower blossoms were strewn over the body. This evidence is difficult to evaluate, as many have argued that the pollen was windblown or tracked in by rodents; since soil samples were not taken from other areas of the site, it is impossible to know if these are dense concentrations of pollen resulting from intentional hominin behavior (Pettitt 2010). What is needed, of course, are other examples of similar burial "offerings" to establish a pattern of behavior.

In Europe, there are a number of Neandertal burials from the MP but an example of a burial with a ritual dimension comes from the site of La Ferrassie which dates to 65,000–70,000 ybp (Zilhão 2007, Pettitt 2010). La

Ferrassie 1 is an adult male who was buried in a shallow pit with a cylindrical bone fragment incised with four sets of parallel lines. La Ferrassie 6 is a 3- or 4-year-old child who was buried in a deep pit covered by a limestone slab decorated with cupules on one side. There are also three flint tools that, according to the excavators, were carefully placed on top of the child's body. For Zilhão (2007), "La Ferrassie suffices to establish a level of symbolic expression among European Neandertals at least identical to that seen in the African lineage at the same time." Similarly, at the Châtelperronian burial site St. Césaire (France), a number of dentalium beads were found in association with the Neandertal remains there, adding an unquestionably ritual dimension to this burial (Zilhão 2007).

The provocative but controversial Neandertal site of La Grotte de Régourdou in France, if correctly interpreted, may be the only known example of a MP "tomb" (Pettitt 2010). At this site, an adult Neandertal is said to be purposefully interred with grave goods and is in association with the nearby interment of a juvenile cave bear. Associated with both skeletons are built features (low walls and ditches). The Neandertal is covered with burnt sand and a tumulus of large stones while the bear is covered with a limestone slab.

Wynn and Coolidge (2004) contrast MP Neandertal burials with the extraordinary AMH triple burial from Sunghir (Russia) where thousands of mammoth ivory beads were found in association with the remains of two children and one adult male. But Wynn and Coolidge (2004) erroneously assign Sunghir to the Aurignacian (i.e., the Early UP) when in fact it is a Gravettian burial (Formicola and Buzhilovo 2004, Formicola 2007, Pettitt 2010). In other words, this is a later UP burial. There are no European AMH burials that are contemporary with those from La Ferrassie or even St. Césaire. As Pettitt (2010:168) notes, there are no known AMH burials in Europe before the Gravettian, only what he calls "funerary caching." Furthermore, there are no richly adorned burials anywhere in the world before this period (Pettitt 2010).

In sum, there is only sporadic evidence of a symbolic dimension to the burials of either AMH or Neandertals in the MP/MSA and EUP. There are two or three provocative examples for each species, but taken as a whole MP/EUP burials are similar to each other and strikingly different from later UP burials (Riel-Salvatore and Clark 2001, d'Errico 2007, Pettitt 2010), particularly those of the Gravettian.

Colorants

Ochre "crayons" have been found at a number of Lower and Middle Paleolithic sites. It is clear that they have been used on hard and soft surfaces (Mellars 1996), but whether these colorants were used for ritual purposes is unknown. Ochre may have been used to tan hides (Keeley 1978), as mosquito repellent, for protection against the sun or against cold, for medicinal purposes (as an astringent, antiseptic, or deodorizer), for use in the extraction or processing of plants (Wadley 2001), for hafting, or for any number of as yet unknown/unimagined tasks (Nowell 2010a). Recently, d'Errico and colleagues (d'Errico and Sorressi 2002, d'Errico et al. 2003a, d'Errico 2007) report on the use of manganese crayons at the Neandertal site of Pech de l'Azé I in southwest France (50–60,000 ybp). Researchers analyzed 500 pigment pieces and grinding stones. They found that the majority of the pigments showed evidence of wear, including rubbing on soft surfaces. An abstract pattern was engraved on two of these pieces using a stone tool. Use-wear and experimental work suggests to these researchers that some of the pieces were sharpened into "pencils" and used to draw on flexible materials such as human or animal skin (d'Errico 2007) and thus may have been used in some type of body painting (Soressi et al. 2002, Zilhão 2007).

At two Spanish Neandertal sites dating to 50,000 ybp, researchers uncovered perforated marine shells, some containing a mixture of pigments, and a white shell with its exterior painted orange. Based on a detailed analysis of the pigment mixture it is likely that Neandertals were following pigment "recipes" and may have used these colorants and perforated shells in body adornment (Zilhão et al. 2010).

Four fragments of pigment were found at the AMH site of Skhul (d'Errico et al. 2010). These fragments not only varied in color and other physical/chemical properties but may have been heat treated to produce a greater range or intensity of color (d'Errico et al. 2010). This is a technique that is known in UP art but is unique in a MP context.

At the 70,000 year old AMH site of Blombos in South Africa, 8,000 fragments of ochre were found. Two of these fragments were engraved with cross-hatched lines. The similarity of the two pieces to each other suggest that the design was deliberate (Henshilwood et al. 2002). According to Klein (2009:535), the engraved pieces of ochre at Pech de l'Azé associated with Neandertals and the ones found at Blombos suggest intent and "represent the most compelling case for art before 50 ka." Also at the site of Blombos,

Abalone shells from a ~100,000 year old layer were found containing evidence of the preparation of an ochre compound made up of finely ground red ochre, charcoal, marrow fat, and an unidentified liquid as indicated by a series of "water marks" (Henshilwood et al., 2011). The use of colorants in Africa can be traced back to the Twin Rivers site (260,000–40,000 ybp). At this site, 176 fragments in 5 different colors were found and there are traces of use on these fragments. Consequently, d'Errico (2007) argues that the use of colorants in Africa predates the emergence of AMH populations and was a behavior characteristic of non-modern populations as well.

Personal Adornment

Perforated tick shells (*Nassarius gibbosulus*) dating to 77,000 ybp that may have been worn as a necklace have been uncovered at Blombos (Henshilwood et al. 2004, d'Errico et al. 2005). Even older evidence of personal adornment comes from the AMH sites of Oued Djebbana in Algeria and Qafzeh in Israel, where a total of three beads have been dated to more than 35,000 ybp and to 100,000–135,000 ybp respectively (Vanhaeren et al. 2006). Interestingly, the beads are manufactured from shells of the same genus as those utilized by hominins at Blombos. Use-wear studies suggest these beads were suspended. Two perforated marine shells of the same species (*N. gibbosulus*) have also been identified at the Skhul cave in Israel, potentially dating to 100,000 BP (Bar-Yosef Mayer, Vandermeersch, and Bar-Yosef 2009; Vanhaeren et al., 2006). Similarly, ochre-covered beads also made from *Nassarius gibbosulus* dating to 82,000 ybp were recovered from the Moroccan site Grotte des Pigeons (Bouzouggar et al. 2007). As R. White (1992) argues, personal adornment in modern societies is one of the most powerful and persuasive ways humans construct meaning and represent beliefs, and it now appears that we have evidence of this behavior in association with modern humans dating to the MSA (see also Vanhaeren 2005). The next evidence comes 60,000–100,000 years later, from Ksar 'Akil (194 beads) and Ucagizli (>90 beads) dating to 39,000 ybp (Kuhn et al. 2001). Another possible personal ornament, assumed to be associated with AMH, is a perforated shark tooth from New Guinea dating to 39,500–28,000 ybp that may have been worn as a pendant (Leavesley 2007).

The earliest personal ornaments in Europe seem to predate the Aurignacian and are associated with the Neandertals (discussed in Zilhão 2007). In addition to the spectacular finds from Spain discussed above, examples

include a spindle-shaped bone pendant and fragments of pierced teeth from
Bacho Kiro (Kozlowski 1982); 24 dentalium beads at the Uluzzian site of
Klisoura 1 in Greece (Koumouzelis et al. 2001); tubular fragments of dentalium beads from the Italian Uluzzian site of Grotta del Cavallo; shell ornaments from other Uluzzian contexts (Riel-Salvatore 2010); a perforated
shell of a fossil gastropod at Willandorf II, and an ivory disk with a hole in
it from Ilsenhöhle in Germany. The majority of Neandertal personal ornaments, however, come from Châtelperronian deposits in France (e.g.,
Caune de Belvis, St. Césaire, Quinçay, and Grotte du Renne at Arcy-sur-
Cure) (details in d'Errico et al. 1998b). At Grotte du Renne, for example,
26 ornaments were uncovered in a secure Châtelperronian context (Zilhão
2007). These ornaments were made following techniques that differ from
those practiced by Aurignacian peoples, suggesting an autonomous origin
for the manufacture and use of personal adornment by Neandertals. More
recently, Peresani et al. (2011) found evidence of the intensive processing
of birds by Neandertals for feathers, based on the location of diagnostic
cut, peeling and scraper marks, and fracture patterns. They suggest that
the feathers were likely used for personal adornment. Similarly, Morin and
Laroulandie (2012) argue for the symbolic use of raptors at numerous sites
in France.

In the Aurignacian, the scale of symbolic behavior increases dramatically with AMH. R. White (2003:68) observes, "it is not an exaggeration to
state that just a few square meters at certain Aurignacian sites have yielded
more representational objects than are known for the entire planet in the
period before 40,000 years ago." It should be noted, however, that the "explosion" of personal adornment and art that characterizes this period is
unevenly distributed and is in fact more geographically circumscribed than
commonly acknowledged (Straus 2009). Possible reasons for this pattern
are discussed below.

Engravings, Figurines, and Musical Instruments

There are few well accepted engravings or figurines prior to the Aurignacian associated with either Neandertal or AMH populations other than
the engraved pieces of ochre at Blombos. There are, however, 2 pieces of
ochre from the site of Piekary IIa that date to 40,000 ybp (Sitlivy et al. 2004,
Zilhão 2007). They have an abstract design engraved on them similar to
that found at Blombos, and because of their age they are associated with

Neandertals. There are also the 2 engraved pieces of ochre from Pech de l'Azé discussed above. Another important example is the bone awls from the Châtelperronian (i.e., Neandertal) levels at Grotte du Renne (Arcy-sur-Cure). One third of the 50 awls and 3 of the 5 bird bone tubes have regular markings on them (d'Errico et al. 2003b). According to these researchers the arrangement and distribution of the lines strongly suggests intentional decoration. Furthermore, as noted, the abstract motifs and techniques of manufacture differ significantly from those used by Aurignacian (AMH) peoples (d'Errico et al. 1998b), suggesting an independent development of a local cultural tradition (d'Errico 2007).

Other possible examples of this behavior include well-known engravings from Molodova I, Layer IV, in the Ukraine that have recently been ascribed to excavation-induced trauma and natural processes such as blood vessel impressions (Nowell and d'Errico 2007); the Neandertal bone "flute" which is best described as a carnivore chewed bone (Chase and Nowell 1998, d'Errico et al. 1998a, Nowell and Chase 2002; but see Turk 1997, Turk et al. 2006); the contentious Neandertal "face" from La Roche-Cotard (France) (Pettitt 2003); the Tata pebble and plaque from Hungary; and the 50,000 year old Quneitra engraving from Syria (Nowell, d'Errico, and Hovers 2001, d'Errico et al. 2003a; see also Goren-Inbar 1990, Marshack 1995). Similar to the Qafzeh engraving, the Quneitra engraving is an incised piece of cortex. This time, however, the lines form a series of nested semi-circles. A re-analysis of the piece (Nowell, d'Errico, and Hovers 2001, d'Errico et al. 2003a) confirms that the lines were made with a stone tool. While the pattern on this piece is more compelling than the Qafzeh cortex, the lack of comparable material makes it difficult to evaluate the degree of intentionality or possible meaning associated with the design. There are no hominin remains associated with this site, and because of its date it could have been made by either Neandertals or modern humans. None of these examples is particularly convincing.

At the AMH site of Diepkloof Rockshelter in South Africa, 270 fragments of incised ostrich eggshell were uncovered, dating to at least 60,000 ybp (Texier et al. 2010). At 35,000–32,000 ybp a number of well-known beautifully made figurines and flutes have been uncovered primarily at the German AMH sites of Vogelherd, Hohlenstein-Stadel, Hohle Fels, and Geissenklösterle (Conard 2003, 2009, Zilhão 2007). Also dating to approximately this time is the spectacular painted cave Chauvet (Clottes 2003).

Other Examples of Ritual

There has been some suggestion that Neandertals practiced ritual and/ or dietary cannibalism with evidence coming from sites such as Krapina (Croatia), Hortus (France), Monte Circeo (Italy), and most recently Moula-Guercy (France) (Defleur et al. 1999). It is difficult to make a strong case for cannibalism when most of these sites were excavated decades ago, often with techniques that do not meet modern standards including the use of dynamite at Krapina. The most convincing evidence comes from Moula-Guercy, an open-air site north of Marseille that was recently excavated. Here 6 Neandertals (2 adults, 2 adolescents, and 2 children) were butchered in the same fashion as the red deer whose fossilized remains were found mixed in with 78 hominin fragments. This suggests dietary rather than ritual cannibalism. A similar pattern was found at Hortus. Speth (2004), however, makes the point that within extant and historic populations virtually all examples of cannibalism have some ritual component to them whether it be the consumption of one's enemies as practiced by the Aztec or ancestor worship as practiced by a number of ethnographically known groups (see also Pettitt 2010). At this point, the evidence for ritual cannibalism is provocative but not conclusive. At the MSA site, Klasies River Mouth, normally associated with AMH (but see above), there is evidence of cannibalism. In this case, as well, the hominin remains are treated in the same fashion as the faunal remains (T.D. White 1987).

In sum, both Neandertals and AMHs have a few examples of burials with a ritual dimension to them, both manufactured items of personal adornment, both notched and engraved ochre and other items, and both used pigments presumably for a variety of purposes including possibly body painting. The archaeological record of both species is very similar for all of the MP and EUP, with the spectacular exception of the Aurignacian of France and the Swabian Jura (German), which are rich in symbolic items.

BEHAVIORAL MODERNITY AND THE ARCHAEOLOGICAL RECORD

Following McBrearty and Brooks' (2000) definition of "behavioral modernity" and their identification of the archaeological signatures of this behavior, it is clear that the archaeological records of AMH and Neandertal populations during the MSA/MP and EUP provide ample evidence for "modern behavior." Abstract thinking, planning depth, behavioral, economic, and technological innovativeness, and symbolic behavior are evident in their subsistence strategies, in their bone, wood, lithic, adhesive, and shell technologies, and in their burials, items of personal adornment, use of colorants, structured use of space, geographic expanses, and other behaviors.

Accordingly, most of the cognitive models discussed at the beginning of this chapter appear to be out of step with current archaeological evidence of Late Pleistocene hominin behavior. It is impossible to reconcile Mithen's (1996, 2005, 2010) assertion that Neandertals were unable to "combine intelligences" with the abundant archaeological evidence to the contrary. Klein's (2000a) model stands or falls on the non-modernity of pre-50,000 ybp AMH populations in Africa and the Levant (Barham and Mitchell 2008). But it is becoming increasingly difficult to maintain that the earliest AMH populations such as those represented by Qafzeh, Skhul, Blombos, Diepkloof Rockshelter, and Pinnacle Point are not behaviorally modern.

Similarly, the vast majority of McBrearty and Brooks' own criteria are met by Neandertals and, in some cases, even older populations, and so the capacity for these modern behaviors could not be the result of a speciation event 160,000 years ago. The validity of Wynn and Coolidge's model (2010) is harder to evaluate because the expression of a final enhancement of working memory may be more subtle than what we can discern in the archaeological record. But if, using modern behavior as our frame of reference, we argue that there is little archaeological evidence of a cognitive difference between Neandertal and AMH populations, the question becomes why did Neandertals go extinct and why is the archaeological record of later UP peoples quantitatively and qualitatively different from the archaeological records of MP / MSA and EUP hominins?

AN ALTERNATIVE MODEL

There is a growing tendency to understand the material culture and lifeways of Late Pleistocene hominins as historically situated phenomena. In other words, many researchers explain perceived behavioral differences between Neandertal and AMH populations as well as the transition from the MSA / MP to the EUP with reference to social, demographic, and cultural factors instead of, or in addition to, newly evolved, biologically based cognitive mechanisms, believing this to be most parsimonious with the archaeological, genetic, paleoneurological, and life history data (e.g., Chase 1999, 2001, 2006, Shennan 2001, Hockett and Haws 2005, Henry et al. 2004, Holloway, Broadfield, and Yuan 2004, Wolpoff et al. 2004, Brumm and Moore 2005, Hovers and Belfer-Cohen 2006, Conard 2006b, O'Connell 2006, d'Errico 2007, Barham 2007, Kuhn and Stiner 2007, Habgood and Franklin 2008, Powell, Shennan, and Thomas 2009, Soffer 2009, Straus 2009, Zilhão et al. 2010). As Hopkinson (2011) observes, "sporadic, localized and ephemeral outbreaks of behaviors and practices that become institutionalized and fixed in hominin behavioral repertoires only many millennia later are very difficult to explain in terms of currently dominant paradigms that refer such institutionalized behavioral shifts to biologically (and therefore innate) advances in hominin cognitive capacities." Accordingly, drawing on Shennan (2001, Powell, Shennan, and Thomas 2009) and Hopkinson (2011), it is possible to propose an alternate model that accounts not only for the seemingly inexplicable flashes of "modern behavior" that we see throughout the Paleolithic that do not persist, but also for the "explosion of art" in parts of Europe in the UP and for Neandertal extinction.

Biological species (including hominins) are distributed across a region in the form of local populations. Taken together, these local populations constitute a species' metapopulation (Hopkinson 2011). Metapopulations experience both successful periods when they expand at the local population level into new habitats, and stressful periods when they contract into refugia (Soffer 2009:48). Sometimes refuging is temporary and populations recover, while in other cases no recovery is possible and local extinctions take place.

The vulnerability of local populations is especially important because innovations occur locally and their fate depends on their spreading from one local population to another within the metapopulation (Hopkinson 2011). As population size increases so does the rate of innovation and the likelihood that a particular innovation will take hold and spread (Shennan 2001). Metapopulation size can remain the same as long as the size of the relevant local populations and the interaction between them increases (Hopkinson 2011). Thus, increase in population size can occur through population growth or when isolated populations come into contact with each other (Shennan 2001). I would add that this could include groups of other hominin species as well.

Based on genetic data, we know that during Oxygen Isotope Stage (OIS) 4 modern human populations fragmented and that some local populations of AMH went extinct (Lahr 1996, Lahr and Foley 1998, Shennan 2001, Kuhn and Stiner 2007). This may have resulted from the global impact of the eruption of Mt. Toba at approximately 71,000 ybp (Ambrose 1998) followed by the onset of harsh glacial conditions or for some as yet unknown reason. It was not until 60,000 ybp that climatic conditions ameliorated enough to allow for population growth and renewal (Lahr 1996, Lahr and Foley 1998) and not until the EUP that long-distance exchange networks may have increased the amount of contact populations had with each other (Shennan 2001). This recovery and expansion in population size is supported not only by genetic data but also by evidence of the broadening of the human diet and increase in the number of archaeological sites (Kuhn and Stiner 2007).

Shennan (2001:13) argues that the population decline at 70,000 ybp would have resulted in a loss of cultural variation as local populations contracted or went extinct. Once the climatic conditions eased at the end of OIS 4, local populations would have begun to increase. Shennan (2001) suggests that cultural innovations would have had greater impact in increasing overall population fitness and that the likelihood that innovations would be maintained and spread leading to dramatic changes in the archaeological record would also increase. Because the rate of innovation retention and spread increases so dramatically as small populations grow this could look like an "explosion" in the archaeological record and thus explain the "explosion" of art and personal adornment in the later Aurignacian. In fact, Kuhn and Stiner argue that

> rather than the appearance of novel cognitive abilities, the integration of beads and other ornaments into the material cultures of both sub-Saharan Africa and Eurasia reflects changing social and demographic concerns. Increasing populations associated with the origins and dispersal of anatomically modern *Homo sapiens* changed the social landscape, putting nearly everyone in frequent contact with strangers. This heightened level of interaction fostered sensitivity to group boundaries as a means of delimiting and defining bodies. (2007:48)

Similarly, Byers (1994) notes what he describes as a Style 1/Style 2 rupture in the archaeological record of the MP to UP transition. For Byers, this represents a transition from a society of non-symbol users (Style 1) to one dominated by symbol users (Style 2) as a minimum threshold of reflexive individuals within a population is surpassed. I believe that Byers is on the right track but that it is not a case of a transition within a population but rather of an overall increase in the sizes, numbers of, and interactions between local populations, the occurrence of cultural mutations, and the spread of new ideas and technologies that led to the rupture. I also think that this "rupture" occurred a few thousand years after the traditional transition of the MP–UP.

As many researchers have recently argued (e.g., Straus 2001:468–69; see also Riel-Salvatore and Clark 2001, Straus 2009), a mounting body of evidence supports "continuity in many aspects of human adaptation across the latter half of the Upper Pleistocene and…an analytical distinction between earlier and later Upper Paleolithic time." For many, the true rupture comes with the Gravettian (28–21,000 ybp). The Gravettian has been referred to as a "Golden" Age because of its innovations in subsistence, technology, and mortuary activity (e.g., double and triple burials), the development of huge regional centers, artistic endeavor (e.g., figurines), and other "non-utilitarian" aspects of behavior (Roebroeks et al. 2000; see also Pettitt 2005, 2010). The Gravettian is not the result of some further "neural mutation" but of population density and historical development.

There is evidence that modern human populations were affected by global climatic conditions after 70,000 ybp and there is no reason to believe that Neandertals were not similarly affected by these conditions even with local ecological variation. If both AMH and Neandertal populations were shrinking (with Neandertal populations in the Levant never recovering; see Shea 2010; Dalén et al. 2012), following Shennan's model we should expect that innovations and evidence of symbolic behavior would decrease and cease to be archaeologically visible. As Mark White and I argue (Nowell and White 2010), there is no need to signal when no one is listening. In fact, in their paper "Now You See It, Now You Don't: Modern Human Behavior in the Middle Paleolithic," Hovers and Belfer-Cohen (2006) argue that the lack of evidence for symbolic behavior in the Levant is a direct result of population size and that due to population instabilities and crashes stored knowledge, including technological and symbolic innovations, must be "re-invented" many times over.

As AMH populations recovered during the late MP and EUP, regional densities increased and contact between groups (of either the same or different species depending on the region) became more frequent, and cultural innovations sped up and spread more widely as a result. Late Neandertals (50,000–25/30,000 ybp) were caught up in this in two ways. First, their own material culture and everyday practices were changing. They were creating more items of personal adornment, expanding their tool industries, and engaging in other kinds of behavior that may have been prompted in part by this same growing sensitivity to group boundaries to which Kuhn and Stiner allude (2007; see also d'Errico et al. 1998a), including encroachment and possible competition from other Neandertal groups or "cultures" (Nowell and Chang 2012). This is not the same as imitating AMH ornament makers without understanding why they were doing so or the power and potential of using these items as a means of communication, as has been suggested by R. White (1992; see discussion in Speth 2004).

Second, the influx of AMHs into Europe and the Levant meant that the Neandertal way of life as "top carnivores" was no longer viable (Stiner and Kuhn 2006, Shea 2010). Kuhn and Stiner (2007:48) "emphasize that these populations were small by modern standards: what is important are relative changes in population densities. The pressures that population density places on human societies depend on the nature of the economies and conditions of the landscape on which people make their livings." The Neandertal strategy could only be sustained with low population densities but as increasing numbers of AMH arrive in Europe they tip the balance against Neandertals (Stiner and Kuhn 2006). But was this because of a cognitive deficiency on the part of Neandertals? Many historic populations have dwindled in size eventually disappearing all together but no one would argue that this was because of some cognitive "inferiority" (O'Connell 2006). The influx of modern human populations appears to have been enough to result in local population extinctions, forcing Neandertals to the fringes of Europe, with the last surviving Neandertals inhabiting Gibraltar ca. 25,000 years ago (Finlayson et al. 2006). This region may have served as a final refugium for them because of its Mediterranean climate and plentiful marine resources (Finlayson et al. 2006). It appears, however, that their population was too small to remain viable in the long term.

Similarly, in the Levant from MIS 4 to MIS 3, increasingly cold and arid conditions reduced the amount of the Levant that was habitable by Neandertals (Shea 2010). Accordingly, there is evidence that the Neandertal range was contracting and that they were undergoing resource stress (Shea 2010 and references therein). Their decrease in population allowed AMH to reoccupy the

Levant from Africa but this time bringing with them a more effective projectile technology and a broader subsistence strategy (Shea 2010). Shea argues that AMH, as an "invader species" armed with new technologies, away from parasites and zoonotic transmitted diseases, would have experienced a tremendous growth in population. It is likely that Neandertals did not develop similar technologies because their strategy of focusing on a limited number of prey and relatively simple tools had been effective for thousands of years. As Shea (2010:141) notes, "it is not easy to explain why Neanderthals did not also develop projectile weaponry and other niche broadening techniques, but it is unlikely to reflect deficient intellect (Speth 2004)." It is more likely that the time and energy investment needed to produce these new technologies was too costly in the context of their overall way of making a living. As Shea (2010:141) concludes, "but for the context of climatically forced habitat degradation around 47/45,000 BP that created selective pressure for niche broadening, Neanderthals might have remained in the Levant indefinitely."

Mithen (2010), Klein (2000a), McBrearty and Brooks (2000), Wynn and Coolidge (2010), and others argue that the perceived behavioral differences between modern humans and Neandertals are so significant that they must be the result of fundamental cognitive differences between these two populations. A careful review of the paleoneurological, genetic, life history, and archaeological data, however, demonstrates the close affinities between Neandertals and AMH populations. Many researchers now argue that differences between them are best explained in terms of social, historical, cultural, and demographic factors. Pulses of modern behavior that appear and disappear only to take hold thousands of years later are the result of innovations occurring in local populations vulnerable to extinction. It is only as population levels increase and contact between local populations (including of other hominin types) increases that there is strong selection for the symbolic behavior that we see among AMH and Late Neandertals. The demise of the Neandertals is likely the result of serial extinctions at the local population level brought about by climatic change with competition from modern humans as the tipping factor. As with many conflicts between modern groups, this outcome was likely the result of a more effective way of life in a particular place and time. Cognitive models must consider the totality of the archaeological record, make comparisons that control for temporal variation, and draw on known mechanisms of human population dynamics when articulating the nature of potential differences between Neandertals and modern humans.

11

Rethinking Paleoanthropology:
A World Queerer Than We Supposed

PETER J. RICHERSON AND ROBERT BOYD

The universe is not only queerer than we suppose, it is queerer than we can suppose.
— J.B.S. Haldane (1927:286)

Advances in paleoclimatology and paleoecology are producing an ever more detailed picture of the environments in which our species evolved, helping us to understand the processes by which our large brain and its productions—toolmaking, complex social institutions, language, art, religion—emerged. Our large brain relative to body mass and the extreme elaboration of our cultures differentiate us from our nearest relatives. We achieved our present anatomy and behavioral repertoire *very* recently. Fossil material attributable to our species goes back perhaps 200,000 years ago (200 kya), by which time the brain of our species and of Neandertals had reached nearly modern proportions. Artifacts that strike us as representing fully modern behavior are rare early in the record of our species, and only become abundant after 50 kya, and then mainly in western Eurasia (Marean et al. 2007, Klein 2009). Our ecological dominance began with the evolution of agriculture starting about 10,000 years ago (Vitousek et al. 1997).

Explaining the late coming of human brains is a major evolutionary puzzle as most important animal adaptations are old. Eyes, internal skeletons, adaptations for terrestrial life and for flight all date back hundreds of millions of years. Many lineages of fully terrestrial animals have re-adapted to fully aquatic life including whales and other mammals, several lineages of mesozoic reptiles, and families from most insect orders. Given that big brains and culture have been such an overwhelming success for us why did they not evolve long ago?

MACROEVOLUTIONARY EXPLANATION

Evolutionary biologists speak of microevolution and macroevolution. While microevolution describes the generation to generation changes that we can observe directly in the field or lab, macroevolution concerns longer time scale changes such as the evolution of new species or the evolution of larger and larger brains in a succession of species.

Evolutionary scholars advance two major sorts of hypotheses—internal and external—to explain big events, such as the rise of modern humans in the late Middle and Late Pleistocene (Boyd and Richerson 1992, Stearns 2002). We might imagine that evolution is a slow, halting, and biased process, limited and directed by *internal* processes. For example, the evolution of the large brains that subserve human technical and social capacities might involve many innovations, each one difficult for evolution to accomplish. Brain size increase might be slow and halting because complex new brain reorganizations cannot occur quickly even if they are strongly favored by selection. The number of mutations and recombinations required may be many. The genotype-to-phenotype mappings may be complex. Once a basic primate template for the brain of a diurnal, arboreal, visually oriented creature was laid down, the path to a larger brain may have been easier. Nevertheless, progress toward the complex human brain may have been slow and halting.

The other class of hypotheses assumes that selection is a powerful force and that genetic constraints on the rate of evolution are of modest importance. At any given time, organisms are close to an evolutionary equilibrium with current environments (Walker and Valentine 1984). According to this model, any major changes in organisms on the geological time scale will be a result of *external* processes of environmental change. Climate might favor small brains in some geological eras (e.g., the relatively small brains of Mesozoic mammals and dinosaurs), while the climates of other eras favor larger brains. Brains have been getting larger and larger in many mammalian lineages for the last 65 million years or so (Jerison 1973), suggesting an external change that parallels the evolution of brain size (Elton, Bishop, and Wood 2001). Bird brain evolution is much less well known than that of mammals because the fragile skeletons of birds rarely fossilize. However, some birds, such as crows, have large brains for their body size and exhibit intelligent behavior comparable to that of apes. Ancient birds had small brains (Emery and Clayton 2004).

Co-evolution is another potential pacemaker of macroevolution. For example, Geerat Vermeij (1987) suggested that the evolution of shelly marine invertebrates was driven by predator-prey arms races. If crabs evolve stronger jaws, their snail prey will evolve stronger shells. If antelope become swifter to avoid predators, cheetah must become swifter still to capture them. Many predators and prey show clear evidence of many rounds of co-evolution to arrive at quite advanced adaptations for offense and defense. If these races unfold slowly, then co-evolutionary processes will have an important macroevolutionary role. Vermeij suggests that the level of energy available in ecosystems governs the equilibrium reached by an arms race when it is finally exhausted. If arms races are as rapid as the races metaphor suggests, then predator-prey arms races will be a microevolutionary phenomenon and the macroevolutionary pattern will be regulated by such external factors as the geochemical and geophysical evolution of the earth. Sometimes, ocean upwelling is active and the ocean is productive, leading to advanced arms races. Other times, the ocean may be stably stratified, keeping predator arms and prey defenses weak and simple.

Co-evolution between two organisms is just a special case of the phenomenon called niche construction (Odling-Smee, Laland, and Feldman 2003). Organisms often modify their physical as well as biological environment and then adapt to the environment they create. Humans build shelters and sew clothing in cold, cloudy environments and then need to evolve light skin to biosynthesize enough vitamin D in the small areas of skin exposed to the infrequent sun (Jablonski and Chaplin 2010). On the other hand, the need for two or more organisms to co-evolve could potentially slow the evolutionary process if both partners are evolving on complex adaptive topographies.

The alert reader will already have noticed that everyone must be an externalist, and internalist, and a co-evolutionist/niche contructionist, depending upon the scale at which the question is asked. Evolution is never instantaneous, so at short enough time scales internal processes must be important. Similarly, at long enough time scales external processes must be important. Surely no advanced animal life was possible until the earth's atmosphere became oxidizing so that oxygen-powered respiration to drive an active life became possible. The Cambrian explosion of animal life was likely a consequence, perhaps a considerably delayed consequence, of an atmosphere with ample oxygen. Similarly, no one doubts that co-evolutionary and niche construction processes are important. The right questions to ask are what processes drive particular evolutionary events on what time scales?

What follows in this chapter is an attempt to stop people thinking in terms of what we call the "naïve internalist" hypothesis. Many students of human evolution seem to assume that the evolution of the world's most complex species must have taken a very long time, as vertebrates generally, then primates, and finally hominins gradually worked their way toward higher relative fitness using ever bigger and more complex brains. In this picture, the external environment itself did not change appreciably while our ancestors became behaviorally more and more sophisticated.

Perhaps this picture is essentially correct, but much evidence casts doubt on it. Past environments were often very different from current ones, as we shall see. At least in some cases, internal constraints do not seem to be limiting except on short time scales. Perhaps when external environments change, some lineages will fairly rapidly evolve to fill every empty ecological niche created by the change. In the last 12,000 years, hundreds of new fish species apparently evolved from a handful of ancestors in Lake Victoria, giving us some idea how fast natural selection can fill new niches (Verheyen et al. 2003).

WHEN WILL SELECTION FAVOR BIG BRAINS AND FANCY CULTURE?

Consider a radically externalist picture. Vertebrate brains are all roughly scale models of one another, differing mainly in size and hence in raw processing power. Relatively few and simple changes may be needed to create larger brains and new functional units, such as vision processing areas, in these larger brains (Krubitzer 1995), contrary to one of the main arguments for the internalist hypothesis. This is especially so within an order, such as the primates (Striedter 2005). Selection can thus plausibly have increased the size of brains and brain components like the cerebral hemispheres of the large-brained birds and mammals in fairly short order. We allow that some time is necessary to fine-tune the functions of large brains, but let us suppose that much can be accomplished in the order of a thousand generations (~25,000 years for humans). Animal breeding for such things as increased milk yield and very large and very small size in dogs get large responses to artificial selection in tens of generations, so if brain evolution is mostly scaling up and scaling down, a thousand generations is actually a generous allocation of time if selection is even moderately strong.

An important consideration is that brains are very expensive organs metabolically. The adult human brain consumes ~16% of total metabolism against perhaps 5% for mammals with average brain sizes and 1% for our smallest brained relatives (Aiello and Wheeler 1995). Humans have plausibly had to sacrifice gut size and hence digestive efficiency to support the evolution of our metabolically costly brain, since gut tissue is even more energy intensive than nervous tissue. All else being equal, selection will favor as small a brain as possible. Think dinosaurs and their famously small brains relative to their body size. If evolution is going to favor big brains, the reason must be that the relevant organisms must live in complex or variable environments that demand big brains. The fact that many lineages of mammals (and probably birds) have undergone recent increases in brain size (Jerison 1973) strongly suggests that a common external environmental change has driven this major macroevolutionary trend.

What sorts of selective pressures would drive the evolution of large brains and, in particular, the extraordinarily large brain and the associated complex culture of humans? Costly systems for phenotypic flexibility—individual learning and social learning are examples—are adaptations to cope with variable environments, as we will argue below. Organisms adapt to very slow environmental change by organic evolution and often to swifter change by range changes. Nonhuman large-brained animals—including other primates, and the crow and parrot families of birds—use large brains to learn how to cope with unpredictable environmental change (Reader and Laland 2002, Sol et al. 2005).

The effect of social learning is to leverage individual learning and decision-making using the inheritance of acquired variation. In a cultural system, a mother can transmit some of her accumulated wisdom to her offspring, sparing them the need to do as much costly trial and error learning as they would otherwise have to do. Many animals use simple systems of social learning to accomplish this trick (Heyes and Galef 1996).

Humans have evolved the capacity for an extremely sophisticated system of cumulative cultural evolution on this simple foundation (Boyd and Richerson 1985, Richerson and Boyd 2005, Tennie, Call, and Tomasello 2009). Humans are quite accurate imitators allowing us to acquire more complex behaviors from others than is possible with simpler forms of social learning not dependent on accurate imitation. Even something as simple as a stone-tipped spear draws upon complex wood-working and stone-working skills and the making of cordage and adhesives. Human individual learning is mainly applied to small improvements in already complex artifacts, leading to the cumulative improvements of toolkits over many generations. No one person invents a fancy skin boat like the Arctic kayak. Rather, kayaks probably evolved over a period of a thousand years or more to judge by the evidence from more durable artifacts (Dumond 1984). Aside from just passing on useful innovations, people can also shop in the marketplace of extant ideas. If we see our neighbors employing a superior new technique, we can borrow it from them, leading to the fairly rapid diffusion of new techniques over wide areas.

Mathematical models suggest that a costly cultural system is adapted to cope with fluctuations of less than a generation (horizontal borrowing of simple innovations) to many tens of generations for the buildup of whole new subsistence systems. On time scales beyond several hundred generations, or around 10,000 years, even humans will begin to respond to variation with genetic rather than cultural adaptations. Thus, humans have undergone massive cultural evolution in the past 10,000 years while the evolution of our genes amounted to some relatively minor tinkering, much of that in response to new diets and new diseases caused by agriculture supplying abundant starchy staples and by the dense populations supported by agriculture (Sabeti et al. 2006, Laland, Odling-Smee, and Myles 2010, Richerson and Boyd 2010). On a time scale of 100,000 years and longer, human populations in the past evolved genetically in ways that paleoanthropologists can easily see in their bones.

Figure 11.1 illustrates these principles with the results of a theoretical study (Boyd and Richerson 1985). Two different stylized populations were pitted against one another in three different environments. One population comprised basic animals that could learn individually and transmit the *starting* point of individual learning genetically. The second population was exactly the same, except that the cultural population transmitted the *end* point

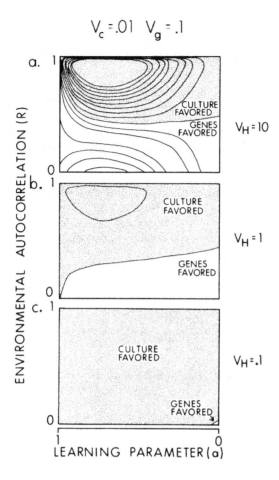

$$V_c = .01 \quad V_g = .1$$

11.1. The results of a mathematical contest between a model of genetic transmission plus individual learning and a model of cultural transmission plus individual learning. The panels should be read as contour plots measuring the difference in fitness of the two populations under different conditions. The learning parameter a measures the importance of inherited initial behavior relative to individual experience. When $a = 1$, individuals don't learn individually but trust their inherited information completely. V_H is the environmental variation, rising in increments of 10 from the bottom to the top panel. The environmental autocorrelation, R, measures the degree to which the environmental variation is organized into multi-generational "waves" in which the parental and offspring environments statistically resemble one another. As is explained in the text, the conspicuous mound in the top panel, where the culture plus learning system is highly fit compared to its genes plus learning alternative, occurs in an environment with extreme, but fairly highly autocorrelated variation. Note that at even higher autocorrelations the genetic system is favored again. (From Boyd and Richerson 1985: chap. 4.)

of their learning to their descendants via social learning. The existence of social learning is one of the most basic differences between a cultural and a genetic evolutionary system. Culture includes the potential to inherit acquired traits and genes do not. The figure is in the form of a contour map that plots the difference in fitness of the two populations as a function of important evolutionary and environmental parameters. The a parameter across the bottom measures the importance of individual learning. When $a = 1$, individuals depend entirely upon their cultural or genetic inheritance and don't learn for themselves. When $a = 0$, they depend entirely upon their own learning and give no weight to what they inherit. The vertical axis is the effect of how organized the variable environment is. The world of the model is noisy, but the noise can be autocorrelated. That is, if $R = 0$, the environmental variation is simple random noise with a variance V_H. As R increases toward 1, a stronger and stronger statistical relationship exists between the environment of mom's generation and offspring's generation, holding the total amount of variation constant. The three panels illustrate the effect of three different amounts of total variance, V_H.

Note that the topography is very flat when the amount of environmental variance is small or moderate. In the model comparison, genes and culture do almost the same work when little evolution is required. If we added a cost to culture, like having a big brain, we would see no culture in the bottom two panels, or only the low-cost culture that many small-brained animals have. Culture has a very big advantage only in one region of the top panel. When the environmental variation is very high, but when that variation is fairly highly autocorrelated, culture is a big advantage. Also, notice that the peak in the top two panels is shifted to the left of center, indicating a substantial dependence on cultural transmission relative to the individual's own experience in the region where culture has its largest advantage. When culture is really important, you should take mom's advice pretty much to heart. If the autocorrelation is too low, listening to mom is not sensible; she is too likely to have lived in a different environment from you. In this situation it makes sense to depend heavily upon individual learning. Although not well displayed in the plot, there is a cliff at the top of each panel. As the environmental autocorrelation becomes very strong, the cultural system becomes a liability again. This result also makes sense. When R is very large, environmental change is very slow, and genes track slow changes under the influence of selection well enough to outweigh the extra costs of the cultural system.

The culture imagined in this model is not only simple but conservative. We allowed only gene-like vertical transmission from one generation to the next. Other aspects of the cultural system, like biased borrowing of useful techniques within a generation will have the effect of making culture useful in more rapidly changing, less autocorrelated environments. Qualitatively, we might say that the more conservative vertical components of culture, especially the building of complex adaptations by many piecemeal innovations, ought to be useful to adapt to changes with autocorrelation out to a few hundred generations. The less conservative mechanisms might be useful to spread new adaptive responses to step-like environmental changes horizontally down to time scales of less than a generation. The Anatomically Modern Human (AMH) cultural system, complete with languages that can accurately and rapidly communicate many ideas, looks like a "tunable" system that could be used to adapt to a broad range of variation from time scales of years to a few millennia. This modeling exercise was completed more than a decade before the climate variation described in the next section was discovered, so the models were not concocted to fit the data!

The human cultural system of adaptation may be thought of as a specific subtype of what Potts (1996, 1998) called "variability selection" (see also Calvin 2002). Potts imagined that a variety of genetic and behavioral adaptive systems would have been favored as environmental variability increased in the last few million years. He discusses environmental variability on a variety of time scales and is not specific about what mechanisms are adapted to which time scales. As the data reviewed below show, the last glacial had high rates of climate change on the millennial and submillennial time scales, exactly those that the theoretical study discussed above flags for special interest.

A reviewer sensibly objected that this explanation for human brain size fails to account for why our brain is so extremely large whereas other species still retain much smaller brains. In his classic study, Jerison (1973) noted that *distributions* of mammal brain sizes increased during the Cenozoic with many mammals retaining small brains. Evolutionary ecologists have long been interested in the effect of environmental variation on species diversity (e.g., Abugov 1982). The general effect is that environmental variation opens niches for "fugitive species" that evade more competitive species by growing quickly in unpredictable patches before superior competitors can build up a population to suppress them. Thus variability tends to increase diversity by creating new ecological niches for species with adaptations keyed on variability.

We imagine that increasingly variable climates diversified niches such that smaller-brained species could still exploit the least variable part of variable environments. Larger-brained species began to use cleverer strategies to exploit windfalls and evade dearths to which smaller-brained species are unable to adapt. The high overhead cost of large brains (Aiello and Wheeler 1995) means that species that exploit resources to some degree protected from environmental fluctuations will be able to outcompete otherwise similar larger-brained species for more stable resources. Sol et al. (2005) provide evidence that the success of introductions of birds to novel environments is correlated with their brain size relative to body size. Reader and Laland's (2002) study of mentions of innovative behavior in the primatological literature finds a strong correlation between innovation and brain size. An increased diversity of brain sizes among otherwise similar taxa at evolutionary equilibrium thus seems a quite plausible result of more variable environments.

Humans in the Pleistocene might well count as a fugitive species exploiting a rather marginal niche. We are not aware of any paleoanthropological evidence that Pleistocene human populations were ever very abundant compared to our smaller-brained competitors. Estimates of effective human population sizes based on mitochondrial coalescence data suggest populations of a few thousand in Africa and perhaps 100,000 in South Asia after 40 kya (Atkinson, Gray, and Drummond 2008). Middle and Lower Pleistocene human abundances seem to have been low relative to competing species (Bobe and Leakey 2009). For example, at the Swartkrans site in South Africa, a large volume of material was excavated, dating between 1.8 and 1 mya. The minimum number of *Homo* individuals recovered was 3 compared to 39 australopithecines, 33 monkeys, 10 large cats, 13 hyenas, and 15 canids (Watson 2004). Given that this is a famous early human site, the number of *Homo* recovered seems rather modest compared to probably competing species, assuming that early *Homo* had an omnivorous diet. The relative abundance of *Homo* in a representative sample of Pleistocene fossil localities would be very interesting. *Homo*'s commitment to large brains and culture did not become a major evolutionary success story until late in our history.

Our stark externalist hypothesis can easily fail in the face of evidence that is currently accumulating regarding past climate variation. If the millennial and submillenial scale variation in the climate record has not changed as the brain sizes and cultural sophistication have increased, allowing for only small lags on the order of at most a few tens of thousands of years, the radical externalist hypothesis is untenable. We can add back more and more internal constraints if lags prove to be longer. If the data eventually show no relationship at all between millennial and submillennial scale variation and the growth of brains and culture, or more decisively yet, an inverse relationship, our theoretical argument must be fatally flawed. Perhaps internal limitations are all that have regulated the growth of nervous systems since the first multicelled animals evolved in the Precambrian—the extreme internal hypothesis. That human brains and culture seem to have evolved in a time of high environmental variation could be a complete coincidence.

EVOLUTION OF THE EARTH'S CLIMATE SYSTEM

The global environment has changed radically over the last 80 million years (Fig. 11.2). Likely enough, environmental change has thrown up vast new ranges of adaptive peaks favoring big brains since the extinction of the dinosaurs (and the ancient small-brained mammals and birds that were their companions). These peaks have probably grown higher in the past few million years. The Holocene geological era (the last 10,000 or so years) has been graced with an unusually stable climate. The Little Ice Age, lasting from ~1100 CE until 1900 CE, turns out to be a polite hiccup compared to the robust climatic belches of the slightly deeper past, although the Little Ice Age hiccup blew a hard wind on some human societies (Fagan 2002). Ruddiman (2007) argues that the long quiet Holocene climate is unusual for an interglacial and that it is a product of gentle anthropogenic increases in atmospheric CO_2 and CH_4 due to releases of these gases from forest clearance and from rice paddies. He attributes the Little Ice Age to Eurasian farm abandonment and forest regrowth in the aftermath of the Bubonic Plague.

Geologists in the 19th century discovered the first hints of dramatically different past climates in the unmistakable signs of several large-scale ice ages in the latter part of the Pleistocene era. Classic geological methods gained a limited insight into these events because each succeeding glacial advance nearly wiped out the evidence of its predecessors. Ocean, lake, and ice coring in the 1960s and 70s, together with the development of dating methods and geochemical, geophysical, and biological proxy measures of past climates, revealed a much richer picture of climate deterioration over the whole Cenozoic ("Age of the Mammals") era (65 mya–present). Under favorable conditions, application of these methods to ice and mud cores enable paleoclimatologists to read a great deal from the material deposited layer by layer by the fall of sediment and snow.

Two of the many paleoclimate proxies are $\delta^{18}O$ and pollen grains (Bradley 1999). $\delta^{18}O$ is the ratio of the main natural heavy isotope of oxygen to the most abundant isotope ^{16}O, expressed as deviations from a standard sample in parts per thousand.

Modern mass spectrometers ionize samples containing isotopes and accelerate them toward an array of detectors in a magnetic field to separate isotopes based on their mass. Small variations in isotope ratios are measured quite accurately by such instruments. The deposition of oxygen isotopes in the shells of common marine amoebae called foraminifera is temperature dependent, providing a paleothermometer for the oceans. The foraminiferal thermometer is complicated by the fact that $H_2^{16/18}O$ water, being a bit heavier than $H_2^{16/16}O$, has a lower vapor pressure. This means that a given molecule of $H_2^{16/18}O$ is less likely than a molecule of $H_2^{16/16}O$ to escape from the ocean surface as water vapor and, if already a vapor molecule, more likely to condense into rain or snow. This condensation discrimination effect is temperature dependent, providing a paleothermometer measuring the temperature at which snow preserved in ice caps condensed.

During ice ages, isotopic discrimination makes the ocean's waters systematically heavier as light water is disproportionately locked up in the glaciers, biasing the foraminiferal thermometer. Hence water vapor evaporated from the heavy oceans will be heavier than during glacials too, biasing the condensation thermometer. These biological and physical isotope discrimination processes have been intensively studied in an effort to calibrate the proxies in terms of actual temperatures. Often, the raw isotopic ratio in ocean carbonate skeletons or ice water is reported without conversion to a possibly problematic paleotemperature. Used in this way, $\delta^{18}O$ is mainly an ice-volume indicator, but ice volume is closely related to global temperature.

Pollen grains are representative of the many biological proxies that are used for inferring past terrestrial climates from lake and coastal ocean sediments. Many plants shed rather copious amounts of pollen, and pollen grains have characteristic cell walls that preserve well in lake- and ocean-bottom muds. As layers of mud accumulate, they roughly record the abundances of pollen-shedding plants. Plants have more or less limited ranges today and the limits are often climatic. Given a suite of plants, and assuming that plants have not evolved much, we can infer past climates from the pollen found in cores. Aside from climate reconstructions, pollen spectra also help paleoecologists reconstruct past ecosystems. Climate and climate variation have direct impacts on human populations, but many of the most important impacts will be felt through impacts on ecosystems which furnish biotic resources to the humans that live in them.

The large-scale history of climates over the Age of the Mammals is that climates became cooler and drier in a series of steplike transitions, culminating in the Plio-Pleistocene ice ages after about 3 mya (Figs. 11.2 and 11.3). The Plio-Pleistocene ice ages themselves are a multistage deterioration that includes three shifts toward higher amplitude, lower frequency ice fluctuations. The first stone tools appear in the paleoanthropological record 2.6 mya, not long after the climate variation began to increase in the late Pliocene (Opdyke 1995). The first signs that hominins start their run toward our extraordinary brain sizes occur slightly later (McHenry and Coffing 2000) (Fig. 11.3). Around a million years ago, 100 ky-year-long glacial cycles of very great amplitude began, the last few wiping out all of the continental evidence of their predecessors. The amplitude of the 100 ky-year-cycles is greater for the last half of their dominance. Up until the advent of ocean core drilling in the mid-20th century, geologists had thus seen only the last three of these big excursions and knew nothing of the longer record.

The low-frequency climate fluctuations are tuned to variations in the earth's orbit. The fluctuations that dominated the record in the late Miocene and early Pliocene (6–3 mya) have a period of around 23 ky and are tuned to the wobble of the earth's axis of rotation. The variation from the late Pliocene to the mid-Pleistocene (3–1 mya) was dominated by a 41 kyr cycle that is tuned to the variation of the inclination of the earth's axis of rotation. In the last half of the Pleistocene, the dominant mode of variation switched again, now to a 100 kyr cycle tuned to the variation in the earth's orbit from being more nearly circular to markedly elliptical.

The causes of this ongoing climate change were not the orbital parameters themselves, since these remain nearly constant for long periods of time. They also cause only relatively small redistributions in the amount of radiation from the sun as a function of latitude and season of the year. Rather, the earth's ocean-atmosphere-ice sheet system seems to have evolved to

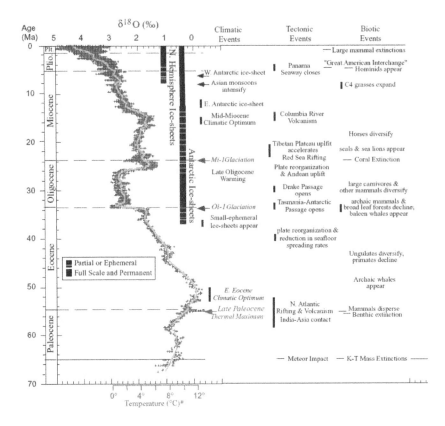

11.2. The record of climate warmth over the last 69 million years based upon the ^{18}O isotope paleoclimate index. The envelope of gray points around the center trend line gives some idea of the increasing amplitude of variation about the trend. Other important events associated with climate change are indicated. The geological events include ones that caused reorganization of air and water flows that may have played a role in causing the climate change. Biotic changes are likely the evolutionary consequences of climate change. For example, as forests contracted because of increased aridity accompanying cooling at the end of the Eocene, archaic mammals were replaced by grazers adapted to more open country. The large carnivores that preyed upon the grazers also diversified. The Miocene expansion of the C4 aridity adapted grasses was probably a consequence of the spread of tropical savannas and temperate steppes. (Modified from Zachos et al. 2001. Reprinted with permission from AAAS.)

"tune in" different orbital frequencies and amplify them. Seafloor spreading has altered the positions of continents, closed seaways, raised mountain ranges, all having the effect of altering wind patterns and ocean currents.

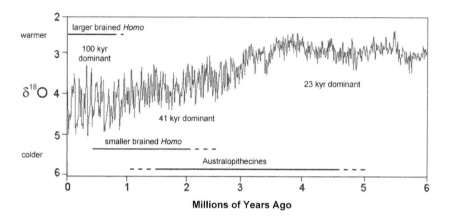

11.3. A composite marine core record of climate deterioration since the mid-Miocene. During cold periods the oceans are enriched in the heavy ^{18}O isotope, a proxy for paleotemperature and ice volume. Periods during which different orbital quasi-cycles dominate the variation in δ^{18}O are indicated. The time lines for important groups of hominine taxa are indicated. Australopithecines include both gracile and robust forms from the early *Australopithecus ramidus* to the late *A. robustus.* The line for small-brained *Homo* includes *H. rudolfensis, erectus,* and *ergaster.* The line for large-brained *Homo* includes *H. heidelbergensis, neanderthalensis,* and *sapiens.* (Redrawn from Opdyke 1995; hominin time lines adapted from Klein 2009. See also deMenocal 2004.)

Ice particularly acts as a feedback mechanism. If cooling causes ice sheets to grow, their bright white surface reflects sunlight back to space, cooling the earth still further. No consensus yet exists on the exact mechanisms involved in the tuning process. The annotations on Figure 11.2 are a clue as to what is on paleoclimatologists' minds.

In the late 1980s and early 1990s two teams of paleoclimatologists, one mostly American (the Greenland Ice Sheet Project 2) and one primarily European (the Greenland Ice Core Project) drilled two 3 km long cores 20 miles apart through the middle of the Greenland Ice Cap (Alley 2000). These teams discovered that last-glacial climates varied sharply on quite short time scales (Fig. 11.4). The cores can resolve the seasons back more than 10 kya and the resolution at 80 kya is only a little more than a decade. Some of the changes in the ice core record are instantaneous within the limits of the record.

Events during the final episodes of warming at the end of the Pleistocene are well resolved in Greenland ice. For example, the Bølling transition is the increase in temperature that produced the last high-amplitude spike before the final end of high amplitude millennial scale variation (just after H1 in Fig. 11.4). This sudden jump from rather cold conditions to intergla-cial warmth began about 14,650 years ago. The climate in Greenland seems to have warmed about 9° C in about 50 years (Severinghaus and Brook 1999). The most extreme event in the Holocene was a two-century-long cold snap about 8,500 years ago when Greenland cooled by about 2.8° C and Central Europe by about 1.7° C (von Grafenstein et al. 1998). This cold event was probably due to a pulse of meltwater from the remnants of the North American or European continental glaciers and can be seen as a sharp downward spike in Figure 11.4.

Exactly what process drove the high-frequency, high-amplitude variation during the last glacial is poorly understood. One of the main mechanisms thought to drive the millennial and submillennial scale variation in climate is variation in heat transport to high latitudes in the Northern Hemisphere by the so-called Atlantic Conveyor (Broecker and Denton 1989). The Atlan-tic Conveyor consists of the Gulf Stream and associated currents of warm, salty water that today flow north of Iceland. At these high latitudes, the

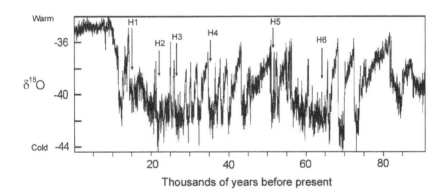

11.4. The Greenland ice paleotemperature proxy record. During periods of high ice volume [18]O is depleted in ice as it accumulates in the ocean. These data are filtered (averaged) using a 150-year low-pass filter so that variations on the time scale of 150 years and less are not portrayed. The Holocene is the little-varying last 11,000 years. The Heinrich events, when large volumes of ice-rafted debris from the North American Glacier were deposited in the western North Atlantic, are noted as H1-H6. (Redrafted after Ditlevsen, Svensmark, and Johnsen 1996 and Bond et al. 1993.)

warm water is cooled in winter by evaporation and conduction of heat to the cold air. It thus becomes sufficiently dense to sink in large volumes to form one of the two major sources of dense bottom water in the Holocene oceans (the other major source is Antarctic Bottom Water, formed in the Southern Ocean along the coast of Antarctica).

These deep-cycling currents are known as the earth's "thermohaline" circulation since the system is driven by temperature and salt effects on density, unlike shallow currents that are wind driven. The sinking of North Atlantic Bottom Water draws the warm water of the tropical and subtropical Atlantic poleward, warming the Northern Hemisphere at high latitudes, preventing continental glaciers from forming in North America and western Europe. During the ice ages, this circulation fails or is driven to lower latitudes, allowing the formation of northern continental glaciers.

One of the sources of instability in the thermohaline circulation is the discharge of fresh water into the North Atlantic. Fresh water is significantly less dense than salty ocean water. If the continental glaciers discharge large volumes of freshwater ice to the high North Atlantic, the conveyor will shut down or shift south. The striking fact is that the continental glaciers, particularly the North American one, discharged vast quantities of ice into the North Atlantic in spasms called Heinrich events (after the German oceanographer who first discovered them).

Icebergs calved from the glacier carried large volumes of sand and pebbles that are recovered in ocean sediment cores and can be traced back to the geological formations over which the glacial parents of the icebergs traveled. Note in Figure 11.4 that much of the variation in the last glacial consists of warm peaks followed by relatively slow cooling punctuated by abrupt warming. Heinrich events are associated with the final part of the cooling in some of these "Bond cycles," followed within a few hundred years by an abrupt warming (Bond et al. 1993). Bundled within the Bond cycles are Dansgaard-Oeschger cycles, again named after the oceanographers who discovered them, with periods of about 1,000 years. Note that the variation is anything but a simple cycle; every Bond cycle has its unique features. Not all Bond cycles are associated with Heinrich events. A vivid picture of the difficulties of disentangling all the feedbacks that might be implicated in the generation of millennial and submillennial scale variation can be found in Broecker (1995).

Since higher latitudes are more affected by glacial variations in temperature than lower latitude regions, one might imagine that the latitudes relevant to human evolution were little influenced by millennial and submillennial scale climate variation. This is clearly not the case. High-resolution lake and ocean cores have turned up considerable evidence that all latitudes were affected. At least in the Northern Hemisphere, the variation was driven by the same processes that affected the high Arctic. The Southern Hemisphere data are complex and controversial. The same sort of millennial and sub-millennial scale variation exists, but the peaks and troughs may not correspond to those in the Northern Hemisphere.

Some notable high-resolution data come from marine cores off the California coast (Hendy and Kennett 2000), the Arabian Sea (Schultz, von Rad, and Erlenkeuser 1998), the tropical Atlantic (Petersen et al. 2000), the South China Sea (Wang et al. 1999), and a lake core from Italy (Allen, Watts, and Huntley 2000). A lake core from Lake Tanganyika in the African Rift resolved some of the millennial and submillennial scale features seen in other cores (Stoltz et al. 2003). In the case of the California coast, the temperature variation between stadials (colder periods) and interstadials (warmer periods) in the last glacial was about 7° C, whereas during the entire Holocene variations have stayed within a 2° C envelope. So far, most of the high-resolution data available are restricted to the last glacial, but reasonably high-resolution data for the last several glacial cycles are becoming available (Martrat et al. 2007, Loulergue et al. 2008). These records suggest that glacial epochs have highly variable climates and that interglacials have less, just as in the last glacial cycle. Larrasoaña et al. (2003) report from a dust record from the Eastern Mediterranean that millennial scale variation increased sharply after the shift of the low frequency variation to dominance of the 100 ky cycle.

Much of the evolutionary trajectory toward modern humans transpired in the last 500 ky or so (Klein 2009, McBrearty and Brooks 2000). An extreme externalist hypothesis postulating short lags between selection and response to selection would require ongoing increases in environmental variability to drive ongoing human evolution between 500 kya and about 50 kya, by which time the paleoanthropological record indicates that humans were cognitively completely modern. The complexity of durable artifacts and the quality of artistic productions from the Upper Paleolithic in western Eurasia (the best-studied region) are on the same level as those collected from living hunter-gatherers.

According to McBrearty and Brooks (2000), during the Middle Paleolithic period, brains got very large and our material culture began to add fancier and fancier elements, culminating in the Upper Paleolithic of western Eurasia. Klein and Edgar (2002) propose a much more abrupt shift from the Middle to Upper Paleolithic cultures, perhaps deriving from a fortuitous mutation enabling symbolic behavior about 50 kya. Could this part of the human evolutionary story have been driven by ongoing increases in high-frequency environmental variation, or was the final modernization a result of internal limitations causing a lag in responses to climate change that occurred earlier, perhaps with the shift to the dominance of the 100 ky glacial cycle beginning about a million years ago?

We currently have two cores with relevant data. One core from the eastern Atlantic off Iberia offers a high-resolution glimpse of the last 420 ky (Martrat et al. 2007). The other is the EPICA Dome C ice core from Antarctica, which samples the last 800 ky (Loulergue et al. 2008). The last glacial cycle was considerably more variable than the second- and third-to-last. Martrat et al. (2007) count 25 stadial-interstadial sub-cycles in the last glacial cycle compared to 15 in the previous two. The earliest glacial cycle in their record counts only 10 sub-cycles. The stadial-interstadial cycles are especially tightly packed between 50 kya and 11 kya. Loulergue et al.'s (2008) core suggests a similar increase in abrupt millennial scale variation over the last 8 glacial-interglacial cycles (Fig. 11.5). This figure includes the data on human brain size increase in the same glacial-cycle time bins based on the data compiled by Ash and Gallup (2007). The fit between the increasing numbers of abrupt climate change events per glacial cycle and brain size increase is as good as one could expect of the so far limited and noisy data.

The big event in human history that occurred about 50 kya was the movement of AMH out of Africa to the rest of the Old World accompanied by the shift from less complex artifacts of the Middle Paleolithic to the more complex ones of the Later Stone Age/Upper Paleolithic. Importantly, *ephemeral* indications of sophisticated artifacts appear in Africa well before 50 kya (Jacobs et al. 2008) and Africa and eastern Eurasia apparently lacked tool traditions of Upper Paleolithic complexity until much after 50 kya (Richerson, Boyd, and Bettinger 2009).

Perhaps the abrupt evolutionary change that Klein and Edgar (2002) postulate was not so much a fortuitous internal event as evolution in response to the up-tempo beat of the Dansgaard-Oeschger cycles after 60 kya, as the two long high-resolution cores indicate. If McBrearty and Brooks (2000) are correct that the evolution of modern behavioral capacities was

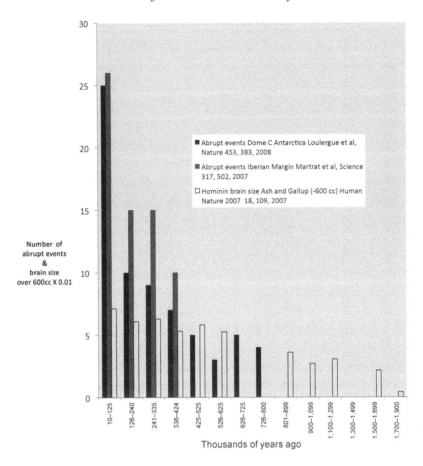

11.5. Number of abrupt events per glacial cycle and human brain size increase. Gray bars: Sea-surface temperature in the Eastern Altantic off Iberia (Martrat et al. 2007). Black bars: Atmospheric methane concentration estimated from bubbles trapped in the EPICA Dome C ice core from Antarctica (Loulergue et al. 2008). Number of abrupt events indicated by original authors in both cases. Open bars: Human brain size increase above ape baseline of 600 cc. Sample sizes per time bin range from 2 to 27. A single outlier in the 726–800 bin not plotted (Ash and Gallup 2007).

stretched out over a longer period in Middle Paleolithic times, the shift from relatively few Dansgaard-Oeschger cycles in the fourth and fifth glacial to more in the second and third might explain a slower pattern of modernization, but one still driven by ongoing environmental deterioration.

We might also imagine that people were biologically, including cognitively, modern for some time before 50 kya, as indicated by brain size, and that the emergence of Upper Paleolithic industries was more a cultural evolutionary than a genetic evolutionary response to the increase in Dansgaard-Oeschger cycles and also to the ecological peculiarities of western Eurasia (Richerson, Boyd, and Bettinger 2009). Perhaps the increasingly variable environment gave highly cultural AMH a decisive competitive advantage over Neandertals and other archaic hominin species living in temperate and colder Eurasian environments. Neandertals and AMH apparently coexisted in the Levant for tens of thousands of years. Perhaps because Neandertals were cold-adapted and AMH a tropical form, AMH remained restricted to what was essentially a subtropical African outpost in far southwestern Asia. Both species apparently made indistinguishable Middle Paleolithic / Mousterian tools during this period (Klein 2009). A highly variable environment might have tipped the competitive balance in favor of the more cultural AMH. Despite their tall lean body form better adapted to lose heat than to retain it, they could use tailored clothing and sophisticated shelters to mitigate this disadvantage while adapting better to variable environments.

The high-resolution paleoclimate evidence currently in hand is still quite sketchy, and the paleoanthropological record could always stand improvement. However, the existing record is certainly sufficient to make a tentative case that increased rapid environmental variation could have driven increased cultural capacities in humans, and increasingly sophisticated cultural systems based on those capacities, over the last few glacial cycles. If the increasing amplitude of the low-frequency climate record outlined in Figure 11.3 was also accompanied by increasing high-frequency variation, then the whole of human evolutionary history might have been driven rather closely by the increasing frequency and amplitude of Dansgaard-Oeschger cycles and higher frequency components of climate. Indeed, the theory illustrated by Figure 11.1 suggests that brain size might itself be a useful paleoclimate index that is sensitive to high-frequency climate change, and that the evolution of human culture in particular evolved in response to Dansgaard-Oeschger cycles and related high-frequency climate variation. The evolution of small-brained members of our own genus, *Homo,* from australopiths coincides roughly with the onset of glacial cycles at the 41 ky-time scale.

The first knapped stone tools also appear in the paleoanthropological record about this time, 2.6 mya. The evolution of larger brained and culturally more sophisticated *Homo* apparently began sometime around 500 kya, perhaps associated with the increase in amplitude of the 100 ky glacial cycle. The bone record and the stone tool record—some index of cultural sophistication—do not match up perfectly. Such evidence as we have (e.g., Fig. 11.5) suggests a degree of independence of the Dansgaard-Oeschger cycles from the glacial cycle period. Clearly, we have much more to learn.

One interesting puzzle is what happens during interglacials. In the cores just reviewed, the last interglacial had long periods of modestly variable environments. If humans are especially adapted to highly variable environments, our hypothesis suggests that interglacials should disfavor humans. In the present interglacial, humans have invented agriculture and become the earth's dominant organism (Richerson, Boyd, and Bettinger 2001), a result contrary to this hypothesis. On the other hand, previous interglacials saw no conspicuous human florescence. Human populations presumably responded to the glacial-interglacial cycle, but these responses are so far unresolved by paleoanthropologists.

RECONSTRUCTING PALEOECOLOGY

Paleoclimate reconstructions are only half the battle in reconstructing the environments and environmental variation that might have affected human evolution. Both the Neandertals and AMH of the last 250 ky appear to have based their subsistence on hunting large mammals, although the Upper Paleolithic people had access to a suite of difficult-to-catch small game that Middle Paleolithic people could not exploit (Stiner et al. 1999). Upper Paleolithic AMH differed from some latest Pleistocene and many Holocene people in that apparently nowhere did they make heavy use of plant resources (Richerson, Boyd, and Bettinger 2001). The transition to the Holocene ushered in climates that were warmer, wetter, and much less variable, and which had higher carbon dioxide concentrations. Such climates apparently favored a higher reliance on plant resources in many parts of the world and the intensification of the use of plant resources led to agriculture in many areas, which in turn spread slowly over the Holocene to most parts of the world (Richerson, Boyd, and Bettinger 2001). Because the climates of the Holocene are so different from the Pleistocene glacial episodes, ethnographically known hunter-gatherers are imperfect models of Pleistocene peoples (Bettinger 2001).

The glacial climatic regimes supported very different plant and animal communities in the last glacial compared to the Holocene (Graham and

Lundelius 1984, Guthrie 1984). Last glacial communities were structured by different forces from those in the Holocene and have no precise analogs in the ecosystems we know from the present. This is so even though the species involved are mostly the same. The difference is in the way species were arranged on the landscape.

Jackson and Williams (2004) review the methods and some of the most significant findings regarding Pleistocene plant communities. Graham et al. (1996) provide a similar review focused on mammals. Both plants and mammals exhibit what were originally termed "disharmonious distributions." In particular, species that today occur in different *biomes* (sub-continental scale biogeographic units) lived in the same biomes in the Pleistocene. In North America, for example, conifers that today live in boreal forests mainly in Canada coexisted with deciduous forest species that today live mainly south of the Canadian border. Animal distributions were similar. As Guthrie (1984) put it, the pattern of the last glacial world was "plaid," while that of the Holocene is "stripes." In the plaid world local diversity was higher, whereas in the stripes world of today species are restricted to their "own" biome, and local community diversity is lower. In the 1980s, paleoecologists attempted to explain disharmonious distributions in terms of less seasonality or less environmental variability of other kinds, allowing local diversity to build up by fine-tuning interactions among species. Since the discovery of millennial and submillennial scale climate variation, explanations have shifted to the hypothesis that plaid distributions reflect out-of-equilibrium conditions.

Allen and Huntley (2000) provide a comparison of the unusual pollen record from Lago Grande di Monticchio in southern Italy with other western European records. The Monticchio record exhibits the pattern of millennial and submillennial climate variation seen in Figures 11.3, 11.4, and 11.5, but the short stadials and interstadials are not reflected in most pollen records. Allen and Huntley argue that Monticchio was near the local forest-grassland community boundary during the last glacial and that the rugged topography surrounding the lake meant that refuge populations of many species existed locally. Hence the pollen rain into the lake could reflect short time scale increases in population density of many species. In other records, long-range dispersal would be required for species favored at any one instant to be reflected in the pollen rain. Coope (1979) showed that fossil beetles whose diets are not tied to specific plants provide a much more sensitive climate indicator than plants normally do. The beetles disperse by flight more rapidly than the plants can manage by more passive means and thus reflect more ephemeral environmental events. Pollen flora normally average over ecological variation that was probably quite relevant to the lives of Pleistocene humans.

The picture that emerges is that the plant and animal communities of last-glacial times were often far out of equilibrium with the climate of the moment. Ranges were expanding or contracting. Ill-adapted species might persist for a bit because they faced no effective competition from better-adapted species that had yet to expand their range into a given location. Woody species might persist for long periods of time in relic stands, diversifying the environment for animals. Ecologists have long suspected that temporal heterogeneity can drive up species diversity. A recent review of this phenomenon suggests that environmental variability can feed variance into chaotic mechanisms that tend to generate endogenous variation even in stable environments (Scheffer et al. 2003). Models of multi-species predator-prey systems suggest that eco-logical dynamics are often chaotic. Thus, ice age ecosystems were probably highly and unpredictably dynamic. Such environments would have imposed novel constraints on hunter-gatherer adaptations.

Elsewhere we argue that such environments are not conducive to in-tensive use of plant resources because a focus on plants implies dietary and processing specializations that require thousands of years to perfect; a span of time far longer than any plant assemblage would persist in a last-glacial plaid world (Richerson, Boyd, and Bettinger 2001). Consistent with this notion, Middle and Upper Paleolithic people seem to have been big game specialists, although Upper Paleolithic peoples were certainly skilled at taking small game and fish and would have no doubt used high quality plant resources, such as fruits and nuts, when available. Perhaps even rela-tively low quality plant resources would have been used when unusually abundant or during times of shortages of better resources (Kislev, Nadel, and Carmi 1992).

Poor quality plant resources, such as grass seeds, can be harvested and made palatable using generalized technologies such as beating ripe seeds into a basket and parching the seeds by tossing them on a tray with live coals (popcorn is a parched-seed product). Holocene peoples used more special-ized techniques to acquire large quantities of seeds (agriculture in many cases) and preparation techniques that increase the nutrients our short gut can absorb from low-quality plant resources (typically, fine grinding and thorough cooking). Evidence for heavy use of these specialized techniques is restricted to the Holocene.

Aside from the *variability* of ice age environments, their *productivity* is also important to understanding Pleistocene hunter-gatherer adaptations. Because ice age environments were on average drier and colder, and had lower carbon dioxide concentrations, than interglacial ones, terrestrial plant productivity must on average have been lower. Indeed, carbon isotope ratio data suggest that this was the case (Beerling 1999).

The data on plant productivity are, however, misleading. The most productive plant communities are closed canopy forests. But forest leaves are held well off the ground and are often defended from browsing by mechanical or chemical means. Hence, forests are much like deserts in terms of the production of animal biomass, particularly large herbivore biomass. By contrast open forests support large browsers like mastodons. Moist grasslands can have almost as high plant production as forests, but the aboveground biomass is all within reach of grazers, making these ecosystems the highest producers of large herbivore biomass. Colder tundra-type vegetation and drier steppe grasslands and shrublands support significant large herbivore biomass despite low plant productivity because what vegetation exists is subject to grazing and browsing.

Thus, in the deserts and arid shrublands of the American West, cattle and sheep ranching are major industries and feral donkeys and horses are abundant enough to be considered pests. Based mainly on the abundance of grazing herbivore fossils, Guthrie (2001) proposed that northern Eurasia was covered by what he called the "Mammoth Steppe" Biome during glacial periods. He reasoned that even when mean temperatures were much like tundra and boreal forest today, the climates were actually much different than these Holocene biomes. Mainly, they were more arid and hence sunnier. They were also at lower latitudes, leading to a longer and warmer summer growing season. Floristically, they were dominated by grasses, sedges, and low shrubs in the sage family. Incidentally, these dominants produce pollen that is not diagnostic at the species level, and they are very diverse groups with species adapted to a very wide variety of habitats. Hence palynology is of relatively little help in reconstructing them. The animal fossil record, dominated by woolly mammoth, horses, and bison, is abundant, consistent with considerably higher herbivore production than would be the case for modern tundra.

Huntley and Allen (2003) make a similar but more general point. Ice age cold and low carbon dioxide concentrations would limit trees more than low growing plants. Ground hugging vegetation benefits from heating of the boundary layer next to the ground even when the air above is cold and soil respiration during the growing season would increase CO_2 in the same microhabitat. Hence, the ice age plaid environment would tend to have many patches with low vegetation of perhaps moderate productivity but very exposed to grazing. At temperate and tropical latitudes, large areas may have been very dry Sahara-like deserts at some points in time. Hyper-arid deserts that sustain little or no human life seem often to be punctuated by wetter "pluvials" with ample surface water and productive grasslands and even forest. Kusimba (1999) gives a scenario for such climate and eco-system variation in East Africa during Later Stone Age times.

Huntley and Allen (2003) attempted to model the impact of climate on vegetation in last glacial Europe. One might hope to use climate reconstructions to drive a regional climate simulation for Europe and then to reconstruct the vegetation living under the climate. This proved impossible to do as the simulated climates during the example stadial used were not cold enough to account for the floras implied by the palynology. They do provide a reconstruction based on the pollen data.

The pollen data indicate that closed canopy forests were of limited distribution in both warm and cold events. They infer that warm events favored more moisture-adapted plants and the cold events more area with plants adapted to arid conditions. Hence plant productivity was higher during warm events and, given that forest expansion was modest, herbivore productivity was probably higher as well. Of course, these reconstructions are quite limited in area. For most of Asia and Africa, even this crude synthetic picture of vegetation dynamics is not yet possible. Clearly, even in the best-studied corner of the world, a high-resolution picture of large herbivore productivity variation in time and space is well beyond our current understanding.

IMPLICATIONS FOR HUMAN EVOLUTION

The Pleistocene Epoch was very different from the Holocene. At least during the glacial phases of the last few glacial-interglacial cycles, high-amplitude millennial and submillennial scale variation was much greater than during the Holocene. Our picture of how this variation evolved is still quite incomplete. It may have become progressively more intense over the last million years. It may have become especially intense in the last glacial, especially after 50 kya when African AMH began to replace more archaic forms like Neandertals in Eurasia. It is potentially correlated with the well-resolved low-frequency orbital scale (Milankovich) variation, which became more intense in three steps dating back approximately 500 kya, 1 mya, and 2.6 mya. The main events of human evolution map onto these events reasonably well. Theoretical models of cultural evolution suggest that culture is adaptation to millennial and sub-millennial scale variation. Two long, high-resolution cores support the hypothesis that increasing climate variation drove the evolution of our brain size right into the last glacial. Decisive tests of the extreme externalist hypothesis will be forthcoming as our understanding of past environmental variation improves.

Paleoecological reconstruction is best developed for Europe for the last glacial cycle, although even there it is much sketchier than we would like. "Disharmonious distributions" with high local diversity suggest that ice age Mammoth Steppe Biomes in northern Eurasia were radically different from those of the Holocene. Closed canopy forest was much reduced and grassy, open biomes dominated most of the area. These open biomes differed greatly in composition under the influence of gradients of temperature and aridity. They were very likely composed of highly dynamic out-of-equilibrium communities whose intrinsic tendency to chaotic variation was pumped by climate variation on time scales too short for range adjustments to lead to Holocene type biomes that are closer to equilibrium.

On the other hand, such open environments, except the very coldest and driest, had medium to very high herbivore productivity. Such sketchy data as are available from lower latitudes also suggest very dynamic ecosystems, a reduction in forest cover, and an expansion of arid grasslands and deserts.

The highly dynamic, but more productive, glacial environments would present three adaptive challenges for big-herbivore hunters. The first would be the ability to take large herbivores on a routine basis. This problem was solved in Middle Paleolithic (MP) times by Mousterian toolmakers. The second would be to cope with the uncertainty of a very noisy environment. Food security on time scales ranging from weeks to years would likely have been more severe than for most ethnographically known hunter-gatherers. Upper Paleolithic/Later Stone Age (UP/LSA) populations were evidently much higher in Europe and Southwest Asia than were the preceding Middle Paleolithic (MP) populations faced with the same suites of game. UP/LSA people must have found solutions to the food security problem that escaped MP people. Social systems for risk reduction are one candidate for such adaptations in accord with evidence for social complexity at least among some UP people. The third challenge would be the problem of maintaining a cultural evolutionary system capable of responding to intense millennial and submillennial scale variation. Even completely modern people appear to lose the more complex elements of their culture when populations become too small. The most expert makers of artifacts are few, and in very small populations they may be lost by chance. The famous case is the Tasmanians, whose toolkit simplified after they were cut off from Australia by rising sea level (Henrich 2004; see also Shennan 2001, Powell, Shennan, and Thomas 2009, Kline and Boyd 2010).

The population on Tasmania at contact times numbered a few thousand. The much more complex mainland toolkit was maintained by a population at contact times of a few hundred thousand. O'Connell and Allen (2007) review evidence that AMH in Australia during the Pleistocene lived at very low population densities and maintained MP style stone tools. (See also Brumm and Moore 2005.) AMH populations in Africa and Southwest Asia also made MP tools for tens of thousands of years leading up to the UP/LSA. The same seems true of South Asia (James and Petraglia 2005) even though the absolute population of southern Asians seems to have been larger than elsewhere after 50 kya (Atkinson, Gray, and Drummond 2008).

On some accounts, more and less complex industries, all made by AMH, coexisted in Africa for several tens of thousands of years (McBrearty and Brooks 2000). Some good evidence suggests that more sophisticated tools were made during brief episodes in Africa (Jacobs et al. 2008). (But equally qualified commentators see a much more abrupt transition from MP to UP/LSA artifacts [Klein 2009].) An artifact assemblage resembling that of the west Eurasian UP does not occur in Australia until the mid Holocene, although we have no reason to think that Australian people were in any way primitive biologically. Some authors interpret the early UP Châtelperronian industry to be a product of diffusion from AMH to Neandertals but some good evidence suggests it to be an indigenous product of Neandertal invention (Zilhão et al. 2010). Perhaps toolkit complexity waxed and waned with the demographic fortunes of populations subject to highly variable conditions and cannot be interpreted uncritically as indicating the raw cognitive sophistication of the toolkit makers.

Populations so small that they lose complex tools would also have a less responsive cultural evolutionary system. Perhaps over a wide range of herbivore productivities, human population densities were bistable. A high population density equilibrium would generate a fancy technology and rapid evolutionary response to millennial and submillennial scale variation. Hence it could maintain high population density. A small population in the same conditions would have a simple toolkit and a slow response to variation and hence would remain small.

Outside this middle range, an especially rich environment might allow a simple system to jump to the complex equilibrium while an especially poor one would reduce a complex population to simplicity. Perhaps in good times in good places AMH (and Neandertals?) could achieve population sizes adequate to sustain more complex toolkits whereas in poorer times and places they could only sustain simpler technologies.

If environments remained poor enough long enough, a population that had achieved UP complexity might suffer a Tasmanian style loss of complexity and drop back to the MP equilibrium. This sort of dynamic is sometimes called a "hysteresis loop." Rather than reacting directly to an environmental change, a population will have a strong tendency to remain either large or small. Given a sufficiently large and persistent change, it will jump to the other equilibrium where it will again persist under environmental conditions where the other equilibrium could be sustained but cannot be attained. This would explain the coexistence of technologies with a LSA cast with those of a MP appearance in Africa during much of the last glacial. AMH appeared in Africa between 200 and 160 kya (White et al. 2003, McDougall, Brown, and Fleagle 2005), long before fully modern suites of artifacts were produced for sustained periods of time.

The ability of AMH to displace (or assimilate; Green et al. 2010) archaic hominin species like the Neandertals may have depended less upon differences in innate abilities and more upon having attained the complex cultural equilibrium and sustaining it long enough to reach such places as Australia, where the environment was so poor that humans tumbled back to the simpler MP equilibrium. Human populations could well have imposed their own chaotic dynamics on ice age systems.

Caspari and Lee (2006) used dental wear to roughly estimate the ratio of old to young adult individuals in hominin fossil death assemblages from the australopiths to the UP. Slight increases are evident at each major change of taxa with one major exception. UP people had an old/young adult ratio of about 2.1, while the European Neandertals had a ratio of only 0.35. In Southwest Asia, where Neandertals and AMH coexisted using Mousterian technology, the small dental sample suggests that both populations had an old/young ratio of about 1. Caspari and Lee suggest that a cultural rather than a genetic change was responsible for this difference. The changes are reciprocal in that older adults can accumulate and transmit more culture than young adults and can accumulate individually acquired knowledge. Culturally more sophisticated societies can support larger populations which will also tend to conserve a more sophisticated cultural repertoire. Caspari and Lee's analysis lends weight to the idea that large-brained hominins of the late Pleistocene had bistable population dynamics.

LARGE-SCALE "ORDERLY ANARCHY"?

The Upper Paleolithic of western Eurasia is theoretically important because the artifacts these people made, such as their famous ivory carvings, cave paintings, and sophisticated stone, bone, and ivory tools, suggest that they were innately essentially identical to ourselves, especially as regards their intelligence and other cognitive attributes. This was the final set of Environments of Evolutionary Adaptedness that shaped human nature, save only whatever fine tuning occurred in the Holocene. Of course, western Eurasia was not the set of environments in which modern behavior arose; that happened in Africa or possibly an African outpost in the Levant. However western and northern Eurasia still have the best archaeological data and hence furnish us with the best picture of what UP/LSA people were capable of. Klein (2009) provides a very useful summary of the available paleoanthropology. In triangulating on the sorts of social systems that might have evolved in the latest Pleistocene, culminating in the evolution of modern artifact kits that characterized the people that spread out of Africa, one useful exercise is to reflect upon the demands a highly variable climate might have made upon social organization. The very different environments of the Pleistocene compared to the Holocene, and the fact that the late Holocene hunter-gatherers were almost all highly specialized in one way or another, means that UP peoples likely lay outside of the en-velope of ethnographically known societies. We here attempt to guess in what direction UP peoples might have departed from the ethnographically known sample.

The reader is warned that attempts to guess the social organization of Pleistocene peoples from the archaeological record is a rather speculative enterprise. Social organization leaves few and ambiguous traces. Other scholars have reached very different conclusions from those argued here. For example, Owens and Hayden (1997; B. Hayden, pers. comm.) compared UP cave art, and its possible use in rituals involving adolescents, with simi-lar practices among ethnographically known hunter-gatherers. They con-cluded that UP societies were "transegalitarian." By this they meant that UP societies were fairly complex politically and had entrepreneurial leaders with higher status than ordinary members of society. Among other things, this analogy requires that UP societies were sufficiently sedentary to accu-mulate material surpluses that leaders used in competition for status. Their ethnographic analogs are people like the Northwest Coast salmon fishing people that lived in permanent plank-house villages of some size.

We argue below that highly variable climates would have prevented UP people from being sedentary, though they may have been politically complex despite being mobile. In general, we think that analogies between UP and Holocene hunter-gatherers are fraught because last glacial envi-ronments were dramatically different from those of the Holocene. Given that the environments of the last glacial were far outside the envelope of Holocene environments, we imagine that social adaptations were likewise probably outside the ethnographic envelope. For other notable attempts to reconstruct UP lifeways see Gamble (1999) and Boehm (2012).

Highly dynamic but locally diverse, disharmonious environments would, in principle, mean that small groups could find a favorable bit of mosaic and settle down and defend it, secure that the variety of resources available in a small area would support a band-sized unit with reasonable security. People using such a strategy might have to have been prepared to move fairly frequently as the mosaic shifted, but perhaps patches would tend to remain more or less the same for a few years or a few generations. Perhaps that is what Neandertals and other makers of MP tools did. They may have chased niches where big game and vulnerable small game were locally unusually abundant as such niches shifted across the landscape.

Studies of the movement of raw materials found in particular camps suggest that MP people moved little and/or traded little compared to UP people in the same environments. In very arid or otherwise spare environments, such as Australia, AMH at very low densities with small, widely separated bands exploiting unusually favorable environments would have been restricted to toolkits of only MP complexity due to the Tasmanian Effect.

The big game that made up the bulk of the herbivore biomass in the size ranges preferred by humans—antelope, red deer, caribou, bison, and horses—were likely very mobile in the last ice age. Certainly the living versions of these species move on a large scale. These animals were probably moving about the landscape to exploit favorable grazing opportunities, avoid humans and other predators, and escape extreme weather. UP people apparently hunted them more effectively than MP people, in part probably because the UP people had access to a broader variety of fall-back resources than MP people (Stiner, Munro, and Surovell 2000). Compared to Neandertals and other Mousterians, UP people could rely on local sedentary resources if their luck failed while they pursued high-risk but high-mean-return migratory big game. Gamble et al. (2004) argue that a difference like this led to a decisive competitive advantage of AMH people over Neandertals in Europe after about 45 kyrs ago. If it proves true that Neandertals were also capable of UP technology and if the evidence for Neandertal genes in Eurasian AMH populations is confirmed, a more complex story of the end of the Neandertals will have to be told.

A possible picture of the UP people at relatively high population densities in western Eurasia is that they were something like the American Great Basin Shoshone (Murphy and Murphy 1986), but with larger bands focused on big game hunting. The Shoshone exploited plant and animal resources in their temperate desert environment, mainly traveling in small independent family groups. The Shoshone did aggregate into multifamily camps in the winter, where they conducted cooperative activities such as rabbit drives, antelope hunts, and ceremonial activities. On the northern edge of their range, they violently contested access to the bison herds with the Blackfeet and their allies. Early accounts state that sometimes as many as 200 warriors were massed for such fights. Leadership for cooperative activities was *ad hoc*.

Because of the simplicity of the Shoshone social system, it is sometimes taken as representing the ancestral state of AMH (Steward 1955). However,

Murphy and Murphy (1986) stress that this system was sophisticated as much as simple. Lone families, often with a store of food that took hundreds of hours to produce, would have been easy prey for larger bands that might want to rob them. Family mobility, and the lack of strong systems of extended kinship often so important in hunter gatherer social structure, meant that winter encampments might contain many strangers. Murphy and Murphy analogize Shoshone life to a modern nation in the sense that highly mobile citizens of these states can move freely within the borders of the state and attach themselves to open task groups wherever they pitch up. To do so required institutions that, among other things, recognized that people had rights to what they produced. Interestingly, the Northern Shoshone were allied with the Bannock, speakers of a mutually unintelligible language. It speaks to the political sophistication of these peoples that they could have an alliance with the Bannock while having a hereditary conflict with the Blackfoot, yet they had no formal leadership or decision-making institutions.

The Shoshone cannot be considered a direct analogy to UP people, much less a homology. Bettinger (2001) points out that the Shoshone, like most ethnographically known hunter-gatherers, are late Holocene people with a high dependence on plant resources compared to Pleistocene analogs, and even their immediate Holocene predecessors in the Great Basin. But the variable environments faced by the Shoshone and their consequent flexibility and opportunism might have some parallels with UP peoples. Shoshonean family bands would have been too small to deal efficiently with big game, so probably kinship- and friendship-based bands built around 5–10 skilled hunters would have been the basic social units of UP people (Hill et al. 2011). The ethnographic sample of big game hunters is dominated by bands of this sort. Hunting with spear throwers requires a collective team of about this size to be effective and a fair number of people are required to eat up a large game carcass before it spoils (Bettinger 2009). In an emergency these basic bands could fission further to exploit small game and plants. In the case of big windfalls or an opportunity to conduct large-scale drive hunts, several bands might aggregate either to exploit the concentrated resource more effectively or to use a windfall to subsidize collective social activities.

The UP focus on big game as a primary target is a little like the late horse-mounted hunters of bison on the American Plains. The mounted bison hunters moved mainly as modest-sized bands much as we infer for UP people, but were prone to fission into family foraging groups at lean times of year and to aggregate opportunistically when large herds were located (Oliver 1962). Interestingly, a group of Shoshone, famously known as the Comanche, very successfully adapted to mounted hunting with minimal changes in their ancestral Shoshone social institutions (Hämäläinen 2008). The UP people were pedestrian, limiting their ability to locate and pursue wide-ranging migratory herds. On the other hand, they enjoyed a quite diverse fauna rather than specializing in one major species. A "plaid" Pleistocene world would likely have sustained a diversity of game with diverse aggregation sizes, whereas a "striped" world would tend to larger, unspecific aggregations. Foot mobility might have sufficed to exploit the sort of ephemeral aggregations existing in a plaid environment. Also a plaid environment with broken woodlands and brushlands in the mosaic would provide the cover needed to deploy ambush tactics based on teams of men using spearthrowers. Excavated UP middens often have a heavily disproportionate representation of the bones of a single species as if UP people often focused on a migration choke-point or other situations where they could harvest game windfalls. Stiner, Munro, and Surovell's (2000) point that UP hunters could take small fleet game using clever tricks probably also implies that they used clever strategies to take large game, for example, using drives and pounds.

Ice age peoples using both MP and UP/LSA technology must have faced severe problems of food security in a dynamic, unpredictable environment. Most likely, MP people could only hope to exploit the less risky of these environments, while UP people likely used intrinsically riskier strategies. For example, UP people pushed further north and east in Eastern Europe and Siberia than Neandertals, eventually reaching North America as the climate warmed at the end of the Pleistocene (Klein 2009: chap. 7; Hoffecker and Elias 2007). The cooperative big game hunting adaptation in ethnographic food foragers relies upon social institutions for risk pooling to mitigate risks of food shortfalls (Winterhalder 1986, Hawkes, O'Connell, and Blurton Jones 2001, Wiessner 2002). If we are correct that climate variability fed through ecosystem processes to create high variation in subsistence resources, UP peoples at population densities necessary to evade the Tasmanian Effect must have had more sophisticated risk management institutions than perhaps any ethnographically known foragers.

One of the interesting features of Shoshone social institutions according to Murphy and Murphy (1986) is that the constituent family bands could move about opportunistically on the landscape with reasonable confidence that they were safe from violence by other Shoshone and Shoshone allies and confident that any resources they produced would not be expropriated by a stronger band. R.L. Bettinger (pers. comm.) has termed this sort of social organization "orderly anarchy" because, in the hunter-gatherer case, it is managed by social institutions other than those of formal leadership. In ethnographic California, orderly anarchy facilitated trade and made armed conflict infrequent at population densities that elsewhere exhibited intense conflict and a tendency for hierarchical political office to arise. Orderly anarchy is a theoretically neglected form for managing social complexity, despite its high profile as a component of modern mobile societies (Putnam, Leonardi, and Nanetti 1993, Ostrom 1990). Imagine the Shoshone with larger constituent bands and perhaps more elaborate social institutions for organizing expedient cooperation in multi-band aggregations.

If large concentrations of game were found, several bands might be recruited for a pound or drive or just for a celebration to help a band eat up a windfall. Young men can run formidable distances carrying messages. If an ever-shifting collection of bands kept in touch with each other in an organized way, the steppe telegraph could probably support a sophisticated fission-fusion system that efficiently found concentrations of big game, assembled the bands needed to exploit them fully, and fissioned to again seek new concentrations of big game, all insured by an ability to exploit small game and plants as necessary, and to receive help from successful bands if a band's subsistence luck failed. Marshack (1971) argued that abstract ladder-like designs inscribed on bone plaques were calendrical devices. Although this suggestion is controversial, we might imagine that bands planned meetings by one means or another.

Some aspects of the paleoanthropological record are consistent with the complexity via orderly anarchy reconstruction. The main named traditions of western and northern Eurasia, the Aurignacian and Gravettian, are very widely distributed in time and space compared to the scale of named archaeological traditions and ethnographically known social systems in the Holocene (van Andel, Davies, and Weninger 2003). These cultural phenomena, marked by both symbolic artifacts like the famous Gravettian "Venus" figurines and utilitarian ones such as Aurignacian split base antler points, are distributed from the Urals to the Atlantic and from the Mediterranean to the highest latitudes from which occupations have been recorded (White

2006). In time, these phenomena last for 10 ky or more. Interestingly, the last glacial record of northwest China does not show any of the distinctive markers of the west Eurasian record (Brantingham et al. 2001). However, Upper Paleolithic people did leave a record even farther north in Baikalian Siberia (Hoffecker and Elias 2007). The west and north Eurasians were perhaps one ethnic group that met other ethnic groups only somewhere in central Eurasia, making the UP transition the original European Union.

Aside from providing scope for operating a highly opportunistic fission-fusion resource acquisition strategy, common ethnicity over a wide area would increase the effective population size for the acquisition and conservation of culture against the Tasmanian Effect. Bocquet-Appel et al. (2005) estimate Upper Paleolithic populations for all of Europe to be in the range of only a few tens of thousands of people. Maintaining the complexity of the UP toolkit with such small populations perhaps required UP Europe to be one society to boost effective population size up to the numbers necessary to support that sophistication (Powell, Shennan, and Thomas 2009).

Indeed, the UP of western and northern Eurasia looks on present evidence to be unique. Perhaps the combination of a large area of productive Mammoth Steppe with a considerable area of maritime climates in the far west supported uniquely dense and/or well connected human populations in this region. In times of warmer climates at least, UP peoples could spread into areas such as the Levant that might have been too dry in colder times to sustain significant populations, and far to the north and east where stadials might have been too cold to permit human occupation. Hoffecker and Elias (2007) argue that a lack of fuelwood would have limited human expansion into northeastern Siberia and Beringia during the colder episodes of the late Pleistocene. Perhaps the sustained sophistication of the west Eurasian UP existed because the eastern part of the Mammoth Steppe Biome acted as a protected area that prevented sophisticated hunters from causing the collapse of exploited species (Richerson, Boyd, and Bettinger 2009).

The Later Stone Age peoples of Africa may prove to have cultures as complex as the Upper Paleolithic (Henshilwood et al. 2003), but on current evidence many diagnostic UP features are episodic in the African late Pleistocene.

Perhaps the analog of the maritime west Eurasian center of cultural complexity in Africa was in equatorial western Africa, an area now covered by tropical forest (Dupont et al. 2000). Southeast Asia might harbor a similar phenomenon as biome reconstructions there also suggest widespread grasslands and dry forests in regions now characterized by wet tropical forests (Hope et al. 2004). These regions have few archaeological sites, perhaps due in part to difficult and hence inadequate exploration. Recent evidence from East Kalimantan (Borneo) suggests that Pleistocene peoples made cave art there (Chazine 2005).

Paleolithic art may contain some information about the social organization of its producers. For example, Owens and Hayden (1997) argue, based on ethnographic analogies, that painted caves were the sites of initiation rites of juveniles into the secret societies of social stratified "transegalitarian" societies. Similarly, Lewis-Williams (2002) uses ethnographic analogies to argue that cave art records the experiences of shamans in altered states of consciousness. Barton, Clark, and Cohen (1994) argue that cave art was produced to symbolically mark group territories during climate downturns when competition for territory became acute in the mild western refuges of UP peoples. However, this interpretation is hardly consistent with the apparent stylistic unity of the Aurignacian and Gravettian traditions noted above. Other students of Paleolithic art are much more skeptical of extracting social information from these productions (Conkey et al. 1997, Bahn and Vertut 1997, Nowell 2006).

Dale Guthrie, the paleontologist who invented the concept of the Mammoth Steppe, is the latest person to attempt a comprehensive analysis of Paleolithic art (2005). Aside from a detailed knowledge of the animals depicted by UP artists, Guthrie is an artist and big game hunter by avocation. He conducted allometric studies of human hands in order to interpret hand and foot prints associated with art in caves. He argues that much UP Pleistocene art, especially the relatively crude pieces, was made by adolescent boys. Many of the hand stencils in caves are the size and shape of those of adolescent males. On Guthrie's interpretations, many of the images are of testosterone-charged themes including naked or provocatively adorned women, crudely rendered vulvas, and big game animals, often big game fatally struck by projectiles and coughing up blood.

Remarkably, no scenes of warfare are present in the rather large corpus of UP art Guthrie reviews, although such scenes are not uncommon in Holocene hunter-gatherer rock art and in the drawings of modern adolescents. Drawings of men carrying shields are also absent from the UP record but are present in Holocene rock art. Warfare is all but universally present among Holocene hunter-gatherers (Otterbein 1985) and shields or parry sticks are very common warriors' gear.

The duration of the Aurignacian and Gravettian traditions in time suggests that the pressure for the generation of stylistic variation was comparatively weak. Guthrie argues that the UP art was dominated by highly naturalistic images (though often crudely rendered images when produced by inexpert juveniles) that incorporate little if any arbitrary stylistic variation. Across the whole UP, art has been impossible to periodize for this reason. This is utterly different from the Holocene where point styles, pottery decoration, and the like are used as time markers on a quite fine scale. The use of symbols to mark group differences leads to distinctive differences in art styles while stylistic similarity and syncretism signal the unity or union of groups (Logan and Schmittou 1998). In Guthrie's interpretation, in striking contrast to that of Lewis-Williams, little if any UP art expresses supernatural themes, and supernatural belief systems typically code symbolic markers of group identity. Since stylistic variation in the Holocene often marks the boundaries between competing social systems, the apparent fact that art was used as a form of personal expression in the UP, but not in its common Holocene function of group badging (Wiessner 1984), suggests that the social organization of UP peoples was strikingly different from those of Holocene hunter-gatherers.

CONCLUSION

The paleoclimatological and paleoecological evidence suggests that Pleistocene people faced very different challenges than did Holocene hunter-gatherers, especially the late, specialized hunter-gatherers of the ethnographic sample. The paleoanthropological and archaeological evidence says much the same thing. Unfortunately, neither body of evidence is sufficient to nail a description (or descriptions) of Paleolithic social life.

We can see fairly clearly that Middle Paleolithic and Upper Paleolithic social systems were quite different. Population densities seem to have increased across the MP/UP transition and raw materials began to be moved impressive distances by UP peoples. Whether the institutions involved in the change took the form of orderly anarchy, transegalitarian leadership and stratification, and/or other social innovations is difficult to verify. Given that ice age climates and biotic environments were clearly outside the envelope of Holocene ones, simple parallels to well-described ethnographic cases are unlikely to be correct.

The puzzle that the stones and the bones of the paleoanthropological record are so weakly correlated illustrates the basic problems of deciphering Late Pleistocene lifeways. Since AMH participated in both MP and UP technologies, a case can be made that cultural differences, driven by something like our bistable population hypothesis or directly by environmental productivity, rather than genes were responsible for the complex interdigitation of MP and UP lifeways. That the Châtelperronean industry, with clear UP elements, might have been made by Neandertals suggests that Neandertals could at least acquire UP traits by diffusion from AMH (Klein 2009:592).

On the other hand, a late, anatomically cryptic modernization of human cognition, perhaps even by a single mutation, might explain the UP "revolution" (Klein [2003a] does not accept that African industries, which seem to some paleoanthropologists to be approaching the UP in complexity, are actually materially different from MP industries). A simple externalist hypothesis invoking genetic evolution is that the onset of high-frequency Dansgaard-Oeschger climate variation after 70 kya favored parallel increases in the innate capacity for culture in both Neandertals and AMH.

One possible picture that seems to be consistent with much of the data is that people could exploit variable Pleistocene environments at low population densities using necessarily simple social and technical strategies by seeking the most stable and most productive environments available. This was perhaps the MP strategy that even quite late AMH used in poor environments. The best-studied case of AMH using MP-level artifacts for prolonged periods is Australia. Alternatively, in environments with high mean herbivore productivity, AMH, and perhaps Neandertals as well, could exploit riskier big game resources using better technology and fancier social organization to increase game take and mitigate risk. Both strategies are potentially self-reinforcing via the Tasmanian Effect. MP strategies are too few to sustain the complex technology the UP strategy requires. An unusual, sustained runup of a MP population would be required to transition to the UP strategy. The palimpsest of MP and UP industries in Africa and Southwest Asia suggests a complex story of gains and losses of the UP strategy during the first half of the last glacial.

Once UP population densities are achieved, complex culturally transmitted technology and social organization can maintain high effective population sizes by sophisticated social institutions (Wiessner 2002, Yengoyan 1968) in the face of considerable environmental variability and at low absolute population densities. At least in western Eurasia the UP strategy was sustained from ca. 40 kya until the onset of the Holocene began to transform hunter-gatherer lifeways. Australians and the peoples of northwestern China seem to have retained MP-level tools much longer, perhaps because of aridity-enforced low effective population sizes.

Our rapidly developing knowledge of ancient climates is working a revolution in how we understand our own past. Quite conceivably, a Plio-Pleistocene pattern of increasing high-frequency climate variability may have driven the pattern of increase in cognitive and cultural sophistication revealed by the paleoanthropological record. At any rate, externalist hypotheses are accumulating some real evidence in their favor.

It is important to note that these are the early days of high-resolution paleoclimate and paleoecological reconstructions. The paleoanthropological record, frustratingly ambiguous about social organization at best, has temporal and spatial gaps that may well mislead us. While we should be modest about any particular hypothesis, it is hard to believe that high-frequency, high-amplitude climate variation played no role in human evolution.

12

Human Behavioral Ecology, Optimality, and Human Action

KIM STERELNY

DOING THE BEST WE CAN

Among the family of evolutionary approaches to human behavior, human behavioral ecology (HBE) is distinctive in emphasizing the adaptive flexibility of human behavior; work in this tradition assumes that our learning and decision mechanisms equip us to respond successfully to a broad range of environments (Smith and Winterhalder 2003). Human behavioral ecologists build models of human action: fertility decisions, food gathering, the shift from foraging to agriculture, resource sharing. These models typically represent agents as doing the best they can: individuals optimize given the constraints imposed by the conditions under which they act; their needs; and, sometimes, the choices of other agents (Winterhalder and Smith 2000, Laland and Brown 2002, Smith and Winterhalder 2003, Laland 2007). In this chapter, I explore the scope and limits of this approach to human behavior.

One aspect of HBE is relatively uncontroversial; models of adaptive decision-making can be used heuristically to identify informational, social, and ecological constraints on decision-making. But there is a more ambitious interpretation of these models: they can be seen as explanations of the cases that confirm them. For example, Rebecca Bliege Bird clearly sees costly signaling models of male hunting (of which, more later) as likely to explain Meriam turtle hunting (Smith, Bliege Bird, and Bird 2003, Bliege

Bird 2007). In the first half of this chapter, my main focus is this more ambitious interpretation of HBE. In the second, my focus switches. Human behavioral ecologists often use models heuristically, and realize that they do (Smith, Borgerhoff Mulder, and Hill 2001, Shennan 2002). But the distinction between explanatory and heuristic approaches is often implicit, and is worth making explicit.

My aim is primarily methodological: to identify the conditions under which these models explain human agency, and to explore further conditions in which HBE models are powerful tools for exposing the limits of our understanding. But in pursuing these methodological objectives, I will also make some substantive conjectures about human evolution, in particular about models of subsistence hunting, and on the fate of the Neandertals.

Human behavioral ecologists portray agents as acting adaptively, given their environments and the options open to them. A life history model might show, for example, that !Kung women's conservative birth spacing pattern optimizes their number of grandchildren by optimizing the trade-off between the number and the quality of their children (see, for example, Kaplan 1996, Blurton Jones, Hawkes, and O'Connell 2006). A foraging model might show that foraging decisions in complex environments come close to maximizing a forager's rate of return per hour invested (Kaplan and Hill 1992, Kelly 1995, Shennan 2002). The idea, though, is not just that some forms of human action are adaptive. Rather, these forms of action occur *because* they are adaptive. There is a systematic connection between environmental challenge and agent response: if we understand the challenge, we can predict and explain the response. Such models of adaptive decision-making have a common structure. They specify the optimal behavior, given a set of assumptions about the environment, the range of options available, the resources that are the target of behavior, and the impact of choice on fitness. Our explanation of (say) a !Kung pattern of birth spacing recognizes that agent choices are constrained by their social and physical environment. !Kung women make choices about birth spacing that are constrained by the objective resource envelop, and also by the choices that others make. For example, if her social group moves, a !Kung mother must move with it. Thus in the rather resource poor and seasonal environments of the !Kung, and given the set of options about birth intervals and child care that are open to them, these women may well maximize fitness by choosing to restrict their fertility, having children at quite long intervals.

Such HBE models *explicitly* represent the objective features of an agent's world. But they *implicitly* rely on agents having the ability to track their world. The explanation of !Kung fertility relies on humans having cognitive mechanisms that allow them to assess the causal structure of their environment, and to recognize the likely consequences of their actions. And it presupposes that subjective utility tracks fitness: the outcomes we prefer increase fitness; those we avoid reduce fitness. This explanation does not presuppose that the immediate, proximate motivation of !Kung women is to maximise the number of their surviving grandchildren. But it does presuppose that their immediate desires (perhaps that they and their children are well-fed) covary systematically with such fitness consequences.

Establishing that a particular pattern of choices maximizes fitness is no easy task. But suppose we can establish that a particular pattern of action is, indeed, actually adaptive. Suppose we can show that (relative to realistic alternatives) fertility decisions in a particular group do maximize fitness. Why should we infer that we observe this pattern *because* it optimizes fitness?

Evolutionary psychologists have been sceptical of HBE modeling in part because they doubted that it was either possible or necessary to show that current behavior is adaptive. (Indeed, in the early days of evolutionary psychology, a special issue of *Ethology and Sociobiology* [11, 3, 1990] was devoted to this issue.) Evolutionary psychologists propose to explain action in contemporary worlds by appeal to cognitive adaptations, and those cognitive adaptations are in turn explained by features of past environments. On this picture, there seems to be no room for current adaptive fit to explain action; at best, adaptive fit shows that contemporary environments are still similar to those historical environments that do explain action. Even correlation will often fail, for we inherit our cognitive machinery from ancestors who lived in a very different world, so there is no reason to suppose that adaptations produce behavior that is now adaptive.

Human behavioral ecologists think otherwise, and their response rests on the idea that unless there were a connection between fitness and our mechanisms of evaluation and motivation, we would not expect agents to systematically act adaptively. So, if we show that behavior is systematically adaptive, we can infer the existence of such a connection between fitness and evaluation. Somehow agents are tracking and responding to their needs and opportunities. To put it in broadly Bayesian terms, the probability that a pattern of action is adaptive is high, given the hypothesis that that pattern is generated by mechanisms of motivation and appraisal that systematically track fitness. It is *not* high on other hypotheses. It would be a *miraculous coincidence* if agents just happened to pick the best, optimal actions available on a regular and repeated basis. Human social and ecological environments vary widely, so showing that a pattern of birth spacing really is adaptive explains that pattern, by showing it to be the result of mechanisms that reliably generate an adaptive fit between action and environment.[1]

This explanatory inference is sound when there is unlikely to be an accidental match between the phenotype of an individual organism and the adaptive demands on that organism. But HBE models are rarely designed to deliver a close quantitative fit between model and observation. For the models are usually simple and general, and so they inevitably suppress some factors causally relevant to decision-making. Foraging models, for example, treat animals and plants merely as food parcels of varying worth. Yet plants and animals provide other resources too: skin, bone, teeth, fiber, and wood are important resources in their own right. Given these simplifying assumptions, we would not expect a precise fit between the model and the actual behavior of foragers in (say) dividing their time between hunting animals and gathering plants. Yet as we move away from a precise fit between model and observation, the "miracle argument" becomes less persuasive. A precise, quantitative fit between model and prediction really would indicate the presence of tracking mechanisms. If, however, all we can show is a qualitative consistency between model and action, then the case for thinking that the model explains the pattern of action is more problematic.

The key problem is that a qualitative fit between model and observation might just signal the presence of ancient mechanisms inherited through deep history. We have motivations we have inherited from deep in the primate and mammalian clade. The existence of these mechanisms, and their importance to our action, is uncontroversial and unproblematic. People eat because they are hungry, get angry when threatened, affiliate with their children, socialize within their groups. There is no live project of explaining (say) why people sometimes have sex. We know the answer to that question. But we do not know the extent to which these ancient mechanisms of desire have been fine-tuned to recent and current environments; the extent to which desire is fine-tuned to the specific circumstances in which agents now find themselves. We need more than a rough qualitative fit between model and world to answer this question. For example, parental uncertainty is a problem for males rather than females. But merely showing that males are more prone to violent sexual jealousy than females would not show that males have adaptive, mate-guarding mechanisms. Over much of hominin evolution, males were more likely to be involved in violent confrontation than females: in dominance interactions; in early hunting and aggressive scavenging; perhaps in joint defense. Consider the greater sexual dimorphism of our remote ancestors and the behavioral differences between male and female chimps. Given these deep-history differences, males and females may well have inherited different motivational packages with respect to violence. So differing levels of sexual violence might reflect deep history rather than mechanisms that adaptively adjust action to the different environmental demands on men and on women. Notoriously, some evolutionary psychologists have argued that jealousy was adaptive in our recent past (Thornhill and Palmer 2001). But that hypothesis demands a tight fit between observed levels of jealous violence and optimal levels. Without a close match between prediction and observation, there is no otherwise-surprising coincidence between observation and model.

Less lurid examples make the same point. Actions can approximate adaptive choice without being the result of mechanisms of evaluation that reliably track the adaptive demands of the local environment. It may well be that the current fad of joining gyms and eating salads (rather than eating spare ribs and watching football) optimizes fitness in western middle-class worlds. But the spread of these practices may not be explained by the fact that they optimize fitness. Rather than being mediated by psychological mechanisms that systematically organize our actions to maximize our fitness, this practice may well have spread by biased cultural transmission. It is the result of emulating those with high prestige (Henrich and Gil-White 2001). This may once have been a good rule of thumb; it was sensible to take your cue from the most successful farmer in your village. But in contemporary environments with open informational networks, imitating celebrities is unlikely to maximize fitness. It is not likely that our daughters optimize their fitness by aping Paris Hilton. If gym-joining is the result of the same mechanisms that induce Hilton-mimicking, then it does not result from mechanisms that reliably adjust actions to local circumstances. Joining gyms is adaptive, but we do not join gyms because it is adaptive. There is, therefore, some tension between HBE's use of simple and general models and the idea that these models explain the actions they model. As we move away from precision, it becomes much less obvious that the observed patterns of action are genuinely surprising except in the light of the model. That is, it becomes less obvious that $\Pr(E/\sim H)$ is low. There is, however, an important class of exceptions to this link between precision and explanatory power.

Sometimes we are puzzled not by the *frequency* of a particular kind of act, nor by the *contexts* in which we observe it. We are puzzled why acts of that kind take place at all. Contrast sex with penis scarification, female genital cutting (FGC), or (less spectacularly) food taboos. One puzzle about FGC is not why it occurs at specific rates, circumstances, and intensity, but why it occurs at all. In contrast with, say, sexual jealousy, a costly signaling model of FGC (to choose the most obvious possibility) that was qualitatively consistent with the data might well explain the phenomenon. Unless the model is roughly right, we do not expect to see any level of FGC. So even for qualitative evidence, if the hypothesis is false, the probability of making the observations is low; that is $\Pr(E/\sim H)$ is low. In the case of these surprising behaviors—behaviors that are in no obvious way expressions of ancient motivational mechanisms—simple models do have explanatory power.

THE SCOPE OF ADAPTIVE MODELING

Above, I discussed an important explanatory strategy of HBE: that of showing that important classes of human action are adaptive, and that they occur because they are adaptive. Obviously, this strategy is in trouble if the acts in question are not adaptive at all. Individual acts of stupidity are legion. Many spectacularly fitness-limiting examples are immortalized in the Darwin awards (http://darwinawards.com/darwin/). However, since HBE models culture-wide patterns of action rather than those of specific agents, these can be regarded as irrelevant noise. Even so, there are many general patterns that seem to reduce fitness. One very general pattern is the great demographic transition. Through the 19th and 20th centuries, Europe saw a sustained fall in female fertility. It is likely that the transition lowered fitness: females refrained from having children that they could have successfully raised, and who would themselves have reproduced (Borgerhoff Mulder 1998; for a dissenting view, see Mace 1998, 2000).

How common are such examples, and how do they impact the utility of HBE models? One famous line of argument suggests that the scope of optimizing decision-making is quite limited. Nativist evolutionary psychology suggests that systematically, resiliently adaptive decision-making depends on special-purpose cognitive adaptations. Problem domain by problem domain, human decision environments are so informationally demanding that we need special equipment—adapted specializations—to make good decisions. (This line of argument was first systematically presented in Barkow, Cosmides, and Tooby 1992, and was extended in Pinker 1997.) We make near-optimal decisions when confronted with problems for which we have such equipment, but in novel environments, or when we confront novel problems, we are unlikely to optimize. Furthermore, many of our current challenges are too new for natural selection to have provided us with the right optimizing tools. As so many of us live in novel environments, human action is adapted but often not adaptive. One plausible example is wealth accumulation (which may well link with the demographic transition mentioned above). Arguably, in contemporary western societies, much wealth accumulation is at the expense of biological fitness. Males and females both limit fertility and delay reproduction until they are well-established in their careers, and have accumulated the material foundations of middle-class life. The result is a small family, and one that reproduces that pattern in the next generation, as doctors and lawyers beget doctors and lawyers. Environmental change has severed the covariation between the immediate focus of motivation and fitness benefit, and selection has not yet had time to respond. In traditional societies (very likely) conservative birth spacing was adaptive, and we have inherited from that social world a willingness to make accumulation/family-size tradeoffs which were once, but are no longer, adaptive.

Nativist evolutionary psychology captures an important insight: much routine human decision-making has a high "cognitive load": effective decisions require an agent to access and use significant amounts of information. Yet there is clearly something wrong with the nativist picture. We are not hopeless enough in novel environments. Hierarchical, state-run societies structured by complex institutions are very new. So too are social worlds in which crucial resources are routinely acquired through trade with strangers, typically using intermediate media with no intrinsic value. Paul Seabright has recently emphasized both the radical way these interactions departed from long-established hominin norms, and the efficiency of trade using money and fixed prices (Seabright 2010). Very often, market life seems to be both adaptive, informationally challenging, and evolutionarily novel—a paradoxical combination for nativist evolutionary psychology. It follows that nativist evolutionary psychology has too limited a conception of how informational resources can be assembled. In earlier works of mine, I argued that both inter-generational cultural transmission and epistemic niche construction play central roles in explaining how agents assemble the cognitive resources they need to act effectively in a complex, informationally translucent environment (Sterelny 2003, 2006a, 2006b, 2011).

Recently, Kevin Laland and Gillian Brown have connected these ideas to human behavioral ecology in arguing that the problem of "adaptive lag" in modern environments is overstated (Laland and Brown 2006). First, they point out that nativist evolutionary psychology (and, for that matter, human behavioral ecology) treats humans as if they merely respond to challenges posed by an autonomous environment: if the environment changes, we must change with it or be punished by fitness decline. But this picture overlooks the ways in which humans engineer their own environment. Organism/environment fit can come about through lineages changing to fit their environment, or by organisms changing their environment to fit their current phenotype. We are not unique in engineering our environment to fit our phenotype, but we are pervasive and incorrigible niche constructors. Most obviously, we marshal our technology in "counter-active niche construction." As the world becomes colder, we use clothes, shelter, fire. As it becomes more seasonal, we make increasing usage of storage. As it becomes drier, we store water in tanks and canteens, and engineer water flow through wells, pumps, irrigation. Our technology makes our experienced environment more stable than the physical environment itself.

Moreover, while it is true that human environments change more rapidly than those of other organisms, it is also true that human evolutionary response is accelerated. For humans inherit novel phenotypic variations from their parents culturally as well as genetically. Adaptive response to change that depends on slow, expensive and imperfect trial-and-error learning can be adopted and fine-tuned by the next generation, who thus escape the costs of failed trials. Moreover, since cultural transmission can be horizontal and oblique, the spread of a successful innovation through a group will typically require far fewer generations than adaptation depending on genetic innovation (Tomasello 1999, Henrich and McElreath 2003, Tomasello 2008). Even though humans live in variable and changing environments, our adaptive response is not severely constrained by limits on our cognitive and informational resources, and so it is reasonable to assume that humans often choose more or less the best of the available options. Models of cultural inheritance explain how agents have the informational resources they need, despite living in labile environments. The human capacity to track and respond to our varying environment, and hence the explanatory scope of HBE, is underwritten by niche construction and cultural inheritance. Action is suited to circumstance, because agents adjust the environment as well as adjusting to the environment. Moreover, though humans live in complex, informationally translucent worlds, cultural inheritance theory shows how informational resources are made available to agents relatively inexpensively.

In my view, Laland and Brown overstate the optimizing power of dual inheritance and niche construction. Some domains are recalcitrant (Sterelny 2007). Think, for example, of threats to health. The threats pathogens pose to human health are both fast-changing and causally complex, and hence effective response is hard to recognize. Pathogens themselves evolve with extraordinary rapidity. Moreover, the suite of pathogens to which we are exposed is very sensitive to demographic, geographic, ecological, and economic changes. For example, human agricultural practices expanded the breeding opportunities of malaria-carrying mosquitoes, thus exposing the population to that pathogen. So it is no surprise (I argue) that folk medicines are much less successful guides to action than folk biology or folk craft lore. Human social and economic life transformed the disease environments, and human response to this change was slow and incomplete. Some 10,000 years or more ago, humans began to shift from mobile foraging lives to village life as sedentary farmers. That shift created a new set of risks; a new set of diseases associated with husbandry; a sedentary lifestyle and larger populations. It has taken 10,000 years for effective public health responses to evolve, and many human collectives still lack those adaptations. Laland and Brown are right that niche construction and cultural inheritance both help in supporting adaptive response to a changing world. They make adaptive response more robust. But some changes overwhelm these mechanisms. Adaptive response is constrained both by rapid environmental change and the informational demands on apt response, and these can interact synergistically.

MODELS AS TOOLS

One way to defend the wide applicability of HBE models, then, is to argue that humans reliably optimize over a wide range of environments, including novel ones. These models are explanatory, if we can establish a close quantitative fit between model and observation. They are explanatory even if the fit is merely qualitative, if the behavior modeled is otherwise surprising. There is an alternative. HBE is heir to the modeling tradition in biology, and many who work within that tradition have emphasized the heuristic role of models in biology, including human behavioral ecology. This perspective is shared widely by those who have reflected on the role of models in science (see Levins 1966, Lewontin 1987, Godfrey-Smith 2001, Smith, Borgerhoff Mulder, and Hill 2001, Shennan 2002). So, for example, Peter Godfrey-Smith has pointed out that we can think of optimality models as tools for identifying the mechanisms that limit adaptive response (Godfrey-Smith 2001). HBE models can be used as tools for discovering hidden features of the selective environment and hidden constraints on agent response to their environment.

To get as much juice out of HBE models as possible, we need to identify the circumstances in which model failures are informative. We can use a model as a discovery strategy, not just as a hypothesis. Thus I have noted, in discussing simple foraging models, that approximate conformity between model and data is not convincing evidence that humans fine-tune foraging to needs, opportunities, and costs. A confirmation of a weak prediction is no surprise. But falsifying a weak prediction is surprising. If we cannot approximately fit a model to apparently unsurprising behavior, we know we are missing some crucial feature of the agent/environment interaction. In some cases, a mismatch brings into focus unexpected features of the fitness environment; the failure to fit model to phenomenon is the result of misconstruing the selective forces in play. In other cases, a mismatch brings into focus the unexpected constraints agents face in recognizing and evaluating the environments in which they act.

In the rest of the chapter, I explore this idea of models as tools through a series of examples. I begin with a puzzle case of polygyny, to illustrate informational constraints on adaptive decision-making. I then turn from psychology to selective environment, discussing male hunting and the idea that we can use model/world mismatch to show the limits of individualist models of selection. In the final section, I discuss the replacement of Neandertals by our species in Europe, and the idea that this replacement was driven by crucial foraging differences between Neandertals and their human competitors. There are many complexities in the Neandertal picture (see Sterelny 2012: chap. 3), but (assuming that crucial ecological and foraging differences have been correctly identified), one element of their decline was their being caught in an ancient fitness trap. If so, we need not suppose they suffered from intrinsic cognitive limits. Such traps are best identified by model failures. I then briefly conclude. But first polygyny, and information constraints on adaptive action.

POLYGYNY

Polygyny is a triumph of HBE. If a women could have a mate of her own (and if sex ratios are typically fairly equal), why would a women consent to be a second wife? Behavioral ecology offers an elegant solution. In humans and other animals, polygyny is a side effect of the unequal control of resources. The basic idea is that females, faced with the immense costs of reproduction, chase resources; males chase females (for the basic model, see Foley 1995; for a readable review, Hrdy 1999:251–57). When resources are scattered in small packages through the territory of a population, females scatter too, and polygyny cannot establish. But when key resources are concentrated in a few large packages, females are concentrated at these resource islands. If one (or a few) males can seize control of these islands, polygyny is favored. By controlling access to the resources females need, a male or a small male coalition can monopolize sexual access to females. This general model, the suggestion goes, applies reasonably well to human cultures. In economically egalitarian social worlds, polygyny is not favored. But as the social world becomes less egalitarian, with differing males having markedly differing access to resources, a polygyny threshold will eventually be reached. As inequality rises, some women will control a greater resource envelop by choosing to become a second wife of a resource-rich male rather than being the only wife of a resource-poor male.

    To treat the polygyny threshold model as applying widely to human societies we cannot be too legalistic in classifying cultures as polygynous; we would have to treat mistress-keeping and serially monogamous marriage as de facto polygyny. That said, this model seems to apply fairly well to many human groups (for both its scope and some limits, see Marlowe 2000, 2003). But there is at least one very puzzling anomaly: an example in which a group of males seems to have used their control of *pseudo-resources* to leverage very unequal sexual access to women. I have in mind a strange feature of Australian Aboriginal life: its sexual gerontocracy. Ian Keen discusses this case in contrasting inequality in Aboriginal cultures with those of the complex forager societies of the Pacific Northwest. The American societies do seem to fit the polygyny threshold model, for they are economically inegalitarian. In the Pacific Northwest, we find foraging societies with quite high population densities, little residential mobility, extensive trade (mediated by precursors to money), significant food storage, and (most saliently), significant and enduring social inequality. The development of enduring inequality seems to depend on an environment where crucial resources are spatially concentrated and can be stored after harvesting. This concentration affords a monopoly opportunity for the strong and ambitious, a monopoly which in turn yields power. High populations in relation to resources, the capacity to store crucial, abundant resources, and the spatial concentration of those crucial resources combine to erode forager egalitarianism.

Keen shows that though Aboriginal forager ecologies were highly variable, none match these conditions of resource anxiety and resource control (2006). So they are not markedly economically unequal. Yet some Aboriginal societies were markedly sexually unequal: they had high, sometimes very high, levels of polygyny. Such groups were sexual gerontocracies in which older males (and sometimes older females) had far greater access to sexual partners than their younger siblings. Strikingly, older males used *pseudo-informational* resources to leverage their sexual access: they controlled ritual knowledge and, via that, they controlled entrée into the adult world. This social structure poses an explanatory challenge. How could such customs be stable in the face of the costs they imposed on younger males? As Brian Hayden points out in commenting on Keen's analysis, we cannot take the kinship and ritual knowledge system of these Aboriginal cultures as explanatorily fundamental in the same way that (say) salmon concentrations in the Pacific Northwest are explanatorily fundamental. He wants to know why these norms were respected; why were they stable? Here we seem to have run into a genuine anomaly: a genuinely opaque behavioral pattern. While the polygyny threshold model does not explain the Aboriginal case, it identifies the puzzle and its shape: the stability of an (apparent) pseudo-resource in the face of the costs that fiction imposes on the many. Without the threshold model, we would not see both the similarity of this case to those we can explain, and the difference. Perhaps these resources are real, with kinship and ritual knowledge coding ecological or social information in a metaphorical way. Perhaps a cognitive constraint is in play: it is possible that the excluded Aboriginals cannot assemble the cognitive resources that would unmask "ritual knowledge" as pseudo-knowledge, perhaps because it is too integrated with real knowledge. Perhaps this is a case where the individualist level of analysis of HBE reaches one of its limits. For the informational resources of these cultures are collective tools; they are built and used collectively, by agents whose interests overlap but which are not identical.

In brief, Aboriginal gerontocracy is seriously anomalous: an example of a behavior for which we have no first-approximation model. Polygyny threshold models underscore just how puzzling this phenomenon is. In the next section, I move from subtle constraints on agents and their cognitive resources to subtle features of the selective environment; complexities that are only evident through data/model mismatch.

FORAGING LIKE A GIRL

HBE models typically assume that agents maximize individual fitness. Yet humans do live in groups, and often seem to act not just cooperatively but altruistically. Furthermore, the conditions that make group selection powerful seem to apply to human life: groups compete, and conformist mechanisms increase uniformity within groups, stabilize differences that arise between them, and make migration between groups less frequent and more expensive. How then would we use HBE's individualist models to detect a signature of group-level selection? We would need to find systematic patterns in action that do not seem adaptive for individuals, but which are adaptive for the groups to which they belong. Male large-game hunting is a plausible candidate. It is pervasive, and often benefits the group. For sharing norms often result in the take from successful hunts being shared: hunters and their families often get no more of the kill than other members of the community. So hunters provide a public good. But for that very reason their actions seem to make no sense at the individual level. Large game are dangerous. So why hunt buffalo if you could go rabbit trapping instead, especially as you get to keep your rabbit.

There seem to be three candidate explanations of large game hunting (together with hybrids and mixed models). On one view, hunters benefit themselves and their immediate family through improved access to food. Hunters cooperate in the hunt itself, because their share of a large catch is more valuable than the small game they could catch themselves. Hunters share food with those outside hunting parties to reduce variance in their access to food. Large game hunting is a boom or bust activity, with occasional successes bringing large rewards, but with many failures. So smoothing variance is important. On a second view, large game hunting is part of a group-level (or perhaps an extended family level) adaptive division of labor. Female foraging (and independent foraging by older children) complements male hunting, for it depends on different skills and equipment; it has fewer troughs and peaks than large game hunting; it is best pursed at different times and places; it reduces risk for the demographic core of the population. The group as a whole harvests more, if different agents (typically of different ages and genders) specialize in different activities. On a third approach, now perhaps the best known, the benefits of hunting do indeed accrue to individual hunters. But the benefits are improved sexual access and higher social status. In hunting, hunters provide a public good, and they do so to send a costly, and hence honest, signal of their quality. The literature on these variant approaches to hunting is large and expanding, and at times acrimonious. The most important defenses of economic approaches to hunting, individual and collective, are Kaplan et al. (2000), Kaplan and Gurven (2005), Marlowe (2005), Gurven and von Rueden (2006), O'Connell (2006), and Gurven and Hill (2009). Kristin Hawkes, with various allies, has been the key figure in developing the signaling, show-off explanation of hunting (see Bliege Bird , Smith, and Bird 2001, Hawkes and Bliege Bird 2002, Smith, Bliege Bird, and Bird 2003, Smith and Bliege Bird 2005, Hawkes, O'Connell, and Coxworth 2010).

I shall focus on the signaling model, since it has been increasingly salient in recent literature (see, for example, Seabright 2010). This model treats large game hunting as sending a costly signal: hunters advertise their quality. The model presupposes a heterogeneous and discretionary environment of social interaction. Agents make choices about their social partners, and those choices matter. Agents do best if they can identify the presence of crucial traits in other agents: foraging ability, fighting power, pathogen resistance. Likewise, agents with these crucial qualities want their quality to be recognized by others. However, the traits in question are not obvious to casual inspection, and there is a temptation to deceive: agents do well if others think they are of high quality, even if they are not.[2] In such circumstances it is sometimes possible to advertise quality by sending a "costly signal" (Zahavi and Zahavi 1997).

A classic example is of a male bird advertising its ability to resist parasites by displaying its showy tail. The crucial idea is that such displays are differentially costly: they impose relatively higher costs on lower quality males—males who do not have the agility or strength of their superiors and who thus do not develop the focal trait in its fullest form. Lower quality agents cannot afford the cost of signaling. Frauds cannot afford the signal, and so its reliability is stabilized by the *differential* cost of sending it (Saunders 2009). The peacock's tail is of no benefit to the local population. But sometimes prosocial acts impose a cost on the agent, and so those acts can be used as signals of agent quality. Amos Zahavi has suggested, for example, that babblers that act as sentries and warn of predators approaching advertise their fine phenotypes. In doing so, they improve their mating prospects. Costly signaling is a natural model of some forms of prosocial behavior in human life[3]: bigman feasts; conspicuous gift-giving to charity; perhaps supererogatory displays of courage in inter-communal conflict (Smith, Bliege Bird, and Bird 2003). Perhaps, likewise, male large-game hunting is also a costly signal of hunter quality (Hawkes 1991, Bliege Bird, Smith, and Bird 2001, Hawkes and Bliege Bird 2002, Smith and Bliege Bird 2005).

Despite its popularity, I think this model is quite unpersuasive. A costly signal is a display of *unusually high quality*. So costly signaling should be an individualistic, *minority* activity—as is, for example, building a new art gallery for a city. But this does not fit the pattern of hunting in forager societies. In some foraging societies, hunting is collective and cooperative rather than individual (see, for example, Alvard and Nolin 2002 on cooperative whale hunting). Indeed, surely only the invention of poison and/or penetrating projectile weapons made individual and small group large-game hunting possible. Such technology is very recent: a recent review lists spearthrowers as dated to 17,000 years ago; bows and poison to around 11,000 ybp (Marlowe 2005:64).[4] Yet there is persuasive evidence that large game hunting played a central role in human economies long before these dates. Hunting must have established itself as a collective, cooperative activity (Foley and Gamble 2009).

Moreover, even when hunting is an individual activity, hunters often contribute their successes—frequent or rare—to the common pool. This collectivization of the take fits the costly signaling framework poorly. We would expect only the best hunters to share. As Smith and Bliege Bird note, when costly signaling is modeled, the stable strategy is: signal only if high quality; respond only to signals (Smith and Bliege Bird 2005:120). But then mediocre-to-poor hunters should *not* share their kills. Poor hunters should keep what they catch and scrounge what they can, or, more likely perhaps, they should abandon hunting altogether and forage like a girl. If hunting and sharing genuinely is individualist signaling for individual advantage, drop-outs need not fear being excluded from the distribution of product. They are not defecting from a cooperative activity: others should welcome their withdrawal from competitive signaling. Hunting should be like playing baseball in America: the best hunt (or hunt intensively, if the rate of hunting is the signal), and the rest watch. But this does not fit forager ethnography: males are notoriously addicted to hunting. The salience of hunting to male life in forager societies is part of Hawkes' reason for thinking that hunting has a more than instrumental role in male life. While that may be right, the show-off hypothesis leaves the hunting and sharing of the less expert unexplained.

In short, I am sceptical about the idea that the main role of hunting is to send signals of quality. But the debates here have certainly not been resolved, and in this context, the main point is that HBE models have identified the crucial empirical issues on which the debate turns. For example, the individual and the group versions of economic explanations of hunting differ on the role of reciprocity. If sharing functions to reduce long-run variation, those who share must be those who receive. If hunting functions to benefit the group, there need be no special return to individually successful hunters. Likewise, as we have seen, one critical empirical issue for the signaling model is to show that male behavior is differential in the way the model predicts (and, of course, that the difference predicts difference in sexual access).

FITNESS TRAPS

Neandertal extinction has been a hugely contentious issue in paleobiology. It has often been suggested that Neandertals disappeared as a consequence of intrinsic cognitive limits that disadvantaged them in competition with *sa-*

piens populations, especially in the tough times of glacial Europe (Klein and Edgar 2002, Wynn and Coolidge 2004, Mithen 2005, Wynn and Coolidge 2007, Klein 2009). They lived in excessively interesting times, and with excessively interesting neighbors. I will finish this chapter by sketching a partial alternative, an explanation that illustrates the role of HBE models in making explicit subtle costs and benefits.

There is very little that is certain about Neandertal extinction. But the basic picture is that somewhere around 45,000 ybp, modern humans expanded into the east and north of Europe (the Aurignacians), coming into contact with Neandertal populations. The Europe of this period was subject to intense climatic variation, with some truly intense cold periods (Finlayson and Carrión 2007). Though climatic change forced frequent shifts in both populations, their habitat preferences overlapped enough so that it is probable but not certain that the two groups remained in at least sporadic contact until the Neandertals disappeared as a distinctive and identifiable population about 30,000 years ago, or perhaps even a little more recently (Finlayson 2009).

Neandertals were an impressive and technologically adept people. In the Levant, Neandertal populations abutted *sapiens* populations around 100,000 years ago, and there is no sign that *sapiens* populations could expand at their expense (Shea 2003a). But there does seem to have been an important difference between Neandertal and *sapiens* foraging systems. Neandertals seem to have specialized in ambush hunting of large- and medium-size game (Finlayson 2009). *Sapiens* seem to have developed a more pursuit hunting technology, but perhaps more importantly, they developed a more robust and efficient sexual division of labor (Kuhn and Stiner 2006, O'Connell 2006, Stiner 2001). So *sapiens* seems to have used a broader range of resources. In contemporary forager societies, the typical pattern is that men hunt and women and children gather. This economic organization is much superior to an all-hunting economy. Competition is reduced; each resource is depleted less. If different resources peak at different times, seasonal variability is reduced. There tends to be less daily variation in gathering and small game hunting, so daily variation is reduced too. Moreover, on the reasonable assumption that large game hunting is more risky than other economic activities, the "reproductive core" of the population is less exposed to risk. Finally, if agents specialize in a particular kind of resource, it is profitable to develop expertise and technology for acquiring that particular resource. So behaviorally modern humans, armed with this division of labor, exploited a wider range of resources. As a consequence, their invasion, with their combination of large and small game hunting and intensive gathering, was multiply bad news for the Neandertals. They depleted the Neandertal resource base through their own hunting. Moreover, because they used a large range of foods, they would continue depleting key Neandertal resources after the supply of large game fell below the crucial threshold needed for Neandertals to be self-sustaining. For *sapiens* could persist in regions from which Neandertals would have to withdraw, and by persisting, make it less likely that Neandertal-friendly conditions would return.

This division of labor seemed not to have established in northern latitudes. There is no evidence of similar niche differentiation among the Neandertals (or in Middle Paleolithic hominins). Remnant late Neandertal populations show some signs of resource expansion, but still seem to focus mostly on large- and medium-size game (Finlayson 2009). We would expect to see archaeological signatures of gathering, if it played a central economic role in Neandertal life. Seeds, nuts, tubers are crucial to modern foragers: they are often abundant and can be stored. But they need to be processed. Grindstones and millstones are durable. Had their use been central to Neandertal lifeways, they would have been found. Neandertals were not restricted to large game, but they seem to have used other resources in small proportions (Kuhn, Brantingham, and Kerry 2004, Kuhn and Stiner 2006, O'Connell 2006). They were not socially organized to systematically exploit small game and river/marine resources. Quite probably, women and children were recruited as look-outs, to beat the bushes to scare and drive the game; even if there was no overall gendered division of labor, there is no reason to suppose that such vulnerable individuals were exposed to direct contact with large dangerous game. Such division of labor, however, cannot eliminate the demographic risks associated with such a narrow resource envelop. Through this specialization, Neandertals placed themselves very high on the food web, with all the risks that follow from this ecological role: high day-to-day and season-to-season variance in success; together with small population sizes and vulnerability to crashes. An economic life dependent on large game hunting would explain why Neandertal populations seem so small. Moreover, if this picture of their default way of life is correct, these technical and behavioral specializations to ambush hunting would make it difficult to switch to pursuit hunting, when in colder periods temperate forest was replaced by open steppe country with its very different herbivore guild.

Fragmentation of a species into small populations is itself a risk factor: small populations are much more likely to fluctuate to extinction in the face of minor disturbance. But for hominins whose lives depend on technology and information, the fragmentation of the species into small groups is especially risky. There is ample evidence that individual by individual, Neandertals were capable of developing and using impressive technologies. This is especially vividly illustrated by their control of fire in cooking birch bark pitch to use as an adhesive, arguably the most complex technology of its time (Nowell, this volume). But lifeways that depend on technology and information have demographic and social preconditions as well as individual cognitive ones. Technique and technology must be reliably transmitted across the generations. The group must support some capacity for innovation in the face of change, together with capacities for recognizing and preserving successful innovation. These collective preconditions of hominin lifeways are fragile in small groups (Powell, Shennan, and Thomas 2009). For one thing, small populations cannot afford specialization, for the market is too small to support specialists. So small populations miss many of the benefits of a division of labor (Ofek 2001). For another, the informational resources of the group are much less well buffered in small populations: they can easily leak away through unlucky accident (Richerson and Boyd, this volume; see also Henrich 2004). The collective informational basis for further innovation in the face of further change is narrower, especially if the time budget of the group is already stressed. In short, small groups lack the benefits of redundancy.

In my view, the differences in material culture between the Neandertals and the *sapiens* populations that replaced them may well reflect nothing more than these impacts of demography and social organization on the generation and maintenance of collective cognitive resources; there may be no significant individual cognitive differences at all. The collective informational resources of small groups are vulnerable, and another puzzling aspect of Neandertal material culture might have demographic origins. Physical symbols of identity and difference are rare, though not unknown (Zilhão et al. 2010). Ornaments, figurines, and local decorative style were becoming prominent features of many *sapiens* populations about this time. While obviously there is a good deal of conjecture in the interpretation of shell necklaces, figurines, ochre, and the like, the most natural interpretation is that these physical symbols are forms of insignia. They are a physical display of group identity and / or role within a group (Kuhn and Stiner 2007). If such "symbolic" material culture does play this role, we would not expect to see it in small groups largely isolated from others, as were the late Neandertals. This interpretation is supported by the Australian experience. Australia has been settled for at least 45,000 years, but physical symbols become common only in the Holocene, when the population begins to expand (d'Errico 2003, Brumm and Moore 2005).

If something like this is right, the crucial question is: why did Neandertals not broaden their resource take too, perhaps via a similar gender and age division of labor? Can resource intensification models illuminate not just what went wrong for the Neandertal, but why it went wrong? Perhaps they can. Humans sometimes respond with remarkable dexterity to novel environmental challenge. But there are other cases in which cultures cling tenaciously to old and failing ways. For example, Jared Diamond in *Collapse* charts the demise of the Greenland Norse, who failed to adopt the cold-climate technology of the Inuit as conditions shifted inexorably against them (Diamond 2005). Elsewhere, I have suggested that the Norse were not being simply pig-headed: they were caught in a fitness trap, marooned on a sinking local optima, and unable to traverse an even deeper valley to reach the survivable peak that their Inuit neighbors represented (Sterelny 2007).

The fate of the Neandertal may be that of the Greenland Norse writ large. Like the Norse, they too were caught in a fitness trap. Imagine a Neandertal community under stress, with its resource take falling towards a critical threshold. Quite likely, a fatally large fitness trench would separate this community on its sinking local optima from nearby peaks occupied by moderns. For suppose (as is plausible) that the ancillary role played by women and older children in hunting mattered to the current, barely adequate, resource flow. Without those roles as lookouts and as agents of distraction, confusion, and panic, still less would be captured. But the women and children could be withdrawn from hunting and encouraged into other activities only if those activities brought immediate reward. That is surely not likely: it understates the skills and the technology needed to find and process plant staples. Even efficient search and processing does not yield a high rate of return per foraging hour.

Indeed, Kuhn and Stiner suggest that the modern division of labor could only be invented in the favorable subtropical regions in which behavioral modernity emerged. In such areas, the small animal fauna and plant-based foods are more diverse and abundant than at higher latitudes, and tropical and subtropical regions often allow children significant foraging opportunities. Children are never fully self-supporting, but in favorable conditions they can make significant contributions to the family economy (Kramer 2005), especially if supplied with appropriate technology (Bock 2005). Once this division of labor was established in favorable places, it was probably self-reinforcing. Local communities would come to be organized around the division of labor and the resource envelop it supplied. Once the mechanisms of cultural inheritance had made this organization of work, from the perspective of the participants, a natural and appropriate part of their life, it could be adapted even to those regions where it would never have been invented, because the forager-gatherer niche was less hospitable. Once it established, it spread risk, by making the human place in the food web more diffuse; as we have seen, the top predator role seized by specialist hunting societies was a risk magnifier, making them especially vulnerable to external shocks disrupting local ecosystems. If these speculations about the origins of the division of labor are right, the fitness valley separating the Neandertals from behavioral modernity might be especially difficult to cross. We do not know the nature of the Neandertal mind. But in contrast to Stephen Mithen (this volume), I see no reason to suppose there were intrinsic limits on Neandertal capacities. Resource intensification models predict shifts from high value large game to small game and plant resources as favored resources become depleted or more difficult to take (Stiner 2001), but these make tacit assumptions about search, pursuit, and handling costs. *Sapiens* populations had the informational resources that enabled them to minimize those costs, and they acquired those resources in circumstances in which the net cost of that information was lower. The Neandertals were not so lucky. When they most needed that information, they could not afford it.

This chapter has defended the broad applicability of HBE models to human action. These models are relevant not only when we can model humans as optimizing machines (even when they seem not to be). HBE models are also insightful, though in a rather different way, when we fail to be optimizing machines. For we can use HBE models to explore the limits on optimality and the reasons for failure.

NOTES

12.1 HBE models are neutral, and are intended to be neutral, on the specificity of these psychological mechanisms. These models are open to the possibility that an appraisal mechanism specific to fertility decisions tracks environmental contingency, but they are not committed to this possibility.

12.2 In contrast, say, to being an airline pilot. It is highly paid, but it is probably not wise to claim to be able to fly when you cannot.

12.3 Though there remains a problem about why the signals should take the form of prosocial behavior. That is not intrinsic to the costly signaling model. The crucial feature of the signal is that it imposes differential costs, not that it provides audience benefit. In their exploration of this model, Smith and Bleige Bird suggest that the benefit attracts an audience and hence amplifies the effect of the signal. But according to the basic model, it is already in the audience's interest to attend to the signals. They deliver valuable information, independently of any public good benefit.

12.4 Of course, these dates are not the true invention of the technology, almost certainly. Rather, they are the first reliable evidence of it, and hence are more likely to be early dates of its widespread use rather than origin.

13

The Distinctively Human Mind:
The Many Pillars of Cumulative Culture

PETER CARRUTHERS

This chapter argues that there are multiple adaptations underlying the distinctiveness of the human mind. Careful analysis of the capacities that are involved in the creation, acquisition, and transmission of culture and cultural products suggests that it is very unlikely that these could be underlain by just one, or even a few, novel cognitive systems. On the contrary, there are at least eight such systems, each of which is largely independent of the others.

INTRODUCTION

What makes human minds distinctive? The question is ambiguous, depending on the extent of the implied contrast. It might mean, "distinctive in relation to the minds of non-human animals, especially the other great apes." Or it might mean, "distinctive in relation to the minds of earlier forms of hominin, especially the Neanderthals." My focus in this chapter will be on the former issue. I am by no means indifferent to questions of hominin cognitive evolution, especially as revealed in the archaeological record. But my main interest, here, is not in the timing and sequencing of the adaptations that led from the last common ancestor of humans and chimpanzees to ourselves, but rather in the question of *how many* distinct capacities are needed to explain the difference. I argue that there are at least a handful of such capacities (probably many more), rather than just one or a few.

Such claims are not new, of course. Evolutionary psychologists often claim that there are multiple adaptations—or "modules"—underlying the distinctiveness of the human mind (Barkow, Cosmides, and Toody 1992, Sperber 1996, Pinker 1997). I have elsewhere endorsed such views, and have laid out the evidence that supports them (Carruthers 2006). But in the present chapter I propose to proceed more negatively, and mostly by way of task analysis (while also drawing on a range of other forms of evidence). I shall consider the views of some of those who have hoped to explain human cognition in terms of one or two major new capacities, arguing not only that these accounts are insufficient, given an analysis of the tasks involved, but also that the specific ways in which they are insufficient demonstrate the need for a number of further adaptations.

What exactly is meant, however, by "explaining human cognition"? And if one is to proceed by way of task analysis, which cognitive tasks are to be analyzed? Ultimately, of course, our goal must be to explain *all* of the ways in which humans are cognitively and behaviorally distinctive. And there are a great many of them. My book, *The Architecture of the Mind* (2006) lists 22, ranging from a capacity for science, through dispositions to sing, dance, and listen to music, to a capacity for humor. But even this catalog is very partial, and should really be much longer. (See Brown 1991 for an extensive list of human universals that are nevertheless unique to the human species.)

Not all of these capacities will be cognitively primitive, of course. Some, at least, will be explicable in terms of others, or in terms of combinations and interactions of others, together with various kinds of learning. But taken in their totality they present a formidable (and in my view insurmountable) challenge to anyone who claims that there is just one adaptation distinctive of the human mind (or even a few such adaptations). Yet this is a challenge that such authors rarely, if ever, attempt to meet. Their explanatory focus is almost always a great deal narrower, often on the distinctively human capacity for cumulative culture. But even in this restricted domain multiple adaptations are required, as we will see.

There is no doubt that our capacity for culture is distinctive in its extent, and that it both underlies our unique adaptability (accommodating ourselves successfully to environments from tropical rainforests to arctic tundra) as well as our most impressive technological and scientific achievements. Tomasello (1999), Donald (2001), and Sterelny (2003) all emphasize the importance, in explaining these facts, of *cumulative* culture. This enables the operation of a "ratchet effect" for human behavioral capacities, as well as for our powers to control, transform, and interact with natural environments. The discoveries and successful practices of one generation can be passed on to the next, providing both the context in which the new generation does its learning, as well as a novel platform from which new discoveries and practices can be developed. In the present chapter I shall join these authors in taking the capacity for cumulative culture as my target for explanation. I shall argue that there are a significant number of adaptations underlying it, rather than just one or two.

A note on terminology before I proceed: although evolutionary psychologists use the language of "modularity," and although my earlier book (2006) is written in defense of a massively modular account of the human mind, I shall not employ that term in the present chapter. This is because too many people have become fixated on what Fodor (1983, 2000b) understands by "module" (and on the requirement that modules should be informationally encapsulated, in particular). Talking in terms of modules would require an extended discussion of the appropriate notion of modularity to employ in the context of an evolutionary psychology, and would distract from the main point at issue. (That discussion is undertaken in the first chapter of Carruthers 2006.) Accordingly, I shall talk of "adaptations" and "systems" instead.

(My use of the former term will be somewhat loose, however. For a case could be made that all of the systems that I shall discuss evolved together in a complex interacting package as the life-history of humans became increasingly social and cultural. In which case they might really constitute a single, complex adaptation. I shall not pursue this question any further.)

It should be stressed, moreover, that most of the systems that I shall be discussing are unlikely to be either unitary (or "atomic") in structure or localized to just one area of the brain. On the contrary, for the most part they possess a complex internal organization, with the various components located in different brain areas. Moreover, those components might initially have evolved for other purposes, and might still also be employed in the service of other systems and other tasks (Anderson 2008). To take just one example: the "mindreading" or "theory of mind" system to be discussed shortly appears to consist of at least four dedicated components distributed in three different areas of the cortex, together with a number of others that are also utilized for other purposes (Frith and Frith 2003, Saxe and Powell 2006). And in the course of its normal operations the mindreading system will need to recruit and interact with multiple other systems also (Nichols and Stich 2003).

One final preparatory comment before we get on with the main business: someone might wonder about the criteria that I have employed when selecting uniquely human capacities as candidates for discussion, since there are a number of other capacities that have also been discussed in this context. A capacity for "mental time travel"—recalling the past and foreseeing the future—would be one. My answer is that I have selected only those capacities that I believe I can defend successfully as being both uniquely human and necessary for cumulative culture. I do not discuss mental time travel, for example, because there is evidence that nonhuman animals can both recall specific events and plan for the future (Clayton, Emory, and Dickinson 2004, Sanz, Morgan, and Gulick 2004, Mulcahy and Call 2006, Correia, Dickinson, and Clayton 2007, Raby et al. 2007).

IMITATION, SHARED INTENTIONALITY, AND MINDREADING

Tomasello (1999) emphasizes the role of true imitation in enabling cultural accumulation. (True imitation is opposed to the forms of goal imitation or emulation-imitation that he says one finds among apes and monkeys. It involves identifying the goals of the actor, as well as a capacity to parse an action into its component parts.) Indeed, he claims that it is sufficient. One aspect of his argument is negative: he asserts that there hasn't been enough time, in the 5 to 7 million years since the hominin line separated from the other great apes, for a suite of multiple cognitive adaptations to evolve; and he claims that the genetic disparities between ourselves and our nearest relatives, the chimpanzees and bonobos, are too minor to explain widespread differences in cognition. These points are supposed to motivate the search for a single major adaptation that can make the difference.

I have replied to this argument elsewhere (Carruthers 2006: chap. 3), explaining how recent research demonstrates that the genetic differences between ourselves and chimpanzees are much more extensive than was previously believed (Ebersberger et al. 2002, Anzai et al. 2003, Pan et al. 2005, ENCODE consortium 2007), and pointing out that since there are a great many physiological differences between humans on the one hand and chimps and bonobos on the other—which have plainly been able to evolve in 5 million years—there is no reason why a significant number of new cognitive capacities should not have appeared also.

In a positive vein Tomasello (1999) argues that the evolution of true imitation resulted in a high-fidelity trans-generational cultural copying mechanism. This enabled humans to gradually ratchet up their behavioral capacities generation by generation. Innovations and improvements created by individuals (often by happenstance or trial and error) could spread through the local population by imitation and thereafter be transmitted to children in the same way. This provided a platform from which new discoveries and improvements could be made, which could in turn be copied and stabilized in the population.

It is natural to wonder why, if this account were correct, we should see such long periods of stasis in the archaeological record, culminating in a veritable "cultural explosion" a mere 40,000 years ago (especially in Europe)—by which time *Homo sapiens* had already been in existence for more than 50,000 years. Two points can be made in reply. One is that the cultural explosion may be partly in the eye of the beholder, resulting from the historical concentration of most archaeological research in Europe. When the full range of data from Africa are examined carefully, in contrast, what emerges is a long period of gradual cultural accumulation of skills and abilities (McBrearty and Brooks 2000). The second point is that the cultural ratchet effect is highly sensitive to population density (Cavalli-Sforza and Feldman 1981, Shennan 2000, 2001). In dispersed populations even successful technologies can be lost, as appears to have happened in the case of Tasmania (Henrich 2004). Hence for long periods of human evolution, cultural progress may have been a fragmentary and local affair, and thus perhaps too ephemeral to show up in the archaeological record. On some accounts human population density passed through an especially tight bottleneck about 70,000 years ago, with the total human population perhaps dropping as low as 10,000 individuals (Ambrose 1998, Lahr and Foley 1998).

Tomasello et al. (2005b) shift the focus of the above account somewhat, since they are more sanguine about the imitative powers of chimpanzees than Tomasello (1999). They cite recent evidence suggesting that chimpanzees are capable of figuring out both the goals and component actions of the activities of others, and that chimpanzees do sometimes engage in true imitation. But they don't do it very often. And chimpanzees show none of the forms of *shared intentionality* that are so distinctive of human infancy and childhood. From an early age, human children will engage in proto-declarative pointing, drawing the attention of a care-giver to interesting objects and events in the environment, seemingly for its own sake. Likewise, they will monitor the patterns of attention and emotional expressions of those around them, whether to check on the safety of a new person or object, or to figure out the meaning of a new word. And they also display a drive towards cooperative activities with others, such as shared pretense and conversational turn-taking, which require them to monitor the goals and intentions of others. Chimpanzees, in contrast, seem only to pay attention to the intentions of others in competitive situations.

According to Tomasello et al. (2005b), then, the single distinctively human cognitive adaptation is actually more motivational than cognitive. It consists in an initial drive to share mental states with others. This sets up a developmental learning sequence that results not only in frequent imitation of the behavior of others (issuing in gradual skill accumulation), but also in full-blown theory of mind a few years later (especially an understanding of false belief). It also results in the acquisition of language. For according to Tomasello et al., language is entirely a cultural product—perhaps the archetypal cultural product, providing the initial "ratchet" for almost everything else that follows. (I shall return to this claim shortly.)

I have no quarrel with this stress on shared intentionality and its facilitatory effect on human imitation abilities, nor with the importance of the latter in enabling cumulative culture. But it is very likely a mistake to think that mature mindreading abilities (including false-belief understanding) are acquired via general learning from an initial starting point of shared intentionality. This is because infants who are a little over a year old (only a few months older than the first emergence of shared intentionality behavior) display an implicit understanding of false belief and its consequences for action in their patterns of expectation and surprise (Onishi and Baillargeon 2005, Southgate, Senju, and Csibra 2007, Surian, Caldi, and Sperber 2007, Song et al. 2008, Scott and Baillargeon 2009), and in their helping behavior (Buttelmann, Carpenter, and Tomasello 2009). The best explanation of young children's failures in explicit false-belief tasks is therefore some variant of what Birch and Bloom (2004) refer to as "the curse of knowledge." It is hard even for adults to set aside their own understanding of a situation and to reason and give answers from the epistemic perspective of another (Keysar, Lin, and Barr 2003). So what probably changes in the first few years of development isn't children's understanding of the mental states of others, as such, but rather an increase in their "executive function" ability to control and suppress responses based on their own view of a situation, together with an increase in working memory capacities.

The above line of criticism has little bearing on the question of the *number* of distinctively human adaptations, however. Whether we think that it is shared intentionality that leads to mature mindreading abilities via general learning (as Tomasello et al. 2005b maintain), or whether we think of the core mindreading system as emerging under maturational constraints over the first year or two of life (as I believe), we still have just a single (albeit complexly structured) distinctively human adaptation for social cognition. Of much more consequence is the question whether natural language is entirely a cultural construct, or whether it, too, has a distinct innate basis. I shall pursue this in the section that follows.

LANGUAGE

Tomasello et al. (2005b) and Donald (2001) argue that language is a cultural product, and that nothing more is needed to explain how children acquire it than general learning abilities combined with capacities for shared intentionality and true imitation. While the former claim is, in some sense, obvious, I shall argue that the later claim is (in part) mistaken, and that humans have a distinct adaptation designed for language learning. I shall begin, however, by outlining the part of the claim that is generally correct.

Bloom (2002) demonstrates in detail how a capacity to read the intentions of others is both necessary and (perhaps) sufficient for the acquisition of the vocabulary of a language. Children learn the meanings of words by figuring out what speakers are intending to refer to, especially by tracking patterns of speakers' attention (in the initial stages at least; later on, contextual cues of other sorts may be sufficient). And one can then imagine a stage in human evolution during which people were able to learn words and to communicate quite successfully with two- or three-word strings, somewhat like the simple sign languages that are created by deaf children who have had no exposure to a language exemplar (Goldin-Meadow and Feldman 1977, Goldin-Meadow and Mylander 1983)—only presumably a good deal more elaborate, since vocabulary would be shared and accumulated culturally over time. But the syntax of language is surely another matter. Here we have every reason to think that there exists a distinct language-specific learning mechanism.

One set of arguments is collected under the title "the poverty of the stimulus" (Laurence and Margolis 2001, Crain, Gualmini, and Pietroski 2005, Segal 2007). Children acquire syntax pretty much effortlessly on the basis of only positive data, and without correction or training. Adult linguists studying the syntax of a new language can elicit data from subjects about what can or—especially—*cannot* be said in that language in order to confirm and disconfirm their hypotheses, but children know, by the age of about 3, more than a linguist will know after a lifetime of theorizing. Moreover, children never make the sorts of mistakes that one would expect them to make if they were inducing the grammar of their language by general-learning methods. Indeed, some principles seem to be acquired unerringly, which would be extremely surprising if they were learning them through the use of some sort of general-purpose system. Moreover, when they do make mistakes, it often turns out that the mistaken grammatical forms that they use would actually be permitted by the grammars of another set of extant languages. Furthermore, there is the evidence that children exposed to extremely impoverished linguistic models (whether pidgin or deaf home sign) will nevertheless acquire a language with all of the syntactic subtlety and complexity possessed by any other natural language (Bickerton 1981, Pinker 1994).

In addition, Valian, Solt, and Stewart (2009) provide a direct test of the general-learning claims made by Tomasello (2000a, 2003). According to the latter, acquisition of syntax proceeds "bottom-up," gradually generalizing from specific examples and formulaic phrases to abstract principles. If there is an innately structured syntax-learning mechanism, in contrast, then abstract syntactic categories should be available from the outset. Valian et al. (2009) set out to test the predictions of these different views in connection with children's understanding of determiners like "a," "the," and "this." On Tomasello's general-learning account, children's understanding should initially be exemplar-based, and generalization to new instances should be slow. If children already possess the abstract category *determiner*, in contrast, then generalization to new cases should be immediate, and the distribution of young children's determiner phrases should closely resemble those of their mothers. While reviewing a range of additional supporting evidence, Valian et al. (2009) were able to show that the predictions of the specialized learning-mechanism account are strongly supported by their data, whereas Tomasello's general-learning approach is disconfirmed.

I think we can assume, then, that our syntactic abilities cannot be explained in terms of our capacity for shared intentionality and/or mindreading combined with general learning. But what about the reverse? Can our distinctive forms of social cognition be explained in terms of our capacity for language? Just such a position has been proposed and defended by Bickerton (1995, 2005), who claims that the evolution of language was the event that explains all other distinctive features of human cognition. Such a position is highly implausible, however, and partly for reasons internal to Bickerton's own theory. He argues persuasively that an intermediate stage in the evolution of a language faculty would have been a capacity for *protolanguage,* which would have consisted in communicative uses of strings of words unregulated by grammar, not unlike those that we see in pidgin languages, or in the home sign languages of the deaf. But it is impossible to see how these protolanguages could be created and sustained without sophisticated forms of social intelligence. It takes mindreading to figure out what someone is trying to communicate to you in protolanguage, and it takes mindreading to use such a language in successful communication. Indeed, the only plausible accounts that we have of the evolution of language presuppose that some form of mindreading was already in existence (Origgi and Sperber 2000).

It appears, then, that we need to postulate at least two distinctively human cognitive capacities: one for shared intentionality and/or mindreading, and one for natural language syntax. And indeed, just as this account would predict, there exist double dissociations between each of these capacities, both in the course of their development in childhood, and in mature individuals. Let me briefly elaborate.

People with disabilities that place them on the autistic spectrum can be deficient in developing social cognition while being normal in their acquisition and use of syntax (but not in the pragmatics of language—Baron-Cohen 1995). And within the set of people diagnosed with Specific Language Impairment (SLI), there exists a subset whose deficit appears to be localized to the acquisition of syntax only, and yet whose mindreading abilities are normal (van der Lely 2005). Moreover, adults suffering from schizophrenia are often deficient in mindreading tasks while being normal in their use of syntax (Pickup and Frith 2001, Sprong et al. 2007). Whereas, in contrast, adults suffering from aphasia can lose all capacity for syntax while still being normal in their social and mindreading abilities (Varley 1998).

Before leaving the topic of language, we should consider whether a capacity for syntax is the *only* novel adaptation associated with it. There is some reason to think that this is not the case. This is because, as soon as linguistic communication became common (especially involving the transmission of information via testimony), there would have been intense pressure to check linguistic messages for accuracy before believing them (Carruthers 2006: chap. 6). One thing we can be certain about is that communication would often have been used for Machiavellian purposes as well as for altruistic ones. Some aspects of the adaptive problem, here, could no doubt have been taken up by the mindreading faculty, which can try to figure out whether the speaker has any motive to deceive, and so forth. But it is very likely that mechanisms for checking consistency and coherence with one's existing beliefs would also have made their appearance. For the absence of such properties would give some indication of likely falsehood, in communication just as in science. It is also very likely that capacities to engage in, and to evaluate, public forms of argumentation would have evolved for the same reason, as Mercier and Sperber (2011) argue.

CREATIVITY

So far I have argued that there are two or three distinct adaptations underlying the human capacity for cumulative culture. But it should be plain, I think, that cultural accumulation wouldn't progress very far without a capacity for creative thought. Sometimes mere happenstance or trial and error can lead to a new discovery, or a new item of technology. But not often. When humans confront problems, they generate new ideas and hypotheses in an attempt to overcome those problems. Even hunters tracking a wounded animal need to think creatively, inventing and debating explanatory hypotheses that might explain the subtle signs available to them (Liebenberg 1990).

Bickerton (1995) suggests that a capacity for creative thought is a by-product of language. This is a natural enough idea, for we know that the large vocabulary and recursive grammar of natural language together provide us with an almost unlimited representational resource (even allowing for limitations in working memory). And we know that we can, at will, combine together words in novel ways—thereby entertaining novel thoughts—and that we often do so, e.g., in humor and in metaphor. However, it is one thing to possess a recursive representational system that makes it *possible* for people to formulate thoughts that neither they, nor anyone else, has entertained before, but it is quite another thing to have a disposition to use it thus, and to use it relevantly. And I can see no way that the former could in any sense be sufficient for the latter.

Notice that any animal that is capable of moving its limbs and torso independently of one another has the wherewithal to string together novel sequences of movement. (Indeed, humans often do precisely this, in creative free dance.) But none does so, except in limited domains. Thus many prey animals will engage in "protean" evasion procedures when being chased by a predator. These are genuinely random sequences of leaps, bounds, and turns that are impossible for a predator to anticipate (Driver and Humphries 1988, Miller 1997). Otherwise, creativity of action seems to be mostly absent from the rest of the animal kingdom, with the possible exception of some limited uses by the other great apes (Carruthers 2006: chap. 2).

I have developed an account of creativity that is action-based (2006, 2007), building on a prior capacity for mental rehearsal of action (which is probably possessed by other apes as well, and hence which isn't itself distinctively human). What evolved at some point in the hominin lineage was a disposition to activate and rehearse combinations of action schemata creatively, sometimes at random (within a certain set of contextual constraints), sometimes utilizing weak semantic associations provided by the context or by current stimuli (as when the curved shape of a banana prompts a child to say, "telephone," and to pretend accordingly). And when this disposition is directed towards linguistic forms of action, the result can be novel rehearsed sentences in "inner speech" that lead the subject to entertain new thoughts. Indeed, I suggest that the proper function of childhood pretend play is to practice the process of creative supposition (especially when resulting from rehearsals of novel natural language sentences), building strategies and heuristics for creative activations of action schemata that will be both fruitful and relevant.

(Notice, by the way, that pretend play is another phenotypic character that is unique to the human species. The proposal sketched here ties that character into the foundations of the human capacity for cumulative culture.)

Whether or not this account is correct, it is surely plain that a capacity for creative thinking would not come free with the capacity for language. It would need to be a separate adaptation—unless, that is, it can be explained as resulting from our capacity for behavioral imitation. Perhaps creative thinking is a culturally constructed behavior, which children have to learn by imitating their elders and/or peers? But this suggestion is quite mysterious. It is one thing to imitate a particular action or sequence of actions—for these are determinate and observable. It is another thing to imitate an inner process of some sort for generating novel combinations and sequences of actions. In this situation it is not the actions themselves that are to be copied, but rather the creative cognitive procedure that generates them, which isn't itself open to observation.

FINE MOTOR COORDINATION

Thus far I have argued that there are a number of distinct "pillars" of cumulative culture. But one doesn't have to reflect very hard to realize that there is also another. This is our remarkable capacity for fine-grained, exact control of movement (Lemon et al. 1999). It is this that enables us to throw a projectile accurately and with force at a moving target, to strike one rock against another at the precise point and at the exact angle needed to detach a sharp flake, and to coordinate our breathing together with movements of mouth, tongue, and larynx in such a way as to produce a smooth stream of speech. And it seems plain that without such control, the basics of material culture could never have got started. There would have been no precision-made stone tools; there would have been no multi-part, finely constructed, specialized hunting weapons; there would have been no sewing of clothes; there would have been no weaving of cloth; and there would have been no pottery or basket making.

Of course, many animals have remarkable physical abilities; and many are capable of fine degrees of physical control of a specialized sort. Think of an elephant picking up a peanut or twisting off a bunch of bananas with its trunk; or think of a hummingbird that maintains its position in front of a nectar-bearing flower while being buffeted by a gusty breeze. But no other animal is capable of anything like the *range* of precise physical skills that we possess. This differential is, no doubt, at least partially explained by the vastly increased size of motor and pre-motor cortex in humans, and also by the unusually extensive projections from the human neocortex to the motor neurons in the medulla and spinal chord (Striedter 2005). In addition, no other animal is similarly motivated to practice and rehearse physical skills in the way that humans do, seemingly taking their own skill-acquisition as an intrinsic goal (Donald 2001).

It is obvious, moreover, that our distinctive motor-control capacities can neither explain, nor be explained by, any of the other distinctively human capacities identified thus far. Although fine-grained motor control may be a necessary condition for smooth and fluent speech, it plainly is, by itself, no guarantor of syntactic abilities. But then neither, obviously, can our possession of language explain our capacity to thread a needle. The same is true for social cognition and for creativity of thought. Motor control is not sufficient for either mindreading or creativity. Nor can mindreading or creativity provide any kind of explanation of our distinctive physical abilities.

PHYSICS

Yet another pillar of cumulative culture is provided by our naïve physics system. Although many animals are adept at tracking causal contingencies among events, it appears that we may be the only species capable of understanding the underlying forces and mechanisms involved (Povinelli 2000). Certainly we are unique in the extent and depth of that understanding. And without it, even the very first steps on the road to cumulative culture—the making of stone handaxes—would not have been possible. For as Mithen explains (1996), we know that the manufacture of such tools would only be possible for people who were capable of appreciating the fracture dynamics of rocks of various types, and of thinking about the physical forces necessary to produce a desired effect. Consistently with these points, attempts to teach chimpanzees to make even the very simplest of Oldowan stone tools have generally been a failure (Toth et al. 1993). It is obvious, likewise, that only a species capable of sophisticated thinking about physical principles would be able to manufacture the sorts of specialized multi-part weapons that are utilized by hunter-gatherers.

It is highly implausible that our naïve physics should be explicable in terms of any of the other distinctively human abilities identified so far, or in terms of any combinations thereof. It is plain that neither syntax, nor creativity, nor fine motor coordination could confer on those that possess them an understanding of physical forces. Nor does it appear plausible that mindreading abilities would be of any help. And even if one believes, as do Gopnik and Schulz (2004), that children's theories of the properties and forces underlying both physical phenomena and human behavior are achieved through the use of powerful Bayesian reasoning mechanisms utilizing directed causal graphs, the distinct starting theories for each of the two reasoning processes would have to be innate.

Moreover, we know that physical understanding emerges early in human childhood. Infants as young as 3 months are surprised if a moving object that disappears behind a screen is later revealed in a position that it could only have reached by passing through a barrier; and they are surprised if an unsupported object doesn't fall. Similarly, by 3 months of age infants expect an object to move when it is struck by another; and by 6 months of age they understand that the amount of displacement of the stationary object is a function of the size of the moving one; and so on and so forth (Baillargeon, Kotovsky, and Needham 1995, Spelke, Phillips, and Woodward 1995). We also know that the development of naïve physics is independent of the development of social cognition, since autistic individuals are normal with respect to the former while being deficient in the latter (Baron-Cohen 1995).

INFERENCE TO THE BEST EXPLANATION

Humans are obviously unique in their capacity for science, and science plainly has a huge impact on culture and cultural products. But—equally obviously—science is not a single, unitary capacity. On the contrary, scientific thinking is the very archetype of a "whole person" activity, involving interactions among virtually all components of the mind. For this reason some have despaired of our ability to understand (in the sense of provide a warranted cognitive-scientific theory of) our own scientific abilities (Pinker 1997, Fodor 2000b, but see Carruthers, Stich, and Siegal 2002 for contrary views). Be that as it may, it is possible to identify, and perhaps understand, some of the components of scientific thinking. One is a capacity for creative thought, which has already been discussed. This is because scientists will frequently need to display creativity in thinking up hypotheses to explain their data, or in arriving at novel ways to test their theories.

Donald (2001) argues that our scientific capacities are themselves a cultural product. There is a great deal of truth in such a claim. Many of the elements of "scientific method" have emerged slowly over the last few centuries, and are now learned by children and young adults, giving rise to novel inferential abilities. And people growing up in a scientific culture will think and reason very differently from someone growing up as a hunter-gatherer, especially if they go on to become scientists themselves (Henrich, Heine, and Norenzayan 2010). There is thus a clear sense in which the contemporary human mind is, to a significant degree, constructed by culture, resulting in further cultural change and cultural products.

These claims comport nicely with an idea that is now widely accepted by those who work on the psychology of reasoning, namely that humans possess two different *types* of cognitive systems for thinking and reasoning (Evans and Over 1996, Sloman 1996, 2002, Stanovich 1999, Kahneman 2002; see also Carruthers 2009 for extended discussion). Most consider that what is generally now called "System 1" is really a collection of different systems that are fast and unconscious, operating in parallel with one another. The principles according to which these systems function are, to a significant extent, universal to humans, and they aren't easily altered (e.g., by verbal instruction). Moreover, the principles via which System 1 systems operate are, for the most part, heuristic in nature ("quick and dirty"), rather than deductively or inductively valid. It is also generally thought that most of the mechanisms constituting System 1 are evolutionarily ancient and shared with other species of animal.

System 2, on the other hand, is generally believed to be a single system that is slow, serial, and conscious. The principles according to which it operates are variable (both across cultures and between individuals within a culture), and can involve the application of valid norms of reasoning. These System 2 principles are malleable and can be influenced by verbal instruction, and they often involve normative beliefs (that is, beliefs about how one *should* reason). Moreover, System 2 is generally thought to be uniquely human. And it is plain that System 2, as instantiated in a trained scientist, will be very different indeed from the System 2 of a hunter-gatherer.

While it is no doubt true that much of our capacity for scientific thinking is socially learned, I believe that there is one key component (in addition to creativity) that long pre-dates the scientific era, and which is probably innate. This is our capacity for inference to the best explanation. Let me elaborate.

Most philosophers of science agree that scientists employ a set of tacit principles for choosing between competing theories—that is, for making an inference to the *best* explanation of the data to be explained. The most plausible way of picturing this, is that contained within the principles employed for *good* explanation are enough constraints to allow one to rank more than one explanation in terms of goodness. While no one any longer thinks that it is possible to codify these principles, it is generally agreed that the good-making features of a theory include such features as the following: *accuracy* (predicting all or most of the data to be explained, and explaining away the rest); *simplicity* (being expressible as economically as possible, and with the fewest commitments to distinct kinds of fact and process); *consistency* (internal to the theory); *coherence* (with surrounding beliefs and theories, meshing together with those surroundings, or at least being consistent with them); *fruitfulness* (making new predictions and suggesting new lines of enquiry); and *explanatory scope* (unifying together a diverse range of data).

Liebenberg (1990) makes a powerful case that at least some of the elements of scientific thinking (including inference to the best explanation) are present among hunter-gatherers, displayed most clearly in their tracking of prey when hunting. As he remarks, it is difficult for a city-dweller to appreciate the subtlety of the signs that can be seen and interpreted by an experienced tracker. Except in ideal conditions (e.g., firm sand or a thin layer of soft snow) a mere capacity to recognize and follow an animal's spoor will be by no means sufficient to find it. Rather, a tracker will need to draw inferences from the precise manner in which a pebble has been disturbed, say, or from the way that a blade of grass has been bent or broken; and in doing so he will have to utilize his knowledge of the anatomy, detailed behavior, and patterns of movement of a wide variety of animals. Moreover, in particularly difficult and stony conditions (or in order to save time during a pursuit) trackers will need to draw on their background knowledge of the circumstances, the geography of the area, and the normal behavior and likely needs of the animal in question to make educated guesses concerning its likely path of travel.

Most strikingly for our purposes, successful hunters will often need to develop speculative hypotheses concerning the likely causes of the few signs available to them, and concerning the likely future behavior of the animal; and these hypotheses are subjected to extensive debate and further empirical testing by the hunters concerned. When examined in detail these activities look a great deal like science, as Liebenberg (1990) demonstrates. First, there is the invention of one or more hypotheses (often requiring considerable imagination) concerning the unobserved (and now unobservable) causes of the observed signs, and the circumstances in which they may have been made. These hypotheses are then discussed and evaluated on the basis of their accuracy, coherence with background knowledge, simplicity, and explanatory and predictive power. One of them may emerge out of this debate as the most plausible, and this can then be acted upon by the hunters, who at the same time search for further signs that might confirm or count against it. In the course of a single hunt one can see the birth, development, and death of a number of different "research programs" in a manner that is at least partly reminiscent of theory-change in science (Lakatos 1970).

Given that they are universal among humans, it is hard to see how the principles of inference to the best explanation could be other than substantially innate (Carruthers 1992). For they are certainly not explicitly taught, at least in hunter-gatherer societies. While nascent trackers may acquire much of their background knowledge of animals and animal behavior by hearsay from adults and peers, very little overt teaching of tracking itself takes place. Rather, young boys will practice their observational and reasoning skills for themselves, first by following and interpreting the tracks of insects, lizards, small rodents, and birds around the vicinity of the campsite, and then in tracking and catching small animals for the pot (Liebenberg 1990). They will, it is true, have many opportunities to listen to accounts of hunts undertaken by the adult members of the group, since these are often reported in detail around the campfire. So there are, in principle, opportunities for learning by imitation. But in fact, without at least a reasonably secure grasp of the principles of inference to the best explanation, it is hard to see how such stories could even be so much as *understood*. Those principles are never explicitly articulated, yet they will be needed to make sense of the decisions reported in the stories; and any attempt to uncover them by inference would need to rely upon the very principles of abductive inference that are in question.

COOPERATION AND NORMS

Sterelny (2003) emphasizes the importance of cooperation among humans, both ancient and modern. This is a pervasive feature of all human cultures, and it has probably played a vital role throughout the course of human evolution. Early forms of it might have included banding together against predators to protect carcasses in the open savannah, sharing of meat, and various kinds of specialized labor and exchange. No doubt, also, successful cooperation played a vital role in agonistic conflicts between groups. What is distinctive of human cooperation isn't just its ubiquity, however. It is also the fact that it is regulated and enforced by systems of norms. Like the kinds of material culture that have formed the focus of most of our discussion up to now, distinct normative systems tend to distinguish different cultures from one another. They are also reliably transmitted between generations.

All human societies are pervaded by beliefs about what people may, may not, and must do (Brown 1991). Indeed, all human activities fall into one of these three categories—they are either permitted, forbidden, or required. And people in all cultures are apt to become angry or indignant if someone does something that is forbidden or fails to do something that is required. They are also apt to become angry when others in the group fail to be suitably disapproving of such breaches of normative rules, thereby engaging in a form of meta-punishment. Moreover, people everywhere experience guilt-like emotions if they themselves should happen to do something that is forbidden, or fail to do something that is required. Furthermore, the motivations involved are intrinsic ones (not merely grounded in fear of punishment or ostracization), since people will pay significant costs to punish others for breaching social norms, even when the punishers have nothing to gain—for example, because those punished are anonymous and won't be interacted with again (Fehr and Gachter 2002).

Reviewing much of the available anthropological and developmental literature, Sripada and Stich (2006) argue that humans possess a distinct multi-part normative reasoning and motivational faculty. One component of the system is concerned with the acquisition and storage of the norms that are current in the surrounding culture. This is by no means a trivial task. For even where explicit instruction is given—e.g., "You mustn't hit your little sister"—the subject generally has to figure out what the real rule is that lies in the background. Another component of the system activates the norms that are appropriate in a given context, and deduces what actions or inactions are necessary to remain in compliance. And then a further component is motivational, issuing in emotions like indignation and guilt. If Sripada and Stich are correct, then it appears that we need to add a further item to our catalogue of the pillars of cumulative culture.

How plausible is it that normative thinking and feeling might be explicable in terms of one or more of the other distinctively human systems distinguished so far? I take it to be obvious that neither language, nor creativity, nor skilled behavior, nor naïve physics, nor any combination thereof is sufficient to explain our normative natures. Tomasello et al. (2005b) claim, however, that both cooperation and the normative aspects of culture can be explained as emerging out of the initial motivation to share mental states, which they think lies at the bottom of our mindreading abilities. Even if we were to grant, though, that the motivational strand in shared intentionality would be sufficient to explain human cooperation (which is actually far from obvious, for the full extent of the latter), there aren't the materials, here, with which to explain normativity. It is one thing, for example, to want (intrinsically) to cooperate with someone, and quite another thing to think and (especially) feel that you *must* do so. And it would be left mysterious why failures to cooperate should result in *guilt* (as opposed to mere disappointment) in one's own case, let alone *indignation* in the case of another.

Just as one would predict if humans possessed some sort of innately channeled normative faculty, there is plenty of evidence that a capacity to reason about rules and obligations is an early emerging one, cross-culturally (Cummins 1996, Harris and Núñez 1996, Núñez and Harris 1998, Harris, Núñez, and Brett 2001). Three-year-old and 4-year-old children are highly reliable at identifying cases where someone has broken a rule, and they are also very good at distinguishing between intentional and accidental non-compliance (categorizing only the former as "naughty"). Moreover, they do this not only in connection with rules imposed by an authority (e.g., a parent or teacher), but also when reasoning about agreements negotiated among the children themselves. And as one might expect, deontic *concepts* are acquired even earlier still. Psycholinguistic research shows that children as young as 2 years of age can make appropriate use of modal terms like "must" and "have to" (Shatz and Wilcox 1991). This latter fact is especially impressive, since few philosophers think that normative concepts can be defined, either ostensively or in terms of others.

FURTHER ADAPTATIONS TO CULTURE

A number of the pillars of culture discussed above are, at the same time, adaptations to social environments in which culture is already important to fitness. Sophisticated forms of mindreading, for example, are surely an adaptation to increasingly complex social groups made possible by simpler varieties of intention-reading. Likewise, the normative faculty discussed earlier would be an adaptation to social groups in which both cooperation and punishment of defectors was becoming progressively more common. But then in addition, of course, as humans became an increasingly cultural species, much of what they needed to learn would have had to be learned from other people—whether by copying their behavior or by believing what others tell them. And this sets up a novel adaptive problem for learners: whom to learn *from*.

One strategy is to imitate the behavior and adopt the beliefs of the majority in your community. Mathematical modeling demonstrates that this is adaptive in a significant range of circumstances (Henrich and Boyd 1998). For individual learning is difficult, error prone, and costly; whereas if the community is a stable one, its beliefs and practices are likely to be adaptive on the whole. This leads Richerson and Boyd (2005) to the claim that there should be a species-unique motivational mechanism in humans that makes us *desire to conform*. Or rather, the mechanism will compute the most frequent variants of behavior and belief in one's environment, and deliver a desire *to behave/believe like that*. And indeed, there are a whole raft of experiments and data in social psychology that demonstrate people's desire to conform, and its powerful effects on behavior (Myers 1993).

Another strategy that one can adopt is to imitate the behavior and assume the beliefs of those who are most successful. Here, too, mathematical modeling shows that there are many circumstances in which the strategy can be adaptive (Boyd and Richerson 1985). And this prompts Henrich and Gil-White (2001) to argue that we have evolved a species-unique motivational mechanism that makes us want to resemble the prestigious. We attempt to get close to those who are prestigious, and we try to learn from them and to model our behavior on theirs. This gives rise to a social dynamic in which those of us who grant prestige to others allow them certain privileges, in return for which they allow us to get close enough to learn from them. And here, too, there is an experimental literature supporting the claim that we have a strong tendency to want to be similar to those who are prestigious (Rogers 1995, Henrich and Gil-White 2001).

In addition to the numerous pillars of culture already identified, therefore, we probably need to add a couple more. These are less fundamental than the others. Much accumulation of culture would surely still be possible without them. But they nevertheless have a significant impact on the ways that cultural practices change and get transmitted over time.

CONCLUSION

I have argued that authors such as Bickerton (1995) and Tomasello (1999) are mistaken in claiming that there is just a single major new adaptation underlying human cognitive uniqueness. Even confining our attention to the uniquely human capacity for cumulative culture (and ignoring the many other respects in which humans are distinctive) there are a significant number of evolutionarily novel cognitive systems underlying it. In fact, there are at least eight. (1) There is a mindreading system for figuring out and as-cribing mental states like belief. (2) There is a language acquisition device, focused on syntax in particular. (3) There are mechanisms that underlie the development of creative forms of thinking and behaving. (4) There are spe-cialized motor control systems that enable fine-grained motor control and support the acquisition of novel skills. (5) There is a naïve physics system that enables us to comprehend simple forces and physical structures. (6) There is a mechanism that enables people to make inferences to the best among two or more competing explanations of some phenomenon. (7) There is a multi-component system for normative learning, reasoning, and motivation. And (8) there are motivational systems that support targeted social learning of cultural practices and cultural information. We can con-clude, therefore, that the cognitive underpinnings of the distinctive human capacity for cumulative culture are multi-faceted, and by no means simple.

Acknowledgments

An early version of this chapter was delivered and discussed at the Evo-lution of Mind, Brain, and Culture workshop held at Penn Museum in Sep-tember 2007. I am grateful to all the participants—and especially to my commentators, Thierry Chaminade and Philip Chase—for their advice and feedback. I am also grateful to two anonymous reviewers for their com-ments and suggestions on an earlier draft, and to Gary Hatfield and Holly Pittman for their advice.

14

Human Culture Is More than Memes and Transmission

PHILIP G. CHASE

In recent years, a particular definition and model of "culture" has become dominant among psychologists, evolutionary biologists, philosophers, primatologists, and evolutionary anthropologists concerned with the evolution of the human mind and human behavior. The underlying concept in this model is the social transmission of information from one individual to another. While this has proven to be a very productive concept, it fails to account for much that is essential to the human way of life. It is my purpose in this chapter to provide an expanded model of culture that includes the process of social transmission but that also accounts for those phenomena that fall outside that process.

The definition of culture that currently prevails in evolutionary thought goes under several rubrics, including "dual inheritance" and "memetics." By whatever name, the model essentially defines culture in terms of group-characteristic social and behavioral variants (specific concepts, ideas, beliefs, values, symbols, technological know-how, songs, myths, and so on and so forth) that exist as information in the minds/brains of individuals, are invented or improved by individuals, and are transmitted by social learning from one individual or group (i.e., population of individuals) to another (Alvard 2003, Boesch and Tomasello 1998, Boyd and Richerson 1985, Cavalli-Sforza and Feldman 1981, Henrich and McElreath 2003, Laland and Hoppitt 2003, Whiten et al. 1999). With "dual inheritance," cultural traits can be inherited through social learning in addition to or instead of through genetic inheritance. Differences of opinion arise in characterizing the units that are socially transmitted. Some authors describe these units as discrete culture particles, called "memes," which are analogous to genes; these authors analyze cultural transmission in terms of genetic transmission (Dawkins 1976, Dennett 1996, Rose 1998). Others, however, don't see the necessity of treating cultural traits as discrete gene-like particles. Richerson and Boyd (2005) reject the meme-based view. They see culture as a population phenomenon that manifests itself in variants between groups; these variants include group-level attitudes such as altruistic moral codes (see also Boyd and Richerson 1985).

The core idea is that the presence of socially transmitted traditions which yield group-distinctive behaviors and attitudes is sufficient for the possession of culture. Accordingly, culture is a set of traditions that vary from one population to another independently of genes and that are transmitted by a system of social inheritance.

One of the most attractive features of this definition is that it permits a Darwinian analysis of culture, in the sense that stability or change in culture can be analyzed statistically in terms of differential transmission (i.e., natural selection) of memes or other cultural variants (Boyd and Richerson 1985, Campbell 1965, Henrich and McElreath 2003, Richerson and Boyd 2005). Culture change may also take place through a "ratchet effect" by which small improvements by successive individuals can accumulate (Tomasello, Kruger, and Ratner 1993). This effect, too, is mediated by individual improvements and their social transmission to other individuals.

However, this model cannot account for a set of phenomena that are of crucial importance to the human way of life. Underlying all such cultural phenomena are agreements or concurrences. These play a major role in governing or informing human behavior. They differ in fundamental ways from memes and individualistic cultural variants, they play either no role or only a very minor role in the lives of nonhuman primates, and they require psychological or mental traits that seem to be less developed in other species than in modern humans. It is my purpose here

1. to describe and analyze concurrences and to explain how they differ from common examples of cultural variants used in transmission models,

2. to create a preliminary synthetic model of culture by analyzing how cultural agreements or concurrences interact with transmission models, and

3. to discuss very briefly the fossil and archaeological evidence pertinent to the evolutionary origins of cultural concurrences.

Because concurrences and social transmission are intimately related, it may appear to some that my discussion is overly technical and of little importance. Nothing could be further from the truth. The ability and willingness to create and to abide by agreements is of major importance to the human way of life and makes possible levels of social organization and social coordination that are impossible for other species. Examples are almost endless, but include phenomena as disparate as language, the use of money, the planning of game drives, the institution of marriage, and the game of football. Any model of human culture that does not account for such phenomena is seriously incomplete.

OTHER DEFINITIONS OF CULTURE

Before proceeding to an analysis of concurrences, it may be worthwhile, as an aside, to point out that the social transmission model of culture is only one of many definitions that have been proposed over many decades of social and anthropological theorizing. In fact, the social transmission definition of culture seems to have been either ignored or rejected by the majority of cultural anthropologists. Recent surveys of anthropological theory either fail to mention it at all (Barnard 2003, Borofsky 1994, Erickson and Murphy 2001, Eriksen and Nielsen 2003, Kuper 1999, Layton 1997, Moore 1997) or dismiss it in a few sentences (Harris 1999). One chapter in an edited volume (McGee and Warms 1996) discussed related topics, but it was omitted completely from a recent critical review of the concept of culture within anthropology (Kuper 1999).

There are probably several reasons why the transmission model of culture has been so largely ignored within anthropology. I suspect, without being able to document it, that one of the most important reasons is that many anthropologists perceive it as arid, overly simplified, and incapable of describing the richness of what they observe in the field. It would be like trying to understand Shakespeare by doing a statistical analysis of his vocabulary.

Much of the richness missed by a transmission model involves agreements within a society: their creation, their effects, and their modification or maintenance. Geertz (1973:6–7), citing Ryle, describes the differences between an involuntary twitch of an eyelid, a wink, and a parody of a wink. The latter two are both created by and caught up in the "webs of significance" that society has created. Such significances are, at their core, social agreements about what the twitch of an eyelid means in contexts that differ in terms of yet other significances in the web of culture. As will be seen below, the bare transmission model cannot account for such phenomena.

Although anthropologists may generally ignore the social transmission model of culture, they are otherwise by no means agreed upon what culture is. In 1952, Kroeber and Kluckhohn surveyed the definitions of "culture" produced within anthropology to that date. They listed no fewer than 154. Just how disparate these definitions were can be illustrated by a few examples:

— "...that complex whole which includes knowledge, belief, art, law, morals, custom, and any other capabilities and habits acquired by man as a member of society..." (Tylor 1871)

— "...any given people's way of life, as distinct from the life-ways of other peoples..." (Kluckhohn and Leighton 1946)

— "...a system of interrelated and interdependent habit patterns of response..." (Willey 1929)

— "Culture is all behavior mediated by symbols." (Bain 1942)

— "Forms of habitual behavior common to a group, community, or society. It is made up of material and non-material traits." (Young 1934)

— "Culture consists in all transmitted social learning." (Kluckhohn 1942:2, as cited in Kroeber and Kluckhohn 1952:58) This is very similar to the transmission model of culture, although Kluckhohn did not analyze it in the same manner.

Nor did the proliferation of definitions end in 1952. New definitions and new analyses have been produced regularly since then (see Kuper 1999 for a recent overview).

— "A society's culture consists of whatever it is one has to know or believe in order to operate in a manner acceptable to its members, and to do so in any role that they accept for any one of themselves." (Goodenough 1964:36)

— "Believing, with Max Weber, that man is an animal suspended in webs of significance he himself has spun, I take culture to be those webs, and the analysis of it to be therefore not an experimental science in search of law but an interpretive one in search of meaning." (Geertz 1973:5)

In spite of the variability among these definitions, it is clear that two concepts underlying the social transmission model of culture have their roots in anthropological thought: the idea that cultures vary independently of genes and that culture in some way depends on social learning. (Hereafter I abbreviate "social transmission model" to "transmission model.")

TOWARD AN EXPANDED MODEL OF CULTURE

Although the transmission model misses some important parts of human social life, it has advantages that most anthropological definitions do not. First, unlike many anthropological definitions, the transmission model is neither an a priori definition based on pure logic nor a product of theory that is to be applied to data. Rather, it arises from observation. (I claim the same advantage for my own model of cultural concurrences.) There can be no doubt that such social transmission exists and that it plays a major role in the human way of life. Second, it is a clearer and more coherent definition of culture than most, and as such it provides a basis for rigorous analysis that many anthropological definitions do not.

The problem with the transmission model of culture is not that it is incorrect or that it is not useful, but that it is incomplete. It does not constitute a complete model of culture, but it must be included as an integral part of any such model. (I say this now in spite of the fact that in Chase 2006 I excluded social transmission from my definition of culture.)

To this end, I will first make a very brief analysis of social transmission from a slightly new perspective. The purpose of this is not to resolve debates about social transmission or to give a complete overview of the model, but merely to look at it in a way that will facilitate the synthesis of transmission with cultural concurrences.

More on Social Transmission

I will start with the assertion that culture resides in the mind, that it does not include behavior. (I will have more to say about this below.) This means that what is transmitted from one individual to another is something in the mind. In my 2006 publication, I called these phenomena "codes" because they code for behavior in a manner analogous to how genes code for phenotypic traits. In other words, what is transmitted is some state of mind that produces behavior.

It seems to me that most—probably all—the codes involved in cultural transmission fall into the category of intentions in the philosophical sense. Intentions are mental states that are about something else (Brentano 1874/1995). I may have a concept of what a dog is, I may know that dogs bite, I may believe that dogs are dangerous, I may fear dogs, etc. This concept, knowledge, belief, and fear are all mental states about dogs, and are therefore intentions in the philosophical sense. (Note that this definition has nothing to do with the common, everyday definition of intention.) Intentions thus include a myriad of kinds of mental states, including beliefs, values, desires, definitions, attitudes, and emotional states such as fear, regret, or pride.

For example, a chimpanzee may have a concept of a termite, a belief that termites are edible, a desire for the taste of a termite, a hope that she will soon be eating termites, and an idea of how to use a stick to get termites out of their mounds. If the chimpanzee's daughter learns from her how to fish for termites, she must create a set of intentions in her own mind that are similar enough to her mother's so that the daughter's behavior, too, will be successful.

(The reason I confine culture to mental, not behavioral, phenomena is as follows: it would be possible to argue that the behavior rather than the intentions has been transmitted, but this would not negate the fact that the individual doing the learning must create a set of intentions. Including both behavior and mental phenomena within culture would make it a hybrid concept that would probably hinder rather than facilitate analysis.)

From this perspective, the evolution of culture in a transmission model may take place in either of, or more likely in both of, two ways. First, some intentions will be transmitted more frequently than others, with the result that the "intention pool" of a population may change. Second, at any step of the way, an individual may alter or improve an intention or set of intentions on his or her own, and then transmit these altered intentions to others. Thus our chimpanzee may learn from watching her mother how to fish for termites, may find a better way of stripping leaves from a twig so that it can fit into a termite hole, and then transmit this altered knowledge to her own daughter—and even back to her mother.

Intentions, which reside in the minds of individuals, can be transmitted from one individual to another. Genes are transmitted by the physical transfer of DNA. Because mental states cannot be transferred physically, they must be transferred by being re-created in the mind of the receiving individual. But the notion of transmission is still valid.

In order to understand how cultural concurrences differ from the transmission of intentions, we must distinguish between intentions and intentional objects. Every intention has an object (or objects)—that which the intention is about. The chimpanzees' intentions are about termites: how they taste, how they behave, etc.

From this perspective, two more facts about cultural transmission should be noted. First, unlike an intention, an intentional object does not reside in the mind of an individual and cannot be transmitted from one mind to another. The behavior of termites is not a property of any individual chimpanzee, and cannot be transferred from one individual to another. Only knowledge of their behavior can be transferred.

Second, the intentional objects discussed so far are things that exist independently of the intentions, regardless of whether the individual has any mental phenomena relating to them. Termites exist whether or not chimpanzees ever think about them, and their behavior exists independently of the intentions of chimpanzees. Even intentions about phenomena in the social world reside at the level of the individual (that is, they belong to individuals) and may therefore be transmitted from one individual to another. If a child learns that adult A is more generous than adult B, or that the best way to get adult C's cooperation is through flattery, these intentions are about characteristics of A, B, and C. Those characteristics do not depend on the child's intentions, and they cannot be transmitted from one child to another—but knowledge of them can be transmitted.

The Nature of Cultural Agreements or Concurrences

Consider something that occurs very frequently among humans. Two people agree to meet at a certain place at a certain time. There are four things to note about this agreement.

1. An anthropologist observing the meeting could not fully account for their behavior without knowing of the agreement.

2. The agreement is the object of identical or very similar intentions in the minds of the two parties to the agreement. Unlike the intentional objects discussed above, it does not exist independently of those intentions; it

is, rather, created by them.

3. The agreement is not a property of either individual. In this it resembles a chemical bond between two atoms. It transcends the individual and belongs to a different, social level of organization.

4. The agreement cannot be changed by differential transmission from one individual to another. It can only be changed by "negotiating" a new agreement, where both parties, through social interaction, create new intentions that redefine the agreement.

The postulated agreement to meet at a given time and place has all these characteristics.

First, an anthropologist or other observer could not accurately account for the behavior of these two individuals without understanding the agreement. This may not be obvious in the case of a simple meeting between two people, but consider that in arranging their meeting, they probably make use of a very important convention: that the day is divided into 24 hours of 60 minutes each. This convention they undoubtedly learned as children from their parents or other adults. In this sense, *knowledge* of the convention was a set of intentions transmitted socially. But the convention itself is of a very different nature. It, too, is an agreement that shares the four characteristics just listed. Understanding the behaviors of people whose actions are governed or coordinated by the 24-hour convention is impossible without knowledge of that set of conventions. When a room full of school children simultaneously jump up from their seats and rush to the door, it is not because of any observable natural cause, but because the clock shows that the school day has ended. (Even if they respond to a bell, the ringing of the bell can only be accounted for if the anthropologist knows about the convention.)

Second, the agreement comes into existence when both parties, through social interaction, create identical (or at least very similar) intentions about it—a belief that an agreement exists, that the agreement is about a meeting, that it will take place at a certain time or place. The agreement is the common intentional object of the individuals' intentions. *It exists only because of those intentions.* In this it differs fundamentally from intentional objects such as the behavior of termites.

Third, the agreement is a social, not an individual phenomenon. It *is* possible to imagine an intentional object that exists only because of the intentions that define it, but that is not social in nature. I might, for example, devise a color coding system for my files that I would use without ever communicating it to anyone else. This system would exist only because I had certain ideas about the relationship between folder color and folder content. However, it would not be an agreement and would not be a cultural phenomenon.

By contrast, an agreement is by its very nature a social phenomenon that exists only because more than one individual believes that it does. As such, it cannot be a property of an individual. It must, rather, be the property of a group consisting of at least two people. It is a social creation, created through social interaction and dependent for its existence on the fact that *more than one* person has intentions that define it. As such, it transcends the individual in the same way that a chemical bond transcends each atom involved.

Fourth, the agreement that a day consists of 24 hours cannot be changed by differential transmission. Both as an intentional object and as a property of a group rather than of an individual, it cannot be transferred from one individual to another. As a creation of social interaction, it can only be modified by social interaction.

If an individual finds a variation on a meme, he or she is free to use it. For example, if I discover the sheet bend, a variation on the square knot, I may or may not decide to use it, but that decision is mine. The knot will work for me regardless of whether others use it. Others who learn about this new knot are likewise free to use it or not, and the knot may become more or less popular. Thus, as regards knots, culture may change by differential transmission.

But imagine a man who decides that dividing the day into 10 hours of 100 minutes each is more logical than dividing it into 24 60-minute hours. If he attempts to use this new system in his dealings with others, nothing but confusion will ensue. The division of the day is a convention, an agreement that coordinates people's actions. He is not therefore free to adopt or reject a new "meme." His clock will not work to coordinate his schedule with others if they do not make use of it. His only recourse is to convince others to accept his new system. Then, when they all, together, accept it *as a new convention or agreement,* it can serve to coordinate their actions. However, this would be a social act of agreement, not an individual act of adoption or non-adoption. The decision to accept or reject such an agreement must be a social decision, because the convention is by its very nature social, not individual.

Another example is the international air traffic control system. This is, in effect, a large and complex set of agreements that coordinate the behaviors of pilots and air traffic controllers in a way intended to avoid collisions and other accidents. As such, it is not an individual but a social phenomenon. The flight and taxiing patterns of aircraft cannot be accounted for without reference to this system of agreements.

Nor can changes in the system be accounted for in terms of differential transmission of observed behaviors that are imitated or not. Even if a pilot is convinced that a different approach to a given runway is better than that agreed upon, acting upon that conviction as an individual would be fatal. The only way to have this change adopted is for the authorities responsible to agree to the change, and for them to mandate it as the new basis for pilot behavior.

Transmission of intentions can account for the spread of the pilot's new idea to others, including those responsible for policy. Transmission is also how pilots and air traffic controllers would learn of an official change of policy. But the change in the agreement itself cannot be accounted for in terms of transmission. This is analogous to one chemical bond being replaced by another. Since neither agreements nor bonds belong to individual humans or atoms, they cannot be transmitted from one individual to another. Knowledge of agreements can and will be transmitted in this way, as will opinions about them. But, as dictated by the very notion of an agreement, the agreements themselves cannot be transmitted from one individual to another, and cannot, therefore, be changed by differential transmission.

To avoid misunderstanding, I should emphasize that only those intentions that *define* an agreement need match for an agreement to exist. The two parties may have very different emotions, attitudes, etc., regarding that agreement. One party to a rendezvous may be looking forward to it, the other may dread it. One may believe that it will serve a highly moral purpose, the other may fear that it constitutes a religious violation. Nevertheless, as long as both understand that there is an agreement to meet at a given time and place, the agreement exists.

I have used the word "agreement," but this word is perhaps a bit misleading, in that it implies that the agreement is (1) negotiated among all the parties, and (2) voluntary on everyone's part. This is not true of all, perhaps even most, cultural agreements. A large number of very important agreements (such as the meanings of words in a language) are inherited by the parties to the agreement (more about this below). Native speakers of English, for example, do not renegotiate the language when they reach the age of two, but rather they learn and accept pre-existing agreements. Moreover, agreements can be imposed. If a supervisor orders his or her subordinates to meet at quitting time, everyone may agree in the sense that they all understand that they are to meet at five o'clock, but they may not have given their willing consent.

What counts, however, is that everyone has the same concept of the meaning of a word, or the same concept of when and where a meeting is to take place. For this reason, from now on I will try to use the word "concurrence" instead of "agreement." The word may be a bit more stilted, but it has fewer misleading overtones.

Of course, there is little or nothing that is new in my concept of concurrence. Searle, for example, wrote that "This book is about a problem that has puzzled me for a long time: there are portions of the real world, objective facts in the world that are only facts by human agreement" (Searle 1995:1); and: "If everybody always thinks that this sort of thing is money, and they use it as money and treat it as money, then it is money. If nobody ever thinks this sort of thing is money, then it is not money. And what goes for money goes for elections, private property, wars, voting, promises, marriages, buying and selling, political offices, and so on" (Searle 1995:32). What Searle calls "institutional facts" are instances of what I call cultural concurrences.

Gilbert analyses one instance of a concurrence, the concept of "taking a walk together" (a notion taken up by Warneken in this volume):

> ...each person expresses a special form of *conditional commitment* such that (as is understood) only when *everyone* has done similarly is *anyone* committed. Thus all the wills are bound simultaneously and interdependently. The character of each one's commitment is then as follows: no one can release himself from the commitment; each is obligated to all the others for performance; each is (thus) entitled to performance from the rest. (1990:7–8, emphasis in the original)

Tomasello et al. (2005b) and Gärdenfors (this volume) describe "joint intentions," where all individuals involved not only have intentions that mesh to accomplish a common goal, but have second order intentions, that is, each intends that the other intends: "...each participant cognitively represent[s] both roles of the collaboration in a single representational format—holistically, from a 'bird's-eye view,' as it were—thus enabling role reversal and mutual helping" (Tomasello et al. 2005:681).

In saying, as I did above, that some human behavior cannot be accounted for without recourse to cultural concurrences, I am saying no more than Gärdenfors said when he wrote that it is necessary to take a "social stance" by ascribing "social intentions":

> The main reason why conventions and other social intentions must be viewed from the social stance is that they are necessary for causal explanations. It is, for example, the existence of certain conventions which I recognize as social intentions that explain why I speak English and drive on the left hand side of the road while I am in Australia. These aspects of my behavior are not explained by the intentions of any individual Australians. (Gärdenfors 1994:91–92)

Thus, there is nothing new to the idea that there are phenomena that exist at the social rather than at the individual level, and that these consist of some kind of meetings of individual minds. Rather, what I wish to emphasize here is that neither the origins of such phenomena nor changes in such phenomena can be accounted for in terms of individual invention (or modification) and subsequent social transmission.

SOCIAL TRANSMISSION AND CONCURRENCES

Nevertheless, transmission of intentions does play a role in human culture, and the two phenomena, social transmission and cultural concurrences, are closely intertwined in the human way of life.

First, as we have seen, knowledge and/or definitions of concurrences may be transmitted from one individual to another.

Second, concurrences themselves may be transmitted, although this transmission must be from one group of people to another group of people, not from one individual to another.

Third, the motivation to enter into concurrences may be transmitted from one individual to another, with implications for the relative frequencies of different concurrences.

Fourth, social transmission and differential selection may in fact cause evolution of a concurrence that permits a degree of latitude with regard to individual concepts of the concurrence.

Group to Group Transmission of Concurrences

Concurrences cannot be transmitted from one individual to another because they are not properties of individuals. However, being properties of groups of individuals they can be transmitted from one group to another. In this sense, they can perhaps be considered as a sort of "social meme" or a "social cultural variant," analogous to other memes but existing at a higher social level of organization. (Richerson and Boyd 2005, despite their emphasis on social imitation between individuals, allow for such social cultural variants, such as group-beneficial sets of attitudes and codes of conduct.)

Until 1967, everyone in Sweden drove on the left side of the road. This was due to a legally binding convention. Other countries (e.g., the United Kingdom and Australia) shared this convention, while in still other countries (e.g., France and Canada), a different convention mandated that drivers stayed to the right. In 1967, Sweden adopted the latter convention. The Swedish government decreed that, as of a given date, everyone would instead drive on the right. This convention was adopted not by the individual choices of those drivers who wished to do so. Rather, it was adopted as a concurrence on the part of Swedish society—through the interactions of Swedish administrative, political, and legal institutions and Swedish drivers. It worked because, and only because, it was accepted—simultaneously—by all Swedish drivers.

This change could not, therefore, be explained by differential transmission of right- versus left-hand driving preferences from one driver to another. Both the old and new conventions were just that—concurrences. The one prevailed over the other not by natural selection but by a change in the concurrence. Prior to this change, the opinion that the convention should be altered was undoubtedly transmitted from one individual to another until it became prevalent, at least among those whose opinion counted in the matter (i.e., those who had the power to impose a new concurrence). After the decision to make the change, *knowledge* of the new convention was transmitted, as a meme, among individuals. But the actual change had to be made at a social level, by concurrence, by the entire body of Swedish drivers.

Nevertheless, the world-wide "concurrence pool" of conventions regarding driving changed on that day in 1967. The drive-on-the-right convention had been adopted in one more country at the expense of the drive-on-the-left convention. One convention became more numerous at the expense of another, by being adopted in place of the other. However, the adoption was made by a social unit (the government and drivers of Sweden) rather than by individuals. Groups may be characterized by properties that exist at the group level, which cannot therefore be transmitted from individual to individual but which *can* be transmitted from group to group (in this case, from other nations to Sweden).

This example allows us to compare my notion of concurrences established at a group level with the ideas of Richerson and Boyd (2005), who are leading proponents of culture as social transmission by imitation. In their scheme, a change of the kind envisioned, when resulting from decision-making, is an instance of "guided variation" (2005:69). They acknowledge that guided variation has no good analogue in genetic evolution (2005:116). As they see it, a change such as occurred in Sweden does not arise through the selective culling of cultural variants (by social-level natural selection), but through psychological processes of decision-making. However, they contend that variations that arise through decision-making are then propagated through imitation (2005:116), and in this way their discussion does not incorporate the notion of a socially instituted concurrence such as I have described. (Swedish drivers did not wake up one day to drive on the right because they were imitating decision-makers or other individual drivers.) The point is that groups may be characterized by properties that exist at the group level, which therefore cannot be transmitted from individual to individual but which *can* be transmitted from group to group.

Selection of Concurrences through Individual Choices

When individuals are free to enter into or to opt out of concurrences, then differential transmission rates that encourage the former will play a role in the survival or popularity of a concurrence. Many cultural concurrences disappear for lack of interest, and may be replaced by other concurrences. This does not change their fundamental nature as concurrences, nor does it change the fact that the concurrences themselves cannot be changed by differential transmission. Only their relative popularity can be changed in this way.

The game of chess consists of a set of conventions—definitions of pieces, of checkmate, etc., and rules for the movement and capture of pieces. These conventions are cultural concurrences with all the characteristics discussed above. First, they are meaningless from the perspective of an individual, since a game requires two players. It is only in the context of the interactions of two players that the conventions have any meaning. Second, it would be impossible, in practical terms, for an anthropologist to explain or account for the behaviors of two chess players without reference to the definitions and rules of the game. Third, both players must have the same conventions in mind if the game is to work. An individual player cannot change the rules without obtaining the concurrence of the other player, or the game simply will not work. Finally, the game of chess is a social creation that exists only to coordinate the behaviors of two players. All this means that the game of chess is a typical cultural concurrence.

However, the chess champion Bobby Fischer created a somewhat different convention that now goes by the name of "Fischer random chess" or "chess960" (Böhm and Jongkind 2004:60; Pritchard 2000:18–20). Bored by the fact that, for expert players, traditional chess relies too much on sheer memory, particularly during the first part of a game, he suggested a new game, in which the pawns would remain in their normal positions, but the rest of the pieces would be arranged randomly behind them (with some limitations).

There are now two variants of chess that can compete for players. (In actuality, many varieties have been proposed; Pritchard 2000.) Each constitutes a cultural concurrence, but they are in competition. If knowledge of random chess is transmitted to enough people, and if enough of them find it preferable to traditional chess, then random chess will eventually supplant the traditional version. In effect, differential transmission of the two versions of chess will affect which one predominates and even which one survives.

However, even if these two sets of conventions seem to be transmitted like memes, this does not change the fact that they *are* conventions and therefore agreements. Before each game, both players must agree on which version they are playing. Still, if a player can find no one to play his or her preferred version of chess, then that version of chess will disappear. Individual decisions to opt into or out of a particular kind of concurrence can thus bring about changes in what concurrences constitute a culture, even if the concurrences themselves cannot be changed, internally, by differential transmission.

Modification of Concurrences through Differential Transmission

There is one kind of cultural concurrence that can be changed by differential transmission. In some cases, the private concepts or definitions of a concurrence are free to differ from one individual to another, within limits, without affecting the functioning of that concurrence.

A good example is language. There are differences in pronunciation among individual speakers of the same language, especially among speakers of different but mutually comprehensible dialects of the same language. These differences, however, do not impede understanding. In effect, each speaker has one concept of how he or she should pronounce a word and a different, broader concept of how others may pronounce the word. The first concept is free to change within the limits of the latter concept, since such variation will not affect mutual comprehension. It is possible, then, that these concepts will be differentially transmitted, and that patterns of actual pronunciation will change through time. It may be that concepts of how others will or should pronounce words respond to the actual patterns of pronunciation, in which case these, too, may change through time in response to differential transmission. Recent studies (Blevins 2004, E. Lieberman et al. 2007) have suggested that at least some phonological and syntactic changes in languages over time take place in just such a way.

WHY IT MATTERS

Cultural concurrences are a major part of the human way of life. One of the most important human adaptations is language, which consists of a complex set of related semantic and syntactic conventions. As Nowak, Komarova, and Niyogi (2002:616) put it, "From a biological perspective, language is not the property of an individual, but the extended phenotype of a population."

But the importance of concurrences does not end with language. For example, the institution of marriage differs from copulation and mating (if by mating we mean some kind of further mutual interaction and cooperation between male and female, such as is typically found in birds). Marriage may involve copulation and mating, but it is actually a cultural institution. It consists of concurrences—definitions, norms, expectations, etc.—that vary from one culture and one society to another. Human societies are invariably organized by means of cultural concurrences, by institutions such as matrilineal clans, patrilineal moieties, or townships with culturally defined residency rules and government offices. Human economic activity is structured by planning for cooperative game drives, by norms for sharing food, by legal conventions, by huge organizations (such as an aircraft manufacturing corporation) that function only by means of culturally defined roles and procedures. In many societies, economic life is also structured by the culturally defined device of money. The human way of life as we know it, be it that of hunter-gatherers or that of urban dwellers, is permeated and shaped by cultural concurrences.

THE ORIGINS AND EXPANSION OF CULTURAL CONCURRENCES

The social creation of concurrences is related to genetic evolution to the extent that certain neural structures are necessary prerequisites—the neural capacity must be present, at least in rudimentary form, before the behavior is possible. It does not necessarily follow that the further development of the phenomenon of concurrences did not take place independently of genetic evolution. Agriculture, for example, was a practice that transformed the adaptive strategies of human populations but that did not arise from genetic evolutionary changes in the human brain (although it did, by changing adaptive pressures, cause subsequent evolutionary changes in physiology).

In previous works (Chase 1999, 2001, 2006), I have pointed out that there are two stages in the development of cultural concurrences that need not have happened simultaneously. First, at some point in primate evolution, the creation of concurrences became part of adaptation, when cultural concurrences guided the behaviors of individuals in particular circumstances. Second, concurrences expanded into ubiquitous webs of symbolic meaning that today permeate the mental and social environments of all human lives, and that not only guide but motivate human behavior.

Humans experience motivational states such as hunger and thirst that are shared with many other animals. These are not cultural in nature. However, cultural concurrences may be used as a tool for satisfying them (as in a cooperative game drive). Human language is a system of concurrences that enhance communication, and enhanced communication makes cooperative activities more effective.

However, among living humans, systems of cultural concurrences, in the form of religious beliefs, codes of conduct, etc., themselves *create* motivations. Symbolic systems have expanded into ubiquitous and all-pervasive webs that affect almost everything we perceive, think, or do and that provide a cultural-symbolic environment in which we live our lives. Perfectly edible food may be seen as inedible because of socially defined food taboos linked to a myriad of interconnected symbolic ideas about society and nature. The cooperative or altruistic behavior usually reserved for kin may be extended to others, even to complete strangers, because of their membership in social groups or alliances created only by social consensus.

I shall review, briefly, the evidence for the origins of each of these phenomena in turn. It should be noted that the evidence is constantly changing as new archaeological sites are excavated and new fossils are found, or as new primatological, genetic, or paleontological studies are carried out.

EVIDENCE FOR THE ORIGINS OF CONCURRENCES

It cannot be assumed that the creation of concurrences is a human rather than a primate (or even mammalian) trait. To determine if this is the case, it is necessary to see if we share this behavior, or the capacity for this behavior, with other primate species. If these species either do not exhibit this trait, or if it is present in only rudimentary form, then we must look to the fossil and archaeological evidence for the evolution of our species for evidence that will help us understand its origins and development.

Evidence of Concurrences among Nonhuman Primates

The evidence for the creation of concurrences among nonhuman primates is scarce and inconclusive. This is somewhat surprising, since at least with regard to linguistic symbols, they seem to be able to enter into concurrences created by humans. In this regard, their capacity seems to outstrip their actual behavior in the wild.

As I have said above, linguistic conventions, including symbolic semantic links between a sign and its reference, are examples *par excellence* of cultural concurrences. Experimental investigation has shown that apes, in a laboratory setting, are able to learn such conventions (e.g., Gardner and Gardner 1978, Greenfield and Savage-Rumbaugh 1991, Ristau and Robbins 1982, Savage-Rumbaugh, Shanker, and Taylor 1998). Initially, skeptics suggested that in these experiments apes did not learn a convention or a symbolic relationship between sign and referent but rather a stimulus and response pairing (Seidenberg and Petitto 1987, Terrace, Petitto, and Bever 1979, Wallman 1992). However, these suggestions stimulated more rigorous experimentation, so that even some skeptics have been satisfied (Snowdon 1990, Tomasello and Call 1997).

Some chimpanzees have been reported to create combinations of symbols to designate things for which their human trainers had provided no signs. For example, after tasting and spitting out a radish, the chimpanzee Lucy signed *cry hurt food*. She also signed *candy drink* or *drink fruit* for watermelon (her vocabulary did not include the symbols *water* and *melon*) (Fouts and Budd 1979:386–87). Miles (1990:535) reported that a language-trained orangutan invented signs for, among other things, contact lenses and for indicating that he would not use his teeth during play. Patterson (1978:191) reported that a gorilla created signs for *bite, stethoscope, tickle,* and *darn.*

Taken at face value, this would imply that chimpanzees are able both to understand the concept of symbolic convention and to create new symbols. Primatologists and psychologists are better qualified than I am to evaluate whether the observations reported do in fact demonstrate this. However, it should be noted that these examples all involve interactions between apes and humans, rather than among apes. A few reports have been made of chimpanzees attempting to teach (human-created) signs to others. For example, Fouts (1987:67) reports that Washoe tried to mold her adopted infants' hands into the sign for food.

These data suggest that at least some apes seem to have the cognitive abilities needed to create or at least to enter into cultural concurrences. However, it should be noted that all of these examples come from captive animals in a laboratory setting. In the wild, nonhuman primates make no use of symbolic language.

There are many examples from wild primates of culture in the memetic sense (Kawamura 1959, Kawai 1965, Nishida 1986, Whiten et al. 1999, Hohman and Fruth 2003, Van Schaik et al. 2003, Nishida, Miktani, and Watts 2004, Lycett, Collard, and McGrew 2007; see Laland and Hoppitt 2003 for a more skeptical view). These do not involve the kind of mutual agreement that concerns us here.

In my opinion, there is no clear evidence for concurrences among nonhuman primates, but there are a few behaviors that are intriguing in this respect.

Take the example of "leaf clip," a behavior whereby chimpanzees bite a leaf into pieces to produce a ripping sound without eating any of the leaf... All males in the Taï forest regularly leaf-clip before drumming. Among Bossou chimpanzees, leaf clip is performed in the context of playing, as a means to enlist a playmate, while Mahale chimpanzees leaf clip as a way to court estrous females. Taï chimpanzees have never been observed to leaf-clip in the context of playing nor in courtship. Similarly, Mahale chimpanzees have never been seen to leaf-clip in the context of playing nor when drumming... Nothing in the form of the behavior or in the noise produced by the leaf clipping indicates that it could mean play rather than courtship. The meaning is adopted collectively and rests on an arbitrary convention shared by group members. Thus, shared meaning and symbolism go together at this level of cultural complexity observed in chimpanzees. (Boesch 2003:86)

As Vishnyatsky (2006) has pointed out, this might be an example of a concurrence among chimpanzees. It is not easy to determine whether leaf-clipping behavior really involves shared meaning or symbolism. Certainly the behavior is intriguing, but it is hard to know exactly what is going on in the minds of these chimpanzees. If leaf-clipping has a shared meaning, what is that meaning? If it is symbolic, in other words, if it is a sign pointing by convention to some referent, then what is the referent? It is difficult, on the basis of this description, either to dismiss or to accept this behavior as definitive evidence of shared meaning in the sense of an agreed-upon convention.

Other behaviors that appear to be cultural (in the sense that they vary from group to group independently of genetics or of environmental determinism) and that involve social interaction are also intriguing in this respect. These include games that are found in some groups but not others, and practices such as mutual hand-sniffing among capuchin monkeys (Perry et al. 2003).

Chimpanzees do hunt "cooperatively" (Goodall 1986:286; Watts and Mitani 2002:13). It might be more accurate, however, to say that they hunt in a coordinated manner. They surround their victim, cutting off possible escape routes. It is not clear that they are doing anything more than observing the behaviors of other chimpanzees, anticipating the possible behavior of the prey, and responding as individuals. Similar behavior has been observed in other species such as lions and wolves (Schaller 1972:249; Kelsall 1968:252; Mech 1970:230). Species other than humans and apes seem to be unaware that other individuals are intentional beings, in the sense that their behavior is governed by mental states (Cheney and Seyfarth 1990, Tomasello and Call 1997). Clearly, one prerequisite for cultural agreements is the recognition that other individuals have minds. This would imply that simple coordinated hunting such as that observed among chimpanzees, lions, and wolves is possible without such concurrences (Chase 2006, Tomasello et al. 2005b pace Boesch 2005; Schuster 2005).

In this volume, Warneken presents experimental evidence that, although chimpanzees may engage in coordinated behavior with others, they apparently do not "view their own and their partner's actions as integral parts of a collaborative activity with a joint goal that they try to reinstate when necessary" (this volume). Tomasello and his colleagues (Tomasello et al. 2005b) have argued that while apes understand others as being intentional agents with mental states that govern their behavior, only our species has the "motivation to share emotions, experience, and activities with other persons," which prevents apes from entering into collaborative activities.

Judging by the comments on Tomasello et al. (2005b), it will be some time before there is a consensus as to whether nonhuman primates are capable of, or even if they engage in, rudimentary forms of cultural concurrence. It may be that there is more continuity between humans and our nearest relatives than Tomasello et al. allow for. However, one thing is clear. Cultural concurrences play at best a minor role in the lives of nonhuman primates; their role in the human way of life is of major importance.

Fossil and Archaeological Evidence for the Origins of Cultural Concurrences

Three lines of evidence all indicate that cultural agreements had come to play an important role in the lives of our ancestors before the end of the Middle Pleistocene, about 127,000 years ago: endocasts of fossil crania, fossil evidence for the evolution of the vocal tract, and archaeological evidence for game drives. There are real problems with all of them, but taken together they are the best evidence we have. (See Chase 2006 for a more complete discussion and evaluation of the evidence.) I will argue below that archaeological data from the Upper Pleistocene (from about 127,000 to 10,000 years ago) probably relates to something other than the origins of cultural concurrences per se.

Endocranial Evidence

When fossil crania are complete enough, it is possible to measure the size of the brain. The interior morphology of the braincase also reflects the external morphology of the brain, allowing for the presence of intervening layers of tissue and fluid. Four lines of evidence may be relevant to the evolution of language, which, of course, consists of cultural conventions: the overall size of the brain, its "reorganization" (i.e., changes in the relative sizes of different parts of the cerebral cortex), the appearance of "language" areas such as Broca's area, and asymmetries of the brain.

The use of brain size as an indicator of language is problematic. Brain size is largely dependent on the size of the body, so that encephalization is usually measured after adjustment for body size (Falk 1980, Jerison 1982, Rightmire 2004). However, body size is often very difficult to estimate for fossil hominins. In addition, there is a great deal of natural variation in the brain sizes of humans living today, variation uncorrelated with linguistic ability. For this reason, the use of brain size alone as an indicator of linguistic ability in fossil hominins has fallen out of favor since Keith's (1948) estimate of the minimum brain size required for language (Falk 1980, Holloway 1966, 1979, Schepartz 1993; cf. Jerison 1976). Deacon (1992, 1997) has argued that encephalization in hominins was achieved by differential growth of different parts of the brain, so that brain size may be taken as an indicator of brain reorganization.

Holloway has argued that brain reorganization toward the modern human state occurs even before the appearance of the genus *Homo.* His reading of the location of the lunate sulcus indicates to him that relative sizes of the parietal association cortex and the primary visual cortex had begun to change between the primitive hominid pattern in *Australopithecus* and early *Homo* (Holloway 1975, 1983, Holloway, Broadfield, and Yuan 2004; but cf. Falk 1980, 1986). Holloway (1975, Holloway et al. 2004) also found differences, relative to apes, in the morphology of both the temporal lobes and the anterior frontal lobes of *Australopithecus* and early *Homo,* while Falk (1983) argued that there were differences between one *Australopithecus* and one *Homo* specimen from Koobi Fora, Kenya, in the form of the frontal lobe. Falk et al. (2000) found gracile *Australopithecus* more similar to *Homo* than to robust *Australopithecus* (= *Paranthropus*) on a number of traits, including the forms of the frontal and temporal lobes. Investigators have also found some evidence of an enlarged Broca's area in *H. habilis* and

H. erectus, and perhaps even in *Australopithecus,* although again there are disagreements about the latter (Holloway 1975, 1983, Holloway, Broadfield, and Yuan 2004, Falk 1983, Tobias 1987).

Further, although the brains of nonhuman primates, particularly those of the great apes, may display asymmetries (LeMay 1976, 1985, Semendeferi 2001), human brains are characterized by both functional and anatomic asymmetries linked to handedness and language. One such asymmetry exhibits a comparative enlargement of the anterior pole of the brain on the right side and of the posterior (occipital) pole on the left. While sometimes observed in other species, the repeated pattern of both asymmetries is distinctively human. Skeletal evidence for this asymmetry has been reported for Neandertals, *H. erectus* and *H. ergaster* (LeMay 1976, Holloway, Broadfield, and Yuan 2004), early *Homo,* and even *Australopithecus* and *Paranthropus* (Holloway et al. 2004).

All of these data indicate that brain reorganization, like encephalization, was underway long before the Middle Pleistocene (more than 780,000 years ago). The problem, however, is linking reorganization to language (and through language to cultural concordances). Neither the causes nor the functional effects of differential growth of different parts of the cortex are clear. Lateralization is associated with both types of handedness (which are probably linked more to toolmaking and tool use than to language), and it is not entirely clear that language areas such as Broca's area originally served their present functions—especially since an area equivalent to Broca's area has been found in nonhuman primates (Deacon 1997:342; Gibson 1996:409). Nevertheless, the data are suggestive. By the end of the Middle Pleistocene, brain endocasts do look quite modern.

Evidence of Fossil Vocal Tracts

Humans today have a rather striking adaptation for speech (Lieberman 1984). Vowels that are acoustically the same are perceived by the brain as being different, depending on the size of the vocal tract that produces them. For example, the "o" in the word "on," when spoken by an adult male, and the "aw" in the word "awl," spoken by an adolescent, are essentially the same. There is also a remarkable adaptation involving stops (consonants such as p, k, or t, where the stream of air from the mouth is momentarily completely blocked). Although each stop is made in the same way the sounds that make up the stop will be acoustically different depending on the vowels that precede or follow it. Yet our brains interpret the different sounds of each stop as being the same. Thus, all the acoustically different forms of p are perceived as being the same sound, because they are made by stopping the air by closing both lips together.

Both these phenomena depend on a vocal tract where the larynx is low, so that the portion below the oral cavity is approximately as long as the oral cavity itself, and is angled sharply below it. This is the case in human adults, but in young children and in other mammals (including adult apes), the larynx is high, and the lower portion of the vocal tract is short and lies at an obtuse angle from the oral cavity.

Although these observations have generally gone unchallenged by human paleontologists, their application to the fossil record has been extremely controversial. Lieberman and his colleagues (Lieberman and Crelin 1971, Lieberman, Klatt, and Wilson 1969, Lieberman, Crelin, and Klatt 1972) attempted to reconstruct the location of the larynx on a Neandertal specimen from La Chapelle-aux-Saints, France, using the angle of the stylohyoid ligaments as indicated by the styloid processes on the base of the cranium. Their reconstruction set off a very heated debate regarding that specimen (Burr 1976, Carlisle and Siegel 1974, Du Brul 1976, Falk 1975, Houghton 1993, LeMay 1975, Morris 1974, Lieberman 1973, 1976, 1991, 2001, Lieberman and Crelin 1974) and their method was not applied to other skulls. A more indirect method has for some reason been less controversial. Laitman and colleagues (Laitman, Heimbuch, and Crelin 1978) measured the "flexion" of the base of the cranium as an indicator of the descent of the larynx. These two phenomena are temporally correlated in the ontogeny of human children (Crelin 1987), but applying this measure to the evolution of speech depends on the assumption that they were correlated in evolution as well. It also assumes that the descent of the larynx was an adaptation for efficient speech, rather than an exaptation or preadaptation. (See Chase 2006 for a much more detailed summary and discussion of this entire topic.) Interestingly enough, while the data on basicranial flexion are rather ambiguous with regard to Neandertals, two skulls, presumed to be of Middle Pleistocene age (from Kabwe, Zambia, and Steinheim, Germany) are modern in this regard (Laitman, Heimbuch, and Crelin 1979).

Like the endocranial evidence, the data regarding fossil vocal tracts depends for its interpretation on a number of assumptions. It, too, points to an adaptation for speech by the end of the Middle Pleistocene. Such an adaptation almost certainly postdates not only the origins of language but the time when language came to play an important role in hominin adaptations. Thus both lines of evidence, while by no means rock solid, point to the conclusion that language, and therefore cultural concurrences, evolved well before the end of the Middle Pleistocene.

Archaeological Evidence

The best archaeological evidence for the origins of cultural concurrences may come from the site of La Cotte de Saint Brelade, Jersey, from the Middle Pleistocene. Here two separate levels contain evidence that mammoths were driven over the edge of a plateau overlooking what was then the coastal plain and into a narrow gap in the face of a cliff. There is little chance that these animals either fell naturally or were killed by carnivores. Their ages are consistent with the driving of an entire mammoth group. Most telling, different kinds of bones were apparently stacked separately, indicating that the mammoths were butchered.

Driving a herd of mammoths is very different from what chimpanzees do, surrounding individual prey animals. Mammoths were large, fast, and intelligent, and driving a herd would require agreeing ahead of time where the herd would be driven, how this would be done, and what each person's role would be. It is very difficult to imagine how this could have been accomplished without (1) agreeing on a plan beforehand, and (2) using language to do so. As Gärdenfors (this volume) puts it,

> For many forms of cooperation among animals, it seems that representations are not needed. If the common goal is *present* in the actual environment, for example food to be eaten or an enemy to be fought, the collaborators need not focus on a *joint* representation of it before acting. If, on the other hand, the goal is detached, that is, distant in time or space, then a joint representation of it must be produced before cooperative action can be taken.

Such a joint representation, of course, is a form of cultural concurrence.

There are a number of other sites from the early Upper Pleistocene where the age profiles of the animals killed may indicate similar drives: eland (*Taurotragus oryx*) at the Klasies River Mouth and Die Kelders Cave 1 sites in South Africa (Klein 1979, 1987, Klein and Cruz-Uribe 1996), aurochs or wild cattle (*Bos primigenius*) at La Borde, France (Jaubert et al. 1990), horses (*Equus*) from beds 14, 22, and 23 of Combe Grenal, France (Levine 1983), and bison (*Bison*) at Il'skaya in the northern Caucasus (Hoffecker, Baryshnikov, and Potapova 1991).

Two hominin crania, from Bodo and Herto in Ethiopia, both dating to the Middle Pleistocene, bear traces of stone tool marks that indicate defleshing (Clark et al. 2003b, White 1986, White et al. 2003). White argues that these traces are not likely to indicate nutrition-oriented cannibalism. If he is right, then these two specimens provide evidence of ritual and, almost certainly, of cultural concurrence in the Middle Pleistocene.

ARCHAEOLOGICAL EVIDENCE FOR THE EXPANSION AND ELABORATION OF SYMBOLIC CULTURE

In its beginning stages, the phenomenon of cultural concurrence was perhaps a simple and probably a practical matter. The organization of a game drive is an excellent example. An agreement that different members of a band of hunter-gatherers would follow different routes in their day's foraging, meeting at a pre-arranged location to exchange food and information would be another example. So too would using language to teach one's offspring how to accomplish practical tasks.

Today, among all living peoples, among all peoples known historically, and among Holocene peoples (those in the last 10,000 years) known only through archaeology, culture has become a very different phenomenon. Almost everything we perceive, think, or do is caught up in a web of symbolic cultural meanings. The moon is no longer simply the moon, but a poetic and often religious symbol and its phases have become the basis of calendrical systems. How we put food in our mouths is dictated not only by functionality but by cultural conventions. Kinship is determined not only by procreation but by legal and social conventions, so that kinship systems and kin-oriented behaviors differ widely from one culture to another. Because of cultural conventions, the cut of one's clothing sends all sorts of social signals to others. I refer to this expansion of symbolic cultural concurrences into overarching, all-encompassing webs as "cultural elaboration."

Once the sphere of symbolic, cultural concurrences has been expanded into ubiquitous webs of meaning, these webs are reflected in people's material culture (i.e., in their artifacts, sensu lato). When an artifact need only fulfill its practical function, its morphology will be determined and limited only by practical considerations. When the way an artifact is made is determined by symbolic cultural norms and carries symbolic cultural meaning, then that fact is likely to be reflected in its appearance. In addition, it is more or less inevitable that artifacts will be made that fulfill *only* symbolic cultural functions—artifacts such as scepters, wedding regalia, or altars.

We have overwhelming evidence for cultural elaboration by 40,000 years ago, in the form of abundant art and highly stylized and decorated artifacts, particularly in Europe. Our task is to assess the evidence for cultural elaboration prior to that time.

As a methodological precept, I have argued that artifacts with a symbolic function will be rare in the absence of cultural elaboration (Chase 1999, 2001, 2006). In the absence of cultural elaborations, the use of symbols would largely be confined to language, and language would be largely confined to practical purposes. In the absence of writing systems, which originate long after the Pleistocene (Nissen et al. 1993), language leaves no direct trace in the archaeological record. However, when the forms of artifacts come to have cultural meanings beyond their practical functions, symbolism may be apparent in the archaeological record. Moreover, in an elaborated symbolic culture, many artifacts will have no function other than the symbolic—as markers of culturally defined status, as ritual objects, etc. Hence, if we find clear evidence of symbolic function in artifacts, especially if these are not unique objects and if more than one artifact type appears to have had a symbolic function, we then have good evidence for cultural elaboration.

In my opinion, most of the archaeological data that have been cited for the origins of symbolism do not reflect the origins of symbolism and cultural concurrences, which probably arose much earlier, in the Middle Pleistocene (with the origin of language and the socially created coding that allowed game drives). Instead, these data provide potential evidence for the elaboration of culture into an all-pervasive web of meaning. In an elaborated culture, the forms of artifacts are constrained not only by their practical functions but by their symbolic functions in a web of cultural meanings, norms, and standards that vary geographically from group to group and that vary over time. The archaeological record reflects this in two ways: through stylistic variation in artifacts that have practical functions and through the presence of artifacts that appear to have a symbolic rather than practical function.

Intergroup differences in cultural and symbolic conventions governing the making of artifacts and in the socially assigned meanings of artifact form should produce a particular patterning of artifacts. Internally, within a social group sharing in the same concurrences, artifacts will be similar. Externally, between social groups, and temporally, as cultures change, there will be marked differences in the appearances of artifacts, differences that cannot be attributed to differences in practical function, to the raw material available to the makers of the artifacts, etc. This is exactly the kind of patterning that archaeologists refer to as style or stylistic variation. It should, then, serve as a marker, not for the origins of symbolism and of cultural concurrences, but for cultural elaboration.

However, there is a problem with the use of style as a way of identifying the origins of cultural elaboration. The only artifacts where style might be recognized before about 40,000 years ago are stone tools and a very few bone tools (Yellen et al. 1995, d'Errico and Henshilwood 2007). Unfortunately, during this period it is virtually impossible, given the nature of the artifacts, to distinguish between style produced by symbolic cultural differences and style produced by memetic differences in technology, that is, by tool-production techniques that are differentially transmitted through imitation and that have nothing to do with cultural concurrences. Further, the persistence of a tool-form over long periods of time, as occurred with the shape of Acheulean handaxes, may represent a technological limitation on the production of the form rather than providing evidence of a rule-bound "style." (See Chase 2006 for a fuller discussion.) This means, in my opinion, that one of the potentially most fruitful lines of evidence is more or less unusable.

The existence of artifacts whose functions are, at least in part, symbolic is a much better marker of cultural elaboration. The problem here lies instead with the criteria for recognizing the symbolic nature of such artifacts. The question has been, to put it mildly, controversial (e.g., Mellars 1973, Chase and Dibble 1987, Bar-Yosef 1988, Belfer-Cohen 1989, Lindly and Clark 1990, Marshack 1990, Duff, Clark, and Chadderdon 1992, Bednarik 1992, Hayden 1993, Knight, Studdert-Kennedy, and Hurford 1995, Mellars 1996, Noble and Davidson 1996, Facchini 1998, Klein 2000a, McBrearty and Brooks 2000, Kaufman 2002, Watts 2002, d'Errico et al. 2003a, Chase 2006, Nowell, this volume). To an unfortunate extent, interpreting an artifact as symbolic or not remains a rather subjective judgment. It is impossible in the space available to provide an adequate survey of the evidence. More-over, new evidence of symbolic artifacts (and of new artifacts for which less than solid claims of symbolic nature are made) are published with remark-able frequency, so that any overview is almost certainly out of date by the time it is published. What follows is an extremely brief and context-oriented summary that hits only a few highlights. (See Nowell, this volume, for ad-ditional information.)

Much of the debate concerns alternative explanations for possibly sym-bolic artifacts. There are, for example, numerous pieces of bone from many sites that bear visually striking patterns of cut marks on their surfaces. How-ever, there are so many bones with so many cut marks in the Paleolithic record, that such patterns are bound to occur occasionally by chance alone. There are also artifacts that have been deliberately perforated or grooved. These have often been interpreted as beads or pendants, but there is no lack of purely practical reasons for grooving or perforating an object (for use as toggles, handles, buttons, etc.).

There are a scattering of early objects whose symbolic nature is prob-ably best considered enigmatic or inconclusive. A piece of metamorphosed quartzite, entirely natural in origin, was recovered from a road cut near Tan-Tan, Morocco, along with Acheulean bifaces (Bednarik 2003, Kucken-burg 2001). It bears a striking resemblance to a human figure, and may or may not have been collected by hominins, who, if they did collect it, may or may not have assigned it some symbolic meaning. The material is tenta-tively dated to 300,000 to 500,000 years ago.

A lapilli tuff pebble was recovered from the Acheulean site of Berekhat Ram in the Golan Heights (d'Errico and Nowell 2000, Feraud et al. 1983, Goren-Inbar 1986, Goren-Inbar and Peltz 1995, Pelcin 1994). It has natu-rally occurring grooves, along with others that were deliberately cut. These grooves give it an appearance that to some resembles a human figure (al-though to my mind its resemblance is not to a human figure per se but to European figurines some 200,000 years younger than Berekhat Ram). It underlay a geological level dated to 233,000 ± 3,000 years ago.

The site of Tata in Hungary produced a plate of mammoth tooth that according to Marshack had been shaped into a rough oval, as well as a fossil nummulite with a crack across its diameter and a scratch running across it at right angles to the crack (Vértes 1959, Vértes 1964, Marshack 1976, 1990, Schwarcz and Skoflek 1982). The site is about 100,000 years old.

After 100,000 years ago, the evidence for an elaboration of culture becomes more conclusive and consistent. Levels in the site of Skhul in Israel dated between 43,000 and 134,000 years (but likely from the earlier part of this range) produced, in addition to hominin fossils, two perforated marine tick (*Nassarius gibbosulus*) shells (Vanhaeren et al. 2006). The perforations may have been either natural or intentional, but the shells were clearly brought to the site by people (they occur naturally between 3 and 20 km from the site) and probably served as beads.

At the site of Grotte des Pigeons, Morocco, 14 marine tick (*N. gibbosulus*) shells were recovered from beds dating to about 82,000 years ago (Bouzoug-gar et al. 2007). (Four of these were from animal burrows that "intersected" one of the beds.) All but two of the beads were perforated, either naturally or by humans. All were clearly brought into the cave by humans, presumably from the coast, which at that time was 40 km away. Wear on the edges of the perforations was consistent with their use as beads. Ten had traces of pigment on them, in locations that the authors interpreted as the result of rubbing against pigment-covered materials such as hide or string.

At Blombos Cave in South Africa, 41 perforated tick (*N. kraussianus*) shells were recovered, two of them from a level dated to 78,000 years, the rest to a layer dated to 75,000 years (Henshilwood et al. 2002:1279; Henshilwood et al. 2004). Also found in the younger level were a fragment of ochre with a pattern of marks whose decorative if not symbolic nature would be difficult to deny, and a piece of bone with similar markings.

Six gastropod (*Littorina*) shells, three of them perforated, were found in the Howiesons Poort and Still Bay levels of Sibudu Cave in South Africa (d'Errico et al. 2008). These layers date to older than 60,000 years and 70,000 years respectively.

Fragments of ostrich eggshell containers bearing geometric engravings have been reported from the Howiesons Poort levels of Diepkloof Rockshelter in South Africa, dating to about 60,000 years ago (Texier et al. 2010).

Going back more than a quarter of a million years, there is evidence for the use of minerals that could have served as pigments. Fragmentary ochre was found in the Karpathian Formation at Baringo, Kenya, with dates going back as far as 284,000 ± 12,000 years (McBrearty and Brooks 2000:528; Tallon 1978:372; Deino and McBrearty 2002), along with hematite-stained grindstones. Hematite and abraded hematite were recovered from levels of Twin Rivers, Zambia, predating 230,000 +35,000/-28,000 years ago (Barham and

Smart 1996). From then on, minerals that could have been used as pigments are reported with increasing frequency in Africa. Some of these show evidence of having been abraded or rubbed, and grindstones with traces of the minerals have also been found. Such data are regularly and not illogically interpreted as evidence that people were decorating either their bodies, their clothes, or their artifacts. However, decorated objects have not been found.

There are other, purely practical uses of materials such as ochre (hematite) that are known either experimentally or ethnographically. These include preserving hides (either by inhibiting the action of collagenase or by drying), protecting the hair or skin from vermin and mosquitoes, protecting the skin from the sun and wind or cold, applying to wounds, neutralizing bad odors, and waterproofing and protecting wood (Mandl 1961, Keeley 1980, Audouin and Plisson 1982, Velo 1986). Ochre was used as a binder in the mastics used to haft stone tools in the Paleolithic of both Africa and Europe (Allain 1979, Allain et al. 1985, Wadley, Williamson, and Lombard 2004). It is thus difficult to know, for any given place or time, the extent to which such minerals were used as pigments rather than for other purely practical purposes. Nonetheless, because it is itself engraved, the ochre from Blombos Cave provides a strong instance of decorative and perhaps symbolic marking.

Implications

In all, the evidence for the elaboration of culture appears to me to point to a gradual development, probably proceeding by fits and starts. The appearance of such evidence in Australia (Brumm and Moore 2005) seems to bear this out. Elaboration here seems to have been unrelated to what happened in Africa and Europe: the archaeological record left by modern humans (*Homo sapiens*) as they spread across southern Asia toward Australia more than 45,000 years ago (the time range for this movement is disputed) does not include symbolic artifacts or evidence of elaborated culture (Petraglia 2007). The kinds of artifacts that elsewhere have been claimed to be symbolic in nature have not, at least to date, been recovered here. (There are two "engravings" of doubtful symbolic intent in India, but these date to before the migration of *Homo sapiens;* Bednarik 2001, 2002; but see Chase 2006:144–45.)

What this seems to imply is that the elaboration of culture was unrelated to either the evolution of the genetically evolved capacity for or the regular use of cultural concurrences, including language. Instead, the elaboration of culture, like the origin of agriculture, appears to have been something that happened at different times and in different places in response to local conditions.

Based on the (admittedly imperfect) data available at present, it would appear that human culture as it is today evolved in three stages. The memetic or bare differential transmission component of culture is ancient. We share it with nonhuman primates and other mammals. Cultural concurrences may have existed in rudimentary form before the hominin lineage split off from the lineages of the apes, but this component of culture became a major part of adaptation only among the hominins, probably only within the genus *Homo*. This seems to have happened before the end of the Middle Pleistocene. The elaboration of cultural concurrences into omnipresent, overarching, all-encompassing systems of symbolic meanings seems to have arisen, independently of genetic changes, during the Upper Pleistocene.

References Cited

Abi-Rached, L., M.J. Jobin, S. Kulkarni, et al. 2011. The Shaping of Modern Human Immune Systems by Multiregional Admixture with Archaic Humans. *Science* 334(6052): 89–94.

Abugov, R. 1982. Species Diversity and Phasing of Disturbance. *Ecology* 63(2): 289–93.

Adachi, I., and K. Fujita. 2007. Cross-modal Representation of Human Caretakers in Squirrel Monkeys. *Behavioural Processes* 74:27–32.

Adachi, I., H. Kuwahata, and K. Fujita. 2007. Dogs Recall Their Owner's Face upon Hearing the Owner's Voice. *Animal Cognition* 10:17–21.

Adams, M.D., S.E. Celniker, R.A. Holt et al. 2000. The Genome Sequence of *Drosophila melanogaster*. *Science* 287(5461): 2185–95.

Adolphs, R. 2002. Neural Systems for Recognizing Emotion. *Current Opinion in Neurobiology* 12(2): 169–77.

Aiello, L.C., and R.I.M. Dunbar. 1993. Neocortex Size, Group Size, and the Evolution of Language. *Current Anthropology* 34:184–93.

Aiello, L.C., and J.C.K. Wells. 2002. Energetics and the Evolution of the Genus *Homo*. *Annual Review of Anthropology* 31:323–38.

Aiello, L.C., and P. Wheeler. 1995. The Expensive-Tissue Hypothesis: The Brain and the Digestive System in Human and Primate Evolution. *Current Anthropology* 36(2): 199–221.

Alexander, R.M. 1992. Human Locomotion. In *The Cambridge Encyclopedia of Human Evolution*, ed. S. Jones, R. Martin, and D. Pilbeam, pp. 80–85. Cambridge: Cambridge University Press.

Allain, J. 1979. L'industrie lithique et osseuse de Lascaux. In *Lascaux Inconnu*, ed. A. Leroi-Gourhan and J. Allain, pp. 87–102. Paris: C.N.R.S.

Allain, J., R. Desbrosse, J. Kozlowski, A. Rigaud, M. Jeannet, and A. Leroi-Gourhan. 1985. Le Magdalénien à navettes. *Gallia Préhistoire* 28(1): 37–124.

Allen, J.R.M., and B. Huntley. 2000. Weichselian Palynological Records from Southern Europe: Correlation and Chronology. *Quaternary International* 73/74:111–25.

Allen, J.R., W.A. Watts, and B. Huntley. 2000. Weichselian Palynostratigraphy, Paleovegetation, and Paleoenvironment: The Record from Lago Monticchio, Southern Italy. *Quaternary International* 73/74:91–110.

Alley, R.B. 2000. *The Two-Mile Time Machine: Ice Cores, Abrupt Climate Change, and Our Future.* Princeton: Princeton University Press.

Allman, J., A. Hakeem, and K. Watson. 2002. Two Phylogenetic Specializations in the Human Brain. *Neuroscientist* 8:335–46.

Alvard, M.S. 2003. The Adaptive Nature of Culture. *Evolutionary Anthropology* 12(3): 136–49.

Alvard, M.S., and D.A. Nolin. 2002. Rousseau's Whale Hunt? Coordination among Big Game Hunters. *Current Anthropology* 43(4): 533–59.

Alvarez Retuerto, A.I., R.M. Cantor, J.G. Gleeson et al. 2008. Association of Common Variants in the Joubert Syndrome Gene (AHI1) with Autism. *Human Molecular Genetics* 17(24): 3887–96.

Ambrose, S. 2001. Paleolithic Technology and Human Evolution. *Science* 291: 1748–53.

Ambrose, S. 1998. Late Pleistocene Human Population Bottlenecks, Volcanic Winter, and Differentiation of Modern Humans. *Journal of Human Evolution* 34:623–51.

Ameloot-van der Heijden, N. 1993. L'industrie laminaire du niveau CA du gisement Paléolithique moyen de Riencourt-les-Baupaume (Pas de Calais). *Bulletin de la Société Préhistoire Française* 90:324–27.

Anderson, M. 2008. Massive Redeployment, Exaptation, and the Functional Integration of Cognitive Operations. *Synthese* 97:329–45.

Andrefsky, W. 2009. Analysis of Stone Tool Procurement, Production, and Maintenance. *Journal of Archaeological Research* 17:65–103.

Anisfeld, M. 1996. Only Tongue Protrusion Modeling Is Matched by Neonates. *Developmental Review* 16:149–61.

Antón, S.C. 2003. Natural History of *Homo erectus. Yearbook of Physical Anthropology* 46:126–70.

Antón, S.C., and C.C. Swisher, III. 2004. Early Dispersals of *Homo* from Africa. *Annual Review of Anthropology* 33:271–96.

Anzai, T., T. Shiina, N. Kimura, et al. 2003. Comparative Sequencing of Human and Chimpanzee MHC Class I Regions Unveils Insertions/Deletions as the Major Path of Genomic Divergence. *Proceedings of the National Academy of Sciences* 100:7708–13.

Arbib, M.A. 2003. The Evolving Mirror System: A Neural Basis for Language Readiness. In *Language Evolution*, ed. M.H. Christiansen and S. Kirby, pp. 182–200.

Oxford: Oxford University Press.

Arnason, U., A. Gullberg, A.S. Burguete, and A. Janke. 2000. Molecular Estimates of Primate Divergences and New Hypotheses for Primate Dispersal and the Origin of Modern Humans. *Hereditas* 133(3): 217–28.

Arnold, K., and K. Zuberbuhler. 2006. Language Evolution: Compositional Semantics in Primate Calls. *Nature* 441:303.

Arp, R. 2006. The Environment of Our Hominin Ancestors: Tool-usage, and Scenario Visualization. *Biology and Philosophy* 21:95–117.

Asfaw, B., T.D. White, O. Lovejoy, et al. 1999. *Australopithecus garhi:* A New Species of Early Hominid from Ethiopia. *Science* 284:629–35.

Ash, J., and G. Gallup. 2007. Paleoclimatic Variation and Brain Expansion during Human Evolution. *Human Nature* 18:109–24.

Atkinson, Q.D., R.D. Gray, and A.J. Drummond. 2008. mtDNA Variation Predicts Population Size in Humans and Reveals a Major Southern Asian Chapter in Human Prehistory. *Molecular Biology and Evolution* 25(2): 468–74.

Audouin, F., and H. Plisson. 1982. Les ocres et leur témoins au paléolithique en France: Enquête et expériences sur leur validité archéologique. *Cahiers du Centre de Recherches Préhistoriques de l'Université de Paris* 8:33–80.

Avital, E., and E. Jablonka. 2000. *Animal Traditions: Behavioural Inheritance in Evolution.* Cambridge: Cambridge University Press.

Backwell, L., F. d'Errico, and L. Wadley. 2008. Middle Stone Age Bone Tools from the Howiesons Poort Layers, Sibudu Cave, South Africa. *Journal of Archaeological Science* 35(6): 1566–80.

Badcock, C. 2000. *Evolutionary Psychology: A Critical Introduction.* Cambridge: Polity Press.

Bahn, P.G., and J. Vertut. 1997. *Journey Through the Ice Age.* Berkeley: University of California Press.

Bailey, J.A., and E.E. Eichler. 2006. Primate Segmental Duplications: Crucibles of Evolution, Diversity and Disease. *Nature Reviews Genetics* 7:552–64.

Bailey, J.A., Z. Gu, R.A. Clark, et al. 2002. Recent Segmental Duplications in the Human Genome. *Science* 297:1003–7.

Bailey, S., and J.-J. Hublin. 2006. Dental Remains from the Grotte du Renne at Arcy-sur-Cure (Yonne). *Journal of Human Evolution* 50:485–508.

Baillargeon, R., L. Kotovsky, and A. Needham. 1995. The Acquisition of Physical Knowledge in Infancy. In *Causal Cognition,* ed. D. Sperber, D. Premack, and A. Premack, pp. 79–116. New York: Oxford University Press.

Bain, R. 1942. A Definition of Culture. *Sociology and Social Research* 27:87–94.

Bakewell, M.A., P. Shi, and J. Zhang. 2007. More Genes Underwent Positive Selection in Chimpanzee Evolution than in Human Evolution. *Proceedings of the National Academy of Sciences USA* 104:7489–94.

Balaban, E. 1988. Bird Song Syntax: Learned Intraspecific Variation Is Meaningful. *Proceedings of the National Academy of Science* 85:3657–60.

Balter, M. 2005. Evolution: Are Human Brains Still Evolving? Brain Genes Show Signs of Selection. *Science* 309:1662–63.

Balter, V., and L. Simon. 2006. Diet and Behavior of the Saint-Césaire Neanderthal Inferred from Biogeochemical Data Inversion. *Journal of Human Evolution* 51:329–38.

Barbas, H., and N. Rempel-Clower. 1997. Cortical Structure Predicts the Pattern of Corticocortical Connections. *Cerebral Cortex* 7(7): 635–46.

Barclay, P. 2005. Reputational Benefits for Altruistic Punishment. *Evolution and Human Behaviour* 27:325–44.

Barham, L.S. 2007. Modern Is as Modern Does? Technological Trends and Thresholds in the South-Central African Record. In *Rethinking the Human Revolution: New Behavioural and Biological Perspectives on the Origin and Dispersal of Modern Humans*, ed. P. Mellars, K. Boyle, O. Bar-Yosef, and C. Stringer, pp. 165–76. Cambridge: McDonald Institute for Archaeological Research.

Barham, L.S., and P. Mitchell. 2008. *The First Africans: African Archaeology from the Earliest Tool-Makers to Most Recent Foragers.* Cambridge: Cambridge University Press.

Barham, L.S., and P. Smart. 1996. An Early Date for the Middle Stone Age of Central Zambia. *Journal of Human Evolution* 30(3): 287–90.

Barkow, J.H., L. Cosmides, and J. Tooby, eds. 1992. *The Adapted Mind: Evolutionary Psychology and the Generation of Culture.* Oxford: Oxford University Press.

Barnard, A. 2003. *History and Theory in Anthropology.* Cambridge: Cambridge University Press.

Baron-Cohen, S. 1995. *Mindblindness.* Cambridge: MIT Press.

Barrett, H.C., L. Cosmides, and J. Tooby. 2007. The Hominid Entry into the Cognitive Niche. In *The Evolution of Mind*, ed. S.W. Gangstead and J.A. Simpson, pp. 241–48. New York: The Guilford Press.

Barrett, L., R. Dunbar, and J. Lycett. 2002. *Human Evolutionary Psychology.* Princeton: Princeton University Press.

Barrett, L., P. Henzi, and D. Rendall. 2007. Social Brains, Simple Minds: Does Social Complexity Really Require Cognitive Complexity? *Philosophical Transactions of the Royal Society B* 362:561–75.

Barsalou, L. 2005. Continuity of the Conceptual System across Species. *Trends in Cog-*

nitive Sciences 9:309–11.

Barton, C.M., G.A. Clark, and A.E. Cohen. 1994. Art as Information: Explaining Upper Paleolithic Art in Western Europe. *World Archaeology* 26(2): 185–207.

Barton, R.N.E. 2000. Mousterian Hearths and Shellfish: Late Neanderthal Activities in Gibraltar. In *Neanderthals on the Edge: 150th Anniversary Conference of the Forbes' Quarry Discovery, Gibraltar,* ed. C.B. Stringer, R.N.E. Barton, and J.C. Finlayson, pp. 211–20. Oxford: Oxbow Books.

Bar-Yosef, O. 1988. Evidence for Middle Palaeolithic Symbolic Behaviour: A Cautionary Note. In *L'Homme de Néandertal.* Vol. 5, *La Pensée,* ed. O. Bar-Yosef, pp. 11–16. Études et Recherches Archéologiques de l'Université de Liège 32.

—— 2002. The Upper Paleolithic Revolution. *Annual Review of Anthropology* 31:395–417.

—— 2004. Eat What Is There: Hunting and Gathering in the World of Neandertals and Their Neighbours. *International Journal of Osteoarchaeology* 14:333–42.

Bar-Yosef, O., and S.L. Kuhn. 1999. The Big Deal about Blades: Laminar Technologies and Human Evolution. *American Anthropologist* 101(2): 322–38.

Bar-Yosef Mayer, D., B. Vandermeersch, and O. Bar-Yosef. 2009. Shells and Ochre in Middle Paleolithic Qafzeh Cave, Israel: Indications for Modern Behavior. *Journal of Human Evolution* 56(3): 307–14.

Bednarik, R.G. 1992. Palaeoart and Archaeological Myths. *Cambridge Archaeological Journal* 2(1): 27–57.

—— 2001. The Oldest Known Rock Art in the World. *Anthropologie (Brno)* 39(2-3): 89–97.

—— 2002. The Oldest Surviving Rock Art: A Taphonomic Review. *Origini* 24:335–49.

—— 2003. A Figurine from the African Acheulian. *Current Anthropology* 44(3): 405–12.

Beehner, J.C., T.J. Bergman, D.L. Cheney, et al. 2005. The Effect of New Alpha Males on Female Stress in Free-Ranging Baboons. *Animal Behaviour* 69:1211–21.

Beerling, D.J. 1999. New Estimates of Carbon Transfer to Terrestrial Ecosystems between the Last Glacial Maximum and the Holocene. *Terra Nova* 11:162–67.

Begun, D.R. 2004. The Earliest Hominins: Is Less More? *Science* 303:1478–80.

Behar, D.M., R.Villems, H. Soodyall, et al. 2008. The Dawn of Matrilineal Diversity. *American Journal of Human Genetics* 82:1130–40.

Belfer-Cohen, A. 1988. The Appearance of Symbolic Expression in the Upper Pleistocene of the Levant as Compared to Western Europe. In *L'Homme de Néandertal.* Vol. 5, *La Pensée,* ed. O. Bar-Yosef, pp. 25–30. Études et Recherches Archéologiques de l'Université de Liège 32.

Belfer-Cohen, A., and E. Hovers. 1992. In the Eye of the Beholder: Mousterian and

Natufian Burials in the Levant. *Current Anthropology* 33:463–67.

Ben-Arie, N., D. Lancet, C. Taylor, et al. 1994. Olfactory Receptor Gene Cluster on Human Chromosome 17: Possible Duplication of an Ancestral Receptor Repertoire. *Human Molecular Genetics* 3:229–35.

Bentley, R.A. 2007. Fashion versus Reason—Then and Now. *Antiquity* 81:1071–73.

Bergman, C.A., and C. Stringer. 1989. Fifty Years Later: Egbert, an Early Upper Paleolithic Juvenile from Ksar Akil, Lebanon. *Paléorient* 15:99–111.

Bergman, T.J., J.C. Beehner, D.L. Cheney, and R.M. Seyfarth. 2003. Hierarchical Classification by Rank and Kinship in Baboons. *Science* 302:1234–36.

Bering, J. 2004. A Critical Review of the "Enculturation Hypothesis": The Effects of Human Rearing on Great Ape Social Cognition. *Animal Cognition* 7(4): 201–12.

Bermúdez de Castro, J.M., M. Martinón-Torres, E. Carbonell, et al. 2004. The Atapuerca Sites and Their Contribution to the Knowledge of Human Evolution in Europe. *Evolutionary Anthropology* 13:25–41.

Bettinger, R.L. 2001. Holocene Hunter-Gatherers. In *Archaeology at the Millennium,* ed. G.M. Feinman and T.D. Price, pp. 137–88. New York: Plenum.

—— 2009. Macroevolutionary Theory and Archaeology: Is There a Big Picture? In *Macroevolution in Human Prehistory,* ed. A. Prentiss, I. Kuijt, J.C. Chatters, and R.L. Bettinger, pp. 275–95. New York: Springer.

Bickerton, D. 1981. *Roots of Language.* Ann Arbor, MI: Karoma.

—— 1990. *Language and Species.* Chicago: University of Chicago Press.

—— 1995. *Language and Human Behaviour.* Seattle, WA: University of Washington Press.

—— 2000. How Protolanguage Became Language. In *The Evolutionary Emergence of Language: Social Function and the Origins of Linguistic Form,* ed. C. Knight, M. Studdert-Kennedy, and J. Hurford, pp. 264–84. Cambridge: Cambridge University Press.

—— 2002. Foraging versus Social Intelligence in the Evolution of Protolanguage. In *The Transition to Language,* ed. A. Wray, pp. 207–25. Oxford: Oxford University Press.

—— 2005. Language First, Then Shared Intentionality, Then a Beneficent Spiral. *Behavioral and Brain Sciences* 28:691–92.

—— 2007. Did Syntax Trigger the Human Revolution? In *Rethinking the Human Revolution: New Behavioural and Biological Perspectives on the Origin and Dispersal of Modern Humans,* ed. P. Mellars, K. Boyle, O. Bar-Yosef, and C. Stringer, pp. 99–105. Cambridge: McDonald Institute for Archaeological Research.

Billard, A., Y. Epars, S. Calinon, et al. 2004. Discovering Optimal Imitation Strategies.

Robotics and Autonomous Systems 47(2-3): 69–77.

Binford, L.R. 1989. Isolating the Transition to Cultural Adaptations: An Organizational Approach. In *The Emergence of Modern Humans: Biocultural Adaptations in the Later Pleistocene,* ed. E. Trinkaus, pp. 18–41. Cambridge: Cambridge University Press.

Binford, S.R., and L.R. Binford, eds. 1968. *New Perspectives in Archeology.* Chicago: Aldine.

Birch, S., and P. Bloom. 2004. Understanding Children's and Adults' Limitations in Mental State Reasoning. *Trends in Cognitive Sciences* 8:255–60.

Birtle, Z., L. Goodstadt, and C. Ponting. 2005. Duplication and Positive Selection among Hominin-specific PRAME Genes. *BMC Genomics* 6:120–25.

Bischof, N. 1978. On the Phylogeny of Human Morality. In *Morality as a Biological Phenomenon,* ed. G. Stent, pp. 53–74. Berlin: Abakon.

Bischof-Köhler, D. 1985. Zur Phylogenese menschlicher motivation. In *Emotion und Reflexivität,* ed. L.H. Eckensberger and E.D. Lantermann, pp. 3–47. Vienna: Urban and Schwarzenberg.

Bishop, D.V.M. 2002. Putting Language Genes in Perspective. *Trends in Genetics* 18:57–59.

Bisson, M., A. Nowell, C. Cordova, and R. Kalchgruber. 2007. Human Evolution at the Crossroads: An Archaeological Survey in NW Jordan. *Near Eastern Archaeology* 69:73–85.

Blakemore, S.J., D. Bristow, G. Bird, et al. 2005. Somatosensory Activations during the Observation of Touch and a Case of Vision-Touch Synaesthesia. *Brain* 128(7): 1571–83.

Blehr, O. 1990. Communal Hunting as a Prerequisite for Caribou (Wild Reindeer) as a Human Resource. In *Hunters of the Recent Past,* ed. L.B. Davis and B.O.K. Reeves, pp. 304–26. London: Unwin Hyman.

Bliege Bird, R. 1999. Cooperation and Conflict: The Behavioral Ecology of the Sexual Division of Labor. *Evolutionary Anthropology* 8(2): 65–75.

—— 2007. Fishing and the Sexual Division of Labor among the Meriam. *American Anthropologist* 109:442–51.

Bliege Bird, R., E.A. Smith, and D.W. Bird. 2001. The Hunting Handicap: Costly Signaling in Human Foraging Strategies. *Behavioral Ecology and Sociobiology* 50(1): 9–19.

Blevins, J. 2004. *Evolutionary Phonology: The Emergence of Sound Patterns.* Cambridge: Cambridge University Press,

Bloom, P. 2002. *How Children Learn the Meanings of Words.* Cambridge: MIT Press.

Blurton Jones, N.G., K. Hawkes, and J. O'Connell. 2006. The Global Process and Local Ecology: How Should We Explain Differences between the Hadza and the !Kung? In *Cultural Diversity among Twentieth Century Foragers: An African Perspective*, ed. S. Kent, pp. 159–87. Cambridge: Cambridge University Press.

Boakes, R. 1984. *From Darwin to Behaviourism: Psychology and the Minds of Animals*. Cambridge: Cambridge University Press.

Bobe, R., and M.G. Leakey. 2009. Ecology of Plio-Pleistocene Mammals in the Omo-Turkana Basin and the Emergence of *Homo*. In *The First Humans: Origins and Early Evolution of the Genus* Homo, ed. F.E. Grine, J.G. Fleagle and R.E. Leakey, pp. 173–84. Dordrecht: Springer.

Bocherens, H., and D.G. Drucker. 2006. Dietary Competition between Neanderthals and Modern Humans: Insights from Stable Isotopes. In *When Neanderthals and Modern Humans Met*, ed. N.J. Conard, pp. 129–43. Tubingen: Kerns Verlag.

Bock, J. 2005. What Makes a Competent Adult Forager? In *Hunter-Gatherer Childhoods: Evolutionary, Developmental, and Cultural Perspectives*, ed. B. Hewlett and M. Lamb, pp. 109–28. New Brunswick, NJ: Transaction.

Bocquet-Appel, J.-P., P.-Y. Demars, L. Noiret, and D. Dobrowsky. 2005. Estimates of Upper Paleolithic Meta-population Size in Europe from Archaeological Data. *Journal of Archaeological Science* 32:1656–68.

Boëda, E., J. Connan, and S. Muhensen. 1998. Bitumen as Hafting Material on Middle Paleolithic Artifacts from the El Koum Basin, Syria. In *Neandertals and Modern Humans in Western Asia*, ed. T. Akazawa, K. Aoki, and O. Bar-Yosef, pp. 181–204. New York: Plenum.

Boehm, Christopher. 2012. *Moral Origins: The Evolution of Virtue, Altruism, and Shame*. New York: Basic Books.

Boesch, C. 1994. Cooperative Hunting in Wild Chimpanzees. *Animal Behaviour* 48(3): 653–67.

—— 2002. Cooperative Hunting Roles among Tai Chimpanzees. *Human Nature* 13(1): 27–46.

—— 2003. Is Culture a Golden Barrier between Human and Chimpanzee? *Evolutionary Anthropology* 12:82–91.

—— 2005. Joint Cooperative Hunting among Wild Chimpanzees: Taking Natural Observations Seriously (Reply to Tomasello et al. 2005b). *Behavioral and Brain Sciences* 28:692–93.

Boesch, C., and H. Boesch. 1989. Hunting Behavior of Wild Chimpanzees in the Tai National Park. *American Journal of Physical Anthropology* 78(4): 547–73.

—— 1990. Tool Use and Tool Making in Wild Chimpanzees. *Folia Primatologica* 54:86–

99.

Boesch, C., and M. Tomasello. 1998. Chimpanzee and Human Cultures. *Current Anthropology* 39:591–604, 610–14.

Boesch, C., G. Hohman, and L.F. Marchant, eds. 2002. *Behavioural Diversity in Chimpanzees and Bonobos.* Cambridge: Cambridge University Press.

Bogin, B. 2001. *The Growth of Humanity.* New York: Wiley-Liss.

Böhm, H., and K. Jongkind. 2004. *Bobby Fischer: The Wandering King.* New York: Sterling.

Bond, G., W. Broecker, S. Johnsen, et al. 1993. Correlations between Climate Records from North Atlantic Sediments and Greenland Ice. *Nature* 365(9 September): 143–46.

Bond, J., E. Roberts, G.H. Mochida, et al. 2002. ASPM Is a Major Determinant of Cerebral Cortical Size. *Nature Genetics* 32:316–20.

Bonner, J.T. 1980. *Evolution of Culture in Animals.* Princeton: Princeton University Press.

Borgerhoff Mulder, M. 1998. Demographic Transition: Are We Any Closer to an Evolutionary Explanation? *Trends in Ecology and Evolution* 13:266–70.

Borofsky, R., ed. 1994. *Assessing Cultural Anthropology.* New York: McGraw-Hill.

Boussaoud, D. 2001. Attention versus Intention in the Primate Premotor Cortex. *Neuroimage* 14(1, Pt. 2): S40–45.

Bouzouggar, A., N. Barton, M. Vanhaeren, et al. 2007. 82,000-year-old Shell Beads from North Africa and Implications for the Origins of Modern Human Behavior. *Proceedings of the National Academy of Sciences* 104:9964–69.

Bower, J. 2005. On "Modern Behavior" and the Evolution of Human Intelligence. *Current Anthropology* 46(1): 121–22. http://www.journals.uchicago.edu.ezproxy.library.uvic.ca/CA/journal/issues/v46n1/051601/051601.text.html - fn1#fn1.

Bowler, J.M., H. Johnston, J.M. Olley, J.R. Prescott, R.G. Roberts, W. Shawcross, and N.A. Spooner. 2003. New Ages for Human Occupation and Climatic Change at Lake Mungo, Australia. *Nature* 421:837–40.

Bowles, S., and H. Gintis. 2003. The Origins of Human Cooperation. In *The Genetic and Cultural Origins of Cooperation,* ed. P. Hammerstein, pp. 429–43. Cambridge: MIT Press.

Boyd, R., and P.J. Richerson. 1985. *Culture and the Evolutionary Process.* Chicago: University of Chicago Press.

—— 1992. How Microevolutionary Processes Give Rise to History. In *History and Evolution,* ed. M.H. Nitecki and D.V. Nitecki, pp. 179–209. Albany: State University of New York Press.

—— 2006. Culture and the Evolution of the Human Social Instincts. In *Roots of Human Sociality*, ed. S. Levinson and N. Enfield, pp. 453–77. Oxford: Berg.

Boyd, R., and J.B. Silk. 2000. *How Humans Evolved*. New York: W.W. Norton.

Bradley, R.S. 1999. *Paleoclimatology: Reconstructing Climates of the Quaternary*. 2nd ed. San Diego: Academic Press.

Braidwood, R.B. 1959. Archeology and the Evolutionary Theory. In *Evolution and Anthropology: A Centennial Appraisal*, ed. B.J. Meggers, pp. 76–89. Washington, DC: Anthropological Society of Washington.

Bramble, D.M., and D.E. Lieberman. 2004. Endurance Running of the Evolution of *Homo. Nature* 432:345–52.

Brantingham, P.J., A.I. Krivoshapkin, J. Li, and Y. Tserendagva. 2001. The Initial Upper Paleolithic in Northeast Asia. *Current Anthropology* 42(5): 735–47.

Brass, M., H. Bekkering, A. Wohlschlager, and W. Prinz. 2000. Compatibility between Observed and Executed Finger Movements: Comparing Symbolic, Spatial, and Imitative Cues. *Brain and Cognition* 44(2): 124–43.

Bratman, M. 1992. Shared Cooperative Activity. *Philosophical Review* 101(2): 327–41.

Brentano, F.C. 1874/1995. *Psychology from an Empirical Standpoint*, ed. L.L. McAlister. New York: Routledge. (Original German edition published in 1874.)

Breuer, T., M. Ndoundou-Hockemba, and V. Fishlock. 2005. First Observation of Tool Use in Wild Gorillas. *PLoS Biology* 3(11): e380.

Brinck, I., and P. Gärdenfors. 2003. Cooperation and Communication in Apes and Humans. *Mind and Language* 18:484–501.

Brodmann, K. 1905. Beiträge zur histologischen Lokalisation der Grosshirnrinde. Dritte Mitteilung: Die Rindenfelder der niederen Affen. *Journal für Psychologie und Neurologie* 4:177–226.

Broecker, W.S. 1995. *The Glacial World According to Wally*. Palisades, NY: Eldigio Press.

Broecker, W.S., and G.H. Denton. 1989. The Role of Ocean-Atmosphere Reorganizations in Glacial Cycles. *Geochimica et Cosmochimica Acta* 53:2465–501.

Brown, D.E. 1991. *Human Universals*. New York: McGraw-Hill.

Brown, K.S, C.W. Marean, A. Herries, et al. 2009. Fire as an Engineering Tool of Early Modern Humans. *Science* 325(5942): 859–62.

Brown, P., T. Sutikna, M.J. Morwood, et al. 2004. A New Small-bodied Hominin from the Late Pleistocene of Flores, Indonesia. *Nature* 431:1055–61.

Brownell, C.A., and M.S. Carriger. 1990. Changes in Cooperation and Self-Other Differentiation during the Second Year. *Child Development* 61(4): 1164–74.

Brownell, C.A., G.B. Ramani, and S. Zerwas. 2006. Becoming a Social Partner with Peers: Cooperation and Social Understanding in One- to Two-year-olds. *Child De-*

velopment 77(4): 803–21.

Brumm, A., and M.W. Moore. 2005. Symbolic Revolutions and the Australian Archaeological Record. *Cambridge Archaeological Journal* 15(2): 157–75.

Brunet, M., F. Guy, D. Pilbeam, et al. 2002. A New Hominid from the Upper Miocene of Chad, Central Africa. *Nature* 418:149–51.

Brunet, M., F. Guy, D. Pilbeam, et al. 2005. New Material of the Earliest Hominid from the Upper Miocene of Chad. *Nature* 434:752–55.

Buccino, G., F. Binkofski, G.R. Fink, et al. 2001. Action Observation Activates Premotor and Parietal Areas in a Somatotopic Manner: An fMRI Study. *European Journal of Neuroscience* 13(2): 400–4.

Buccino, G., S. Vogt, A. Ritzl, et al. 2004. Neural Circuits Underlying Imitation Learning of Hand Actions: An Event-related fMRI Study. *Neuron* 42(2): 323–34.

Buller, D.J. 2005. *Adapting Minds: Evolutionary Psychology and the Persistent Quest for Human Nature.* Cambridge: MIT Press.

Burke, A. 2004. The Ecology of Neandertals: Preface. *International Journal of Osteoarchaeology* 14:155–61.

Burling, R. 2005. *The Talking Ape.* Oxford: Oxford University Press.

Burr, D.B. 1976. Neandertal Vocal Tract Reconstructions: A Critical Appraisal. *Journal of Human Evolution* 5:285–90.

Buss, D.M. 1989. Sex Differences in Human Mate Preferences: Evolutionary Hypotheses Tested in 37 Cultures. *Behavioral and Brain Sciences* 12:1–49.

Buss, D.M., M.G. Haselton, T.K. Shackelford, et al. 1998. Adaptations, Exaptations, and Spandrels. *American Psychologist* 53:533–48.

Bustamante, C.D., A. Fledel-Alon, S. Williamson, et al. 2005. Natural Selection on Protein-coding Genes in the Human Genome. *Nature* 437:1153–57.

Buttelmann, D., M. Carpenter, and M. Tomasello. 2009. Eighteen-month-old Infants Show False Belief Understanding in an Active Helping Paradigm. *Cognition* 112:337–42.

Byers, M. 1994. Symboling and the Middle to Upper Paleolithic Transition: A Theoretical and Methodological Critique. *Current Anthropology* 35:369–99.

Byrne, R.W. 1995. *The Thinking Ape: Evolutionary Origins of Intelligence.* Oxford: Oxford University Press.

—— 1996. Machiavellian Intelligence. *Evolutionary Anthropology* 5:172–80.

Byrne, R.W., and L.A. Bates. 2007. Sociality, Evolution, and Cognition. *Current Biology* 17:R714–23.

Byrne, R.W., and A. Whiten. 1988. *Machiavellian Intelligence: Social Expertise and the Evolution of Intellect in Monkeys, Apes and Humans.* Oxford: Clarendon Press.

Byrne, R.W., P.J. Barnard, I. Davidson, et al. 2004. Understanding Culture across Species. *Trends in Cognitive Science* 8(8): 341–46.

Byrne, R.W., and L.A. Bates. 2007. Sociality, Evolution, and Cognition. *Current Biology* 17:R714–23

Calcott, B. 2008. The Other Cooperation Problem: Generating Benefit. *Biology and Philosophy* 23:179–203.

Call, J., and M. Tomasello. 1996. The Effect of Humans on the Cognitive Development of Apes. In *Reaching into Thought: The Minds of the Great Apes,* ed. A.E. Russon and K.A. Bard, pp. 371–403. Cambridge: Cambridge University Press.

—— (1999). A Nonverbal False Belief Task: The Performance of Children and Great Apes. *Child Development* 70(2): 381–95.

Call, J., M. Carpenter, and M. Tomasello. 2005. Copying Results and Copying Actions in the Process of Social Learning: Chimpanzees (*Pan troglodytes*) and Human Children (*Homo sapiens*). *Animal Cognition* 8:151–63.

Calvin, W.H. 2002. *A Brain for All Seasons.* Chicago: University of Chicago Press.

Calvin, W.H., and D. Bickerton. 2000. *Lingua Ex Machina: Reconciling Darwin with the Human Brain.* Cambridge, MA: MIT Press.

Campanella, S., and P. Belin. 2007. Integrating Face and Voice in Person Perception. *Trends in Cognitive Sciences* 11:535–43.

Campbell, A.W. 1905. *Histological Studies on the Localisation of Cerebral Function.* Cambridge: Cambridge University Press.

Campbell, B.G., J.D. Loy, and K. Cruz-Uribe. 2006. *Humankind Emerging.* Boston: Allyn and Bacon.

Campbell, D.T. 1965. Variation and Selective Retention in Socio-cultural Evolution. In *Social Change in Developing Areas: A Reinterpretation of Evolutionary Theory,* ed. H.R. Barringer, G.I. Blanksten, and R.W. Mack, pp. 19–48. Cambridge, MA: Schenkman.

Caramelli, D., C. Lalueza-Fox, C. Vernesi, et al. 2003. Evidence for a Genetic Discontinuity between Neandertals and 24,000-year-old Anatomically Modern Europeans. *Proceedings of the National Academy of Sciences USA* 100(11): 6593–97.

Carbonell, E., J.M. Bermúdez de Castro, J.M. Parés, et al. 2008. The First Hominin of Europe. *Nature* 452:465–70.

Carey, S. 1985. *Conceptual Development in Childhood.* Cambridge, MA: MIT Press.

—— 2011. Précis of *The Origin of Concepts. Behavioral and Brain Sciences* 34(3): 113–24.

Carlisle, R.C., and M. Siegel. 1974. Some Problems in the Interpretation of Neanderthal Speech Capabilities: A Reply to Lieberman. *American Anthropologist* 76:319–22.

Carroll, S.B., J.K. Grenier, and S.D. Weatherbee. 2005. *From DNA to Diversity: Molecular Genetics and the Evolution of Animal Design.* 2nd ed. Malden, MA: Blackwell.

Carruthers, P. 1992. *Human Knowledge and Human Nature.* New York: Oxford University Press.

—— 2002. The Cognitive Functions of Language. *Brain and Behavioral Sciences* 25:657–726.

—— 2006. *The Architecture of the Mind: Massive Modularity and the Flexibility of Thought.* Oxford: Oxford University Press.

—— 2007. The Creative-action Theory of Creativity. In *The Innate Mind.* Vol. 3, *Foundations and the Future,* ed. P. Carruthers, S. Laurence, and S. Stich, pp. 254–71. New York: Oxford University Press.

—— 2009. An Architecture for Dual Reasoning. In *In Two Minds: Dual Processes and Beyond,* ed. J. Evans and K. Frankish, pp. 109–27. New York: Oxford University Press.

Carruthers, P., S. Stich, and M. Siegal, eds. 2002. *The Cognitive Basis of Science.* Cambridge: Cambridge University Press.

Casey, B.J., J.N. Giedd, and K.M. Thomas. 2000. Structural and Functional Brain Development and Its Relation to Cognitive Development. *Biological Psychology* 54:241–57.

Caspari, R., and S.-H. Lee. 2006. Is Human Longevity a Consequence of Cultural Change or Modern Biology? *American Journal of Physical Anthropology* 129:512–17.

Catani, M., D.K. Jones, and D.H. ffytche. 2005. Perisylvian Language Networks of the Human Brain. *Annals of Neurology* 57(1): 8–16.

Cavalli-Sforza, L., and M. Feldman. 1981. *Cultural Transmission and Evolution: A Quantitative Approach.* Princeton: Princeton University Press.

Chagnon, N.A., and W. Irons, eds. 1979. *Evolutionary Biology and Human Social Behavior: An Anthropological Perspective.* North Scituate, MA: Duxbury Press.

Chaminade, T., and J. Decety. 2001. A Common Framework for Perception and Action: Neuroimaging Evidence. *Behavioral and Brain Sciences* 24(5): 879–82.

Chaminade, T., D. Meary, J.P. Orliaguet, and J. Decety. 2001. Is Perceptual Anticipation a Motor Simulation? A PET Study. *Neuroreport* 12(17): 3669–74.

Chaminade, T., A.N. Meltzoff, and J. Decety. 2002. Does the End Justify the Means? A PET Exploration of the Mechanisms Involved in Human Imitation. *Neuroimage* 15(2): 318–28.

Chaminade, T., E. Oztop, G. Cheng, and M. Kawato. 2008. From Self-Observation to Imitation: Visuomotor Association on a Robotic Hand. *Brain Research Bulletin* 75(6): 775–84.

Chaminade, T., M. Zecca, S.-J. Blakemore, et al. 2010. Brain Response to a Humanoid Robot in Areas Implicated in the Perception of Human Emotional Gestures. *PLoS One* 5(7): e11577.

Chao, L.L., and A. Martin. 2000. Representation of Manipulable Man-made Objects in the Dorsal Stream. *Neuroimage* 12(4): 478–84.

Chartrand, T.L., and J.A. Bargh. 1999. The Chameleon Effect: The Perception-Behavior Link and Social Interaction. *Journal of Personality and Social Psychology* 76(6): 893–910.

Chase, P.G. 1999. Symbolism as Reference and Symbolism as Culture. In *The Evolution of Culture: An Interdisciplinary View*, ed. R.I.M. Dunbar, C. Knight, and C. Power, pp. 34–49. Edinburgh: Edinburgh University Press.

—— 2001. "Symbolism" Is Two Different Phenomena: Implications for Archaeology and Paleontology. In *Humanity from African Naissance to Coming Millennia*, ed. P.V. Tobias, M.A. Raath, J. Moggi-Cecchi, and G.A. Doyle, pp. 199–212. Florence: Firenze University Press.

—— 2006. *The Emergence of Culture: The Evolution of a Uniquely Human Way of Life*. New York: Springer.

—— 2007. The Significance of Acculturation Depends on the Meaning of Culture. In *Rethinking the Human Revolution: New Behavioural and Biological Perspectives on the Origin and Dispersal of Modern Humans*, ed P. Mellars, K. Boyle, O. Bar-Yosef, and C. Stringer, pp. 55–66. Cambridge: McDonald Institute for Archaeological Research.

Chase, P.G., and A. Nowell. 1998. Taphonomy of a Suggested Middle Paleolithic Bone Flute from Slovenia. *Current Anthropology* 39(4): 549–53.

Chase, P.G., and H. Dibble. 1987. Middle Paleolithic Symbolism: A Review of Current Evidence and Interpretations. *Journal of Anthropological Archaeology* 6:263–96.

Chazine, J.-M. 2005. Rock Art, Burials, and Habitations: Caves in East Kalimantan. *Asian Perspectives* 44(1): 219–30.

Chen, F.C., and W.H. Li. 2001. Genomic Divergences between Humans and Other Hominoids and the Effective Population Size of the Common Ancestor of Humans and Chimpanzees. *American Journal of Human Genetics* 68:444–56.

Chen, Y.S., A. Olckers, T.G. Schurr, et al. 2000. Mitochondrial DNA Variation in the Southern African Kung and Khwe, and Their Genetic Relationships to Other African Populations. *American Journal of Human Genetics* 66(4): 1362–83.

Chen, F.C., E.J. Vallender, H. Wang, et al. 2001. Genomic Divergence between Human and Chimpanzee Estimated from Large-scale Alignments of Genomic Sequences. *Journal of Heredity* 92(6): 481–89.

Cheney, D.L., and R.M. Seyfarth. 1990. *How Monkeys See the World: Inside the Mind of Another Species.* Chicago: University of Chicago Press.

——— 1997. Reconciliatory Grunts by Dominant Female Baboons Influence Victims' Behaviour. *Animal Behaviour* 54:409–18.

——— 1998. Why Monkeys Don't Have Language. In *The Tanner Lectures on Human Values,* Vol. 19, ed. G. Petersen, pp. 175–219. Salt Lake City, UT: University of Utah Press.

——— 1999. Recognition of Other Individuals' Social Relationships by Female Baboons. *Animal Behaviour* 58:67–75.

——— 2007. *Baboon Metaphysics: The Evolution of a Social Mind.* Chicago: University of Chicago Press.

Cheney, D.L., R.M Seyfarth, and J.B. Silk. 1995a. The Responses of Female Baboons to Anomalous Social Interactions: Evidence for Causal Reasoning? *Journal of Comparative Psychology* 109:134–41.

——— 1995b. The Role of Grunts in Reconciling Opponents and Facilitating Interactions among Adult Female Baboons. *Animal Behaviour* 50:249–57.

Cheney, D.L., R.M. Seyfarth, J. Fischer, et al. 2004. Factors Affecting Reproduction and Mortality among Baboons in the Okavango Delta, Botswana. *International Journal of Primatology* 25:401–28.

Cheng, Z., M. Ventura, X. She, et al. 2005. A Genome-wide Comparison of Recent Chimpanzee and Human Segmental Duplications. *Nature* 437:88–93.

Childe, V.G. 1936. *Man Makes Himself.* London: Watts.

Chimpanzee Sequencing and Analysis Consortium. 2005. Initial Sequence of the Chimpanzee Genome and Comparison with the Human Genome. *Nature* 437:69–87.

Chomsky, N. 1980. *Rules and Representations.* New York: Columbia University Press.

——— 1982. *Noam Chomsky on the Generative Enterprise: A Discussion with Riny Huybregts and Henk van Riemsdijk.* Dordrecht: Foris.

——— 1984. *Modular Approaches to the Study of the Mind.* San Diego: San Diego State University Press.

Christiansen, M.H., and S. Kirby, eds. 2003. *Language Evolution.* Oxford: Oxford University Press.

Ciccarelli, F.D., C. von Mering, M. Suyama, et al. 2005. Complex Genomic Rearrangements Lead to Novel Primate Gene Function. *Genome Research* 15:343–51.

Clark, A. 1993. Symbolic Invention: The Missing (Computational) Link? *Behavioral and Brain Sciences* 16:753–54.

——— 1997. *Being There: Bringing Brain, Body and World Together Again.* Cambridge: MIT

Press.

Clark, A., and D.J. Chalmers. 1998. The Extended Mind. *Analysis* 58:7–19.

Clark, A.G., S. Glanowski, R. Nielsen, et al. 2003a. Inferring Nonneutral Evolution from Human-Chimp-Mouse Orthologous Gene Trios. *Science* 302:1960–63.

Clark, J.D., Y. Beyene, G. WoldeGabriel, et al. 2003b. Stratigraphic, Chronological and Behavioural Contexts of Pleistocene *Homo sapiens* from Middle Awash, Ethiopia. *Nature* 423(6941): 747–52.

Clayton, N., N. Emory, and A. Dickinson. 2004. *The Rationality of Animal Memory: The Cognition of Caching.* In *Rational Animals?*, ed. S. Hurley and M. Nudds, pp. 197–216. New York: Oxford University Press.

Clegg, M., and L. Aiello. 1999. A Comparison of the Nariokotome *Homo erectus* with Juveniles from a Modern Human Population. *American Journal of Physical Anthropology* 110:81–93.

Clottes, J. 2003. *Chauvet: Art of the Earliest Times.* Salt Lake City: University of Utah Press.

Collard, M.C., and B.A. Wood. 2000. How Reliable Are Human Phylogenetic Hypotheses? *Proceedings of the National Academy of Sciences USA* 97:5003–6.

Conard, N.J. 1990. Laminar Lithic Assemblages from the Last Interglacial Complex in Northwestern Europe. *Journal of Anthropological Research* 46:243–62.

—— 2003. Paleolithic Ivory Sculptures from Southwestern Germany and the Origins of Figurative Art. *Nature* 426:830–32.

—— 2006a. Changing Views of the Relationship between Neanderthals and Modern Humans. In *When Neanderthals and Modern Humans Met*, ed. N.J. Conard, pp. 5–20. Tübingen: Kerns Verlag.

—— ed. 2006b. *When Neanderthals and Modern Humans Met.* Tübingen: Kerns Verlag.

—— 2009. Female Figurine from the Basal Aurignacian of Hole Fels Cave Southwestern Germany. *Nature* 459:248–52.

Condillac, E. Bonnot de. [1746] 1756. *An Essay on the Origin of Human Knowledge, Being a Supplement to Mr. Locke's Essay on Human Understanding*, trans. T. Nugent. London: J. Nourse. Originally published in French.

Conkey, M.W., O. Soffer, D. Stratmann, and N.G. Jablonski. 1997. *Beyond Art: Pleistocene Image and Symbol.* Memoirs of the California Academy of Sciences 23. San Francisco: California Academy of Sciences.

Coolidge, F.L., and T. Wynn. 2001. Executive Functions of the Frontal Lobes and the Evolutionary Ascendancy of *Homo sapiens. Cambridge Archaeological Journal* 11:255–60.

—— 2005. Working Memory, Its Executive Functions, and the Emergence of Modern

Thinking. *Cambridge Archaeological Journal* 15:5–26.

—— 2007. The Working Memory Account of Neandertal Cognition: How Phonological Storage Capacity May Be Related to Recursion and the Pragmatics of Modern Speech. *Journal of Human Evolution* 52:707–10.

—— 2009. *Rise of* Homo sapiens: *The Evolution of Modern Thinking.* Malden, MA: Wiley-Blackwell.

Coope, G.R. 1979. Late Cenozoic Fossil Coleoptera: Evolution, Biogeography, and Ecology. *Annual Review of Ecology and Systematics* 10:247–67.

Correia, S.P.C., A. Dickinson, and N.S. Clayton. 2007. Western Scrub-Jays Anticipate Future Needs Independently of Their Current Motivational State. *Current Biology* 17:856–61.

Cosmides, L., and J. Tooby. 1987. From Evolution to Behavior: Evolutionary Psychology as the Missing Link. In *The Latest on the Best: Essays on Evolution and Optimality,* ed. J. Dupré, pp. 277–306. Cambridge, MA: MIT Press.

Crain, S., A. Gualmini, and P. Pietroski. 2005. Brass Tacks in Linguistic Theory: Innate Grammatical Principles. In *The Innate Mind: Structure and Contents,* ed. P. Carruthers, S. Laurence, and S. Stich, pp. 175–97. New York: Oxford University Press.

Crelin, E.S. 1987. *The Human Vocal Tract: Anatomy, Function, Development, and Evolution.* New York: Vintage Press.

Cremaschi, M., S.D. Lernia, and E.A.A. Garcee. 1998. Some Insights into the Aterian in the Libyan Sahara: Chronology, Environment, and Archaeology. *African Archaeological Review* 15(4): 261–86.

Crockford, C., R. Wittig, P. Whiten, et al. 2008. Social Stressors and Coping Mechanisms in Wild Female Baboons. *Hormones and Behavior.* 53:254–65.

Cross, I. 1999. Is Music the Most Important Thing We Ever Did? Music, Development and Evolution. In *Music, Mind and Science,* ed. S.W. Yi, pp. 10–39. Seoul: Seoul National University Press.

Cross, I. 2001. Music, Mind and Evolution. *Psychology of Music* 29:95–102.

Cummins, D. 1996. Evidence of Deontic Reasoning in 3- and 4-year-old Children. *Memory and Cognition* 24:823–29.

Curtiss, S. 1977. *Genie: A Linguistic Study of a Modern-Day "Wild Child."* New York: Academic Press.

Dalén L., L. Orlando, B. Shapiro, et al. 2012. Partial Genetic Turnover in Neandertals: Continuity in the East and Population Replacement in the West. *Molecular Biology and Evolution* 29(8):1893–97.

Daly, M., and M. Wilson. 1985. Child Abuse and Other Risks of Not Living with Both Parents. *Ethology and Sociobiology* 6:197–210.

—— 1988. Evolutionary Social Psychology and Family Homicide. *Science* 242:519–24.

Darwin, C. 1838 [1987]. Notebook M. In *Charles Darwin's Notebooks, 1836–1844,* ed. P.H. Barrett, P.J. Gautrey, S. Herbert, D. Kohn, and S. Smith, pp. 517–62. Ithaca, NY: Cornell University Press.

—— 1842 [1909]. Essay of 1842. In *Foundations of the Origin of Species: Two Essays Written in 1842 and 1844 by Charles Darwin,* ed. Francis Darwin, pp. 1–53. Cambridge: University Press. Ms. first published in 1909.

—— 1844 [1909]. Essay of 1844. In *Foundations of the Origin of Species: Two Essays Written in 1842 and 1844 by Charles Darwin,* ed. Francis Darwin, pp. 57–255. Cambridge: University Press. Ms. first published in 1909.

—— 1859. *On the Origin of Species by Means of Natural Selection.* London: John Murray.

—— 1871. *The Descent of Man and Selection in Relation to Sex.* London: John Murray.

—— 1872. *The Expression of the Emotions in Man and Animals.* New York: Appleton.

Dasser, V. 1988. Mapping Social Concepts in Monkeys. In *Machiavellian Intelligence: Social Expertise and the Evolution of Intellect in Monkeys, Apes, and Humans,* ed. R.W. Byrne and A. Whiten, pp. 85–93. Oxford: Oxford University Press.

Davidson, I., and W. Noble. 1989. The Archaeology of Perception: Traces of Depiction and Language. *Current Anthropology* 30(2): 125–56.

—— 1993. Tools and Language in Human Evolution. In *Tools, Language and Cognition in Human Evolution,* ed. K.R. Gibson and T. Ingold, pp. 363–88. Cambridge: Cambridge University Press.

Dawkins, R. 1976. *The Selfish Gene.* Oxford: Oxford University Press.

Day, M. 2004. Religion, Off-line Cognition and the Extended Mind. *Journal of Cognition and Culture* 4:101–21.

Deacon, H., and S. Wurz. 2001. Middle Pleistocene Populations of Southern Africa and the Emergence of Modern Behavior. In *Human Roots: Africa and Asia in the Middle Pleistocene,* ed. L. Barham and K. Robson-Brown, pp. 55–63. Bristol: West. Acad. Spec. Press.

Deacon, T.W. 1992. The Neural Circuitry Underlying Primate Calls and Human Language. In *Language Origin: A Multidisciplinary Approach,* ed. J. Wind, B.H. Bichakjian, A. Nocentini, and B. Chiarelli, pp. 121–62. Dordrecht: Kluwer Academic Publishers.

—— 1997. *The Symbolic Species: The Co-evolution of Language and the Brain.* New York: W.W. Norton.

Dean, C.M., and H.B. Smith. 2009. Growth and Development of the Nariokotome Youth, KNM-WT 15000. In *The First Humans: Origin and Early Evolution of the Genus* Homo, ed. F.E. Grine, J.G. Fleagle, and R.E. Leakey, pp. 101–20. New York:

Springer.

Decety, J., and T. Chaminade. 2003. When the Self Represents the Other: A New Cognitive Neuroscience View on Psychological Identification. *Consciousness and Cognition* 12(4): 577–96.

Decety, J., T. Chaminade, J. Grezes, and A.N. Meltzoff. 2002. A PET Exploration of the Neural Mechanisms Involved in Reciprocal Imitation. *Neuroimage* 15(1): 265–72.

Deci, E.L. 1971. Effects of Externally Mediated Rewards on Intrinsic Motivation. *Journal of Personality and Social Psychology* 18(1): 105–15.

Defleur, A., T. White, P. Valensi, et al. 1999. Neanderthal Cannibalism at Moula-Guercy, Ardeche, France. *Science* 286(5437): 128–31.

de Heinzelin, J., J.D. Clark, T.D. White, et al. 1999. Environment and Behavior of 2.5-million-year-old Bouri Hominids. *Science* 284:625–29.

Deininger, W., M. Fuhrmann, and P. Hegemann. 2000. Opsin Evolution: Out of the Wild Green Yonder? *Trends in Genetics* 16:158–59.

Deino, A.D., and S. McBrearty. 2002. 40Ar/39Ar Dating of the Kapthurin Formation, Baringo, Kenya. *Journal of Human Evolution* 42(1): 185–210.

deMenocal, P.B. 1995. Plio-Pleistocene African Climate. *Science* 270:53–59.

—— 2004. African Climate Change and Faunal Evolution during the Plio-Pleistocene. *Earth and Planetary Letters* 220:3–24.

Dennell, R.W. 1997. The World's Oldest Spears. *Nature* 385:767–68.

Dennett, D.C. 1988. Why Creative Intelligence Is Hard to Find. *Behavioral and Brain Sciences* 11:253.

—— 1996. *Darwin's Dangerous Idea: Evolution and the Meanings of Life*. New York: Touchstone; Simon and Schuster.

d'Errico, F. 2003. The Invisible Frontier: A Multiple Species Model for the Origin of Behavioural Modernity. *Evolutionary Anthropology* 12:188–202.

—— 2007. The Origin of Humanity and Modern Cultures: Archaeology's View. *Diogenes* 54:122–33.

d'Errico, F., and C.S. Henshilwood. 2007. Additional Evidence for Bone Technology in the Southern African Middle Stone Age. *Journal of Human Evolution* 52:142–63.

d'Errico, F., and A. Nowell. 2000. A New Look at the Berekhat Ram Figurine: Implications for the Origin of Symbolism. *Cambridge Archaeological Journal* 10:123–67.

d'Errico, F., and M. Soressi. 2002. Systematic Use of Pigment by Pech-de-l'Azé Neandertals: Implications for the Origin of Behavioral Modernity. Paleoanthropology Society Meeting (abstracts), March 19–20, Denver, CO. *Journal of Human Evolution* 42(3): A13.

d'Errico, F., M. Vanhaeren, and L. Wadley. 2008. Possible Shell Beads from the Middle Stone Age Layers of Sibudu Cave, South Africa. *South African Journal of Archaeological Science* 35:2675–85.

d'Errico, F., P. Villa, A. Pinto, and R. Idaragga. 1998a. A Middle Paleolithic Origin of Music? Using Cave Bear Bone Accumulations to Assess the Divje Babe I "Flute." *Antiquity* 72:65–79.

d'Errico, F., J. Zilhão, D. Baffier, et al. 1998b. Neanderthal Acculturation in Europe? A Critical Review of the Evidence and Its Interpretation. *Current Anthropology* 39:S1–S44.

d'Errico, F., C. Henshilwood, G. Lawson, et al. 2003a. Archaeological Evidence for the Emergence of Language, Art and Symbolism and Music: An Alternative Multidisciplinary Perspective. *Journal of World Prehistory* 17:1–70.

d'Errico, F., M. Julien, D. Liolios, et al. 2003b. Many Awls in Our Argument: Bone Tool Manufacture and Use in the Châtelperronian and Aurignacian Levels at Grotte de Renne at Arcy-sur-Cure. In *Chronology of the Aurignacian and the Transitional Technocomplexes: Dating, Stratigraphies, Cultural Implications.* Trabalhos de Arqueologia 33, ed. J. Zilhão and F. d'Errico, pp. 247–70. Lisbon: Portuguese Institute of Archaeology.

d'Errico, F., C. Henshilwood, M. Vanhaeren, and K. Van Neikerk. 2005. Nassarius kraussianus Shell Beads from Blombos Cave: Evidence for Symbolic Behavior in the Middle Stone Age. *Journal of Human Evolution* 48:3–24.

d'Errico, F., H. Salomon, C. Vignaud, and C. Stringer. 2010. Pigments from the Middle Paleolithic Levels of Es-Skhul (Mount Carmel, Israel). *Journal of Archaeological Science* 37:3099–110.

Dessalles, J.-L. 2007. *Why We Talk.* Oxford: Oxford University Press.

de Waal, F.B.M. 1996. *Good Natured.* Cambridge: Harvard University Press.

de Waal, F.B.M., and S.F. Bosnan. 2006. Simple and Complex Reciprocity in Primates. In *Cooperation in Primates and Humans,* ed. P.M. Kappeler and C.P. Van Schaik, pp. 85–105. Berlin: Springer.

Dewey, J. 1894. The Theory of Emotion (I). Emotional Attitudes. *Psychological Review* 1:553–69.

—— 1895. The Theory of Emotion (II). The Significance of Emotions. *Psychological Review* 2:13–32.

Dewsbury, D.A. 1984. *Comparative Psychology in the Twentieth Century.* Stroudsburg, PA: Hutchinson Ross.

Diamond, J. 2005. *Collapse: How Societies Choose to Fail or Survive.* London: Penguin-Allen Lane.

Dinstein, I., U. Hasson, N. Rubin, and D.J. Heeger. 2007. Brain Areas Selective for Both Observed and Executed Movements. *Journal of Neurophysiology* 98:1415–27.

di Pellegrino, G., L. Fadiga, L. Fogassi, et al. 1992. Understanding Motor Events: A Neurophysiological Study. *Experimental Brain Research* 9:176–80.

Ditlevsen, P.D., H. Svensmark, and S. Johnsen. 1996. Contrasting Atmospheric and Climate Dynamics of the Last-Glacial and Holocene Periods. *Nature* 379(29 Feb.): 810–12.

Dominguez-Rodrigo, M., and T.R. Pickering. 2003. Early Hominid Hunting and Scavenging: A Zooarcheological Review. *Evolutionary Anthropology* 12:275–82.

Donald, M. 1991. *Origins of the Modern Mind: Three Stages in the Evolution of Culture and Cognition.* Cambridge: Harvard University Press.

—— 1998a. Hominid Enculturation and Cognitive Evolution. In *Cognition and Culture: The Archaeology of Symbolic Storage,* ed. C. Renfrew and C. Scarre, pp. 17–29. Cambridge University: Monographs of the McDonald Institute for Archaeological Research.

—— 1998b. Mimesis and the Executive Suite: Missing Links in Language Evolution. In *Approaches to the Evolution of Language: Social and Cognitive Biases,* ed. J.R. Hurford, M. Studdert-Kennedy, and C. Knight, pp. 44–67. Cambridge: Cambridge University Press.

—— 1999. Preconditions for the Evolution of Protolanguages. In *The Descent of Mind,* ed. M.C. Corballis and S.E.G. Lea, pp. 355–65. Oxford: Oxford University Press.

—— 2001. *A Mind So Rare: The Evolution of Human Consciousness.* New York: W.W. Norton.

—— 2004. The Virtues of Rigorous Interdisciplinarity. In *The Development of the Mediated Mind: Sociocultural Context and Cognitive Development,* ed. J. Lucariello, J. Hudson, R. Fivush, and P. Bauer, pp. 245–56. Cambridge: Cambridge University Press.

Driver, P., and N. Humphries. 1988. *Protean Behavior: The Biology of Unpredictability.* New York: Oxford University Press.

Duarte, C., J. Maurício, P. Pettitt, et al. 1999. The Early Upper Paleolithic Human Skeleton from the Abrigo do Lagar Velho (Portugal) and Modern Human Emergence in Iberia. *Proceedings of the National Academy of Sciences USA* 96:7604–9.

Du Brul, E.L. 1976. Biomechanics of Speech Sounds. In *Origins and Evolution of Language and Speech,* ed. H.B. Steklis, S.R. Harnad, and J. Lancaster, pp. 631–42. New York: Annals of the New York Academy of Sciences.

Duff, A.I., G.A. Clark, and T.J. Chadderdon. 1992. Symbolism in the Early Paleolithic: A Conceptual Odyssey. *Cambridge Archaeological Journal* 2:211–29.

Dumond, D.E. 1984. Prehistory: Summary. In *Handbook of North American Indians*. Vol. 5, *Arctic*, ed. D. Damas, pp. 72–79. Washington, DC: Smithsonian Institution.

Dunbar, R.I.M. 1992. Neocortex Size as a Constraint on Group Size in Primates. *Journal of Human Evolution* 22:469–93.

—— 1993. Coevolution of Neocortical Size, Group Size and Language in Humans. *Behavioral and Brain Sciences* 16(4): 681–735.

—— 1995. Neocortex Size and Group Size in Primates: A Test of the Hypothesis. *Journal of Human Evolution* 28:287–96.

—— 1996. *Grooming, Gossip and the Evolution of Language*. London: Faber and Faber.

—— 1998. The Social Brain Hypothesis. *Evolutionary Anthropology* 6:178–90.

—— 2003. The Origin and Subsequent Evolution of Language. In *Language Evolution*, ed. M.H. Christiansen and S. Kirby, pp. 219–34. Oxford: Oxford University Press.

Dunbar, R.I.M., and L. Barrett. 2007. Evolutionary Psychology in the Round. In *Oxford Handbook of Evolutionary Psychology*, ed. R.I.M. Dunbar and L. Barrett, pp. 3–9. Oxford: Oxford University Press.

Dupont, L., S. Jahns, F. Marret, and S. Ning. 2000. Vegetation Change in Equatorial West Africa: Time-slices for the Last 150 ka. *Paleogeography, Paleoclimatology, Paleoecology* 155:95–122.

Ebersberger, I., D. Metzler, C. Schwarz, and S. Pääbo. 2002. Genome-wide Comparison of DNA Sequences between Humans and Chimpanzees. *American Journal of Human Genetics* 70:1490–97.

Eichler, E.E. 2006. Widening the Spectrum of Human Genetic Variation. *Nature Genetics* 38:9–11.

Eisenberg, N. 1992. *The Caring Child*. Cambridge, MA: Harvard University Press.

Eisenberg, N., R.A. Fabes, and T. Spinrad. 2006. Prosocial Development. In *Handbook of Child Psychology: Social, Emotional, and Personality Development*, 6th ed., 4 vols., Vol. 3, ed. W. Damon, R.M. Lerner, and N. Eisenberg, pp. 646–718. Hoboken, NJ: John Wiley and Sons.

Ellen, P., and C. Thinus-Blanc, eds. 1987. *Cognitive Processes and Spatial Orientation in Animal and Man*. Vol. I, *Experimental Animal Psychology and Ethology*. Leiden: Martinus Nijhoff Publishers.

Elston, G.N., R. Benavides-Piccione, A. Elston, et al. 2005. Specialization in Pyramidal Cell Structure in the Sensory-Motor Cortex of the Chacma Baboon (*Papio ursinus*) with Comparative Notes on Macaque and Vervet Monkeys. *The Anatomical Record Part A: Discoveries in Molecular, Cellular, and Evolutionary Biology* 286(1): 854–65.

Elton, S., L.C. Bishop, and B. Wood. 2001. Comparative Context of Plio-Pleistocene

Hominin Brain Evolution. *Journal of Human Evolution* 41:1–27.

Emery, N.J. 2000. The Eyes Have It: The Neuroethology, Function and Evolution of Social Gaze. *Neuroscience and Biobehavioral Reviews* 24:581–604.

Emery, N.J., and N.S. Clayton. 2004. The Mentality of Crows: Convergent Evolution of Intelligence in Corvids and Apes. *Science* 306:1903–7.

Enard, W., and S. Pääbo. 2004. Comparative Primate Genomics. *Annual Review of Genomics and Human Genetics* 5:351–78.

Enard, W., M. Przeworski, S.E. Fisher, et al. 2002. Molecular Evolution of FOXP2, a Gene Involved in Speech and Language. *Nature* 418:869–72.

ENCODE Project Consortium. 2007. Identification and Analysis of Functional Elements in 1% of the Human Genome by the ENCODE Pilot Project. *Nature* 447:799–816.

Endler, John A. 1986. *Natural Selection in the Wild.* Monographs in Population Biology 21. Princeton: Princeton University Press.

Engh, A.L., J.C. Beehner, T.J. Bergman, et al. 2006a. Behavioural and Hormonal Responses to Predation in Female Chacma Baboons (*Papio hamadryas ursinus*). *Proceedings of the Royal Society of London B* 273:707–12.

—— 2006b. Female Hierarchy Instability, Male Immigration, and Infanticide Increase Glucocorticoid Levels in Female Chacma Baboons. *Animal Behaviour* 71:1227–37.

Engh, A.E., R.R. Hoffmeier, D.L. Cheney, and R.M. Seyfarth. 2006c. Who, Me? Can Baboons Infer the Target of Vocalisations? *Animal Behaviour* 71:381–87.

EPICA, Community Members. 2004. Eight Glacial Cycles from an Antarctic Ice Core. *Nature* 429:623–28.

Eriksen, T.H., and F.S. Nielsen. 2003. *A History of Anthropology.* London: Pluto Press.

Erickson, P.A., and L.D. Murphy, eds. 2001. *Readings for a History of Anthropological Theory.* Peteborough, Ontario: Broadview Press.

Erlandson, J.M. 2001. The Archaeology of Aquatic Adaptations, Paradigms for a New Millennium. *Journal of Anthropological Research* 9(4): 287–348.

Evans, J., and D. Over. 1996. *Rationality and Reasoning.* Hove, UK: Psychology Press.

Evans, P.D., J.R. Anderson, E.J. Vallender, et al. 2004a. Adaptive Evolution of ASPM, a Major Determinant of Cerebral Cortical Size in Humans. *Human Molecular Genetics* 13:489–94.

—— 2004b. Reconstructing the Evolutionary History of Microcephalin, a Gene Controlling Human Brain Size. *Human Molecular Genetics* 13:1139–45.

Evans, P.D., S.L. Gilbert, N. Mekel-Bobrov, et al. 2005. Microcephalin, a Gene Regulating Brain Size, Continues to Evolve Adaptively in Humans. *Science* 309(5741): 1717–20.

Evans, P.D., N. Mekel-Bobrov, E.J. Vallender, et al. 2006. Evidence that the Adaptive Allele of the Brain Size Gene Microcephalin Introgressed into *Homo sapiens* from an Archaic *Homo* Lineage. *Proceedings of the National Academy of Sciences USA* 103(48): 18178–83.

Facchini, F. 1998. Il simbolismo nell'uomo preistorico: Aspetti ermeneutici e manifestazioni. *Rivista di Scienze Preistoriche* 49:651–71.

Fagan, B.M. 2002. *The Little Ice Age: How Climate Made History, 1300–1850.* 1st pbk. ed. New York: Basic Books.

Falk, D. 1975. Comparative Anatomy of the Larynx in Man and the Chimpanzee: Implications for Language in Neanderthal. *American Journal of Physical Anthropology* 43:123–32.

—— 1980. A Re-analysis of the South African Australopithecine Natural Endocasts. *American Journal of Physical Anthropology* 53:525–40.

—— 1983. Cerebral Cortices of East African Early Hominids. *Science* 221:1072–74.

—— 1986. Endocast Morphology of Hadar Hominid AL 162-28 (Reply to Holloway and Kimbel). *Nature* 321:536–37.

Falk, D., J.C. Redmond, Jr., J. Guyera, et al. 2000. Early Hominid Brain Evolution: A New Look at Old Endocasts. *Journal of Human Evolution* 38(5): 695–717.

Fan, Y., E. Linardopoulou, C. Friedman, et al. 2002. Genomic Structure and Evolution of the Ancestral Chromosome Fusion Site in 2q13–2q14.1 and Paralogous Regions on Other Human Chromosomes. *Genome Research* 2:1651–62.

Fay, J.C., and C.I. Wu. 2000. Hitchhiking under Positive Darwinian Selection. *Genetics* 155:1405–13.

Fehr, E., and S. Gächter. 2002. Altruistic Punishment in Humans. *Nature* 415: 137–40.

Feraud, G., D. York, C.M. Hall, et al. 1983. 40Ar/39Ar Age Limit for an Acheulean Site in Israel. *Nature* 304:263–5.

Ferguson-Smith, M.A., and V. Trifonov. 2007. Mammalian Karyotype Evolution. *Nature Reviews Genetics* 8(12): 950–62.

Ferland, R.J., W. Eyaid, R.V. Collura, et al. 2004. Abnormal Cerebellar Development and Axonal Decussation Due to Mutations in AHI1 in Joubert Syndrome. *Nature Genetics* 36(9): 1008–13.

Ferrari, P.F., V. Gallese, G. Rizzolatti, and L. Fogassi. 2003. Mirror Neurons Responding to the Observation of Ingestive and Communicative Mouth Actions in the Monkey Ventral Premotor Cortex. *European Journal of Neuroscience* 17(8): 1703–14.

Ferrari, P.F., S. Rozzi, and L. Fogassi. 2005. Mirror Neurons Responding to Observation of Actions Made with Tools in Monkey Ventral Premotor Cortex. *Journal of Cognitive Neuroscience* 17(2): 212–26.

Feuk, L., J.R. MacDonald, T. Tang, et al. 2005. Discovery of Human Inversion Polymorphisms by Comparative Analysis of Human and Chimpanzee DNA Sequence Assemblies. *PLoS Genetics* 1(4): e56. doi:10.1371/journal.pgen.0010056

Finlayson, B., and S.J. Mithen, eds. 2007. *The Early Prehistory of Wadi Faynan, Southern Jordan.* Oxford: Oxbow Books/CBRL.

Finlayson, C. 2009. *The Humans Who Went Extinct: Why Neanderthals Died Out and We Survived.* Oxford: Oxford University Press.

Finlayson, C., F. Giles Pacheco, J. Rodríguez-Vidal, et al. 2006. Late Survival of Neanderthals at the Southernmost Extreme of Europe. *Nature* 443:850–53.

Finlayson, C., and J.S. Carrión. 2007. Rapid Ecological Turnover and Its Impact on Neanderthal and Other Human Populations. *Trends in Ecology and Evolution* 22:213–22.

Fisher, C., and L.R. Gleitman. 2002. Language Acquisition. In *Stevens Handbook of Experimental Psychology.* Vol. 3, *Learning and Motivation,* ed. H.F. Pashler and C.R. Gallistel, pp. 445–96. New York: Wiley.

Fisher, S.E., and G.F. Marcus. 2006. The Eloquent Ape: Genes, Brains and the Evolution of Language. *Nature Reviews Genetics* 7:9–20.

Fitch, W.T. 2004. Kin Selection and "Mother Tongues": A Neglected Component in Language Evolution. In *The Evolution of Communication Systems,* ed. K. Oller and U. Griebel, pp. 275–96. Cambridge, MA: MIT Press.

—— 2010. *The Evolution of Language.* Cambridge: Cambridge University Press.

Fitch, W.T., and M.D. Hauser. 2004. Computational Constraints on Syntactic Processing in a Nonhuman Primate. *Science* 303(5656): 377–80.

Fitch, W.T., M.D. Hauser, and N. Chomsky. 2005. The Evolution of the Language Faculty: Clarifications and Implications. *Cognition* 97:179–210.

Fitzpatrick, R.C., J.E. Butler, and B.L. Day. 2006. Resolving Head Rotation for Human Bipedalism. *Current Biology* 16(15): 1509–14.

Flannery, K.V. 1972. *The Origins of the Village as a Settlement Type in Mesoamerica and the Near East: A Comparative Study.* London: Duckworth.

Fodor, J.A. 1983. *The Modularity of Mind: An Essay on Faculty Psychology.* Cambridge, MA: MIT Press.

—— 2000a. *In Critical Condition.* Cambridge, MA: MIT Press.

—— 2000b. *The Mind Doesn't Work That Way.* Cambridge, MA: MIT Press.

Fogassi, L., P.F. Ferrari, B. Gesierich, et al. 2005. Parietal Lobe: From Action Organization to Intention Understanding. *Science* 308(5722): 662–67.

Foley, R., ed. 1984. *Hominid Evolution and Community Ecology.* London: Academic Press.

—— 1995. *Humans Before Humanity.* Oxford: Blackwell.

—— 2002. Adaptive Radiations and Dispersals in Hominin Evolutionary Ecology. *Evolutionary Anthropology* 11:32–37.

Foley, R., and C. Gamble. 2009. The Ecology of Social Transitions in Human Evolution. *Philosophical Transactions of the Royal Society of London B* 364:3267–79.

Foley, R., and M.M. Lahr. 2003. On Stony Ground: Lithic Technology, Human Evolution, and the Emergence of Culture. *Evolutionary Anthropology* 12:109–22.

Formicola, V. 2007. From the Sunghir Children to the Romito Dwarf: Aspects of the Upper Paleolithic Funerary Landscape. *Current Anthropology* 48:446–54.

Formicola, V., and A.P. Buzhilovo. 2004. Double Child Burial from Sunghir (Russia): Pathology and Inferences for Upper Paleolithic Funerary Practices. *American Journal of Physical Anthropology* 124:189–98.

Forrester, G.S. 2008. A Multidimensional Approach to Investigations of Behaviour: Revealing Structure in Animal Communication Signals. *Behaviour* 76(5): 1749–60.

Forster, P. 2004. Ice Ages and the Mitochondrial DNA Chronology of Human Dispersals: A Review. *Philosophical Transactions of the Royal Academy of Sciences B* 359:255–62.

Fortna, A., Y. Kim, E. MacLaren, et al. 2004. Lineage-specific Gene Duplication and Loss in Human and Great Ape Evolution. *PLoS Biology* 2:e207.

Fouts, R.S. 1987. Chimpanzee Signing and Emergent Levels. In *Cognition, Language, and Consciousness: Integrative Levels,* ed. G. Greenberg and E. Tobach, pp. 57–84. Hillsdale, NJ: Erlbaum Associates.

Fouts, R.S., and R.L. Budd. 1979. Artificial and Human Language Acquisition in a Chimpanzee. In *The Great Apes,* ed. D.A. Hamburg and E.R. McCown, pp. 375–92. Menlo Park, CA: Benjamin Cummings.

Fox, E.A., A.F. Sitompul, and C.P. van Schaik. 1999. Intelligent Tool Use in Wild Sumatran Orangutans. In *The Mentalities of Gorillas and Orangutans: Comparative Perspectives,* ed. S.T. Parker, R.W. Mitchell, and H.L. Miles, pp. 99–116. Cambridge: Cambridge University Press.

Fragaszy, D.M., and S. Perry, eds. 2003. *Biology of Traditions: Models and Evidence.* Cambridge: Cambridge University Press.

Franz, H., C. Ullmann, A. Becker, et al. 2005. Systematic Analysis of Gene Expression in Human Brains Before and After Death. *Genome Biology* 6:R112.

Frazer, K.A., X. Chen, D.A. Hinds, et al. 2003. Genomic DNA Insertions and Deletions Occur Frequently between Humans and Nonhuman Primates. *Genome Research* 13:341–46.

French, C.A., M. Groszer, C. Preece, et al. 2007. Generation of Mice with a Conditional FOXP2 Null Allele. *Genesis* 45:440–46.

Friederici, A.D., J. Bahlmann, S. Heim, et al. 2006. The Brain Differentiates Human and Non-human Grammars: Functional Localization and Structural Connectivity. *Proceedings of the National Academy of Sciences USA* 103(7): 2458–63.

Frith, U., and C. Frith. 2003. Development and Neurophysiology of Mentalizing. *Philosophical Transactions of the Royal Society of London B* 358:459–73.

Fulton, J.F. 1935. A Note on the Definition of the Motor and Premotor Areas. *Brain* 58(2): 311–16.

Gabunia, L., S.C. Antón, D. Lordkipanidze, et al. 2001. Dmanisi and Dispersal. *Evolutionary Anthropology* 10:158–70.

Gagneux P., C. Wills, U. Gerloff, et al. 1999. Mitochondrial Sequences Show Diverse Evolutionary Histories of African Hominoids. *Proceedings of the National Academy of Sciences USA* 96:5077–82.

Galef, B.G. 1992. The Question of Animal Culture. *Human Nature* 3:157–78.

—— 1996. Social Enhancement of Food Preferences in Norway Rats: A Brief Review. In *Social Learning in Animals: The Roots of Culture,* ed. C.M. Heyes and B.G. Galef, pp. 49–64. San Diego: Academic Press.

—— 2009. Culture in Animals? In *The Question of Animal Culture,* ed. K.N. Laland and B.G. Galef, pp. 222–46. Cambridge, MA: Harvard University Press.

Gallese, V., L. Fadiga, L. Fogassi, and G. Rizzolati. 1996. Action Recognition in the Premotor Cortex. *Brain* 119:593–609.

Gamble, C. 1999. *The Paleolithic Societies of Europe.* Cambridge: Cambridge University Press.

—— 2007. *Origins and Revolutions: Human Identity and Prehistory.* Cambridge: Cambridge University Press.

Gamble, C., W. Davies, P. Pettitt, and M. Richards. 2004. Climate Change and Evolving Human Diversity in Europe during the Last Glacial. *Philosophical Transactions of the Royal Society of London B* 359:243–54.

Gärdenfors, P. 1994. The Social Stance. *Protosoziologie* 6:91–94.

—— 1996. Cued and Detached Representations in Animal Cognition. *Behavioural Processes* 36:263–73.

—— 2001. Slicing the Theory of Mind. *Danish Yearbook for Philosophy* 36:7–34.

—— 2003. *How Homo Became Sapiens: On the Evolution of Thinking.* Oxford: Oxford University Press.

—— 2004. Cooperation and the Evolution of Symbolic Communication. In *The Evolution of Communication Systems,* ed. K. Oller and U. Griebel, pp. 237–56. Cambridge, MA: MIT Press.

—— 2007a. The Cognitive and Communicative Demands of Cooperation. In the electronic *Festschrift Hommage à Wlodek: Philosophical Papers Dedicated to Wlodek Rabinowicz.* http://www.fil.lu.se/hommageawlodek/.

—— 2007b. Cognitive Semantics and Image Schemas with Embodied Forces. In *Embodiment in Cognition and Culture,* ed. J.M. Krois, M. Rosengren, A. Steidele, and D. Westerlamp, pp. 57–76. Amsterdam: John Benjamins.

—— 2008. Evolutionary and Developmental Aspects of Intersubjectivity. In *Consciousness Transitions: Phylogenetic, Ontogenetic and Physiological Aspects,* ed. H. Liljenström and P. Århem, pp. 281–385. Amsterdam: Elsevier.

Gärdenfors, P., and M. Osvath. 2010. The Evolution of Anticipatory Cognition as a Precursor to Symbolic Communication. In *Evolution of Language: Biolinguistic Approaches,* ed. R. Larson, V. Déprez, and H. Yamakido, pp. 103–14. Cambridge: Cambridge University Press.

Gardner, B.T., and R.A. Gardner. 1978. Comparative Psychology and Language Acquisition. In *Psychology: The State of the Art,* ed. K. Salzinger and F.L. Denmark, pp. 37–76. Annals of the New York Academy of Sciences 309.

Gardner, H. 1983. *Frames of Mind: The Theory of Multiple Intelligences.* New York: Basic Books.

—— 1993. *Multiple Intelligences: The Theory in Practice.* New York: Basic Books.

Gaudzinski, S., and W. Roebroeks. 2000. Adults Only: Reindeer Hunting at the Middle Paleolithic Site Salzgitter Lebenstedt, Northern Germany. *Journal of Human Evolution* 38:497–521.

Gazzaniga, M.S., R.B. Ivry, and G.R. Mangun. 1998. *Cognitive Neuroscience: The Biology of the Mind.* New York: W.W. Norton.

Geertz, C. 1962. The Growth of Culture and the Evolution of Mind. In *Theories of Mind,* ed. J.M. Scher, pp. 713–40. New York: Free Press.

—— 1966. The Impact of the Concept of Culture on the Concept of Man. In *New Views of the Nature of Man,* ed. J. Platt, pp. 93–118. Chicago: University of Chicago Press.

—— 1973. Thick Description: Toward an Interpretive Theory of Culture. In *The Interpretation of Cultures: Selected Essays,* ed. C. Geertz, pp. 3–30. New York: Basic Books.

Gelman, S., J.D. Coley, and G. Gottfried. 1994. Essentialist Beliefs in Children: The Acquisition of Concepts and Theories. In *Mapping the Mind,* ed. L.A. Hirschfeld and S.A. Gelman, pp. 341–66. Cambridge: Cambridge University Press.

Gerard, R.W., and I. Veith, eds. 1960. Panel Four: The Evolution of Mind. In *Evolution after Darwin,* 3 vols., vol. 3, ed. S. Tax, (co-edited with C. Callendar), pp. 175–206. Chicago: University of Chicago Press.

Ghazanfar, A., and N. Logothetis. 2003. Facial Expressions Linked to Monkey Calls. *Nature* 423:937–38.

Ghazanfar, A., J.X. Maier, K.L. Hoffman, and N. Logothetis. 2005. Multisensory Integration of Dynamic Faces and Voices in Rhesus Monkey Auditory Cortex. *Journal of Neuroscience* 25:5004–12.

Gibbard, P.L., and M.J. Head. IUGS Ratification of the Quaternary System/Period and the Pleistocene Series/Epoch with a Base at 2.58 MA. *Quaternaire* 20:411–12.

Gibson, J.J. 1966. *The Senses Considered as Perceptual Systems.* Boston: Houghton Mifflin.

Gibson, K.R. 1996. The Ontogeny and Evolution of the Brain, Cognition, and Language. In *Handbook of Human Symbolic Evolution,* ed. A. Lock and C.R. Peters, pp. 407–31. Oxford: Clarendon Press.

Gilad, Y., C.D. Bustamante, D. Lancet, et al. 2003a. Natural Selection on the Olfactory Receptor Gene Family in Humans and Chimpanzees. *American Journal of Human Genetics* 73:489–501.

Gilad, Y., O. Man, S. Pääbo, et al. 2003b. Human Specific Loss of Olfactory Receptor Genes. *Proceedings of the National Academy of Sciences USA* 100(6): 3324–27.

Gilad, Y., O. Man, and G. Glusman. 2005. A Comparison of the Human and Chimpanzee Olfactory Receptor Gene Repertoires. *Genome Research* 15:224–30.

Gilbert, M. 1990. Walking Together: A Paradigmatic Social Phenomenon. In *The Philosophy of the Human Sciences. Midwest Studies in Philosophy XV,* ed. P.A. French, pp. 1–14. Notre Dame, IN: Notre Dame University Press.

Gil-da-Costa, R., A. Braun, M. Lopes, et al. 2004. Toward an Evolutionary Perspective on Conceptual Representation: Species-specific Calls Activate Visual and Affective Processing Systems in the Macaque. *Proceedings of the National Academy of Sciences USA* 101:17516–21.

Gil-da-Costa, R., A. Martin, M.A. Lopes, et al. 2006. Species-specific Calls Activate Homologs of Broca's and Wernicke's Areas in the Macaque. *Nature Neuroscience* 9:1064–70.

Godfrey-Smith, P. 2001. Three Kinds of Adaptationism. In *Adaptation and Optimality,* ed. S. Orzack and E. Sober, pp. 335–57. Cambridge: Cambridge University Press.

Gogtay, N., J.N. Giedd, L. Lusk, et al. 2004. Dynamic Mapping of Human Cortical Development during Childhood through Early Adulthood. *Proceedings of the National Academy of Sciences USA* 101(21): 8174–9.

Goldin-Meadow, S., and H. Feldman. 1977. The Development of Language-like Communication without a Language Model. *Science* 197:401–3.

Goldin-Meadow, S., and C. Mylander. 1983. Gestural Communication in Deaf Children: The Non-effects of Parental Input on Language Development. *Science* 221:372–74.

Gomez, J.C. 2004. *Apes, Monkeys, Children, and the Growth of Mind*. Cambridge, MA: Harvard University Press.

Gonder, M.K., H.M. Mortensen, F.A. Reed, et al. 2007. Whole-mtDNA Genome Sequence Analysis of Ancient African Lineages. *Molecular Biology and Evolution* 24(3): 757–68.

Goodall, J. 1986. *The Chimpanzees of Gombe: Patterns of Behavior*. Cambridge: The Belknap Press of Harvard University Press.

Goodenough, O. 1995. Mind Viruses: Culture, Evolution and the Puzzle of Altruism. *Social Science Information* 34:287–320.

Goodenough, W.H. 1964. Culture, Anthropology, and Linguistics. In *Language in Culture and Society. A Reader in Linguistics*, ed. D. Humes. New York: Harper and Row.

Gopnik, A., and A. Meltzoff. 1997. *Words, Thoughts, and Theories*. Cambridge, MA: MIT Press.

Gopnik, A., and H. Wellman. 1994. The Theory Theory. In *Mapping the Mind*, ed. L.A. Hirschfeld and S.A. Gelman, pp. 257–93. Cambridge: Cambridge University Press.

Gopnik, A., and J.W. Astington. 1988. Children's Understanding of Representational Change, and Its Relation to the Understanding of False Belief and the Appearance-Reality Distinction. *Child Development* 59:26–37.

Gopnik, A., and L. Schulz. 2004. Mechanisms of Theory Formation in Young Children. *Trends in Cognitive Sciences* 8:371–77.

Goren-Inbar, N. 1986. A Figurine from the Acheulian Site of Berekhat Ram. *Mitekufat Haeven* 19:7–12.

———, ed. 1990. *Quneitra: A Mousterian Site on the Golan Heights*. Qedem 31. Jerusalem: Institute of Archaeology, Hebrew University of Jerusalem.

Goren-Inbar, N., and S. Peltz. 1995. Additional Remarks on the Berekhat Ram Figurine. *Rock Art Research* 12(2): 131–32.

Gradstein, F.M., J.G. Ogg, and A.G. Smith, eds. 2004. *A Geologic Time Scale 2004*. Cambridge: Cambridge University Press.

Graham, R.W., and E.L. Lundelius, Jr. 1984. Coevolutionary Disequilibrium and Pleistocene Extinctions. In *Quaternary Extinctions. A Prehistoric Revolution*, ed. P.S. Martin and R.G. Klein. Tucson, AZ: University of Arizona Press.

Graham, R.W., E.L. Lundelius, Jr., M.A. Graham, et al. 1996. Spatial Response of Mammals to Late Quaternary Environmental Fluctuations. *Science* 272(5268): 1601–6.

Gravina, B., P. Mellars, and C.B. Ramsey. 2005. Radiocarbon Dating of Interstratified Neanderthal and Early Modern Human Occupations at the Châtelperronian Type-Site. *Nature* 438:51–56.

Green, R.E., J. Krause, S.E. Ptak, et al. 2006. Analysis of One Million Base Pairs of Neanderthal DNA. *Nature* 44:330–36.

Green, R.E., A.-S. Malaspinas, J. Krause, et al. 2008. A Complete Neandertal Mitochondrial Genome Sequence Determined by High-throughput Sequencing. *Cell* 134:416–26.

Green, R.E., J. Krause, A.W. Briggs, et al. 2010. A Draft Sequence of the Neandertal Genome. *Science* 328(5979): 710–22.

Greenfield, P.M. 1991. Language, Tools, and Brain: The Ontogeny and Phylogeny of Hierarchically Organized Sequential Behavior. *Behavioral and Brain Sciences* 14(4): 531–50.

Greenfield, P.M., and E.S. Savage-Rumbaugh. 1991. Imitation, Grammatical Development, and the Invention of Protogrammar by an Ape. In *Biological and Behavioral Determinants of Language and Development,* ed. N.A. Krasnegor, D.M. Rumbaugh, R.L. Schieffelbusch, and M. Studdert-Kennedy, pp. 235–58. Hillsdale, NJ: Lawrence Erlbaum Associates.

Grezes, J., J.L. Armony, J. Rowe, and R.E. Passingham. 2003. Activations Related to "Mirror" and "Canonical" Neurons in the Human Brain: An fMRI Study. *Neuroimage* 18(4): 928–37.

Groszer, M., D.A. Keays, R.M.J. Deacon, et al. 2008. Impaired Synaptic Plasticity and Motor Learning in Mice with a Point Mutation Implicated in Human Speech Deficits. *Current Biology* 18:354–62.

Grün, R., and C. Stringer. 2000. Tabun Revisited: Revised ESR Chronology and New ESR and U-Series Analyses of Dental Material from Tabun C1. *Journal of Human Evolution* 39:601–12.

Grush, R. 1997. The Architecture of Representation. *Philosophical Psychology* 10:5–23.

Gulz, A. 1991. *The Planning of Action as a Cognitive and Biological Phenomenon.* Lund University Cognitive Studies 2. Lund.

Gurven, M., and C. von Rueden. 2006. Hunting, Social Status and Biological Fitness. *Social Biology* 53:81–99.

Gurven, M., and K. Hill. 2009. Why Do Men Hunt? A Re-evaluation of "Man the Hunter" and the Sexual Division of Labor. *Current Anthropology* 50(1): 51–74.

Guthrie, R.D. 1984. Mosaics, Allelochemics and Nutrients. In *Quaternary Extinctions. A Prehistoric Revolution,* ed. P.S. Martin and R.G. Klein, pp. 259–98. Tucson, AZ: University of Arizona Press.

—— 2001. Origin and Causes of the Mammoth Steppe: A Story of Cloud Cover,

Woolly Mammoth Tooth Pits, Buckles, and Inside-Out Beringia. *Quaternary Science Reviews* 20:549–74.

—— 2005. *The Nature of Paleolithic Art*. Chicago: Chicago University Press.

Habgood, P.J., and N.R. Franklin. 2008. The Revolution that Didn't Arrive: A Review of Pleistocene Sahul. *Journal of Human Evolution* 55(2): 187–222.

Hagoort, P. 2005. On Broca, Brain, and Binding: A New Framework. *Trends in Cognitive Science* 9(9): 416–23.

Haidle, M.N. 2010. Working-memory Capacity and the Evolution of Modern Cognitive Potential: Implications from Animal and Early Human Tool Use. *Current Anthropology* 51(suppl. 1): S149–66.

Haile-Selassie, Y. 2001. Late Miocene Hominoids from the Middle Awash, Ethiopia. *Nature* 412:178–81.

Haile-Selassie, Y., G. Suwa, and T.D. White. 2004. Late Miocene Teeth from Middle Awash, Ethiopia, and Early Hominid Dental Evolution. *Science* 303(5663): 1503–7.

Haldane, J.B.S. 1927. *Possible Worlds and Other Essays*. London: Chatto and Windus.

Hallowell, A.I. 1955. *Culture and Experience*. Philadelphia: University of Pennsylvania Press.

Hämäläinen, Pekka. 2008. *The Comanche Empire*. New Haven: Yale University Press.

Hamdan, F.F., H. Daoud, D. Rochefort, et al. 2010. De Novo Mutations in FOXP1 in Cases with Intellectual Disability, Autism, and Language Impairment. *American Journal of Human Genetics* 87:671–78.

Hamilton, W.D. 1964. The Genetical Evolution of Social Behavior. *Journal of Theoretical Biology* 7(1): 1–16.

Hammerschmidt, K., and J. Fischer. 2008. Constraints in Primate Vocal Production. In *The Evolution of Communicative Creativity: From Fixed Signals to Contextual Flexibility*, ed. U. Griebel and K. Oller, pp. 93–119. Cambridge, MA: MIT Press.

Hamzei, F., M. Rijntjes, C. Dettmers, et al. 2003. The Human Action Recognition System and Its Relationship to Broca's Area: An fMRI Study. *Neuroimage* 19(3): 637–44.

Hardy, B. 2010. Climatic Variability and Plant Food Distribution in Pleistocene Europe: Implications for Neanderthal Diet and Subsistence. *Quaternary Science Reviews* 29:662–79.

Hare, B., A.P. Melis, V. Woods, et al. 2007. Tolerance Allows Bonobos to Outperform Chimpanzees in a Cooperative Task. *Current Biology* 17:619–23.

Harris, M. 1999. *Theories of Culture in Postmodern Times*. Walnut Creek, CA: Altamira Press.

Harris, P., and M. Núñez. 1996. Understanding of Permission Rules by Pre-school

Children. *Child Development* 67:1572–91.

Harris, P., M. Núñez, and C. Brett. 2001. Let's Swap: Early Understanding of Social Exchange by British and Nepali Children. *Memory and Cognition* 29:757–64.

Harvati, K., S.R. Frost, and K.P. McNulty. 2004. Neanderthal Taxonomy Reconsidered: Implications of 3D Primate Models of Intra- and Interspecific Differences. *Proceedings of the National Academy of Sciences USA* 101(5): 1147–52.

Harvey, P.H., and T.H. Clutton-Brock. 1985. Life History Variation in Primates. *Evolution* 39:559–81.

Hauk, O., I. Johnsrude, and F. Pulvermuller. 2004. Somatotopic Representation of Action Words in Human Motor and Premotor Cortex. *Neuron* 41(2): 301–7.

Hauser, M. 2000. *Wild Minds: What Animals Really Think*. London: Penguin Books.

Hauser, M.D., N. Chomsky, and W.T. Fitch. 2002. The Faculty of Language: What Is It, Who Has It, and How Did It Evolve? 10.1126/science.298.5598.1569. *Science* 298(5598): 1569–79.

Hawkes, J. 2012. Dynamics of Genetic and Morphological Variability within Neandertals. *Journal of Anthropological Sciences* 90:1–17.

Hawkes, K. 1991. Showing Off: Tests of Another Hypothesis about Men's Foraging Goals. *Ethology and Sociobiology* 11:29–54.

Hawkes, K., and R. Bliege Bird. 2002. Showing Off, Handicap Signaling and the Evolution of Men's Work. *Evolutionary Anthropology* 11(1): 58–67.

Hawkes, K., J.F. O'Connell, and N.G. Blurton Jones. 2001. Hadza Meat Sharing. *Evolution and Human Behavior* 22:113–42.

Hawkes K., J.F. O'Connell, and J.E. Coxworth. 2010. Family Provisioning Is Not the Only Reason Men Hunt. *Current Anthropology* 51(2): 259–64.

Hawkes, K., J.F. O'Connell, N.G. Blurton Jones, et al. 1998. Grandmothering, Menopause, and the Evolution of Human Life Histories. *Proceedings of the National Academy of Sciences USA* 95:1336–39.

Hayden, B. 1993. The Cultural Capacities of Neandertals: A Review and Reevaluation. *Journal of Human Evolution* 24:113–46.

Heesy, C.P. 2008. Ecomorphology of Orbit Orientation and the Adaptive Significance of Binocular Vision in Primates and Other Mammals. *Brain, Behavior and Evolution* 71:54–67.

Hemmer, Helmut. 2007. Estimation of Basic Life History Data of Fossil Hominoids. In *Handbook of Paleoanthropology*. Vol. I, *Principles, Methods and Approaches*, ed. W. Henke, I. Tattersall, and T. Hardt, pp. 587–619. Berlin: Springer.

Hendy, I.L., and J.P. Kennett. 2000. Dansgaard-Oeschger Cycles and the California Current System: Planktonic Foraminiferal Response to Rapid Climate Change in Santa Barbara Basin, Ocean Drilling Program Hole 893A. *Paleooceanography* 15(1): 30–42.

Henrich, J. 2004. Demography and Cultural Evolution: Why Adaptive Cultural Processes Produced Maladaptive Losses in Tasmania. *American Antiquity* 69(2): 197–214.

Henrich, J., and F. Gil-White. 2001. The Evolution of Prestige: Freely Conferred Deference as a Mechanism for Enhancing the Benefits of Cultural Transmission. *Evolution and Human Behavior* 22:165–96.

Henrich, J., and R. Boyd. 1998. The Evolution of Conformist Transmission and the Emergence of Between-Group Differences. *Evolution and Human Behavior* 19:215–41.

Henrich, J., and R. McElreath. 2003. The Evolution of Cultural Evolution. *Evolutionary Anthropology* 12:123–35.

Henrich, J., S. Heine, and A. Norenzayan. 2010. The Weirdest People in the World? *Behavioral and Brain Sciences* 33:61–83.

Henrich, J., R. Boyd, S. Bowles, et al. 2005. "Economic Man" in Cross-cultural Perspective: Behavioral Experiments in 15 Small-scale Societies. *Behavioral and Brain Sciences* 28:795–855.

Henry, A.G., A.S. Brooks, and D.R. Piperno. 2011. Microfossils in Calculus Demonstrate Consumption of Plants and Cooked Foods in Neanderthal Diets (Shanidar III, Iraq; Spy I and II, Belgium). *Proceedings of the National Academy of Sciences USA* 108:486–91.

Henry, D.O. 1995. *Prehistoric Cultural Ecology and Evolution: Insights from Southern Jordan.* New York: Plenum.

—— 2012. The Palimpsest Problem, Hearth Pattern Analysis and Middle Paleolithic Site Structure. *Quaternary International* 247:246–66.

Henry, D.O., H.J. Hietala, A.M. Rosen, et al. 2004. Human Behavioral Organization in the Middle Paleolithic: Were Neanderthals Different? *American Anthropologist* 106:17–31.

Henshilwood, C.S., and C.W. Marean. 2006. Remodelling the Origins of Modern Human Behavior. In *The Human Genome and Africa. Part One: History and Archaeology.* ed. H. Soodyall, pp. 31–46. Pretoria: Human Sciences Research Council.

Henshilwood, C.S., C.W. Marean, and commentators. 2003. The Origin of Modern Human Behavior. *Current Anthropology* 44(5): 627–51.

Henshilwood, C.S., and J. Sealy. 1995. Bone Artefacts from the Middle Stone Age at Blombos Cave, Southern Cape, South Africa. *Current Anthropology* 38:890–95.

Henshilwood, C.S., F. d'Errico, R. Yates, et al. 2002. Emergence of Modern Human

Behavior: Middle Stone Age Engravings from South Africa. *Science* 295 (5558): 1278–80.

Henshilwood, C.S., F. d'Errico, M.Vanhaeren, et al. 2004. Middle Stone Age Shell Beads from South Africa. *Science* 304 (5669): 404.

Henshilwood, C.S., F. d'Errico, K.L. van Niekerk, et al. 2011. A 100,000-Year-Old Ochre-Processing Workshop at Blombos Cave, South Africa. *Science* 334:219–22.

Hernandez-Aguilar, R.A., J. Moore, and T.R. Pickering. 2007. Savanna Chimpanzees Use Tools to Harvest the Underground Storage Organs of Plants. *Proceedings of the National Academy of Sciences USA* 104:19210–13.

Heyes, C.M. 2000. Evolutionary Psychology in the Round. In *The Evolution of Cognition,* ed. C.M. Heyes and L. Huber, pp. 3–22. Cambridge, MA: MIT Press.

—— 2001. Causes and Consequences of Imitation. *Trends in Cognitive Science* 5(6): 253–61.

Heyes, C.M., and B.G. Galef, eds. 1996. *Social Learning in Animals: The Roots of Culture.* San Diego: Academic Press.

Higham, T., T. Compton, C. Stringer, et al. 2011. The Earliest Evidence for Anatomically Modern Humans in Northwestern Europe. *Nature* 479:521–24.

Higuchi, S., T. Chaminade, H. Imamizu, and M. Kawato. 2009. Shared Neural Correlates for Language and Tool Use in Broca's Area. *Neuroreport* 20(15): 1376–81.

Hikosaka, O., K. Sakai, S. Miyauchi, et al. 1996. Activation of Human Presupplementary Motor Area in Learning of Sequential Procedures: A Functional MRI Study. *Journal of Neurophysiology* 76(1): 617–21.

Hill, K. 2009. Animal "Culture"? In *The Question of Animal Culture,* ed. K.N. Laland and B.G. Galef, pp. 269–87. Cambridge, MA: Harvard University Press.

Hill, K., R.S. Walker, M. Božičević, J. Eder, et al. 2011. Co-residence Patterns in Hunter-Gatherer Societies Show Unique Human Social Structure. *Science* 331:1286–89.

Hill, R.S., and C.A. Walsh. 2005. Molecular Insights into Human Brain Evolution. *Nature* 437:64–67.

Hinde, R.A. 1970. *Animal Behaviour: A Synthesis of Ethology and Comparative Psychology.* 2d ed. New York: McGraw-Hill.

—— 1982. *Ethology: Its Nature and Relations with Other Sciences.* New York: Oxford University Press.

Hoberg, E.P., N.L. Alkire, A. de Queiroz, et al. 2001. Out of Africa: Origins of the *Taenia* Tapeworms in Humans. *Proceedings of the Royal Society of London B* 268:781–87.

Hobolth, A., O.F. Christensen, T. Mailund, and M.H. Schierup. 2007. Genomic Relationships and Speciation Times of Human, Chimpanzee, and Gorilla Inferred from a Coalescent Hidden Markov Model. *PLoS Genetics* 3:e7.

Hockett, B., and J.A. Haws. 2005. Nutritional Ecology and the Human Demography of Neandertal Extinction. *Quaternary International* 137:21–34.

Hockett, C.F. 1960. Logical Considerations in the Study of Animal Communication. In *Animal Sounds and Communication,* ed. W.E. Lanyon and W.N. Tavolga, pp. 392–430. Washington, DC: American Institute of Biological Sciences.

Hodder, I. 1985. Post-processual Archaeology. *Advances in Archaeological Method and Theory* 8:1–26.

Hoffecker J.F. 2002. *Desolate Landscapes: Ice Age Settlement in Eastern Europe.* Piscataway, NJ: Rutgers University Press.

Hoffecker, J.F., and S.A. Elias. 2007. *Human Ecology of Beringia.* New York: Columbia University Press.

Hoffecker, J.F., G. Baryshnikov, and O. Potapova. 1991. Vertebrate Remains from the Mousterian Site of Il'skaya I (Northern Caucasus, U.S.S.R.): New Analysis and Interpretation. *Journal of Archaeological Science* 18:113–47.

Hoffman, M.L. 1981. Is Altruism Part of Human Nature? *Journal of Personality and Social Psychology* 40(1): 121–37.

—— 2000. *Empathy and Moral Development: Implications for Caring and Justice.* New York: Cambridge University Press.

Hohmann, G., and B. Fruth. 2003. Culture in Bonobos? Between-Species and Within-Species Variation in Behavior. *Current Anthropology* 44(4): 563–71.

Holloway, R.L. 1966. Cranial Capacity, Neural Reorganization, and Hominid Evolution: A Search for More Suitable Parameters. *American Anthropologist* 68:103–21.

—— 1975. Early Hominid Endocasts: Volumes, Morphology, and Significance for Hominid Evolution. In *Primate Functional Morphology and Evolution,* ed. R. Tuttle, pp. 393–415. The Hague: Mouton.

—— 1979. Brain Size, Allometry and Reorganization: Toward a Synthesis. In *Development and Evolution of Brain Size: Behavioral Implications,* ed. M.E. Hahn, C. Jensen, and B.C. Dudeck, pp. 59–89. New York: Academic Press.

—— 1983. Human Paleontological Evidence Relevant to Language Behavior. *Human Neurobiology* 2:105–14.

—— 1999. Evolution of the Human Brain. In *Handbook of Human Symbolic Evolution,* ed. A. Lock and C.R. Peters, pp. 74–125. Malden, MA: Blackwell.

Holloway, R.L., D.C. Broadfield, and M. Yuan. 2004. *The Human Fossil Record.* Vol. 3, *Brain Endocasts: The Paleoneurological Evidence.* Hoboken, NJ: Wiley-Liss.

Hollox, E.J., J.A. Armour, and J.C. Barber. 2003. Extensive Normal Copy Number Variation of a β-defensin Antimicrobial-Gene Cluster. *American Journal of Human*

Genetics 73:591–600.

Hope, G., A.P. Kershaw, S. van der Kaars, et al. 2004. History of Vegetation and Habitat Change in the Austral-Asian Region. *Quaternary International* 118-119:103–26.

Hopkinson, T. 2011. The Transmission of Technological Skills in the Palaeolithic: Insights from Metapopulation Ecology. In *Investigating Archaeological Cultures: Cultural Transmission and Material Culture Variability*, ed. B. Roberts and M. Vander Linden, pp. 229–44. New York: Springer.

Horner, V., D. Proctor, K.E. Bonnie, et al. 2010. Prestige Affects Cultural Learning in Chimpanzees. *PLoS ONE* 5(5): e10625.

Hoshi, E., and J. Tanji. 2004. Differential Roles of Neuronal Activity in the Supplementary and Presupplementary Motor Areas: From Information Retrieval to Motor Planning and Execution. *Journal of Neurophysiology* 92(6): 3482–99.

Houghton, P. 1993. Neandertal Supralaryngeal Vocal Tract. *American Journal of Physical Anthropology* 90:139–46.

Hovers, E., and A. Belfer-Cohen. 2006. Now You See It, Now You Don't: Modern Human Behavior in the Middle Paleolithic. In *Transitions before the Transition: Evolution and Stability in the Middle Paleolithic and Middle Stone Age,* ed. E. Hovers and S.L. Kuhn, pp. 295–304. New York: Springer.

Hovers, E., and S.L. Kuhn, eds. 2006. *Transitions before the Transition: Evolution and Stability in the Middle Paleolithic and Middle Stone Age.* New York: Springer.

Hrdy, S.B. 1999. *Mother Nature: A History of Mothers, Infants, and Natural Selection.* New York: Pantheon Books.

Hublin, J.J. 2009. The Origin of Neandertals. *Proceedings of the National Academy of Sciences USA* 106(38): 16022–27.

Hudjashov, G., T. Kivisild, P.A. Underhill, et al. 2007. Revealing the Prehistoric Settlement of Australia by Y Chromosome and mtDNA Analysis. *Proceedings of the National Academy of Sciences USA* 104:8726–30.

Hughes, A.L., and M. Nei. 1988. Pattern of Nucleotide Substitution at Major Histocompatibility Complex Class in Loci Reveals Overdominant Selection. *Nature* 335:167–70.

Humphrey, N.K. 1976. The Social Function of Intellect. In *Growing Points in Ethology,* ed. P.P.G. Bateson and R.A. Hinde, pp. 303–17. Cambridge: Cambridge University Press.

—— 1993. *A History of the Mind.* London: Vintage Books.

Hunt, G.R., and R.D. Gray. 2003. Diversification and Cumulative Evolution in New Caledonian Crow Tool Manufacture. *Proceedings of the Royal Society of London B* 270:867–74.

—— 2007. Parallel Tool Industries in New Caledonian Crows. *Biology Letters* 3:173–75.

Hunt, K.D. 1996. The Postural Feeding Hypothesis: An Ecological Model for the Evolution of Bipedalism. *South African Journal of Science* 92:77–90.

Huntley, B., and J.R.M. Allen. 2003. Glacial Environments III: Paleo-vegetation Patterns in Last Glacial Europe. In *Neanderthals and Modern Humans in the European Landscape During the Last Glaciation: Archaeological Results of the Stage 3 Project,* ed. T.H. van Andel, W. Davies, and L. Aiello, pp. 79–102. Cambridge: McDonald Institute for Archaeological Research.

Hurford, J.R. 1990. Beyond the Roadblock in Linguistic Evolution Studies. *Behavioral and Brain Sciences* 13:736–37.

—— 1998. Introduction: The Emergence of Syntax. In *Approaches to the Evolution of Language: Social and Cognitive Biases,* ed. J.R. Hurford, M. Studdert-Kennedy, and C. Knight, pp. 299–304. Cambridge: Cambridge University Press.

—— 2003. The Neural Basis of Predicate-Argument Structure. *Behavioral and Brain Sciences* 26(3): 261–83.

—— 2007. *The Origins of Meaning.* Oxford: Oxford University Press.

Hurford, J.R., M. Studdert-Kennedy, and C. Knight, eds. 1998. *Approaches to the Evolution of Language: Social and Cognitive Biases.* Cambridge: Cambridge University Press.

Hutchison, W.D., K.D. Davis, A.M. Lozano, et al. 1999. Pain-related Neurons in the Human Cingulate Cortex. *Nature Neuroscience* 2(5): 403–5.

Iacoboni, M., R.P. Woods, M. Brass, et al. 1999. Cortical Mechanisms of Human Imitation. *Science* 286(5449): 2526–28.

Iafrate, A.J., L. Feuk, M.N. Rivera, et al. 2004. Detection of Large-scale Variation in the Human Genome. *Nature Genetics* 36:949–51.

Ingason, A., T. Sigmundsson, S. Steinberg, et al. 2007. Support for Involvement of the AHI1 Locus in Schizophrenia. *European Journal of Human Genetics* 15:988–91.

Ingman, M., H. Kaessmann, S. Pääbo, and U. Gyllensten. 2000. Mitochondrial Genome Variation and the Origin of Modern Humans. *Nature* 408:708–13.

International Human Genome Sequencing Consortium (IHGSC). 2004. Finishing the Euchromatic Sequence of the Human Genome. *Nature* 431:931–45.

Irons, W., and L. Cronk. 2000. Two Decades of a New Paradigm. In *Adaptation and Human Behavior: An Anthropological Perspective,* ed. L. Cronk, N. Chagnon, and W. Irons, pp. 3–26. New York: Aldine de Gruyter.

Isaac, G.L. 1976. Stages of Cultural Elaboration in the Pleistocene: Possible Archaeological Indicators of the Development of Language Capabilities. *Annals of the New York Academy of Sciences* 280:275–88.

—— 1977. *Olorgesailie: Archaeological Studies of a Middle Pleistocene Lake Basin in Kenya.* Chicago: University of Chicago Press.

—— 1983. Bones in Contention: Competing Explanations for the Juxtaposition of Early Pleistocene Artifacts and Faunal Remains. In *Animals and Archaeology.* Vol. 1, *Hunters and Their Prey,* ed. J. Clutton-Brock and C. Grigson, pp. 3–20. Oxford: British Archaeological Reports.

Jablonski, N.G. 2004. The Evolution of Human Skin and Skin Color. *Annual Review of Anthropology* 33:585–623.

Jablonski, N.G., and G. Chaplin. 1993. Origin of Habitual Terrestrial Bipedalism in the Ancestor of the *Hominidae. Journal of Human Evolution* 24:259–80.

—— 2010. Skin Pigmentation as an Adaptation to UV Radiation. *Proceedings of the National Academy of Sciences USA* 107 (Suppl. 2): 8962–68.

Jackendoff, R. 1987. *Consciousness and the Computational Mind.* New York: Basic Books.

—— 1999. Possible Stages in the Evolution of the Language Capacity. *Trends in Cognitive Science* 3:272–79.

—— 2002. *Foundations of Language.* Oxford: Oxford University Press.

Jackendoff, R., and S. Pinker. 2005. The Nature of the Language Faculty and Its Implications for Evolution of Language (Reply to Fitch, Hauser, and Chomsky). *Cognition* 97:211–25.

Jackson, S.T., and J.W. Williams. 2004. Modern Analogs of Quaternary Paleoecology: Here Today, Gone Yesterday, Gone Tomorrow? *Annual Review of Earth and Planetary Sciences* 32:495–537.

Jacob, P., and M. Jeannerod. 2005. The Motor Theory of Social Cognition: A Critique. *Trends in Cognitive Sciences* 9(1): 21–25.

Jacobs, Z., R.G. Roberts, R.F. Galbraith, et al. 2008. Ages for the Middle Stone Age of Southern Africa: Implications for Human Behavior and Dispersal. *Science* 322:733–35.

James, H.V.A., and M.D. Petraglia. 2005. Modern Human Origins and the Evolution of Behavior in the Later Pleistocene Record of South Asia. *Current Anthropology* 46:S3–27.

James, W. 1890. *Principles of Psychology.* New York: Holt.

Jaubert, J., M. Lorblanchet, H. Laville, et al. 1990. *Les Chasseurs d'Aurochs de La Borde. Un Site du Paléolithique Moyen (Livernon, Lot).* Documents d'Archéologie Française, No. 27. Editions de la Maison des sciences de l'Homme, Paris.

Jensen, K., B. Hare, J. Call, and M. Tomasello. 2006. What's in It for Me? Self-regard Precludes Altruism and Spite in Chimpanzees. *Proceedings of the Royal Society of London B* 273:1013–21.

Jerison, H.J. 1973. *Evolution of the Brain and Intelligence.* New York: Academic Press.

—— 1976. Discussion Paper: The Paleoneuraology of Language. In *Origins and Evolution of Language and Speech,* ed. H.B. Steklis, S.R. Harnad, and J. Lancaster, pp. 370–82. Annals of the New York Academy of Sciences 280.

—— 1982. The Evolution of Biological Intelligence. In *Handbook of Human Intelligence,* ed. R.J. Sternberg, pp. 723–91. Cambridge: Cambridge University Press.

Jespersen, O. [1895]1983. *Progress in Language.* Amsterdam Classics in Linguistics 17. Amsterdam: John Benjamins Publishing.

Johansen-Berg, H., T.E. Behrens, M.D. Robson, et al. 2004. Changes in Connectivity Profiles Define Functionally Distinct Regions in Human Medial Frontal Cortex. *Proceedings of the National Academy of Sciences USA* 101(36): 13335–40.

Johansson, S. 2005. *Origins of Language: Constraints on Hypotheses.* Philadelphia: John Benjamins Publishing.

Johnson, M.E., L. Viggiano, J.A. Bailey, et al. 2001. Positive Selection of a Gene Family during the Emergence of Humans and African Apes. *Nature* 413:514–19.

Johnson-Frey, S.H. 2004. The Neural Bases of Complex Tool Use in Humans. *Trends in Cognitive Sciences* 8(2): 71–8.

Jolly, A. 1966. Lemur Social Behavior and Primate Intelligence. *Science* 153:501–6.

Kahneman, D. 2002. Maps of Bounded Rationality: A Perspective on Intuitive Judgment and Choice. Nobel laureate acceptance speech. Available at http://nobelprize.org/economics/laureates/2002/kahneman-lecture.html.

Kaminski, J., J. Riedel, J. Call, and M. Tomasello. 2005. Domestic Goats, *Capra hircus,* Follow Gaze Direction and Use Social Cues in an Object Task. *Animal Behaviour* 69:11–18.

Kaplan, H. 1996. A Theory of Fertility and Parental Investment in Traditional and Modern Human Societies. *American Journal of Physical Anthropology* 101(S23): 91–135.

Kaplan, H., and M. Gurven. 2005. The Natural History of Human Food Sharing and Cooperation: A Review and a New Multi-Individual Approach to the Negotiation of Norms. In *Moral Sentiments and Material Interests: On the Foundations of Cooperation in Economic Life,* ed. H. Gintis, S. Bowles, R. Boyd, and E. Fehr, pp. 75–114. Cambridge, MA: MIT Press.

Kaplan, H., and K. Hill. 1992. The Evolutionary Ecology of Food Acquisition. In *Evolutionary Ecology and Human Behavior,* ed. E.A. Smith and B. Winterhalder, pp. 167–201. New York: Aldine.

Kaplan, H., K. Hill, J. Lancaster, and A. Hurtado. 2000. A Theory of Human Life History Evolution: Diet, Intelligence, and Longevity. *Evolutionary Anthropology*

9:156–85.

Kappelman, J. 1996. The Evolution of Body Mass and Relative Brain Size in Fossil Hominids. *Journal of Human Evolution* 30:243–76.

Karkanas, P., J.-P. Rigaud, J.F. Simek, et al. 2002. Ash, Bones and Guano: A Study of the Minerals and Phytolithis in the Sediments of Grotte XVI, Dordogne, France. *Journal of Archaeological Science* 29:721–32.

Karmiloff-Smith, A. 1992. *Beyond Modularity: A Developmental Perspective on Cognitive Science*. Cambridge, MA: MIT Press.

Kaufman, D. 2002. Redating the Social Revolution: The Case for the Middle Paleolithic. *Journal of Anthropological Research* 58(4): 477–92.

Kawai, M. 1965. Newly Acquired Pre-cultural Behavior of the Natural Troop of Japanese Monkeys on Koshima Islet. *Primates* 6(1): 1–30.

Kawamura, S. 1959. The Process of Sub-culture Propagation among Japanese Macaques. *Primates* 2(1): 43–60.

Keeley, L.H. 1978. Preliminary Microware Analysis of the Meer Assemblage. In *Les chasseurs de Meer*, ed. F. van Noten, pp. 73–86. Brugge: De Tempel.

—— 1980. *Experimental Determination of Stone Tool Uses*. Chicago: University of Chicago Press.

Keen, I. 2006. Constraints on the Development of Enduring Inequalities in Late Holocene Australia. *Current Anthropology* 47(1): 7–38.

Keil, F. 1989. *Concepts, Kinds, and Cognitive Development*. Cambridge, MA: MIT Press.

—— 1994. The Birth and Nurturance of Concepts by Domains: The Origins of Concepts of Living Things. In *Mapping the Mind*, ed. L.A. Hirschfeld and S.A. Gelman, pp. 234–54. Cambridge: Cambridge University Press.

Keith, A. 1948. *A New Theory of Human Evolution*. London: Watts.

Kelly, R. 1995. *The Foraging Spectrum*. Washington, DC: Smithsonian Institution Press.

Kelsall, J.P. 1968. *The Migratory Barren-Ground Caribou of Canada*. Canadian Wildlife Service Monograph 3. Ottawa: Queen's Printer.

Kenward, B., C. Rutza, A.A.S. Weira, and A. Kacelnik. 2006. Development of Tool Use in New Caledonian Crows: Inherited Action Patterns and Social Influences. *Animal Behaviour* 72:1329–43.

Keysar, B., S. Lin, and D. Barr. 2003. Limits on Theory of Mind Use in Adults. *Cognition* 89:25–41.

Keysers, C., and D.I. Perrett. 2004. Demystifying Social Cognition: A Hebbian Perspective. *Trends in Cognitive Science* 8(11): 501–7.

Keysers, C., B. Wicker, V. Gazzola, et al. 2004. A Touching Sight: SII/PV Activation during the Observation and Experience of Touch. *Neuron* 42(2): 335–46.

Khaitovich, P., B. Muetzel, X. She, et al. 2004. Regional Patterns of Gene Expression in Human and Chimpanzee Brains. *Genome Research* 14:1462–73.

Kilner, J.M., Y. Paulignan, and S.J. Blakemore. 2003. An Interference Effect of Observed Biological Movement on Action. *Current Biology* 13(6): 522–25.

Kilner, J.M., A. Neal, N. Weiskopf, et al. 2009. Evidence of Mirror Neurons in Human Inferior Frontal Gyrus. *Journal of Neuroscience* 29(32): 10153–59.

Kimbel, W.H., D.C. Johanson, and Y. Rak. 1997. Systematic Assessment of a Maxilla of *Homo* from Hadar, Ethiopia. *American Journal of Physical Anthropology* 103:235–62.

Kirby, S. 1998. Fitness and the Selective Adaptation of Language. In *Approaches to the Evolution of Language: Social and Cognitive Biases,* ed. J.R. Hurford, M. Studdert-Kennedy, and C. Knight, pp. 359–83. Cambridge: Cambridge University Press.

——— 2000. Syntax without Natural Selection: How Compositionality Emerges from Vocabulary in a Population of Learners. In *The Evolutionary Emergence of Language: Social Function and the Origins of Linguistic Form,* ed. C. Knight, M. Studdert-Kennedy, and J. Hurford, pp. 303–23. Cambridge: Cambridge University Press.

——— 2001. Spontaneous Evolution of Linguistic Structure: An Iterated Learning Model of the Emergence of Regularity and Irregularity. *IEEE Journal of Evolutionary Computation* 5:101–10.

Kislev, M.E., D.I. Nadel, and I. Carmi. 1992. Epipalaeolithic (19,000 BP) Cereal and Fruit Diet at Ohalo II, Sea of Galilee, Israel. *Review of Palaeobotany and Palynology* 73:161–66.

Kitcher, P. 1985. *Vaulting Ambition: Sociobiology and the Quest for Human Nature.* Cambridge, MA: MIT Press.

Kivisild, T., P. Shen, D.P. Wall, et al. 2006. The Role of Selection in the Evolution of Human Mitochondrial Genomes. *Genetics* 172(1): 373–87.

Klein, J., and N. Takahata. 2002. *Where Do We Come From? The Molecular Evidence for Human Descent.* Berlin: Springer-Verlag.

Klein, R.G. 1979. Stone Age Exploitation of Animals in Southern Africa. *American Scientist* 67:151–60.

——— 1987. Reconstructing How Early People Exploited Animals: Problems and Prospects. In *The Evolution of Human Hunting,* ed. H. Nitecki and D.V. Nitecki, pp. 11–46. New York: Plenum Press.

——— 2000a. Archeology and the Evolution of Human Behavior. *Evolutionary Anthropology* 9(1): 17–36.

——— 2000b. The Earlier Stone Age of Southern Africa. *South African Archaeology Bulletin* 55:107–22.

——— 2003a. Commentary. *Current Anthropology* 44(5): 640–1.

—— 2003b. Whither the Neandertals? *Science* 299:1525–27.

—— 2009. *The Human Career: Human Biological and Cultural Origins.* 3rd ed. Chicago: University of Chicago Press.

Klein, R.G., and K. Cruz-Uribe. 1996. Exploitation of Large Bovids and Seals at Middle and Later Stone Age Sites in South Africa. *Journal of Human Evolution* 31(4): 315–34.

Klein, R.G., and B. Edgar. 2002. *The Dawn of Human Culture: A Bold New Theory on What Sparked the "Big Bang" of Human Consciousness.* New York: John Wiley.

Klein, R.G., K. Allwarden, and C. Wolf. 1983. Calculation and Interpretation of Ungulate Age Profiles from Dental Crown Heights. In *Hunter-Gatherer Economy in Prehistory: A European Perspective,* ed. G. Bailey, pp. 47–57. Cambridge: Cambridge University Press.

Kline, M.A., and R. Boyd. 2010. Population Size Predicts Technological Complexity in Oceania. *Proceedings of the Royal Society B* 277:2559–64.

Kluckhohn, C. 1942. Report to the Sub-Committee on Definitions of Culture. Committee on Conceptual Integration. Mimeographed.

—— 1949. *Mirror for Man: The Relation of Anthropology to Modern Life.* New York: Whittlesey House.

—— 1959. The Role of Evolutionary Thought in Anthropology. In *Evolution and Anthropology: A Centennial Appraisal,* ed. B.J. Meggers, pp. 144–57. Washington, DC: Anthropological Society of Washington

Kluckhohn, C., and D.C. Leighton. 1946. *The Navaho.* Oxford: Oxford University Press.

Knappet, C., ed. 2005. *Thinking Through Material Culture: An Inter-disciplinary Perspective.* Pittsburgh: University of Pennsylvania Press.

Knight, C., C. Power, and I. Watts. 1995. The Human Symbolic Revolution: A Darwinian Account. *Cambridge Archaeological Journal* 5(1): 1–27.

Knight, C., M. Studdert-Kennedy, and J. Hurford, eds. 2000. *The Evolutionary Emergence of Language: Social Function and the Origins of Linguistic Form.* Cambridge: Cambridge University Press.

Koechlin, E., and T. Jubault. 2006. Broca's Area and the Hierarchical Organization of Human Behavior. *Neuron* 50(6): 963–74.

Kohler, E., C. Keysers, M.A. Umilta, et al. 2002. Hearing Sounds, Understanding Actions: Action Representation in Mirror Neurons. *Science* 297(5582): 846–48.

Köhler, W. 1925. *Mentality of Apes,* trans. Ella Winter. London: Routledge and Kegan Paul.

Kohn, M., and S.J. Mithen. 1999. Handaxes: Products of Sexual Selection? *Antiquity* 73:518–26.

Koller, J., U. Baumer, and D. Mania. 2001. High-tech in the Middle Paleolithic: Neandertal Manufactured Pitch Identified. *European Journal of Archaeology* 4:385–97.

Konopka, G., J.M. Bomar, K. Winden, et al. 2009. Human-specific Transcriptional Regulation of CNS Development Genes by FOXP2. *Nature* 462:213–17.

Kornack, D.R., and P. Rakic. 1998. Changes in Cell-cycle Kinetics during the Development and Evolution of Primate Neocortex. *Proceedings of the National Academy of Sciences USA* 95:1242–46.

Koumouzelis, M., B. Ginter, J. Kozlowski, et al. 2001. The Early Upper Paleolithic in Greece: The Excavations in Klisoura Cave. *Journal of Archaeological Science* 28:515–39.

Kouprina, N., A. Pavlicek, G.H. Mochida, et al. 2004. Accelerated Evolution of the ASPM Gene Controlling Brain Size Begins Prior to Human Brain Expansion. *PLoS Biology* 2:e126.

Kozlowski, J. 1982. *Excavation in the Bacho Kiro Cave (Bulgaria) Final Report.* Warsaw: Polish Scientific Publishers.

Kramer, K. 2005. Children's Help and the Pace of Reproduction: Cooperative Breeding in Humans. *Evolutionary Anthropology* 14:224–37.

Krause, J., C. Lalueza-Fox, L. Orlando, et al. 2007a. The Derived FOXP2 Variant of Modern Humans Was Shared with Neandertals. *Current Biology* 17:1908–12.

Krause, J., L. Orlando, D. Serre, et al. 2007b. Neandertals in Central Asia and Siberia. *Nature* 449:902–4.

Krawczyk, D.C. 2002. Contributions of the Prefrontal Cortex to the Neural Basis of Human Decision Making. *Neuroscience and Biobehavioral Reviews* 26(6): 631–64.

Kroeber, A.L. 1923. *Anthropology.* New York: Harcourt, Brace.

—— 1928. Sub-human Culture Beginnings. *Quarterly Review of Biology* 3:325–42.

Kroeber, A.L., and C. Kluckhohn. 1952. *Culture: A Critical Review of Concepts and Definitions.* Cambridge, MA: Peabody Museum.

Krubitzer, L. 1995. The Organization of Neocortex in Mammals: Are Species Differences Really So Different? *Trends in Neuroscience* 18(9): 408–17.

Kruger, A.C., and M. Tomasello. 1996. Cultural Learning and Learning Culture. In *Handbook of Education and Human Development: New Models of Learning, Teaching and Schooling,* ed. D.R. Olson and N. Torrance, pp. 369–87. Cambridge, MA: Blackwell.

Kuckenburg, M. 2001. *Als der Mensch zum Schöpfer wurde: An den Wurzeln der Kultur.* Stuttgart: Klett-Cotta.

Kuhn, S.L., P.J. Brantingham, and K.W. Kerry. 2004. The Early Upper Paleolithic and the Origins of Modern Human Behavior. In *The Early Upper Paleolithic beyond*

Western Europe, ed. P.J. Brantingham, S.L. Kuhn, and K.W. Kerry, pp. 242–48. Berkeley, CA: University of California Press.

Kuhn, S.L., and M. Stiner. 2006. What's a Mother To Do? *Current Anthropology* 47(6): 953–80.

—— 2007. Paleolithic Ornaments: Implications for Cognition, Demography and Identity. *Diogenes* 54:40–48.

Kuhn, S.L., M. Stiner, S. Reese, and E. Güleç. 2001. Ornaments of the Earliest Upper Paleolithic: New Insights from the Levant. *Proceedings of the National Academy of Sciences USA* 98:7641–46.

Kuper, A. 1999. *Culture: The Anthropologist's Account.* Cambridge, MA: Harvard University Press.

Kusimba, S.B. 1999. Hunter-Gatherer Land Use Patterns in Late Stone Age East Africa. *Journal of Anthropological Archaeology* 18:165–200.

Lahr, M.M. 1996. *The Evolution of Modern Human Diversity.* Cambridge: Cambridge University Press.

Lahr, M.M., and R.A. Foley. 1998. Towards a Theory of Modern Human Origins: Geography, Demography, and Diversity in Recent Human Evolution. *Yearbook of Physical Anthropology* 41:137–76.

Lai, C.S.L., S.E. Fisher, J.A. Hurst, et al. 2001. A Forkhead-domain Gene Is Mutated in a Severe Speech and Language Disorder. *Nature* 413:519–23.

Laitman, J.T., R.C. Heimbuch, and E.S. Crelin. 1978. Developmental Change in a Basicranial Line and Its Relationship to the Upper Respiratory System in Living Primates. *American Journal of Anatomy* 152:467–82.

—— 1979. The Basicranium of Fossil Hominids as an Indicator of Their Upper Respiratory Systems. *American Journal of Physical Anthropology* 51:15–34.

Lakatos, I. 1970. Falsification and the Methodology of Scientific Research Programmes. In *Criticism and the Growth of Knowledge,* ed. I. Lakatos and A. Musgrave, pp. 91–196. Cambridge: Cambridge University Press.

Lakoff, G., and M. Johnson. 1999. *Philosophy in the Flesh: The Embodied Mind and Its Challenge to Western Thought.* New York: Basic Books.

Laland, K.N. 2007. Niche Construction, Human Behavioural Ecology and Evolutionary Psychology. In *Oxford Handbook of Evolutionary Psychology,* ed. R. Dunbar and L. Barrett, pp. 35–48. Oxford: Oxford University Press.

Laland, K.N., and B.G. Galef, eds. 2009. *The Question of Animal Culture.* Cambridge, MA: Harvard University Press.

Laland, K.N., and G. Brown. 2002. *Sense and Nonsense: Evolutionary Perspectives on Human Behaviour.* Oxford: Oxford University Press.

—— 2006. Niche Construction, Human Behavior and the Adaptive-lag Hypothesis. *Evolutionary Anthropology* 15:96–104.

Laland, K.N., J. Odling-Smee, and S. Myles. 2010. How Culture Shaped the Human Genome: Bringing Genetics and the Human Sciences Together. *Nature Reviews Genetics* 11(2): 137–48.

Laland, K.N., J.R. Kendal, and R.L. Kendal. 2009. Animal Culture: Problems and Solutions. In *The Question of Animal Culture,* ed. K.N. Laland and B.G. Galef, pp. 174–97. Cambridge, MA: Harvard University Press.

Laland, K.N., and W. Hoppitt. 2003. Do Animals Have Culture? *Evolutionary Anthropology* 12:150–59.

Lander, E.S., L.M. Linton, B. Birren, et al. 2001. Initial Sequencing and Analysis of the Human Genome. *Nature* 409(6822): 860–921.

Lari, M., E. Rizzi, L. Milani, et al. 2010. The Microcephalin Ancestral Allele in a Neanderthal Individual. *PLoS ONE* 5:e10648.

Larick, R., and R.L. Ciochon. 1996. The African Emergence and Early Asian Dispersals of the Genus *Homo. American Scientist* 84:538–51.

Larrasoaña, J.C., A.P. Roberts, E.J. Rohling, et al. 2003. Three Million Years of Monsoon Variability over the Northern Sahara. *Climate Dynamics* 21:689–98.

Laurence, S., and E. Margolis. 2001. The Poverty of the Stimulus Argument. *British Journal for the Philosophy of Science* 52:217–76.

Layton, R.H. 1997. *An Introduction to Theory in Anthropology.* Cambridge: Cambridge University Press.

Leakey, L.S.B. 1934. *Adam's Ancestors: An Up-to-Date Outline of What Is Known about the Origin of Man.* London: Longmans.

Leakey, L.S.B., P.V. Tobias, and J. Napier. 1964. A New Species of Genus *Homo* from Olduvai Gorge. *Nature* 6(4): 424–27.

Leakey, M.G., F. Spoor, F.H. Brown, et al. 2001. New Hominin Genus from Eastern Africa Shows Diverse Middle Pliocene Lineages. *Nature* 410:433–40.

Leavesley, M.G. 2007. A Shark-Tooth Ornament from Pleistocene Sahul. *Antiquity* 81(312): 308–15.

Lebedev, M.A., A. Messinger, J.D. Kralik, and S.P. Wise. 2004. Representation of Attended versus Remembered Locations in Prefrontal Cortex. *PLoS Biology* 2(11): e365.

Leigh, S. 1996. Evolution of Human Growth Spurts. *American Journal of Physical Anthropology* 101:455–74.

Leimar, O., and P. Hammerstein. 2001. Evolution of Cooperation through Indirect Reciprocation. *Proceedings of the Royal Society of London B* 268:745–53.

LeMay, M. 1975. The Language Capability of Neanderthal Man. *American Journal of Physical Anthropology* 42(1): 9–14.

—— 1976. Morphological Cerebral Asymmetries of Modern Man, Fossil Man, and Nonhuman Primates. In *Origins and Evolution of Language and Speech,* ed. H.B. Steklis, S.R. Harnad, and J. Lancaster, pp. 289–311. Annals of the New York Academy of Sciences 280.

—— 1985. Asymmetries of the Brains and Skulls of Nonhuman Primates. In *Cerebral Lateralization in Nonhuman Species,* ed. S.D. Glick, pp. 233–45. Orlando, FL: Academic Press.

Lemon, R., J. Armand, E. Olivier, and S. Edgley. 1999. Skilled Action and the Development of the Corticospinal Tract in Primates. In *Neurophysiology and Neuropsychology of Motor Development,* ed. K. Connolly and H. Forssberg, pp. 162–76. Cambridge: Cambridge University Press.

Leonard, W., and M.L. Robertson. 2000. Ecological Correlates for Home Range Variation in Primates: Implications for Human Evolution. In *On the Move: How and Why Animals Travel in Groups,* ed. S. Boinski and P.A. Garber, pp. 628–48. Chicago: University of Chicago Press.

Lepper, M.R. 1981. Intrinsic and Extrinsic Motivation in Children: Detrimental Effects of Superfluous Social Controls. In *Minnesota Symposium on Child Psychology,* Vol. 14, ed. W.A. Collins, pp. 155–214. Hillsdale, NJ: Erlbaum.

Lepper, M.R., D. Greene, and R.E. Nisbett. 1973. Undermining Children's Intrinsic Interest with Extrinsic Reward: A Test of the "Overjustification" Hypothesis. *Journal of Personality and Social Psychology* 28(1): 129–37.

Leroi-Gourhan, A. 1998. Shanidar et ses fleurs. *Paléorient* 24:79–88.

Lev, E., M. Kislev, and O. Bar-Yosef. 2005. Mousterian Vegetal Foods in Kebara Cave, Mt. Carmel. *Journal of Archaeological Science* 32:473–84.

Lévêque, F., and B. Vandermeersch. 1980. Découvertes de restes humains dans une niveau Castelperronien à St. Césaire (Charente-Maritime). *Comptes Rendus de l'Académie des Sciences de Paris* 291:187–89.

Levine, M.A. 1983. Mortality Models and the Interpretation of Horse Population Structure. In *Hunter-Gatherer Economy in Prehistory: A European Perspective,* ed. G. Bailey, pp. 23–46. Cambridge: Cambridge University Press.

Levins, R. 1966. The Strategy of Model-Building in Population Biology. *American Scientist* 54:421–31.

Lewis-Williams, D. 2002. *The Mind in the Cave: Consciousness and the Origins of Art.* London: Thames and Hudson.

Lewontin, R.C. 1987. Polymorphism and Heterosis: Old Wine in New Bottles and

Vice Versa. *Journal of the History of Biology* 20(3): 337–49.

Liberman, A.M., and I.G. Mattingly. 1985. The Motor Theory of Speech Perception Revised. *Cognition* 21:1–36.

Liebenberg, L. 1990. *The Art of Tracking: The Origin of Science.* Cape Town: David Philip.

Lieberman, D.E. 1999. Homology and Hominid Phylogeny: Problems and Potential Solutions. *Evolutionary Anthropology* 7(4): 142–51.

—— 2000. Ontogeny, Homology and Phylogeny in the Hominid Craniofacial Skeleton: The Problem of the Browridge. In *Development, Growth and Evolution: Implications for the Study of the Hominid Skeleton,* ed. P. O'Higgins and M.J. Cohn, pp. 85–122. London: Academic.

—— 2007. Homing In on Early *Homo. Nature* 449:291–92.

Lieberman, E., J.-B. Michel, J. Jackson, T. Tang, and M.A. Nowak. 2007. Quantifying the Evolutionary Dynamics of Language. *Nature* 449:713–16.

Lieberman, P. 1973. On the Evolution of Language: A Unified View. *Cognition* 2(1): 59–94.

—— 1975. *On the Origins of Language: An Introduction to the Evolution of Human Speech.* New York: Macmillan.

—— 1976. Structural Harmony and Neanderthal Speech: A Reply to LeMay. *American Journal of Physical Anthropology* 43:496.

—— 1984. *The Biology and Evolution of Language.* Cambridge, MA: Harvard University Press.

—— 1991. *Uniquely Human: The Evolution of Speech, Thought, and Selfless Behavior.* Cambridge, MA: Harvard University Press.

—— 2001. On the Neural Bases of Spoken Language. In *In the Mind's Eye: Multidisciplinary Approaches to the Evolution of Human Cognition,* ed. A. Nowell, pp. 172–86. Archaeology Series 13. Ann Arbor, MI: International Monographs in Prehistory.

—— 2007. The Evolution of Human Speech: Its Anatomical and Neural Bases. *Current Anthropology* 48(1): 39–66.

Lieberman, P., D.H. Klatt, and W.H. Wilson. 1969. Vocal Tract Limitations on the Vowel Repertoires of Rhesus Monkey and Other Nonhuman Primates. *Science* 164:1184–87.

Lieberman, P., and E.S. Crelin. 1971. On the Speech of Neanderthal Man. *Linguistic Inquiry* 2:203–22.

—— 1974. Speech and Neanderthal Man: A Reply to Carlisle and Siegel. *American Anthropologist* 76:323–25.

Lieberman, P., E.S. Crelin, and D.H. Klatt. 1972. Phonetic Ability and Related Anatomy of the Newborn and Adult Human, Neanderthal Man, and the Chimpanzee. *American Anthropologist* 74:287–307.

Lieberman, P., and J. Shea. 1994. Behavioral Differences between Archaic and Modern Humans in the Levantine Mousterian. *American Anthropologist* 96:300–32.

Liegeois, F., T. Baldeweg, A. Connelly, et al. 2003. Language fMRI Abnormalities Associated with FOXP2 Gene Mutation. *Nature Neuroscience* 6:1230–37.

Lindgren, K. 1997. Evolutionary Dynamics in Game-theoretic Models. In *The Economy as an Evolving Complex System* II, ed. B. Arthur, S. Durlauf, and D. Lane, pp. 337–67. Reading, MA: Addison-Wesley.

Lindly, J.M., and G.A. Clark. 1990. Symbolism and Modern Human Origins. *Current Anthropology* 31:233–61.

Liu, G., NISC Comparative Sequencing Program, S. Zhao, et al. 2003. Analysis of Primate Genomic Variation Reveals a Repeat Driven Expansion of the Human Genome. *Genome Research* 13:358–68.

Logan, M.H., and D.A. Schmittou. 1998. The Uniqueness of Crow Art: A Glimpse into the History of an Embattled People. *Montana: The Magazine of Western History* (summer): 58–71.

Lonsdorf, E.V. 2005. Sex Differences in the Development of Termite-fishing Skills in the Wild Chimpanzees, *Pan troglodytes schweinfurthii*, of Gombe National Park, Tanzania. *Animal Behaviour* 70:673–83.

Lordkipanidze, D., T. Jashashvili, A. Vekua, et al. 2007. Postcranial Evidence from Early *Homo* from Dmanisi, Georgia. *Nature* 449:305–10.

Loulergue, L., A. Schilt, R. Spahni, et al. 2008. Orbital and Millennial-scale Features of Atmospheric CH_4 over the Past 800,000 Years. *Nature* 453(7193): 383–86.

Lovejoy, C.O. 1981. The Origin of Man. *Science* 211:341–50.

Lycett, S.J., M. Collard, and W.C. McGrew. 2007. Phylogenetic Analyses of Behavior Support Existence of Culture among Wild Chimpanzees. *Proceedings of the National Academy of Sciences* 104:17588–92.

Macaulay, V., C. Hill, A. Achilli, et al. 2005. Single, Rapid Coastal Settlement of Asia Revealed by Analysis of Complete Mitochondrial Genomes. *Science* 308:1034–36.

Mace, R. 1998. The Coevolution of Human Fertility and Wealth Inheritance Strategies. *Philosophical Transactions of the Royal Society of London, Series B* 353:389–97.

—— 2000. An Adaptive Model of Human Reproductive Rate Where Wealth Is Inherited: Why People Have Small Families. In *Adaptation and Human Behaviour*, ed. L. Cronk, N. Chagnon, and W. Irons, pp. 261–82. New York: Aldine de Gruyter.

Madella, M., M. Jones, P. Goldberg, et al. 2002. The Exploitation of Plant Resources by Neanderthals in Amud Cave (Israel): The Evidence from Phytolith Studies.

Journal of Archaeological Science 29:703–19.

Mandl, I. 1961. Collagenases and Elastases. *Advances in Enzymology and Related Subjects of Biochemistry* 23:164–264.

Manica, A., W. Amos, F. Balloux, and T. Hanihara. 2007. The Effect of Ancient Population Bottlenecks on Human Phenotypic Variation. *Nature* 448:346–48.

Maravita, A., and A. Iriki. 2004. Tools for the Body (Schema). *Trends in Cognitive Sciences* 8(2): 79–86.

Marean, C.W., M. Bar-Mathews, J. Bernatchez, et al. 2007. Early Human Use of Marien Resources and Pigment in South Africa during the Middle Pleistocene. *Nature* 449:905–8.

Marin-Padilla, M. 1992. Ontogenesis of the Pyramidal Cell of the Mammalian Neocortex and Developmental Cytoarchitectonics: A Unifying Theory. *Journal of Computational Neurology* 321:223–40.

Marks, J. 1992. Chromosomal Evolution in Primates. In *Cambridge Encyclopedia of Human Evolution,* ed. S. Jones, R.D. Martin, and D.R. Pilbeam, pp. 298–302. Cambridge: Cambridge University Press.

Marlowe, F.W. 2000. Paternal Investment and the Human Mating System. *Behavioural Processes* 51:45–61.

—— 2003. The Mating System of Foragers in the Standard Cross-cultural Sample. *Cross-Cultural Research* 37:282–306.

—— 2005. Hunter-Gatherers and Human Evolution. *Evolutionary Anthropology* 14:54–67.

Marshack, A.A. 1971. *The Roots of Civilization: The Cognitive Beginnings of Man's First Art, Symbol, and Notation.* New York: McGraw-Hill.

—— 1976. Some Implications of the Paleolithic Symbolic Evidence for the Origins of Language. *Current Anthropology* 17:274–82.

—— 1990. Early Hominid Symbol and Evolution of the Human Capacity. In *The Emergence of Modern Humans: An Archaeological Perspective,* ed. P. Mellars, pp. 457–98. Ithaca, NY: Cornell University Press.

—— 1995. A Middle Paleolithic Symbolic Composition from the Golan Heights: The Earliest Known Depictive Image. *Current Anthropology* 37:356–65.

Martin, R.D. 1990. *Primate Origins and Evolution: A Phylogenetic Reconstruction.* Princeton: Princeton University Press.

Martrat, B., J.O. Grimalt, N.J. Shackleton, et al. 2007. Four Climate Cycles of Recurring Deep and Surface Water Destabilizations on the Iberian Margin. *Science* 317(5837): 502–7.

Matsuzawa, T. 1994. Field Experiments on Use of Stone Tools in the Wild. In *Chim-*

panzee Cultures, ed. R.W. Wrangham, W.C. McGrew, F. de Waal, and P. Heltne, pp. 351–70. Cambridge, MA: Harvard University Press.

Maynard Smith, J., and J. Haigh. 1974. The Hitch-hiking Effect of a Favourable Gene. *Genetical Research, Cambridge* 23:23–35.

Mayr, E. 1961. Cause and Effect in Biology. *Science* 134:1501–6.

McBrearty, S., and A. Brooks. 2000. The Revolution that Wasn't: A New Interpretation of the Origin of Modern Behavior. *Journal of Human Evolution* 39:453–563.

McDougall, I., F.H. Brown, and J.G. Fleagle. 2005. Stratigraphic Placement and Age of Modern Humans from Kibish, Ethiopia. *Nature* 433:733–36.

McGee, R.J., and R.L. Warms. 1996. *Anthropological Theory: An Introductory History.* Mountain View, CA: Mayfield.

McGrew, W.C. 1994. Tools Compared: The Material of Culture. In *Chimpanzee Cultures,* ed. R.W. Wrangham, W.C. McGrew, F. de Waal, and P. Heltne, pp. 25–40. Cambridge, MA: Harvard University Press.

—— 2004. *The Cultured Chimpanzee: Reflections on Cultural Primatology.* Cambridge: Cambridge University Press.

McHenry, H.M., and K. Coffing. 2000. *Australopithecus* to *Homo*: Transformations in the Body and Mind. *Annual Review of Anthropology* 29:125–46.

McKusik, V.A. 1998. *Mendelian Inheritance in Man: A Catalog of Human Genes and Genetic Disorders.* Baltimore: Johns Hopkins University Press.

McNeill, A.R. 1992. Human Locomotion. In *The Cambridge Encyclopedia of Human Evolution,* ed. S. Jones, R. Martin, and D. Pilbeam, pp. 80–85. Cambridge: Cambridge University Press.

McPherron, S.P., Z. Alemseged, C.W. Marean, et al. 2010. Evidence for Stone-Tool-Assisted Consumption of Animal Tissues before 3.39 Million Years Ago at Dikika, Ethiopia. *Nature* 466:857–60.

Mech, L.D. 1970. *The Wolf: The Ecology and Behavior of an Endangered Species.* Garden City, NY: Natural History Press.

Medin, D. 1989. Concepts and Conceptual Structure. *American Psychologist* 44:1469–81.

Meggers, B.J., ed. 1959. *Evolution and Anthropology: A Centennial Appraisal.* Washington, DC: Anthropological Society of Washington.

Mekel-Bobrov, N., D. Posthuma, S.L. Gilbert, et al. 2007. The Ongoing Adaptive Evolution of Aspm and Microcephalin Is Not Explained by Increased Intelligence. 10.1093/hmg/ddl487. *Human Molecular Genetics* 16:600–608.

Melis, A.P., B. Hare, and M. Tomasello. 2006a. Chimpanzees Recruit the Best Collaborators. *Science* 311:1297–1300.

—— 2006b. Engineering Cooperation in Chimpanzees. *Animal Behaviour* 72:275–86.

Mellars, P. 1973. The Character of the Middle–Upper Palaeolithic Transition in Southwest France. In *The Explanation of Culture Change,* ed. C. Renfrew, pp. 255–76. London: Duckworth.

—— 1989. Major Issues in the Emergence of Modern Humans. *Current Anthropology* 30:349–85.

—— 1996. *The Neanderthal Legacy: An Archaeological Perspective from Western Europe.* Princeton: Princeton University Press.

—— 2005. The Impossible Coincidence: A Single-Species Model for the Origins of Modern Human Behavior in Europe. *Evolutionary Anthropology* 14:12–27.

—— 2006. Going East: New Genetic and Archaeological Perspectives on the Modern Human Colonization of Eurasia. *Science* 313:796–800.

Mellars, P., and C. Stringer, eds. 1989. *The Human Revolution: Behavioural and Biological Perspectives in the Origins of Modern Humans.* Edinburgh: Edinburgh University Press.

Mellars, P., K. Boyle, O. Bar-Yosef, and C. Stringer, eds. 2007. *Rethinking the Human Revolution: New Behavioural and Biological Perspectives on the Origin and Dispersal of Modern Humans.* Cambridge: McDonald Institute for Archaeological Research.

Meltzoff, A.N. 1995. Understanding the Intentions of Others: Re-enactment of Intended Acts by 18-month-old Children. *Developmental Psychology* 31(5): 1–16.

Meltzoff, A.N., and M.K. Moore. 1977. Imitation of Facial and Manual Gestures by Human Neonates. *Science* 198(4312): 74–78.

Mercader, J., H. Barton, J. Gillespie, et al. 2007. 4,300-year-old Chimpanzee Sites and the Origins of Percussive Stone Technology. *Proceedings of the National Academy of Sciences USA* 104(9): 3043–48.

Mercier, H., and D. Sperber. 2011. Why Do Humans Reason? Arguments for an Argumentative Theory. *Behavioral and Brain Sciences* 34:57–74.

Mesoudi, A., A. Whiten, and K.N. Laland. 2004. Perspective: Is Human Cultural Evolution Darwinian? Evidence Reviewed from the Perspective of *The Origin of Species. Evolution* 58:1–11.

Miles, H.L.W. 1990. The Cognitive Foundations for Reference in a Signing Orangutan. In *"Language" and Intelligence in Monkeys and Apes: Comparative Developmental Perspectives,* ed. S.T. Parker and K.R. Gibson, pp. 511–39. Cambridge: Cambridge University Press.

Miller, E.K., and J.D. Cohen. 2001. An Integrative Theory of Prefrontal Cortex Function. *Annual Review of Neurosciences* 24:167–202.

Miller, G. 1997. Protean Primates: The Evolution of Adaptive Unpredictability in

Competition and Courtship. In *Machiavellian Intelligence* II, ed. R. Byrne and A. Whiten, pp. 312–40. Cambridge: Cambridge University Press.

—— 2000. Evolution of Human Music through Sexual Selection. In *The Origins of Music,* ed. N.L. Wallin, B. Merker, and S. Brown, pp. 329–60. Cambridge: MIT Press.

Milton, K. 1987. Primate Diets and Gut Morphology: Implications for Hominid Evolution. In *Food and Evolution: Toward a Theory of Human Food Habits,* ed. M. Harris and E.B. Ross, pp. 93–113. Philadelphia: Temple University Press.

—— 1999. A Hypothesis to Explain the Role of Meat-eating in Human Evolution. *Evolutionary Anthropology* 8:1–21.

Mitchell, P. 1997. *Introduction to Theory of Mind: Children, Autism and Apes.* London: Arnold.

Mithen, S.J. 1990. *Thoughtful Foragers: A Study of Prehistoric Decision Making.* Cambridge: Cambridge University Press.

—— 1996. *The Prehistory of the Mind: A Search for the Origins of Art, Religion, and Science.* London: Thames and Hudson.

—— 1998. The Supernatural Beings of Prehistory and the External Storage of Religious Ideas. In *Cognition and Material Culture: The Archaeology of Symbolic Storage,* ed. C. Renfrew and C. Scarre, pp. 97–106. Cambridge: McDonald Institute of Archaeological Research.

—— 2003. *After the Ice: A Global Human History, 20,000–5000 BC.* London: Weidenfeld and Nicolson; Cambridge: Harvard University Press.

—— 2005. *The Singing Neandertals: The Origins of Music, Language, Mind and Body.* London: Weidenfeld and Nicolson.

—— 2007. Did Farming Arise from a Misapplication of Social Intelligence? *Philosophical Transactions of the Royal Society* 362(1480): 705–18.

—— 2010. Excavating the Prehistoric Mind: The Brain as Cultural Artifact and Material Culture as Biological Extension. In *Social Brain, Distributed Mind,* ed. R. Dunbar, C. Gamble, and J. Gowlett, pp. 481–504. Oxford: Oxford University Press.

Mitteroecker, P., P. Gunz, M. Bernhard, et al. 2004. Comparison of Cranial Ontogenetic Trajectories among Great Apes and Humans. *Journal of Human Evolution* 46:679–98.

Mizutani, A., A. Matsuzaki, M.Y. Momoi, et al. 2007. Intracellular Distribution of a Speech/Language Disorder Associated FOXP2 Mutant. *Biochemical and Biophysical Research Communications* 353:869–74.

Moore, J.D. 1997. *Visions of Culture: An Introduction to Anthropological Theories and Theorists.* Thousand Oaks, CA: Altamira Press.

Morgan, C.L. 1894. *Introduction to Comparative Psychology.* London: Walter Scott.

Morin, E., and V. Laroulandie. 2012. Presumed Symbolic Use of Diurnal Raptors by Neanderthals. *PLoS ONE* 7(3): e32856. doi:10.1371/journal.pone.0032856.

Morris, D.H. 1974. Neanderthal Speech. *Linguistic Inquiry* 5:144–50.

Morwood, M.J., P.B. O'Sullivan, F. Aziz, and A. Raza. 1998. Fission-track Ages of Stone Tools and Fossils on the East Indonesian Island of Flores. *Nature* 392:173–76.

Morwood, M.J., R.P. Soejono, R.G. Roberts, et al. 2004. Archaeology and the Age of a New Hominin from Flores in Eastern Indonesia. *Nature* 431:1087–91.

Mourre, V., P. Villa, and C.S. Henshilwood. 2010. Early Use of Pressure Flaking on Lithic Artifacts at Blombos Cave, South Africa. *Science* 330:659–62.

Mulcahy, N.J., and J. Call. 2006. Apes Save Tools for Future Use. *Science* 312:1038–40.

Mulcahy, N., J. Call, and R.I.M. Dunbar. 2005. Gorillas (*Gorilla gorilla*) and Orangutans (*Pongo pygmaeus*) Encode Relevant Problem Features in a Tool-Using Task. *Journal of Computational Psychology* 119:23–32.

Muller, M.N., and J.C. Mitani. 2005. Conflict and Cooperation in Wild Chimpanzees. In *Advances in the Study of Behavior,* ed. P.J.B. Slater, J. Rosenblatt, C. Snowdon, T. Roper, and M. Naguib, pp. 275–331. New York: Elsevier.

Munn, N.L. 1971. *Evolution of the Human Mind.* Boston: Houghton Mifflin.

Murphy, R.F., and Y. Murphy. 1986. Northern Shoshone and Bannock. In *Handbook of North American Indians: Great Basin,* ed. W.L. d'Azevedo, pp. 284–307. Washington, DC: Smithsonian Institution Press.

Murray, J.A.H., ed. 1933. *The Oxford English Dictionary.* 13 vols. Oxford: Clarendon Press.

Myers, D. 1993. *Social Psychology.* 4th ed. New York: McGraw-Hill.

Nakamura, K., K. Sakai, and O. Hikosaka. 1998. Neuronal Activity in Medial Frontal Cortex during Learning of Sequential Procedures. *Journal of Neurophysiology* 80(5): 2671–87.

Nelissen, K., G. Luppino, W. Vanduffel, et al. 2005. Observing Others: Multiple Action Representation in the Frontal Lobe. *Science* 310(5746): 332–36.

Nelson, K. 1986. *Event Knowledge: Structure and Function in Development.* Hillsdale, NJ: Lawrence Erlbaum.

—— 1996. *Language in Cognitive Development: Emergence of the Mediated Mind.* New York: Cambridge University Press.

—— 2007. *Young Minds in Social Worlds: Experience, Meaning and Memory.* Cambridge, MA: Harvard University Press.

Newmeyer, F. 1991. Functional Explanations in Linguistics and the Origins of Language. *Language and Communication* 11:3–28.

—— 2003. Grammar Is Grammar and Usage Is Usage. *Language* 79:682–707.

Nichols, S., and S. Stich. 2003. *Mindreading: An Integrated Account of Pretence, Self-Awareness, and Understanding Other Minds.* New York: Oxford University Press.

Nielsen, R., C. Bustamante, A.G. Clark, et al. 2005. A Scan for Positively Selected Genes in the Genomes of Humans and Chimpanzees. *PLoS Biology* 3:e170.

Nishida, T. 1986. Local Traditions and Cultural Transmission. In *Primate Societies,* ed. B. Smuts, D.L. Cheney, R.M. Seyfarth, R.W. Wrangham, and T.T. Struhsaker, pp. 462–74. Chicago: University of Chicago Press.

Nishida, T., J.C. Mitani, and D.P. Watts. 2004. Variable Grooming Behaviours in Wild Chimpanzees. *Folia Primatologica* 75(1): 31–36.

Nissen, H.J., P. Damerow, and R.K. Englund. 1993. *Archaic Bookkeeping: Writing and Techniques of Economic Administration in the Ancient Near East,* trans. Paul Larsen. Chicago: University of Chicago Press.

Noble, W., and I. Davidson. 1996. *Human Evolution, Language and Mind: A Psychological and Archaeological Inquiry.* Cambridge: Cambridge University Press.

Noonan, J.P., G. Coop, S. Kudaravalli, et al. 2006. Sequencing and Analysis of Neanderthal Genomic DNA. *Science* 17 November 314:1113–18.

Nowak, M.A., and K. Sigmund. 2005. Evolution of Indirect Reciprocity. *Nature* 437:1291–98.

Nowak, M.A., N.L. Komarova, and P. Niyogi. 2002. Computational and Evolutionary Aspects of Language. *Nature* 417:611–17.

Nowell, A. 2001. The Re-emergence of Cognitive Archaeology. In *In the Mind's Eye: Multidisciplinary Perspectives on the Evolution of Human Intelligence,* ed. April Nowell, pp. 20–32. Ann Arbor, MI: International Monographs in Prehistory.

—— 2006. From a Paleolithic Art to Pleistocene Visual Cultures (Introduction to Two Special Issues on Advances in the Study of Pleistocene Imagery and Symbol Use). *Journal of Archaeological Method and Theory* 13(4): 239–49.

—— 2010a. Defining Behavioral Modernity in the Context of Neandertal and Anatomically Modern Human Populations. *Annual Review of Anthropology* 39:437–52.

—— 2010b. Working Memory and the Speed of Life. *Current Anthropology* 51(S1): S121–33.

Nowell, A., and F. d'Errico. 2007. The Art of Taphonomy and the Taphonomy of Art. *Journal of Archaeological Method and Theory* 14:1–26.

Nowell, A., F. d'Errico, and E. Hovers. 2001. Origin of Symbolism in the Near East: A New Analysis of the Evidence. Poster presented at the Society for American Archaeology meetings. New Orleans, LA.

Nowell, A., and M.L. Chang. 2012. Symbolism in Late European Neanderthals: Detection and Evolutionary Context. Paper presented at American Association of Physical Anthropologists meetings, Portland, OR.

Nowell, A., and M. White. 2010. Growing Up in the Middle Pleistocene: Life History Strategies and Their Relationship to Acheulian Industries. In *Stone Tools and the Evolution of Human Cognition,* ed. A. Nowell and I. Davidson, pp. 67–82. Boulder: University Press of Colorado.

Nowell, A., and P.G. Chase. 2002. Is a Cavebear Bone from Divje Babe I, Slovenia, a Neandertal Flute? In *The Archaeology of Early Sound: Origin and Organization,* 2nd Symposium of the Study Group on Music Archaeology, ed. E. Hickmann and R. Eichmann, pp. 69–81. Berlin: Orient-Archäologie 12.

Núñez, M., and P. Harris. 1998. Psychological and Deontic Concepts: Separate Domains or Intimate Connection? *Mind and Language* 13:153–70.

Obayashi, S., T. Suhara, K. Kawabe, et al. 2001. Functional Brain Mapping of Monkey Tool Use. *Neuroimage* 14(4): 853–61.

Obayashi, S., T. Suhara, Y. Nagai, et al. 2002. Macaque Prefrontal Activity Associated with Extensive Tool Use. *Neuroreport* 13(17): 2349–54.

O'Connell, J.F. 2006. How Did Modern Humans Displace Neanderthals? Insights from Hunter-Gatherer Ethnography and Archaeology. In *When Neanderthals and Modern Humans Met,* ed. N.J. Conard, pp. 43–64. Tübingen: Kerns Verlag.

O'Connell, J.F., and J. Allen. 2007. Pre-LGM Sahul (Pleistocene Australia–New Guinea) and the Archaeology of Early Modern Humans. In *Rethinking the Human Revolution: New Behavioural and Biological Perspectives on the Origin and Dispersal of Modern Humans,* ed. P. Mellars, K. Boyle, O. Bar-Yosef, and C. Stringer, pp. 395–410. Cambridge: McDonald Institute for Archaeological Research.

O'Connell, J.F., K. Hawkes, and N.G. Blurton Jones. 1999. Grandmothering and the Evolution of *Homo erectus. Journal of Human Evolution* 27:77–87.

Odling-Smee, F.J., K.N. Laland, and M.W. Feldman. 2003. *Niche Construction: The Neglected Process in Evolution.* Princeton: Princeton University Press.

Ofek, H. 2001. *Second Nature: Economic Origins of Human Evolution.* Cambridge: Cambridge University Press.

Oldroyd, D.R. 1980. *Darwinian Impacts: An Introduction to the Darwinian Revolution.* Atlantic Highlands, NJ: Humanities Press.

Oliver, Symmes C. 1962. *Ecology and Cultural Continuity as Contributing Factors in the Social Organization of the Plains Indians.* Publications in American Archaeology and Ethnology 48(1). Berkeley: University of California Press.

Olszewski, D., and H.L. Dibble. 1994. The Zagros Aurignacian. *Current Anthropology* 35(1): 68–75.

Onishi, K., and R. Baillargeon. 2005. Do 15-month-olds Understand False Beliefs? *Science* 5719:255–58.

Opdyke, N.D. 1995. Mammalian Migration and Climate over the Last Seven Million Years. In *Paleoclimate and Evolution, with Emphasis on Human Origins,* ed. E.S. Vrba, G.H. Denton, T.C. Partridge, and L.H. Burckle, pp. 109–14. New Haven: Yale University Press.

Orban, G.A., K. Claeys, K. Nelissen, et al. 2005. Mapping the Parietal Cortex of Human and Non-human Primates. *Neuropsychologia* 44:2647–67.

Origgi, G., and D. Sperber. 2000. Evolution, Communication, and the Proper Function of Language. In *Evolution and the Human Mind,* ed. P. Carruthers and A. Chamberlain, pp. 140–69. Cambridge: Cambridge University Press.

Orschiedt, J. 2008. Der Fall Krapina—Neue Ergebnisse zur Frage von Kannibalismus beim Neandertaler. *Quartär* 55:63–81.

Orzack, S.H., and E. Sober. 1994. Optimality Models and the Test of Adaptationism. *American Naturalist* 143:361–80.

Ostrom, E. 1990. *Governing the Commons: The Evolution of Institutions for Collective Action.* Cambridge: Cambridge University Press.

Osvath, M., and P. Gärdenfors. 2005. *Oldowan Culture and the Evolution of Anticipatory Cognition.* Lund University Cognitive Studies 122. Lund.

Osvath, M., and H. Osvath. 2008. Chimpanzee and Orangutan Forethought: Self-control and Pre-experience in the Face of Future Tool Use. *Animal Cognition* 11:661–74.

Otterbein, K.F. 1985. *The Evolution of War: A Cross-Cultural Study.* New Haven, CT: Human Relations Area Files Press.

Owens, D'A., and B. Hayden. 1997. Prehistoric Rites of Passage: A Comparative Study of Transegalitarian Hunter-Gatherers. *Journal of Anthropological Archaeology* 16(2): 121–61.

Owren, M.J., R.M. Seyfarth, and D.L. Cheney. 1997. The Acoustic Features of Vowel-like Grunt Calls in Chacma Baboons (*Papio cynocephalus ursinus*): Implications for Production Processes and Functions. *Journal of the Acoustical Society of America* 101:2951–63.

Oztop, E., D. Franklin, T. Chaminade, and C. Gordon. 2005. Human-Humanoid Interaction: Is a Humanoid Robot Perceived as a Human? *International Journal of Humanoid Robotics* 2(4): 537–59.

Pan, Q., M. Bakowski, Q. Morris, et al. 2005. Alternative Splicing of Conserved Exons Is Frequently Species-Specific in Human and Mouse. *Trends in Genetics* 21:73–77.

Panger, M.A., A.S. Brooks, B.G. Richmond, and B. Wood. 2002. Older than the Oldowan? Rethinking the Emergence of Hominin Tool Use. *Evolutionary Anthropology* 11:235–45.

Passingham, R.E. 1993. *The Frontal Lobe and Voluntary Action.* Oxford University Press: Oxford.

Patterson, F.G. 1978. Linguistic Capabilities of a Lowland Gorilla. In *Sign Language and Language Acquisition in Man and Ape,* ed. F.C.C. Peng, pp. 161–201. Boulder: Westview Press.

Patterson, F.G., and E. Linden. 1981. *The Education of Koko.* New York: Holt, Rinehart and Winston.

Patterson, N., D.J. Richter, S. Gnerre, et al. 2006. Genetic Evidence for Complex Speciation of Humans and Chimpanzees. *Nature* 441:1103–8.

Pavlov, P., J.I. Svendsen, and S. Indrelid. 2001. Human Presence in the European Arctic Nearly 40,000 Years Ago. *Nature* 413:64–67.

Payne, K. 1999. The Progressively Changing Songs of Humpback Whales: A Window on the Creative Process in a Wild Animal. In *The Origins of Music,* ed. N.L. Wallin, B. Merker, and S. Brown, pp. 135–50. Cambridge, MA: MIT Press.

Pearson, O.M. 2000. Postcranial Remains and the Origin of Modern Humans. *Evolutionary Anthropology* 9:229–47.

Peirce, C.S. 1931–35. *The Collected Papers of Charles Sanders Peirce.* 4 vols. Cambridge, MA: Harvard University Press.

Pelcin, A. 1994. A Geological Explanation for the Berekhat Ram Figurine. *Current Anthropology* 35:674–75.

Penn, D.C., and D.J. Povinelli. 2007. On the Lack of Evidence that Non-human Animals Possess Anything Remotely Resembling a 'Theory of Mind.' *Philosophical Transactions of the Royal Society B* 362:731–44.

Peresani, M., I. Fiore, M. Gala, et al. 2011. Late Neandertals and the Intentional Removal of Feathers as Evidenced from Bird Bone Taphonomy at Fumane Cave 44 ky B.P., Italy. *Proceedings of the National Academy of Science USA* DOI: 10.1073/pnas.1016212108.

Perner, J., S. Leekam, and H. Wimmer. 1987. Three-year-olds' Difficulty with False Belief: The Case for a Conceptual Deficit. *British Journal of Developmental Psychology* 5:125–37.

Perry, G.H., J. Tchinda, S.D. McGrath, et al. 2006. Hotspots for Copy Number Variation in Chimpanzees and Humans. *Proceedings of the National Academy of Sciences USA* 103:8006–11.

Perry, G.H., F. Yang, T. Marques-Bonet, et al. 2008. Copy Number Variation and Evolution in Humans and Chimpanzees. *Genome Research* 18:1698–1710.

Perry, S.E. 2006. What Cultural Primatology Can Tell Anthropologists about the Evolution of Culture. *Annual Review of Anthropology* 35:171–90.

—— 2009. Are Nonhuman Primates Likely to Exhibit Cultural Capacities Like Those of Humans? In *The Question of Animal Culture,* ed. K.N. Laland and B.G. Galef, pp. 247–68. Cambridge, MA: Harvard University Press.

Perry, S.E., M. Baker, L. Fedigan, et al. 2003. Social Conventions in Wild White-faced Capuchin Monkeys: Evidence for Traditions in a Neotropical Primate. *Current Anthropology* 44:241–68.

Petersen, L.C., G.H. Haug, K.A. Hughen, and U. Roehl. 2000. Cycle of the Tropical Atlantic during the Last Glacial. *Science* 290:1947–51.

Petraglia, M.D. 2007. Factoring the Arabian Peninsula and the Indian Subcontinent into Out of Africa Models. In *Rethinking the Human Revolution: New Behavioural and Biological Perspectives on the Origin and Dispersal of Modern Humans,* ed. P. Mellars, K. Boyle, O. Bar-Yosef, and C. Stringer, pp. 383–94. Cambridge: McDonald Institute for Archaeological Research.

Petrides, M. 2005. Lateral Prefrontal Cortex: Architectonic and Functional Organization. *Philosophical Transactions of the Royal Society of London B* 360(1456): 781–95.

Petrides, M., G. Cadoret, and S. Mackey. 2005. Orofacial Somatomotor Responses in the Macaque Monkey Homologue of Broca's Area. *Nature* 435(7046): 1235–38.

Pettigrew, J.D. 1991. Evolution of Binocular Vision. In *Evolution of the Eye and Visual System,* ed. J.R. Cronly-Dillon and R.L. Gregory, pp. 271–83. Boca Raton, FL: CRC Press.

Pettitt, P.B. 2003. Is This the Infancy of Art or the Art of an Infant? A Possible Neanderthal Face from la Roche Cotard, France. *Before Farming* 11:1–3.

—— 2005. The Rise of Modern Humans. In *The Human Past: World Prehistory and the Development of Human Societies,* ed. C. Scarre, pp. 124–73. New York: Thames and Hudson.

—— 2010. *Paleolithic Origins of Human Burial.* New York: Routledge.

Picard, N., and P.L. Strick. 2001. Imaging the Premotor Areas. *Current Opinion in Neurobiology* 11(6): 663–72.

Pickford, M., B. Senut, D. Gommery, et al. 2002. Bipedalism in *Orrorin tugenensis* Revealed by Its Femora. *Comptes Rendus Palevol* 1(4): 191–203.

Pickup, G., and C. Frith. 2001. Theory of Mind Impairments in Schizophrenia: Symptomatology, Severity, and Specificity. *Psychological Medicine* 31:207–20.

Pilbeam, D., and N. Young. 2004. Hominoid Evolution: Synthesizing Disparate Data. *Comptes Rendus Palevol* 3:303–19.

Pinker, S. 1994. *The Language Instinct: The New Science of Language and Mind.* London:

Penguin Press.

—— 1997. *How the Mind Works.* New York: W.W. Norton.

Pinker, S., and P. Bloom. 1990. Natural Language and Natural Selection. *Behavioral Brain Science* 13:707–83.

Pinker, S., and R. Jackendoff. 2005. The Faculty of Language: What's Special about It? *Cognition* 95:201–36.

Plotkin, H. 2004. *Evolutionary Thought in Psychology: A Brief History.* Malden, MA: Blackwell.

Plummer, T. 2004. Flaked Stones and Old Bones: Biological and Cultural Evolution at the Dawn of the Dawn of Technology. *Yearbook of Physical Anthropology* 47:118–64.

Plutchik, R. 1980. *Emotion: A Psychoevolutionary Synthesis.* New York: Harper and Row.

Pollick, A.S., and F.B. de Waal. 2007. Ape Gestures and Language Evolution. *Proceedings of the National Academy of Sciences USA* 104(19): 8184–89.

Ponce de León, M.S., and C.P.E. Zollikofer. 2001. Neanderthal Cranial Ontogeny and Its Implications for Late Hominid Diversity. *Nature* 412:534–38.

Ponce de León, M., L. Golovanova, V. Doronichev, et al. 2008. Neanderthal Brain Size at Birth Provides Insights into the Evolution of Human Life History. *Proceedings of the National Academy of Sciences USA* 105:13764–68.

Pontzer, H., and R.W. Wrangham. 2004. Climbing and the Daily Energy Cost of Locomotion in Wild Chimpanzees: Implications for Hominoid Locomotor Evolution. *Journal of Human Evolution* 46:315–33.

Potts, R. 1987. Reconstructions of Early Hominid Sociology: A Critique of Primate Models. In *Evolution of Human Behavior: Primate Models,* ed. W.G. Kinzey, pp. 28–47. Albany: State University of New York Press.

—— 1996. *Humanity's Descent: The Consequences of Ecological Instability.* New York: Avon Books.

—— 1998. Environmental Hypotheses of Hominin Evolution. *Yearbook of Physical Anthropology* 41:93–136.

Povinelli, D.J. 2000. *Folk Physics for Apes: The Chimpanzee's Theory of How the World Works.* Oxford: Oxford University Press.

Povinelli, D.J., and J. Vonk. 2003. Chimpanzee Minds: Suspiciously Human? *Trends in Cognitive Sciences* 7(4): 157–60.

Powell, A., S. Shennan, and M.G. Thomas. 2009. Late Pleistocene Demography and the Appearance of Modern Human Behavior. *Science* 324:1298–1301.

Premack, D. 1993. Prolegomenon to Evolution of Cognition. In *Exploring Brain Functions: Models in Neuroscience,* ed. T.A. Poggio and D.A. Glaser, pp. 269–90. New York: John Wiley.

—— 2004. Is Language the Key to Human Intelligence? *Science* 303:318–20.

Premack, D., and G. Woodruff. 1978. Does the Chimpanzee Have a Theory of Mind? *Behavioral and Brain Sciences* 4:515–26.

Preston, S.D., and F. de Waal. 2003. Empathy: Its Ultimate and Proximal Bases. *Behavioral and Brain Sciences* 25:1–72.

Pritchard, D.B. 2000. *Popular Chess Variants.* New York: Sterling Publishing.

Proops, L., K. McComb, and D. Reby. 2008. Cross-modal Individual Recognition in Domestic Horses (*Equus caballus*). *Proceedings of the National Academy of Sciences USA* 106:947–51.

Putnam, R.D., R. Leonardi, and R. Nanetti. 1993. *Making Democracy Work: Civic Traditions in Modern Italy.* Princeton: Princeton University Press.

Raby, C., D. Alexis, A. Dickinson, and N. Clayton. 2007. Planning for the Future by Western Scrub-Jays. *Nature* 445:919–21.

Raff, R.A. 1996. *The Shape of Life: Genes, Development, and the Evolution of Animal Form.* Chicago: University of Chicago Press.

Rakoczy, H. 2006. Pretend Play and the Development of Collective Intentionality. *Cognitive Systems Research* 7:113–27.

Ramirez Rossi, F.V., and J.M. Bermúdez de Castro. 2004. Surprisingly Rapid Growth in Neanderthals. *Nature* 428:936–39.

Rat Genome Sequencing Project Consortium. 2004. Genome Sequence of the Brown Norway Rat Yields Insights into Mammalian Evolution. *Nature* 428(6982): 493–521.

Reader, S.M., and K.N. Laland. 2002. Social Intelligence, Innovation, and Enhanced Brain Size in Primates. *Proceedings of the National Academy of Sciences USA* 99:4436–41.

Rendall, D. 2003. Acoustic Correlates of Caller Identity and Affect Intensity in the Vowel-like Grunt Vocalizations of Baboons. *Journal of the Acoustical Society of America* 113:3390–402.

Renfrew, C. 1982. *Towards an Archaeology of Mind.* Cambridge: Cambridge University Press.

—— 1998. Mind and Matter: Cognitive Archaeology and External Symbolic Storage. In *Cognition and Material Culture: The Archaeology of Symbolic Storage,* ed. C. Renfrew and C. Scarre, pp. 1–6. Cambridge: McDonald Institute for Archaeological Research.

—— 2009. Neuroscience, Evolution and the Sapient Paradox: The Factuality of Value and of the Sacred. In *The Sapient Mind: Archaeology Meets Neuroscience,* ed. C. Renfrew, C. Firth, and L. Malafouris, pp. 165–75. Oxford: Oxford University Press.

Renfrew, C., and C. Scarre, eds. 1998. *Cognition and Material Culture: The Archaeology of Symbolic Storage.* Cambridge: McDonald Institute for Archaeological Research.

Rhesus Macaque Genome Sequencing and Analysis Consortium. 2007. Evolutionary and Biomedical Insights from the Rhesus Macaque Genome. *Science* 316:222–34.

Rice, P.C., and N.H. Moloney. 2008. *Biological Anthropology and Prehistory.* Boston: Allyn and Bacon.

Richards, R.J. 1987. *Darwin and the Emergence of Evolutionary Theories of Mind and Behavior.* Chicago: University of Chicago Press.

Richardson, R.C. 2007. *Evolutionary Psychology as Maladapted Psychology.* Cambridge, MA: MIT Press.

Richerson, P.J., and R. Boyd. 2005. *Not by Genes Alone: How Culture Transformed Human Evolution.* Chicago: Chicago University Press.

—— 2010. Gene-Culture Coevolution in the Age of Genomics. *Proceedings of the National Academy of Science USA* 107 (Suppl. 2): 8985–92.

Richerson, P.J., R. Boyd, and R.L. Bettinger. 2001. Was Agriculture Impossible during the Pleistocene but Mandatory during the Holocene? A Climate Change Hypothesis. *American Antiquity* 66(3): 387–411.

Richerson, P.J., R.L. Bettinger, and R. Boyd. 2005. Evolution on a Restless Planet: Were Environmental Variability and Environmental Change Major Drivers of Human Evolution? In *Handbook of Evolution.* Vol. 2, *The Evolution of Living Systems Including Hominids,* ed. F.M. Wuketits and F.J. Ayala, pp. 223–42. New York: Wiley.

Richerson, P.J., R. Boyd, and R.L. Bettinger. 2009. Cultural Innovations and Demographic Change. *Human Biology* 81(2-3): 211–35.

Richmond, B.G., D.R. Begun, and D.S. Strait. 2001. Origin of Human Bipedalism: The Knuckle-Walking Hypothesis Revisited. *Yearbook of Physical Anthropology* 116:70–105.

Richmond, B.G., and W.L. Jungers. 2008. *Orrorin tugenensis* Femoral Morphology and the Evolution of Hominin Bipedalism. *Science* 319:1662–65.

Riel-Salvatore, J. 2010. A Niche Construction Perspective on the Middle–Upper Paleolithic Transition in Italy. *Journal of Archaeological Method and Theory* DOI: 10.1007/s10816-010-9093-9.

Riel-Salvatore, J., and G. Clark. 2001. Grave Markers: Middle and Early Upper Paleolithic Burials and the Use of Chronotypology in Contemporary Paleolithic Research. *Current Anthropology* 42:449–80.

Rightmire, G.P. 1998. Human Evolution in the Middle Pleistocene: The Role of *Homo heidelbergensis. Evolutionary Anthropology* 6:218–27.

—— 2004. Brain Size and Encephalization in Early to Mid-Pleistocene *Homo. American*

Journal of Physical Anthropology 124(2): 109–23.

Rilling, J.K. 2006. Human and Non-human Primate Brains: Are They Allometrically Scaled Versions of the Same Design? *Evolutionary Anthropology* 15:65–77.

Ristau, C.A., and D. Robbins. 1982. Language in the Great Apes: A Critical Review. *Advances in the Study of Behavior* 12:141–255.

Rizzolatti, G., and M.A. Arbib. 1998. Language within Our Grasp. *Trends in Neurosciences* 21(5): 188–94.

Rizzolatti, G., and L. Craighero. 2004. The Mirror-Neuron System. *Annual Review of Neuroscience* 27:169–92.

Rizzolatti, G., G. Luppino, and M. Matelli. 1998. The Organization of the Cortical Motor System: New Concepts. *Electroencephalography and Clinical Neurophysiology* 106(4): 283–96.

Rizzolatti, G., R. Camarda, L. Fogassi, et al. 1988. Functional Organization of the Inferior Area 6 in the Macaque Monkey. II Area F5 and the Control of Distal Movements. *Experimental Brain Research* 71:491–507.

Rizzolatti, G., L. Fadiga, M. Matelli, et al. 1996a. Localization of Grasp Representations in Humans by PET: 1. Observation versus Execution. *Experimental Brain Research* 111(2): 246–52.

Rizzolatti, G., L. Fadiga, V. Gallese, and L. Fogassi. 1996b. Premotor Cortex and the Recognition of Motor Actions. *Cognitive Brain Research* 3(2): 131–41.

Robson, S.L., and B. Wood. 2008. Hominin Life History: Reconstruction and Evolution. *Journal of Anatomy* 212:394–425.

Roe, A., and G.G. Simpson, eds. 1958. *Behavior and Evolution.* New Haven, CT: Yale University Press.

Roebroeks, W., M. Mussi, J. Svoboda, and K. Fennema, eds. 2000. *Hunters of the Golden Age: The Mid Upper Paleolithic of Eurasia 30,000–20,000 BP.* Leiden: Leiden University Press.

Rogers, E. 1995. *Diffusion of Innovations.* 4th ed. New York: Free Press.

Roitblat, H.L. 1982. The Meaning of Representation in Animal Memory. *Behavioral and Brain Sciences* 5:353–72.

Romanes, G.J. 1889. *Mental Evolution in Man: Origin of Human Faculty.* New York: Appleton.

Rose, N. 1998. Controversies in Meme Theory. *Journal of Memetics* 2(1): [http://jom-emit.cfpm.org/].

Rossano, M. 2009. Ritual Behavior and the Origins of Modern Cognition. *Cambridge Archaeological Journal* 19(2): 243–56.

Rothi, L.J.G., C. Ochipa, and K.M. Heilman. 1991. A Cognitive Neuropsychological

Model of Limb Praxis. *Cognitive Neuropsychology* 8:443–58.

Roux, V., and B. Bril, eds. 2005. *Stone Knapping: The Necessary Conditions for a Uniquely Hominin Behaviour.* Cambridge: McDonald Institute for Archaeological Research.

Ruddiman, W.F. 2007. The Early Anthropogenic Hypothesis: Challenges and Responses. *Reviews of Geophysics* 45 (RG4001): 1–37.

Ruff, C. 2002. Variation in Human Body Size and Shape. *Annual Review of Anthropology* 31:211–32.

—— 2008. Femoral/Humeral Strength in Early African *Homo erectus. Journal of Human Evolution* 54:383–90.

Rushworth, M.F.S., M.E. Walton, S.W. Kennerley, and D.M. Bannerman. 2004. Action Sets and Decisions in the Medial Frontal Cortex. *Trends in Cognitive Sciences* 8(9): 410–17.

Russell, M. 1987a. Bone Breakage in the Krapina Hominid Collection. *American Journal of Physical Anthropology* 72:373–79.

—— 1987b. Mortuary Practice at the Krapina Neandertal Site. *American Journal of Physical Anthropology* 72:381–97.

Russon, A., and D. Begun, eds. 2004. *The Evolution of Thought: The Evolutionary Origins of Great Ape Intelligence.* Cambridge: Cambridge University Press.

Sabeti, P.C., S.F. Schaffner, B. Fry, et al. 2006. Positive Natural Selection in the Human Lineage. *Science* 312:1614–20, plus supplementary material online.

Sahlins, M. 1976. *The Use and Abuse of Biology: An Anthropological Critique of Sociobiology.* Ann Arbor: University of Michigan Press.

—— 1999. Two or Three Things that I Know about Culture. *Journal of the Royal Anthropological Institute* 5:399–421.

Sakai, K.L. 2005. Language Acquisition and Brain Development. *Science* 310(5749): 815–19.

Sanz, C.M., and D.B. Morgan. 2007. Chimpanzee Tool Technology in the Goualougo Triangle, Republic of Congo. *Journal of Human Evolution* 52(4): 420–33.

Sanz, C.M., D.B. Morgan, and S. Gulick. 2004. New Insights into Chimpanzees, Tools, and Termites from the Congo Basin. *American Naturalist* 164(5): 567–81.

Sapolsky, R. 2002. Endocrinology of the Stress Response. In *Behavioral Endocrinology,* ed. J.B. Becker, S.M. Breedlove, D. Crews, and M.M. McCarthy, pp. 409–50. Cambridge, MA: MIT Press.

Sargeant, B.L., and J. Mann. 2009. From Social Learning to Culture: Intrapopulation Variation in Bottlenose Dolphins. In *The Question of Animal Culture,* ed. K.N. Laland and B.G. Galef, pp. 152–73. Cambridge, MA: Harvard University Press.

Sarnecki, J., and M. Sponheimer. 2002. Why Neanderthals Hate Poetry: A Critical

Notice of Steven Mithen's *The Prehistory of the Mind*. *Philosophical Psychology* 15:173–84.

Saunders, S. 2009. Costly Signalling: A Work in Progress. Review of Searcy and Nowicki, *Evolution of Animal Communication*. *Biology and Philosophy* 24:405–16.

Savage-Rumbaugh, E.S. 1986. *Ape Language: From Conditioned Response to Symbol*. New York: Columbia University Press.

—— 1994. Hominid Evolution: Looking to Modern Apes for Clues. In *Hominid Culture in Primate Perspective*, ed. D. Quiatt and J. Itani, pp. 7–49. Niwot, CO: University Press of Colorado.

Savage-Rumbaugh, E.S., D.M. Rumbaugh, and K. McDonald. 1985. Language Learning in Two Species of Apes. *Neuroscience and Biobehavioral Reviews* 9:653–65.

Savage-Rumbaugh, E.S., K. McDonald, R.A. Sevcik, et al. 1986. Spontaneous Symbol Acquisition and Communicative Use by Pygmy Chimpanzees (*Pan paniscus*). *Journal of Experimental Psychology: General* 115(3): 211–35.

Savage-Rumbaugh, E.S., S.G. Shanker, and T.J. Taylor. 1998. *Apes, Language, and the Human Mind*. New York: Oxford University Press.

Saxe, R., and L. Powell. 2006. It's the Thought That Counts: Specific Brain Regions for One Component of Theory of Mind. *Psychological Science* 17:692–99.

Saygin, A.P. 2007. Superior Temporal and Premotor Brain Areas Necessary for Biological Motion Perception. *Brain* 130(9): 2452–61.

Schaffner, S.F. 2004. The X Chromosome in Population Genetics. *Nature Reviews Genetics* 5:43–51.

Schaller, G.B. 1972. *The Serengeti Lion: A Study of Predator-Prey Relations*. Wildlife Behavior and Ecology Series. Chicago: University of Chicago Press.

Scheffer, M., S. Rinaldi, J. Huisman, and F.J. Weissing. 2003. Why Plankton Communities Have No Equilibrium: Solutions to the Paradox. *Hydrobiologia* 491:9–18.

Scheopartz, L.A. 1993. Language and Modern Human Origins. *Yearbook of Physical Anthropology* 36:91–126.

Schillaci, M.A. 2006. Sexual Selection and the Evolution of Brain Size in Primates. *PLoS One* 1:e62.

Schoenemann, P.T. 2006. Evolution of the Size and Functional Areas of the Human Brain. *Annual Review of Anthropology* 35:379–406.

Schoenemann, P.T., M.J. Sheehan, and L.D. Glotzer. 2005. Prefrontal White Matter Volume Is Disproportionately Larger in Humans than in Other Primates. *Nature Neuroscience* 8:242–52.

Schöning, C., T. Humle, Y. Möbius, and W.C. McGrew. 2008. The Nature of Culture: Technological Variation in Chimpanzee Predation on Army Ants Revisited. *Jour-*

nal of Human Evolution 55(1): 48–59.

Schultz, H., Ul. von Rad, and H. Erlenkeuser. 1998. Correlation between Arabian Sea and Greenland Climate Oscillations of the Past 110,000 Years. *Nature* 116(6680): 54–57.

Schuster, R. 2005. Why Not Chimpanzees, Lions, and Hyenas Too? (Reply to Tomasello et al. 2005b). *Behavioral and Brain Sciences* 28:716–17.

Schwarcz, H.P., and I. Skoflek. 1982. New Dates from the Tata, Hungary, Archaeological Site. *Nature* 295:590–91.

Schwartz, P. 2002. The Continuing Usefulness Account of Proper Function. In *Functions: New Essays in the Philosophy of Psychology and Biology,* ed. A. Ariew, R. Cummins, and M. Perlman, pp. 244–60. Oxford: Oxford University Press.

Scott, K. 1980. Two Hunting Episodes of Middle Palaeolithic Age at La Cotte de Saint-Brelade, Jersey (Channel Islands). *World Archaeology* 12:137–52.

Scott, R., and R. Baillargeon. 2009. Which Penguin Is This? Attributing False Beliefs about Object Identity at 18 Months. *Child Development* 80:1172–96.

Seabright, P. 2010. *The Company of Strangers: A Natural History of Economic Life.* 2nd ed. Princeton, NJ: Princeton University Press.

Searle, J.R. 1990. Collective Intentions and Actions. In *Intentions in Communication,* ed. P. Cohen, J. Morgan, and M. Pollack, pp. 401–15. Cambridge, MA: MIT Press.

—— 1995. *The Construction of Social Reality.* New York: Free Press.

—— 2005. What Is an Institution? *Journal of Institutional Economics* 1(1): 1–22.

Sebat, J., B. Lakshmi, J. Troge, et al. 2004. Large-scale Copy Number Polymorphism in the Human Genome. *Science* 305:525–28.

Segal, G. 2007. Poverty of Stimulus Arguments Concerning Language and Folk Psychology. In *The Innate Mind.* Vol. 3, *Foundations and the Future,* ed. P. Carruthers, S. Laurence, and S. Stich, pp. 90–105. Oxford: Oxford University Press.

Seidenberg, M.S., and L.A. Petitto. 1987. Communication, Symbolic Communication, and Language: Comment on Savage-Rumbaugh, McDonald, Sevcik, Hopkins, and Rupert (1986). *Journal of Experimental Psychology: General* 116(3): 279–87.

Sellers, W.I., G.M. Cain, W. Wang, and R.H. Crompton. 2005. Stride Lengths, Speed and Energy Costs in Walking of *Australopithecus afarensis:* Using Evolutionary Robotics to Predict Locomotion of Early Human Ancestors. *Journal of the Royal Society Interface* 2:431–41.

Semaw, S. 2000. The World's Oldest Stone Artefacts from Gona, Ethiopia: Their Implications for Understanding Stone Technology and Patterns of Human Evolution between 2.6–1.5 Million Years Ago. *Journal of Archaeological Science* 27:1197–1214.

Semaw, S., S.W. Simpson, J. Quade, et al. 2005. Early Pliocene Hominids from Gona,

Ethiopia. *Nature* 433:301–5.

Semendeferi, K. 2001. Before or After the Split? Hominid Neural Specializations. In *In the Mind's Eye: Multidisciplinary Approaches to the Evolution of Human Cognition,* ed. A. Nowell. Archaeology Series 13. Ann Arbor, MI: International Monographs in Prehistory.

Semendeferi, K., E. Armstrong, A. Schleicher, et al. 2001. Prefrontal Cortex in Humans and Apes: A Comparative Study of Area 10. *American Journal of Physical Anthropology* 114:224–41.

Semendeferi, K., H. Damasio, R. Frank, and G.W. Van Hoesen. 1997. The Evolution of the Frontal Lobes: A Volumetric Analysis Based on Three-Dimensional Recon- structions of Magnetic Resonance Scans of Human and Ape Brains. *Journal of Human Evolution* 32(4): 375–88.

Semmann, D., H.-J. Krambeck, and M. Milinski. 2005. Reputation Is Valuable Within and Outside One's Own Social Group. *Behavioral Ecology and Sociobiology* 57:611– 16.

Semple, C.A., M. Rolfe, and J.R. Dorin. 2003. Duplication and Selection in the Evolu- tion of Primate β-defensin Genes. *Genome Biology* 4:R31.

Senut, B., M. Pickford, D. Gommery, et al. 2001. First Hominid from the Miocene (Lukeino Formation, Kenya). *Comptes Rendus de l'Académie des Sciences de Paris, Série 2A* 332:137–44.

Serre, D., A. Langaney, M. Chech, et al. 2004. No Evidence of Neandertal mtDNA Contribution to Early Modern Humans. *PLoS Biology* 2(3): 313–17.

Severinghaus, J.P., and E.J. Brook. 1999. Abrupt Climate Change at the End of the Last Glacial Period Inferred from Trapped Air in Polar Ice. *Science* 286(29 Oct.): 930–34.

Seyfarth, R.M., and D.L. Cheney. 2003. Signalers and Receivers in Animal Communi- cation. *Annual Review of Psychology* 54:145–73.

––––– 2008. Primate Vocal Communication. In *Primate Neuroethology,* ed. M. Platt and A.A. Ghazanfar, pp. 84–97. Oxford: Oxford University Press.

Sharp, A.J., D.P. Locke, S.D. McGrath, et al. 2005. Segmental Duplications and Copy Number Variation in the Human Genome. *American Journal of Human Genetics* 77:78–88.

Shatz, M., and S. Wilcox. 1991. Constraints on the Acquisition of English Modals. In *Perspectives on Language and Thought,* ed. S. Gelman and J. Byrnes, pp. 319–53. Cambridge: Cambridge University Press.

Shea, J. 2003a. Close Encounters: Neandertals and Modern Humans in the Middle Paleolithic Levant. *The Review of Archaeology* 24:42–55.

—— 2003b. Neandertals, Competition and the Origin of Modern Human Behavior in the Levant. *Evolutionary Anthropology* 12:173–87.

—— 2003c. The Middle Paleolithic of the East Mediterranean Levant. *Journal of World Prehistory* 17:313–94.

—— 2006. The Middle Paleolithic of the Levant: Recursions and Convergence. In *Transitions before the Transition: Evolution and Stability in the Middle Paleolithic and Middle Stone Age,* ed. E. Hovers and S.L. Kuhn 2006, pp. 189–212. New York: Springer.

—— 2010. Neanderthals and Early *Homo sapiens* in the Levant. *South-Eastern Mediterranean Peoples between 130,000 and 10,000 Years Ago,* ed. E. Garcea, pp. 126–43. Oxford: Oxbow Books.

Shennan, S. 2000. Population, Culture History, and the Dynamics of Culture Change. *Current Anthropology* 41:811–35.

—— 2001. Demography and Cultural Innovation: A Model and Its Implications for the Emergence of Modern Human Culture. *Cambridge Archaeological Journal* 11:5–16.

—— 2002. *Genes, Memes and Human History: Darwinian Archaeology and Cultural Evolution.* London: Thames and Hudson.

—— 2009. Pattern and Process in Cultural Evolution: An Introduction. In *Pattern and Process in Cultural Evolution,* ed. S. Shennan, pp. 1–18. Berkeley: University of California Press.

Shi, P., M.A. Bakewell, and J. Zhang. 2006. Did Brain-specific Genes Evolve Faster in Humans than in Chimpanzees? *Trends in Genetics* 22:608–13.

Shipp, S. 2005. The Importance of Being Agranular: A Comparative Account of Visual and Motor Cortex. *Philosphical Transactions of the Royal Society London B* 360(1456): 797–814.

Sigmund, K., C. Hauert, and M. Nowak. 2001. Reward and Punishment. *Proceedings of the National Academy of Sciences USA* 98:10757–62.

Silk, J.B., D.L. Cheney, and R.M. Seyfarth. 1996. The Form and Function of Post-conflict Interactions between Female Baboons. *Animal Behaviour* 52:259–68.

Silk, J.B., J. Altmann, and S.C. Alberts. 2006a. Social Relationships among Adult Female Baboons (*Papio cynocephalus*). I. Variation in the Strength of Social Bonds. *Behavioral Ecology and Sociobiology* 61:183–95.

—— 2006b. Social Relationships among Adult Female Baboons (*Papio cynocephalus*). II: Variation in the Quality and Stability of Social Bonds. *Behavioral Ecology and Sociobiology* 61:197–204.

Silk, J.B., J.C. Beehner, T. Bergman, et al. 2009. The Benefits of Social Capital: Close

Social Bonds among Female Baboons Enhance Offspring Survival. *Proceedings of the Royal Society of London B* 276:3099–104.

Silk, J.B., J.C. Beehner, T. Bergman, et al. 2010. Strong and Consistent Social Bonds Enhance the Longevity of Female Baboons. *Current Biology* 20:1359–61.

Silk, J.B., R.M. Seyfarth, and D.L. Cheney. 1999. The Structure of Social Relationships among Female Savannah Baboons in Moremi Reserve, Botswana. *Behaviour* 136:679–703.

Silk, J.B., S. Brosnan, J. Vonk, et al. 2005. Chimpanzees Are Indifferent to the Welfare of Unrelated Group Members. *Nature* 437:1357–59.

Silk, J.B., S.C. Alberts, and J. Altmann. 2003. Social Bonds of Female Baboons Enhance Infant Survival. *Science* 302:1231–34.

Singer, R., and J. Wymer. 1982. *The Middle Stone Age at Klasies River Mouth in South Africa*. Chicago: University of Chicago Press.

Sitlivy, V., K. Sobczyk, C. Escutenaire, et al. 2004. Late Middle Paleolithic Complexes of Cracow Region, Poland. In *Actes de XIVème Congrès UISPP, Section 6, Le Paléolithique Supérieur*, ed. M. Dewez and P. Noiret, pp. 305–17. BAR International Series 1240. Oxford: Archaeopress.

SLI Consortium. 2002. A Genomewide Scan Identifies Two Novel Loci Involved in Specific Language Impairment. *American Journal of Human Genetics* 70:384–98.

Slimak, L., J.I. Svendsen, J. Mangerud, et al. Late Mousterian Persistence Near the Arctic Circle. *Science* 332(6031): 841–45.

Sloman, S. 1996. The Empirical Case for Two Systems of Reasoning. *Psychological Bulletin* 119:3–22.

—— 2002. Two Systems of Reasoning. In *Heuristics and Biases: The Psychology of Intuitive Judgment*, ed. T. Gilovich, D. Griffin, and D. Kahneman, pp. 379–96. Cambridge: Cambridge University Press.

Smith, E.A. 1983. Anthropological Application of Optimal Foraging Theory: A Critical Review. *Current Anthropology* 24:625–51.

—— 2000. Three Styles in the Evolutionary Analysis of Human Behavior. In *Adaptation and Human Behavior: An Anthropological Perspective*, ed. L. Cronk, N. Chagnon, and W. Irons, pp. 27–46. New York: Aldine de Gruyter.

Smith, E.A., and B. Winterhalder, eds. 1992. *Evolutionary Ecology and Human Behavior*. New York: Aldine de Gruyter.

—— 2003. Human Behavioral Ecology. In *Encyclopedia of Cognitive Science* 2, ed. L. Nadel, pp. 377–85. London: Nature Publishing Group.

Smith, E.A., M. Borgerhoff Mulder, and K. Hill. 2001. Controversies in the Evolutionary Social Sciences: A Guide for the Perplexed. *Trends in Ecology and Evolution*

16:128–34.

Smith, E.A., and R. Bliege Bird. 2005. Costly Signaling and Cooperative Behavior. In *Moral Sentiments and Material Interests: The Foundations of Cooperation in Economic Life,* ed. H. Gintis, S. Bowles, R. Boyd, and E. Fehr, pp. 115–48. Cambridge, MA: MIT Press.

Smith, E.A., R. Bliege Bird, and D.W. Bird. 2003. The Benefits of Costly Signaling: Meriam Turtle Hunters. *Behavioral Ecology* 14(1): 116–26.

Smith, T.M., P. Tafforeau, D.J. Reidd, et al. 2010. Dental Evidence for Ontogenetic Differences between Modern Humans and Neanderthals. *Proceedings of the National Academy of Science USA* 107(49): 20923–28.

Snowdon, C.T. 1990. Language Capacities of Nonhuman Animals. *Yearbook of Physical Anthropology* 33:215–43.

Sober, E. 2002. The ABC of Altruism. In *Altruism and Altruistic Love,* ed. S.G. Post, L.G. Underwood, J. Schloss, et al, pp. 17–28. Oxford: Oxford University Press.

Sockol, M.D., D.A. Raichlen, and H. Pontzer. 2007. Chimpanzee Locomotor Energetics and the Origin of Human Bipedalism. *Proceedings of the National Academy of Sciences USA* 104:12265–69.

Soffer, O. 2009. Defining Modernity, Establishing Rubicons, Imagining the Other— and the Neanderthal Enigma. In *Sourcebook of Paleolithic Transitions,* ed. M. Camps and P. Chauhan, pp. 43–64. New York: Springer.

Sol, D., R.P. Duncan, T.M. Blackburn, et al. 2005. Big Brains, Enhanced Cognition, and Response of Birds to Novel Environments. *Proceedings of the National Academy of Science USA* 102(15): 5461–65.

Song, H., K. Onishi, R. Baillargeon, and C. Fisher. 2008. Can an Actor's False Belief Be Corrected by an Appropriate Communication? Psychological Reasoning in 18.5-month-old Infants. *Cognition* 109:295–315.

Soriano, S., P. Villa, and L. Wadley. 2007. Blade Technology and Tool Forms in the Middle Stone Age of South Africa: The Howiesons Poort and Post-Howiesons Poort at Rose Cottage Cave. *Journal of Archaeological Science* 34:681–703.

Soressi, M., D. Armand, F. d'Errico, et al. 2002. Pech-de-l'Azé I (Carsac, Dordogne): Nouveaux travaux de recherche sur le Moustérien de tradition Acheuléenne. *Bulletin de la Société Préhistorique Française* 99:5–11.

Southgate, V., A. Senju, and G. Csibra. 2007. Action Anticipation through Attribution of False Belief by 2-year-olds. *Psychological Science* 18:587–92.

Specific Language Impairment Consortium. 2002. A Genomewide Scan Identifies Two Novel Loci Involved in Specific Language Impairment. *American Journal of Human Genetics* 70:384–98.

Speigel on-line. Stone Age Camp Found in Germany. February 6, 2007.

Spelke, E., A. Phillips, and A. Woodward. 1995. Infants' Knowledge of Object Motion and Human Action. In *Causal Cognition,* ed. D. Sperber, D. Premack, and A. Premack, pp. 44–78. Oxford: Oxford University Press.

Sperber, D. 1996. *Explaining Culture: A Naturalistic Approach.* Oxford: Blackwell.

Speth, J. 2004. News Flash: Negative Evidence Convicts Neanderthals of Gross Mental Incompetence. *World Archaeology* 36:519–26.

—— 2006. Housekeeping, Neandertal Style: Hearth Placement and Midden Formation in Kebara Cave (Israel). In *Transitions before the Transition: Evolution and Stability in the Middle Paleolithic and Middle Stone Age,* ed. E. Hovers and S.L. Kuhn, pp. 171–88.

Speth, J., and E. Tchernov. 2002. Middle Paleolithic Tortoise Use at Kebara Cave (Israel). *Journal of Archaeological Science* 29:471–83.

Spikins, P. 2009. Autism, the Integrations of "Difference" and the Origins of Modern Human Behavior. *Cambridge Archaeological Journal* 19(2): 179–201.

Spoor, F., B. Wood, and F. Zonnveld. 1994. Implications of Early Hominid Labyrinthine Morphology for Evolution of Human Bipedal Locomotion. *Nature* 369:645–48.

—— 1996. Evidence for a Link between Human Semicircular Canal Size and Bipedal Behaviour. *Journal of Human Evolution* 30:183–87.

Spoor, F., M.G. Leakey, P.N. Gathogo, et al. 2007. Implications of New Early *Homo* Fossils from Ileret, East of Lake Turkana, Kenya. *Nature* 448:688–91.

Sprong, M., P. Schothorst, E. Vos, et al. 2007. Theory of Mind in Schizophrenia: Meta-analysis. *British Journal of Psychiatry* 191:5–13.

Spuhler, J.N., ed. 1959. *The Evolution of Man's Capacity for Culture.* Detroit: Wayne State University Press.

Sripada, C.S., and S. Stich. 2006. A Framework for the Psychology of Norms. In *The Innate Mind.* Vol. 2, *Culture and Cognition,* ed. P. Carruthers, S. Laurence, and S. Stich, pp. 280–301. Oxford: Oxford University Press.

Standen, V., and R. Foley, eds. 1989. *Comparative Socioecology: The Behavioural Ecology of Humans and Other Animals.* Oxford: Blackwell.

Stanford, C.B. 2001. A Comparison of Social Meat-Foraging by Chimpanzees and Human Foragers. In *Meat-Eating and Human Evolution,* ed. C.B. Stanford and H.T. Bunn, pp. 122–40. Oxford: Oxford University Press.

Stanley, H.M. 1895. *Studies in the Evolutionary Psychology of Feeling.* London: Swan Sonnenschein.

Stanley, S.M. 1992. An Ecological Theory for the Origin of *Homo. Paleobiology* 18:237–

57.

Stanovich, K. 1999. *Who Is Rational? Studies of Individual Differences in Reasoning.* Mahwah, NJ: Lawrence Erlbaum.

Stearns, S.C. 1992. *The Evolution of Life Histories.* Oxford: Oxford University Press.

—— 2002. Less Would Have Been More. *Evolution* 56(11): 2339–45.

Stedman, H.H., B.W. Kozyak, A. Nelson, et al. 2004. Myosin Gene Mutation Correlates with Anatomical Changes in the Human Lineage. *Nature* 428:415–18.

Steiper, M.E., N.M. Young, and T.Y. Sukarna. 2004. Genomic Data Support the Hominoid Slowdown and an Early Oligocene Estimate for the Hominoid-Cercopithecoid Divergence. *Proceedings of the National Academic of Sciences USA* 101:17021–26.

Sterelny, K. 2003. *Thought in a Hostile World: The Evolution of Human Cognition.* Malden, MA: Blackwell.

—— 2004. Externalism, Epistemic Artefacts and the Extended Mind. In *The Externalist Challenge,* ed. R. Schantz, pp. 239–54. New York: de Gruyter.

—— 2006a. The Evolution and Evolvability of Culture. *Mind and Language* 21(2): 137–65.

—— 2006b. Cognitive Load and Human Decision, or, Three Ways of Rolling the Rock Uphill. In *The Innate Mind.* Vol. 2, *Culture and Cognition,* ed. P. Carruthers, S. Laurence, and S. Stich, pp. 218–33. Oxford: Oxford University Press.

—— 2007. SNAFUS: An Evolutionary Perspective. *Biological Theory* 2:317–28.

—— 2011. From Hominins to Humans: How *sapiens* Became Behaviourally Modern. *Philosophical Transactions of the Royal Society B* 366(1566): 809–22.

—— 2012. *The Evolved Apprentice: How Evolution Made Humans Unique.* Cambridge, MA: MIT Press.

Steudel-Numbers, K.L. 2006. Energetics in *Homo erectus* and Other Early Hominins: The Consequences of Increased Lower-Limb Length. *Journal of Human Evolution* 51:445–53.

Stevens, J.R., and M. Hauser. 2004. Why Be Nice? Psychological Constraints on the Evolution of Cooperation. *Trends in Cognitive Science* 8:60–65.

Steward, J.H. 1955. *Theory of Culture Change: The Methodology of Multilinear Evolution.* Urbana: University of Illinois Press.

Stiner, M.C. 2001. Thirty Years on the "Broad Spectrum Revolution" and Paleolithic Demography. *Proceedings of the National Academy of Sciences USA* 98(13): 6993–96.

—— 2002. Carnivory, Coevolution, and the Geographic Spread of the Genus *Homo*. *Journal of Archaeological Research* 10(1): 1–63.

Stiner, M.C., N.D. Munro, T.A. Surovell, et al. 1999. Paleolithic Population Growth Pulses Evidenced by Small Animal Exploitation. *Science* 283(8 Jan.): 190–94.

Stiner, M.C., N.D. Munro, and T.A. Surovell. 2000. The Tortoise and the Hare: Small-Game Use, the Broad-Spectrum Revolution, and Paleolithic Demography. *Current Anthropology* 41(1): 39–73.

Stiner, M., and S.L. Kuhn. 2006. Changes in Connectedness and Resilience of Paleolithic Societies in Mediterranean Ecosystems. *Human Ecosystems* 34(5): 693–712.

Stoltz, C.A., J.W. King, G.S. Ellis, et al. 2003. Paleolimnology of Lake Tanganyika, East Africa, over the Past 100 K Yr. *Journal of Paleolimnology* 30:139–59.

Stone, C.P. 1943. Multiply, Vary, Let the Strongest Live and the Weakest Die—Charles Darwin. *Psychological Bulletin* 40:1–24.

Stout, D. 2005. The Social and Cultural Context of Stone-knapping Skill Acquisition. In *Stone Knapping: The Necessary Conditions for a Uniquely Hominin Behaviour,* ed. V. Roux and B. Bril, pp. 331–40. Cambridge: McDonald Institute for Archaeological Research.

Stout, D., N. Toth, K. Schick, and T. Chaminade. 2008. Neural Correlates of Early Stone Age Toolmaking: Technology, Language and Cognition in Human Evolution. *Philosophical Transactions of the Royal Society of London B* 363(1499): 1939–49.

Stout, D., R. Passingham, C. Frith, J. Apel, and T. Chaminade. 2011. Technology, Expertise, and Social Cognition in Human Evolution. *European Journal of Neuroscience* 33(7):1328–38.

Stout, D., and T. Chaminade. 2007. The Evolutionary Neuroscience of Tool Making. *Neuropsychologia* 45(5): 1091–100.

—— 2009. Making Tools and Making Sense: Complex, Intentional Behaviour in Human Evolution. *Cambridge Archaeological Journal* 19(1): 85–96.

Straus, L.G. 2001. Comment, on Grave Markers: Middle and Upper Paleolithic Burials and the Use of Chronotypology in Contemporary Paleolithic Research, by J. Riel-Salvatore and G. Clark. *Current Anthropology* 42:468–69.

—— 2009. Has the Notion of "Transitions" Outlived Its Usefulness? The European Record in Wider Context. In *Sourcebook of Paleolithic Transitions,* ed. M. Camps and P. Chauhan, pp. 3–18. New York: Springer.

Striedter, G.F. 2005. *Principles of Brain Evolution.* Sunderland, MA: Sinauer.

Stringer, C.B. 2002a. Modern Human Origins: Progress and Prospects. *Philosophical Transactions of the Royal Society of London B* 357:563–79.

—— 2002b. The Morphological and Behavioural Origins of Modern Humans. *Proceedings of the British Academy* 106:23–30.

Stringer, C.B., and C. Gamble. 1993. *In Search of the Neanderthals: Solving the Puzzle of Human Origins.* New York: Thames and Hudson.

Stringer, C., J.C. Finlayson, R.N.E. Barton, et al. 2008. Neanderthal Exploitation of

Marine Mammals in Gibraltar. *Proceedings of the National Academy of Sciences* 105(38): 14319–24.

Stuss, D., and F. Benson. 1986. *The Frontal Lobes.* New York: Raven Press.

Suddendorf, T., and J. Busby. 2003. Mental Time Travel in Animals? *Trends in Cognitive Sciences* 7:391–96.

Suddendorf, T., and M.C. Corballis. 1997. Mental Time Travel and the Evolution of the Human Mind. *Genetic, Social and General Psychology Monographs* 123:133–67.

Sugden, R. 1986. *The Economics of Rights, Co-operation and Welfare.* Oxford: Blackwell.

Surian, L., S. Caldi, and D. Sperber. 2007. Attribution of Beliefs by 13-month-old Infants. *Psychological Science* 18:580–86.

Tabourin, Y. 2003. La mer et les premiers hommes modernes. In *Échanges et Diffusion dans la Préhistoire Méditerranéenne,* ed. B. Vandermeersch, pp. 113–22. Paris: CTHS.

Taglialatela, J.P., J.L. Russell, J.A. Schaeffer, and W.D. Hopkins. 2008. Communicative Signaling Activates "Broca's" Homolog in Chimpanzees. *Current Biology* 18:343–48.

Tallon, P.W. J. 1978. Geological Setting of the Hominid Fossils and Acheulean Artifacts from the Kapthurin Formation, Baringo District, Kenya. In *Geological Background to Fossil Man,* ed. W.W. Bishop, pp. 361–73. Edinburgh: Scottish Academic Press.

Talmy, L. 1988. Force Dynamics in Language and Cognition. *Cognitive Science* 12:49–100.

—— 2006. Recombinance in the Evolution of Language. Paper presented at the 6th International Conference on the Evolution of Language, Rome.

Tattersall, I., and J.H. Schwartz. 1999. Commentary: Hominids and Hybrids: The Place of Neanderthals in Human Evolution. *Proceedings of the National Academy of Sciences USA* 96:7117–19.

Tax, S., ed. 1960. *Evolution after Darwin.* 3 vols. Chicago: University of Chicago Press. (Vol. 3 co-edited with C. Callendar.)

Teaford, M.F., P.S. Ungar, and F.E. Grine. 2000. Paleontological Evidence for the Diets of African Plio-Pleistocene Hominins with Special Reference to Early *Homo.* In *Human Diet: Its Origin and Evolution,* ed. P.S. Ungar and M.F. Teaford, pp. 143–66. New York: Praeger.

Tenesa, A., P. Navarro, B.J. Hayes, et al. 2007. Recent Human Effective Population Size Estimated from Linkage Disequilibrium. *Genome Research* 17(4): 520–26.

Tennie, C., J. Call, and M. Tomasello. 2009. Ratcheting Up the Ratchet: On the Evolution of Cumulative Culture. *Philosophical Transactions of the Royal Society B: Bio-*

logical Sciences 364:2405–15.

Terrace, H.S., L.A. Petitto, and T.G. Bever. 1979. Can an Ape Create a Sentence? *Science* 206:891–900.

Tettamanti, M., G. Buccino, M.C. Saccuman, et al. 2005. Listening to Action-related Sentences Activates Fronto-Parietal Motor Circuits. *Journal of Cognitive Neuroscience* 17(2): 273–81.

Texier, P.-J., G. Porraz, J. Parkington, et al. 2010. A Howiesons Poort Tradition of Engraving Ostrich Eggshell Containers Dated to 60,000 Years Ago at Diepkloof Rock Shelter, South Africa. *Proceedings of the National Academy of Sciences USA* 107(14): 6180–85.

Thatch, W.T. 1998. What Is the Role of the Cerebellum in Motor Learning and Cognition? *Trends in Cognitive Sciences* 2:331–37.

Thieme, H. 1997. Lower Palaeolithic Hunting Spears from Germany. *Nature* 385:807–10.

—— 1999. Altpaläolithische Holzgeräte aus Schöningen, lkr. Helmstedt, *Germania* 77 / 2:451–87.

Thomas, D.A. 1995. *Music and the Origins of Language: Theories from the French Enlightenment.* Cambridge: Cambridge University Press.

Thornhill, R., and C.T. Palmer. 2001. *A Natural History of Rape: Biological Bases of Sexual Coercion.* Cambridge, MA: MIT Press.

Thorpe, S.K., R.L. Holder, and R.H. Crompton. 2007. Origin of Human Bipedalism as an Adaptation for Locomotion on Flexible Branches. *Science* 316:1328–31.

Thorpe, W.H. 1963. *Learning and Instinct in Animals.* Cambridge, MA: Harvard University Press.

Tibbetts, E.A., and J. Dale. 2007. Individual Recognition: It Is Good To Be Different. *Trends in Ecology and Evolution* 22:529–37.

Tinbergen, N. 1963. On Aims and Methods of Ethology. *Zeitschrift für Tierpsychologie* 20:410–33.

Tobach, E. 1976. Evolution of Behavior and the Comparative Method. *International Journal of Psychology* 11:185–201.

Tobias, P.V. 1987. The Brain of *Homo habilis:* A New Level of Organization in Cerebral Evolution. *Journal of Human Evolution* 16(7-8): 741–61.

—— 1991. *The Skulls, Endocasts, and Teeth of* Homo habilis. Cambridge: Cambridge University Press.

Tolman, E.C. 1932. *Purposive Behavior in Animals and Men.* New York: Century.

Tomasello, M. 1990. Cultural Transmission in the Tool Use and Communicatory Signaling of Chimpanzees? In *"Language" and Intelligence in Monkeys and Apes: Com-*

parative Developmental Perspectives, ed. S.T. Parker and K.R. Gibson, pp. 274–311. Cambridge: Cambridge University Press.

——— 1999. *The Cultural Origins of Human Cognition.* Cambridge, MA: Harvard University Press.

——— 2000a. Do Young Children Have Adult Syntactic Competence? *Cognition* 74(3): 209–53.

——— 2000b. Two Hypotheses about Primate Cognition. In *The Evolution of Cognition,* ed. C. Heyes and L. Huber, pp. 165–83. Cambridge, MA: MIT Press.

——— 2003. *Constructing a Language: A Usage-based Theory of Language Acquisition.* Cambridge, MA: Harvard University Press.

——— 2008. *The Origins of Human Communication.* Cambridge, MA: MIT Press.

Tomasello, M., and J. Call. 1997. *Primate Cognition.* New York: Oxford University Press.

——— 2004. The Role of Humans in the Cognitive Development of Apes Revisited. *Animal Cognition* 7:213–15.

Tomasello, M., A.C. Kruger, and H.H. Ratner 1993. Cultural Leaning. *Behavioral and Brain Sciences* 16:495–511.

Tomasello, M., M. Carpenter, and R.P. Hobson. 2005a. *The Emergence of Social Cognition in Three Young Chimpanzees.* Monographs of the Society for Research in Child Development 70(1), Serial No. 279. Boston: Blackwell.

Tomasello, M., M. Carpenter, J. Call, et al. 2005b. Understanding and Sharing Intentions: The Origins of Cultural Cognition. *Behavioral and Brain Sciences* 28:675–91.

Tooby, J., and L. Cosmides. 1989. Evolutionary Psychology and the Generation of Culture. Part 1: Theoretical Considerations. *Ethology and Sociobiology* 10:29–49.

——— 1992. The Psychological Foundations of Culture. In *The Adapted Mind: Evolutionary Psychology and the Generation of Culture,* ed. J.H. Barkow, L. Cosmides, and J. Tooby, pp. 19–136. New York: Oxford University Press.

——— 1995. Mapping the Evolved Functional Organization of Mind and Brain. In *The Cognitive Neurosciences,* ed. Michael Gazzaniga, pp. 1185–97. Cambridge, MA: MIT Press.

Toth, N. 1985. The Oldowan Reassessed: A Close Look at Early Stone Artifacts. *Journal of Archaeological Science* 12:101–20.

Toth, N., and K. Schick. 1993. Early Stone Industries and Inferences Regarding Language and Cognition. In *Tools, Language and Cognition in Human Evolution,* ed. K. Gibson and T. Ingold, pp. 346–62. Cambridge: Cambridge University Press.

Toth, N., K. Schick, E. Savage-Rumbaugh, R. Sevcik, and D. Rumbaugh. 1993. *Pan* the Tool-maker: Investigations into the Stone Tool-making and Tool-using Capabilities of a Bonobo (*Pan paniscus*). *Journal of Archaeological Science* 20:81–91.

Toth, N., K. Schick, and S. Semaw. 2003. A Comparative Study of the Toolmaking Skills of *Pan, Australopithecus,* and *Homo sapiens.* In *The Oldowan: Case Studies into the Earliest Stone Age,* ed. K. Schick and N. Toth, pp. 155–222. Bloomington, IN: Craft Press.

Trevathan, W.R. 1987. *Human Birth: An Evolutionary Perspective.* New York: Aldine de Gruyter.

Trinkaus, E. 1983. *The Shanidar Neandertals.* New York: Academic Press.

—— 1995. Neanderthal Mortality Patterns. *Journal of Archaeological Science* 22:121–42.

—— 2005. Early Modern Humans. *Annual Review of Anthropology* 34:207–30.

—— 2007. Human Evolution: Neandertal Gene Speaks Out. *Current Biology* 17(21): R917–19.

Trinkaus, E., O. Molodovan, S. Milota, et al. 2003. An Early Modern Human from Peştera cu Oase, Romania. *Proceedings of the National Academy of Sciences USA* 100(20): 11231–36.

Trivers, R.L. 1971. The Evolution of Reciprocal Altruism. *Quarterly Review of Biology* 46:35–57.

Tulving, E. 1985. How Many Memory Systems Are There? *American Psychologist* 40:385–98.

Turk, I., ed. 1997. *Mousterian Bone Flute and Other Finds from Divje Babe I Cave Site in Slovenia.* Ljubljana: Institut za Arhaeologijo.

Turk, I., B.A.B. Blackwell, J. Turk, and M. Pflaum. 2006. Résultats de l'analyse tomographique informatisée de la plus ancienne flûte découverte à Divje babé I (Slovénie) et sa position chronologique dans le contexte des changements paléoclimatiques et paléoenvironnementaux au cours du dernier glaciaire. *L'Anthropologie* 110:293–317.

Tuzun, E., A.J. Sharp, J.A. Bailey, et al. 2005. Fine-scale Structural Variation of the Human Genome. *Nature Genetics* 37:727–32.

Tylor, E.B. 1871. *Primitive Culture: Researches into the Development of Mythology, Philosophy, Religion, Art, and Culture.* London: John Murray.

Tzedakis, P.C., K.A. Hughen, I. Cacho, and K. Harvati. 2007. Placing Late Neanderthals in a Climatic Context. *Nature* 449:206–8.

Umilta, M.A., E. Kohler, V. Gallese, et al. 2001. I Know What You Are Doing: A Neurophysiological Study. *Neuron* 31(1): 155–65.

Ungar, P.S., F.E. Grine, and M.F. Teaford. 2006. Diet in Early *Homo*: A Review of the Evidence and a New Model of Adaptive Versatility. *Annual Review of Anthropology* 35:209–28.

Valian, V., S. Solt, and J. Stewart. 2009. Abstract Categories or Limited-scope Formulae? The Case of Children's Determiners. *Journal of Child Language* 36:743–78.

Vallverdú, J., M. Vaquero, I. Caceres, et al. 2010. Sleeping Activity Area within the Site Structure of Archaic Human Groups: Evidence from Abric Romani Level N Combustion Activity Areas. *Current Anthropology* 51(1): 137–45.

van Andel, T.H., W. Davies, and B. Weninger. 2003. The Human Presence in Europe during the Last Glacial Period I: Human Migrations and the Changing Climate. In *Neanderthals and Modern Humans in the European Landscape during the Last Glaciation: Archaeological Results of the Stage 3 Project,* ed. T.H. van Andel and W. Davies, pp. 31–56. Oxford: MacDonald Institute for Archaeological Research.

van der Lely, H. 2005. Domain-specific Cognitive Systems: Insights from SLI. *Trends in Cognitive Sciences* 9:53–59.

Vanhaeren, M. 2005. Speaking with Beads: The Evolutionary Significance of Personal Ornaments. In *From Tools to Symbols: From Early Hominids to Modern Humans,* ed. F. d'Errico and L. Backwell, pp. 525–53. Johannesburg: Witwatersrand University Press.

Vanhaeren, M., F. d'Errico, C. Stringer, et al. 2006. Middle Paleolithic Shell Beads in Israel and Algeria. *Science* 312:1785–87.

van Schaik, C.P., M. Ancrenaz, G. Borgen, et al. 2003. Orangutan Cultures and the Evolution of Material Culture. *Science* 299(5603): 102–5.

van Schaik, C.P., and P.M. Kappeler. 2006. Cooperation in Primates and Humans: Closing the Gap. In *Cooperation in Primates and Humans,* ed. C.P. van Schaik and P.M. Kappeler, pp. 85–105. Berlin: Springer.

Vargha-Khadem, F., D.G. Gadian, A. Copp, and M. Mishkin. 2005. FOXP2 and the Neuroanatomy of Speech and Language. *Nature Reviews Neuroscience* 6:131–38.

Varley, R. 1998. Aphasic Language, Aphasic Thought. In *Language and Thought,* ed. P. Carruthers and J. Boucher, pp. 128–45. Cambridge: Cambridge University Press.

Vauclair, J. 1990. Primate Cognition: From Representation to Language. In *Language and Intelligence in Monkeys and Apes,* ed. S.T. Parker and K.R. Gibson, pp. 312–29. Cambridge: Cambridge University Press.

Vekua, A., D. Lordkipanidze, G.P. Rightmire, et al. 2002. A New Skull of Early *Homo* from Dmanisi, Georgia. *Science* 297:85–89.

Velo, J. 1986. The Problem of Ochre. *Mankind Quarterly* 26:229–37.

Verheyen, E., W. Salzburger, J. Snoeks, and A. Meyer. 2003. Origin of the Superflock of *Cichlid* Fishes from Lake Victoria, East Africa. *Science* 300(5617): 325–29.

Verhoeven, K., L. Van Laer, K. Kirschhofer, et al. 1998. Mutations in the Human Alpha-tectorin Gene Cause Autosomal Dominant Non-syndromic Hearing Impairment. *Nature Genetics* 19(1): 60–62.

Vermeij, G.J. 1987. *Evolution and Escalation: An Ecological History of Life.* Princeton: Princeton University Press.

Vértes, L. 1959. Churinga de Tata. *Bulletin de la Société Préhistorique Française* 56:604–11.

—— 1964. *Tata—eine mittelpaläolitische Travertin-Seidlung in Ungarn.* Budapest: Akadémia Kiadó.

Villa, P. 1983. *Terra Amata and the Middle Pleistocene Archaeological Record of Southern France.* Berkeley: University of California Press.

Visalberghi, E., D. Fragaszy, E. Ottoni, et al. 2007. Characteristics of Hammer Stones and Anvils Used by Wild Bearded Capuchin Monkeys (*Cebus libidinosus*) to Crack Open Palm Nuts. *American Journal of Physical Anthropology* 132:426–44.

Vishnyatsky, L.B. 2006. Review of *The Emergence of Culture. The Evolution of a Uniquely Human Way of Life,* by Philip G. Chase. *PaleoAnthropology* 2006:95–97.

Vitousek, P.M., H.A. Mooney, J. Lubchenco, and J.M. Melillo. 1997. Human Domination of Earth's Ecosystems. *Science* 277(25 July): 494–99.

Vogt, O., and C. Vogt. 1919. Ergebisse unserer Hirnforschung. *Journal für Psychologie und Neurologie* 25:277–462.

von Grafenstein, U., H. Erlenkeuser, J. Muller, et al. 1998. The Cold Event 8200 Years Ago Documented in Oxygen Isotope Records of Precipitation in Europe and Greenland. *Climate Dynamics* 14:73–81.

Vrba, E.S. 1985. African *Bovidae:* Evolutionary Events since the Miocene. *South African Journal of Science* 81:263–66.

—— 1994. An Hypothesis of Heterochrony in Response to Climatic Cooling and Its Relevance to Early Human Evolution. In *Integrative Paths to the Past. Paleoanthropological Advances in Honor of F. Clark Howell,* ed. R.S. Corruccini and R.L. Ciochon, pp. 345–76. Englewood Cliffs, NJ: Prentice Hall.

Vygotsky, L.S. 1978. *Mind in Society: The Development of Higher Psychological Processes.* Cambridge, MA: Harvard University Press.

Wadley, L. 2001. What Is Cultural Modernity? A General View and a South African Perspective from Rose Cottage Cave. *Cambridge Archaeological Journal* 11:201–21.

—— 2005. Putting Ochre to the Test: Replication Studies of Adhesives that May Have Been Used for Hafting Tools in the Middle Stone Age. *Journal of Human Evolution* 49:587–601.

Wadley, L., B. Williamson, and M. Lombard. 2004. Ochre in Hafting in Middle Stone Age Southern Africa: A Practical Role. *Antiquity* 78(301): 661–75.

Wagner, M., and D.A. Owens. 1992. Introduction: Modern Psychology and Early Functionalism. In *Progress in Modern Psychology: The Legacy of American Functional-*

ism, ed. D.A. Owens and M. Wagner, pp. 3–16. Westport, CT: Praeger Publishers.

Walker, A., and R. Leakey, eds. 1993. *The Nariokotome* Homo erectus *Skeleton.* Cambridge: Harvard University Press.

Walker, M., S. Johnsen, S.O. Rasmussen, et al. 2009. Formal Definition and Dating of the GSSP (Global Stratotype Section and Point) for the Base of the Holocene Using the Greenland HGRIP Ice Core, and Selected Auxiliary Records. *Journal of Quaternary Science* 24:3–17.

Walker, T.D., and J.W. Valentine. 1984. Equilibrium Models of Evolutionary Species Diversity and the Number of Empty Niches. *American Naturalist* 124:887–99.

Wall, J.D. 2003. Estimating Ancestral Population Sizes and Divergence Times. *Genetics* 163:395–404.

Wall, J.D., and M. Przeworski. 2000. When Did the Human Population Size Start Increasing? *Genetics* 155:1865–74.

Wallin, N.L., B. Merker, and S. Brown, eds. 2000. *The Origins of Music.* Cambridge, MA: MIT Press.

Wallman, J. 1992. *Aping Language. Themes in the Social Sciences.* Cambridge: Cambridge University Press.

Walsh, D.M. 1996. Fitness and Function. *British Journal for the Philosophy of Science* 47:553–74.

Wang, L., M. Sarnthein, H. Ehrlenkeuser, et al. 1999. East Asian Monsoon Climate during the Late Pleistocene: High-resolution Sediment Records from the South China Sea. *Marine Geology* 156:245–384.

Wang, Y.Q., and B. Su. 2004. Molecular Evolution of Microcephalin, a Gene Determining Human Brain Size. *Human Molecular Genetics* 13(11): 1131–37.

Warden, C.J., T.N. Jenkins, and L.H. Warner. 1934. *Introduction to Comparative Psychology.* New York: Ronald Press.

Warneken, F., and M. Tomasello. 2006. Altruistic Helping in Human Infants and Young Chimpanzees. *Science* 311:1301–3.

—— 2007. Helping and Cooperation at 14 Months of Age. *Infancy* 11(3): 271–94.

—— 2008. Extrinsic Rewards Undermine Altruistic Tendencies in 20-month-olds. *Developmental Psychology* 44(6): 1785–8.

Warneken, F., B. Hare, A.P. Melis, et al. 2007. Spontaneous Altruism by Chimpanzees and Young Children. *PLoS Biology* 5:1414–20.

Warneken, F., F. Chen, and M. Tomasello. 2006. Cooperative Activities in Young Children and Chimpanzees. *Child Development* 77(3): 640–63.

Washburn, S.L. 1953. The Strategy of Physical Anthropology. In *Anthropology Today: An Encyclopedic Inventory,* ed. A.L. Kroeber, pp. 714–27. Chicago: University of

Chicago Press

Washburn, S.L., and F.C. Howell. 1960. Human Evolution and Culture. In *Evolution after Darwin,* 3 vols., vol. 2, ed. S. Tax, pp. 33–56. Chicago: University of Chicago Press.

Watanabe, K. 1994. Precultural Behavior of Japanese Macaques: Longitudinal Studies of the Koshima Troop. In *The Ethological Roots of Culture,* ed. R.A. Gardner, B.T. Gardner, B. Chiarelli, and F.X. Plooji, pp. 81–94. Boston: Kluwer Academic Press.

Watson, V. 2004. Composition of the Swartkrans Bone Accumulations, in Terms of Skeletal Parts and Animals Represented. In *Swartkrans: A Cave's Chronicle of Early Man,* ed. C.K. Brain, pp. 35–73. Pretoria: Transvaal Museum.

Watts, D.P., and J.C. Mitani. 2002. Hunting Behavior of Chimpanzees at Ngogo, Kibale National Park, Uganda. *International Journal of Primatology* 23(1): 1–28.

Watts, I. 2002. Ochre in the Middle Stone Age of Southern Africa: Ritualized Display or Hide Preservative? *South African Archaeological Bulletin* 57(117): 1–14.

Weaver, T.D., C.C. Roseman, and C.B. Stringer. 2008. Close Correspondence between Quantitative- and Molecular-Genetic Divergence Times for Neandertals and Modern Humans. *Proceedings of the National Academy of Sciences USA* 105:4645–49.

Weidenreich, F. 1946. *Apes, Giants and Man.* Chicago: University of Chicago Press.

Wellman, H.M., and D. Liu. 2004. Scaling of Theory-of-Mind Tasks. *Child Development* 75:523–41.

Weniger, G.-C. 2006. Neandertals and Early Moderns: Human Contacts on the Borderline of Archaeological Visibility. In *When Neanderthals and Modern Humans Met,* ed. N.J. Conard, pp. 21–32. Tübingen: Kerns Verlag.

Wheeler, P.E. 1984. The Evolution of Bipedality and Loss of Functional Body Hair in Hominids. *Journal of Human Evolution* 13:91–98.

——1991. The Thermoregulatory Advantages of Hominid Bipedalism in Open Equatorial Environments: The Contribution of Increased Convective Heat Loss and Cutaneous Evaporative Cooling. *Journal of Human Evolution* 21(2): 107–15.

Whitcome, K.K., L.J. Shapiro, and D.E. Lieberman. 2007. Fetal Load and the Evolution of Lumbar Lordosis in Bipedal Hominins. *Nature* 450:1075–78.

White, L. 1949. *Science of Culture: A Study of Man and Civilization.* New York: Farrar, Straus and Giroux.

White, R. 1992. Beyond Art: Toward an Understanding of the Origins of Material Representation in Europe. *Annual Review of Anthropology* 21:537–64.

—— 2003. *Prehistoric Art: The Symbolic Journey of Humankind.* New York: Harry N. Abrams.

—— 2006. The Women of Brassempouy: A Century of Research and Interpretation.

Journal of Archaeological Method and Theory 13(4): 251–304.

White, T.D. 1986. Cut Marks on the Bodo Cranium: A Case of Prehistoric Defleshing. *American Journal of Physical Anthropology* 69:503–9.

—— 1987. Cannibalism at Klasies? *Sagittarius* 2:6–9.

White, T.D., G. Suwa, S. Simpson, et al. 2000. Jaws and Teeth of *Australopithecus afarensis* from Maka, Middle Awash, Ethiopia. *American Journal of Physical Anthropology* 111:45–68.

White, T.D., B. Afshaw, D. DeGusta, et al. 2003. Pleistocene *Homo sapiens* from Middle Awash, Ethiopia. *Nature* 423(6941): 742–47.

White, T.D., G. WoldeGabriel, B. Asfaw, et al. 2006. Asa Issie, Aramis and the Origin of *Australopithecus*. *Nature* 440:883–89.

Whiten, A. 2005. The Second Inheritance System of Chimpanzees and Humans. *Nature* 437:52–55.

—— 2009. The Identification and Differentiation of Culture in Chimpanzees and Other Animals: From Natural History to Diffusion Experiments. In *The Question of Animal Culture,* ed. K.N. Laland and B.G. Galef, pp. 97–124. Cambridge, MA: Harvard University Press.

Whiten, A., and R.W. Byrne. 1988. Tactical Deception in Primates. *Behavioral and Brain Sciences* 11:233–44.

——, eds. 1997. *Machiavellian Intelligence* II. Cambridge: Cambridge University Press.

Whiten, A., and C.P. van Schaik. 2007. The Evolution of Animal "Cultures" and Social Intelligence. *Philosophical Transactions of the Royal Society B* 362:603–20.

Whiten, A., D.M. Custance, J.C. Gomez, et al. 1996. Imitative Learning of Artificial Fruit Processing in Children (*Homo sapiens*) and Chimpanzees (*Pan troglodytes*). *Journal of Comparative Psychology* 110(1): 3–14.

Whiten, A., V. Horner, and S. Marshall-Pescini. 2003. Cultural Panthropology. *Evolutionary Anthropology* 12:92–105.

—— 2004. How Do Apes Ape? *Learning and Behavior* 32:36–52.

Whiten, A., J. Goodall, W.C. McGrew, et al. 1999. Cultures in Chimpanzees. *Nature* 399(6737): 682–85.

Whiten, A., J. Goodall, W.C. McGrew, et al. 2001. Charting Cultural Variation in Chimpanzees. *Behaviour* 138:1481–1516.

Wicker, B., C. Keysers, J. Plailly, et al. 2003. Both of Us Disgusted in My Insula: The Common Neural Basis of Seeing and Feeling Disgust. *Neuron* 40(3): 655–64.

Wiessner, P. 1984. Reconsidering the Behavioral Basis for Style: A Case Study among the Kalahari San. *Journal of Anthropological Archaeology* 3:190–234.

—— 2002. Hunting, Healing, and Hxaro Exchange: A Long-term Perspective on

!Kung (Ju/'hoansi) Large-game Hunting. *Evolution and Human Behavior* 23(6): 407–36.

Wilkins, J. 1998. What's in a Meme? Reflections from the Perspective of the History and Philosophy of Evolutionary Biology. *Journal of Memetics* 2(1): [http://jom-emit.cfpm.org/].

Wilkinson, G.S. 1984. Reciprocal Food Sharing in the Vampire Bat. *Nature* 308:181–84.

Willey, G.R. 1960. Historical Patterns and Evolution in Native New World Cultures. In *Evolution after Darwin,* 3 vols., ed. S. Tax, vol. 2, pp. 111–41. Chicago: University of Chicago Press.

Willey, M.M. 1929. The Validity of the Culture Concept. *American Journal of Sociology* 35:204–19.

Williamson, S.H., M.J. Hubisz, A.G. Clark, et al. 2007. Localizing Recent Adaptive Evolution in the Human Genome. *PLoS Genetics* 3:e90.

Wilson, E.O. 1975. *Sociobiology: The New Synthesis.* Cambridge, MA: Harvard University Press.

Wilson, S.M., A.P. Saygin, M.I. Sereno, and M. Iacoboni. 2004. Listening to Speech Activates Motor Areas Involved in Speech Production. *Nature Neuroscience* 7(7): 701–2.

Winter, H., L. Langbein, M. Krawczak, et al. 2001. Human Type I Hair Keratin Pseudogene phihHaA Has Functional Orthologs in the Chimpanzee and Gorilla: Evidence for Recent Inactivation of the Human Gene after the *Pan-Homo* Divergence. *Human Genetics* 108(1): 37–42.

Winterhalder, B. 1986. Diet Choice, Risk, and Food Sharing in a Stochastic Environment. *Journal of Anthropological Archaeology* 5:369–92.

Winterhalder, B., and E.A. Smith, eds. 1981. *Hunter-Gatherer Foraging Strategies.* Chicago: University of Chicago Press.

—— 2000. Analyzing Adaptive Strategies: Human Behavioral Ecology at Twenty-five. *Evolutionary Anthropology* 9(2): 51–72.

Wise, S.P. 1985. The Primate Premotor Cortex: Past, Present, and Preparatory. *Annual Review of Neuroscience* 8:1–19.

Wittig, R.M., C. Crockford, E. Wikberg, et al. 2007. Kin-mediated Reconciliation Substitutes for Direct Reconciliation in Baboons. *Proceedings of the Royal Society of London B* 274:1109–15.

Wittig, R.M., C. Crockford, J. Lehman, et al. 2008. Focused Grooming Networks and Stress Alleviation in Wild Female Baboons. *Hormones and Behavior* 54(1): 170–7.

Wolpert, L. 2003. Causal Belief and the Origins of Technology. *Philosophical Transactions of the Royal Society of London A* 361:1709–19.

Wolpoff, M.H., J. Hawks, D.W. Frayer, et al. 2001. Modern Human Ancestry at the Peripheries: A Test of the Replacement Theory. *Science* 291:293–97.

Wolpoff, M.H., B. Senut, P. Pickford, et al. 2002. Palaeoanthropology: Sahelanthropus or "Sahelpithecus"? *Nature* 419:581–82.

Wolpoff, M.H., B. Mannnheim, A. Mann, et al. 2004. Why Not the Neandertals? *World Archaeology* 36:527–46.

Wood, B. 2002. Hominid Revelations from Chad. *Nature* 418:133–35.

Wood, B., and D. Strait. 2004. Patterns of Resource Use in Early *Homo* and *Paranthropus*. *Journal of Human Evolution* 46:119–62.

Wood, B., and M. Collard. 1999. The Changing Face of Genus *Homo*. *Evolutionary Anthropology* 8(9): 195–207.

Woolsey, C.N., P.H. Settlage, D.R. Meyer, et al. 1952. Patterns of Localization in Precentral and "Supplementary" Motor Areas and Their Relation to the Concept of a Premotor Area. *Research Publications: Association for Research in Nervous and Mental Disease* 30:238–64.

Worden, R.P. 1998. The Evolution of Language from Social Intelligence. In *Approaches to the Evolution of Language: Social and Cognitive Biases*, ed. J.R. Hurford, M. Studdert-Kennedy, and C. Knight, pp. 148–66. Cambridge: Cambridge University Press.

Wray, A. 1998. Protolanguage as a Holistic System for Social Interaction. *Language and Communication* 18:47–67.

—— 2000. Holistic Utterances in Protolanguage: The Link from Primates to Humans. In *The Evolutionary Emergence of Language: Social Function and the Origins of Linguistic Form*, ed. C. Knight, M. Studdert-Kennedy, and J. Hurford, pp. 285–302. Cambridge: Cambridge University Press.

——, ed. 2002. *The Transition to Language*. Oxford: Oxford University Press.

Wynn, T., and F.L. Coolidge. 2003. The Role of Working Memory in the Evolution of Managed Foraging. *Before Farming* 2:1–16.

—— 2004. The Expert Neandertal Mind. *Journal of Human Evolution* 46:467–87.

—— 2007. Did a Small but Significant Enhancement in Working Memory Capacity Power the Evolution of Modern Thinking? In *Rethinking the Human Revolution: New Behavioural and Biological Perspectives on the Origin and Dispersal of Modern Humans*, ed. P. Mellars, K. Boyle, O. Bar-Yosef, and C. Stringer, pp. 79–90. Cambridge: McDonald Institute for Archaeological Research.

—— 2010. Beyond Symbolism and Language: An Introduction to Supplement 1, Working Memory. *Current Anthropology* 51 (Suppl. 1): S5–16.

Yamakoshi, G. 2001. Ecology of Tool Use in Wild Chimpanzees: Toward Reconstruction of Early Hominid Evolution. In *Primate Origins of Human Cognition and Behavior,* ed. T. Matsuzawa, pp. 537–56. Tokyo: Springer.

Yang, M.A., A.-S. Malaspinas, E.Y. Durand, and M. Slatkin. 2012. Ancient Structure in Africa Unlikely to Explain Neanderthal and Non-African Genetic Similarity. *Molecular Biology and Evolution* 29(10): 2987–95.

Yellen, J.E., A.S. Brooks, E. Cornelissen, et al. 1995. A Middle Stone Age Worked Bone Industry from Katanda, Upper Semliki Valley, Zaire. *Science* 268(5210): 553–56.

Yengoyan, A.A. 1968. Demographic and Ecological Influences on Aboriginal Australian Marriage Systems. In *Man the Hunter,* ed. R.B. Lee and I. DeVore, pp. 185–99. Chicago: Aldine.

Yesner, D.R. 1981. Archaeological Applications of Optimal Foraging Theory: Harvest Strategies of Aleut Hunter-Gatherers. In *Hunter-Gatherer Foraging Strategies,* ed. B. Winterhalder and E.A. Smith, pp. 148–70. Chicago: University of Chicago Press.

Young, K. 1934. *An Introductory Sociology.* New York: American Book Co.

Zachos, J., M. Pagani, L. Sloan, et al. 2001. Trends, Rhythms, and Aberrations in Global Climate 65 Ma to Present. *Science* 292(5517): 686–93.

Zahavi, A., and A. Zahavi. 1997. *The Handicap Principle: A Missing Piece of Darwin's Puzzle.* Oxford: Oxford University Press.

Zajonc, R.B. 1965. Social Facilitation. *Science* 149:269–74.

Zhang, J., D.M. Webb, and O. Podlaha. 2002. Accelerated Protein Evolution and Origins of Human-specific Features: Foxp2 as an Example. *Genetics* 162:1825–35.

Zhivotovsky, L.A., N.A. Rosenberg, and M.W. Feldman. 2003. Features of Evolution and Expansion of Modern Humans, Inferred from Genome-wide Microsatellite Markers. *American Journal of Human Genetics* 72(5): 1171–86.

Zietkiewicz, E., V. Yotova, M. Jarnik, et al. 1998. Genetic Structure of the Ancestral Population of Modern Humans. *Journal of Molecular Evolution* 47:146–55.

Zilhão, J. 2006. Neandertals and Moderns Mixed, and It Matters. *Evolutionary Anthropology* 15:183–95.

—— 2007. The Emergence of Ornaments and Art: An Archaeological Perspective on the Origins of Behavioral Modernity. *Journal of Archaeological Research* 15:1–54.

Zilhão, J., and F. d'Errico. 1999. The Chronology and Taphonomy of the Earliest Aurignacian and Its Implications for the Understanding of Neanderthal Extinction. *Journal of World Prehistory* 13:1–68.

Zilhão, J., F. d'Errico, J.-G. Bordes, et al. 2006. Analysis of Aurignacian Intrastratification at the Châtelperronian Type Site and Implications for the Behavioral Modernity of Neandertals. *Proceedings of the National Academy of Sciences USA* 103(33): 12643–48.

Zilhão, J., D. Angelucci, E. Badal-Garcia, et al. 2010. Symbolic Use of Marine Shells and Mineral Pigments by Iberian Neandertals. *Proceeding of the National Academy of Science USA* 107(3): 1023–28.

Zimmerman, E., and U. Radespiel. 2007. Primate Life Histories. In *Handbook of Paleoanthropology*. Vol. 2, *Primate Evolution and Human Origins,* ed. W. Henke, I. Tattersall, and T. Hardt, pp. 1163–1205. Berlin: Springer.

Zlatev, J., T. Persson, and P. Gärdenfors. 2005. *Bodily Mimesis as the "Missing Link" in Human Cognitive Evolution.* Lund University Cognitive Studies 121. Lund.

Zollikofer, C.P., M.S. Ponce de León, D.E. Lieberman, et al. 2005. Virtual Cranial Reconstruction of *Sahelanthropus tchadensis. Nature* 434:755–59.

Zuberbuhler, K. 2002. A Syntactic Rule in Forest Monkey Communication. *Animal Behaviour* 63:293–99.

Index

(Page numbers in italics indicate figures)